T0137440

Lecture Notes in Computer Science 2610
Edited by G. Goos, J. Hartmanis, and J. van Leeuwen

Springer
Berlin
Heidelberg
New York
Barcelona
Hong Kong
London
Milan
Paris
Tokyo

Conor Ryan   Terence Soule
Maarten Keijzer   Edward Tsang
Riccardo Poli   Ernesto Costa (Eds.)

Genetic Programming

6th European Conference, EuroGP 2003
Essex, UK, April 14-16, 2003
Proceedings

Volume Editors

Conor Ryan
University of Limerick, Computer Science and Information Systems
Limerick, Ireland
E-mail: conor.ryan@ul.ie

Terence Soule
University of Idaho, Department of Computer Science
Moscow, ID 83844-1010, USA
E-mail: tsoule@cs.uidaho.edu

Maarten Keijzer
Free University of Amsterdam, Department of Computer Science
1081 HV Amsterdam, The Netherlands
E-mail: mkeijzer@cs.vu.nl

Edward Tsang
Riccardo Poli
University of Essex, Department of Computer Science
Wivenhoe Park, Colchester CO4 3SQ, United Kingdom
E-mail:{edward, rpoli}@essex.ac.uk

Ernesto Costa
University of Coimbra, Department of Computer Science
Polo II, Pinhal Marrocos, 3030-290 Coimbra, Portugal
E-mail: ernesto@dei.uc.pt

Cataloging-in-Publication Data applied for

A catalog record for this book is available from the Library of Congress

Bibliographic information published by Die Deutsche Bibliothek
Die Deutsche Bibliothek lists this publication in the Deutsche Nationalbibliographie; detailed bibliographic data is available in the Internet at <http://dnb.ddb.de>.

CR Subject Classification (1998): D.1, F.1, F.2, I.5, I.2, J.3

ISSN 0302-9743
ISBN 3-540-00971-X Springer-Verlag Berlin Heidelberg New York

Springer-Verlag Berlin Heidelberg New York
a member of BertelsmannSpringer Science+Business Media GmbH

http://www.springer.de

Printed in Germany

Typesetting: Camera-ready by author, data conversion by Olgun Computergrafik
Printed on acid-free paper SPIN: 10872831 06/3142 5 4 3 2 1 0

Preface

In this volume we present the accepted contributions to the Sixth European Conference on Genetic Programming (EuroGP 2003) which took place at the University of Essex, UK on 14-16 April 2003. EuroGP is now a well-established conference and, without any doubt, the most important international event devoted to Genetic Programming occurring in Europe. The proceedings have all been published by Springer-Verlag in the LNCS series. EuroGP began as an international workshop in Paris, France in 1998 (14–15 April, LNCS 1391). Subsequently the workshop was held in Göteborg, Sweden in 1999 (26–27 May, LNCS 1598) and then EuroGP became an annual conference: in 2000 in Edinburgh, UK (15–16 April, LNCS 1802), in 2001 in Lake Como, Italy (18–19 April, LNCS 2038) and in 2002 in Kinsale, Ireland (3–5 April, LNCS 2278). From the outset, there have always been specialized workshops, co-located with EuroGP, focusing on applications of evolutionary algorithms (LNCS 1468, 1596, 1803, 2037, and 2279). This year was no exception and EvoWorkshops 2003, incorporating EvoBIO, EvoCOP, EvoIASP, EvoMUSART, EvoSTIM and EvoROB, took place at the University of Essex (LNCS 2611).

Genetic Programming (GP) is that part of Evolutionary Computation which solves particular complex problems or tasks by evolving and adapting populations of computer programs, using Darwinian evolution and Mendelian genetics as a source of inspiration. Some of the 45 papers included in these proceedings address foundational and theoretical issues, and there is also a wide variety of papers dealing with different applications areas, such as computer science, engineering, finance, medicine or robotics, demonstrating that GP is a powerful and practical problem-solving paradigm.

A rigorous, double-blind, peer-review selection mechanism was applied to the 61 submitted papers. This resulted in 24 plenary talks (39% of those submitted) and 21 research posters. Every paper was reviewed by at least three members of the International Program Committee who were carefully selected for their knowledge and competence, and, as far as possible, papers were matched with the reviewer's particular interests and special expertise. The results of this careful process can be seen here in the high quality of the contributions published within this volume.

Of the 45 accepted papers, a large majority came from European countries (about 75%), confirming the strong European character of the conference. Nevertheless, we should emphasize the fact that the other 25% came from many different countries around the world with a clear predominance by the US.

We would like to express our sincere thanks especially to the two internationally renowned invited speakers who gave keynote talks at the conference: Prof. David E. Goldberg of the University of Illinois at Urbana-Champaign, USA and Prof. Chris Stephens of the Universidad Nacional Autónoma de México, México.

The success of any conference results from the input of many people, to whom we would like to express our gratitude. Firstly, we would like to thank the members of the Program Committee for their attentiveness, perseverance and willingness to provide high-quality reviews. We would also like to thank EvoNet, the Network of Excellence in Evolutionary Computing, for its support, in particular to Jennifer Willies and Chris Osborne for their valuable and professional help with all the organizational and logistical aspects. Last, but not least, we would like to thank the members of EvoGP, the EvoNet working group on Genetic Programming.

April 2003

Conor Ryan
Terence Soule
Maarten Keijzer
Edward Tsang
Riccardo Poli
Ernesto Costa

Organization

EuroGP 2003 was organized by EvoGP, the EvoNet Working Group on Genetic Programming.

Organizing Committee

Program co-chairs:	Conor Ryan (University of Limerick, Ireland) Terence Soule (University of Idaho, USA)
Publicity chair:	Maarten Keijzer (Free University, The Netherlands)
Local co-chairs:	Edward Tsang (University of Essex, UK) Riccardo Poli (University of Essex, UK)
Publication chair:	Ernesto Costa (University of Coimbra, Portugal)

Program Committee

Vladan Babovic, DHI Water and Environment, Denmark
Wolfgang Banzhaf, University of Dortmund, Germany
Bertrand Braunschweig, Institut Français du Pétrole, France
Stefano Cagnoni, University of Parma, Italy
Jean-Jacques Chabrier, University of Bourgogne, France
Shu-Heng Chen, National Chengchi University, Taiwan
Pierre Collet, Ecole Polytechnique, France
Marco Dorigo, Free University of Brussels, Belgium
Malachy Eaton, University of Limerick, Ireland
Marc Ebner, University of Würzburg, Germany
Aniko Ekart, University of Birmingham, UK
Francisco Fernández, University of Extremadura, Spain
Cyril Fonlupt, University of Littoral, Côte d'Opale, France
James A. Foster, University of Idaho, USA
Frank Francone, Chalmers University of Technology, Sweden
Wolfgang Golubsky, University of Münster, Germany
Steven Gustafson, University of Nottingham, UK
Jin-Kao Hao, University of Angers, France
Robert Heckendorn, University of Idaho, USA
Hitoshi Iba, University of Tokyo, Japan
Christian Jacob, University of Calgary, Canada
Colin Johnson, University of Kent at Canterbury, UK
Maarten Keijzer, Free University, The Netherlands
Didier Keymeulen, Jet Propulsion Laboratory, USA

William B. Langdon, University College London, UK
Jean Louchet, INRIA, France
Evelyne Lutton, INRIA, France
Peter Martin, University of Essex, UK
Julian Miller, University of Birmingham, UK
Peter Nordin, Chalmers University of Technology, Sweden
Michael O'Neill, University of Limerick, Ireland
Una-May O'Reilly, Massachusetts Institute of Technology, USA
Riccardo Poli, University of Essex, UK
Philippe Preux, University of Littoral, Côte d'Opale, France
Jonathan Rowe, University of Birmingham, UK
Conor Ryan, University of Limerick, Ireland
Bart Rylander, University of Portland, USA
Kazuhiro Saitou, University of Michigan, USA
Marc Schoenauer, INRIA, France
Michele Sebag, University of Paris-Sud, France
Alexei Skourikhine, Los Alamos National Laboratory, USA
Terence Soule, University of Idaho, USA
Adrian Stoica, Jet Propulsion Laboratory, USA
Adrian Thompson, University of Sussex, UK
Andy Tyrell, University of York, UK
Gilles Venturini, University of Tours, France
Krister Wolff, Chalmers University of Technology, Sweden

Sponsoring Institutions

University of Essex, UK
EvoNet: The Network of Excellence in Evolutionary Computing, funded by the European Commission's IST Programme

Table of Contents

Talks

Posters

Evolving Cellular Automata to Grow Microstructures

David Basanta[1], Peter J. Bentley[2], Mark A. Miodownik[1], and Elizabeth A. Holm[3]

[1] Department of Mechanical Engineering, Kings College London, The Strand, London
{david.basanta,mark.miodownik}@kcl.ac.uk
[2] Department of Computer Science, University College London, Gower St. London
p.bentley@cs.ucl.ac.uk
[3] Sandia National Laboratories, Albuquerque, New Mexico, USA
eaholm@sandia.gov

Abstract. The properties of engineering structures such as cars, cell phones or bridges rely on materials and on the properties of these materials. The study of these properties, which are determined by the internal architecture of the material or microstructure, has significant importance for material scientists. One of the things needed for this study is a tool that can create microstructural patterns. In this paper we explore the use of a genetic algorithm to evolve the rules of an effector automata to recreate these microstructural patterns.

1 Introduction

Materials science is the study of materials and their properties. Most materials are crystalline and so have a regular periodic crystal structure at the atomic scale. But a brick or a spanner are not made of one single perfect crystal. They are made from billions of small crystals. Each crystal is not the same shape or composition, and they often exist as a nested structure in which one crystal will contain many types of smaller crystal. This complicated multiscale pattern is called the microstructure. The microstructure has long been recognised as the origin for the wealth of different types of materials that we see around us. The term is not limited to describe the structure of crystalline materials, it is used to describe the internal patterns of all materials.

What makes a wine glass brittle and an optical fibre strong is not explained in terms of the strength of atomic bonds, which are chemically identical. The extraordinary difference in properties is entirely attributable to the different types of microstructure in the two products [1]. Changing the microstructure changes the properties. This is the origin of 'heat treatment' in metallurgy. A sword can be made brittle and weak, or strong and tough by simply putting it in a fire. The heat treatment produces a different microstructure. The materials for jet engines, silicon chips, batteries, and even concrete building foundations are engineered to have specific microstructures to give specific properties. The study of these microstructures, these patterns, is therefore a major area of research. Figure 3 (left) illustrates the microstructure of a jet engine alloy, showing small spherical alumina crystals embedded in a bigger nickel-aluminium crystal. The size and dispersion of the alumina crystals is one of the major controlling factors of the high temperature strength of the material.

C. Ryan et al. (Eds.): EuroGP 2003, LNCS 2610, pp. 1–10, 2003.

There is a major effort to design new materials with special properties [2]. This involves investigating new types of microstructure and using computer simulation to test the properties. One of the first steps along this road is to develop a tool that can create microstructural patterns [3]. This paper deals with this issue and introduces a new method to create microstructural patterns using a genetic algorithm (GA) to evolve a type of cellular automaton (CA).

2 Background

2.1 Introduction to Microstructures

All materials have internal architectures that determine their properties, known as *microstructures.* Details of specific microstructures are normally obtained using one of the different microscopy techniques available. Among the features that can be found in a microstructure are grains, grain boundaries and phases.

Most materials are composed of various crystals or grains and are separated by grain boundaries. Inside these grains, there can be more crystals or particles of different types and orientations. Each different type of particle constitutes a phase in the grain [4].

2.2 Cellular Automata

Cellular automata (CA) are mathematical tools that can be used to model physical systems. A CA consists of cells usually arranged in a square grid and communicating with each other [5]. There are two features that differentiate CAs: the initial configuration (IC) and the rule set. The IC determines the dimensions of the lattice and the state of each automaton at the initial stage. The rule set is the set of rules that will be applied to the lattice each iteration, starting from the IC. The initial state of the lattice will change following the dictate of these rules.

CA are being used in a number of different fields and applications ranging from materials science [6] to the evolution of "artificial brains" [7]. In most of these applications, the rules of the CA are designed by humans but there is a growing interest in using evolutionary computing techniques to automate rule generation. Some examples of this trend are the use of GAs [8] and GP [9] to evolve CAs for the density classification problem or the use of a "Selfish Gene" algorithm to evolve a CA that can test digital circuits [10]. Closer to the task of evolving shapes, work performed by Kumar and Bentley [11] used GAs to evolve and compare different developmental processes, including CAs, by evolving specific bitmaps. Also relevant to this research is the evolution of CA and pheromonal agent systems to explore pattern formation described in [12].

2.3 Effector Automata

Effector automata (EfA) are a type of CA introduced in [13] in which the cells of the lattice represent only locations in the space and automata are entities that can occupy those cells. The rules of an EfA are different from those in a standard CA (see Fig. 1). In a standard CA the rules specify the state of the automaton in the next time step whereas in an EfA the rules specify the location of a moving automaton in the next time step. Regardless of the differences, the EfA retains most of the properties of CA like strictly local interactions among automata, and a high degree of parallelism.

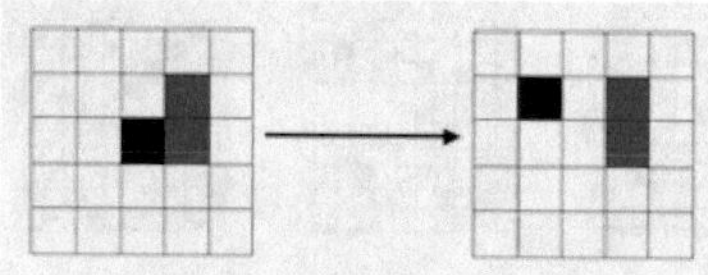

Fig. 1. The first 2D lattice represents the EfA at time step t, the second lattice represents how the darker cell (automaton) would move at time step t+1 if the rule "`if (neighbours<=3) then move`" was applied. The direction of movement is not specified in the rule; the EfA will choose randomly a direction in which the automaton will not collide with any of its neighbours.

3 Using GAs to Grow Microstructures with Effector Automata

3.1 Effector Automata Rules

The rules of the EfA used in this work differ significantly from other implementations of EfA. They can fall in one of two types:

```
If (number_of_neighbours ≥ threshold) then move, else stay.
If (number_of_neighbours ≤ threshold) then move, else stay.
```

The neighbours of an automaton are the automata that occupy contiguous cells. In a 2D EfA, an automaton may have a maximum of eight neighbours so there are sixteen possible rules, eight of the first type and eight of the second. Rules have been numbered from zero to fifteen so rule zero stands for a rule of the first type with threshold equal to zero and rule eight stands for rule of the second type with threshold zero.

The direction of movement is not specified in the rules, it is chosen randomly between all the neighbouring cells that do not contain another automaton. Experiments previously conducted with this type of rules have shown that the random movement of the automata has little effect in the overall distribution of the automata if the number of these automata is sufficiently big.

An EfA was chosen instead of the standard CA for several reasons. First, the number of automata to deal with is reduced from all the cells in the lattice to all the cells that actually contain automata. Second, the GA doesn't have to spend time finding the right value for the number of active automata in the lattice. These two things make EfA more computationally efficient than standard CA. The effects of using different rules with two ICs can be seen in Fig. 2.

3.2 Genetic Algorithm

In this work a genetic algorithm grows two-phase single-crystal microstructures. This kind of microstructure can be represented with lattices with cells in one of two different states, Fig. 3.

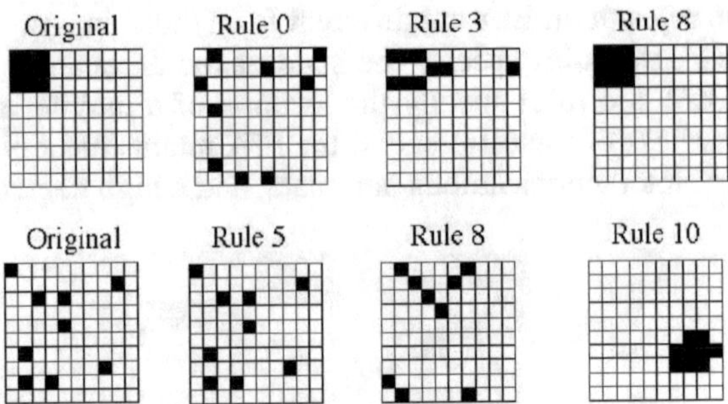

Fig. 2. The two lattices in the first column represent the ICs of the CA. The rest of the lattices represent the IC to their left after being iterating it for a number of times with different rules. Some rules, e.g., rule 1 and rule 10, can produce large changes to the IC.

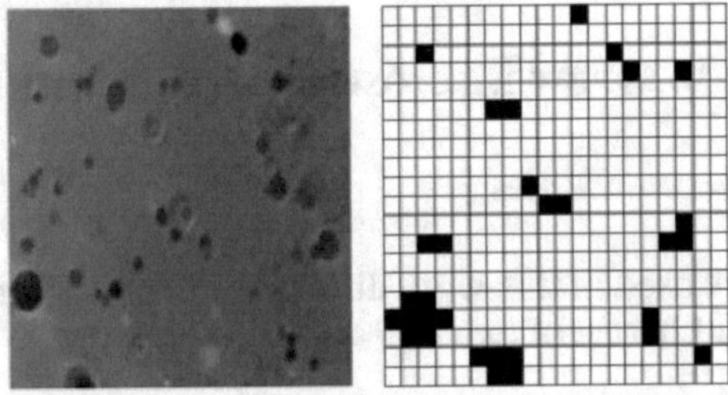

Fig. 3. Part the microstructure of an ODS ferritic superalloy (left). The discretisation into a 20x20 lattice that will be used as a target by the GA (right).

The GA reconstructs microstructures in 2D but the method described in this paper works in exactly the same fashion regardless of the dimensionality of the microstructure being reconstructed. It uses the same information needed to reconstruct microstructures in 3D. The only difference between 2D and 3D is the size of the search space. To enable easier experimentation, this work focuses on 2D reconstruction.

A fairly standard generational GA with elitism is used. Selection is performed through tournaments with two contestants per tournament; selected candidates are combined using a two point crossover operator and each chromosome has a probability of 0.1 of being mutated. There is one slot for elitism so the best candidate of each generation passes directly to the next generation without modifications.

The GA evolves a population of EfA rule sets. Every gene in the genome represents one of the 16 possible rules and is coded as an integer in the range 0-15. The length of the genome is fixed by the user, the bigger this number, the more rules in the rule set.

Each of these rule sets, together with an IC, is used to create the EfA. The IC is common to all EfA created during the run and is randomly generated. To construct an EfA using the rule set, every automaton (filled cell in the IC) is assigned one rule randomly chosen from the rule set. Once an automaton is assigned a rule, it follows that rule alone for the duration of the execution of the EfA. After iterating each EfA for a fixed number of times, the resulting lattice is input to the fitness function.

3.3 Fitness Function

The fitness function examines the distribution of automata on the lattice and compares it to the distribution of the target provided to the GA. Fitter individuals have distributions of automata that match the target more closely.

To obtain the distribution of automata along the lattice, a distance is obtained for every pair of automata in the lattice. Using this information a distribution of automata and distances is built for every automaton. The following two-point correlation function was used:

$$f(d) = \frac{1}{N^2} \sum_{i=1}^{i=N} n_d \qquad (1)$$

where d is the correlation distance, N is the total number of automata in the system and n_d is the number of automata at distance d from automaton i. This distribution relates a given automaton with any other automaton in the lattice and the Euclidean distance that separates them. The distribution obtained as a result of averaging the distributions of all automata in the lattice is used to compare different lattices with the target lattice provided to the GA.

4 Experiments

The objective of these experiments is to see if it is possible to reconstruct shapes of different levels of complexity using EfA whose rules have been evolved by a GA.

In addition, the impact of two system parameters on the GA was investigated. To measure this impact, two different experiments, one for each parameter, were devised. For each experiment, a number of different variations of the parameters were tried. Every variation of the parameters was tested ten times with three different target lattices (see Fig. 4). Each lattice represents shapes of increasing complexity and though they are unlikely to represent real microstructures, the results of the GA with these lattices will be a good indicator of the capabilities of the GA to create shapes of microstructures.

Experiment 1: *Size of rule set.* Tests evolving rule sets of sizes: 1, 2, 3, 4, 5 and 10.

Experiment 2: *Maximum number of iterations.* Tests iterating the EfA for 100, 1000 and 100000 time steps.

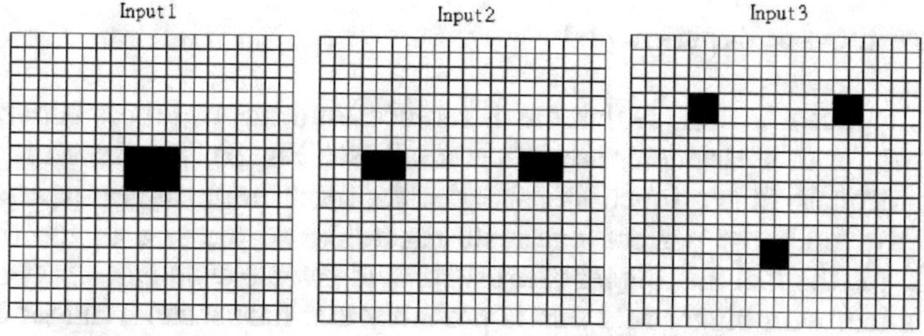

Fig. 4. The three input 2D lattices used as targets for the GA in the tests. Though the number of clusters increases in each target and so does the difficulty of finding a solution, the number of automata remains the same in all cases.

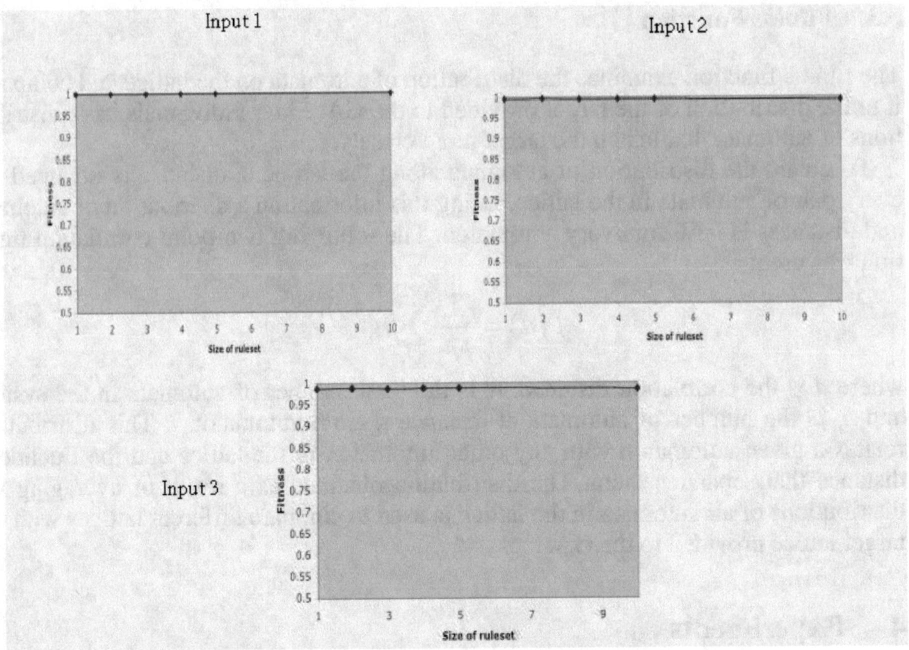

Fig. 5. Average fitness obtained by the GA with different values for the size of the rule set. When the target is simple, like in target 1, the GA always finds a perfect match regardless of the number of rules.

The GA population size for all the experiments was 20 individuals. This population size is quite small when compared to the populations sizes used in other GAs but EfA's fitness are much harder to evaluate so smaller populations are needed in order to have a more efficient system. The GA terminated when it found a perfect match according to the fitness function, otherwise it evolved up to 500 generations and returned the best candidate found. In experiment 1 each EfA was iterated a maximum of 10000 times. In experiment 2 the size of the rule set was 5.

5 Results

5.1 Results for Experiment 1

The first noticeable thing is that the differences in terms of fitness between the different values for this parameter are rather small (see Fig. 5). This result is probably due to an inadequate fitness function. As expected, for a simple target such as the first, the GA always finds the perfect candidate regardless of the size of the rule set. More surprising is the fact that bigger rule sets provide worse candidates for targets 2 and 3. The problem with bigger rule sets is probably that they mean a bigger or more difficult search space for the GA.

The size of the rule set has also a noticeable impact on the rules that are used to reconstruct shapes (see Fig. 6). If the size of the rule set is small, the range of possible

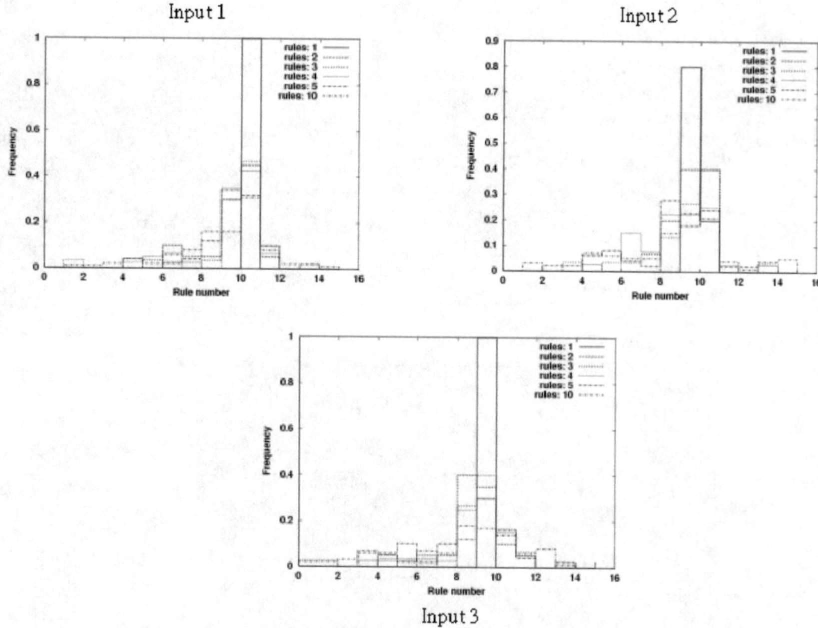

Fig. 6. Rules used to reconstruct the inputs in the first experiment.

rules is only 2, rule 9 and rule 10. As the size of the rule set increases, so does the range of possible rules. Still, it is clear that rules in the range 8-11 have better chances of being included in a given rule set than rules outside this range. There is a good reason for that; other experiments performed with these rules have shown that rules in the range 8-11 are the most likely to create clusters of automata when the automata are originally dispersed which is the case in most of the ICs.

5.2 Results for Experiment 2

In the second experiment, the performance of the GA as the EfA iteration variable increases seems to improve in target 1 and 2 but not in 3 (see Fig. 7).

Another interesting result from this experiment is that only rules in the range 8-11 have a chance of appearing in the rule set of a good candidate for a solution in the later stages of the evolution of the GA.

6 Analysis

In terms of performance, the experiments suggest that there are no major differences between the different parameters used for both experiments. It is conceivable that this result may be affected by the fitness function, which may be allocating good fitness ratings for too many individuals.

Nevertheless, the results show that the GA converges, on average, to an optimal solution in fewer generations when the EfA runs for more time steps. This advantage

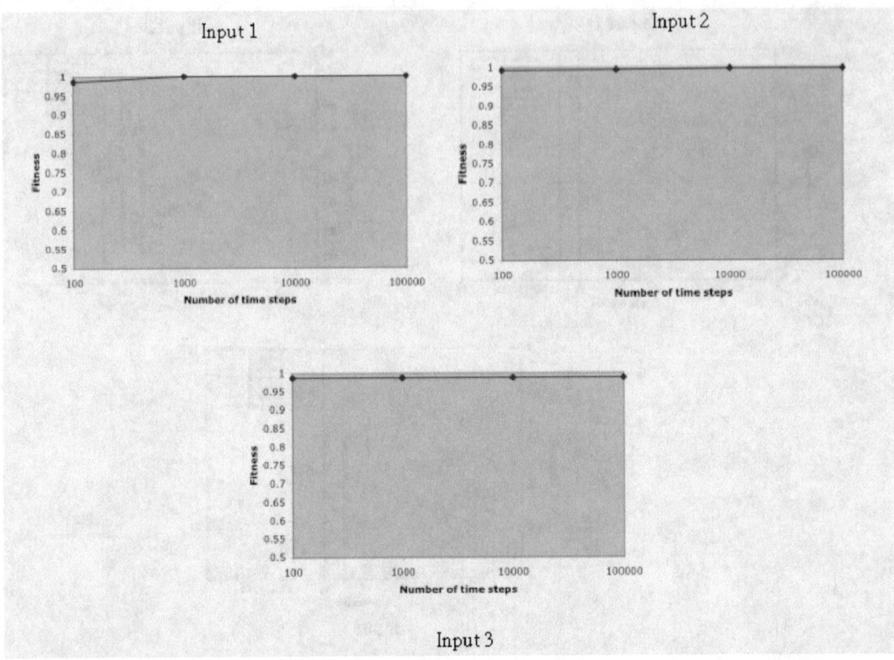

Fig. 7. Fitness of the best candidates for each input in the second experiment.

has to be offset with the fact that the GA normally evolves faster with EfA running for fewer iterations. When the GA evolves larger rule sets it can potentially construct shapes with richer complexity, but this advantage turns to be a disadvantage when the target to be reconstructed is simple. In these cases, the fact that the search-space increases as the size of the rule set gets bigger, is enough to give smaller rule sets an edge in terms of performance.

Another observation from these tests is that of all the 16 potential rules, there is a small subset (rule numbers in the range 8-11) that are much more likely to be included in the rule set of a fit candidate. Previous analysis has shown that these particular rules tend to cluster the IC they are provided with. Since the ICs are randomly generated and on average contain no clusters, is not surprising that rules that create clusters are popular. The reason why rules with numbers greater than 11 are not usually included in the rule sets of fit candidates is that automata using these rules need a large number of automata as their neighbours so they stop moving around. Also, previous analysis has shown that these rules need more iterations before reaching a stable situation. Therefore, it is likely that automata that follow rules with numbers larger than 11 would be more successful in an EfA with a high proportion of automata over empty cells, that were iterated a huge number of time steps.

7 Conclusion

This paper has demonstrated that it is possible to reconstruct shapes of some complexity using a GA that evolves rules of an effector automata. The system we described takes advantage of the features of emergence and self-organisation of CA. Though none of the automata have a plan of how the lattice should look at the end, they manage to move to appropriate new positions by interacting with each other and following their evolved rules. By doing this they ensure that the resulting pattern in the lattice looks similar to the target that the system wants to recreate, regardless of the position they occupied at the beginning.

These results are interesting by themselves and could be very significant for material scientists. A system able to interpolate 3D microstructures from 2D cross-sections is important, and could enable new materials to be engineered that will be used to build things like smaller mobile phones, faster engines or safer cars. The system shown in this paper can easily be extended to create 3D shapes starting from 2D images as the information it uses to reconstruct them is the same. The only change needed is that the lattice of the EfA has three dimensions instead of two since the fitness function uses non-dimensional information to compare the solutions provided by the GA to the original input.

Acknowledgements

This work was supported by Sandia National Laboratories, a multiprogram laboratory operated by Sandia Corporation, a Lockheed Martin Company, for the United States Department of Energy under Contract DE-AC04-94AL85000. It was also supported by the U.S. Department of Energy Office of Basic Energy Sciences New Initiative program and by a grant from the Nuffield Foundation, and by the Computational Materials Science Network, a program of the Office of Science, U.S. Department of Energy.

References

1. Gordon G. E. *Structures or Why Things Don't Fall Down*, Pelican Books, London. (1978)
2. Raabe D. *Computational Materials Science: The simulation of materials, microstructures and properties*, Wiley, Weinheim.. (1998)
3. Basanta D., Miodownik M. A., Holm E. A., and Bentley P. J. Designing the Internal Architecture of Metals using a Genetic Algorithm. *Computer-Based Design. Engineering Design Conference 2002. Professional Engineering Publishing Ltd, London, UK. pp. 349-355.* (2002)
4. Brandon, D., Kaplan, W. D. Microstructural characterization of materials. Wiley, Weinheim, (1999)
5. Ulam, S. On some mathematical properties connected with patterns of growth of figures. In Proceedings of Symposia on Applied Mathematics, volume 14, pages 215-224. American Mathematical Society. (1962.)
6. Raabe D. Cellular automata in materials science with particular reference to recrystallization simulation. Annual review of materials research. (2002)
7. De Garis, H. The Evolutionary Engineering of a Billion Neuron Artificial Brain by 2001 Which Grows/Evolves at Electronic Speeds Inside a Cellular Automata Machine. Published in Sanchez, E., and Tomassini, M. Towards Evolvable Hardware; The Evolutionary Engineering Approach. Springer. (1996)
8. Mitchell M., Crutchfield J. P., Das R. Evolving Cellular Automata to perform computations. Published in Baeck T., Fogel D., and Michalewicz (Eds.), Handbook of Evolutionary Computation. The institute of physics. (1997)

9. Andre, D., Bennett, F., Koza, J. Discovery by genetic programming of a cellular automata rule that is better than any known rule for the majority classification problem. Published in Koza, J.R, Goldberg, D.E., Fogel, D.B., Riolo, R.L., Genetic Programming 1996: Proceedings of the First Annual Conference, MIT Press. (1996.)
10. Corno, F., Reorda, M. S., and Squillero, G. Exploiting the Selfish Gene Algorithm for Evolving Hardware Cellular Automata. Proceedings of the 2000 Congress on Evolutionary Computation CEC00. IEEE press. (2000).
11. Kumar, S., Bentley, P. The ABCs of evolutionary design. Investigating the evolvability of embryogenies for morphogenesis. Genetic and Evolutionary Computation Conference (GECCO '99) RN/99/2. (1999)
12. Bentley K. A. (2002). Exploring aesthetic pattern formation. Generative Art 2002 conference proceedings. (2002)
13. Lohn, J. and Reggia., J. Discovery of Self-Replicating Structures using a Genetic Algorithm. In 1995 IEEE International Conference on Evolutionary Computing. (1995)

An Innovative Application of a Constrained-Syntax Genetic Programming System to the Problem of Predicting Survival of Patients

Celia C. Bojarczuk[1], Heitor S. Lopes[2], and Alex A. Freitas[3]

[1] Departamento de Eletrotecnica, CEFET-PR
Av. 7 de setembro, 3165, Curitiba, 80230-901, Brazil
celia@cpgei.cefetpr.br

[2] CPGEI, CEFET-PR
Av. 7 de setembro, 3165, Curitiba, 80230-901, Brazil
hslopes@cpgei.cefetpr.br

[3] Computing Laboratory, University of Kent
Canterbury, CT2 7NF, UK
A.A.Freitas@ukc.ac.uk
www.cs.ukc.ac.uk/people/staff/aaf

Abstract. This paper proposes a constrained-syntax genetic programming (GP) algorithm for discovering classification rules in medical data sets. The proposed GP contains several syntactic constraints to be enforced by the system using a disjunctive normal form representation, so that individuals represent valid rule sets that are easy to interpret. The GP is compared with C4.5 in a real-world medical data set. This data set represents a difficult classification problem, and a new preprocessing method was devised for mining the data.

1 Introduction

Classification is an important problem extensively studied in several research areas, such as statistical pattern recognition, machine learning and data mining [Hand 1997]. The basic idea is to predict the class of an instance (a record of a given data set), based on the values of predictor attributes of that instance.

This paper proposes a genetic programming (GP) system for discovering simple classification rules in the following format: IF (a-certain-combination-of-attribute-values-is-satisfied) THEN (predict-a-certain-class). Each individual represents a set of these IF-THEN rules. This rule format has the advantage of being intuitively comprehensible for the user. Hence, he/she can combine the knowledge contained in the discovered rules with his/her own knowledge, in order to make intelligent decisions about the target classification problem – for instance, medical diagnosis.

The use of GP for discovering comprehensible IF-THEN classification rules is relatively little explored in the literature, by comparison with more traditional rule induction and decision-tree-induction methods [Witten and Frank 2000]. We believe such a use of GP is a promising research area, since GP has the advantage of performing a global search in the space of candidate rules. In the context of classification

C. Ryan et al. (Eds.): EuroGP 2003, LNCS 2610, pp. 11–21, 2003.

rule discovery, in general this makes it cope better with attribute interaction than conventional, greedy rule induction and decision-tree-building algorithms [Freitas 2002], [Dhar et al. 2000], [Papagelis and Kalles 2001].

The GP algorithm proposed in this paper is a constrained-syntax one. The idea of constrained-syntax GP is not new [Montana 1995]. However, we believe this paper has the contribution of proposing a constrained-syntax GP tailored for the discovery of simple classification rules. That is, it enforces several syntactic constraints, so that individuals represent rule sets that are valid and easy to interpret, due to the use of a disjunctive normal form representation.

The remainder of this paper is organized as follows. Section 2 describes the proposed constrained-syntax GP for discovering classification rules. Section 3 reports the results of computational experiments comparing the GP with C4.5. Finally, section 4 presents the conclusions and future research.

2 A Constrained-Syntax GP for Discovering Classification Rules

An individual can contain multiple classification rules, subject to the restriction that all its rules have the same consequent – i.e., they predict the same class. In other words, an individual consists of a set of rule antecedents and a single rule consequent. The rule antecedents are connected by a logical OR operator, and each rule antecedent consists of a set of conditions connected by a logical AND operator. Therefore, an individual is in disjunctive normal form (DNF) – i.e., an individual consists of a logical disjunction of rule antecedents, where each rule antecedent is a logical conjunction of conditions (attribute-value pairs). The rule consequent specifies the class to be predicted for an instance that satisfies all the conditions of any of the rule antecedents.

The terminal set consists of the attribute names and attribute values of the data set being mined. The function set consists of logical operators (AND, OR) and relational operators ("=", "≠", "≤", ">").

Figure 1 shows an example of the genetic material of an individual. Note that the rule consequent is not encoded into the genetic material of the individual. Rather, it is chosen by a deterministic procedure, as will be explained later. In the example of Figure 1 the individual contains two rules, since there is an OR node at the root of the tree. Indeed, the tree shown in that figure corresponds to the following two rule antecedents: IF $(A_1 \leq 2)$ OR IF $((A_3 \neq 1)$ AND $(A_5 > 1))$.

Once the genetic material (set of rule antecedents) of an individual is determined, the rule consequent (predicted class) associated with the individual is chosen in such a way that the fitness of the individual is maximized. More precisely, for each class, the system computes what would be the fitness of the individual if that class were chosen to be the class predicted by the individual. Then, the system chooses the class that leads to the best fitness value for the individual.

As mentioned above, all the rules of an individual have the same rule consequent – i.e., they predict the same class. This leaves us with the problem of how to discover

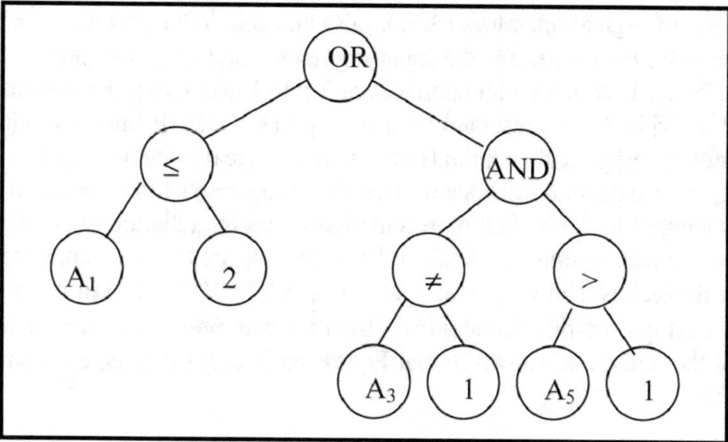

Fig. 1. Example of an individual

rules predicting different classes. The most common solution for this problem in the literature is to run the GP *k* times, where *k* is the number of classes [Kishore et al. 2000]. In the *i-th* (*i=1,...,k*) run, the GP discovers rules predicting the *i-th* class. Instead of using this conventional approach, our system works with a population of individuals where different individuals may have different rule consequents. Hence, in our approach an entire solution for the classification problem consists of *k* individuals, each of them predicting a different class. In other words, at the end of the evolution, the solution returned by GP will consist of *k* individuals, each of them being the best individual (the one with the best fitness value) for a different class.

To summarize, in our individual representation each individual consists of a set of rules predicting a given class, and an entire solution for the classification problem consists of *k* individuals, each of them predicting a different class.

One advantage of this approach, by comparison with the previously mentioned conventional approach of running the GP once for each class, is that in the former we need to run the GP just once to discover rules predicting different classes. Therefore, our approach is considerably more efficient, in terms of computational time.

2.1 Syntactic Constraints on the Individual Representation

Conventional GP systems must satisfy the property of closure, which means that the output of any function of the function set can be used as the input for any other function of that set. This property is satisfied, for instance, if the function set contains only mathematical operators (like +, -, /, *) and all terminal symbols are real-valued variables or constants. However, in a typical data mining scenario the situation is more complex, since we often want to mine a data set with a mixing of categorical (nominal) and continuous (real-valued) attributes. Hence, our individual representation includes several constraints useful for data mining applications, as follows.

First, we specify, for each function of the function set, what are the data types valid for the input arguments and the output of the function. The function set of our

GP consists of logical operators (AND, OR) and relational operators ("=", "≠", "≤", ">"). The valid data types for the input arguments and output of these operators are shown in Table 1. Note that all operators of Table 1 take two input arguments, so that each GP individual is represented by a binary tree. Our GP can cope with attributes that are either categorical (nominal) or continuous (real-valued), which is a desirable flexibility in a data mining system. The data type restrictions specified in Table 1 naturally suggest an individual representation based on a hierarchy of operators, consisting of boolean operators (AND, OR) at the top of the tree, attributes and their values at the leaves, and relational operators ("=", "≠","≤", ">") in the middle of the tree. An example of this hierarchical structure was previously shown in Figure 1. Note that the individual shown in that Figure satisfies all data type constraints specified in Table 1.

Table 1. Valid data types for each operator's input arguments and output

Operator	Input arguments	Output
AND, OR	(boolean, boolean)	boolean
"=", "≠"	(categorical, categorical)	boolean
"≤", ">"	(real, real)	boolean

In addition to the data type constraints of Table 1, our GP system enforces two other constraints. First, an AND node cannot be an ancestor of an OR node. Although this is not essential for producing syntactically-valid individuals, it enforces the restriction that every individual represents a set of rule antecedents in (DNF). The DNF representation is not only intuitively simple, but also facilitates the enforcement of the second additional constraint, called "attribute-uniqueness constraint". This constraint means that an attribute can occur at most once in a rule antecedent. This constraint avoids invalid rule antecedents like: IF (*Sex* = *male*) AND (*Sex* = *female*).

2.2 Genetic Operators

Our GP uses reproduction and crossover operators. The reproduction operator consists of passing a copy of an individual to the next generation. The crossover operator used here is a variant of the standard tree-crossover operator. In our system that crossover operator is adapted to our constrained-syntax individual representation, as follows.

First, a crossover point (a tree node) is randomly selected in one of the parent individuals, here called the first parent. Then the crossover point (tree node) of the other parent individual, here called the second parent, is randomly selected among the nodes that are compatible with the crossover point of the first parent, i.e., among the nodes that return the same data type as the data type returned by the crossover point of the first parent. Then the crossover is performed by swapping the subtrees rooted at the crossover points of the two parent individuals, as usual.

Our GP also uses a form of elitism that we call classwise elitism. The basic idea of elitism is that the best (or a small set of best) individual(s) of a generation is passed unchanged to the next generation, to prevent the stochastic process of evolution from losing that individual. Recall that the population contains individuals predicting different classes. In our classwise elitism the best individual of each of the k classes is chosen to be passed unchanged to the next generation. In other words, k elite individuals are passed unaltered to the next generation. The *i-th* elite individual ($i = 1,...,k$) is the best individual among all individuals predicting the *i-th* class. The motivation for this classwise elitism is to avoid that the population converges to a state where all individuals represent rule sets predicting the same class. Without classwise elitism this would tend to happen, because in general some classes are easier to predict than others, i.e., individuals predicting the easiest class would dominate the population.

2.3 Fitness Function

The fitness function used in this work is the same as the fitness function proposed in [Bojarczuk et al. 2000]. Note, however, that [Bojarczuk et al. 2000] used a simple individual representation, working only with boolean attribute values. This required all attributes to be booleanized in a preprocessing step, which significantly reduces the flexibility and autonomy of the algorithm. By contrast, this work uses a considerably more flexible and elaborate individual representation, as discussed earlier.

The fitness function evaluates the quality of each individual (a rule set where all rules predict the same class) according to two basic criteria, namely its predictive accuracy and its simplicity. Predictive accuracy is measured by the product $Se \cdot Sp$, where Se (the sensitivity) is given by $Se = tp / (tp + fn)$ and Sp (the specificity) is given by $Sp = tn / (tn + fp)$, where tp, fp, tn and fn denote respectively the number of true positives, false positives, true negatives and false negatives observed when a rule is used to classify a set of instances [Hand 1997].

The second criterion used in the fitness function is the simplicity (Sy) of the rule set represented by an individual, given by: $Sy = (maxnodes - 0.5 \cdot numnodes - 0.5) / (maxnodes - 1)$ where *numnodes* is the current number of nodes (functions and terminals) of an individual (tree), and *maxnodes* is the maximum allowed size of a tree (empirically set to 45). The inclusion of a simplicity term in the fitness function helps to produce simpler (shorter) rule sets to be shown to the user, and it also helps to avoid code bloat. Finally, the entire fitness function is given by the product of the indicators of predictive accuracy and simplicity, i.e.: $fitness = Se \cdot Sp \cdot Sy$. The motivation for this fitness function is explained in [Bojarczuk et al. 2000].

2.4 Classification of New Instances

Recall that, after the GP run is over, the result returned by GP consists of a set of k individuals, where k is the number of classes. The *i-th* returned individual (i=1,...,k) consists of a set of rules predicting the *i-th* class for a data instance (record) that satisfies the rule set associated with the individual. An instance is said to satisfy a rule set if it satisfies all the conditions of at least one of the rules contained in the rule set. Recall that an individual contains a rule set in disjunctive normal form.

When the set of returned individuals is used to classify a new instance (in the test set), the instance will be matched with all the *k* individuals, and one of the following three situations will occur:

(a) The instance satisfies the rule set of exactly one of the *k* individuals. In this case the instance is simply assigned the class predicted by that individual;

(b) The instance satisfies the rule set of two or more of the *k* individuals. In this case the instance is assigned the class predicted by the individual with the best fitness value (computed in the training set, of course);

(c) The instance does not satisfy the rule set of any of the *k* individuals. In this case the instance is assigned a default class, which is the majority class, that is the class of the majority of the instances in the training set.

3 Computational Results

In this section we compare the results of our GP with C4.5, a very well-known decision tree algorithm [Quinlan 1993], in a new data set, called Pediatric Adrenocortical Tumor, which has not been previously used in any computational classification experiment reported in the literature. We emphasize that preparing this data set for data mining purposes was a considerable challenge. We had to carry out a significant preprocessing of the available data, as described in the following. The data set used in our experiments consisted of 124 instances (records) and 10 attributes.

The first step was to decide which attribute would be used as the goal (or class) attribute, to be predicted. Discussing with the user, it was decided to predict how long a patient will survive after undergoing a surgery. The corresponding goal attribute is hereafter called *Survival*. The values of this attribute for the instances were not directly available in the original data set. It had to be computed in an elaborate way, as follows.

First the system computed, for each instance (patient), the number of days between the date of the surgery and the date of the last follow up of the patient. Then the system checked, for each instance, the value of another attribute called *Status*, whose domain contained four values. One of these values indicated that the patient was *dead*, whereas the other three values indicated that the patient was still *alive*. (The difference in the meaning of those three values indicating *alive* patient reflect different stages in the progress of the disease, but this difference is not relevant for our discussion here.)

A major problem in predicting *Survival* is that, if the *Status* of a patient (as recorded in the hospital's database) is different from *dead*, this does not necessarily means that patient is still *alive* in real life. Maybe the patient actually died, but this information was not yet included in the database, due to a loss of contact between the family of the patient and the hospital. On the other hand, if the value of *Status* recorded in the hospital's database is *dead*, this *Status* is presumably true. As a result, for many of the patients, one cannot be sure about the true value of the *Survival* attribute. One can be sure about this value only when the value of the *Status* attribute is *dead*. When *Status* is different from *dead*, the value of *Survival* computed as described above is just an underestimate of the true value of that attribute. Hence, any attempt to directly predict the value of *Survival* would be highly questionable.

To circumvent this problem, we transformed the original problem of predicting *Survival* for all patients into three separate problems, each of them carefully defined to lead, at least in principle, to more reliable results. We try to predict the value of *Survival* for each of three classes of this attribute separately. These three classes were defined by discretizing the *Survival* attribute (which was previously measured in number of days) into three ranges of values, namely less than one year, between one and two years, between two and five years. These intervals were determined by the user, a medical expert on Pediatric Adrenocortical Tumor. Hereafter these ranges are called class 1, class 2 and class 3, respectively, for short.

This leads to three classification experiments, each of them aiming at discriminating between two classes, a "positive" class and a "negative" class. In the *i-th* experiment, $i = 1,2,3$, the instances having class i are considered as positive-class instances, and all the other instances are considered as negative-class instances.

The reason why we need to perform three separate classification experiments is as follows. As mentioned above, when the patient's *Status* is different from *dead*, one cannot be sure about the true value of the *Survival* attribute. For instance, suppose that a patient underwent surgery one and a half year ago. One cannot be sure if the patient has class 2 or 3, since (s)he might or not live until (s)he completes two years of survival after surgery. However, one can be sure that this patient does not have class 1. So, its corresponding instance can be used as a negative-class instance in the first classification experiment, aiming at predicting whether or not a patient has class 1. On the other hand, that instance cannot be used in the second or third classification experiments, because in those experiments there would be no means to know if the instance had a positive class or a negative class.

The key idea is that an instance is used in a classification experiment only when one can be sure that it is either definitely a positive-class instance or definitely a negative-class instance, and for some instances (those having *Status* different from *dead*) this depends on the classification experiment being performed. Finally, we now precisely specify how we have defined which instances were used as positive-class or negative-class instances in each of the three classification experiments.

The first experiment consists of predicting class 1, i.e. *Survival* less than one year. In this experiment the positive-class instances are the patients whose *Status* is *dead* and whose *Survival* is less than or equal to one year. The negative-class instances are the patients whose *Survival* is greater than one year. After this instance-filtering process the data set contained 22 positive-class instances and 83 negative-class instances.

The second experiment consists of predicting class 2, i.e. *Survival* between one and two years. In this experiment the positive-class instances are the patients whose *Status* is *dead* and *Survival* is greater than one year and less than or equal to two years. The negative-class instances are the patients whose *Status* is *dead* and *Survival* is either less than one year or greater than two years. After this instance-filtering process the data set contained 8 positive-class instances and 86 negative-class instances.

The third experiment consists of predicting class 3, i.e. *Survival* between two years and five years. In this experiment the positive-class instances are the patients whose *Status* is *dead* and *Survival* is greater than two years and less than or equal to five years. The negative-class instances are the patients whose *Status* is *dead* and *Survival* is either less than two years or greater than five years. After this instance-filtering process the data set contained 6 positive-class instances and 62 negative-class instances.

Table 2 reports the accuracy rate obtained by C4.5 and the GP in each of the three classification experiments. The numbers after the "±" symbol denote standard deviations. In all the experiments we have used the default parameters of C4.5 and the GP, making no attempt to optimize the parameters of the two systems. The default parameters of the GP are: population size of 500 individuals, 50 generations, crossover probability of 95%, reproduction probability of 5%, initial population generated by the ramped half and half method, maximum tree size of 45 nodes. We used roulette wheel selection. All results were obtained by performing a 5-fold cross-validation procedure [Hand 1997], where each of the 5 iterations of the cross-validation procedure involved a single run of both the GP and C4.5.

Based on the results reported in Table 2, at first glance C4.5 seems to outperform our GP system in this data set. In two out of the three classes (namely, classes 2 and 3) the accuracy rate of C4.5 is significantly better than the one of the GP – since the corresponding accuracy rate intervals (taking into account the standard deviations) do not overlap. However, this conclusion would be premature, as we now show.

Table 2. Classification accuracy rate (%) on the test set

Class	C4.5	GP
1	75.7 ± 1.22	73.3 ± 2.43
2	88.2 ± 0.77	78.8 ± 2.81
3	87.3 ± 1.01	67.8 ± 6.82

Table 3. Sensitivity (*Se*) and Specificity (*Sp*) on the test set

Class	C4.5			GP		
	Se	*Sp*	*Se* · *Sp*	*Se*	*Sp*	*Se* · *Sp*
1	0.1	0.916	0.079	0.79	0.725	0.560
2	0	1	0	0.9	0.781	0.693
3	0	1	0	0.1	0.735	0.067

The problem with the results of Table 2 is that they are based on classification accuracy rate. Although this measure of predictive accuracy is still the most used in the literature, it has some drawbacks [Hand 1997]. The most important one is that it is relatively easy to achieve a high value of classification accuracy when one class (the majority class) has a high relative frequency in the data set, which is the case in our data set. In one extreme, suppose that 99% of the examples have a given class c_l. In this case one can trivially achieve a classification accuracy rate of 99% by "predicting" class c_l for all examples. Does that mean that the classification algorithm (a trivial majority classifier) is doing a good job? Of course not. What this means is that the measure of classification accuracy rate is too weak in this case, in the sense that it is too easy to get a very high value of this measure. One needs a more demanding measure of predictive accuracy, which emphasizes the importance of correctly classifying examples of all classes, regardless of the relative frequency of each class.

Indeed, an analysis of the trees induced by C4.5 shows that the results of the last two rows of Table 2 (referring to classes 2 and 3) are very misleading. In particular, C4.5 is *not* discovering better rules for these classes. When predicting class 2 and class 3, C4.5 induces a degenerate, "empty" tree with no internal node; i.e., a tree containing only one leaf node, predicting the majority class. This has consistently occurred in all the five folds of the cross-validation procedure. Clearly, C4.5 opted for an "easy solution" for the classification problem, favoring the correct prediction of the majority of the examples at the expense of making an incorrect prediction of all the minority-class examples. Such an easy solution is useless for the user, since it provides no rules (i.e., no knowledge) for the user. Only when predicting class 1 C4.5 was able to induce a non-degenerate, non-empty tree on average. And even for this class an empty tree was induced in some folds of the cross-validation procedure.

By contrast, our GP system discovered, on average, rules with 2, 1.7 and 1.9 conditions, for rules predicting classes 1, 2 and 3, respectively, which constitute a simple rule set to be shown to the user. Overall, the rules were considered comprehensible by the user. We now need to evaluate these rules according to a more demanding measure of predictive accuracy, emphasizing the importance of correctly classifying examples of all classes, as mentioned above. Hence, we report in Table 3 the values of sensitivity (Se), specificity (Sp), and the product $Se \cdot Sp$ (see section 2) obtained by C4.5 and our GP system in the Pediatric adrenocortical tumor data set.

As can be observed in this table, both C4.5 and our GP failed to discover good rules predicting class 3 but, unlike C4.5, our GP succeeded in discovering good rules (with relatively good values of Se and Sp) predicting classes 1 and 2. In addition, in all the three classes, the value of the product $Se \cdot Sp$ obtained by our GP considerably outperforms the one obtained by C4.5.

4 Conclusions and Future Research

As mentioned in the introduction, the idea of constrained-syntax GP is not new. However, we believe this paper has the contribution of proposing a constrained-syntax GP tailored for the discovery of simple classification rules. This was achieved by incorporating into the GP the following mechanisms:

(a) An individual representation based on disjunctive normal form (DNF). As mentioned in section 2.1, the use of DNF has two advantages. First, it is an intuitively simple form of rule set presentation to the user. Second, it facilitates the enforcement of the attribute-uniqueness constraint – i.e., an attribute can occur at most once in a rule antecedent. (In passing note that, although most of the data type constraints enforced by our GP could alternatively be represented in a grammar-based GP, the attribute-uniqueness constraint cannot be directly represented in a grammar-based GP.)

(b) A result designation scheme where the solution for the classification problem consists of k individuals (where k is the number of classes), each of them predicting a different class, and all of them produced in the same run of the GP. This makes the GP more efficient, avoiding the need for k runs of the GP, as usual in the literature.

(c) Classwise elitism, an extension of the basic idea of elitism to the framework of classification. In this kind of elitism the best individual of each of the k classes is chosen to be passed unchanged to the next generation. This avoids that the population converges to a state where all individuals represent rule sets predicting the "easiest class", and guarantees that the result designation procedure works properly.

Although each of these ideas is perhaps relatively simple, their combination effectively produces a GP tailored for the discovery of classification rules.

In addition, this paper also offers a contribution from the data mining perspective. We have proposed a new way of preprocessing a medical data set for the purpose of predicting how long a patient will survive after a surgery.

The proposed preprocessing method was applied to the Pediatric Adrenocortical Tumor data set, but it is a relatively generic method, which could be also applied to other medical data sets where one wants to predict how long a patient will survive after a given event such as a major surgery. (Of course, the method is not generic enough to cover other kinds of prediction, such as medical diagnosis.)

Furthermore, the GP was compared with C4.5 in a difficult medical classification problem. The accuracy rate of C4.5 was found to be significantly better than the one of the GP at first glance. However, an analysis of the trees built by C4.5 showed that it was *not* discovering better classification rules. It was just building a degenerate, empty tree, predicting the majority class for all data instances. We then performed a more detailed analysis of the predictive accuracy of both systems, measuring the sensitivity and the specificity rates for each class separately, and showed that, according to this measure of predictive accuracy, overall the GP obtained considerably better results than C4.5.

We are currently applying our GP to other data sets. A future research direction might consist of performing experiments with other function sets and evaluate the influence of the function set of the GP in its performance, across several data sets.

References

[Bojarczuk et al. 2000] C.C. Bojarczuk, H.S. Lopes, A.A. Freitas. Genetic programming for knowledge discovery in chest pain diagnosis. IEEE Engineering in Medicine and Biology magazine - special issue on data mining and knowledge discovery, 19(4), 38-44, July/Aug. 2000.

[Dhar et al. 2000] V. Dhar, D. Chou and F. Provost. Discovering interesting patterns for investment decision making with GLOWER – a genetic learner overlaid with entropy reduction. *Data Mining and Knowledge Discovery Journal 4* (2000), 251-280.

[Freitas 2002] A.A. Freitas. *Data Mining and Knowledge Discovery with Evolutionary Algorithms.* Springer, 2002.

[Hand 1997] D.J. Hand. *Construction and Assessment of Classification Rules.* Chichester: John Wiley & Sons, 1997.

[Kishore et al. 2000] J.K. Kishore, L.M. Patnaik, V. Mani and V.K. Agrawal. Application of genetic programming for multicategory pattern classification. *IEEE Transactions on Evolutionary Computation 4(3)* (2000), 242-258.

[Montana 1995] D.J. Montana. Strongly typed genetic programming. *Evolutionary Computation 3* (1995), 199-230.

[Papagelis and Kalles 2001] A. Papagelis and D. Kalles. Breeding decision trees using evolutionary techniques. *Proc. 18th Int. Conf. on Machine Learning*, 393-400. San Mateo: Morgan Kaufmann, 2001.

[Quinlan 1993] J.R. Quinlan. *C4.5: Programs for Machine Learning.* San Mateo, CA: Morgan Kaufmann, 1993.

[Witten and Frank 2000] I.H. Witten and E. Frank. *Data Mining: practical machine learning tools and techniques with Java implementations.* San Mateo: Morgan Kaufmann, 2000.

New Factorial Design Theoretic Crossover Operator for Parametrical Problem

Kit Yan Chan, M. Emin Aydin, and Terence C. Fogarty

Faculty of Engineering, Science and Technology
South Bank University, 103 Borough Road
London, SE1 0AA
{chankf,aydinme,fogarttc}@sbu.ac.uk

Abstract. Recent research shows that factorial design methods improve the performance of the crossover operator in evolutionary computation. However the methods employed so far ignore the effects of interaction between genes on fitness, i.e. "epistasis". Here we propose the application of a systematic method for interaction effect analysis to enhance the performance of the crossover operator. It is shown empirically that the proposed method significantly outperforms existing crossover operators on benchmark problems with high interaction between the variables.

1 Introduction

Evolutonary algorithms imitate the idea of natural selection with random individuals, applying crossover and mutation operators. They are very effective and efficient search techniques used in optimization and machine learning for poorly understood, irregular and complex spaces [2]. However, one of the main drawbacks of evolutionary algorithms is their premature convergence. Recent research [2,4,5,12] has shown that the searching performance of an evolutionary algorithm can be improved when factorial design methods are integerated into the crossover operator.

Leung [5,12] developed a crossover operator using an factorial design method called orthogonal crossover (OC). Its salient feature is to incorporate orthogonal design [1], into the crossover operator. In this approach values of the genes in the chromosome are grouped into an orthogonal array. However, in this approach, only a limited number of combinations are considered by the orthogonal array rather than undertaking a full factorial design. It may not be applicable for parametrical problem as the optimal combination may not be included in the orthogonal array.

Another factorial design method, main effect analysis [7], has been proposed to improve the crossover operator [3]. Main effect orthogonal crossover, MC in this paper, uses main effect analysis to consider combinations which are not included in the orthogonal array. In this crossover operator the children are formed from the best combinations of the genes with the best main effect. Thus all the combinations are considered, which is more promising for parametric problems than OC on its own. By

C. Ryan et al. (Eds.): EuroGP 2003, LNCS 2610, pp. 22–33, 2003.

solving a set of GA benchmark problem, experimental results show that MC outperforms OC in solution quality.

MC allows us to approximate the main effect on each gene accurately, but it ignores linkage in the form of interaction effects between genes. If strong interaction exists in localized features of the search space, misleading results may be obtained [8]. In this paper, a new crossover operator using interaction effect analysis is proposed. It employs the approach of the interaction plot [10] to analyze the interaction between genes. From the interaction plot, a clear picture of the interaction effects between genes can be obtained. In the crossover operator the children can be produced by considering both the main effect and the interaction effect in the genes. By solving a set of GA benchmark problems, it is shown empirically that the proposed crossover operator aids the search for the optimal solution. Significant results can be found on parametrical optimization problems with high interaction effects between variables, i.e. non-separable problems.

This paper is organized as follows. In section two, a brief explanation of factorial design methods is given. In section three, previous crossover operators which utilized factorial design methods are discussed. In section four, the proposed crossover operator which utilizes consideration of interaction effect is presented. In section five, performance comparisons between the proposed crossover operator and the existing operators are described. Finally, a conclusion is given in section six.

2 Orthogonal Arrays and Factorial Design Methods (Preliminary)

In factorial design, our aim is to find the best combination of parameter levels for optimum yield. A "full factorial" approach where all possible combinations of parameter levels are tried, may be necessary to determine the optimum conditions. In general, when there are *k* factors and each factor has *n* levels, the number of combinations for the "full factorial" approach is n^k. Unfortunately, when the number of factors and the number of levels are large, it is almost impossible to test all the combinations. For example, if the designer is studying 13 design parameters at three levels, a full factorial approach would require studying 1594323 (3^{13}) experimental configurations, which is prohibitive.

Orthogonal design is a method in which certain subsets of the full dimensional search are used to optimize the process [1]. It employs orthogonal arrays (OA) from the theory of the design of experiments to study the parameter space with a small number of experiments [9]. It provides the designer with a systematic and efficient method for conducting experiments to determine near optimum settings of design parameters [10]. For instance, four input parameters, each with three level settings, fortuitously fit the orthogonal array $L_9(3^4)$ shown in Table 1.

In the orthogonal array $L_9(3^4)$, each element in the top row represents an independent input parameter, and each element in the left-hand column represents an experimental run. The elements at the intersections indicate the level settings that apply to that input parameter for that experimental run. Using an orthogonal array $L_9(3^4)$ means that only 9 experiments are carried out in search of the 81 (3^4) design parameter combinations required by a full factorial design.

Table 1. The orthogonal array $L_9(3^4)$

Run	Input parameter			
	1st parameter	*2nd parameter*	*3rd parameter*	*4th parameter*
1	1	1	1	1
2	1	2	2	2
3	1	3	3	3
4	2	1	2	3
5	2	2	3	1
6	2	3	1	2
7	3	1	3	2
8	3	2	1	3
9	3	3	2	1

3 Crossover Operators with Factorial Design Methods

The efficiency of the crossover operator has been improved by incorporating orthogonal design [5,12]. Experimental results show that the resulting operators aid the classical evolutionary algorithm in searching for the optimal solution with respect to both convergence speed and accuracy.

A crossover operator, called orthogonal crossover (OC) in this paper, has been developed using orthogonal design for parametrical problem [5]. In this approach, orthogonal design has been integrated into the classical crossover operator, so that two parents can be used to generate a small but representative set of sampling points as children.

In a similar way to classical crossover, two parents $\mathbf{p}_1$ and $\mathbf{p}_2$ are selected randomly from the population. Both $\mathbf{p}_1$ and $\mathbf{p}_2$ are divided into N genes i.e. $\mathbf{p}_1 = (p_{1,1}, p_{1,2}, \ldots, p_{1,N})$ and $\mathbf{p}_2 = (p_{2,1}, p_{2,2}, \ldots, p_{2,N})$. The lower and upper levels of the orthogonal design are defined as $\mathbf{Level(1)}$ and $\mathbf{Level(Q)}$ respectively, where

$\mathbf{Level(1)} = \left[\min(p_{1,1}, p_{2,1}), \min(p_{1,2}, p_{2,2}), \ldots \min(p_{1,N}, p_{2,N})\right]$ and

$\mathbf{Level(Q)} = \left[\max(p_{1,1}, p_{2,1}), \max(p_{1,2}, p_{2,2}), \ldots \max(p_{1,N}, p_{2,N})\right]$.

Q is the number of levels of the orthogonal design. We quantify each gene of $\mathbf{Level(1)}$ and $\mathbf{Level(Q)}$ into Q levels such that the difference between any two successive levels is the same. We denote the ith level to be $\mathbf{Level(i)} = [\beta_{i,1}, \beta_{i,2}, \ldots \beta_{i,N}]$, where i=1,2,…,Q. And $\beta_{i,j}$ is denoted as:

$$\beta_{i,j} = \begin{cases} \min(p_{1,i}, p_{2,i}) & \text{for } j = 1 \\ \min(p_{1,i}, p_{2,i}) + (j-1) \cdot \left(\dfrac{|p_{1,i} - p_{2,i}|}{Q-1} \right) & \text{for } 2 \le j \le Q-1 \\ \max(p_{1,i}, p_{2,i}) & \text{for } j = Q. \end{cases} \quad (1)$$

After quantifying $\mathbf{Level(1)}$ and $\mathbf{Level(Q)}$, we sample the Q levels into M potential offspring based on the combinations of the M rows of factor levels in orthogonal array $\mathbf{L_M(Q^N)}$. For $i = 1,2,\ldots M$, the ith offspring $\mathbf{o_i}$ is produced as $\mathbf{o_i} = [\beta_{a_1(i),1}, \beta_{a_2(i),2}, \ldots, \beta_{a_N(i),N}]$, where the combination of the ith row of $\mathbf{L_M(Q^N)}$ is denoted as $\mathbf{a(i)} = [a_1(i), a_2(i), \ldots, a_N(i)]$. Since $\mathbf{o}_1$ is equal to the first parent string $\mathbf{p_1}$, we evaluate the cost value f_i of each offspring $(\mathbf{o_i} \text{ for } i = 2,3,\ldots, M)$ according to the cost function; i.e. $f_i = fun(\mathbf{o_i})$, where $fun(\ )$ is denoted as the cost function. Then we select the two offspring with the smallest cost value to be the two children. In this approach, N-1 function evaluations are carried out in each operation.

For $i = 1,2,\ldots,M$, the ith offspring $\mathbf{o_i}$ are allocated according to the ith combination of the orthogonal array $\mathbf{L_M(Q^N)}$. N offspring have been produced meaning that M combinations are explored inside the orthogonal array $\mathbf{L_M(Q^N)}$. However, the total number of combinations of N genes with Q levels is N^Q. In this approach, only M combinations have been considered, so $N^Q - M$ combinations have not been explored through the operator. It may not be applicable for parametrical problem as the optimal combination may not be included in the orthogonal array.

Another factorial design method has also been used in the crossover operator [3]. We call this approach main effect orthogonal crossover (MC) in this paper. In this approach, the combinations, which are not included in the orthogonal array, are considered by main effect analysis. The children are formed from the best combinations of the genes with lowest main effect in minimization problem. Thus all the combinations are considered in this approach and it is more promising for parametric problem than orthogonal crossover on its own.

The main steps of MC are similar to those of OC. In OC, we select the two offspring with the smallest cost to be the two children after evaluating the cost value of each offspring $(o_i \text{ for } i = 1,2,\ldots M)$. In MC, we further analyze the cost values of each offspring and estimate the best combination of the genes in each offspring based on their main effect rather than selecting the two offspring with the smallest cost to be the two children.

For i=1,2,…,M, f_i is denoted to be the cost value of the ith offspring $\mathbf{o_i}$; i.e.: $f_i = fun(\mathbf{o_i})$, where $fun(\ )$ is the cost function. In other word, f_i represents as the function evaluation value of ith row in the orthogonal array. The main effect of the jth gene with level k is defined as:

$$S_{jk} = \frac{1}{Q}\sum_{i=1}^{N} f_i \cdot \left[\text{the level of the } i^{th} \text{ experiment of } j^{th} \text{ gene is } k\right] \quad (2)$$

where

$$\left[\text{condition}\right] = \begin{cases} 1 \text{ if the condition is true} \\ 0 \text{ otherwise.} \end{cases}$$

For a minimization problem, if the main effect of the jth gene is $S_{j1} > S_{j2}$, the level 2 of the jth gene is better than the level 1 of the jth gene on the contribution. Otherwise, level 1 is better. The first child is formed from the best combinations with the best level on each gene. Note that the main effect reveals the individual effect of a gene. The most effective gene has the largest main effect difference (MED). The main effect difference on the ith gene is denoted as:

$$MED_j = \left|\max(S_{ji}) - \min(S_{ji})\right|, \text{ for } i = 1,2,\ldots,M. \quad (3)$$

The second child is formed in a similar way to the first child except that the gene with the lowest main effect difference in the other level is chosen. It should be emphasized that main effect analysis is the simplest approach to data analysis. However, it is common for two of the genes to interact and yield a result that is more dependent upon the interaction effect of the two genes than on the main effect of either individual gene [8]. Based on experimental design methods, further analysis, which gives insights into interaction effect and main effect inside the chromosome, has been done by Reeves [8]. His central idea is to perform an 'Analysis of Variance', whereby the variability of the fitness value of the chromosome (measured by sums of squared deviations from mean fitness, and denoted by SS) is partitioned into main effect and interaction; i.e.:

$$\text{Total SS} = \text{Main effects SS} + \text{Interactions SS}$$

Based on this observation, the lack of provision for adequately dealing with potential interactions between the genes is a major weakness of MC. If a string exhibits very low interaction between the genes, it could probably be processed more efficiently by main effect analysis. Otherwise, the predicted optimal combination may not be reproducible if strong interaction exists between the genes. It is necessary to check the interaction effect between the genes. MC could be further improved, if the concept of interaction effect analysis is integrated into the operator.

4 Crossover Operation with Interaction Effect Analysis

We propose a new crossover operator called Interaction Effect Orthogonal Crossover (IC) which considers the interaction effect between the genes to extend the application of factorial design methods to improve the performance of the crossover operator in an evolutionary algorithm. The main steps of IC are similar to the MC. In MC, the children are formed by estimating the best combination of the genes based on the their main effect. In IC, we further analyze the interaction between the genes by performing interaction effect analysis. We use the approach of the interaction plot, which is commonly used to analyze interaction between factors in quality control in industry [10]. From the interaction plot [7], a clear picture of the interaction effect between the genes can be indicated.

To estimate the interaction effect between the ith and j^{th} gene, first we prepare an interaction response matrix, which can be expressed as:

$$\mathbf{I}_{ij} = \left[I_{ij}(m,n);\ \text{for } 1 \le m,n \le Q \right]_{QxQ}$$

where the Q rows and Q columns of $\mathbf{I}_{ij}$ corresponds to the Q levels of the ith gene and the Q levels of the jth gene respectively. $I_{ij}(m,n)$, which represents the interaction effect between the ith gene with level k_i and the jth gene with level k_j, is defined as:

$$I_{ij}(k_i,k_j) = \sum_{p=1}^{N} f_p \cdot \left[\text{the level of the } p^{th} \text{ experiment of } i^{th} \text{ gene } k_i \text{ and } j^{th} \text{ gene is } k_j\right]$$
$$\text{where } [\text{condition}] = \begin{cases} 1 \text{ if the condition is true} \\ 0 \text{ otherwise.} \end{cases} \tag{4}$$

Then we check whether the interaction between the ith and j^{th} gene is strong or not by using the approach of interaction plot [7]. The rth line of the interaction plot is defined as:

$$\mathbf{Line}_{ij}\ (\mathbf{r}) = \left[I_{ij}(1,r), I_{ij}(2,r), \ldots, I_{ij}(Q,r) \right];\ \text{for } 1 \le r \le Q$$

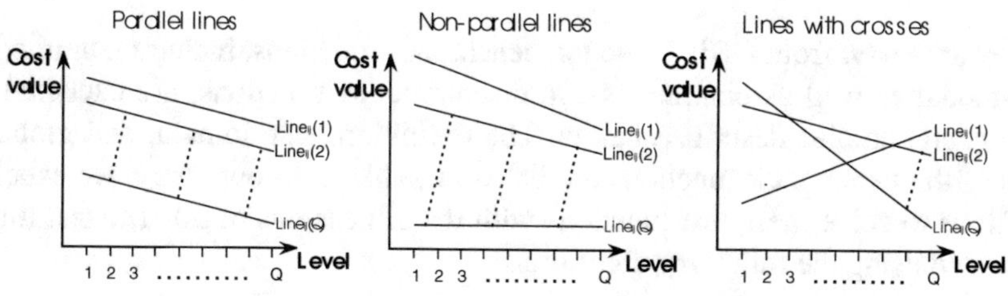

Fig. 1a. No interaction exists between the ith and j^{th} gene

Fig. 1b. Interaction occurs between the ith and j^{th} gene

Fig. 1c. Strong interaction occurs between the ith and j^{th} gene

If the lines on the interaction plots (as shown in Figure 1a) are parallel, no interaction exists between the ith and j^{th} gene. If the lines on the interaction plots are nonparallel (as shown in Figure 1b), interaction occurs and if the lines cross (as shown in Figure 1c), strong interaction occurs. Then, we rank the gene pair, which has parallel lines, non-parallel lines and lines crossing in the interaction plot, to have the lowest rank, higher rank and highest rank respectively.

When interaction exists between the ith and j^{th} gene, the two-gene level combination, which gives the lowest cost value, is chosen as the best. For example, $I_{ij}(1,2)$ is the average of cost corresponding to the ith gene at level 1 and the jth gene at level 2; $I_{ij}(2,1)$ is the average of cost corresponding to the ith gene at level 2 and the jth gene at level 1. For minimization problem, if $I_{ij}(1,2) > I_{ij}(2,1)$, the level 1 of the ith gene and level 2 of the jth gene is better than the level 2 of the ith gene and the level 1 of the jth gene on the contribution for the optimization problem.

If strong interaction does not exist, it is possible to separate out the main effect on each gene and the best combination can be formed by main effect analysis. If strong interaction does exist, the child is formed in two parts. The first part is the genes without strong interaction between each other and the second part is the genes carried strong interaction between each other. For the first part, the best combination is formed with the best main effect. For the second part, the best combination is formed by using the interaction effect analysis.

The procedures of the three crossover operators (OC, MC and IC) are summarized in Figure 2.

5 Numerical Experiments and Results

We execute the algorithms to solve the benchmark functions ($f_1 - f_{10}$) shown in Table 2.

They are taken from [13]. These ten benchmark functions, including unimodal and multi-modal as well as continuous and discontinuous functions, are executed in the experimental studies described below. The definition, test domain, and global optimums of the benchmark functions are listed in Table 2. In our study, we execute the algorithms to solve these test functions with the dimensions of 30. The test functions were tested using the following algorithms:

1) Orthogonal genetic algorithm (OGA): The basic process of OGA is similar to the classical genetic algorithm [2] except crossover utilizes the orthogonal crossover (OC) [5].
2) Main effect orthogonal genetic algorithm (MGA): The basic process of MGA is similar to the classical genetic algorithm except crossover utilizes the main effect orthogonal crossover (MC) [3].
3) Interaction effect orthogonal genetic algorithm (IGA): The basic process of IGA is similar to the classical genetic algorithm except crossover utilizes the interaction effect orthogonal crossover (IC), which has been discussed in Section 4.
4) Standard genetic algorithm (SGA): The basic process of SGA is similar to the classical genetic algorithm [2] except the crossover operator. In its crossover op-

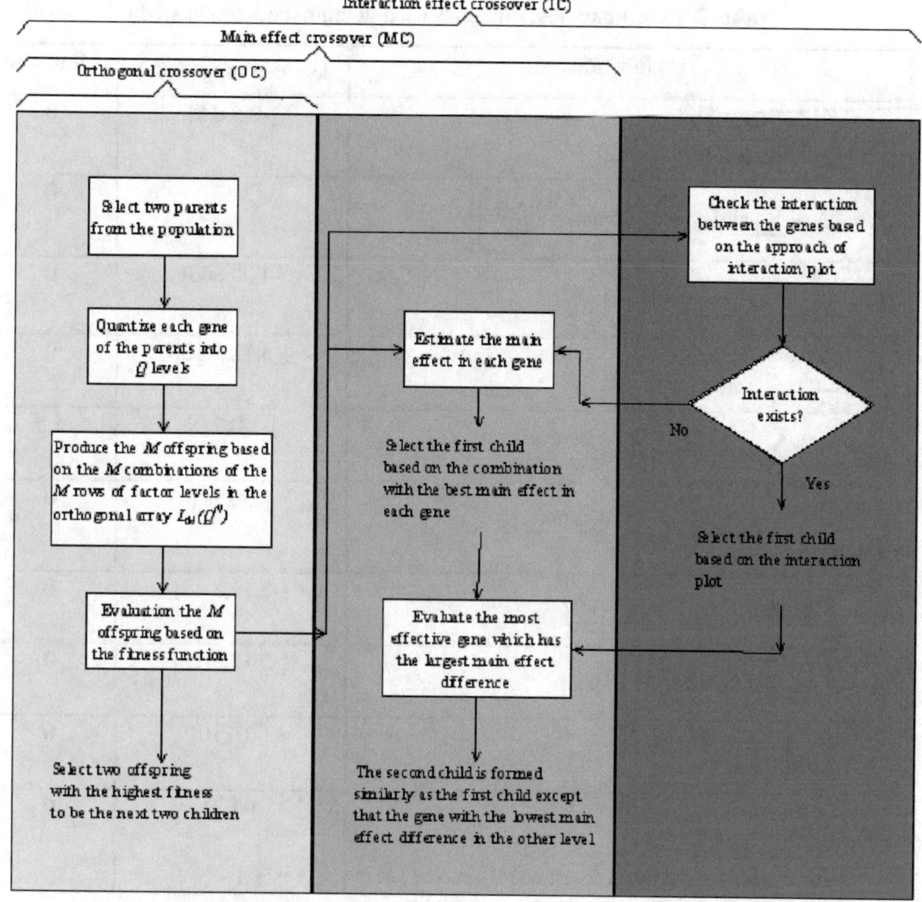

Fig. 2. A brief summary of procedures of OC, MC and IC

erator, we randomly select nine parents from the current generation, Then we perform 3-points crossover on the two best parents to generate two offspring for the next generation.

Orthogonal array $L_9(3^4)$ is used in the OC, MC and IC. We adopt the following parameter values or scheme. For the crossover rate, we choose 0.2 in OGA, MGA and IGA, and 1.0 in SGA. For the mutation rate, we choose 1/30 in all algorithms. For the number of generations, we choose 2000 in all algorithms. For the population size of OGA, MGA and IGA, we choose 200. For the population size of SGA, we choose 380 for fair comparison. Thus the total number function evaluations in all algorithms are the same. We performed 50 independent runs for each algorithm on each test function and recorded: 1) the mean best function value (i.e., the mean of the function values found in the 50 runs), 2) the standard deviation of the function values. Table 3 summarizes the results and the ranks of the mean best function value for all test functions using the different algorithms.

Table 2. Benchmark test functions used in our experimental study

Test functions	Domain range (x_i)	Minimum
$f_1 = \sum_{i=1}^{N} \left\| \frac{\sin(10x_i\pi)}{10x_i\pi} \right\|$	[-0.5,0.5]	0
$f_2 = 2N + \sum_{i=1}^{N-1} \left[\sin(x_i + x_{i+1}) + \sin\left(\frac{2x_i x_{i+1}}{3} \right) \right]$	[3,13]	0
$f_3 = \frac{1}{4000} \sum_{i=1}^{N} x_i^2 - \prod_{i=1}^{N} \cos\left(\frac{x_i}{\sqrt{i}} \right) + 1$	[-600,600]	0
$f_4 = \sum_{i=1}^{N} x_i^2$	[-5.12,5.12]	0
$f_5 = 2N - \sum_{i=1}^{N} [x_i \sin(10\pi x_i)]$	[-1.0,2.0]	4.5
$f_6 = 20 + e - 20e^{-0.2\sqrt{\frac{\sum_{i=1}^{N} x_i^2}{N}}} - e^{\sum_{i=1}^{N} \frac{\cos(20\pi x_i)}{N}}$	[-30,30]	0
$f_7 = \sum_{i=1}^{N-1} \left[100(x_{i+1} - x_i^2)^2 + (x_i - 1)^2 \right]$	[-5.12,5.12]	0
$f_8 = \sum_{i=1}^{N} \left[x_i^2 - 10\cos(2\pi x_i) + 10 \right]$	[-5.12,5.12]	0
$f_9 = \sum_{i=1}^{N} \|x_i\| + \prod_{i=1}^{N} \|x_i\|$	[-10,10]	0
$f_{10} = \sum_{i=1}^{N} r_i x_i^2$ where r_i is a randomly shuffled integer between 1 to N.	[-1,1]	0

We can see from Table 3 that IGA outperforms the other algorithms on the ten benchmark functions. MGA is better than OGA, which is better than SGA. However, it is very hard to evaluate how well the proposed algorithm IGA outperforms the others. We employ the t-test to assess whether the performance of the algorithm are statistically different from others. Table 4 shows the t-value between IGA on the one hand and OGA, MGA and SGA on the other. We can see from Table 4 that IGA is significantly better than OGA in all ten benchmark functions. It is also significantly better than SGA on all ten benchmark functions except f_1. The performances of both algorithms are the same in f_1. In general, we can conclude that IGA is significantly better than OGA and SGA.

We can see from Table 4 that the performance of IGA is significantly better than that of MGA in f_2, f_3, f_7 and f_9. The benchmark functions can be divided into two classes – separable function and non-separable function. For separable function, like f_1, f_4, f_5, f_6, f_8 and f_{10}, the optimal value for each parameter can be determined independently of all other parameters. It can be decomposed into a linear combination of independent sub-functions. For example, a separable function can be expressed as:

Table 3. Comparison between the algorithms on $f_1 - f_{10}$. The results are averaged over 50 runs. 'Mean Best' indicates the mean best function values found in algorithm. 'Std. Dev.' stands for the standard deviation. 'Rank' represents the rank of the mean best function for the algorithms

Test fun.	SGA		OGA		MGA		IGA	
	mean best (std. dev.)	rank	mean best (std. dev.)	rank	mean best (std. dev.)	rank	mean best (std. dev.)	rank
f_1	1.1695e-5 (5.9765e-61)	1	1.2346e-7 (0.3706e-6)	2	1.1695e-15 (5.9765e-31)	1	1.1695e-15 (5.9765e-31)	1
f_2	11.4379 (1.6682)	4	9.9545 (1.3819)	3	9.7185 (1.3466)	2	9.2823 (1.5890)	1
f_3	3.6298e-2 (2.3554e-2)	3	1.6071e-1 (9.2195e-3)	4	2.5579e-2 (2.7997e-4)	2	2.3410e-2 (3.1301e-4)	1
f_4	2.6331e-5 (2.1242e-5)	4	2.5156e-4 (0.1307e-3)	3	1.8652e-6 (2.0298e-6)	2	1.7246e-6 (2.0380e-6)	1
f_5	10.0526 (1.7231)	3	12.2229 (1.6369)	4	8.1280 (1.2438)	2	7.9584 (1.3503)	1
f_6	2.6344e-2 (1.7988e-2)	4	2.6142e-2 6.4883e-3	3	3.3567e-3 (2.4818e-3)	2	2.8256e-3 (1.4289e-3)	1
f_7	1000.5020 (6.1062)	4	30.9190 (3.3334)	2	31.9761 (3.7992)	3	28.1299 (2.8437)	1
f_8	27.0152 (6.3197)	4	11.2942 (4.1570)	3	10.7239 (2.9388)	2	9.8174 (2.9264)	1
f_9	1.2425e-2 (5.6384e-3)	3	2.1123e-2 (7.3232e-3)	4	1.0182e-3 (7.428e-4)	2	7.5812e-4 (5.0251e-4)	1
f_{10}	1.7673e-2 (6.0468e-3)	3	4.6557e-2 (1.7254e-4)	4	1.5867e-3 (4.5988e-4)	2	1.5434e-3 (5.4753e-4)	1
ave. ranks	3.3		3.2		1.9		1	
Final ranks	4		3		2		1	

Table 4. The t-value between IGA to OGA, MGA and SGA

Test functions	IGA to OGA	IGA to MGA	IGA to SGA
f_1	2.3309^{+}	0	0
f_2	2.2343^{+}	1.4659^{++}	6.5495^{+}
f_3	2.0335^{+}	1.5300^{++}	17.2858^{+}
f_4	13.3721^{+}	0.3422	8.0717^{+}
f_5	14.0692^{+}	0.6468	6.6966^{+}
f_6	24.4224^{+}	0.8876	9.0598^{+}
f_7	1.4207^{+}	1.6273^{+}	13.2784^{+}
f_8	9.8513^{+}	0.3409	2.2799^{+}
f_9	19.4162^{+}	1.9640^{+}	14.3888^{+}
f_{10}	23.9626^{+}	0.2790	18.6249^{+}

$^{+}$ The value of t with 49 degree of freedom is significant at $\alpha = 0.05$ by a two tailed test

$^{++}$ The value of t with 49 degree of freedom is significant at $\alpha = 0.075$ by a two tailed test

$$F(x_1, x_2, ..., x_n) = \sum_{i=1}^{n} S_i(x_i)$$

where $S_i()$ is defined to be the n separate sub-functions. Each subspace can be completely enumerated, thereby avoiding local optima. This characteristic often allows stochastic search methods to move the search into the basin of attraction of the global optimum of that sub-function. That kind of functions may produce misleading results and may lead experimental researchers to draw dubious conclusions about the relative merits of various types of evolutionary algorithm [11]. For non-separate functions, like f_2, f_3, f_7 and f_9, they cannot be decomposed into a linear combinations of independent sub-functions since the variables are interacting with each other. Each variable is interacting with each other one and cannot be enumerated completely.

Due to the strong interaction among variables of functions, f_2, f_3, f_7 and f_9, the performance of MGA is significantly poorer than that of IGA. It demonstrates that the lack of provision for adequately dealing with potential interactions between the genes is a major weakness of MGA. If the function carries a very low interaction between the variables such as f_1, f_4, f_5, f_6, f_8 and f_{10}, the performances MGA and IGA are not significantly different.

Recalling that the steps of the three algorithms are similar, except that they use different crossover operator. In OGA, the crossover operation is integrated with orthogonal design. In MGA and IGA, the crossover operation is integrated with main effect analysis and interaction effect analysis. These results indicate that IGA can give better mean solution quality than OGA. In addition, IGA outperform MGA when the function carries high interaction between the variables. These results indicate that interaction effect analysis can improve the crossover operator.

6 Conclusion

In this paper, a new crossover operator (IC) using experimental design methods is presented. The principle of IC is to consider the contribution of main effect in each individual gene and interaction effect between genes. It compensates for the potential drawbacks of the existing operators, which ignore the interaction effect between the genes. A set of GA benchmark functions has been employed to compare the performance of the proposed operator with the existing operators - standard crossover, orthogonal crossover (OC) and main effect orthogonal crossover (MC). It is shown empirically that the proposed IC outperforms the standard crossover and OC on all benchmark functions. Furthermore, the proposed IC outperforms all the tested operators for solving parametrical problem with high interaction effect between the variables. For further investigation, we will further evaluate the performance of our proposed operator by solving the problems that have high epistasis between the genes.

Acknowledgment

The authors sincerely thank James Werner for his helpful comments and his suggestions on improving the presentation for this paper.

References

1. G.E.P. Box, W.G. Hunter, J.S. Hunter, *Statistics for Experimenters*. John Wiley, 1978.
2. D.E. Goldberg, *Genetic Algorithms in Search, Optimization and Machine Learning*. United States of America: Addison Wesley Longman, Inc, 1989.
3. S.Y. Ho, L.S. Shu, H.M. Chen, Intelligent genetic algorithm with a new intelligent crossover using orthogonal arrays. *Proceedings of the Genetic and Evolutionary Computation Conference*, vol. 1, pp. 289-296, 1999.
4. S.Y. Ho, H.M. Chen, A GA-based systematic reasoning approach for solving traveling salesman problems using an orthogonal array crossover, *Proceeding of the Fourth International Conference on High Performance Computing in the Asia Pacific Region*, vol. 2, pp. 659-663, 2000.
5. Y.W. Leung, Y. Wang, An orthogonal genetic algorithm with quantization for global numerical optimization. *IEEE Transactions on Evolutionary Computation*, vol. 5, No. 1, pp. 41-53, 2001.
6. D.C. Montgomery, *Design and Analysis of Experiments*. New York: John Wiley and Sons, Inc, 1997.
7. M.S. Phadke, *Quality engineering using robust design*. New York: Prentice Hall, 1987.
8. C.R. Reeves, C.C. Wright, Epistasis in Genetic Algorithms: An Experimental Design Perspective. *Proceedings of the 6th International Conference on Genetic Algorithms*, pp. 217-224, 1995.
9. G. Taguchi, S. Konishi, *Orthogonal Arrays and Linear Graphs*. Dearbon, MI: American Supplier Institute, 1987.
10. R. Unal, D.O. Stanley, C.R. Joyner, Propulsion system design optimization using the Taguchi Method. *IEEE Transactions on Engineering Management*, vol. 40, no. 3, pp. 315-322, August 1993.
11. D. Whitley, K. Mathias, S. Rana and J. Dzubera, Building better test function, *Proceedings of the 6th International Conference on Genetic Algorithms*, pp. 239-246, 1995.
12. Q. Zhang, Y.W. Leung, An orthogonal genetic algorithm for multimedia multicast routing. *IEEE Transactions on Evolutionary Computation*, Vol. 3, No. 1, pp. 53-62, 1999.
13. X. Yao, Y. Lin and G. Lin, Evolutionary programming made faster, *IEEE Transactions on Evolutionary Computation*, Vol. 3, No. 2, pp. 82-102, 1999.

Overfitting or Poor Learning: A Critique of Current Financial Applications of GP

Shu-Heng Chen and Tzu-Wen Kuo

AI-ECON Research Center, Department of Economics
National Chengchi University, Taipei, Taiwan 11623
chchen@nccu.edu.tw, kuo@aiecon.org

Abstract. Motivated by a measure of predictability, this paper uses the extracted signal ratio as a measure of the degree of overfitting. With this measure, we examine the performance of one type of overfitting-avoidance design frequently used in financial applications of GP. Based on the simulation results run with the software Simple GP, we find that this design is not effective in avoiding overfitting. Furthermore, within the range of search intensity typically considered by these applications, we find that underfitting, instead of overfitting, is the more prevalent problem. This problem becomes more serious when the data is generated by a process that has a high degree of algorithmic complexity. This paper, therefore, casts doubt on the conclusions made by those early applications regarding the poor performance of GP, and recommends that changes be made to ensure progress.

1 Motivation and Introduction

Overfitting is one of the most intensively addressed issues in data mining ([2], [6], [8], [9], [14]). A great many techniques have been developed over the past decade, and some of these techniques have also been applied to the financial applications of genetic programming ([4]). For example, the use of *cross-validation* now seems to have become a standard procedure followed by many financial GP users. This has become particularly so following a series of prestigious journal publications that have recommended this way of preventing overfitting ([1], [10], [11], and [16]). By this procedure, one run of GP uses two time periods. The first period is called the *training period* and is used to train the genetic programs. The second period is referred to as the *selection period*, which is used to select the best performing programs and decide when to stop the training. For example, in [10], the termination criterion is achieved if no new best rule appears for 25 generations.

As opposed to the problem of overfitting, *poor learning* (*underfitting*) has received much less attention. The asymmetry seems to be natural. Given the rich expressive power of the heavy data-mining machinery, people tend to believe that they may easily abuse the power if caution is not well taken. Validation is a classical tool for resolving this issue and has also become one of the common overfitting-avoidance designs ([15]). This validation scheme has been used as if

C. Ryan et al. (Eds.): EuroGP 2003, LNCS 2610, pp. 34–46, 2003.

it will make learning stop at a right moment, no more (overfitting) and no less (underfitting). However, *is that really so*? It may not surprise us if this scheme fails to avoid overfitting, as already suggested by some empirical studies ([12]). Nonetheless, it may surprise us if we are told that this design can also result in underfitting.

In this paper, we shall show that underfitting can occur mainly due to our ignorance of the extremely large search space extended by the primitives of GP. Coming with this ignorance is the causal design of search intensity, e.g., a causal combination of the population size and the number of generations. Little attention has been paid to whether the resultant search intensity is good enough. Under such circumstances, worrying about abusing the expressive power of GP may be a little far-fetched, and adding a validation scheme may make things even worse.

To show this, we introduce a technical notion of overfitting based on the *signal ratio*. Then, by artificially generating time-series data with different signal ratios and different *algorithmic complexity* (*node complexity*), we test how likely it is that a standard GP may overfit the data. We first start the experiments (Experiment Series 1) without imposing any overfitting-avoidance design, and then examine how serious is the overfitting problem that may arise. In this series of experiments, we find that even with a moderate degree of search intensity, overfitting is in effect not a serious problem. On the contrary, for most of the cases, the real concern is underfitting. In another series of experiments (Experiment Series 3), we heighten the search intensity by doubling the population size. As one may expect, this will result in the problem of overfitting becoming more likely to appear. That is true. Nevertheless, our results show that what bothers us more is still the problem of underfitting. Given this situation, introducing an overfitting-avoidance design can do more harm than good. The last point is exactly what we show in the other two series of experiments (Experiment Series 2 and 4).

The rest of the paper is organized as follows. Section 2 proposes a technical and practical notion of overfitting. Section 3 gives the details of the experimental designs. Section 4 presents the simulation results with accompanying discussions, and is followed by the concluding remarks in Section 5.

2 Signal Ratio and Overfitting

Motivated by [7], we apply the *signal ratio* as a measure of overfitting. The idea is straightforward. Consider a series $\{y_t\}$. Its signal-noise orthogonal decomposition can be written as

$$y_t = x_t + \epsilon_t, \tag{1}$$

where the *signal* x_t follows a deterministic process, whereas the noise ϵ_t is an identically independently distributed process with a mean zero and a variance σ_ϵ^2. The variance decomposition of y_t can then be written as follows.

$$\sigma_y^2 = \sigma_x^2 + \sigma_\epsilon^2, \tag{2}$$

where σ_y^2 is the variance of y_t. However, rigorously speaking, σ_x^2 is not the variance of x_t, since by the signal we mean that x_t is not random but deterministic. Therefore, σ_x^2 should be interpreted as the *fluctuation* of an ensemble of the deterministic process of $\{x_t\}$ [1]. With the decomposition (2), the *signal ratio*, denoted by θ, is defined as

$$\theta = \frac{\sigma_x^2}{\sigma_y^2} = 1 - \frac{\sigma_\epsilon^2}{\sigma_y^2}. \tag{3}$$

With this definition of the signal ratio, the problem of *overfitting* can then be stated as follows. Let $\hat{y}_t$ be the signal extracted by a machine learning tool, say, GP. Then we say that the problem of overfitting is detected if

$$\hat{\theta} = \frac{\sigma_{\hat{y}}^2}{\sigma_y^2} > \theta. \tag{4}$$

In other words, overfitting is detected if the information (signal) extracted by GP is even greater than the maximum information which we actually have from y_t. When Equation (4) is satisfied, this means that GP has learned more than it should and, as a result, has started to mistake noise as a signal. Similarly, if the inequality is turned the other way around, i.e. $\hat{\theta} < \theta$, then we say that GP has not learned enough so that some information is left unexploited. Contrary to the case of overfitting, here we encounter the problem of *underfitting*.

3 Experimental Designs

3.1 Data

Based on the notion of overfitting discussed in Section 2, we propose the following data-generation mechanism. First, we start with the generation process for signals, $\{x_t\}$. [3] examined the predictability of the chaotic time series with GP. The three chaotic time series considered by them are

$$x_t = f(x_{t-1}) = 4x_{t-1}(1 - x_{t-1}), \quad x_0 \in [0,1], \tag{5}$$

$$x_t = f(x_{t-1}) = 4x_{t-1}^3 - 3x_{t-1}, \quad x_0 \in [-1,1], \tag{6}$$

and

$$x_t = f(x_{t-1}) = 8x_{t-1}^4 - 8x_{t-1}^2 + 1, \quad x_0 \in [-1,1]. \tag{7}$$

We choose these three chaotic time series as the signal generation processes. Since neither can we control the signal ratio nor can we know the true signal ratio in real financial time series, the test proposed in this paper will be conducted by using only these deterministic chaotic series. Certainly, as the title of the paper suggests, to be a genuine critique of current financial applications, we shall extend our tests to real financial data in the future.

[1] We shall be more specific on this when we come to the design of the experiments.

These three laws of motion are different in terms of their *algorithmic size*, i.e. the *length* of their symbolic expression. To see this, we rewrite each of the equations above into the corresponding LISP S-expression:

$$(* (4 * (x_t (- 1 x_t)))) \tag{8}$$

$$(- (* 4 (* x_t (* x_t x_t))) (* 3 x_t)) \tag{9}$$

$$\begin{array}{l}(+ (- (* 8 (* x_t (* x_t (* x_t x_t)))) \\ (* 8 (* x_t x_t))) 1)\end{array} \tag{10}$$

The *length* of a LISP S–expression is determined by counting from the leftmost to the rightmost position the number of elements (atoms) in the string that makes up the S–expression. From Eqs. (8) to (10), the lengths of the LISP S-expression are 7, 11, and 17, respectively. Therefore, in terms of algorithmic complexity, Eq. (5) is the simplest, while Eq. (7) is the most complex expression.

In addition to the signal, an *i.i.d.* noise is added to obscure the observation series $\{y_t\}$.

$$y_t = x_t + \epsilon_t = f(x_{t-1}) + \epsilon_t. \tag{11}$$

GP is applied to fit the hidden relationship between y_t and x_{t-1}, and the predicted value of y_t is

$$\hat{y}_t = \hat{f}(x_{t-1}). \tag{12}$$

Based on Equation (3), different signal ratios can be derived by manipulating σ_ϵ^2. In this study, we consider five values of θ, ranging from a very high noise ratio $\theta = 0.05$, to 0.15, 0.25, and 0.35, and to a high signal ratio of 0.5. Therefore, a total of 15 different time series of $\{y_t\}$ are generated from the signal series depicted in Eqs. (5) to (7) with five different values of θ.

3.2 Genetic Programming

The genetic programming software used in this paper is **Simple GP**, developed by the AI-ECON Research Center[2]. All of the main GP control parameters can be set by directly inputting the values into the main menu, shown in Figure 1[3].

The validation scheme, used in [1], [10], [11], and [16], is incorporated into **Simple GP**. This can be seen from Figure 2. In the top half of the menu, there is a place for users to indicate whether they wish to impose the validation scheme as an early termination criterion. This can be done by simply answering how many pieces of the data are to be divided (the first box, Figure 2) and by showing how these pieces of data are to be distributed to be used for training, validating, and testing. In the example in Figure 2, [3]-(1,1,1) states that the data are to be divided into three equal parts, and that the first part will be used

[2] Some detailed descriptions of it can be found in [5].

[3] The purpose of indicating this software is mainly for those interested readers who would like to replicate or validate the results obtained in this paper.

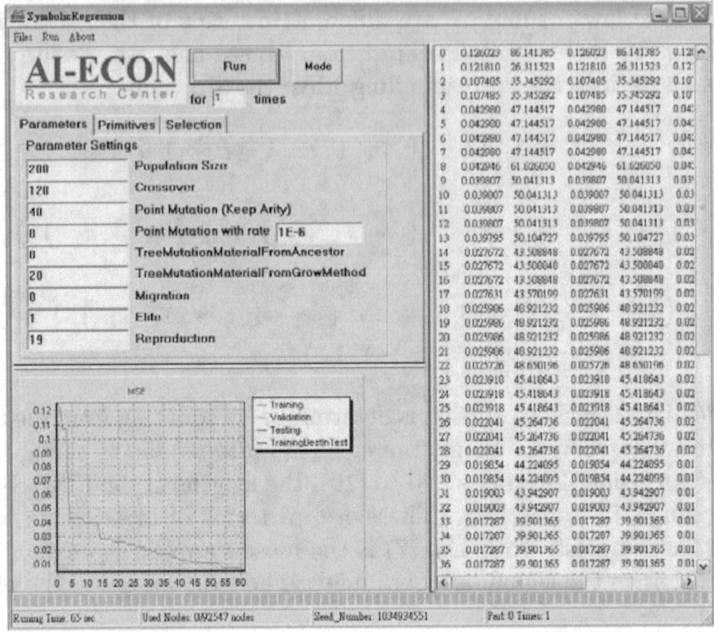

Fig. 1. Simple GP: Main Menu 1

for training, the second for validation, and the third for testing. By inserting a zero number into the validation place, one can in effect turn off the validation scheme. For example, [1]-(1,0,0) means that there is only one training set. This specification is exactly what we were faced with when doing the first and the third series of experiments, while for the second and fourth series of experiments the validation scheme is added.

The steps involved in **Simple GP** are detailed as follows:

1. Create an initial generation of *Pop* random forecasting models using the *ramp-half-and-half* method.
2. Measure the fitness of each model over the *training set* and rank according to fitness.
3. Select the top-ranked k models and calculate its fitness over the validation set. Save it as the initial best k models.
4. Implement all genetic operators in the standard way, and a new generation of models will be born.
5. Measure the fitness of each model in the new generation over the training set. The best k models are selected, and their fitness over the *validation set* is calculated and compared with that of the previously saved best k models. Then a $(k+k)$-selection scheme is applied to select the best k models, and they are saved as the *new* best k models.
6. Stop if none of these best k models are replaced for g generations, or after *Gen* generations. Otherwise, return to step 4.

Step 5 is the validation scheme used in [1], [10], [11], and [16].

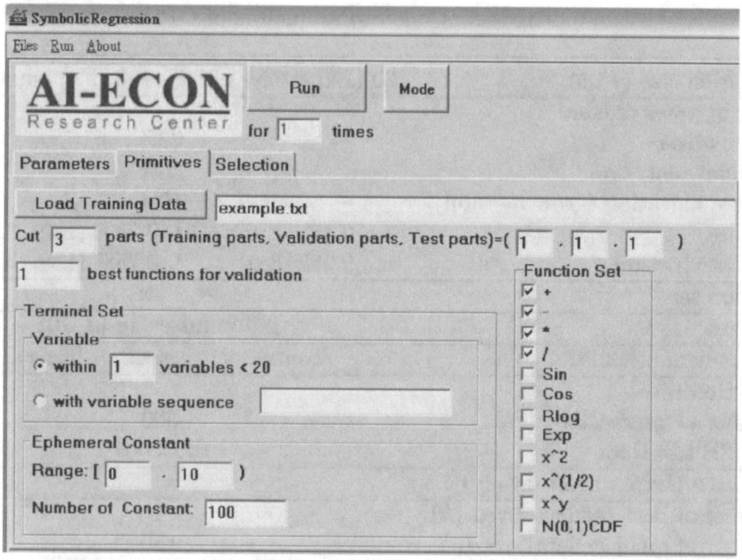

Fig. 2. Simple GP: Main Menu 2

Four series of experiments were conducted. Experiments 1 and 3 did not include the validation scheme. They differed in search intensity characterized by population size. The one set in Experiment Series 1 was 200, and the one set in Experiment Series 3 was 400. Validation was involved in Experiments 2 and 4. In each series of experiments, a hundred runs of GP were implemented for each chaotic time series with each of the five signal ratios. In other words, there were in total 1,500 (=15 $\times$ 100) independent runs conducted in each series of experiments. The values of the control parameters are summarized in Table 1.

4 Results

One interesting thing to observe is whether overfitting can easily appear when validation is not imposed (Experiment Series 1). To see this we average the $\hat{\theta}$ obtained from 100 runs, called $\bar{\theta}$. They are reported in the first block of Table 2. Since we have 100 runs (a large sample), $\bar{\theta}$ can be regarded as a reasonable estimate of the corresponding *population* "signal ratio", extracted by GP, referred to as θ^*. Furthermore, by applying the central limit theorem, one can decide whether there is either overfitting or underfitting by testing the following null hypothesis:

$$H_0 : \theta^* = \theta. \tag{13}$$

GP correctly extracts what it is supposed to extract if the null fails to be rejected; otherwise overfitting is found if $\theta^* > \theta$ significantly or underfitting is found if $\theta^* < \theta$ significantly. In Table 2, immediately below $\bar{\theta}$, is the test statistic, which is followed by the *p-value*.

Table 1. Control Parameters of GP

Population size (*Pop*)	200 (Experiment 1, 2), 400 (Experiment 3, 4)
Offspring trees created	
by crossover	60%
by point mutation	20%
by tree mutation (grow method)	10%
by elite	0.5% (Exp. 1, 2), 0.25% (Exp. 3, 4)
by reproduction	9.5% (Exp. 1, 2), 9.75% (Exp. 3, 4)
Function set	$+, -, \times, \div$
Constant	100 numbers in [0, 10)
Replacement scheme	Tournament selection (size=2)
Stop criterion	
number of generations (*Gen*)	300
or MSE less than	0.000001
Validation (Experiment 3 only)	
number of best models saved (k)	1
number of quiet generations (g)	150

From these results, we can see that the null is rejected in 13 out of the 15 designs. Of the 13 cases, only one design (the design with Eq. 5 and $\theta = 0.05$) is proved to be an example of overfitting, and all others belong to the case of underfitting. It is then obvious that *overfitting turns out not to be a serious issue even though the validation design is not imposed.* Here, what concerns us more is just the opposite, i.e. the issue of underfitting. This result is particularly striking since the search intensity ($Pop = 200, Gen = 300$) is by no means low as opposed to most financial applications of GP[4].

In this case, if one just follows convention ([1], [10], [11], and [16]) and adds a validation step (Experiment Series 2), what will happen? Basically, nothing changes, and we benefit little from this setting. First, the validation step is an overfitting-avoidance design, and is therefore not supposed to solve the problem of underfitting. The second block in Table 2 confirms this: those 13 designs that were shown to be underfitting in Experiment 1, remain the same in Experiment 2. Second, as for the design in which overfitting is detected, imposing validation does not help either: it remains overfitting, while the over-extracted signal ratio declines from 0.0849 to 0.0808.

The evidence presented so far raises two questions. First, when shall we expect the problem of overfitting to appear? Second, is validation an effective overfitting-avoidance design? The next two series of experiments are designed to address these two questions. In Experiment 3, search intensity was enhanced by increasing the population size from 200 to 400 (Table 1). Would this more intensive search lead to a higher risk of overfitting? The third block in Table 2 seems to suggest so. Out of the 15 designs, which have the same settings

[4] For example, the population size set in [10], [11] and [16] is just 100, and the number of generations is also just 100.

Table 2. Simulation Results

Exp \ θ			0.05	0.15	0.25	0.35	0.5
1	eq1	$\bar{\theta}$	0.0849	0.1413	0.2560	0.3091	0.4191
		z	11.9532	-1.5340	0.7095	-3.5711	-5.0880
		p	0.0000	0.0625	0.2390	0.0002	0.0000
	eq2	$\bar{\theta}$	0.0352	0.1386	0.2323	0.3029	0.3998
		z	-12.5330	-3.0916	-2.9883	-5.3213	-9.6061
		p	0.0000	0.0010	0.0014	0.0000	0.0000
	eq3	$\bar{\theta}$	0.0438	0.0868	0.1760	0.1850	0.2947
		z	-3.5610	-15.2165	-11.3537	-20.4669	-18.8052
		p	0.0002	0.0000	0.0000	0.0000	0.0000
2	eq1	$\bar{\theta}$	0.0808	0.1411	0.2450	0.2893	0.3821
		z	10.1044	-1.5189	-0.4152	-4.9791	-5.7578
		p	0.0000	0.0644	0.3390	0.0000	0.0000
	eq2	$\bar{\theta}$	0.0301	0.1348	0.2298	0.3119	0.4156
		z	-16.4007	-4.0032	-3.5421	-4.5439	-8.7157
		p	0.0000	0.0000	0.0002	0.0000	0.0000
	eq3	$\bar{\theta}$	0.0425	0.0853	0.1758	0.1988	0.2866
		z	-4.1114	-15.5164	-12.7027	-16.9850	-18.7969
		p	0.0000	0.0000	0.0002	0.0000	0.0000
3	eq1	$\bar{\theta}$	0.0944	0.1587	0.2829	0.3332	0.4801
		z	20.0965	2.3321	6.4594	-2.2650	-1.5415
		p	0.0000	0.0098	0.0000	0.0118	0.0616
	eq2	$\bar{\theta}$	0.0407	0.1476	0.2559	0.3458	0.4317
		z	-7.7766	-0.7945	1.2601	-0.6809	-7.5529
		p	0.0000	0.2134	0.1038	0.2480	0.0000
	eq3	$\bar{\theta}$	0.0520	0.1056	0.1843	0.2346	0.3398
		z	1.2838	-10.8656	-10.1204	-14.3101	-14.1068
		p	0.0996	0.0000	0.0002	0.0000	0.0000
4	eq1	$\bar{\theta}$	0.0902	0.1588	0.2758	0.3219	0.4842
		z	19.8840	2.2404	4.8728	-3.0996	-1.1045
		p	0.0000	0.0125	0.0000	0.0010	0.1347
	eq2	$\bar{\theta}$	0.0345	0.1546	0.2514	0.3388	0.4471
		z	-11.2780	1.9955	0.2991	-1.6719	-6.1439
		p	0.0000	0.0230	0.1912	0.0473	0.0000
	eq3	$\bar{\theta}$	0.0477	0.1053	0.1836	0.2250	0.3267
		z	-1.2219	-11.0175	-10.0111	-15.6075	-14.7593
		p	0.1109	0.0000	0.0000	0.0000	0.0000

$\bar{\theta}$ denotes the sample average of $\hat{\theta}$ (extracted signal ratio) over 100 runs. z refers to the test statistic derived from the central limit theorem. p is the p-value of the associated test statistic that is more extreme in the direction of the alternative hypothesis ($\theta^* \neq \theta$) when H_0 is true.

as those in Experiment 1 except for population size, the number of overfitting cases increases from one to three. The evidence based on the designs that use Equation (5) and where $\theta = 0.05$, 0.15 and 0.25 is now in favor of overfitting. Equally interesting is that the null of just fitting (Equation 13) has now failed to be rejected in five of the designs, a jump from the original two.

Nevertheless, what seems to be most disappointing is that the majority of them (7 out of 15) still exhibit the feature of underfitting. If we look at the distribution of these seven designs, most of them, four out of the seven, come from the one using Equation (7), which is the one with the highest degree of algorithmic complexity (node complexity) ([3]). This finding is very plausible. As analyzed by [5], laws of motion with a higher degree of algorithmic complexity generally require more intensive searches than those with less complexity. As a result, such a design is less likely to abuse the power of curve fitting when the data is generated by a process with a high degree of algorithmic complexity.

Since the risk of overfitting increases with search intensity, it is crucial to know how effectively an overfitting design can ameliorate the situation. Therefore, in Experiment 4, we add back the validation design as we did in Experiment 2, and test its performance. The results are shown in the last block in Table 2. Our attention is particularly drawn to the design where the problem of overfitting is found, i.e. the three designs mentioned before. Unfortunately, from Table 2, we can see that the problem of overfitting remains in all of these three designs. In two of the three cases, we do see the decrease in the extracted signal ratio, one in its decreasing from 0.0944 to 0.0902, and the other in its falling from 0.2829 to 0.2758. However, these changes are not enough given that the true signal ratios θ are just only 0.05 and 0.25, respectively. Furthermore, it is interesting to notice that in one case the problem even gets worse, i.e. the design using Equation (6) where $\theta = 0.15$. In that case, originally, GP extracted a signal ratio with $\bar{\theta} = 0.1476$, which is significantly below the threshold $\theta = 0.15$. However, when the validation design is imposed, the extracted signal ratio goes significantly beyond 0.15 to 0.1546; and hence exhibits the feature of overfitting.

5 Two Further Tests

In addition to the test of the null (13), we also carried out two examinations pertaining to the effect of *search density* and *validation* upon the degree of fitting (the signal ratio extracted by GP). We first conducted a statistical test for the hypothesis that *intensifying search shall increase the degree of fitting.* Let θ_i^* be the population signal ratio extracted by GP under Experiment Series i ($i = 1, 2, 3, 4$). The effect of search density can be analyzed by testing the null

$$\theta_1^* = \theta_3^*, \tag{14}$$

and

$$\theta_2^* = \theta_4^*, \tag{15}$$

separately. (14) is the null of equal fitting when validation is not imposed, whereas (15) is the null of equal fitting when validation is imposed. If these two null hypotheses fail to be rejected, then intensifying search intensity has little effect on the degree of fitting. As before, the large sample theorem is applied to these two tests. The test results of the null (14) and (15) are shown in the first and second block of Table 3 respectively. Form the corresponding Z statistics, the number of rejections is very high for both tests, if one takes the usual critical region $\mid Z \mid > Z_{0.025} = 1.96$.

In the first block of Table 3 , θ_3^* is bigger than θ_1^* in all of the fifteen cases, and the null (14) is rejected at a total of twelve times. In the second block of the Table, θ_4^* is also bigger than θ_2^* in all of the fifteen cases, and the null (15) has failed to be rejected only in one case. *As a result, it is quite evident that search intensity has a positive effect on the degree of fitting, and hence will contribute to a risk of overfitting.*

We then turn to see the effect of validation on the degree of overfitting. The two null hypotheses to test are

$$\theta_1^* = \theta_2^*, \tag{16}$$

and

$$\theta_3^* = \theta_4^*. \tag{17}$$

The test results are reported in the third and the fourth block of Table 3. For both tests, the null of equal fitting has failed to be rejected in only one out of the fifteen cases, if the same critical region is applied. Therefore, even though numerically θ_1 (θ_3) has a larger degree of fitting than θ_2 (θ_4), the difference is statistically negligible. *This finding may surprise many of us, who believe that validation shall help to avoid overfitting.*

One possible explanation for this seemingly surprising finding is as follows. When the algorithmic complexity associated with the problem is high, the desired termination point may be farther than what our designated search density may reach. In this case, the termination condition set by the validation design will rarely be met. Hence, using or not using the validation design would not make much difference. This explanation may apply to the cases of Equations (6) and (7) where the problem of underfitting is severe. However, it remains to be a puzzle why the design also failed to work for the case of Equation (5)[5].

6 Conclusion: Implications for Financial Applications

For most financial engineers, financial data are usually assumed to be *highly complex* (nonlinear) but also *informative.* The first assumption implies that the algorithmic complexity of the data generation process can be quite high, whereas the second assumption indicates a moderate level for the signal ratio. If these two properties are correct, then our simulation results seem to suggest that the problem of and the caution associated with overfitting may be exaggerated given the usual search intensity frequently set in many financial applications of GP. In this case, adding a validation design may actually make the hidden information in

[5] One conjecture is that the validation parameter g (see Table 1) may not be set appropriately. One of our next studies is to examine the role of this parameter.

Table 3. Significance of Search Intensity and Validation

Null \ θ			0.05	0.15	0.25	0.35	0.5
$\theta_1^* = \theta_3^*$	eq1	θ_1^*	0.0849	0.1413	0.2560	0.3091	0.4191
		θ_3^*	0.0944	0.1587	0.2829	0.3332	0.4801
		z	2.5983	2.5624	2.7387	1.7624	2.9742
	eq2	θ_1^*	0.0352	0.1386	0.2323	0.3029	0.3998
		θ_3^*	0.0407	0.1476	0.2559	0.3458	0.4317
		z	3.2509	1.8926	3.1265	3.9871	2.3133
	eq3	θ_1^*	0.0438	0.0868	0.1760	0.1850	0.2947
		θ_3^*	0.0520	0.1056	0.1843	0.2346	0.3398
		z	3.5101	3.2295	0.8971	4.3496	2.8683
$\theta_2^* = \theta_4^*$	eq1	θ_2^*	0.0808	0.1411	0.2450	0.2893	0.3821
		θ_4^*	0.0902	0.1588	0.2758	0.3219	0.4842
		z	2.5599	2.5072	2.3340	2.1508	4.0907
	eq2	θ_2^*	0.0301	0.1348	0.2298	0.3119	0.4156
		θ_4^*	0.0345	0.1546	0.2514	0.3388	0.4471
		z	2.4027	4.4574	2.9530	2.5051	2.4323
	eq3	θ_2^*	0.0425	0.0853	0.1758	0.1988	0.2866
		θ_4^*	0.0477	0.1053	0.1836	0.2250	0.3267
		z	2.0218	3.4492	0.8918	2.1906	2.4568
$\theta_1^* = \theta_2^*$	eq1	θ_1^*	0.0849	0.1413	0.2560	0.3091	0.4191
		θ_2^*	0.0808	0.1411	0.2450	0.2893	0.3821
		z	0.9647	0.0208	0.7456	1.1840	1.4263
	eq2	θ_1^*	0.0352	0.1386	0.2323	0.3029	0.3998
		θ_2^*	0.0301	0.1348	0.2298	0.3119	0.4156
		z	3.0306	0.7202	0.3008	-0.7408	-1.1133
	eq3	θ_1^*	0.0438	0.0868	0.1760	0.1850	0.2947
		θ_2^*	0.0425	0.0853	0.1758	0.1988	0.2866
		z	0.5065	0.2661	0.0311	-1.1474	0.5112
$\theta_3^* = \theta_4^*$	eq1	θ_3^*	0.0944	0.1587	0.2829	0.3332	0.4801
		θ_4^*	0.0902	0.1588	0.2758	0.3219	0.4842
		z	1.4089	-0.0094	0.9590	0.9575	-0.2164
	eq2	θ_3^*	0.0407	0.1476	0.2559	0.3458	0.4317
		θ_4^*	0.0345	0.1546	0.2514	0.3388	0.4471
		z	3.3936	-1.8452	0.6938	0.7738	-1.2350
	eq3	θ_3^*	0.0520	0.1056	0.1843	0.2346	0.3398
		θ_4^*	0.0477	0.1053	0.1836	0.2250	0.3267
		z	1.7624	0.0530	0.0693	0.8434	0.8029

The first two blocks are the test results of the null hypotheses (14) and (15), whereas the last two blocks are the test results of the null hypotheses (16) and (17). The Z statistic is the corresponding test statistic.

financial data even less exploited. This underfitting may partially be responsible for the inferior performance observed in [1], [16] and many other studies. This may also help explain why, in some applications, we found that the post-sample performance was even better than the in-sample performance ([13]).

On the other hand, the ability to use cross-validation to resolve the problem of overfitting may be overestimated. As we have seen from our simulations, the validation design cannot effectively prevent any of the four overfitting cases detected in the designs without the use of the validation sample. Under these circumstances, using the validation design may mislead one to believe that the overfitting problem has been well taken care of, while in fact it has not ([12]).

In conclusion, the essence and the implication of this paper is a call for a prudent use of the overfitting-avoidance design in financial data mining. Instead of taking it for granted, this paper provides a thorough analysis of the validation design frequently used in financial applications of GP. Our results lead us to be very suspicious of its contribution. Our analysis also points out another weakness of existing financial applications of GP, i.e. the causal design of search intensity. So far, few studies have carefully documented the effect of different population sizes and different numbers of generations on information exploitation. Using the production theory from economics, [5] showed that what matters is the *combined effect* of *Pop* and *Gen*. Studies which change only *Pop* or *Gen* at one time may underestimate the significance of search intensity. We believe that a proper addressing of search intensity with a more effective overfitting-avoidance design may give rise to another series of interesting financial applications of GP, which is the direction for the next study.

Acknowledgements

The authors are grateful to two anonymous referees for their comments and suggestions.

References

1. Allen, F., Karjalainen, R.: Using Genetic Algorithms to Find Technical Trading Rules. Journal of Financial Economics **51**(2) (1999) 245–271
2. Bender, E.: Mathematical Methods in Artificial Intelligence. IEEE, Los Alamitos, Calif. (1996)
3. Chen, S.-H., Yeh, C.-H.: Toward a Computable Approach to the Efficient Market Hypothesis: An Application of Genetic Programming. Journal of Economic Dynamics and Control **21**(6) (1997) 1043–1063
4. Chen, S.-H. (ed.): Genetic Algorithms and Genetic Programming in Computational Finance. Kluwer Academic Publishers (2002)
5. Chen, S.-H., Kuo, T.-W.: Genetic Programming: A Tutorial with the Software Simple GP. In: Chen, S.-H. (ed.), Genetic Algorithms and Genetic Programming in Computational Finance, Kluwer Academic Publishers (2002) 55–77
6. Geman, S., Bienenstock, E., Doursat, R.: Neural Networks and the Bias/Variance Dilemma. Neural Computation **4**(1) (1992) 1–58

7. Kaboudan, M. A.: A Measure of Time Series's Predictability Using Genetic Programming Applied to Stock Returns. Journal of Forecasting **18** (1999) 345–357
8. Kecman, V.: Learning and Soft Computing: Support Vector Machines, Neural Networks, and Fuzzy Logic Models. MIT Press (2001)
9. Mehrotra, K., Mohan, C., Ranka, S.: Elements of Artificial Neural Networks. MIT Press, Cambridge, Mass. (1997)
10. Neely, C., Weller, P., Ditmar, R.: Is Technical Analysis in the Foreign Exchange Market Profitable? A Genetic Programming Approach. Journal of Financial and Quantitative Analysis **32**(4) (1997) 405–427
11. Neely, C. J., Weller, P. A.: Technical Trading Rules in the European Monetary System. Journal of International Money and Finance **18**(3) (1999) 429–458
12. Neely, C. J., Weller, P. A.: Using GP to Predict Exchange Rate Volatility. In: Chen, S.-H. (ed.): Genetic Algorithms and Genetic Programming in Computational Finance. Kluwer Academic Publishers, Boston Dordrecht London (2002) 263–279
13. Noe, T. H., Wang, J.: The Self-Evolving Logic of Financial Claim Prices. In: Chen, S.-H. (ed.): Genetic Algorithms and Genetic Programming in Computational Finance. Kluwer Academic Publishers, Boston Dordrecht London (2002) 249–262
14. Smith, M.: Neural Networks for Statistical Modeling. Van Nostrand Reinhold, New York (1993)
15. Stone, M.: Cross-Validatory Choice and Assessment of Statistical Predictors. Journal of the Royal Statistical Society **B36** (1974) 111–147
16. Wang, J.: Trading and Hedging in S&P 500 Spot and Futures Markets Using Genetic Programming. Journal of Futures Markets **20**(10) (2000) 911–942

Evolutionary Design of Objects Using Scene Graphs

Marc Ebner

Universität Würzburg, Lehrstuhl für Informatik II
Am Hubland, 97074 Würzburg, Germany
ebner@informatik.uni-wuerzburg.de
http://www2.informatik.uni-wuerzburg.de/staff/ebner/welcome.html

Abstract. One of the main issues in evolutionary design is how to create three-dimensional shape. The representation needs to be general enough such that all possible shapes can be created, yet it has to be evolvable. That is, parent and offspring must be related. Small changes to the genotype should lead to small changes of the fitness of an individual. We have explored the use of scene graphs to evolve three-dimensional shapes. Two different scene graph representations are analyzed, the scene graph representation used by OpenInventor and the scene graph representation used by VRML. Both representations use internal floating point variables to specify three-dimensional vectors, rotation axes and rotation angles. The internal parameters are initially chosen at random, then remain fixed during the run. We also experimented with an evolution strategy to adapt the internal variables. Experimental results are presented for the evolution of a wind turbine. The VRML representation produced better results.

1 Motivation

Evolutionary algorithms can be used to find structures which are optimal for a given problem. In evolutionary design [4–6], each individual represents a particular shape. Genetic operators are used to change these shapes. Selection is used to find structures which are suited for the given problem. The main question to address is which representation to use. Which representation is best suited to find shape? The representation has be be able to create all possible shapes. In addition to this requirement the representation should be chosen such that parent and offspring are closely related. If the fitness of parent and offspring are completely uncorrelated we have a random fitness landscape and evolution degrades to random search.

So far, a number of different representations have been used in evolutionary design. They range from direct encoding of shapes to generative encodings such as L-Systems [7–9, 13]. Several different representations for three-dimensional objects are known from the field of computer graphics [17]. Those representations were created to model three-dimensional objects and visualize them in a virtual environment. Some of these representations may also be used for evolutionary

C. Ryan et al. (Eds.): EuroGP 2003, LNCS 2610, pp. 47–58, 2003.

design. In addition to being able to create any possible shape these representations need to be evolvable, that is, parent and child have to be related. We are investigating a representation known from computer graphics, a scene graph, for evolutionary design.

2 Scene Graph

A computer graphics object or entire scene can be stored in a scene graph. A scene graph is an ordered collection of nodes. Several different types of nodes such as shape nodes, property nodes, transformation nodes, and group nodes exist. Shape nodes are used to define elementary shapes such as spheres, cubes, cylinders and cones. Property nodes can be used to define the look of the elementary shapes. The shapes are placed at the origin of a local coordinate system. In order to combine different shapes and to position these shapes relative to each other we need transformation and group nodes. Transformation nodes change the current coordinate system. Using transformation nodes we can rotate, translate or scale the coordinate system any way we like. Group nodes can be used to merge different scene graphs. The contents of the individual scene graphs are placed in the same coordinate system.

Two different types of scene graphs are commonly used. One is used by OpenInventor [18], an object-oriented library for 3D graphics, the other one is used in the virtual reality modeling language (VRML) [1]. In OpenInventor transformation nodes are used as outer nodes of the tree. The scene graph is displayed by executing the action stored in the root node and then traversing each child in turn. Transformation nodes change the current coordinate system. All nodes which are executed after a particular transformation node are influenced by this transformation. To limit the influence of the transformation nodes a special type of group node, called separator node, exists. This group node stores the current coordinate system on a stack before traversing its children. After all children have been traversed, the current coordinate system is restored. Objects commonly have a separator at the root of the tree. Thus, such objects can be combined easily to create a larger scene.

The scene graph used in VRML differs from the one used by OpenInventor in that transformation nodes are also separator nodes. In VRML transformation nodes are used as inner nodes of the tree. They change the current coordinate system but this change only affects the children of the transformation node. Thus, the distinction between separator nodes and group nodes is not necessary in VRML. Figure 1 shows the differences between an OpenInventor and a VRML scene graph which represent the same object. Let us start with the VRML scene graph. The object consists of 4 cubes (A, B, C, and D). In VRML the object is constructed by positioning cube A (node 5) using a transformation node (node 2). Next, cube B (node 3) is placed at the origin. The transformation stored in node 2 only affects node 5 but does not affect any other nodes. Cube C is positioned relative to cube B and cube D is positioned relative to cube B. This is achieved by positioning cube C (node 6) using a transformation node (node 4)

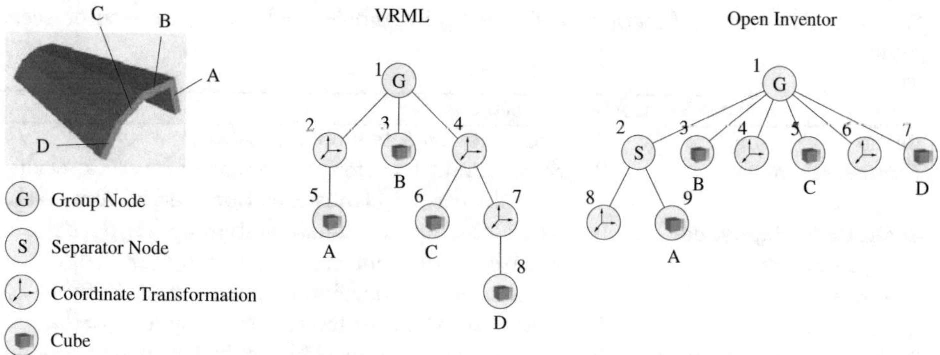

Fig. 1. Differences in the representation of the same object between VRML and OpenInventor. The same object is represented once with a VRML scene graph and once with an OpenInventor scene graph.

followed by an additional transformation node (node 7) which positions cube D (node 8) relative to the coordinate system of cube C. The transformation stored in node 4 affects all nodes below it (nodes 6, 7, and 8). Thus, cube D (node 8) is affected by two transformations (node 4 and 7).

The OpenInventor scene graph has a different structure. Cube A (node 9) is positioned using a transformation node (node 8). The effect of this transformation is encapsulated using a separator node (node 2). Thus, the transformation stored in node 8 only affects node 9. It does not affect any other nodes. Next, cube B (node 3) is positioned at the origin. Cube C is positioned relative to cube B and cube D is positioned relative to cube D. The transformation stored at node 4 changes the coordinate system and affects nodes 5, 6, and 7. The transformation stored at node 6 only affects node 7. Thus, cube C (node 5) is only affected by the transformation node 4, whereas cube D (node 7) is affected by both transformations (node 4 and 6).

Both scene graphs are trees and of course we can use genetic programming to evolve such scene graphs.

3 Evolving Scene Graphs

We have used genetic programming [3, 10–12] to evolve scene graphs. Each node is either a terminal symbol or an elementary function depending on the number of arguments. Table 1 shows the elementary functions and terminal symbols used for the OpenInventor scene graphs. The elementary functions and terminal symbols used for the VRML scene graphs are similar except that the group node is not used and nodes `Translate`, `TranslateX`, `TranslateY`, `TranslateZ`, `Rotate`, `RotateX`, `RotateY`, `RotateZ` take two arguments. These transformations save the current transformation matrix on a stack, evaluate their children and then restore the original transformation matrix. In a sense, they work like combined separator and transformation nodes. We also added a no-operation node to be able to add only a single subtree to a transformation node.

Table 1. Elementary functions and terminal symbols used for OpenInventor scene graphs.

Name	Internal Vars.	Args.	Function
`Group`	none	2	Combines objects stored in subtrees.
`Separator`	none	2	Save current transformation matrix on stack, evaluate subtrees, pop transformation matrix from stack.
`Translate`	dx, dy, dz	0	Translates the coordinate system by $[dx, dy, dz]^T$.
`TranslateX`	dx	0	Translates the coordinate system by $[dx, 0, 0]^T$.
`TranslateY`	dy	0	Translates the coordinate system by $[0, dy, 0]^T$.
`TranslateZ`	dz	0	Translates the coordinate system by $[0, 0, dz]^T$.
`Rotate`	`nx, ny, nz, a`	0	Rotates the coordinate system by the angle `a` around the vector $[nx, ny, nz]^T$.
`RotateX`	`a`	0	Rotates the coordinate system around the X-Axis.
`RotateY`	`a`	0	Rotates the coordinate system around the Y-Axis.
`RotateZ`	`a`	0	Rotates the coordinate system around the Z-Axis.
`Cube`	`w, h, d`	0	Places a cube with dimensions `w`×`h`×`d` at the current position.
`Sphere`	`r`	0	Places a sphere with radius `r` at the current position.
`Cylinder`	`r, h`	0	Places a cylinder with radius `r` and height `h` at the current position.

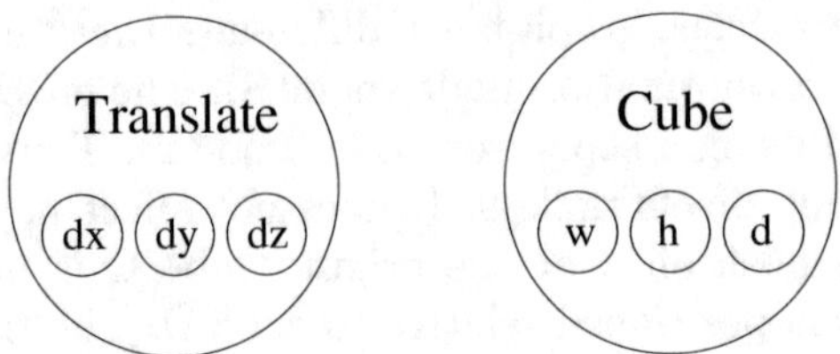

Fig. 2. Each node also contains a number of internal variables. For instance, a translation node contains a vector and a shape node describing a cube contains the size of the cube.

Floating point variables may be stored inside each node (Figure 2). For a shape node describing a cube, these variables are used to specify the width, height, and depth of the cube. For a transformation node the variables are used to specify the vector which translates the coordinate system. Thus, the topology of the object is defined by the tree structure of the individual which is evolved using genetic programming. The internal variables are initially selected from a random range suitable for each node. The values are set whenever a new node is created and then left unchanged during the course of the run. If a new subtree is created by the mutation operator, new nodes with new internal variables are generated. These variables are thus similar to the standard ephemeral constants except that they are internal to a node. The internal variables are always exchanged with the node during crossover.

Mutation, and crossover operators are defined as usual. The mutation operator first selects an individual. Next, a node is randomly selected. Internal nodes

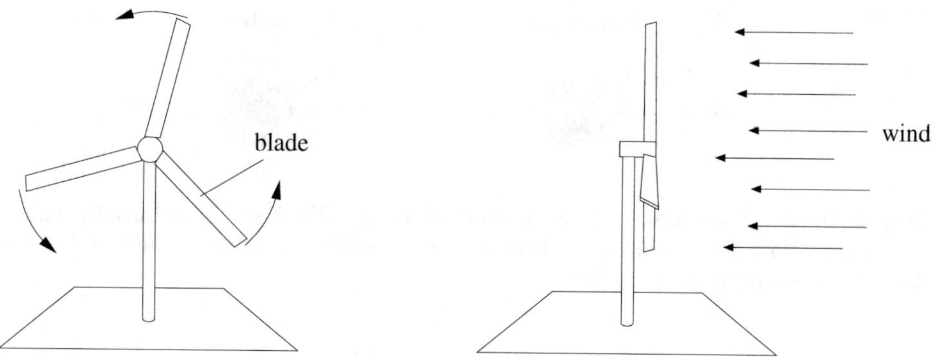

Fig. 3. A wind turbine is constructed from three blades which are rotated around a center.

are selected with a probability of 90%, external nodes are selected with a probability of 10%. Then this node is replaced by a newly generated subtree. The subtree is generated with the grow method with a maximum depth of 6. If the number of nodes of the resulting individual is larger than 1000 or the depth of the tree is larger than 17, we add the parent to the next population instead. The crossover operator chooses two individuals. A random node is selected in each individual and the two subtrees are swapped. Again, internal nodes are selected with a probability of 90%, external nodes are selected with a probability of 10%. Constraints are imposed on the size of the individuals. If the number of nodes of an offspring is larger than 1000 or the depth of the tree is larger than 17, we add the parent to the next population instead.

4 Evolving the Blades of a Wind Turbine

As a sample problem we have chosen to evolve the blades of a horizontal-axis wind turbine. We should note that our goal is to investigate the evolvability of different representations for evolutionary design. We are not interested in actually finding an optimal shape which can be used for a real wind turbine. Indeed, the resulting shape looks more like a water than a wind turbine.

To simulate the virtual mechanics we have used ODE (Open Dynamics Engine) which was developed by Smith [16]. ODE is a library for simulating rigid body dynamics in VR environments. ODE supports collision detection and collision response of primitive geometry objects such as cubes, spheres, capped cylinders and planes. A capped cylinder is a cylinder with a half-sphere cap at each end. This type of cylinder is used by ODE because it makes collision detection easier.

A single individuals represents the shape of a blade of the turbine. The turbine is constructed by adding three of the blades to a base (Figure 3). Each blade is rotated by 120°compared to the previous bade. A real turbine is moved by wind passing over both surfaces of an airfoil shaped blade [2]. This causes

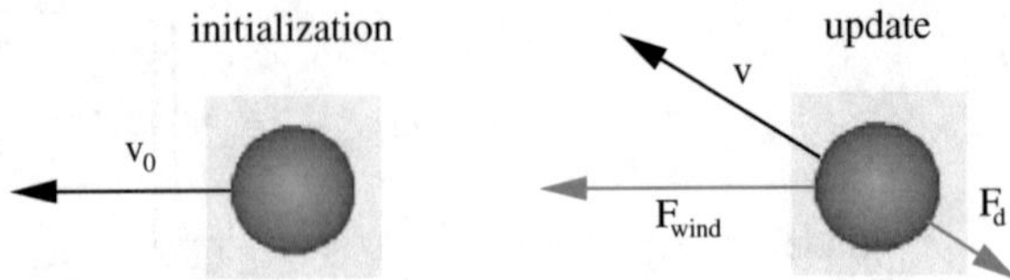

Fig. 4. Initialization and update of wind particles. Wind particles initially have a starting velocity of v_0. During each time step we apply a force F_{wind} and a damping force $F_d = -\alpha_d v$ to the particle.

pressure differences between the top and the bottom surfaces of the blades. We model wind as a fixed number of small spherical particles. The particles are placed in front of the blade at random locations within a certain radius around the axis of the turbine.

Each particle initially has a starting velocity of v_0 (Figure 4). The simulation is carried out for a fixed number of steps. During each step we apply a force F_{wind} to each wind particle. A damping force F_d is also applied. This damping force is directly proportional to the velocity of the particle $F_d = -\alpha_d v$. Thus, the total force acting on a single wind particle is given by

$$F = F_{\text{wind}} + F_d = F_{\text{wind}} - \alpha_d v.$$

Collisions between wind particles and the turbine's blades are detected by ODE. ODE calculates forces in response to collisions between the blades and the wind particles. We don't allow collisions between wind particles as this is computationally intractable. The wind particles are only allowed to move within the volume of a virtual cylinder placed around the turbine. If a wind particle leaves this cylinder it is again placed at a random location in front of the turbine. Fitness of an individual is defined as the average rotational energy of the rotor:

$$\text{fitness} = \frac{1}{\text{steps}} \sum_{i=1}^{\text{steps}} \frac{1}{2} \omega_i I \omega_i$$

where steps is the number of steps the simulation was done, I is the inertia matrix of the turbine's rotor, and ω_i is the rotational velocity of the rotor at time step i.

5 Experiments

Experiments were carried out with the following parameters. The rotor was placed at a height of 15 units above the ground plane. Maximum wind radius was set to 10 units. Wind particles were created 6 units in front of the rotor. Blades whose bounding box extends outside the virtual cylinder receive a fitness of zero. Blades which are thicker than 4 units also receive a fitness of zero. Spheres with radius 0.1 units were used as wind particles. The number of wind

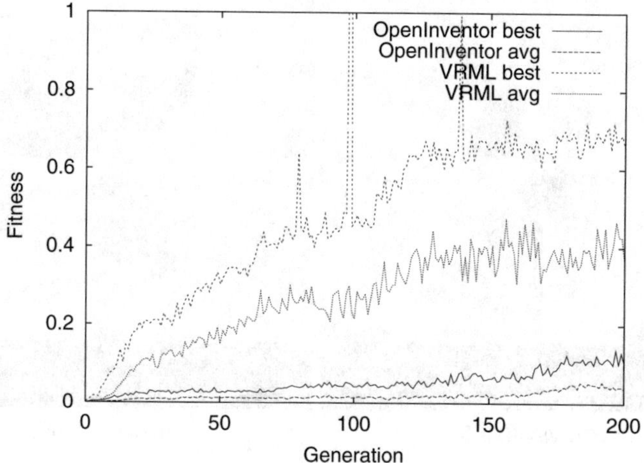

Fig. 5. Fitness statistics are shown for two experiments with a population size of 50 individuals. One experiment used the OpenInventor scene graph to represent the blades of a wind turbine. The other experiment used the VRML scene graph. The peak at generation 98 (maximum fitness of 1.957) resulted from a wind particle being caught between the blade and the base of the wind turbine. This led to a large rotational velocity of the rotor as the wind particle was freed.

particles was set to 100. Each particle has a starting velocity $v_0 = 1.5$. Wind force F_{wind} was set to 0.03 units and α_d, which defines the amount of drag, was set to 0.02. The simulation was carried out for 3000 steps.

A population size of 50 individuals with tournament selection of size 7 was used. The best individual was always copied into the next generation. The population was initialized using ramped half-and-half initialization with maximum depths between 2 and 6. Mutation and crossover were applied with a probability of 50% each. Figure 5 shows the results for both representations. Two evolved wind turbine designs are shown in Figure 6. The wind turbine on the left was evolved using the OpenInventor representation, the wind turbine on the right was evolved using the VRML representation. The wind turbine which was evolved using the VRML representation has a much higher fitness (0.652) in comparison to the turbine which was evolved using the OpenInventor representation (0.105). We then performed additional experiments to see if the VRML representation is significantly better than the OpenInventor representation. To exclude the possibility that a particle was caught between the blade and the base of the wind turbine we increased the distance between the base and the rotor. Due to the amount of time required to evaluate a single run we were only able to perform 10 runs for the OpenInventor representation and 10 runs for the VRML representation. A single run takes between one and three days to complete. For each setup we compared the maximum fitness achieved after 200 generations with a population size of 50 individuals. A t-test was applied to analyze the results. The results with the VRML representation were significantly better than the OpenInventor representation (t=2.413).

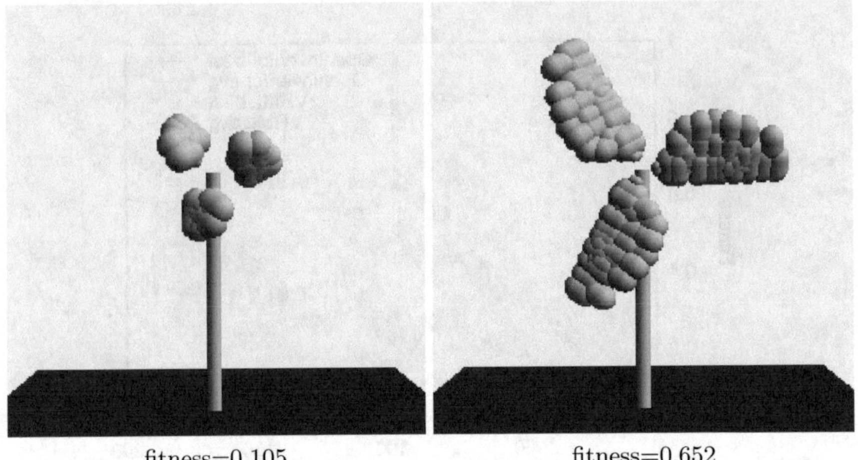

Fig. 6. Two evolved designs for the blades of a wind turbine. The one on the left was evolved using the OpenInventor scene graph. The one on the right was evolved using the VRML scene graph.

Each subtree of the VRML scene graph is a substructure of the blade which is encapsulated and can be exchanged using the crossover operation. With the OpenInventor representation the entire design may be disrupted by a single mutation if group nodes are used instead of separator nodes. A single mutation can have a large impact because transformations may influence other subtrees.

We also experimented with the use of an evolution strategy [14, 15] to adapt the values of the internal parameters. The evolution strategy was nested inside a genetic programming loop. Rechenberg [14] describes a method called structure evolution, where continuous parameters are adapted in an inner loop and discrete parameters are adapted in an outer loop. The same approach was followed here. Genetic programming is used to adapt the topology of the objects and an evolution strategy is used to make small changes to the structure. The genetic programming loop was executed every n-th time step. We denote this type of algorithm as GP_n/ES.

Evolution strategies use Gaussian mutations to change the variables. Let $[v_1, ..., v_n]$ be n real valued variables. This vector is mutated by adding a vector of Gaussian mutations. Each variable v_i has an additional parameter δ_i which specifies the standard deviation which will be used to mutate the variable. The standard deviations are adapted by multiplying the standard deviations with $e^{N(0,\tau)}$ where $N(0, \tau)$ is a Gaussian distributed random number with standard deviation τ. For our experiments we have set $\tau = 0.05$. This process automatically adapts the step size of the mutation. Step sizes which lead to large improvements are propagated into the next generation.

Figure 7 shows the results for wind turbines which were evolved using the nested GP/ES algorithm. The wind turbine on the left was evolved using a GP_{10}/ES-algorithm, the wind turbine on the right was evolved using a GP_{20}/ES-algorithm. We again performed 10 runs for each setup. The full set of statistics

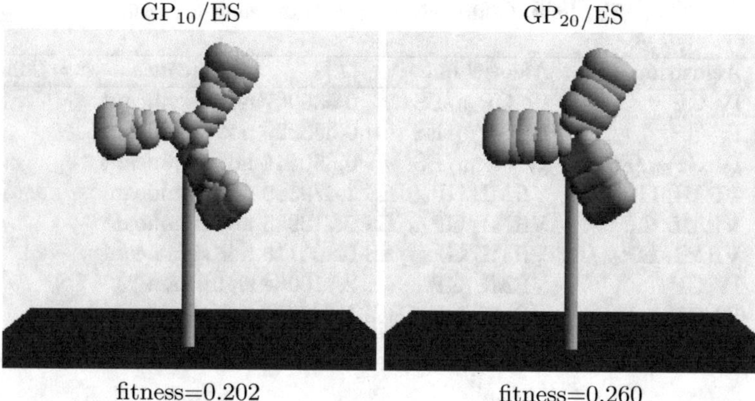

Fig. 7. Evolved wind turbines using a mixed GP/ES algorithm for 200 generations.

Table 2. Average and standard deviation of maximum fitness achieved. Only 10 runs could be performed for each algorithm due to the amount of time required to complete a single run.

Algorithm	μ	σ
IV GP	0.146944	0.051362
IV GP_{10}/ES	0.130383	0.083100
IV GP_{20}/ES	0.162535	0.129536
VRML GP	0.341237	0.249383
VRML GP_{10}/ES	0.205339	0.148970
VRML GP_{20}/ES	0.269060	0.200728

is shown in Table 2. The results of different setups were compared using a t-test. Table 3 shows if differences were significant at $\alpha = 0.05$.

Figure 8 shows the maximum fitness for all ten runs for each setup. A possible explanation for these results is that bigger improvements could be achieved by varying the topology of the shape as opposed to fine-tuning the shape. If we apply an ES-mutation, all internal parameters are mutated at the same time. This causes the overall shape to change a little from one generation to the next. However, if we apply a GP-mutation, the change is local to a subtree. A part of the structure may be added or removed. Larger fitness gains could be achieved by locally changing the shape as opposed to varying the entire structure.

Additional experiments were made with a population size of 100 individuals. Figure 9 shows evolved wind turbines after 100 generations. The first wind turbine was evolved using the OpenInventor representation. The second, third, and fourth wind turbines were evolved using the VRML representation. The second wind turbine was evolved using the simple GP algorithm with fixed internal variables. The third wind turbine was evolved using a GP_{10}/ES-algorithm. The fourth wind turbine was evolved using a GP_{20}/ES-algorithm.

Table 3. Comparison of results using a t-test.

Algorithm 1	Algorithm 2	$\|T\|$	significance at $\alpha = 0.05$
IV GP	IV GP_{20}/ES	0.536067	not significant
IV GP	IV GP_{10}/ES	0.353820	not significant
IV GP_{20}/ES	IV GP_{10}/ES	0.660644	not significant
VRML GP	VRML GP_{20}/ES	1.479385	not significant
VRML GP	VRML GP_{10}/ES	0.712965	not significant
VRML GP_{20}/ES	VRML GP_{10}/ES	0.806116	not significant
IV GP	VRML GP	2.413064	significant
IV GP_{20}/ES	VRML GP_{20}/ES	1.389561	not significant
IV GP_{10}/ES	VRML GP_{10}/ES	1.410075	not significant

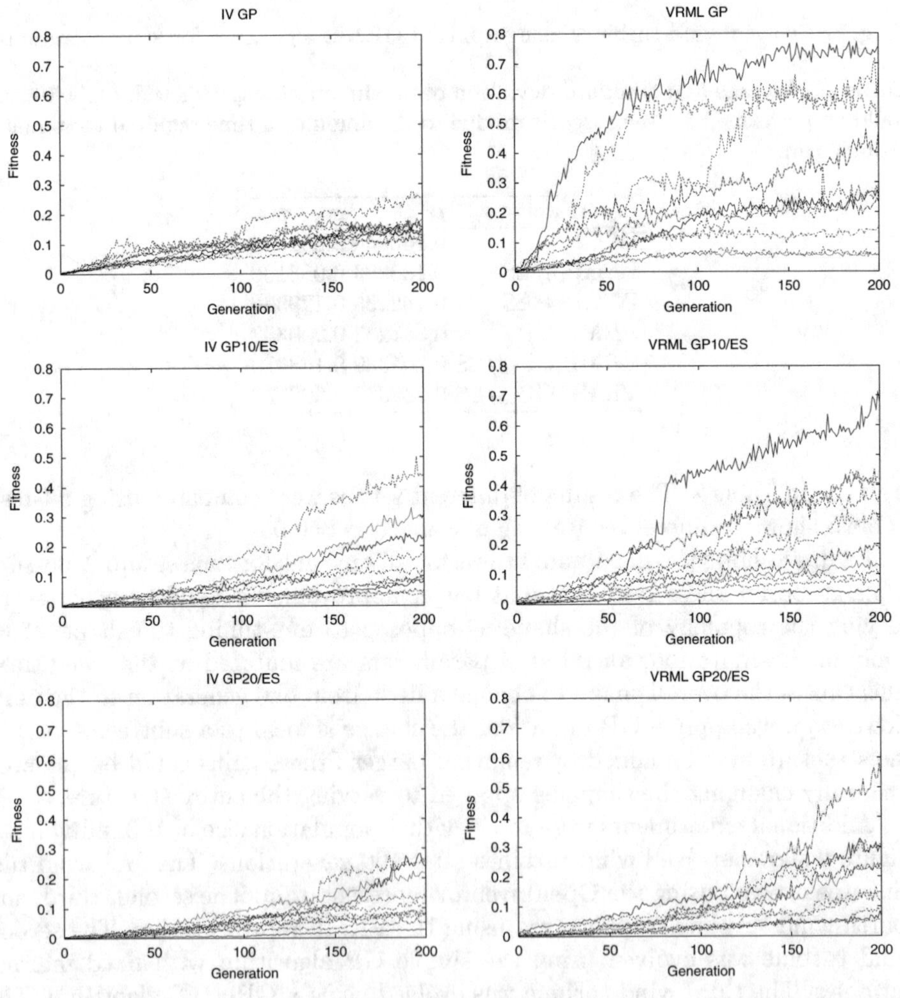

Fig. 8. Fitness of best individual. Ten runs were performed for each setup.

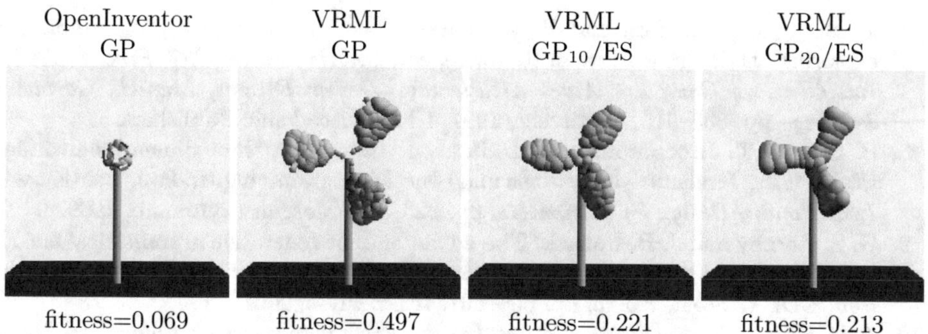

Fig. 9. Results for a population size of 100 individuals after 100 generations.

6 Conclusion

Two different scene graph representations for evolutionary design were analyzed. OpenInventor's scene graph is more volatile in comparison to a VRML scene graph. If group nodes are used, a single mutation may completely change the overall shape of the object. Subtrees of a VRML representation are automatically encapsulated and may be extracted and placed at other locations of the structure. Floating point variables which specify three-dimensional vectors, rotation axis or rotation angles are stored inside the nodes of the tree representation. These variables are initialized with random values from a specific range. After initialization, they remain unchanged for the life of the node. Significantly better results were achieved with the VRML representation in comparison to the OpenInventor representation if fixed internal variables were used.

We also experimented with a mixed GP/ES algorithm where the values of the internal variables are evolved using an evolution strategy. The overall topology of the shape was evolved using genetic programming. However, this approach did not lead to significantly better results.

References

1. A. L. Ames, D. R. Nadeau, and J. L. Moreland. *VRML 2.0 Sourcebook.* John Wiley & Sons, Inc., NY, 2nd edition, 1997.
2. American Wind Energy Association. The most frequently asked questions about wind energy, 2002.
3. W. Banzhaf, P. Nordin, R. E. Keller, and F. D. Francone. *Genetic Programming - An Introduction: On The Automatic Evolution of Computer Programs and Its Applications.* Morgan Kaufmann Publishers, San Francisco, CA, 1998.
4. P. J. Bentley, ed. *Evolutionary Design by Computers.* Morgan Kaufmann Publishers, May 1999.
5. P. J. Bentley and D. W. Corne, eds. *Creative Evolutionary Systems.* Morgan Kaufmann Publishers, Jan. 2001.
6. P. J. Bentley. *Generic Evolutionary Design of Solid Objects using a Genetic Algorithm.* PhD thesis, Division of Computing and Control Systems, School of Engineering, The University of Huddersfield, 1996.

7. T. Broughton, A. Tan, and P. S. Coates. The use of genetic programming in exploring 3D design worlds. In R. Junge, ed., *CAAD futures 1997. Proc. of the 7th Int. Conf. on Computer Aides Architectural Design Futures, Munich, Germany, 4-6 Aug.*, pp. 885–915, Dordrecht, 1997. Kluwer Academic Publishers.
8. P. Coates, T. Broughton, and H. Jackson. Exploring three-dimensional design worlds using Lindenmeyer systems and genetic programming. In P. J. Bentley, ed., *Evolutionary Design by Computers*, pp. 323–341. Morgan Kaufmann, 1999.
9. G. S. Hornby and J. B. Pollack. The advantages of generative grammatical encodings for physical design. In *Proc. of the 2001 Congress on Evolutionary Computation, COEX, Seoul, Korea*, pp. 600–607. IEEE Press, 2001.
10. J. R. Koza. *Genetic Programming. On the Programming of Computers by Means of Natural Selection.* The MIT Press, Cambridge, MA, 1992.
11. J. R. Koza. *Genetic Programming II. Automatic Discovery of Reusable Programs.* The MIT Press, Cambridge, MA, 1994.
12. J.R. Koza, F.H. Bennett III, D. Andre, and M.A. Keane. *Genetic Programming III. Darwinian Invention and Problem Solving.* Morgan Kaufmann Publishers, 1999.
13. S. Kumar and P. Bentley. The ABCs of evolutionary design: Investigating the evolvability of embryogenies for morphogenesis. In *GECCO-99 Late Breaking Papers*, pp. 164–170, 1999.
14. I. Rechenberg. *Evolutionsstrategie '94.* frommann-holzboog, Stuttgart, 1994.
15. H.-P. Schwefel. *Evolution and Optimum Seeking.* John Wiley & Sons, NY, 1995.
16. R. Smith. *Open Dynamics Engine v0.03 User Guide*, Dec. 2001.
17. A. Watt. *3D Computer Graphics.* Addison-Wesley, Harlow, England, 2000.
18. J. Wernecke. *The Inventor Mentor: Programming Object-Oriented 3D Graphics with Open Inventor, Release 2.* Addison-Wesley, Reading, MA, 1994.

Ensemble Techniques for Parallel Genetic Programming Based Classifiers

Gianluigi Folino, Clara Pizzuti, and Giandomenico Spezzano

ICAR-CNR
c/o DEIS, Univ. della Calabria
87036 Rende (CS), Italy
{folino,pizzuti,spezzano}@icar.cnr.it

Abstract. An extension of Cellular Genetic Programming for data classification to induce an ensemble of predictors is presented. Each classifier is trained on a different subset of the overall data, then they are combined to classify new tuples by applying a simple majority voting algorithm, like bagging. Preliminary results on a large data set show that the ensemble of classifiers trained on a sample of the data obtains higher accuracy than a single classifier that uses the entire data set at a much lower computational cost.

1 Introduction

Genetic programming (*GP*) [16] is a general purpose method that has been successfully applied to solve problems in different application domains. In the data mining field [8], *GP* has showed to be a particularly suitable technique to deal with the task of data classification [13,19,22,17,9,10,12] by evolving decision trees. Many data mining applications manage databases consisting of a very large number of objects, each having several attributes. This huge amount of data (gigabytes or even terabytes of data) is too large to fit into the memory of computers, thus it causes serious problems in the realization of predictors, such as decision trees [20]. One approach is to partition the training data into small subsets, obtain an ensemble of predictors on the basis of each subset, and then use a voting classification algorithm to predict the class label of new objects [5,4,6]. The main advantage of this approach is that accuracy comparable to that of a single predictor trained on all the training set can be obtained, but at a much lower computational cost.

Bagging [2] is one of the well known ensemble techniques that builds *bags* of data of the same size of the original data set by applying random sampling with replacement. It has been shown that bagging improves the accuracy of decision tree classifiers [2,21]. Quinlan [21], for example, over 27 databases, experimented that bagging reduces the classification error by about 10% on average and that it is superior to C4.5 on 24 of the 27 data sets. However, when the data set is too large to fit into main memory, bags are also too large, thus, constructing and elaborating many bags of the same size of the entire data set is not feasible. In this

C. Ryan et al. (Eds.): EuroGP 2003, LNCS 2610, pp. 59–69, 2003.

case data reduction through the partitioning of the data set into smaller subsets seems a good approach, though an important aspect to consider is which kind of partitioning has the minimal impact on the accuracy of results. Furthermore, to speed up the overall predictor generation process it seems straightforward to consider a parallel implementation of bagging.

In this paper we present an extension of Cellular Genetic Programming for data classification to induce an ensemble of predictors, each trained on a different subset of the overall data, and then combine them together to classify new tuples by applying a simple majority voting algorithm, like bagging. Preliminary results on a large data set show that the ensemble of classifiers trained on a subset of the data set obtains higher accuracy than a single classifier that uses the entire data set.

The paper is organized as follows. In section 2 a brief overview of the ensemble techniques is given. In section 3 the cellular parallel implementation of GP for data classification is presented. Section 4 proposes an extension of cellular genetic programming with ensemble techniques. In section 5, finally, the results of the method on some standard problems are presented.

2 Ensemble Techniques

Let $S = \{(x_i, y_i) | i = 1, \ldots, n\}$ be a training set where x_i, called example, is an attribute vector with m attributes and y_i is the class label associated with x_i. A predictor, given a new example, has the task to predict the class label for it. Ensemble techniques build K predictors, each on a different subset of the training set, then combine them together to classify the test set.

Bagging (bootstrap aggregating) was introduced by Breiman in [2] and it is based on bootstrap samples (replicates) of the same size of the training set S. Each bootstrap sample is created by uniformly sampling instances from S with replacement, thus some examples may appear more than once while others may not appear in it. K bags $B_1, \ldots, B_K$ are generated and K classifiers $C_1, \ldots, C_K$ are built on each bag B_i. The number K of predictors is an input parameter. A final classifier classifies an example by giving as output the class predicted most often by $C_1, \ldots, C_K$, with ties solved arbitrarily.

More complex techniques such as boosting [14] and arching [3] adaptively change the distribution of the sample depending on how difficult each example is to classify. Bagging, boosting and variants have been studied and compared, and shown to be successful in improving the accuracy of predictors [7,1]. These techniques, however, requires that the entire data sets be stored in main memory. When applied to large data sets this kind of approach could be impractical.

Breiman in [4] suggested that, when data sets are too large to fit into main memory, a possible approach is to partition the data in small pieces, build a predictor on each piece and then paste these predictors together. Breiman obtained classifiers of accuracy comparable if all the data set had been used. Similar results were found by Chan and Stolfo in [5]. In [6] Chawla et al. on a very large data set with a committee of eight classifiers trained on different partitions of the data attained accuracy higher than one classifier trained on the entire data set.

Regarding the application of ensemble techniques to Genetic Programming, Iba in [15] proposed to extend Genetic Programming to deal with bagging and boosting. A population is divided in a set of subpopulations and each subpopulation is evolved on a training set sampled with replacement from the original data,. The size of the sampled training set is the same of the entire training set. Best individuals of each subpopulation participate in voting to give a prediction on the testing data. Experiments on some standard problems using ten subpopulations showed the effectiveness of the approach.

3 Data Classification Using Cellular Genetic Programming

Approaches to data classification through genetic programming involve a lot of computation and their performances may drastically degrade when applied to large problems because of the intensive computation of fitness evaluation of each individual in the population. High performance computing is an essential component for increasing the performances and obtaining large-scale efficient classifiers. To this purpose, several approaches have been proposed. The different models used for distributing the computation and to ease parallelize genetic programming, cluster around two main approaches [23]: the well-known *island model* and the *cellular model*. In the island model several isolated subpopulations evolve in parallel, periodically exchanging by migration their best individuals with the neighboring subpopulations. In the cellular model each individual has a spatial location on a low-dimensional grid and the individuals interact locally within a small neighborhood. The model considers the population as a system of active individuals that interact only with their direct neighbors. Different neighborhoods can be defined for the cells and the fitness evaluation is done simultaneously for all the individuals. Selection, reproduction and mating take place locally within the neighborhood. In [11] a comparison of cellular genetic programming with both canonical genetic programming and the island model using benchmark problems of different complexity is presented and the the superiority of the cellular approach is shown.

Cellular genetic programming (*CGP*) for data classification was proposed in [9]. The method uses cellular automata as a framework to enable a fine-grained parallel implementation of GP through the diffusion model.The main advantages of parallel genetic programming for classification problems consist in handling large populations in a reasonable time, enabling fast convergence by reducing the number of iterations and execution time, favoring the cooperation in the search for good solutions, thus improving the accuracy of the method. The algorithm, in the following referred as *CGPC* (*Cellular Genetic Programming Classifier*, is described in figure 1.

At the beginning, for each cell, an individual is randomly generated and its fitness is evaluated. Then, at each generation, every tree undergoes one of the

```
Let p_c, p_m be crossover and mutation probability
for each point i in grid do in parallel
    generate a random individual t_i
    evaluate the fitness of t_i
end parallel for
while not MaxNumberOfGeneration do
    for each point i in grid do in parallel
        generate a random probability p
        if (p < p_c)
            select the cell j, in the neighborhood of i,
            such that t_j has the best fitness
            produce the offspring by crossing t_i and t_j
            evaluate the fitness of the offspring
            replace t_i with the best of the two offspring
            evaluate the fitness of the new t_i
        else
        if ( p < p_m + p_c) then
            mutate the individual
            evaluate the fitness of the new t_i
        else
            copy the current individual in the population
        end if
        end if
end parallel for
end while
```

Fig. 1. The algorithm CGPC

genetic operators (reproduction, crossover, mutation) depending on the probability test. If crossover is applied, the mate of the current individual is selected as the neighbor having the best fitness, and the offspring is generated. The current string is then replaced by the best of the two offspring if the fitness of the latter is better than that of the former. The evaluation of the fitness of each classifier is calculated on the entire training data. After the execution of the number of generations defined by the user, the individual with the best fitness represents the classifier. The parallel implementation of the algorithm has been realized using a partitioning technique based upon a domain decomposition in conjunction with the Single-Program-Multiple-Data (SPMD) programming model. Furthermore, a parallel file system for partitioning the data set on different processors to obtain an efficient data access time was adopted. Figure 2 shows the software architecture of the implementation. On each processing element (PE) is allocated a process that contains a slice (SP_i) of the population and operates on all the data thought the parallel file system transferring the partitioned data set into the memory of the computer. In this way all the individuals of a subpopulation can operate on the training data without the need to request the transfer of the data many times. The size of the subpopulation of each slice process is

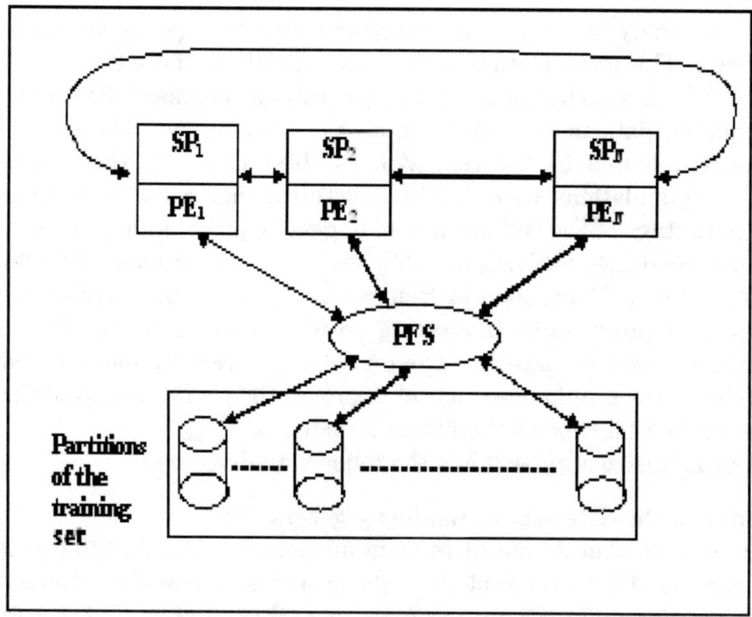

Fig. 2. Software architecture of CGPC

calculated by dividing the population for the number of processors of the parallel machine and ensuring that the size of each subpopulation be greater then a threshold determined from the granularity supported by the processor. For efficiency reasons, the individuals within a slice are combined into a single process that sequentially updates each individual. This reduces the amount of internal communication on each process, increasing the granularity of the application. Communication between processors is local, all that needs to be communicated between slices are the outermost individuals. The configuration of the structure of the processors is based on a ring topology and a slice process is assigned to each.

4 Ensemble of Classifiers in CGP

Although *CGPC* allows the construction of accurate decision trees, the performance of the algorithm is strongly depending on the size of the training set. In fact, in this model, one of the most expensive operation is the evaluation of the fitness of each decision tree: the entire data set is needed to compute the number of examples that are correctly classified, thus it must be replicated for each subpopulation. One approach to improve the performance of the model is to build an ensemble of classifiers, each working on a different subset of the original data set, then combine them together to classify the test set.

In this paper we propose an extension of *CGPC* to generate an ensemble of classifiers, each trained on a different subset of the overall data and then use them together to classify new tuples by applying a simple majority voting algorithm, like bagging. The main feature of the new model, in the following referred as *BagCGPC*, is that each subpopulation generates a classifier working on a sample of the training data instead of using all the training set. The single classifier is always represented by the tree with the best fitness in the subpopulation. With K subpopulations we obtain K classifiers that constitute our ensemble. To take advantage of the cellular model of genetic programming subpopulations are not independently evolved, but they exchange the outmost individuals in an asynchronous way. Experimental results show that communication among the subpopulations produces an interesting positive result since the diffusion effect, that allows to transfer classifiers from a subpopulation to another, reduces the average size of trees and consequently improves the performances of the method since the evaluation time of the fitness is reduced.

This cooperative approach has the following advantages :

- samples of the data set are randomly generated;
- large data set that do not fit in main memory can be taken in consideration;
- the method is fault tolerant since the ensemble of classifiers has a collective fault masking ability operating with a variable number of classifiers.

Preliminary experiments on a large data set show that the ensemble of classifiers trained on a subset of the data set obtains higher accuracy than a single classifier the uses the entire data set.

Notice that our approach substantially differs from Iba's scheme [15] that extends genetic programming with bagging, since we use a parallel genetic programming model, we make cooperate the subpopulations to generate the classifiers and each subpopulation does not use the overall training set.

5 Experimental Results

In this section we present preliminary experiments and results of *BagCGPC* on a large data set taken from the UCI Machine Learning Repository [18], the *Cens* data set, and compare them with *CGPC*. The parameters used for the experiments are shown in table 1. Both algorithms run for 100 generations with a population size depending on the number of classifiers. We experimented *BagCGPC* with 2, 3, 4, 5, 10, 15, and 20 classifiers. Every classifier, with its subpopulation, runs on a single processor of the parallel machine. The size of a subpopulation was fixed to 100, thus *CGPC* used a population size of $100 \times number\ of\ classifiers$. For example, if an ensemble of 5 classifiers is considered, the population size for *CGPC* is 500 (and the number of processors on which *CGPC* is executed is 5) while, if the number of classifiers is 20, *CGPC* used a population of 2000 elements (and executed on 20 processors). All results were obtained by averaging 10-fold cross-validation runs. The experiments were performed on a Linux cluster with 16 dual-processor 1,133 Ghz Pentium III nodes having 2 Gbytes of memory connected by Myrinet and running Red Hat v7.2.

Table 1. Main parameter used in the experiments

Name	Value
max_depth_for_new_trees	6
max_depth_after_crossover	6
max_mutant_depth	2
grow_method	RAMPED
selection_method	GROW
crossover_func_pt_fraction	0.7
crossover_any_pt_fraction	0.1
fitness_prop_repro_fraction	0.1
parsimony_factor	0

Table 2. Comparing accuracy for BagCGP and CGPC

Num. proc.	BagCGP				CGPC
	6000	15000	30000	50000	All dataset
1	5,992	5,831	5,770	5,687	5,582
2	5,823	5,779	5,638	5,404	5,407
3	5,662	5,516	5,428	5,375	5,349
4	5,536	5,372	5,254	5,205	5,278
5	5,439	5,338	5,108	5,072	5,244
10	5,359	5,215	5,068	5,040	5,211
15	5,340	5,207	5,060	5,028	5,185
20	5,322	5,183	5,020	5,004	5,127

In our experiments we wanted to investigate the influence of the sample sizes on the accuracy of the method. To this end we used the *Cens* data set, a large real data set containing weighted census data extracted from the 1994 and 1995 current population surveys conducted by the U.S. Census Bureau. The data set consists of 299285 tuples, 42 attributes and two classes.

Figure 3, and the corresponding table 2, show the effect of different sample sizes on accuracy as the number of classifiers increases. For each ensemble, the error of *CGPC* and *BagCGPC* with sample size of 6000, 15000, 30000, and 50000 are shown. From the figure we can note that when the sample size is 6000, *BagCGPC* is not able to outperform the single classifier working on the entire data set. The same effects is obtained when the number of classifiers is less then three. But, as the sample size or the number of classifiers increases, *BagCGPC* is able to obtain an error lower than *CGPC*. An ensemble of four classifiers using a subset of the data of size 30000 obtains higher accuracy. Augmenting the sample size and the number of classifiers a further increase can be attained, though a saturation point stops this effect. Another positive result regards the computation time. In fact *BagCGPC* is much more efficient than *CGPC*. Table 3 shows the the execution times of *CGPC* and *BagCGPC* for each sample. For example, *CGPC* required 6053 seconds to run on the Cens data set for 100 generations with a population size of 500 elements. When five classifiers

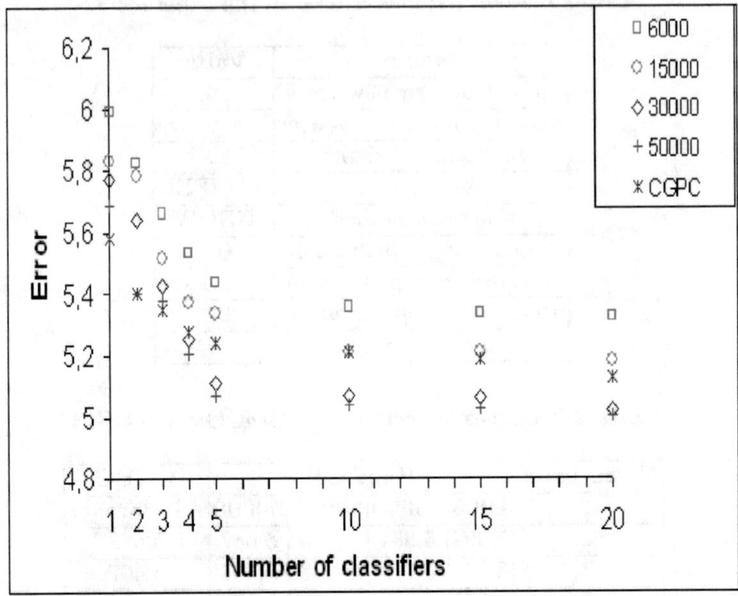

Fig. 3. Error for different sample sizes of training set vs number of classifiers used. (Cens dataset)

Table 3. Comparing execution times for BagCGP and CGPC

Num. proc.	**BagCGP**				**CGPC**
	6000	**15000**	**30000**	**50000**	**All dataset**
1	588	633	783	841	3760
2	596	654	823	976	4051
3	612	719	980	1022	4233
4	635	725	965	1056	5598
5	668	843	1064	1117	6053
10	799	902	1116	1278	6385
15	823	922	1226	1316	8026
20	964	1055	1456	1621	9161

are employed, each using 50000 tuples and a population size of 100 elements, *BagCGPC* needed 1117 seconds of computation time.

As already stated in the previous section, communication among the subpopulations has a positive impact on the average size of the trees and consequently improves the performances of the method since the evaluation time of the fitness is reduced. This effect can be seen in figure 4, where the average length of the trees is shown when the algorithm ran with 5 classifiers and 50000 tuple, in case of communication of the border trees among the subpopulations and no communication, respectively. After 100 generations, in the former case the average size is 900 and the computation time is 1117 seconds, as already said, while in the

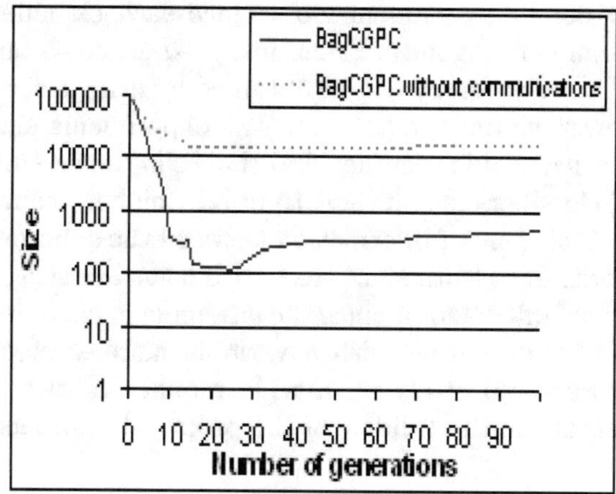

Fig. 4. Average length of the trees for the Cens dataset (5 classifiers, 50000 tuples) with and without communications

Table 4. Comparing execution times and accuracy of *CGPC*, *BagCGPC* and *BagCGPC* without communication using 5 classifiers and 1/5 of the training tuples running on 5 processors

Dataset	CGPC		BagCGPC		BagCGPC without com.	
	Test Error	Time (sec)	Test Error	Time (sec)	Test Error	Time (sec)
Adult	17,26	717	16,58	209	18,26	364
Mushroom	0,35	143	0,43	52	1,23	80
Sat	23,04	228	23,63	30	24,23	47
Shuttle	5,18	729	5,37	151	8,54	174

latter the average size is about 10000 and the time needed by the method was 4081 seconds. In the lack of communication also accuracy worsened, going from 5,07 to 5,56.

A confirmation of this behavior was obtained for other 4 data sets of small-medium size, shown in table 4, where the execution time and the error on the test set for *CGPC* and *BagCGPC* (with and without communications) algorithms are reported, in case of 5 classifiers and a sample of size 1/5 the overall training set. In all the four data sets we obtained a lower execution time and a higher accuracy using the committee of classifiers generated by the *BagCGPC* algorithm with communication with respect to no communication, though in this case the misclassification error is not always lower than that of the single classifier generated by *CGPC*.

6 Conclusions and Future Work

An extension of Cellular Genetic Programming for data classification to induce an ensemble of predictors was presented. The approach is able to deal with large data set that do not fit in main memory since each classifier is trained on a subset of the overall training data. Preliminary experiments on a large real data set showed that higher accuracy can be obtained by using a sample of reasonable size at a much lower computational cost. The experiments showed that sample size influences the achievable accuracy and that, choosing a suitable sample size, a low number of classifiers is sufficient to obtain higher accuracy. Furthermore we showed that the sharing of information between the subpopulations improves the ability of algorithm to learn since trees with a smaller size are produced. The method proposed is fault tolerant since the ensemble of classifiers has a collective fault masking ability operating with a variable number of classifiers. We are planning an experimental study on a wide number of very large benchmark problems to substantiate the validity of the proposed approach.

References

1. Eric Bauer and Ron Kohavi. An empirical comparison of voting classification algorithms: Bagging, boosting, and variants. *Machine Learning*, (36):105–139, 1999.
2. Leo Breiman. Bagging predictors. *Machine Learning*, 24(2):123–140, 1996.
3. Leo Breiman. Arcing classifiers. *Annals of Statistics*, 26:801–824, 1998.
4. Leo Breiman. Pasting small votes for classification in large databases and on-line. *Machine Learning*, 36(1,2):85–103, 1999.
5. P. K. Chan and S.J. Stolfo. A comparative evaluation of voting and meta-learning on partitioned data. In *International Conference on Machine Learning ICML95*, pages 90–98, 1995.
6. N. Chawla, T.E. Moore, W. Bowyer K, L.O. Hall, C. Springer, and P. Kegelmeyer. Bagging-like effects for decision trees and neural nets in protein secondary structure prediction. In *BIOKDD01: Workshop on Data mining in Bioinformatics (SIGKDD01)*, 2001.
7. Thomas G. Dietterich. An experimental comparison of three methods for costructing ensembles of decision trees: Bagging, boosting, and randomization. *Machine Learning*, (40):139–157, 2000.
8. U.M. Fayyad, G. Piatesky-Shapiro, and P. Smith. From data mining to knowledge discovery: an overview. In U.M. Fayyad & al. (Eds), editor, *Advances in Knowledge Discovery and Data Mining*, pages 1–34. AAAI/MIT Press, 1996.
9. G. Folino, C. Pizzuti, and G. Spezzano. A cellular genetic programming approach to classification. In *Proc. Of the Genetic and Evolutionary Computation Conference GECCO99*, pages 1015–1020, Orlando, Florida, July 1999. Morgan Kaufmann.
10. G. Folino, C. Pizzuti, and G. Spezzano. Genetic programming and simulated annealing: A hybrid method to evolve decision trees. In Riccardo Poli, Wolfgang Banzhaf, William B. Langdon, Julian Miller, Peter Nordin, and Terence C. Fogarty, editors, *Proceedings of EuroGP'2000*, volume 1802 of *LNCS*, pages 294–303, Edinburgh, UK, 15-16 April 2000. Springer-Verlag.
11. G. Folino, C. Pizzuti, and G. Spezzano. Cage: A tool for parallel genetic programming applications. In Julian F. Miller, Marco Tomassini, Pier Luca Lanzi, Conor Ryan, Andrea G. B. Tettamanzi, and William B. Langdon, editors, *Proceedings of EuroGP'2001*, volume 2038 of *LNCS*, pages 64–73, Lake Como, Italy, 18-20 April 2001. Springer-Verlag.

12. G. Folino, C. Pizzuti, and G. Spezzano. Parallel genetic programming for decision tree induction. In *Proceedings of the 13th IEEE International Conference on Tools with Artificial Intelligence ICTAI01*, pages 129–135. IEEE Computer Society, 2001.
13. A.A. Freitas. A genetic programming framework for two data mining tasks: Classification and generalised rule induction. In *Proceedings of the 2nd Int. Conference on Genetic Programming*, pages 96–101. Stanford University, CA, USA, 1997.
14. Y. Freund and R. Scapire. Experiments with a new boosting algorithm. In *Proceedings of the 13th Int. Conference on Machine Learning*, pages 148–156, 1996.
15. Hitoshi Iba. Bagging, boosting, and bloating in genetic programming. In *Proc. Of the Genetic and Evolutionary Computation Conference GECCO99*, pages 1053–1060, Orlando, Florida, July 1999. Morgan Kaufmann.
16. J. R. Koza. *Genetic Programming: On the Programming of Computers by means of Natural Selection.* MIT Press, Cambridge, MA, 1992.
17. R.E. Marmelstein and G.B. Lamont. Pattern classification using a hybbrid genetic program - decision tree approach. In *Proceedings of the Third Annual Conference on Genetic Programming*, Morgan Kaufmann, 1998.
18. C.J. Merz and P.M. Murphy. In *UCI repository of Machine Learning*, http://www.ics.uci/mlearn/MLRepository.html, 1996.
19. N.I. Nikolaev and V. Slavov. Inductive genetic programming with decision trees. In *Proceedings of the 9th International Conference on Machine Learning*, Prague, Czech Republic, 1997.
20. J. Ross Quinlan. *C4.5 Programs for Machine Learning.* Morgan Kaufmann, San Mateo, Calif., 1993.
21. J. Ross Quinlan. Bagging, boosting, and c4.5. In *Proceedings of the 13th National Conference on Artificial Intelligence AAAI96*, pages 725–730. Mit Press, 1996.
22. M.D. Ryan and V.J. Rayward-Smith. The evolution of decision trees. In *Proceedings of the Third Annual Conference on Genetic Programming*, Morgan Kaufmann, 1998.
23. M. Tomassini. Parallel and distributed evolutionary algorithms: A review. In P. Neittaanmki K. Miettinen, M. Mkel and J. Periaux, editors, *Evolutionary Algorithms in Engineering and Computer Science*, J. Wiley and Sons, Chichester, 1999.

Improving Symbolic Regression with Interval Arithmetic and Linear Scaling

Maarten Keijzer

Computer Science Department, Free University Amsterdam
mkeijzer@cs.vu.nl

Abstract. The use of protected operators and squared error measures are standard approaches in symbolic regression. It will be shown that two relatively minor modifications of a symbolic regression system can result in greatly improved predictive performance and reliability of the induced expressions. To achieve this, interval arithmetic and linear scaling are used. An experimental section demonstrates the improvements on 15 symbolic regression problems.

1 Introduction

Two commonly used methods in symbolic regression are the focus of this work: the use of protected operators and of error measures. It will be shown that although protected operators avoid undefined mathematical behaviour of the function set by defining some ad-hoc behaviour at those points, the technique has severe shortcomings in the vicinity of mathematical singularities. An approach using interval arithmetic is proposed to provably induce expressions that do not contain undefined behaviour anywhere in their output range, both for training and unseen data.

Although error measures (particularly squared error measures) often satisfactorily determine the goal of a symbolic regression run, they can in many circumstances be very difficult for genetic programming. Here the use of linear scaling, prior to calculating the error measure, is examined. This scaling takes the form of a simple and efficient linear regression that is used to find the optimal slope and intercept of the expressions against the target. In effect, the use of linear scaling is a fast method to calculate two constants that otherwise would have to be found during the run of the genetic programming system. This enables the system to concentrate on the more important problem of inducing an expression that has the desired shape.

This paper demonstrates that the use of these techniques in combination provide a very effective method of performing symbolic regression that produces solutions that provably avoid undefined behaviour on both training and test set, and which performs better than a more standard approach. The runtime overhead for the two techniques is minimal: in the case of interval arithmetic a single evaluation of the tree suffices, while the linear scaling approach can be done in time linear with the number of cases. It is also demonstrates that the implementation of these techniques is, if not trivial, particularly easy to achieve in most

C. Ryan et al. (Eds.): EuroGP 2003, LNCS 2610, pp. 70–82, 2003.

tree-based genetic programming systems. Overall, the work demonstrates to the genetic programming community that it is possible to dramatically improve the reliability and performance of a symbolic regression system without resorting to exotic measures.

2 Why Protected Operators Do Not Help

In standard genetic programming, Koza identified the need for *closure* in the set of primitives: functions and terminals. Every function is defined in such a way that it can handle every possible input value. For symbolic regression, this means that some ad-hoc values need to be defined to avoid division by zero, taking the logarithm of zero or a negative number or taking the square root of a negative number[1]. For example: Koza chose to return the value 1 in the case of a division by zero to make it possible for genetic programming to synthesize constants by using x/x [10]. Likewise, exception values can be defined for other functions that have a limited range of applicability such as the logarithm and the square root. Another approach is to delete proposed solutions when they perform a mathematically unsound operation. Although this might avoid destructive operations on the training set, the practitioner still has to protect the operators when applied to unseen data. A third approach is to restrict the function set to those functions that do not have undefined behaviour, for instance the set of polynomial functions, possibly augmented with trigonometry and exponentiation. Systems based on the induction of polynomials, have been used for symbolic regression with success [6,1]. However, even though the set of polynomials can approximate any function, it does do this at the possible cost of increasing the size of the solutions[2]. By limiting the expressiveness of genetic programming one might miss out on that particular expression that combines representational clarity with low error. Especially when there are reasons to assume that particular functions are valid in the application domain, restricting oneself to polynomials might be a suboptimal choice.

Howard and Roberts [5], identified another problem with protected division. In their problem setting, the arbitrary values a division operator can induce led very quickly to a local optimum that used these values. Their solution was to sacrifice the division operator and continue with attempting to find an polynomial.

Although protection of operators at undefined values will make sure that the function that is evolved using symbolic regression will always return a numerical value on any input, it can lead to undesired phenomena in the output range of such a function. Consider for instance the functions induced by genetic programming in Figure 1. Although these functions are well-behaved on the training set, examining their range on all possible inputs reveals the use of asymptotes in

[1] Assuming that symbolic regression is performed on the set of reals instead of the set of complex numbers.

[2] As an example, consider the polynomial Taylor expansion of the exponentiation function. With every decrease in error an extra polynomial term needs to be added.

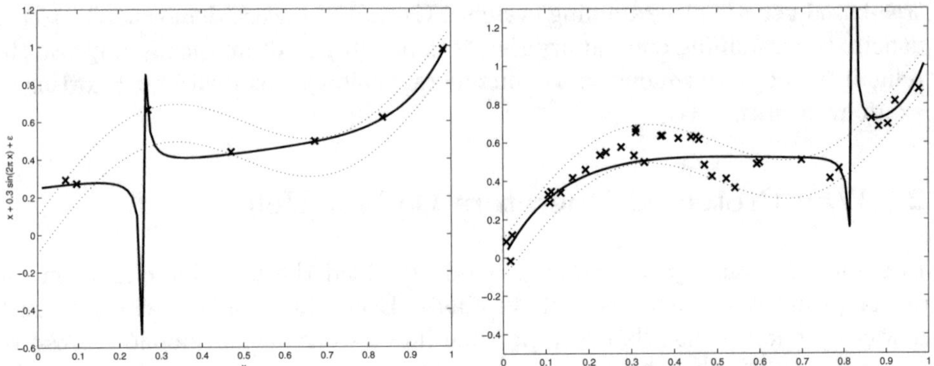

Fig. 1. Two examples where genetic programming induces an asymptote to fit the data: (a) a situation with sparse data and (b) a situation with a more dense covering. The set of training points are depicted with crosses. The function set included the protected division operator.

regions of the input space that are not covered by the training points. When using this function on unseen data, it is quite possible that a prediction will be requested for a point that lies on this asymptote. In that case the function identified by genetic programming can return arbitrarily high or low values. Note that protection only holds for the point where the actual division by zero occurs: there the function will return the ad hoc value defined by the protection rule.

3 Static Analysis through Interval Arithmetic

Interval arithmetic is a general method for calculating the bounds for an operation of arithmetic, given the bounds of the input arguments. It is often used to give reliable bounds on the value of mathematical functions calculated on hardware of finite precision, or in global optimization [2]. Given for instance that an input variable x has values in the range $[-1, 1]$, and another input variable y consists of values in the range $[0, 2]$, it is possible to deduce that the addition function $x + y$ will necessarily output values that lie in the range $[-1, 3]$. Similarly, a division by a variable that has the value 0 as a possibility, will result in infinite bounds, as division by zero is a possibility.

Sanchez used interval arithmetic to force genetic programming to output bounds as the output for cases, rather than point predictions [14] . Here we will focus on a very basic use of interval arithmetic: making sure that the mathematical function defined by a genetic programming system does not contain any undefined values. It then functions as a pre-processing step for the acceptance of a solution to be submitted to evaluation for performance. This can be viewed as a form of static analysis. For a different problem setting than symbolic regression, Johnson [8] attempts to replace evaluation over fitness cases with a more rigorous framework of static analysis techniques. A complete replacement of evaluation by static analysis does not seem to be feasible for symbolic regression due to the high dimensionality of the input space. Here static analysis in the form of interval arithmetic is used as a fast and simple test of the feasibility of solutions. To use interval arithmetic, an extra demand is placed on the definition of the terminal set, namely the theoretical range of the input variables. Many variables have such a known range: a percentage measurement is forced to lie in the interval [0,1], while a standard deviation is necessarily positive. If the theoretical range is unknown, or if it is infinite, the training data itself can be used to define these bounds. Given that each variable x is accompanied with its lower bound x_l and its upper bound x_u, all operations of arithmetic can be defined as recursive operations on the lower and upper bound of the interval. Some examples:

$$x + y \quad \begin{cases} \text{lower}: & x_l + y_l \\ \text{upper}: & x_u + y_u \end{cases}$$

$$-x \quad \begin{cases} \text{lower}: & -x_u \\ \text{upper}: & -x_l \end{cases}$$

$$x \times y \quad \begin{cases} \text{lower}: & \min(x_l y_l, x_l y_u, x_u y_l, x_u y_u) \\ \text{upper}: & \max(x_l y_l, x_l y_u, x_u y_l, x_u y_u) \end{cases}$$

$$e^x \quad \begin{cases} \text{lower}: & e^{x_l} \\ \text{upper}: & e^{x_u} \end{cases}$$

And for division:

$$1/x \quad \begin{cases} \text{lower}: & \min(1/x_l, 1/x_u) \\ \text{upper}: & \max(1/x_l, 1/x_u) \end{cases}$$

if $\text{sign}(x_l) = \text{sign}(x_u)$, and none of the bounds are zero.

Similar bounds can be defined for functions such as sqrt and the logarithm, whose monotonic behaviour make the definition equivalent to the application of the operators on the bounds. Checking whether the bounds fall into the well-defined area of the range is then trivial. Periodic functions such as sine and cosine take a bit more work, as the output range is defined by the exact periods that are in use in the input range[3].

By calculating the bounds recursively through a symbolic expression, possible problem with undefined values are identified at the node where the violation can occur. Here it is suggested that when this occurs, the individual is either assigned the worst possible performance value, or that it is simply deleted. As this procedure involves a single evaluation of the tree, it is a cheap method to make sure that all individuals are well-defined for all possible input values. Tree based GP systems that use a recursive or stack based approach to evaluation, could easily accommodate the evaluation of the theoretical bounds of the algorithm.

Although in mathematical notation, the implementation of interval arithmetic may seem trivial, it is found that to use the definitions straightforwardly can lead to numerically unstable results. Small roundoff errors at the start of

[3] Calculating tight bounds for these trigonometric functions is however expensive. Therefore, in the experimental section, the loose bounds of [-1,1] are always returned for the sine and cosine functions.

a big calculation can propagate in such a way that subsequent interval calculations become wrong. To counter this, a library for interval arithmetic is used that uses the underlying hardware to provably make sure that the intervals that are defined include all possible floating point numbers in the interval.

Even though the algorithm sketched above will return the theoretical range for the entire function if it is well defined, this information is not used, because the bounds are not necessarily tight. Consider for example the expression $x * x$, with bounds $x_l = -1$ and $x_u = 1$. Application of the interval arithmetic rule for multiplication will lead to an output range of $[-1, 1]$, while a tighter bound of $[0, 1]$ can be deduced. In general the effects of a multiple occurrence of a single variable in the expression, will lead to larger bounds than necessary. For this reason, it can be necessary to include the function $\mathrm{sqr}(x) = x{*}x$ with appropriate interval calculations next to the usual binary multiplication, to make it possible that the formula $1/(1 + \mathrm{sqr}(x))$ is not discarded when x is bounded below by a value smaller than -1.

4 Minimization of Error Can Deceive Genetic Programming

Practitioners of symbolic regression usually use absolute or squared error measures to calculate the performance of a solution. Due to the straightforward comparison of the predicted value and the target value when using error measures, a genetic programming system is forced to first get the range right before any solutions can be considered. Consider for example the two target functions $t = x^2$ and $t = 100 + x^2$. When using standard symbolic regression to find these functions, a large difference in search efficiency can be observed. Whereas the first target function is readily found (often even in the initial generation), the second target function is usually not found at all. Table 1 shows the results of experiments with these two different target functions. When floating point constants are used, genetic programming routinely converges on the average of the training data: a value of 100.37. Only in 8 cases out of the 50 runs that were performed did the particular genetic programming system find something that had a better performance than this average. The selection pressure on getting the range right is so high in this case, that the system spends most effort in finding that particular value. Once found, diversity has dropped to such a point that the additional square of the inputs is no longer found.

5 Linear Scaling

The use of linear scaling (regression) is by no means new to genetic programming. Iba, Nikolaev and others routinely use multiple linear regression for finding coefficients in polynomial regression models [6,7,12]. Hiden, McKay and other have researched many different forms of multiple linear regression for combining several expressions created by GP [11,4,3]. However, multiple linear regression is

Table 1. Number of successes of a genetic programming system on two simple problems. For each problem the system was run 50 times for 20 generations using a population size of 500 individuals. The function set consisted of simple arithmetic. The inputs consisted of 21 regularly spaced points between -1 and 1. A solution was considered a success if its mean squared error was smaller than 0.001.

Target	**Success Rate**
x^2	98%
$x^2 + 100$	16%

a fairly costly procedure as it involves a matrix inversion either over the covariance matrix, or over the data set itself. Another problem with multiple linear regression lies in the need to specify the number of coefficients that are used. If this number increases, the likeliness of overfitting increases as well. Topchy and Punch [16] go so far as to extend linear regression to a more general gradient search. With their approach, coefficients appearing inside non-linear function are optimized. They also use a protected operator, namely division. A full gradient descent is computationally even more expensive than multiple linear regression, therefore Topchy and Punch limit the number of gradient steps for each individual to 3 [16]. They also report that the individuals undergoing gradient search tend to increase the number of coefficients to be able to get a better performance on the training set.

Here the use of the simplest form of regression is examined: the calculation of the slope and intercept of a formula. Given that $y = \text{gp}(x)$ is the output of an expression induced by genetic programming on the input data x, a linear regression on the target values t can be performed using the equations:

$$b = \frac{\sum[(t - \bar{t})(y - \bar{y})]}{\sum[(y - \bar{y})^2]} \tag{1}$$

$$a = \bar{t} - b\bar{y} \tag{2}$$

where n is the number of cases, and $\bar{y}$ and $\bar{t}$ denote the average output and average target value respectively. These expressions calculate the *slope* and *intercept* respectively of a set of outputs y, such that the sum of squared errors between t and $a + by$ is minimized. The operations defined by Equation 1 and 2 can be done in $O(N)$ time.

After this any error measure can be calculated on the scaled formula $a + by$, for instance the mean squared error (MSE):

$$MSE(t, a + by) = \frac{1}{N}\sum_{i}^{N}(a + by - t)^2 \tag{3}$$

If a is different from 0 and b is different from 1, the procedure outlined above is guaranteed to reduce the MSE for any formula $y = \text{gp}(x)$. The cost of calculating the slope and intercept is linear in the size of the dataset. By efficiently calculating the slope and intercept for each individual, the need to search for these two constants is removed from the genetic programming run. Genetic programming is then free to search for that expression whose *shape* is most similar to that of the target function.

To ensure numerical stability in the calculation of the slope, the variance of the outputs y is measured. If this value exceeds 10^7 or is lower than 10^{-7}, the individual gets deleted. Note that an expression that evaluates to a constant will lead to a denominator of 0 in Equation 1. In this case the expression will also get deleted.

6 Demonstration

To demonstrate the use of both proposed improvements a number of experiments are performed. To test the claim that the use of interval arithmetic removes one source of overfitting, a genetic programming system with and without interval checks is used. Two things need to be ascertained: first and foremost, it needs to be shown that the use of interval arithmetic indeed produces solutions that perform better on unseen data than solutions produced without such interval checks. Secondly, it needs to be ascertained if there is a price to pay for using interval arithmetic. It could be possible that deleting individuals that are possibly undefined, precludes a genetic programming system of performing optimally. To test the claim that the use of scaling reduces underfitting, it would be sufficient to show that it will produce better solutions on the training data. Although it seems vacuous to perform these experiments as it is a priori known that the use of scaling will reduce the training error, even for random search, it is still instructive to see the amount of improvement that can be achieved using this method. At this point, no effort is undertaken to estimate the generalization performance of the scaled and unscaled variants. The genetic programming system that is used does not use any form of regularization, and the expressions are allowed to grow to a size of 1024 nodes. Error on a separate testset is only used to estimate the likeliness of the systems to produce destructive overfitting behaviour.

These questions inspired three settings for the experiments: (a) one where both interval arithmetic and linear scaling are used; (b) one for which linear scaling is not used but interval arithmetic is; and (c) one for which linear scaling is used, but interval arithmetic is not. The use of interval arithmetic is checked by comparing the performance on both test and training set of the two systems that both use linear scaling, while the use of linear scaling is checked by comparing the training set performance of the two systems that both use interval arithmetic instead of protected operators.

Choosing a good set of problems for testing symbolic regression is difficult, especially because no established set of benchmark problems has been established. To prevent the bias inherent in an ad-hoc definition of testing functions, most problems are taken from other papers that apply or propose improvements on symbolic regression. Where possible the results produced by the improvements suggested in this paper will be compared to the results in the papers that are used. The target expressions defined below are preceded with a reference to the originating paper. In one case there is no such reference, this is the rational function using three variables.

$$[9] : f(x) = 0.3x \sin(2\pi x) \tag{4}$$

$$[13] : f(x) = x^3 \exp^{-x} \cos(x) \sin(x)(\sin^2(x) * \cos(x) - 1) \tag{5}$$

$$[] : f(x, y, z) = \frac{30xz}{(x-10)y^2} \tag{6}$$

$$[15] : f(x) = \sum_i^x 1/i \tag{7}$$

$$[15] : f(x) = logx \tag{8}$$

$$[15] : f(x) = \sqrt{x} \tag{9}$$

$$[15] : f(x) = \text{arcsinh}(x) \tag{10}$$

$$[15] : f(x, y) = x^y \tag{11}$$

$$[16] : f(x, y) = xy + sin((x-1)(y-1)) \tag{12}$$

$$[16] : f(x, y) = x^4 - x^3 + y^2/2 - y \tag{13}$$

$$[16] : f(x, y) = 6sin(x)cos(y) \tag{14}$$

$$[16] : f(x, y) = 8/(2 + x^2 + y^2) \tag{15}$$

$$[16] : f(x, y) = x^3/5 + y^3/2 - y - x \tag{16}$$

The aim of this set of experiments is to demonstrate the practical implications of the use of the two methods studied here. Being of low dimensionality does not make the problems easy however. Many of the problems above mix trigonometry with polynomials, or make the problems in other ways highly non-linear. The description of the sampling strategy and other problem specific details can be found in Table 3. It is attempted to mimic the problem setup from the originating papers as closely as possible. The genetic programming system that is used in the experiments, is a steady state algorithm, that uses subtree crossover and node mutation as its genetic operators. Parents are chosen using tournament selection. A child is created using crossover, and is subsequently mutated. The child replaces an individual that is chosen using a third independent (but inverse) tournament. Crossover points are chosen using a heuristic similar to the 90/10 rule [10] by giving the uniform node selection routine three tries to select a non-terminal. Random constants are ephemeral, but with a small twist. The system uses one byte per node, where all values not taken up by functions or variables are used as constants. After random initialization of the constants using a normal distribution with standard deviation 5, the constants are sorted. This sort order is used by node mutation to select a single increment or decrement of the index to the ephemeral constant in 50% of the cases, otherwise a uniform index mutation is used. This allows for small changes in the constant value to take place more regularly than otherwise. The parameters for the system can be found in Table 2.

Table 4 shows the amount of destructive overfitting that occurs with each of the three training setups. It is clear from the table that the approach that

Table 2. Parameter settings for the genetic programming system. Unless noted otherwise in Table 3 these settings are used for each run.

Population Size	500
Function Set	$\{\ x+y,\ x \times y,\ 1/x,\ -x,\ \text{sqrt}(x)\ \}$
Tournament Size	5
Number of Evaluations	25,000
Maximum Genome Size	1024
Number of Runs	50

Table 3. Problem settings for the 15 problems tackled in this paper. The training and testing ranges are denoted using *[start:step:stop]* notation when the set is created using regular intervals. The notation $rnd(min, max)$ defines random (uniform) sampling in the range, while the mesh([start:step:stop]) defines regular sampling in two dimension.

Problem	Equation	range (train)	range (test)	note
1	Eq 4	x = [-1:0.1:1]	[-1:0.001:1]	
2	Eq 4	x = [-2:0.1:2]	[-2:0.001:2]	
3	Eq 4	x = [-3:0.1:3]	[-3:0.001:3]	
4	Eq 5	x = [0:0.05:10]	[0.05:0.05:10.05]	{exp, log, sin, cos}
				100000 evals
5	Eq 6	x,z = rnd(-1,1)	idem	Train: 1000 cases
		y = rnd(1,2)	idem	Test: 10000 cases
6	Eq 7	x = [1:1:50]	[1:1:120]	extrapolation
7	Eq 8	x = [1:1:100]	[1:0.1:100]	
8	Eq 9	x = [0:1:100]	[0:0.1:100]	
9	Eq 10	x = [0:1:100]	[0:0.1:100]	
10	Eq 11	x,y = rnd(0,1)	x,y = mesh([0:0.01:1])	Train: 100 cases
11	Eq 12	x,y = rnd(-3,3)	x,y = mesh([-3:0.01:3])	Train: 20 cases
12	Eq 13	x,y = rnd(-3,3)	x,y = mesh([-3:0.01:3])	Train: 20 cases
13	Eq 14	x,y = rnd(-3,3)	x,y = mesh([-3:0.01:3])	Train: 20 cases
14	Eq 15	x,y = rnd(-3,3)	x,y = mesh([-3:0.01:3])	Train: 20 cases
15	Eq 16	x,y = rnd(-3,3)	x,y = mesh([-3:0.01:3])	Train: 20 cases

Table 4. Amount of destructive overfitting over 50 runs for each of the 15 problems. For each run, the best of run result is evaluated over the test data, and the number of times the MSE exceeds 10000 is recorded.

problem	1	2	3	4	5	6	7	8	9	10	11	12	13	14	15
no interval	6	11	25				1			49	31	30	36	23	40
no scaling			2									1	15		1
interval + scaling												1	3		1

only uses protected operators is much more likely to produce expressions that generalize so badly that they are useless in prediction. Both methods that do use interval arithmetic instead of protected operators are much less susceptible to the problem of destructive overfitting. On Problem 10, genetic programming without interval checks consistently uses asymptotes to model the training data. This leads to a very poor generalization performance.

The performance over the training data for the three methods can be found in Table 5. For comparative purposes, the training error is stated in the percentage points of the Normalized Root Mean Square Error (NRMS), which is calculated as $100\% \times sqrt(N/(N-1) \times MSE)/\sigma_t$, where N is the number of cases, and σ_t

Table 5. Mean training performance of the best of run individuals produced by the three methods on 50 runs. The figures are stated in percentage points of the normalized root mean squared error, for which a value of 100 is equal to the performance of the mean target value and an error of 0 corresponds with a perfect fit. A more detailed comparison between the scaled and unscaled variant for the problems stated in boldface can be found in Figure 2.

problem	1	2	**3**	**4**	5	6	7	**8**	9	10	11	12	**13**	14	15
no interval	20	54	76	22	2	2	2	2	2	11	12	4	30	15	10
no scaling	50	78	88	46	22	49	50	56	93	54	19	4	63	91	23
interval + scaling	8	34	62	15	1	1	1	1	1	7	11	1	25	1	7

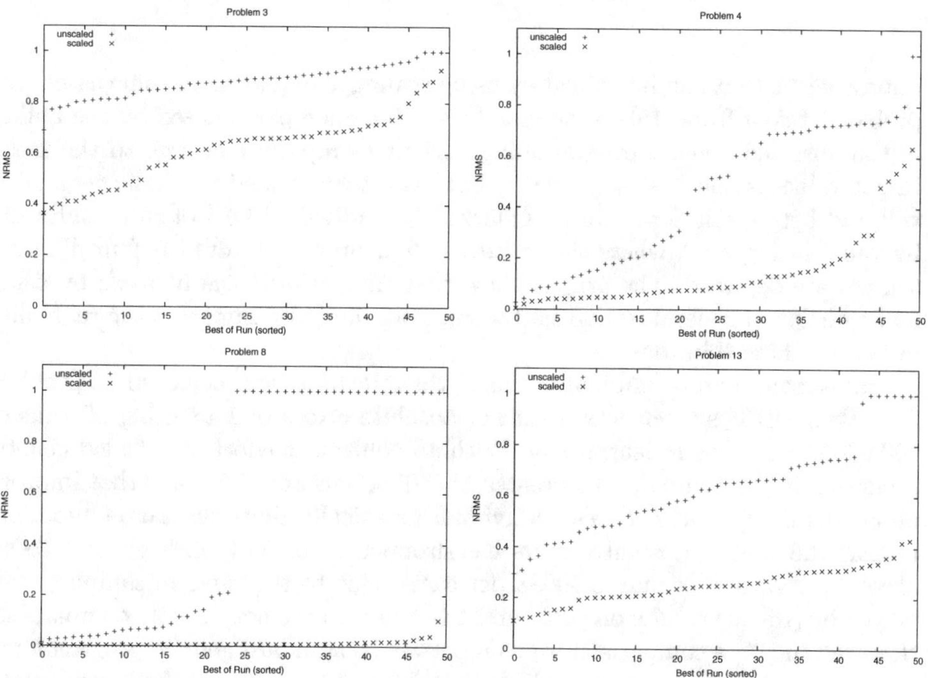

Fig. 2. Plot of the errors of the best of run individuals on the training set for 4 selected problems. Depicted are the NRMS errors for the scaled and the unscaled variant. An error of 1.0 usually means that the run has converged to a constant.

the standard deviation of the target values. This measure assigns the value 100 to an expression that performs equivalent with the mean target value. A perfect fit is obtained when the NRMS error reaches 0.

Interestingly, the comparison between the use of protected operators and interval arithmetic (that both use scaling), reveals that the exclusion of individuals that can have undefined values on unseen data actually improves the ability to fit the data. It was already observed by Howard and Roberts that the use of the division operator near the value zero is a source for premature convergence [5]. The findings in this work give additional support for this claim. The performance

Table 6. Performance difference (MSE) between standard (unscaled) GP, gradient descent GP (HGP), and scaled GP on the 5 problems taken from [16]. The first two columns of results are taken from [16] and represent the mean MSE on 10 runs, each run taking 30,000 evaluations. The results in the last two columns are performed using 50 runs, and represent the experiments performed here on 25,000 evaluations.

Problem	unscaled GP [16]	HGP [16]	unscaled GP	scaled GP
11	0.8	0.47	0.37	0.11
12	2.18	1.03	2.80	0.10
13	6.59	5.98	2.74	0.43
14	4.41	4.06	0.47	0.001
15	0.78	0.27	1.60	0.12

improvement that can be gained by using scaling is high, and in some cases (the problems taken from [15]), extreme. This is for some part caused by the ability of the unscaled genetic programming variant to rapidly converge to the mean target value as the best expression, but even then, scaled symbolic regression will find better solutions more regularly. The individual best of run results can be found in Figure 2, where the results on four problems from the four different sources are depicted. The graphs show that the performance increase by using scaling helps in general to find better solutions, and also improves the reliability in finding these solutions.

Salustowicz and Schmidhuber report that the best error achieved on problem 4 by their PIPE system was a sum of absolute errors of 1.18 using 20 runs of 100,000 evaluations in length [13]. With an equivalent effort, the scaled genetic programming system not only creates 11 individuals out of 50 runs that improve upon this figure, but the best individual practically finds the target function, in that the sum of absolute errors has dropped to 0.098 (which equates to an absolute deviation of only 0.00098 per case). Due to the random sampling employed by [16] the results on problem 11 through 15 are not directly comparable. However, in [16] a comparison is given between a standard genetic programming approach and their use of a gradient descent routine. These differences is what is used here to give an estimate of the difference between the use of gradient descent and the scaling method used here, by comparing using the unscaled genetic programming system as a baseline for comparison. The results are tabulated in Table 6. Even though the results are not directly comparable, the magnitude of the differences indicate that scaled GP performs at the very least as good as the use of gradient descent. It is however left as future work to compare simple linear scaling as is done here with more involved coefficient fitting methods as multiple linear regression and gradient descent.

7 Conclusion

The use of interval arithmetic on the theoretical range of the input values for symbolic regression, is an efficient way to induce functions that will provably avoid the use of mathematical functions at undefined values on unseen data.

This completely circumvents the need to protect mathematical operators and avoids the induction of asymptotes in areas of the input range that are not covered by the training examples. It was demonstrated that the use of protected operators do not help in avoiding the use of asymptotes. For all 15 problems tried here, the use of interval arithmetic in itself already helps in performing better.

The use of scaling prior to evaluation is an efficient way to promote solutions that have the overall shape of the target function right, but miss the appropriate scale. In effect, the scaling method is used to calculate the two linear constants for each individual in time linear with the number of cases. The improvement achieved by using this simple form of scaling is often dramatic when compared to an unscaled variant.

The experiments point out that the combination of interval arithmetic and linear scaling provides a safe and effective method of performing symbolic regression, without introducing additional parameters and also without sacrificing runtime efficiency.

References

1. J. W. Davidson, D. A. Savic, and G. A. Walters, *Method for the identification of explicit polynomial formulae for the friction in turbulent pipe flow*, Journal of Hydroinformatics 1 (1999), no. 2, 115–126.
2. Eldon Hansen, *Global optimization using interval analysis*, Dekker, New York, 1992.
3. Hugo Hiden, Ben McKay, Mark Willis, and Gary Montague, *Non-linear partial least squares using genetic programming*, Genetic Programming 1998: Proceedings of the Third Annual Conference (University of Wisconsin, Madison, Wisconsin, USA) (John R. Koza, Wolfgang Banzhaf, Kumar Chellapilla, Kalyanmoy Deb, Marco Dorigo, David B. Fogel, Max H. Garzon, David E. Goldberg, Hitoshi Iba, and Rick Riolo, eds.), Morgan Kaufmann, 22-25 July 1998, pp. 128–133.
4. Hugo Hiden, Mark Willis, Ming Tham, Paul Turner, and Gary Montague, *Non-linear principal components analysis using genetic programming*, Second International Conference on Genetic Algorithms in Engineering Systems: Innovations and Applications, GALESIA (University of Strathclyde, Glasgow, UK) (Ali Zalzala, ed.), Institution of Electrical Engineers, 1-4 September 1997.
5. Daniel Howard and Simon C. Roberts, *Genetic programming solution of the convection-diffusion equation*, Proceedings of the Genetic and Evolutionary Computation Conference (GECCO-2001) (San Francisco, California, USA) (Lee Spector, Erik D. Goodman, Annie Wu, W. B. Langdon, Hans-Michael Voigt, Mitsuo Gen, Sandip Sen, Marco Dorigo, Shahram Pezeshk, Max H. Garzon, and Edmund Burke, eds.), Morgan Kaufmann, 7-11 July 2001, pp. 34–41.
6. Hitoshi Iba, Hugo de Garis, and Taisuke Sato, *Genetic programming using a minimum description length principle*, Advances in Genetic Programming (Kenneth E. Kinnear, Jr., ed.), MIT Press, 1994, pp. 265–284.
7. Hitoshi Iba and Nikolay Nikolaev, *Genetic programming polynomial models of financial data series*, Proceedings of the 2000 Congress on Evolutionary Computation CEC00 (La Jolla Marriott Hotel La Jolla, California, USA), IEEE Press, 6-9 July 2000, pp. 1459–1466.

8. Colin Johnson, *Deriving genetic programming fitness properties by static analysis*, Genetic Programming, Proceedings of the 5th European Conference, EuroGP 2002 (Kinsale, Ireland) (James A. Foster, Evelyne Lutton, Julian Miller, Conor Ryan, and Andrea G. B. Tettamanzi, eds.), LNCS, vol. 2278, Springer-Verlag, 3-5 April 2002, pp. 298–307.
9. Maarten Keijzer and Vladan Babovic, *Genetic programming, ensemble methods and the bias/variance tradeoff - introductory investigations*, Genetic Programming, Proceedings of EuroGP'2000 (Edinburgh) (Riccardo Poli, Wolfgang Banzhaf, William B. Langdon, Julian F. Miller, Peter Nordin, and Terence C. Fogarty, eds.), LNCS, vol. 1802, Springer-Verlag, 15-16 April 2000, pp. 76–90.
10. John R. Koza, *Genetic programming: On the programming of computers by means of natural selection*, MIT Press, Cambridge, MA, USA, 1992.
11. Ben McKay, Mark Willis, Dominic Searson, and Gary Montague, *Non-linear continuum regression using genetic programming*, Proceedings of the Genetic and Evolutionary Computation Conference (Orlando, Florida, USA) (Wolfgang Banzhaf, Jason Daida, Agoston E. Eiben, Max H. Garzon, Vasant Honavar, Mark Jakiela, and Robert E. Smith, eds.), vol. 2, Morgan Kaufmann, 13-17 July 1999, pp. 1106–1111.
12. Nikolay Y. Nikolaev and Hitoshi Iba, *Regularization approach to inductive genetic programming*, IEEE Transactions on Evolutionary Computing 54 (2001), no. 4, 359–375.
13. R. P. Salustowicz and J. Schmidhuber, *Probabilistic incremental program evolution*, Evolutionary Computation 5 (1997), no. 2, 123–141.
14. Luciano Sanchez, *Interval-valued GA-P algorithms*, IEEE Transactions on Evolutionary Computation 4 (2000), no. 1, 64–72.
15. Matthew Streeter and Lee A. Becker, *Automated discovery of numerical approximation formulae via genetic programming*, Proceedings of the Genetic and Evolutionary Computation Conference (GECCO-2001) (San Francisco, California, USA) (Lee Spector, Erik D. Goodman, Annie Wu, W. B. Langdon, Hans-Michael Voigt, Mitsuo Gen, Sandip Sen, Marco Dorigo, Shahram Pezeshk, Max H. Garzon, and Edmund Burke, eds.), Morgan Kaufmann, 7-11 July 2001, pp. 147–154.
16. Alexander Topchy and W. F. Punch, *Faster genetic programming based on local gradient search of numeric leaf values*, Proceedings of the Genetic and Evolutionary Computation Conference (GECCO-2001) (San Francisco, California, USA) (Lee Spector, Erik D. Goodman, Annie Wu, W. B. Langdon, Hans-Michael Voigt, Mitsuo Gen, Sandip Sen, Marco Dorigo, Shahram Pezeshk, Max H. Garzon, and Edmund Burke, eds.), Morgan Kaufmann, 7-11 July 2001, pp. 155–162.

Evolving Hierarchical and Recursive Teleo-reactive Programs through Genetic Programming

Mykel J. Kochenderfer

Department of Computer Science
Stanford University
Stanford, California 94305
mykel@cs.stanford.edu

Abstract. Teleo-reactive programs and the triple tower architecture have been proposed as a framework for linking perception and action in agents. The triple tower architecture continually updates the agent's knowledge of the world and evokes actions according to teleo-reactive control structures. This paper uses block stacking problems to demonstrate how genetic programming may be used to evolve hierarchical and recursive teleo-reactive programs.

1 Introduction

It is important that the control programs for intelligent agents be easy for humans to write and for machines to generate and modify through learning and planning. Nils Nilsson has proposed the teleo-reactive program structure as a possible candidate for representing these programs [4,5]. Teleo-reactive programs are hierarchical and consist of ordered lists of production rules whose conditions are continuously evaluated with reference to the agent's perceptions, thereby enabling the creation of intelligent and robust mobile robots that are highly reactive and adaptable in dynamic environments.

Teleo-reactive programs make up the "action tower" of Nilsson's triple tower architecture for autonomous agents [7]. The other two towers maintain the agent's understanding of the world, which is used by the teleo-reactive programs to evoke the appropriate actions. The "perception tower" contains rules that create an increasingly abstract description of the world based on the primitive predicates perceived by the agent. These descriptions of the world are then deposited in the "model tower" and kept faithful to the environment through a truth-maintenance system. Nilsson illustrated the performance of the triple tower architecture and teleo-reactive programs in the blocks-world domain. He created a system capable of stacking any specified tower of blocks on a table from any configuration without search[1].

[1] A link to an animated Java applet demonstrating the use of teleo-reactive programs and the triple tower architecture in the blocks-world domain may be found online here: `http://cs.stanford.edu/~nilsson/trweb/tr.html`.

C. Ryan et al. (Eds.): EuroGP 2003, LNCS 2610, pp. 83–92, 2003.

While other learning techniques for teleo-reactive programs have been proposed [6], this paper expands upon previous work by the author [1] and is the first to demonstrate the suitability of genetic programming for the automatic creation of hierarchical and recursive teleo-reactive programs. To make it easy to compare the evolved teleo-reactive programs with Nilsson's human-designed block stacking system, the same predicates available in Nilsson's "perception tower" are used along with the same primitive actions, *pickup*(x) and *putdown*(x) [7]. This paper presents novel teleo-reactive programs created through genetic programming that are simpler than the solution published by Nilsson.

Some of the relevant details of teleo-reactive programs and a discussion of their incorporation into genetic programming are found in the next section. The methods used in evolving teleo-reactive programs for block stacking are explained in section 3. A report of the results follows in section 4, and conclusions are drawn from these results in section 5. Further work is discussed in the final section.

2 Teleo-reactive Programs

A teleo-reactive program, as proposed by Nilsson [4,5], is an ordered list of production rules, as shown below:

$$K_1 \to a_1$$
$$\vdots$$
$$K_i \to a_i$$
$$\vdots$$
$$K_m \to a_m$$

The K_i's are conditions that are evaluated with reference to a world model, and the a_i's are actions on the world. The conditions may contain free variables that are bound when the teleo-reactive program is called. Actions may be primitives, they may be sets of actions to be executed in parallel, or they may be calls to other teleo-reactive programs (thereby enabling hierarchy and recursion). Typically, K_1 is the goal condition, a_1 is the nil action, and K_m is true.

The rules are scanned from top to bottom for the first condition that is satisfied, and then the corresponding action is taken. Since the rules are scanned continuously, *durative* actions are possible in addition to *discrete* actions. In the version of block stacking discussed in this paper, only *discrete* actions are used.

In order to use the standard genetic programming algorithms [2] to evolve teleo-reactive programs, they must be represented as trees. Teleo-reactive programs may be thought of as a list of condition trees and action trees. Fig. 1 shows a sample condition tree and action tree.

The variable-length list structure of a single teleo-reactive program may be represented as a larger tree containing these condition trees and action trees. In this paper, the `trprog` function, `if` function, and `end` terminal are used to enforce this tree structure, as illustrated in Fig. 2. These functions and terminals are described in Sect. 3.1.

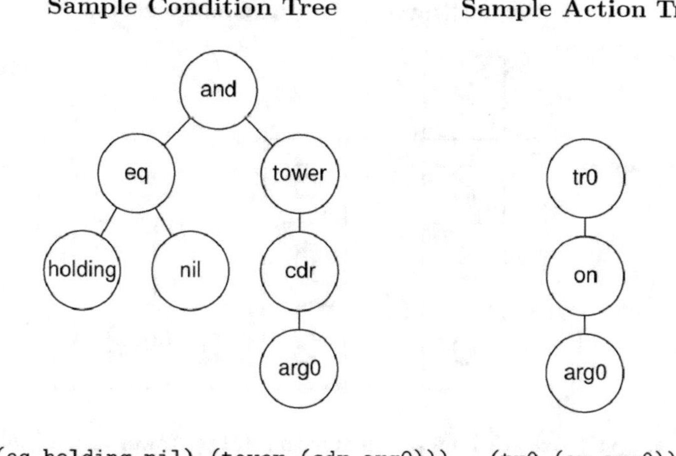

`(and (eq holding nil) (tower (cdr arg0)))` `(tr0 (on arg0))`

Fig. 1. Sample condition and action trees and their corresponding LISP-style symbolic expressions.

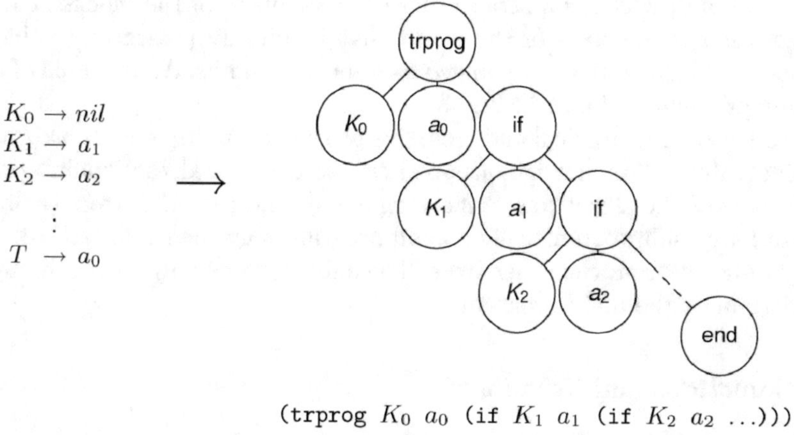

Fig. 2. A tree representation for the variable length list of condition (K_i) and action (a_i) subtrees.

3 Methods

The teleo-reactive tree structures described in the previous section proved easy to implement using the strongly-typed version of LIL-GP made available by Sean Luke[2]. This section explains the setup for the genetic programming experiments.

Before discussing the functions and terminals, it is important to understand how a block stacking problem is specified. Each blocks-world problem consists

[2] Sean Luke's strongly-typed kernel is based on the LIL-GP Genetic Programming System from Michigan State University. The source is freely available here: `http://www.cs.umd.edu/~seanl/gp/patched-gp`.

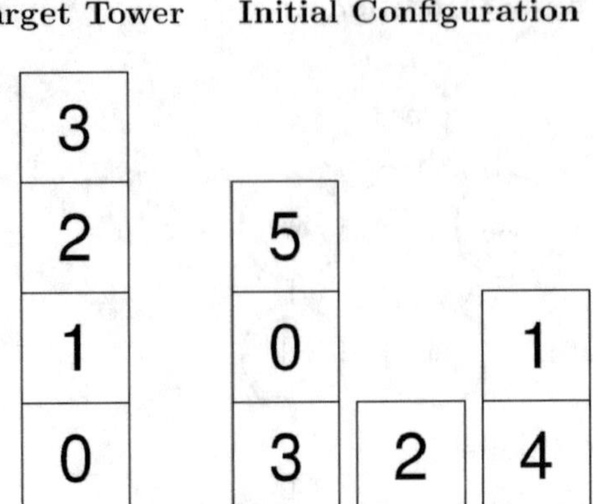

Fig. 3. A sample block stacking problem with a target tower and initial configuration.

of a target tower that is passed as an argument to the program and an initial configuration of blocks. The target tower is simply the tower that the agent wishes to build, which is a strict ordering of a subset of the blocks. The initial configuration is the state of the world that is initially presented to the agent. The state contains n blocks arranged as a set of columns. An example of a block stacking problem is shown in Fig. 3.

To allow for hierarchical and recursive programs, multiple trees are grown for each individual. The first tree (named $tr0$) is considered the "main" program, which receives the target tower as an argument, and the other trees (named $tr1$, $tr2$, etc.) are "subprograms." The main program may then call itself recursively or any program from the other trees. The subprograms may then call any other subprogram or the main program.

3.1 Functions and Terminals

The functions and terminals were designed to resemble the predicates available to the block stacking agent from the perception tower in Nilsson's triple-tower architecture [7]. The only significant difference in this paper is that the functions that only work on lists with single elements have an implicit "car" in their definition.

The teleo-reactive structures use four types in the strongly-typed genetic programming system: *TR*, *Boolean*, *List*, and *Action*. Every tree has as its root the function `trprog`, which takes a *Boolean*, an *Action*, and a *TR* as arguments. The `trprog` function evaluates its first argument, and if it evaluates to true the program will terminate. Otherwise, the function will evaluate its third argument. If the third argument is evaluated and returns `end`, the action specified by the second argument is taken.

The *TR* type consists of the three-argument `if` function and the terminal `end`. The `if` function takes a *Boolean*, an *Action*, and a *TR*. It evaluates the first argument and will then evaluate the second argument if it is true and the third argument if it is false. The `trprog` and `if` functions enforce a linear tree structure with condition and action subtrees as explained earlier.

The *Boolean* type consists of the `true` terminal, three standard boolean functions, and three functions based on the predicates available from Nilsson's perception tower. They are explained below.

- The function `and` takes two *Boolean* arguments and returns *true* if both arguments evaluate to *true*, otherwise it returns *false*.
- The function `not` takes one *Boolean* argument and returns *false* if the argument evaluates to *true*, otherwise it returns *true*.
- The function `eq` takes two *List* arguments and returns *false* if the *car* (i.e. the first element) of both arguments are not equal, otherwise it returns *true*.
- The function `tower` takes one *List* argument and returns *true* if the argument is `ordered` and `clear`, otherwise it returns *false*.
- The function `ordered` takes one *List* argument and returns *true* if there exists a stack of blocks on the table having a substack with an order corresponding to the argument, otherwise it returns *false*. As specified in Nilsson's paper, `(ordered nil)` evaluates to *false*.
- The function `clear` takes one *List* argument and returns *true* if the first element of the list is the table or if the first element of the list is a block that does not have a block on top of it, otherwise it returns *false*.

The *List* type consists of the following terminals and functions.

- The terminal `nil` is the empty list.
- The terminal `table` is a list consisting of one element representing the table.
- The terminal `holding` is a list consisting of the block that is currently being held by the agent. If the agent is not holding a block, then this terminal is an empty list.
- The function `cdr` takes one *List* argument and returns the list with the first element removed. If the argument is `nil`, this function returns `nil`.
- The function `on` takes one *List* argument and returns the block that is directly on top of the first block in the list. If the first element in the list is not a block or if the block is clear, then this function returns `nil`.
- The function `under` takes one *List* argument and returns the block that is directly under the first block in the list. If the block is on top of the table, then the function returns `table`. Otherwise, this function returns `nil`.

In addition to the *List* terminals specified above, there are other terminals representing the arguments to the teleo-reactive programs, which are called `arg`x. The main program has one argument, `arg0`, which is the list specifying the target tower.

The *Action* type has one terminal, `terminate`, which simply terminates the agent. The agent has two primitive actions available, namely, `pickup` and `putdown`. Both functions take one *List* argument. The action `pickup` can be applied if no block is on the first element of the argument and the agent is not currently holding anything. The result is that the agent is holding the block.

The action putdown can be applied if the agent is holding a block and the first element of the argument specifies a block that is clear. The result is that the agent is no longer holding the block and that the block that was held by the agent is placed on top of the specified block.

Notice that if the agent ever takes an action that has no effect on the environment, all future actions will be the same and, hence, will have no effect on the environment. The same action will be taken in the teleo-reactive tree because only the agent may change the environment. Therefore, an experiment terminates as soon as the agent takes an action that has no effect on the world.

3.2 Evaluation of Fitness

The most natural way to measure fitness is to count the number of blocks that were stacked correctly by the agent by the time the agent decides to stop or within a certain number of operations. Evaluating a teleo-reactive stacking program on a single test case is unlikely to produce a solution to the general block-stacking problem. Therefore, it is best to evaluate the fitness of a particular teleo-reactive program on a collection of fitness cases involving a variety of target towers and initial configurations with varying numbers of blocks.

The number of initial configurations for a given number of blocks may be extremely large. The number of possible configurations is given by the "sets of lists" sequence, which counts the number of partitions of $\{1,\ldots,n\}$ into any number of lists [3]. Starting with $n = 2$, the sequence proceeds: 3, 13, 73, 501, 4051, 37633, 394353, 4596553, ..., according to the recursive formula:

$$a(n) = (2n-1)a(n-1) - (n-1)(n-2)a(n-2)$$

The number of configurations grows extremely quickly. For 18 blocks, there are 588,633,468,315,403,843 possible arrangements.

It is necessary, therefore, to rely on random samples of this space for the fitness cases. Using the BWSTATES program made available by John Slaney[3], samples were selected randomly from a uniform distribution of blocks-world states. It is also important that the fitness cases include target towers consisting of varying numbers of blocks. The target towers ranged from one block to all of the blocks. Two fitness case collections were generated for the experiments, each consisting of 100 blocks-world problems. One collection consists of problems with the number of blocks ranging from three to seven, and the other collection consists of problems with the number of blocks ranging from three to twelve.

During the genetic programming run, the teleo-reactive programs were evaluated on each fitness case. The agent is allocated a certain number of steps to solve each problem or to give up. The agent was also allowed a maximum recursion depth that varied with the number of blocks in the world. The raw fitness is the sum of the number of blocks stacked correctly in all the fitness cases, minus half a point for every block on top of an otherwise correct tower. The standardized fitness is simply the sum of all the target tower sizes minus the raw fitness. The number of hits is the number of problems that were solved by the agent.

[3] Freely available here: http://arp.anu.edu.au/~jks/bwstates.html.

3.3 Parameters

The experiments used a population size of 60,000. The "grow" method [2] of generating the initial random population was used with a depth ramp ranging from 3 to 9 for each of the trees.

There were two breeding phases: crossover (90%) and mutation (10%). Breeding was fitness proportionate. The maximum depth for evolved trees was 12.

The individuals were allowed to have four program trees, meaning that an individual may use up to three subprograms in addition to its main program. One of the subprograms was allowed two arguments, but the other subprograms were allowed only one. All subprograms were allowed to call each other and the main program.

3.4 Human-Designed Solution

A version of Nilsson's hierarchical teleo-reactive program that solves the block-stacking problem [7] is shown in Fig. 4. This program uses the functions and terminals defined in this paper to make it easy to compare the evolved programs presented later.

4 Results and Discussion

The experiments were run on shared dual-processor Sun UltraSPARC III+ 900MHz workstations. Several completely fit individuals evolved within 300 generations, which took a few days of processing time. To determine whether the fully fit individuals could solve block stacking problems they had not seen before, the evolved programs were tested on a collection of 11,500 randomly generated problems with the number of blocks ranging from three to twenty-five. Most evolved programs solved at least 99% of these new problems. Two individuals were able to solve all of them, and they are believed to be completely general solutions for block stacking.

The evolved programs generally consisted of a lot of code that never gets executed for a variety of reasons. Frequently, most likely because of crossover, there are redundant conditions. The evolved programs listed in this section have been stripped of their "dead code" and some of the conditions were replaced by equivalent, more reader-friendly conditions.

The first individual that solved the collection of 11,500 test problems was evolved in generation 272. It used the 100 fitness cases with the number of blocks ranging from three to seven. The individual consists of only the main program and one subprogram, and contains fewer rules than the human designed solution. The individual is reproduced in Fig. 5. The program effectively terminates when it reaches the goal by making infinite recursive calls between the two program trees. Although infinite recursion might not be desirable, it only occurs when the agent has completed its task.

Another individual that solved all of the test problems used the 100 fitness cases with the number of blocks ranging from three to twelve. It was produced

$$\mathbf{tr0}(\mathbf{arg0}):$$

$$\begin{aligned} tower(arg0) &\rightarrow nil \\ ordered(arg0) &\rightarrow tr3(arg0) \\ cdr(arg0) = nil &\rightarrow tr1(arg0) \\ tower(cdr(arg0)) &\rightarrow tr2(arg0, cdr(arg0)) \\ T &\rightarrow tr0(cdr(arg0)) \end{aligned}$$

$$\mathbf{tr1}(\mathbf{arg0}):$$

$$\begin{aligned} under(arg0) = table &\rightarrow nil \\ holding \neq nil &\rightarrow putdown(table) \\ clear(arg0) &\rightarrow pickup(arg0) \\ T &\rightarrow tr3(arg0) \end{aligned}$$

$$\mathbf{tr2}(\mathbf{arg0}, \mathbf{arg1}):$$

$$\begin{aligned} on(arg1) = arg0 &\rightarrow nil \\ holding = arg0 \wedge clear(arg1) &\rightarrow putdown(arg1) \\ holding \neq nil &\rightarrow putdown(table) \\ clear(arg0) \wedge clear(arg1) &\rightarrow pickup(arg0) \\ clear(arg1) &\rightarrow tr3(arg0) \\ T &\rightarrow tr3(arg1) \end{aligned}$$

$$\mathbf{tr3}(\mathbf{arg0}):$$

$$\begin{aligned} clear(arg0) &\rightarrow nil \\ T &\rightarrow tr1(on(arg0)) \end{aligned}$$

Fig. 4. A version of Nilsson's hierarchical teleo-reactive program that solves the block stacking problem using the function and terminals defined in this paper.

$$\mathbf{tr0}(\mathbf{arg0}):$$

$$\begin{aligned} holding \neq nil \wedge on(arg0) = nil \wedge \neg(under(arg0) = table \wedge tower(cdr(arg0))) &\rightarrow tr1(cdr(arg0)) \\ holding \neq on(arg0) &\rightarrow tr1(on(arg0)) \\ tower(arg0) &\rightarrow tr1(arg0) \\ under(arg0) = table \wedge \neg tower(cdr(arg0)) &\rightarrow tr1(cdr(arg0)) \\ T &\rightarrow pickup(arg0) \end{aligned}$$

$$\mathbf{tr1}(\mathbf{arg0}):$$

$$\begin{aligned} arg0 = holding &\rightarrow tr0(arg0) \\ holding = nil &\rightarrow tr0(arg0) \\ tower(arg0) &\rightarrow putdown(arg0) \\ under(arg0) = table &\rightarrow tr0(arg0) \\ T &\rightarrow putdown(table) \end{aligned}$$

Fig. 5. An evolved program that solves arbitrary block stacking problems.

in generation 286. This hierarchical and recursive individual uses only the main program, and it is reproduced in Fig. 6. The program terminates when it reaches the goal by taking the action *putdown*($arg0$), which does not change the state of the world.

tr0(arg0):

$$\neg ordered(arg0) \wedge holding = nil \wedge clear(arg0) \wedge under(arg0) \neq table \rightarrow pickup(arg0)$$
$$tower(cdr(arg0)) \wedge holding = nil \wedge clear(arg0) \wedge arg0 \neq nil \rightarrow pickup(arg0)$$
$$arg0 = nil \rightarrow putdown(table)$$
$$\neg tower(cdr(arg0)) \wedge \neg clear(arg0) \rightarrow tr0(on(arg0))$$
$$tower(arg0) \rightarrow putdown(arg0)$$
$$tower(cdr(arg0)) \wedge clear(arg0) \rightarrow tr0(on(arg0))$$
$$holding = nil \wedge tower(cdr(arg0)) \rightarrow tr0(on(arg0))$$
$$T \rightarrow tr0(cdr(arg0))$$

Fig. 6. An evolved program that solves arbitrary block stacking problems.

5 Conclusions

This paper has demonstrated how genetic programming may be used to evolve teleo-reactive programs. Teleo-reactive programs may be represented as symbolic expressions that are recombined and mutated according to fitness through the standard strongly-typed genetic programming procedures. The block stacking problem has demonstrated how genetic programming is capable of evolving hierarchical and recursive teleo-reactive programs.

It is remarkable that hierarchical and recursive programs are able to successfully evolve when both the calls to other programs and the programs themselves are evolving in parallel with only the guidance of fitness-proportionate selection. The standard genetic programming technique was able to evolve novel solutions to the block stacking problem for an arbitrary number of blocks in any configuration. Not only do the evolved solutions not resemble the human-designed solution, they use completely different approaches. The evolved programs are simpler and have fewer rules and subprograms than the one produced by a human programmer.

It is rather surprising that only one hundred fitness cases selected randomly from the extremely vast state space of problems can guide genetic programming to evolve general plans for stacking blocks. The preliminary results presented in this paper indicate that genetic programming is well suited for learning teleo-reactive programs.

6 Further Work

Further work will be done using genetic programming to evolve teleo-reactive programs. Certainly, it would be interesting to see if genetic programming can evolve teleo-reactive programs for use in other, more complex domains.

The obvious next step is to evolve the rules that produce the higher-order predicates, such as *clear* and *ordered*, from the primitive predicate *on*. These rules would be evolved in parallel with the teleo-reactive programs that use these predicates, just as the main program and the three subprograms were evolved in parallel. In other words, the perception tower and action tower of the triple tower architecture would be evolved together.

Acknowledgments

I would like to thank Nils Nilsson and John Koza for their suggestions and encouragement.

References

1. M. Kochenderfer. Evolving teleo-reactive programs for block stacking using indexicals through genetic programming. In J. R. Koza, editor, *Genetic Algorithms and Genetic Programming at Stanford*, pages 111–118. Stanford Bookstore, Stanford University, 2002.
2. J. R. Koza. *Genetic Programming: On the Programming of Computers by Means of Natural Selection.* MIT Press, Cambridge, Massachusetts, 1992.
3. T. S. Motzkin. Sorting numbers for cylinders and other classification numbers. *Combinatorics, Proceedings of Symposia in Pure Mathematics*, 19:167–176, 1971.
4. N. Nilsson. Toward agent programs with circuit semantics. Technical Report STAN-CS-92-1412, Department of Computer Science, Stanford University, 1992.
5. N. Nilsson. Teleo-reactive programs for agent control. *Journal of Artificial Intelligence Research*, 1:139–158, 1994.
6. N. Nilsson. Learning strategies for mid-level robot control. Unpublished memo, Department of Computer Science, Stanford University, May 2000.
7. N. Nilsson. Teleo-reactive programs and the triple-tower architecture. *Electronic Transactions on Artificial Intelligence*, 5:99–110, 2001.

Interactive GP for Data Retrieval in Medical Databases*

Yann Landrin-Schweitzer, Pierre Collet, and Evelyne Lutton

INRIA - Rocquencourt, B.P. 105, 78153 LE CHESNAY Cedex, France
{Yann.Landrin-Schweitzer,Pierre.Collet,Evelyne.Lutton}@inria.fr
http://www-rocq.inria.fr/fractales/

Abstract. We present in this paper the design of ELISE, an interactive GP system for document retrieval tasks in very large medical databases. The components of ELISE have been tailored in order to produce a system that is capable of suggesting documents related to the query that may be of interest to the user, thanks to evolved profiling information. Tests on the "Cystic Fibrosis Database" benchmark [2] show that, while suggesting original documents by adaptation of its internal rules to the context of the user, ELISE is able to improve its recall rate.

1 Introduction

Medical databases of large pharmaceutical companies are becoming really huge, not only in a linear or polynomial way, but by discrete steps each time a new company is absorbed that already had its own database. The result is a patchwork of smaller databases that each have their own structure and format, focussed on different fields and in possibly different languages.

However, modern search engines have very impressive precision and recall rates meaning that they manage to retrieve nearly all the relevant documents for a specific query.

This leads to the paradoxical problem that for each query, the user gets back hundreds if not thousands of documents so precisely focussed on his query that all first documents contain more or less the same data in a way that may recall convergence in evolutionary algorithms. After a certain rank, precision decreases rapidly and documents become only very loosely related to the user query.

The new difficult challenge for search engines operating on such databases is to introduce diversity in the retrieved documents, while keeping at the same time a high relevance to the original query.

One way of achieving this feat is to take into account some kind of user profiling, based on the history of the previous requests made by the user, with the aim of retrieving data both of interest to a specific user and at the same time matching his query.

This remains however quite deterministic, and other methods are seeked to introduce more diversity and randomness in the results, so as to mimic lateral thinking.

* This research is partly funded by Novartis-Pharma (IK@N/KE)

C. Ryan et al. (Eds.): EuroGP 2003, LNCS 2610, pp. 93–106, 2003.

These specifications triggered the idea to use evolutionary algorithms, and more precisely genetic programming to evolve a user profile and use it to rewrite user queries that may retrieve documents of interest of the user, even if they do not absolutely exactly correspond to his query.

The ELISE (Evolutionary Learning Interactive Search Engine) uses the specificities of a Parisian Approach to cut down the number of necessary evaluations to see an evolution in the model.

Section 2 presents an overview of the ELISE system. The genome and structure of the GP on which ELISE is based are detailed in section 3, with special focus on the structure of the rewriting language used to encode the profile and on the Parisian approach scheme. Section 4 presents the characteristics of the evolutionary engine used in ELISE and experiments are analysed in section 5. Conclusion and future works are described in section 6.

2 ELISE: An Evolutionary Learning Interactive Search Engine

ELISE relies on an interactive EA that evolves a "user profile" with a *Parisian Approach*[4] —i.e. represented by the whole population of the EA. This profile determines the process that translates user queries into an alternate form taking into account user specificities. A new generation is produced with each query and fitness is computed by the analysis of the user's behaviour.

Experience and earlier tests on ELISE have shown that the choice of this particular structure is more convenient than other potential strategies of queries rewriting, like the exploitation of user-specific thesauri (as in a classical semantic expansion) or the deterministic use of one or several complete rewriting rules.

A set of small parts of rewriting rules, hereafter referred to as *modules*, is evolved by the system. The evolution relies on a Parisian EA: some modules are extracted out of a population of modules by a ranking selection and fit into templates to produce a fixed number of rewriting rules. Each new query obtained by applying a rule to the original query is then passed on to the boolean search engine and results lists are merged and reordered to be presented to the user. Among the list returned by the engine, documents that are actually viewed by the user translate into an external fitness bonus to any rule that triggered the apparition of this document and by extension to any module involved in the production of this rule. A proportion of the individuals, with lower fitnesses, is then replaced by new individuals produced through mutation and crossover from the best part of the population.

ELISE can be used as an improving mechanism on top of any kind of boolean search engine. The one used for experiments (see section 5) is SWISH++, [19], a basic public-domain boolean search engine, without any semantic expansion or stemming tool. Independantly it needs a semantic network to perform semantically sound term replacement. As the test where performed on a medical database, the EMBase thesaurus was used [6].

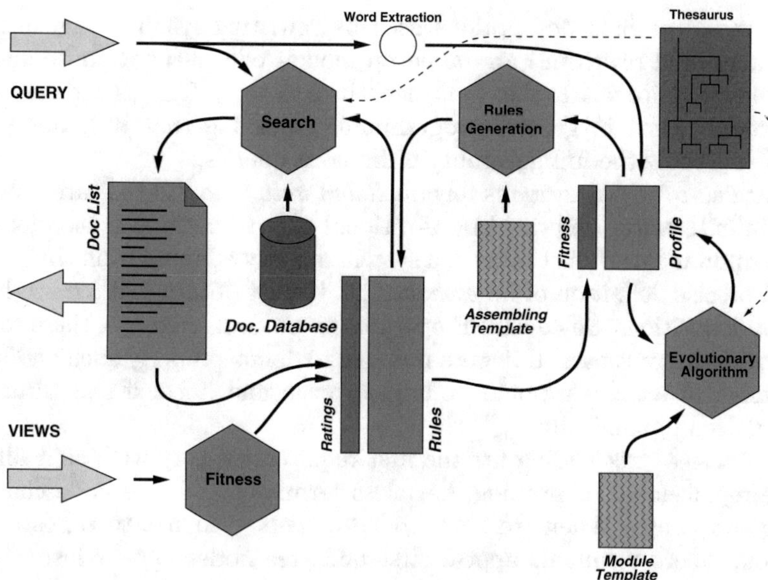

Fig. 1. ELISE evolves a set of rewriting modules, the "user profile." Queries are rewritten by rules derived from this profile and returned documents are displayed to the user. Fitness functions of modules are then updated and activate a new generation of the EA

3 Genome and Structure

3.1 Rewriting Language

The way the modules are coded and their expressive capabilities (i.e. complexity) have a deep impact on the depth and generality of the rules that can be evolved. These must meet two main requirements in order to be used within ELISE:

– The first requirement is a structure constraint. Since modules are basic *components* of more elaborate structures, they must be assembled together in a flexible, yet reliable way: the resulting rule must be valid, whatever modules it is made of. In order to support genetic operators, both local modifications (mutations) and global relocations (implied by recombination) must not violate syntax and must be compatible with the main part of the data implicitely encoded into the module. Moreover, relocations must be made at a small computational cost.
– The second requirement is a power requirement. These structures need to operate efficiently, although with enough generality, on boolean queries. A boolean query is essentially a tree, where leaves are query terms and nodes are boolean operators. There is no theoretical limit on the complexity of such trees (i.e. depth) and no meaningful empirical limit either —as common web search-engine practice reveals. This implies that the rules must be able to process arbitrarily large sets of data.

The most common descriptions used by rewriting systems (e.g. in regular-expression-based rewriting) are based on models equivalent to finite automata, operating on finite words (i.e. finite length data sets). This is the case of tree-based coding used in genetic programming, meaning that it is not powerful enough to handle the full generality of boolean queries.

Extended rewriting systems rely on *Rabin automata* [15] that are able to recognize infinite words described by ω-rational expressions which therefore fit the power requirement. Unfortunately, a system directly adapted from this paradigm needs a precise definition of its *alphabet*, i.e. the set of terminal *letters* that trigger state transitions. Since ELISE operates on natural language, these terminals would be terms or senses. If it were possible to define properly such an alphabet, the number of terminals would be huge or even undefined, if new terms are to be recognized dynamically.

The classical tree coding fits the first requirement very well, as it allows for subtree replacement or pruning, harmless terminals and tree node changes, or subtree swappings. When trees are coded as lists —thanks to a postfix representation, where terminals appear first and tree nodes appear last—, genetic operations become list cutting, splicing and replacement. (Such coding is a particular case of concatenative language.)

The descriptive power of these list-coded programs can be enhanced to equal that of Rabin automata by providing them with looping capabilities to fulfill the second requirement. The result is close enough to the classical tree representation to make it possible to reuse an important part of the theoretical and practical tools developed throughout the history of genetic programming.

3.2 Language Structure

Generality and description capacity is a common problem in GP program coding. A generic set of tools was therefore developed to handle this kind of representation, independently of the text-retrieval context[14]. A library was written that provides a generic parser, and memory management systems —necessary in a stack-based language and execution tools. This allowed to reuse such coding to evolve rules in other contexts. In this model, programs are lists, containing either atoms or sublists. Two types of atoms are available: instructions, taking arguments and putting back results on a stack and character strings, that are simply added onto the stack when the program is run. No distinction is made between data (lists of strings, for instance) and program parts.
A program written with this language may therefore look like:

```
[ [ "hickory" "dickory" "dock" ] <DUP> <CAT> ]
```

If strings are delimited by quotes, instructions by angle brackets and lists by square brackets, if the `DUP` instruction duplicates the top item of the stack and the `CAT` instruction concatenates two lists, executing this program would put the list `[ "hickory" "dickory" "dock" ]` on the stack, duplicate it and concatenate the two identical lists.
After execution, the top stack item would contain the list:

```
[ "hickory" "dickory" "dock" "hickory" "dickory" "dock" ]
```

The lax syntax of concatenative languages allows for the construction of syntactically valid programs from simple operations such as cut and paste or replacement, thanks to the fact that on the stack, data and instruction code are similar and interchangeable. However, this has a drawback: some programs produced this way can not be guaranteed to run. But evolutionary optimization has a wide range of tools to deal with invalid individuals, and allowing for such transgressions in many cases actually benefits to the efficiency of optimisation algorithms.

The instruction set is specifed on a per-application basis, within a general framework. Tools and information necessary to design efficient genetic operators and "repair" systems are available using instruction signatures (arity, input and output type requirements).

3.3 Instruction Set

If the representation is general enough to be usable in most genetic programming cases, the necessary adaptation to the specificities of the problem lies mainly in the creation of an appropriate set of instructions. While wide enough to allow for all meaningful rewriting method to be evolved, it must be specific enough so as to limit the size of the representation space.

In most applications, basic stack operations are needed (e.g, duplication or deletion of an element on the stack, list cutting and pasting operations, etc...). Other instructions need to be tailored to operate on the particular data the genetic algorithm deals with.

In ELISE, this mainly consists in terms and senses or query parts. So semantic instructions (sense or concept lookups in a semantic network, returning sets of terms) and tree operations (since queries have a tree structure) have been developed to handle this data.

Semantic instructions actually reflect the different flavours of term expansion that can be built over a semantic network. As these depend heavily on the actual capabilities of the semantic network used, they will not be listed here, but among them are generally available: several flavours of synonymy, hypernyms and hyponyms, and sometimes meronyms and holonyms when those are defined.

Tree operations consist of:

- conditionals, based on a particular value of the root node,
- splitting instructions, capable to break a tree into subtrees,
- grouping instructions, that join two subtrees into a single one with a given root node value, one of the boolean operators used by the search engine.

However, the main purpose of this language, compared to classical tree structures, is to obtain more descriptive power, which is usually provided by looping or recursive instructions. However a completely general loop instruction (i.e, *do* `instructions` *while* `condition`) considerably enlarges the description space of the coding, which is also the search space of the ELISE learning machine.

A *mapping* instruction is used instead. This restricted version of loops takes advantage of the fact that there is no difference between data (terminals) and

instruction code : the *mapping* instruction applies a program to each and every node of the list.
For instance, [["hickory" "dickory" "dock"] ["mouse" <#AND>] <MAP>] executes the subprogram ["mouse" <#AND>] on each element of the first list, to produce the new list:
[["hickory" "#and" "mouse"]["dickory" "#and" "mouse"]
["dock" "#and" "mouse"]]
where "#and" refers to the operator used by the boolean search engine.

3.4 Derived Rewriting Rules

Modules such as the one described above may perform adequate transcriptions for the task at hand, but there is not much chance that a single module represents the solution that is sought. Therefore, following the Parisian approach[4], many modules are merged into complete rewriting rules through a set of templates that perform various combinations of two or three modules via a set of boolean operators available in the underlying search engine (for example "AND," "OR," "NO" and possibly "NEAR" or "LIKE" if they are available). Plausibly meaningful combinations of evolved modules can be randomly built this way, without *a priori* preference for any particular combination. From a higher viewpoint, modules contain evolved user-specific knowledge, while templates represent possible combinations of elementary rewriting procedures that use the boolean system.

Templates need some *a priori* designer input into the learning system and need to be carefully constructed. But they enable the human supervisor to finely tune the system behaviour and its reaction to query structures, as well as to adapt to particular quirks of the underlying search engine. Obviously, the quality and the number of templates available influences the performance of the system.

4 Evolving a User Profile: GP Genetic Operators

The paradigm of genetic algorithms was originally developped to deal with bit-string individuals, on which the definition of genetic operators —mutation and crossover— is straightforward. However, when working on more complex genome structures, an important part of the EA performance is linked to the accurate tailoring of these operators to the problem that needs to be solved.

As explained earlier, a module (the ELISE genome) is a small program part. Even with the lax syntax that is adopted, some of the modules fail to run. While this is desirable, to move more easily between basins of attraction in fitness landscape, the occurrence of such individuals should remain low. Consequently, genetic operators must be designed in order to produce valid structures most of the time. This means essentially taking into account instruction arity and input types when doing mutations or crossover and "repairing" discrepancies when needed by introducing extra arguments or ignoring some, as required to keep the overall input and output signature of genetically modified (mutated or recombined) instructions.

Therefore, three types of mutation operators are used, with distinct probabilities:

- Local, intra-class mutation
- Local, cross-class mutation
- Global (structural) mutation

The intra-class mutation operates on atoms, albeit in differents ways depending on the type of the atoms. When it operates on strings, it replaces a term by another connected to it in the semantic network used. When instructions are mutated, it replaces one instruction by another with the same prototype: same number and types of required arguments and same number and types of returned values.

The cross-class mutation changes an instruction into another, with a different prototype or turns an atom into another atom of a different sort altogether: in other words it changes an instruction into a terminal or the opposite. These operations are followed by a specific repair phase, aiming at keeping input and output signatures coherence. For instance, replacing an instruction taking two arguments with one taking three, the first of which being a string, will call for the insertion of an additional string, to preserve input consistency. This string comes from a bank of terms used in the queries.

The global mutation changes the structure itself of the genome, by replacing an atom by a list or the reverse. When mutating a string, as no prior arity information is available, no reparation is attempted (resulting in numerous infeasible individuals). When mutating an instruction, conserving the number of arguments and results is attempted. This calls upon the notion of "arity" of a list, defined —in much the same way as for instructions— as the number and types of objects needed on the stack for a correct execution. However, since complex switches and conditions can be implemented in a subprogram, "arity" is not always unique and generally tricky to determine, resulting in possibly incomplete repair.

Following the same idea, two types of crossover are used. The local version will not descend into sublists (from a functional point of view, these are subprograms), leaving them unchanged, while the global version will also apply a crossover in sublists when possible. These crossovers rely on the same mechanisms as those used for bit strings (remember that genomes are lists, too): cut points are positioned randomly along the two parents' lists and list sections are exchanged in alternance. One of the modified lists is then taken as result of the crossover.
Here is an example of these operators in action for the two following modules:

```
[ <VOCGEN> "metabolic disorder" <VOCSYN> <#AND> ]
[ [ <SPLIT> "acetic acid" <VOCGEN> <#AND> <#OR> ] <IFOR> ]
```

The first module applies <VOCGEN> (generalisation operator) to the query terms (that are by default on top of the stack) and puts the result back onto the stack. Then, "metabolic disorder" is added on the stack and <VOCSYN>

(synonym expansion) is applied to it. Finally an #<AND> operator is applied to the two results. All in all, only documents containing terms common to the generalisation of the original query and metabolic disorder synonyms will be retrieved.

The second module restricts the set of documents retrieved by the second part of an <#OR> query to those having to do with generalisations of "acetic acid."

A crossover between both modules could read:

```
[ [ <SPLIT> "acetic acid" <VOCGEN> <#AND> <#OR> ] <IFOR> <VOCSYN> <#AND> ]
```

A mutation on the resulting module could be:

```
[ [ <SPLIT> "paramyxoviridae infections" <VOCGEN> <#AND> <#OR> ] <IFOR>
<VOCSYN> <#AND> ]
```

4.1 Fitness Function and User Interaction

One of the main problems encountered in interactive EAs is to build a reliable and appropriate fitness function out of user input, i.e. data that by essence is relatively noisy and not always translatable into numeric values. In the context of ELISE, a simple measurement of the "user satisfaction" quality was available as the time spent browsing documents among those proposed in a result list. In a Parisian perspective, this is a global efficiency measurement, from which a local fitness value must be derived for each module.

However, in test settings, this "spent time" notion was not available and was replaced by a formula based on the *recall rate* and the *precision* of rules[1], as these are quantities commonly used to evaluate the performance of search engines and were easily computable with the used datasets. In effect, the fitness of a module is thus the ratio of $Recall\_rate + \alpha * Precision$ over the total number of documents returned for rules using this module.

4.2 Initialisation and Parameters

To avoid a "slow start" syndrome, where the 30 or so first queries return very frustrating answers, as the user's profile is still in the first stages of evolution, a minimal (at least 30%) proportion of the initial modules is created from an initialisation template, containing modules performing "reasonable" rewritings, such as thesaurus-based term expansion, boolean form weakening, sense disjunction, etc... The rest of the population is made of randomly generated modules, with a preset ratio of instructions over strings, and subprograms depth.

To cope with noisy fitness evaluations and to stay within the Parisian paradigm, a slow evolution process is applied: only a small part of the population

[1] The recall rate is the percentage of returned documents that match the target with respect to the total size of the target. The precision is the percentage of relevant documents in the document set, returned by the system.

(the 15% individuals of lower fitness) is updated with each generation, with a 80% probability of Xover and using a very high mutation rate (at much as 30% local intra-class mutations per gene and only around 5% local cross-class and global mutation) to improve "creativity."

Those figures come from the fact that most functional modules contain around 5 genes (below, they do not get high enough rewards, and above, they rapidly become infeasible).

The typical population size used in experiments is 50 individuals, from which an equal number of rules is derived.

5 Experiments and Analysis

Tests presented below have been performed automatically on the Cystic Fibrosis Database (CFD)[2], using the SWISH++ [19] basic boolean search engine. The semantic operators are based on a medical oriented thesaurus: MeSH [13].

Of course, it is very difficult to automatically test such an interactive system (especially with respect to the "satisfaction of the user" quantity). Results remains however interesting in the sense that they allow to gather statistics rather easily. The CFD test consists of 1239 documents published from 1974 to 1979 on a specific topic (Cystic Fibrosis Aspects) and a set of 100 queries with the respective relevant documents as answers. For each query, the global recall rate and precision of the system can be precisely measured by comparing the returned document set to the relevant registered answers that have been determined by experts of the field.

Figure 2 presents three curves: the cumulated mean[2] recall rate of the basic boolean search engine (less than 10%), the cumulated mean recall rate of ELISE using the same boolean engine (around 45% after 18 queries only and constantly growing until the end of the test of 140 queries, i.e. 140 generations of the EA). A learning behaviour can be seen on this curve, resulting on a definite increase of the recall rate.

This behaviour is even more obvious on the middle curve, showing ELISE results on queries where the underlying boolean search engine returns no relevant document: even in this extremely unfavourable case, ELISE is able to obtain interesting recall rates.

Figure 3 presents the same set of cumulated mean curves but for the precision measurement. ELISE comes up with a much lower precision than the basic seach engine, which is an expected result, showing that diversity is increased: all modules of the user-profile need to be evaluated at least once, even if they are the result of a recent mutation. The fact that they may very well return random answers lowers the global precision of ELISE, but knowing that the module contains bad genes is a crucial information to evolve the whole system.

Figure 4 shows the evolution of best and mean fitness of the modules: the fitness function is very noisy, even if it is itself a mean evaluation of the efficiency of a module over several evaluations.

---

[2] This is the mean value computed on all queries tested so far, implying that the first values of the curves are not significant, the size of the sample being too small.

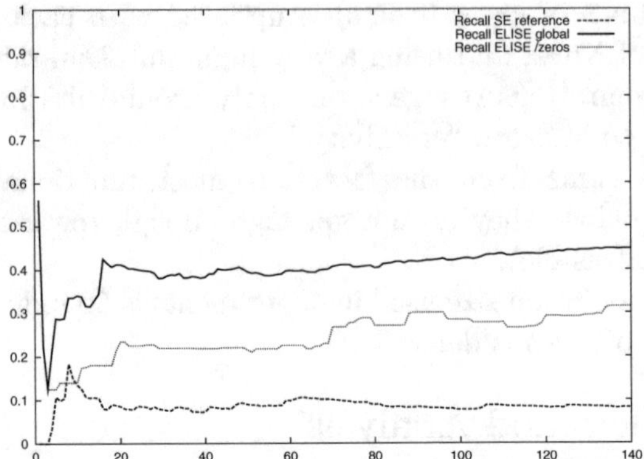

Fig. 2. Cumulated mean recall rates of the underlying boolean search engine (dashes, bottom curve), of ELISE (solid line, top curve) and of ELISE for queries for which the underlying search engine returns no answer (dots, middle curve)

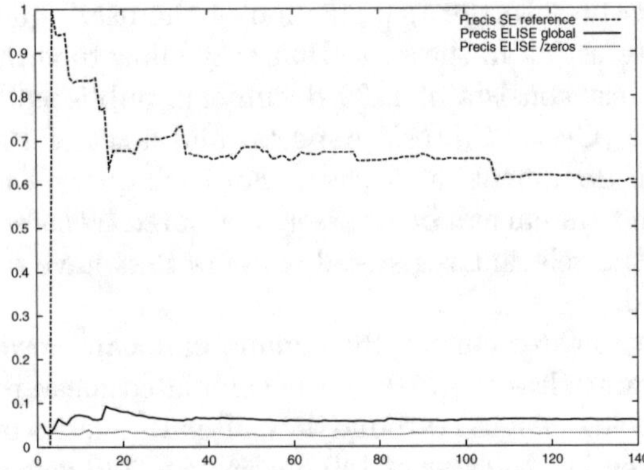

Fig. 3. Cumulated mean precisions of the underlying boolean search engine (dashes, top curve), of ELISE (solid line, middle curve) and of ELISE for queries for which the underlying search engine returns no answer (dots, bottom curve)

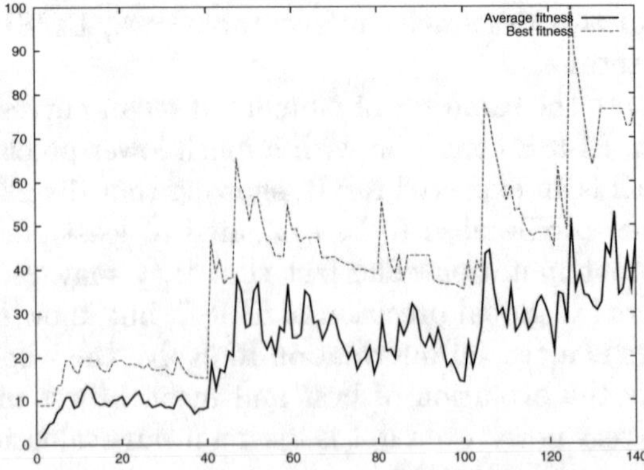

Fig. 4. Evolution of the fitness of the modules : best individual (dashes, top curve) and mean fitness for the whole population(solid line, bottom curve)

Some of the best modules of the final population (after 140 generations) of the run that produced the curves are explained below.

["artery, ciliary" <#OR>] Returns documents obtained from the original query, plus documents about "ciliary arteries." This is a generalisation (extension of the scope) of the original query.

[<#NOT> "ananase" <SPLIT>] Performs a search for documents about "ananase," while ignoring the original query (!)

["arteries, ciliary" <#AND>] Among documents obtained from the original query, this module returns only those about "ciliary arteries." This is a restriction of the original query.

["artery, ciliary" <VOCGEN>] Performs a search for documents having to do with "ciliary arteries" or generalisations of this concept, in the set of documents returned by the original query.

["dayto anase" <#OR>] Performs a search for documents about "dayto anase," and appends them to those returned by the original query.

[<SPLIT> "bromelain" <#VOID>] Uses the implicit operator of boolean search engines (that is, generally a loose "and") to restrict the scope of the right part of the original query (i.e. at the right of the root boolean operator).

The evolved modules, along with the submitted queries, have been presented to medical practitioners. Their analysis shows that after 140 generations, the modules contain a whole set of enzymes that are used as anti-inflammatory agents, related to CF only at a secondary degree. The recurrent apparition of the term "ciliary arteries" is stranger, although a hypothesis can be formulated: ciliary arteries are localised in the eyes, and ocular arterial disease is frequent in diabetes, itself frequent in CF.

This far-fetched explanation, plus a couple of other such findings seem to show that ELISE would exhibit some "lateral-thinking" abilities that were sought in this research. This same conclusion also seems to arise from a global analysis of the terms that appear in the modules, as shown in the tests below.

In order to evaluate more precisely the character strings that are evolved in the user profile after a given set of questions the questions of the CFD have been classified in several sub-classes by the same medical practitioners (see table 1). Two types of tests have been performed, see table 2:

1. with a set of questions presented to ELISE, restricted to a specific sub-class,
2. by first evolving the profile during 100 generations on the whole set of questions of the CFD, except a given sub-class of questions (learning set) and then specialise the profile on this sub-class during 50 generations (test set).

Evolved terms have been sorted in 4 relevance categories, see table 2. This second analysis seems to confirm that the ELISE system hosts unexpected keywords in its modules, that might potentially provide lateral thinking capabilities to conventional search engines.

Table 1. Query sets classification key: subsets of the CFD and sub-subsets

Set n^o	Classification 1: CF afflictions and consequences by organ or function
10	respiratory system
11	epithelia or secretions in the respiratory tract
12	infectious pathologies and immunologic mecanisms in the lung
13	treatment of respiratory system damage
14	other respiratory afflictions
20	gastrointestinal and hepatic consequences of CF
21	pancreatic pathologies
22	other gastrointestinal and hepatic pathologies
30	physiologic and biochemical consequences of CF in other organs
40	epidemiology and genetics of CF
50	diagnosis of CF

Set n^o	Classification 2: specialities
10	diagnosis of CF or of CF-related pathologies
20	epidemiology and genetics of CF
30	clinical features of CF
40	biochemical and physiologic manifestations of CF
41	in the respiratory system
42	other
50	CF treatments
51	treatment of pulmonary manifestations
52	treatment of digestive consequences
53	other treatments
60	other pathologies and manifestations

Table 2. Runs performance and relevance classification of the vocabulary extracted from final modules

Test run number	Run 1	Run 2	Run 3	Run 4	Run 5
Learning set[1]	1-13	1-12	1-!12	2-50	2-!50
Number of terms in learning set	14	14	85	21	81
Test set[1]	1-13	1-12	1-12	2-50	2-50
Number of terms in test set	14	13	13	21	21
Recall rate	38.1	38.4	42.3	33.3	35.4
Precision	9.8	10.4	12.2	12.0	9.1
% of terms directly related to the test set	19.2	28.6	26.6	20.0	28.6
% of terms undirectly related to the test set	19.2	57.1	40.0	10.0	42.8
% of terms related to the CF but not the test set	11.6	0	20.0	30.0	5.7
% of unrelated terms	50.0	14.3	13.3	40.0	22.8

Note: The "N-S" notation means "Class N, subset S." "N-!S" means "Class N, all the CFD [illegible] subset S," see table 1

6 Conclusion and Future Works

In this paper, research was carried by adding ELISE on top of an extremely basic boolean search engine, meaning that results discussed above can only be improved, not only in terms of recall rate but also in precision if a state of the art engine is used by ELISE.

Right now, however, tests are quite promising in that the performance of the boolean engine is quite enhanced while at the same time rewriting queries with related terms that did not appear in any previous request. Evolution takes place at a reasonable pace which is compatible with a human user (nice results begin to show up after around 20 queries).

ELISE is currently being ported to ULIX[22], the state of the art search engine of Novartis-Pharma. Future work will consist in analysing and tuning ELISE in real-world conditions and with real users (among others, diversity of the relevant returned documents will be precisely analysed, as well as systems response time and load issues). The conditions being different, it is very likely that this feedback will bring many changes to the present prototype. Future papers on ELISE will discuss this issue.

Acknowledgements

The authors are grateful to Thierry PROST (M.D. PhD), for his educated analysis of the innards of ELISE and to Gilles ROGER (M.D. PhD), for his help as Cystic Fibrosis specialist.

References

1. E. Cantu-Paz and C. Kamath, "On the use of evolutionary algorithms in data mining," In Abbass, H., Sarker, R. and Newton, C. (Eds.) *Data Mining: a Heuristic Approach*, pp. 48-71. Hershey, PA: IDEA Group Publishing, 2002.
2. Cystic Fibrosis Collection, `http://www.sims.berkeley.edu/~hearst/irbook/cfc.html`
3. Y. Landrin-Schweitzer, E. Lutton, P. Collet "Interactive Parisian GP for an Evolutionary Search Engine", submitted.
4. P. Collet, E. Lutton, F. Raynal, M. Schoenauer, "Polar IFS + Parisian Genetic Programming = Efficient IFS Inverse Problem Solving," In *Genetic Programming and Evolvable Machines Journal*, Volume 1, Issue 4, pp. 339-361, October, 2000.
5. A. Dix, "Interactive Querying, locating and dicovering information," *Second Workshop on Information Retrieval and Human Computer Interaction*, Glasgow, 11th September 1998, `http://www.hiraeth.com/alan/topics/QbB/`
6. EMBASE, the Excerpta Medica database Elsevier Science, Secondary Publishing Division, New York
7. D. J. Foskett. "Thesaurus," *Readings in Information Retrieval*, K. S. Jones, P. Willet, M. Kaufmann Publishers, San Fransisco, 1997
8. A.A. Freitas, "Data Mining with Evolutionary Algorithms: Research Directions," AAAI Worshop, Tech. Report WS-99-06, The AAAI Press, 1999.
9. A.A. Freitas, "A survey of evolutionary algorithms for data mining and knowledge discovery," in: A. Ghosh and S. Tsutsui. (Eds.) *Advances in Evolutionary Computation*, Springer-Verlag, 2002.
10. M. D. Gordon, "Probabilistic and Genetic Algrithms for Document Retrieval," *Communications of the ACM* 31, pp 1208-1218, 1988.
11. J.-T. Horng and C.-C. Yeh, "Applying Genetic Algorithms to Query Optimisation in Document Retrieval," *Information Processing and Management* 36, 2000
12. Y.-H. Kim, S. Kim, J.-H. Eom and B.-T. Zhang, "SCAI Experiments on TREC-9," Proceedings of the *Ninth Text REtrieval Conference* (TREC-9), pp. 392-399, 2000.
13. "MeSH (Medical Subject Headings), a controlled vocabulary thesaurus" `http://www.nlm.nih.gov/pubs/factsheets/mesh.html` National Library of Medicine (NLM), National Institutes of Health, Bethesda, Maryland

14. Y. Landrin-Schweitzer, "OKit, a Virtual Machine and Compiler for Concatenative Languages." `http://varkhan.free.fr/Software/OKit`
15. R. McNaughton, "Testing and generating infinite sequences by a finite automaton," *Information and Control*, vol 9, 1966, pp 521–530.
16. R. Poli and S. Cagnoni, "Genetic Programming with User-Driven Selection : Experiments on the Evolution of Algorithms for Image Enhancement," in *2nd Annual Conf. on Genetic Programming*, pp 269-277, 1997.
17. D.-H. Shin , Y.-H. Kim, S. Kim, J.-H. Eom, H.-J. Shin and B.-T. Zhang, "SCAI TREC-8 Experiments," Proceedings of TREC 8, pp. 511-518, 1999.
18. W. M. Spears "Adapting crossover in a Genetic Algorithm," *ICGA '91, International Conference on Genetic Algorithms*, 1991.
19. SWISH++, Simple Web Indexing System for Humans: C++ version, `http://homepage.mac.com/pauljlucas/software/swish/`
20. H. Takagi, " Interactive Evolutionary Computation : System Optimisation Based on Human Subjective Evaluation," *IEEE Int. Conf. on Intelligent Engineering Systems* (INES'98), Vienna, Austria, pp 1-6, Sept 17-19, 1998.
21. The Text REtrieval Conference (TREC) homepage `http://trec.nist.gov/`
22. T. Vachon, N. Grandjean, P. Parisot, "Interactive Exploration of Patent Data for Competitive Intelligence: Applications in Ulix (Novartis Knowledge Miner)," *International Chemical Information Conference and Exhibition*, Nîmes, France, 21-24 October 2001. `http://www.infonortics.com/chemical/ch01/01chempro.html`
23. D. Vrajitoru, "Genetic Algorithms in Information Retrieval," *AIDRI97*, Learning; From Natural Principles to Artificial Methods , Genve, June 1997.
24. D. Vrajitoru, "Large Population or Many Generations for Genetic Algorithms ? Implications in Information Retrieval", In F. Crestani, G. Pasi (eds.): *Soft Computing in Information Retrieval. Techniques and Applications*, Physica-Verlag, Heidelberg, pp 199-222, 2000.
25. G. A. Miller, C. Fellbaum, R. Tengi, P. Wakefield, "WordNet, an Electronic Lexical Database for the English language: `http://www.cogsci.princeton.edu/~wn/`" Cognitive Science Laboratory, Princeton University.
26. J. Yang, R. R. Korfhage and E. Rasmussen, "Query Improvement in Information Retrieval using Genetic Algorithms: A Report on the Experiments of the TREC project", The first Text Retrieval Conference (TREC-1), 1993.

Parallel Programs Are More Evolvable than Sequential Programs

Kwong Sak Leung[1], Kin Hong Lee[1], and Sin Man Cheang[2]

[1] Department of Computer Science and Engineering
The Chinese University of Hong Kong
Shatin, Hong Kong, China
{ksleung,khlee}@cse.cuhk.edu.hk
[2] Department of Computing
Hong Kong Institute of Vocational Education (Kwai Chung)
20 Hing Shing Road, Kawi Chung, Hong Kong, China
smcheang@vtc.edu.hk

Abstract. This paper presents a novel phenomenon of the *Genetic Parallel Programming (GPP)* paradigm – the *GPP accelerating phenomenon*. GPP is a novel Linear Genetic Programming representation for evolving parallel programs running on a *Multi-ALU Processor (MAP)*. We carried out a series of experiments on GPP with different number of ALUs. We observed that parallel programs are more evolvable than sequential programs. For example, in the Fibonacci sequence regression experiment, evolving a 1-ALU sequential program requires 51 times on average of the computational effort of an 8-ALU parallel program. This paper presents three benchmark problems to show that the GPP can accelerate evolution of parallel programs. Due to the accelerating evolution phenomenon of GPP over sequential program evolution, we could increase the normal GP's evolution efficiency by evolving a parallel program by GPP and if there is a need, the evolved parallel program can be translated into a sequential program so that it can run on conventional hardware.

1 Introduction

Genetic Programming (GP) [1], a branch of the Evolutionary Computation, employed Genetic Algorithms [2] to evolve computer programs as its phenotype. GP has been widely applied on different areas [3,4,5]. There are two main streams in GP, the tree-based GP (TGP) [6,7] and Linear GP (LGP) [8]. In TGP, a program is represented in a tree structure, similar to the S-expression structure using in LISP. Genetic operations manipulate branches and leave nodes of the program tree, e.g. swap two subtrees within a program tree. The main advantage of TGP is that it can maintain the correctness of evolved offspring without syntax error. The main disadvantage is its inefficiency in fitness evaluation because of the pointer representation of the tree structure. Running a program tree on a classical Von Neumann machine involves very computationally intensive operations, e.g. stack operations, recursive function calls, and program tree interpretation. Pointer machines [9] can speed up program tree execution but it is not a cost-effective solution.

C. Ryan et al. (Eds.): EuroGP 2003, LNCS 2610, pp. 107–118, 2003.

In LGP, a program is represented in linear list of operations, either in machine codes or in high-level language statements [10,11]. LGP directly evolves program instructions that read and write values from and to variables or registers. LGP is based on the principle of the register machines. Evolved genetic programs can be run on a real machine directly without any additional translation process. Since all genetic evolutionary techniques spend a large portion of the processing time on fitness evaluation, direct instruction execution in LGP instead of program tree interpretation in TGP results in higher efficiency. In LGP, crossovers swap segments of codes of two individuals, and mutations modify opcodes/operands inside an individual. LGP has been adopted in different real-life applications, e.g. Medical Data Mining [3], recursive sequence learning [12], and speech recognition [13].

The proposed *Genetic Parallel Programming (GPP)* paradigm is a hardware/software cooperating system. GPP evolves parallel programs which run on a general-purpose, tightly coupled, Multiple Instruction-streams Multiple Data-streams (MIMD) register machine, called *Multi-ALU Processor (MAP)*. With the advances in semiconductor technologies, more components can be fabricated in a chip. A high capacity integrated circuit allows us to implement tightly coupled multi-processor architecture, such as MAP, on a single chip with minimal inter-component delays. Re-programmable devices, e.g. Field Programmable Gate Arrays (FPGA), are flexible for genetic program evaluation because of their rapid prototyping capability. For example, different MAP configurations, e.g. different number of ALUs, can be programmed on FPGAs to perform fitness evaluations.

GPP has been used to evolve parallel programs for symbolic regression, recursive function regression, and artificial ant problems. It has been reported in papers [14,15] that GPP can evolve optimal parallel programs to make use of the parallelism of the MAP.

In order to investigate the evolvabilities of GPP with different number of ALUs, we performed a series of experiments. Surprisingly, we observed a novel phenomenon – *parallel programs are more evolvable than sequential programs.* From all of our experiments, it is more efficient to evolve parallel programs (using multiple ALU) than sequential programs (using one ALU). For example, in the Fibonacci sequence regression experiment, evolving a 1-ALU sequential program requires 51 times on average of the computational effort of an 8-ALU parallel program. We call this phenomenon the *GPP accelerating phenomenon.* This hypothesis opens up a new approach to evolve a satisfactory solution program (algorithm) in two stages: 1) evolve a highly parallel MAP program; and 2) translate the parallel program to a sequential program. De-compiling a parallel program is straightforward and spends linear order of processing time to the size of the parallel program.

The rest of the paper is organized as follows: section 2 contains a description of the GPP and the MAP; section 3 describes the GPP accelerating phenomenon; sections 4 and 5 present the experiments and results; and finally, section 6 concludes our work.

2 Genetic Parallel Programming (GPP)

The GPP system is a novel LGP system that evolves parallel machine codes for an optimal designed MIMD architecture with multiple arithmetic/logic units (ALUs).

Fig. 1 below shows the framework of the GPP system. It consists of two core components: 1) an Evolution Engine (EE); and 2) a Multi-ALU Processor (MAP). The EE manipulates the population, performs GP operations (selection, mutation and crossover) and de-assembles the solution program to symbolic assembly codes.

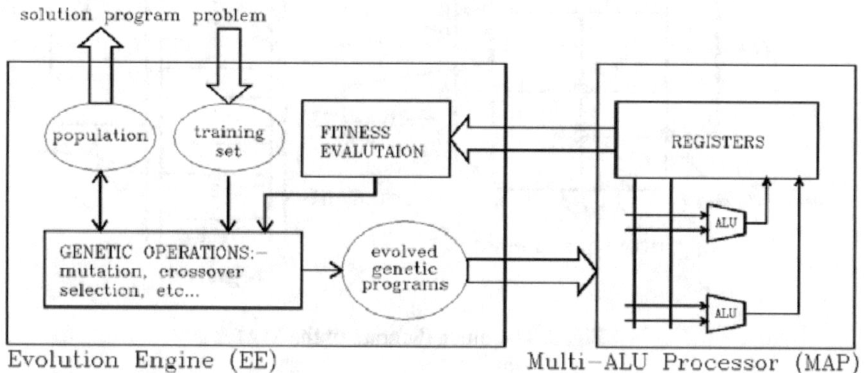

Fig. 1. The GPP system framework

2.1 The Multi-ALU Processor (MAP)

As shown in Fig. 2, multiple ALUs access a shared register-file through a crossbar switching network. We define a MAP by

$$\mathcal{M} = <\mathbf{A}, \mathbf{R}, \mathbf{P}, \mathbf{C}, \mathbf{B}, \{\mathbf{F}_0, \ldots, \mathbf{F}_{n(\mathbf{A})-1}\}, \{\mathbf{O}_0, \ldots, \mathbf{O}_{n(\mathbf{A})-1}\}, \mathbf{N}> \quad (1)$$

where $\mathbf{A} = \{a_0, \ldots, a_{n(\mathbf{A})-1}\}$, the set of ALUs
$\mathbf{R} = \{r_0, \ldots, r_{n(\mathbf{R})-1}\}$, the set of registers
$\mathbf{P} = \{p_0, \ldots, p_{n(\mathbf{P})-1}\}$, the set of ports
$\mathbf{C} \subset \mathbf{R}$, the set of constant registers
$\mathbf{B} = \{b_0, \ldots, b_{n(\mathbf{B})-1}\}$, the branch function set
$\mathbf{F}_i = \{f_0, \ldots, f_{n(\mathbf{F}i)-1}\}$, the ALU function set of the ith ALU, $0 \le i \le n(\mathbf{A})-1$
$\mathbf{O}_i \subset \mathbf{R}-\mathbf{C}$, the output register set of the ith ALU, $0 \le i \le n(\mathbf{A})-1$
$\mathbf{I}_i = \{i^A_i, i^B_i\}$, the input port set of the ith ALU, $0 \le i \le n(\mathbf{A})-1$
$\mathbf{N} \subseteq (\bigcup_{i=0}^{n(A)-1} \mathbf{I}_i) \times \mathbf{P}$, the set of connected cross-points in the crossbar-network

Every ALU maintains two status flags, Zero and Negative flags, for determining program flow. All data are stored in **R**. **C** is a subset of **R** for storing program constant values. All registers in **C** are read-only and their values are manipulated by the EE of the GPP. All remaining registers (**R**–**C**) can be modified by ALUs. ALUs receive register values through a programmable crossbar-network (**N**) and n(**P**) ports. Each port can be connected to the output of any one register in **R** in order to pass values to the crossbar-network (**N**). At most n(**P**) values can be supplied to ALUs' inputs ($\bigcup_{i=0}^{n(A)-1} \mathbf{I}_i$). A port's value can be shared by more than one ALU input. In order to prevent multiple ALUs from writing to the same register simultaneously, we restrict

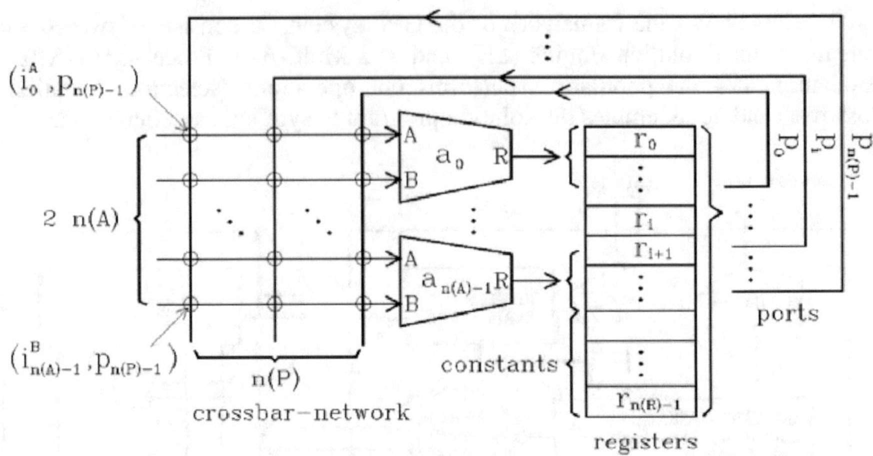

Fig. 2. The block diagram of the MAP

each ALU to write to a subset of registers in **R**–**C**. Each ALU output register set $\mathbf{O}_i$ is mutually exclusive to all other ALUs' output sets, i.e. $\mathbf{O}_i \cap \mathbf{O}_j = \phi$ ($\forall i,j,\ i \neq j$). The MAP is designed to decode any bit pattern as a valid instruction without causing processor fatal errors, e.g. invalid opcodes. This closure property is especially important for GPP because of its random nature based on genetic evolutionary techniques. Using this architecture, no pre-evaluation repairing process is needed before execution.

For the proposed MAP architecture, the numbers of ALUs (n(**A**)) and ports (n(**P**)) are two important parameters which affect the parallelism of the evolved programs. n(**A**) limits the maximum number of parallel operations which are executed in a MAP clock cycles. Note that when n(**A**)=1, the MAP evolves sequential programs. n(**P**) limits the maximum number of registers' values that can be passed to ALUs. Obviously, we have $1 \leq n(\mathbf{P}) \leq 2n(\mathbf{A})$ because there are two inputs in each ALU. Too many ports consume unnecessary hardware resources but too few ports hamper the degree of parallelism. The number of cross-points in the crossbar-network is equal to $2 \times n(\mathbf{A}) \times n(\mathbf{P})$.

2.2 The Evolution Engine (EE)

The EE is the software component of the GPP. It manipulates the population of individuals, performs genetic operations (selection, mutation and crossover), loads individuals to the MAP for fitness evaluations and de-assembles the final solution program to symbolic assembly codes. The genotype of an individual is the control codes of parallel instructions. For example, a MAP ($\mathcal{M}^*$) with 4-ALU, 4-port, 16-register, 8-constant and a fully connected crossbar-network, is defined by

$$\begin{aligned}\mathcal{M}^* = <\ & \{a_0,a_1,a_2,a_3\}, \{r_0, \ldots, r_{15}\}, \{p_0,p_1,p_2,p_3\}, \{r_8, \ldots, r_{15}\}, \\ & \{b_0, \ldots, b_7\}, \{\{f_0, \ldots, f_{15}\}, \{f_0, \ldots, f_{15}\}, \{f_0, \ldots, f_{15}\}, \{f_0, \ldots, f_{15}\}\}, \\ & \{\{r_0,r_1\}, \{r_2,r_3\}, \{r_4,r_5\}, \{r_6,r_7\}\}, \Big(\bigcup_{i=0}^{n(A)-1} \mathbf{I}_i\Big) \times \{p_0,p_1,p_2,p_3\} >\end{aligned} \quad (2)$$

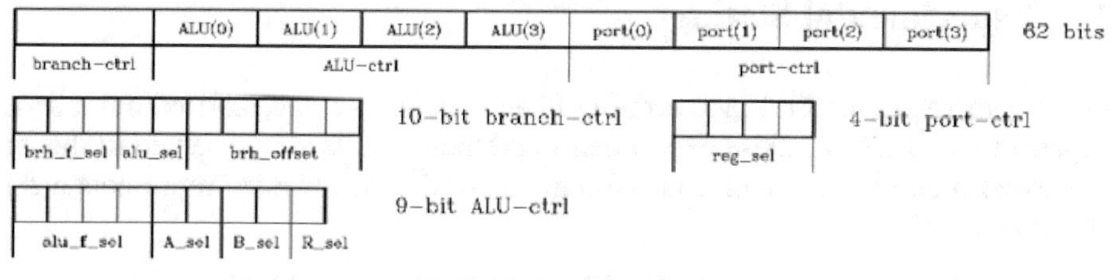

(a) 62-bit control codes

```
jgt 3 4, nop,add r02 r02 r03,mov r06 r05,shr r06 r07
```

(b) an example assembly instruction

Fig. 3. An $\mathcal{M}$* parallel instruction

Fig. 3(a) above shows the format of a parallel instruction of $\mathcal{M}$*. Each parallel instruction occupies 62 bits. A 32-instruction $\mathcal{M}$* parallel program is encoded with 62×32 (=1984) bits. A 5-bit branch offset, *brh_offset*, is used for relative branching. 5-bit is enough for a 32-instruction program because it can access ±16 relative address locations. Fig. 3(b) above shows an example of a 5-subinstruction parallel instruction. The branch sub-instruction (`jgt 3 4`) controls the program to jump forward 4 address locations if the last calculation result of a_3 is greater than zero. The ALU sub-instructions perform arithmetic/logic operations.

3 The GPP Accelerating Phenomenon

Writing a sequential program on a single ALU MAP is as simple as writing a program on a conventional sequential processor. Nevertheless, writing a fully optimal parallel program that can make use of all the parallelism of a multiple-ALU MAP is a difficult task. It involves complicated tasks: 1) write a sequential algorithm for the problem; 2) find out dependences of sequential instructions; 3) resolve processor resources constraints, e.g. n(**P**) and n(**A**); and 4) assign multiple sub-instructions to parallel instructions. Besides, the physical connections of the programmable crossbar-network (**N**) are needed to be considered. This gives us the first impression that evolving a parallel program is more difficult than evolving a sequential program. However, experimental results contradict our intuition. After performing a series of preliminary experiments on some benchmark problems with different number of ALUs, we observed that the evolutionary efficiency increases (the computational effort decreases) when the number of ALUs increases.

We call this the *GPP accelerating phenomenon*. If this hypothesis is right, GPP opens up a new approach to evolve a sequential program (algorithm) in two stages: 1) evolve a highly parallel program with the GPP in less CPU time; and 2) de-compile the evolved parallel program into a sequential program of the target program language. Obviously, the first stage takes up a large portion of the processing time. De-compiling a parallel program into a sequential program is straightforward and spends linear processing time with respect to the parallel program's size. Thus, the whole evolutionary process can be sped up significantly.

4 Experimental Settings

In order to verify the GPP accelerating phenomenon, we have carried out a series of experiments. Three of these experiments and their results are presented in this paper. The experiments were run on four 16-register MAPs, $\mathcal{M}_{i,j}$, where i represents n(**A**) and j represents n(**P**).

$$\mathcal{M}_{1,2} = \langle \{a_0\}, \mathbf{R'}, \{p_0,p_1\}, \mathbf{C'}, \mathbf{B'}, \{\mathbf{F'}\}, \{\{r_0,r_1,r_2,r_3,r_4,r_5,r_6,r_7\}\}, \mathbf{N'} \rangle$$
$$\mathcal{M}_{2,4} = \langle \{a_0,a_1\}, \mathbf{R'}, \{p_0,p_1,p_2,p_3\}, \mathbf{C'}, \mathbf{B'}, \{\mathbf{F'},\mathbf{F'}\}, \{\{r_0,r_1,r_2,r_3\},\{r_4,r_5,r_6,r_7\}\}, \mathbf{N'} \rangle$$
$$\mathcal{M}_{4,4} = \langle \{a_0,a_1,a_2,a_3\}, \mathbf{R'}, \{p_0,p_1,p_2,p_3\}, \mathbf{C'}, \mathbf{B'}, \{\mathbf{F'},\mathbf{F'},\mathbf{F'},\mathbf{F'}\}, \{\{r_0,r_1\},\{r_2,r_3\},\{r_4,r_5\},\{r_6,r_7\}\}, \mathbf{N'} \rangle$$
$$\mathcal{M}_{8,8} = \langle \{a_0,a_1,a_2,a_3,a_4,a_5,a_6,a_7\}, \mathbf{R'}, \{p_0,p_1,p_2,p_3,p_4,p_5,p_6,p_7\}, \mathbf{C'}, \mathbf{B'}, \{\mathbf{F'},\mathbf{F'},\mathbf{F'},\mathbf{F'},\mathbf{F'},\mathbf{F'},\mathbf{F'},\mathbf{F'}\}, \{\{r_0\},\{r_1\},\{r_2\},\{r_3\},\{r_4\},\{r_5\},\{r_6\},\{r_7\}\}, \mathbf{N'} \rangle$$
$$\mathbf{R'}=\{r_0, \ldots, r_{15}\},\ \mathbf{C'}=\{r_8, \ldots, r_{15}\},\ \mathbf{B'}=\{b_0, \ldots, b_7\},\ \mathbf{F'}=\{f_0, \ldots, f_{15}\},\ \mathbf{N'}=\Big(\bigcup_{i=0}^{n(A)-1} \mathbf{I}_i\Big)\times\mathbf{P}$$

Table 1. GP parameters for all experiments

crossover probability	1.0
instruction bit mutation probability	0.02
constant mutation probability	0.05
population size	2000
program size	maximum 32 parallel instructions
selection method	tournament (size=10)
experiments	10 independent runs

Table 1 above shows the common GP parameters for all experiments. All ALU's function sets are identical. All experiments were run on a software emulator of the GPP system written in C. The three GP benchmark problems, i.e. the Sextic polynomial, the Fibonacci sequence and the Santa Fe Ant Trail [6], were tested with $\mathcal{M}_{1,2}$, $\mathcal{M}_{2,4}$, $\mathcal{M}_{4,4}$, and $\mathcal{M}_{8,8}$. Having investigated the difficulties of the benchmark problems, we set the maximum program size to 32 parallel instructions that provide enough instructions to evolve solution programs.

Table 2. GP parameters for the Sextic polynomial regression

ALU function set (**F'**)	+, –, ×, %, mov, nop
branch function set (**B'**)	nxt, end
terminal set	$r_0 \leftarrow x$, $r_4 \rightarrow y$
Constants	[-1.0,1.0]
training samples	50 random values of x from [-1.0,1.0]
raw fitness	total absolute error
success predicate	a program with raw fitness < 0.01
data type	floating-point
maximum individual evaluation time	32 MAP clock cycles

The first problem is a symbolic regression of the Sextic polynomial ($y=x^6-2x^4+x^2$). The objective is to evolve a parallel program which optimizes the total absolute error to 0.01, as shown in Table 2 above. All ALUs contain six functions: 1) four arithmetic functions, i.e. +, –, × and %; 2) one data movement function, *mov*; and 3) one no-operation function, *nop*. Since the problem is a simple function regression, no conditional branch function is included in the branch function set. The *nxt* sub-instruction controls the program to advance the program counter by one. Parallel instructions are executed in serial until an *end* sub-instruction is encountered or the 32nd instruction is arrived.

Table 3. GP parameters for the Santa Fe Ant Trail

ALU function set (**F'**)	–, mov, lft, rgt, wlk, nop
branch function set (**B'**)	nxt, jeq, end
terminal set	$r_0 \leftarrow$ 1(*food-ahead*), 0(*no_food_ahead*) $r_4 \rightarrow$ 'L'(*left*), 'R'(*right*), or 'W'(*walk*)
constants	all set to zero
training samples	89 food pellets on a 32×32 plane
raw fitness	number of food pellets remained
success predicate	a program with raw fitness = 0
data type	32-bit signed integer
maximum individual evaluation time	- 500 ant actions on the plane - no pellet eaten in 50 consecutive actions - 64 MAP clock cycles per action

The second problem is the Santa Fe Ant Trail [6]. The objective is to determine the shortest path, the Santa Fe Trail, for an artificial ant to eat all the 89 food pellets lying along an irregular winding trail on a 32×32 cells plane. GPP evolves a Finite State Machine (FSM) with two inputs, i.e. *food_ahead* and *no_food_ahead*, from the front sensor of the ant and three outputs, i.e. *turn_left*, *turn_right* and *go_ahead*. Three new constant assignment functions, as shown in Table 3 above, are included in the ALUs' function sets: 1) *lft* moves 'L' to a register; 2) *rgt* moves 'R' to a register; and 3) *wlk* moves 'W' to a register. These commands control the ant to perform respective actions. For this problem, a solution program needs to be called repeatedly to guide the ant to move and to eat food pellets on the plane step-by-step. For each call, the program gets the front sensor's input, i.e. *food_ahead* or *no_food_ahead*, through r_0, and then determines the next action based on the current input and the previous state (values stored in registers). The action command is stored in r_4. We do not use any specific output instruction. Thus, GPP needs to learn the FSM and to put the action command in r_4. A satisfactory program must show that all 89 food pellets are eaten within 500 actions. The maximum execution time for each action call is limited to 64 cycles to prevent infinite loop. An evaluation always stops after 500 actions even if the ant cannot eat all food pellets. In order to save evolutionary time, an evaluation will be stopped if the ant does not eat any food pellets within 50 consecutive actions.

The last problem is a symbolic regression of the Fibonacci sequence ($T_1=T_0=1$ & $T_i=T_{i-1}+T_{i-2}$). It is a recursive sequence. A solution program is very difficult to be evolved because it includes program loops. As shown in Table 4 above, three new branch control sub-instructions are added: 1) *jmp* for *unconditional_jump*; 2) *jep* for *jump_if_equal*; and 3) *jgt* for *jump_if_greater*. We also relax the maximum individual evaluation time to 200 MAP clock cycles for program loops evolution.

Table 4. GP parameters for the Fibonacci sequence regression

ALU function set (**F'**)	+, −, ×, %, shr, inc, dec, mov, nop
branch function set (**B'**)	nxt, jmp, jeq, jgt, end
terminal set	$r_0 \leftarrow i$, $r_4 \rightarrow T_i$
constants	0 or 1
training samples	10 random values of *i* from [0,24]
raw fitness	Total absolute error
success predicate	a program with raw fitness = 0
data type	32-bit signed integer
maximum individual evaluation time	200 MAP clock cycles

4.1 Computational Effort Measurement

In order to compare the computational effort of GPP with different MAP configurations, we adopt Koza's computational effort measurement (E-measure) method [6]. It estimates the number of individuals which would have to be processed to give a certain probability (z) of success.

$$R(M,i,z)=\begin{cases} 1 & \text{if } P(M,i)=1.0 \\ \left\lceil \dfrac{\log(1-z)}{\log[1-P(M,i)]} \right\rceil & \text{otherwise} \end{cases} \tag{3}$$

$$I(M,i,z)=(i+M)R(z) \tag{4}$$

$$E=I(M,i^*,z)=(i^*+M)R(z) \tag{5}$$

$$C=E\times\frac{\textit{total no. MAP cycles consumed for all success runs}}{\textit{total tournaments evolved for all success runs}} \tag{6}$$

$$T=E\times\frac{\textit{total GPP software emulator execution time for all success runs}}{\textit{total tournaments evolved for all success runs}} \tag{7}$$

In equation (3) above, $P(M,i)$ is the experimental cumulative probability of success for a run to yield satisfactory solution at or before the tournament i. M represents the population size. In equation (4) above, $R(z)$ represents the number of independent runs required to satisfy the success predicate by tournament i with the probability of z. $I(M,i,z)$ represents the minimum number of individuals that needs to be processed in order to yield a satisfactory solution at tournament i with a specific value of z=0.99. In equation (5) above, the computational effort (E) required to yield a satisfactory solution for the problem is the minimal value of $I(M,i,z)$ over all the tournaments i between 0 and the maximum allowed tournament i_{max}. Let the tournament i^* at which $I(M,i^*,z)$ has the minimum value. The E is equal to $I(M,t^*,z)$ (equation (5) above). We can also calculate the computational effort in terms of MAP clock cycles (C) and CPU time (T) (equations (6) and (7) above). The E assesses the evolvability of the GPP. The C assesses the potential speedup of the hardware-assisted MAP. The T assesses the pure software speedup of the GPP paradigm.

5 Results and Evaluations

We performed ten runs on each of the three problems with four different configurations of MAPs, i.e. $\mathcal{M}_{1,2}$, $\mathcal{M}_{2,4}$, $\mathcal{M}_{4,4}$ and $\mathcal{M}_{8,8}$. The three performance indicators (*E*, *C* and *T*) are shown in Tables 5 to 7 below. The (*E*) columns represent the computational effort for evolving the first satisfactory program based on equation (5) above with z=0.99. The (*C*) columns represent the estimated computational effort in terms of MAP clock cycles (equation (6) above). The (*T*) columns represent the computational effort in terms of CPU time of the GPP emulator running on a 2.1GHz Intel Pentium 4 PC (equation (7) above). For easy comparison, three ratio columns are included. Each ratio value is calculated by dividing its corresponding indicator value by the $\mathcal{M}_{8,8}$ indicator value, as shown in the last row of each table (in italic).

Table 5. Experimental results of Sextic polynomial regression

MAP	computational effort (*E*) ($\times 10^6$)	*ratio*	MAP clock cycles (*C*) ($\times 10^6$)	ratio	CPU Time(*T*) (min)	ratio
$\mathcal{M}_{1,2}$	5.31	9.8	111.84	13.7	59.5	5.5
$\mathcal{M}_{2,4}$	2.26	4.2	46.14	5.7	36.6	3.4
$\mathcal{M}_{4,4}$	0.45	0.8	7.60	0.9	6.3	0.6
$\mathcal{M}_{8,8}$	*0.54*	1.0	*8.16*	1.0	*10.7*	1.0

Table 5 above shows the experimental results of the Sextic polynomial regression. Except $\mathcal{M}_{4,4}$, all the three performance indicators (*E*, *C* and *T*) decrease while n(**A**) increases. The values of $\mathcal{M}_{4,4}$ are slightly smaller than that of $\mathcal{M}_{8,8}$. It is because this problem is too simple to fully utilize parallelism of $\mathcal{M}_{8,8}$. The relatively large search space of $\mathcal{M}_{8,8}$ to $\mathcal{M}_{4,4}$ increases the effort of evolution; even so $\mathcal{M}_{8,8}$ maintains an effort level as low as that of the $\mathcal{M}_{4,4}$. The *E*, *C* and *T* ratios of evolving an $\mathcal{M}_{1,2}$ sequential program to an $\mathcal{M}_{8,8}$ parallel program are 9.8, 13.7 and 5.5 respectively. The *T* ratios show that it is more efficient to evolve a parallel program even without the hardware-assisted MAP. Furthermore, the total MAP clock cycles (*C*) for fitness evaluation decreases while n(**A**) increases. In the software emulator of the GPP, a parallel instruction is executed in sequential manner. For example, an $\mathcal{M}_{4,4}$ instruction consists of five sub-instructions, i.e. one branch sub-instruction and four arithmetic/logic sub-instructions. We can imagine that the hardware-assisted GPP can further speed up parallel programs evolution because all sub-instructions will be executed in parallel in a single MAP clock cycle.

Table 6. Experimental results of Santa Fe Ant Trail

MAP	computational effort (*E*) ($\times 10^6$)	*ratio*	MAP clock cycles (*C*) ($\times 10^9$)	ratio	CPU time (*T*) (min)	ratio
$\mathcal{M}_{1,2}$	17.16	5.2	24.55	11.4	221.3	6.3
$\mathcal{M}_{2,4}$	6.24	1.9	6.07	2.8	58.9	1.7
$\mathcal{M}_{4,4}$	5.22	1.6	4.21	1.9	62.3	1.8
$\mathcal{M}_{8,8}$	*3.30*	1.0	*2.16*	1.0	*35.0*	1.0

Table 6 above shows similar experimental results for the Santa Fe Ant Trail problem. All the three performance indicators (*E*, *C* and *T*) decrease while n(**A**) increases.

The E, C and T ratios of evolving an $\mathcal{M}_{1,2}$ sequential program to an $\mathcal{M}_{8,8}$ parallel program are 5.2, 11.4 and 6.3 respectively.

Table 7. Experimental results of Fibonacci sequence regression

MAP	computational effort (E) ($\times 10^6$)	*ratio*	MAP clock cycles (C) ($\times 10^9$)	ratio	CPU time (T) (min)	ratio
$\mathcal{M}_{1,2}$	332.74	50.7	24.15	52.5	1565.5	27.9
$\mathcal{M}_{2,4}$	134.26	20.5	10.14	22.0	786.4	14.0
$\mathcal{M}_{4,4}$	21.89	3.3	1.77	3.8	139.1	2.5
$\mathcal{M}_{8,8}$	*6.56*	1.0	*0.46*	1.0	*56.0*	1.0

Table 7 above also shows the speed up phenomenon for the Fibonacci sequence regression problem. All the three performance indicators (E, C and T) decrease while n(**A**) increases. The E, C and T ratios for evolving an $\mathcal{M}_{1,2}$ sequential program to an $\mathcal{M}_{8,8}$ parallel program are 50.7, 52.5 and 27.9 respectively. These figures reflect that GPP is more efficient in evolving parallel programs than sequential programs.

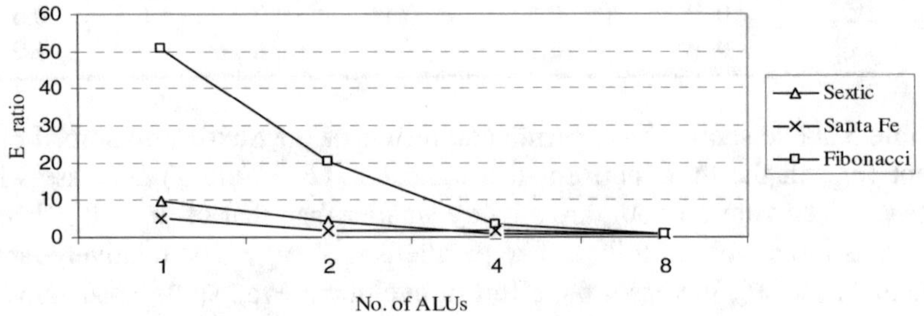

Fig. 4. Computational effort (E) vs. n(**A**)

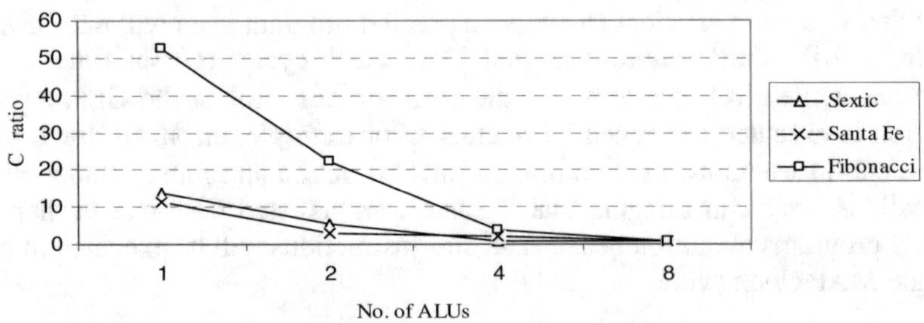

Fig. 5. MAP clock cycles (C) vs. n(**A**)

Fig. 4 above shows the relative computational effort (E), i.e. amount of genetic operations, of the three presented problems with different number of processors (n(**A**)). Undoubtedly, all curves show a general trend of decreasing E with an increasing n(**A**) up to 4 ALUs but the E ratio of $\mathcal{M}_{8,8}$ to $\mathcal{M}_{4,4}$ is not so significant. An $\mathcal{M}_{4,4}$ consists of 2×4×4 (=32) cross-points in its crossbar-network. An $\mathcal{M}_{8,8}$ consists of 2×8×8 (=128) cross-points in its crossbar-network. An $\mathcal{M}_{8,8}$ consumes 4 times hardware resources of an $\mathcal{M}_{4,4}$. Hardware resource of the crossbar-network is very sensitive to the number of cross-point. It designates that an $\mathcal{M}_{4,4}$ is more cost-effective than an $\mathcal{M}_{8,8}$ for the tested

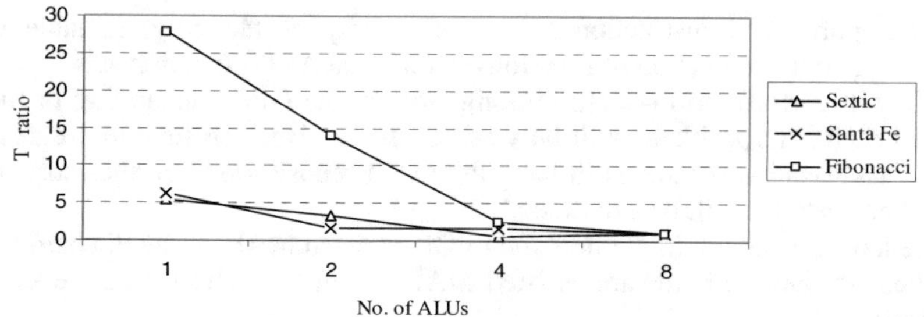

Fig. 6. Emulator CPU time (*T*) vs. n(**A**)

problems. Fig. 5 above shows the relative MAP clock cycles (*C*), i.e. amount of fitness evaluations. It shows that fitness evaluation effort also decreases while n(**A**) increases.

One worry of GPP is that the complicated steps in evaluating a parallel program will cancel out the cycle gained. However, Fig. 6 above shows that the pure software CPU time (*T*) also decreases with n(**A**). It demonstrates the effectiveness and efficiency of our GPP paradigm with a parallel program representation. It also shows that GPP speed up GP evolution not only by hardware-assisted fitness evaluations but also by its internal robust evolvability. It opens up a new opportunity for us to use GPP to solve more complicated problems by including higher-level functions, e.g. problem specific modules. Even if these higher-level functions may not be implemented in parallel hardware, the pure software speedup of GPP also benefits the evolution.

6 Conclusions and Further Work

This paper has reported a novel Genetic Parallel Programming (GPP) paradigm based on Linear Genetic Programming (LGP) that can be used to evolve optimal parallel program for a parallel architecture. It has also presented the GPP accelerating phenomenon – "parallel programs are more evolvable than sequential programs". The phenomenon shows that GPP does not only evolve parallel program automatically, but it also speeds up the evolution process. Experimental results on the three benchmark problems in this work indicate that GPP is more efficient in evolving parallel programs than sequential programs. The rationale behind the GPP accelerating phenomenon is that the more the number of parallel ALUs, the higher the probability of an expected operation to be hit. Similar to flipping coins, if we flip one coin, the probability of coming up with "head" is 0.5. However, if we flip two coins simultaneously, the probability of coming up with "head(s)" increases to 0.75. This hypothesis opens up a new approach to evolve a parallel program with an optimal MIMD processor, the Multi-ALU Processor (MAP). This conjecture will have significant impact on GP evolution research. An entirely new approach is to evolve a satisfactory solution in parallel program representation and then de-compile the evolved parallel program to sequential codes of conventional program languages. The effort for de-compiling a parallel MAP program is much lower than that of the evolutionary process. Thus, the whole evolution can be sped up significantly.

We are going to develop de-compilers for different high-level languages in order to port evolved algorithms to other systems. Further studies should be conducted to explore the effect of different settings on MAP configurations, e.g. the numbers of register, ports, and instructions, the connectivity of the programmable crossbar-network, and the allocation of functions to different ALUs function sets.

We will perform an in-depth investigation on the GPP accelerating phenomenon. More benchmark problems will be worked on, e.g. Boolean function regression and Data Classification databases in the public UCI repositories. Furthermore, the theoretical background will be examined.

We have planned to implement the FPGA-assisted MAP on the Pilchard Card [16]. We believe that the hardware-assisted MAP can further speed up the evolution significantly.

Apart from the above, we are going to apply GPP to real-life problems, e.g. solve more complicated problems with higher-level function sets.

References

1. Banzhaf, W., Koza, J.R., Ryan, C., Spector, L., Jocob, C.: Genetic Programming. IEEE Intelligent Systems Journal, Vol. 17, No. 3 (2000) 74-84
2. Goldberg, D.E.: Genetic Algorithm in Search, Optimization and Machine Learning. Addison-Wesley (1989)
3. Brameier, M., Banzhaf, W.: A Comparison of Linear Genetic Programming and Neural Networks. IEEE Trans. on Evolutionary Computation, Vol. 5, No. 1 (2001) 17-26
4. Kishore, J.K., Patnaik, L.M., Mani, V., Agrawal, V.K.: Application of Genetic Programming for Multicategory Pattern Classification. IEEE Trans. on Evolutionary Computation, Vol. 4, No. 3 (2000) 242-258
5. Wong, M.L., Leung, K.S.: Data Mining Using Grammar Based Genetic Programming and the Applications. Kluwer Academic (2001)
6. Koza, J.R.: Genetic Programming: On the Programming of Computers by Means of Natural Selection. MIT Press (1992)
7. Koza, J.R.: Genetic Programming II: Automatic Discovery of Reusable Programs. MIT Press (1994)
8. Banzhaf, W., Nordin, P., Keller, R.E., Francone, F.D.: Generic Programming: An Introduction on the Automatic Evolution of Computer Programs and its Applications. Morgan Kaufmann (1998)
9. Lee, K.H., Leung, K.S., Cheang, S.M.: A Microprogrammable List Processor for Personal Computers. IEEE Micro, Vol. 10, No. 4 (1990) 50-61
10. Nordin, P., Hoffmann, F., Francone, F.D., Brameier, M., Banzhaf, W.: AIM-GP and Parallelism. Proc. of IEEE Congress on Evolutionary Computation (1999) 1059-1066
11. Heywood, M.I., Zincir-Heywood, A.N.: Dynamic Page Based Crossover in Linear Genetic Programming. IEEE Trans. on Systems, Man, and Cybernetics. Vol. 23, No. 3 (2002) 380-388
12. Huelsbergen, L.: Learning Recursive Sequences via Evolution of Machine-Language Programs. Proc. of the 2nd Annual Genetic Programming Conf. (1997) 186-194
13. Conrads, M., Nordin, P., Banzhaf, W.: Speech Sound Discrimination with Genetic Programming. Proc. of the 1st European Workshop on Genetic Programming (1998) 113-129
14. Leung, K.S., Lee, K.H., Cheang, S.M.: Evolving Parallel Machine Programs for a Multi-ALU Processor. Proc. of IEEE Congress on Evolutionary Computation (2002) 1703-1708
15. Leung, K.S., Lee, K.H., Cheang, S.M.: Genetic Parallel Programming - Evolving Linear Machine Programs Codes on a Multi-ALU Processor. Proc. of Int. Conf. on Artificial Intelligence in Engineering and Technology (2002) 207-213
16. Leong, P.H.W., Leong, M.P., Cheung, O.Y.H., Tung, T., Kwok, C.M., Wong, M.Y. and Lee, K.H.: Pilchard – A reconfigurable computing platform with memory slot interface. Proc. of the 8th Annual IEEE Symposium on Field Programmable Custom Computing Machines (2001)

Genetic Programming with Meta-search: Searching for a Successful Population within the Classification Domain

Thomas Loveard

School of Computer Science
RMIT University
GPO Box 2476V, Melbourne Victoria 3001, Australia
toml@cs.rmit.edu.au

Abstract. The genetic programming (GP) search method can often vary greatly in the quality of solution derived from one run to the next. As a result, it is often the case that a number of runs must be performed to ensure that an effective solution is found. This paper introduces several methods which attempt to better utilise the computational resources spent on performing a number of independent GP runs. Termed meta-search strategies, these methods seek to search the space of evolving GP populations in an attempt to focus computational resources on those populations which are most likely to yield competitive solutions.

Two meta-search strategies are introduced and evaluated over a set of classification problems. The meta-search strategies are termed a pyramid search strategy and a population beam search strategy. Additional to these methods, a combined approach using properties of both the pyramid and population beam search methods is evaluated.

Over a set of five classification problems, results show that meta-search strategies can substantially improve the accuracy of solutions over those derived by a set of independent GP runs. In particular the combined approach is demonstrated to give more accurate classification performance whilst requiring less time to train than a set of independent GP runs, making this method a promising approach for problems for which multiple GP runs must be performed to ensure a quality solution.

1 Introduction

Often when faced with a difficult problem in genetic programming, the traditional method of overcoming the difficulties of such a problem is seen to be the investment of large amounts of computational resources for very large population sizes or many generations [1,7]. However, some recent research has shown that in many cases, computational resources can often be better applied by performing GP runs with moderate parameter choices [5,6]. By using moderate choices it is possible to perform a number of independent GP runs in isolation, and select the better performing run, which will usually give overall better performance than performing fewer runs which use much larger parameter choices [8,11].

C. Ryan et al. (Eds.): EuroGP 2003, LNCS 2610, pp. 119–129, 2003.

Given the variability of any independent GP run and the need to perform many runs to ensure a quality solution is found for some problems, it can be argued that for such problems, each evolving run is not searching the global search space. Each GP run is instead reaching some localised outcome. By evolving multiple populations we seek to cover as many local search areas as possible, with the hope that one such local search will eventuate in a solution which is globally competitive. A higher level search is being performed, and this search is over the space of evolving populations.

Within the space of evolving populations it is possible to use strategies other than simply evaluating a number of GP runs from beginning to end. It is possible to choose to end a GP run which is proving to be unfruitful, and to allot more computational resources to runs which are performing well, and in effect perform a higher level search over the space of evolving populations. Work by [12] in the field of genetic algorithms is the only other example in the field of evolutionary computation where such a higher level search over populations has been implemented. This investigation used a factor termed "utility" to identify promising populations to focus evolutionary search upon. This investigation gave promising results for the potential of a meta-search method within the field of evolutionary computation, although this method was only applied to one optimisation problem in the field of genetic algorithms.

This paper extends this small body of work by introducing a number of new meta-search methods to perform a higher level search over the space of evolving populations, and by the application of such meta-search methods to the domain of GP and tasks involving classification. The aim of this work is to develop meta-search methods which can improve the accuracy of classifiers trained using GP while keeping the computational expense of the search process equivalent to a method that simply evolves a number of GP populations to completion.

2 Meta-search: A Pyramid Strategy

Work from [8] showed that at some number of generations, runs for a given problem will tend to be predisposed towards success or failure. If runs are predisposed to fail, and such runs can be identified at an early stage of evolution, then much wasteful evaluation could be saved by terminating the run. In such an instance, the sooner runs which will prove to be unsuccessful can be terminated, the greater the savings of computational expenditure will be. With the savings gained from terminating poorly performing runs, more resources are made available for widening the search for a successfully evolving population.

The pyramid meta-search method was developed from this principle of terminating populations that appear to be performing poorly as the search progress. Because many populations will be terminated before the maximum number of generations are reached the pyramid search method re-invests the computational savings by evolving a larger number of initial populations. Populations which appear to be performing the worst are terminated, based upon the current best fitness of individuals within the population. As the search progresses, more and

Table 1. Three Pyramid Meta-Search Strategies, Each Using 4000 Generations in Total, Compared With a Standard Set of 40 Runs

Pyramid Stage	Generations	Populations Evolving Per Stage: Conventional GP of 40 Runs	Wide-Based Pyramid	Medium-Based Pyramid	Small-Based Pyramid
1	Gens 0-10	40	240	120	65
2	Gens 11-20	40	40	75	65
3	Gens 21-30	40	30	50	65
4	Gens 31-40	40	20	40	65
5	Gens 41-50	40	15	30	45
6	Gens 51-60	40	15	25	30
7	Gens 61-70	40	10	20	22
8	Gens 71-80	40	10	16	18
9	Gens 81-90	40	10	14	15
10	Gens 91-100	40	10	10	10

more populations are terminated. As a result of the termination of poor populations, the number of evolving populations is reduced from a large number of populations at the start, or base, of a pyramid search, to a small number of populations at the end point. It is hoped that the computational resources invested in evolving a larger number of populations in early stages of the pyramid search will result in more populations with overall potential to effectively solve the problem at hand. These populations should be the least likely to be terminated due to poor performance and so should result in highly effective solutions.

Three pyramid structures are developed for testing in this paper. These consist of a wide-based, medium-based and smaller-based pyramid structures, each designed to run for 100 generations in total. Table 1 outlines the number of runs which are being pursued at each stage of the pyramid. In each case the pyramid search is designed to evaluate the same number of generations as would a conventional set of 40 independent GP populations, run for 100 generations. The wide-based pyramid evaluates a very large number of populations for the first 10 generations, seeking to find the very best runs to continue. By eliminating all the worst performing runs at an early stage we save a great amount of computational resources, and evolve only those runs with the very best potential. In contrast in the small-based pyramid gives populations more time to establish a tendency to succeed before elimination occurs. In this case we are less likely to eliminate a population which could have otherwise led to a globally competitive solution, but where this potential does not become evident until later stages of a run.

3 Meta-search: Population Beam Search

The pyramid structure of populations given above is one method in which computational effort can be directed away from poorly performing populations. In the case of the pyramid search, savings in computational effort are reinvested in broadening the search for a good population in the initial stages of GP runs.

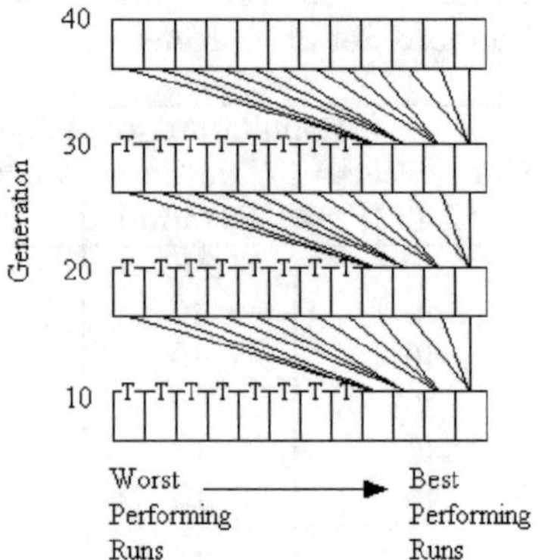

Fig. 1. A Population Beam Search: Width = 12 populations, w = 4 and Replacement Interval = 10 Generations. "T" Indicates a Terminated Run

In contrast, a population beam search is a meta-search strategy which seeks to maintain a constant number of evolving populations for the total number of generations run. Unlike the conventional GP method of running many populations from start to finish however, the population beam search seeks to divert computational focus away from poorly performing populations, and invest more heavily in those populations which are performing well.

At any given point of a run, a number of possible paths of evolution can be taken. A given population may be predisposed to leading in good or bad evolutionary directions for solving the target problem, but neither direction is completely assured. The exact course of evolution is decided by the random choices of which individuals are selected, biased by fitness, and the choices of which individuals are used together in crossover operations, and which individuals are used for mutation and reproduction operations. Every move from one generation to the next involves thousands of random choices and each one of these random choices has the ability to move the evolving population in a direction that is moving towards, away from, or neutral to a globally optimal outcome.

The population beam search approach seeks to use the computational resources saved by terminating poorly performing populations to evaluate multiple copies of populations which are performing well. In doing so this approach attempts to maximise the chance that a successful path of evolution will be followed in at least one of the population copies. Figure 1 shows this meta-search strategy where twelve populations are being evolved. In this case, at the end of every ten generations, the eight populations which are performing the worst are terminated. With the computational resources saved, this allows for the four best performing populations to evolve in a number of separate directions, each running in three population coppies to give a total of twelve populations overall. At the end of another ten generations the populations are sorted from the best to the worst performing, with the worst 8 populations being terminated once more to allow the best performing populations to explore multiple run paths.

The population beam search strategy can be implemented with a number of configurations. The number of populations being evolved within the meta-search is one key parameter. In Figure 1, twelve populations make up the beam search. We term this parameter of the number of populations in the meta-search the *width* of the search. Another key parameter is the number of populations which are terminated at each stage, and in direct relation, the number of populations which are duplicated in a subsequent stage of a run. The value for the number of populations which are retained for duplication at the end of each stage is generally known in a beam search as the beam width and is given the symbol w. The final key parameter of a population beam search is how regularly populations are terminated and replaced with copies of better performing populations. Over 100 generations in total, replacement could occur every ten generations, twenty generations or even every single generation. The regularity at which populations are terminated and replaced is termed the *replacement interval.*

In this paper, three alternative population beam search parameter sets are implemented to give an indication of the performance of the population beam search over a range of parameters. Runs are compared with the performance of 40 independent GP runs, and so in each case the overall number of populations making up a population beam search will be 40. In each case a replacement interval of 10 generations was seen to be appropriate. The three alternative beam search methods are: A) $Width = 10$, $w = 1$. Evaluated 4 Times to give a total of 40 populations. B) $Width = 10$, $w = 5$. Evaluated 4 Times to give a total of 40 populations. C) $Width = 40$, $w = 20$. Evaluated once to give a total of 40 populations. Search method A actually performs a greedy search, which is a special case of a beam search where $w = 1$.

4 A Combined Approach: A Pyramid Search and Population Beam Search

If the pyramid search and population beam search strategies can be used to make effective use of evolving GP populations, then it may be possible to use these two search strategies in combination. A large number of populations can be used at earlier stages of evolution, with elimination of many runs early on, as occurs with the pyramid search approach. At each stage of the pyramid however, sufficient runs can be eliminated such that the remaining runs can be duplicated multiple times at the next stage of the pyramid. The combination strategy of a pyramid search and population beam search used in this paper is shown in Table 2. In this method, each level of the pyramid reduces the number of populations which continue to evolve. The number of runs which are able to continue evolution (the value of w) is at a level such that each population can be duplicated twice at the next level of the pyramid.

The parameters for the combined search strategy given in Table 2 are again only one of many possible parameter options possible for such a combined search method. This combined search method uses moderate parameter choices from both the pyramid and population beam search methods to give a middle-of-the-road solution for the combined strategy for this investigation.

Table 2. A Combined Pyramid Search and Population Beam Search

Stage	Generations	*Width*	*w*
1	Gens 0-10	120	37
2	Gens 11-20	74	25
3	Gens 21-30	50	20
4	Gens 31-40	40	15
5	Gens 41-50	30	13
6	Gens 51-60	26	10
7	Gens 61-70	20	8
8	Gens 71-80	16	7
9	Gens 81-90	14	5
10	Gens 91-100	10	–

Table 3. Datasets

Dataset	Training Set Size	Test Set Size	Number of Classes
Satlog Satellite Image	4435	2000	6
Satlog Image Segmentation	2310	1000	7
Thyroid Disease	3772	3428	3
Adult	4884	4884	2
Splice Gene Sequences	2000	1175	3

5 Experimental Configuration

Five classification datasets taken from the UCI Machine Learning Repository [2] were selected to test the various meta-search methods against. These datasets are shown in Table 3. The test and training datasets used for the Satlog Image Segmentation, Adult and Splice Gene Sequences datasets were sampled from the original, larger datasets by random selection without replacement.

Each meta-search strategy is applied to all five datasets and compared with the best result achieved by a standard set of forty independent GP runs. All GP populations consist of 500 individuals and are run for a maximum of 100 generations. Tournament selection was used for selection of individuals, with a tournament size of 4 individuals. When moving to a new generation, crossover was used to generate 89% of new individuals and mutation accounted for 10%. Elitist reproduction accounted for the remaining 1% of individual being transferred to the next generation. Initially, GP program trees were limited to a maximum tree depth of 6 nodes, with an overall maximum tree depth for the run set at 17 nodes.

The dynamic range selection method introduced in [9] was used to allow GP programs to perform classification of the datasets. For those runs which involve the use of nominal attributes (Adult and Spice datasets), the binary conversion method introduced in [10] was used to represent nominal attributes. The GP function set consisted of the arithmetic operations { +, -, *, / } and the conditional operations { IF_LTE, IF_GTE, IF_EQ }. The terminal set consisted

Table 4. Best Test Error Produced From The Evaluation of 4000 Generations

	Satlog Satellite Image	Satlog Image Segment.	Thyroid Disease Dataset	Adult Dataset	Splice Dataset
Conventional GP: 40 Runs	0.161	0.073	0.015	0.144	0.058
Wide-Based Pyramid	0.155	0.061	0.009	0.144	0.054
Medium-Based Pyramid	0.162	0.063	0.014	0.143	0.053
Small-Based Pyramid	0.159	0.066	0.013	0.144	0.056
Beam Search: 4 X Width=10,w=1	0.162	0.070	0.009	0.144	0.058
Beam Search: 4 X Width=10,w=5	**0.146**	0.054	0.015	0.148	0.050
Beam Search: 1 X Width=40,w=20	0.150	0.068	**0.007**	**0.142**	**0.048**
Combined: Beam and Pyramid	0.150	**0.052**	**0.007**	0.145	0.051

of randomly assigned constant values within the range of -1 to 1, and terminals for the attributes of the classification dataset.

One implication of the population beam meta-search method with any of the parameter settings used in this paper is that the runs at the end point of the search will not be independently arrived at classifiers. Unlike a standard set of GP runs performed in isolation and the pyramid search where every run is independent, many runs at the end of a population beam search will have been derived from the same genetic material at some stage of the run. Because of this, we cannot meaningfully derive average fitness values for the populations within a population beam search or the combined meta-search methods. As a result of this, we compare only the single best classifier from all populations of any search method within this paper.

6 Results

Table 4 shows the results for the best test error rate achieved by each search method for the five datasets. The error rate of the best classifier from each method was selected through the performance of that classifier on the training data. This is because the selection of the best performing classifier based on the test data would be making use of some aspect of the test data for the training (selection) of classifiers and this would invalidate the results.

From the results in Table 4 it can be seen that the performance of the various meta-search methods are very encouraging when compared with the use of a conventional set of 40 GP runs. The three pyramid search methods generally always produced a classifier more accurate (making less errors) than did the best result from a standard set of 40 populations run for 100 generations. In particular, the wide-based pyramid appears to perform well, being able to produce a classifier more accurate than the standard set of runs in four of the five datasets, and for the Adult dataset the performance of the wide based pyramid was equal to that of the standard set of 40 runs.

The population beam search using parameters of $width = 10$ and $w = 1$ was generally able to produce a classifier more accurate classification than the con-

Table 5. Total Training Time (HH:MM) For 4000 Generations Using Meta-Search Methods Over Five Datasets

	Satlog Satellite Image	Satlog Image Segmet.	Thyroid Disease Dataset	Adult Dataset	Splice Dataset
Conventional GP	22:43	7:59	17:48	20:34	11:47
Wide-Based Pyramid	14:42	5:02	13:24	15:12	8:09
Medium-Based Pyramid	17:16	5:40	15:15	17:26	9:25
Small-Based Pyramid	20:21	6:30	16:25	18:22	10:38
Beam Search: 4 X Width=10,w=1	28:49	8:36	25:48	23:50	13:39
Beam Search: 4 X Width=10,w=5	21:52	7:44	19:43	26:11	13:13
Beam Search: 1 X Width=40,w=20	22:35	7:51	30:37	27:39	13:39
Combined: Beam and Pyramid	18:16	6:52	17:36	18:26	9:45

ventional 40 GP runs. However, the performance of the population beam search methods using a larger value of w were generally able to produce more accurate results again. The population beam search which uses a value of $w = 1$ chooses a narrow focus for computational effort, with only one population being replicated at each stage of the search. This may lead to the overall search becoming too specialised. The results for the two population beam search methos which use larger values of w are most encouraging. For parameter values of $width = 10$ and $w = 5$ the method is able to perform classification with substantially reduced errors for the Satlog Satellite Image and Satlog Image Segmentation datasets. With parameters of $Width = 40$, $w = 20$ the method is able to produce a classifier which outperforms the best classifier from the conventional GP method in every case, with substantially reduced errors for the Satlog Satellite Image, Satlog Image Segmentation datasets and Thyroid Disease datasets. From these results it would appear that a population beam search is able to produce highly effective solutions when compared to a standard set of populations evolving from beginning to end. This is particularly so when the search width is large and the beam width is large enough so as not to make the search too specialised.

The accuracy of the combined meta-search method was generally very high when compared with the best accuracy achieved by a conventional set of GP runs. In only one case, that of the Adult dataset, was the test error rate of the combined meta-search method less than that of a conventional set of 40 runs, but this was only by a very small margin. It is interesting to note that the combined search method was also generally able to perform more accurate classification than the pyramid search methods over any given dataset.

6.1 Training Times

While each search method was designed so that 4000 generations in total were evaluated, some substantial differences in training times were found, as can be seen in Table 5. This was mainly the case in the pyramid search strategies, where each method required less training time than did the conventional set of

40 GP runs. The savings in training times were due to the fact that the pyramid search strategies (particularly the wide based pyramid) evaluate the majority of the 4000 generations between the stages of generation 0 to 10 or generations 10 to 20. This gives substantial reductions in training time because GP program trees tend to be smaller in the earlier generations of a run and require less time to execute. This cost saving also applies to the combined meta-search method which requires less training time than the conventional set of runs for all five datasets.

The population beam search methods which run a consistent number of runs for the entire 100 generations tended to have similar run times to the conventional GP of 40 runs. There are a number of cases where the population beam search does require longer training times than the conventional set of GP populations, but this is not always the case. There appears to be no general pattern for training times for the population beam search methods when compared with a conventional set of GP populations.

6.2 Future Directions for Meta-search Methods

The work in this paper has implemented a number of search strategies which search through the space of evolving populations. Both pyramid and population beam search methods have shown promise for improving the performance of GP when compared to a conventional set of GP populations.

Given that the population beam search and combined meta-search methods result in populations that are not independent from other populations, it has not been possible to perform statistical validation of the results given in this paper. Future work will involve the use of many independent meta-search runs with comparison to the use of a standard set of GP populations.

Additionally, In the methods of meta-search used in this paper there is no transfer of genetic material between the evolving populations. This is because it was desirable to separate each population so that those leading towards sub-optimal solutions would not affect the performance of the populations evolving in a good evolutionary path. However, much work has been performed in the area of multiple population GP where genetic material is transferred at some interval between populations [3,4]. The classical implementation of these models is the island model of populations, where each population is seen as an island, isolated for the other populations, where some small number of individuals migrate between the islands over the course of a run.

In addition to this, both the pyramid and population beam search strategies discard much genetic material which might possibly lead to globally competitive solutions. At each stage of both meta-search methods, a number of poorly performing populations are terminated. However, this is somewhat of a waste of computational effort in itself, as some reasonable amount of computation will have been invested in each terminated population.

Future directions for the meta-search methods implemented within this paper will use the transfer of genetic material between populations in the meta-search. Also of interest is the idea that instead of terminating populations which are performing poorly, these populations could be truncated substantially by killing many individuals within the population, but retaining some number of individuals. Such truncated populations could be combined with other populations in a transfer of genetic material so that the computational effort spent upon evaluating the terminated population would not be entirely lost. Such a strategy could be seen as a "sinking island" model, where available resources diminish during the course of the run and populations compete for these resources through their potential for evolutionary success as a population as a whole. The possibilities for this line of thought could even stretch to strategies using a form of "meta-evolution" where populations compete for probabilistic selection, crossover (transfer of individuals between populations) and attempt to avoid extinction through termination.

One final factor for consideration is that in this paper we measure how well a population is performing simply by the fitness value of the best of population individual at a given point in the run. However, other measures exist which could well combine to give a better overall judgement of how well we can expect a population to perform in the future. Factors such as diversity and the fitness increase in recent generations could be used in combination with the best of population fitness to derive a measure for how well we can expect a population to perform. Another possible factor could also be the use of a validation set of data to select populations which are generalising well over data not used for training. All such factors could be combined to allow populations to be much more accurately distinguished for the potential for success, and the appropriate terminations or truncations could be made with less risk of eliminating a population with potential to reach a globally competitive solution. This could give substantially improved performance for the meta-search methods implemented within this paper.

6.3 Conclusions

This paper has implemented two meta-search methods of the pyramid search and population beam search methods, and has additionally developed a meta-search method which combines the two approaches. Results for all the meta-search methods show these approaches to be capable of producing generally more accurate classifiers than a conventional set of GP populations. In particular, the combined search method of pyramid search and population beam search has shown to be generally capable of generating more accurate classifiers than a standard set of evolving populations (in some cases substantially more accurate) while using a lesser amount of training time. These results clearly demonstrate the feasibility of meta-search methods for GP and leave such methods with great potential for further investigation.

References

1. Wolfgang Banzhaf, Peter Nordin, Robert E. Keller, and Frank D. Francone. *Genetic Programming – An Introduction; On the Automatic Evolution of Computer Programs and its Applications.* Morgan Kaufmann, dpunkt.verlag, January 1998.

2. C.L. Blake and C.J. Merz. UCI repository of machine learning databases, 1998.
3. Erick Cantu-Paz. Topologies, migration rates, and multi-population parallel genetic algorithms. In *Proceedings of the Genetic and Evolutionary Computation Conference*, volume 1, pages 91–98, Orlando, Florida, USA, 13-17 July 1999. Morgan Kaufmann.
4. F. Fernandez, M. Tomassini, W. F. Punch III, and J. M. Sanchez. Experimental study of multipopulation parallel genetic programming. In *Genetic Programming, Proceedings of EuroGP'2000*, volume 1802 of *LNCS*, pages 283–293, Edinburgh, 15-16 April 2000. Springer-Verlag.
5. Matthias Fuchs. Large populations are not always the best choice in genetic programming. In *Proceedings of the Genetic and Evolutionary Computation Conference*, volume 2, pages 1033–1038, Orlando, Florida, USA, 13-17 July 1999. Morgan Kaufmann.
6. Chris Gathercole and Peter Ross. Small populations over many generations can beat large populations over few generations in genetic programming. In *Genetic Programming 1997: Proceedings of the Second Annual Conference*, pages 111–118, Stanford University, CA, USA, 13-16 July 1997. Morgan Kaufmann.
7. John R. Koza. *Genetic Programming: On the Programming of Computers by Means of Natural Selection.* MIT Press, 1992.
8. Thomas Loveard and Vic Ciesielski. Genetic programming for classification: An analysis of convergence behaviour. *Lecture Notes in Computer Science*, 2557:309–320, 2002.
9. Thomas Loveard and Victor Ciesielski. Representing classification problems in genetic programming. In *Proceedings of the Congress on Evolutionary Computation*, volume 2, pages 1070–1077, COEX, Seoul, Korea, 27-30 May 2001. IEEE Press.
10. Thomas Loveard and Victor Ciesielski. Employing nominal attributes in classification using genetic programming. In *Proceedings of the 4th Asia-Pacific Conference on Simulated Evolution and Learning (SEAL02)*, volume 2, pages 487–491, Orchid Country Club, Singapore, 2002.
11. Sean Luke. When short runs beat long runs. In *Proceedings of the Genetic and Evolutionary Computation Conference (GECCO-2001)*, pages 74–80, San Francisco, California, USA, 7-11 July 2001. Morgan Kaufmann.
12. Louis Steinberg and Khaled Rasheed. Optimization by searching a tree of populations. In *Proceedings of the Genetic and Evolutionary Computation Conference*, volume 2, pages 1723–1730, Orlando, Florida, USA, 13-17 July 1999. Morgan Kaufmann.

Evolving Finite State Transducers: Some Initial Explorations

Simon M. Lucas

Dept. of Computer Science
University of Essex, Colchester CO4 3SQ, UK
sml@essex.ac.uk

Abstract. Finite state transducers (FSTs) are finite state machines that map strings in a source domain into strings in a target domain. While there are many reports in the literature of evolving general finite state machines, there has been much less work on evolving FSTs. In particular, the fitness functions required for evolving FSTs are generally different to those used for FSMs. This paper considers three string-distance based fitness functions. We compute their fitness distance correlations, and present results on using two of these (Strict and Hamming) to evolve FSTs. We can control the difficulty of the problem by the presence of short strings in the training set, which make the learning problem easier. In the case of the harder problem, the Hamming measure performs best, while the Strict measure performs best on the easier problem.

1 Introduction

Finite State Machines(FSMs) have been evolved for various problems by many researchers. Finite State Transducers (FSTs), by contrast, have received very little attention from the evolutionary computing community. The distinction between a finite state machine and a finite state transducer lies in how the behaviour of the machine is interpreted, rather than the inherent nature of the machine. In general the behaviour of an FSM is judged by the net effect of a sequence of actions (outputs) on its containing environment. With an FST, however, the exact order of the sequence of outputs is important.

Work on evolving FSMs dates back to the 1960's and the work of Fogel *et al* [1] where FSMs were evolved for predicting symbol sequences. More recent work includes that of Chellapilla and Czarnecki [2] where modular FSMs were evolved for the "food trail" problem of Jefferson *et al* [3]. Hybrid systems are also possible, for example Benson [4] evolved an augmented type of FSM where each node had an associated GP-evolved program. Finite state automata (FSA) (equivalent to regular grammars) are a class of FSM that produce no output symbols, but instead have accepting and rejecting states which are used to decide whether a string belongs to a particular regular language. There has also been interest in evolving context-free grammars [5,6], or their equivalent pushdown automata [7].

C. Ryan et al. (Eds.): EuroGP 2003, LNCS 2610, pp. 130–141, 2003.

While FSTs have received little attention from the evolutionary computation community, they are frequently used elsewhere. String transduction problems arise naturally when mapping from one domain to another, and have many applications within speech and language processing, for example. FSTs have been learned from sample data for applications such as restricted domain machine translation [8] and text-to-speech pronunciation [9].

There exist some efficient algorithms for inducing a certain class of FST known as subsequential transducers, in particular the onward subsequential transducer induction algorithm (OSTIA) [10], and its improved data driven version that can work on smaller samples of data [8]. It would be interesting to make a comparison of these algorithms versus evolutionary methods; this will be reported in a future paper.

1.1 Relevance to Genetic Programming

The problem of evolving FSTs is related to Genetic Programming in two ways. Firstly, an FST is a simple form of computing machine. Therefore, by evolving the states and the transition matrices, we are evolving a form of program, albeit a rather different one to the usual Lisp S-expression. FSTs offer compact, elegant and highly efficient solutions to interesting problems, and are easily implemented both in hardware and software. The time-complexity of transforming a string using a deterministic FST (such as the ones evolved in this paper) depends only on the length of the string, and it is linear with respect to this length. Importantly, the time complexity is independent of the size of the input alphabet, the size of the output alphabet, and the number of states in the machine.

Secondly, the problems that can be tackled with FSTs are also relevant to GP, and it will be interesting to see which paradigm is better able to solve this class of problem. The answer to this is not obvious. On the one hand, where a compact FST is known to exist, it might appear that performing evolution in a space restricted to representing FSTs would be advantageous. On the other hand, GP is free to use all kinds of tricks and shortcuts denied to FSTs, so which method works best may be highly problem dependent, and sensitive to the GP function set used.

2 Motivation

The original motivation for this work came from chain-code based recognition of binary images. Chain codes represent a 2-d image as a sequence of symbols [11] where each symbol represents a move around the contour of an image. Some example 4-direction chain codes are shown in Figure 1. Each chain code begins with the (x, y) location of the start of the chain, which is followed by the sequence of movement vectors encoded as symbols $\{0, 1, 2, 3\}$. Small differences in the image can lead to significantly different chain codes, as shown here, though they share long common subsequences.

Any string classification method can be used to build a chain-coded image recognizer [12]. An efficient method introduced by Lucas [13] is the scanning

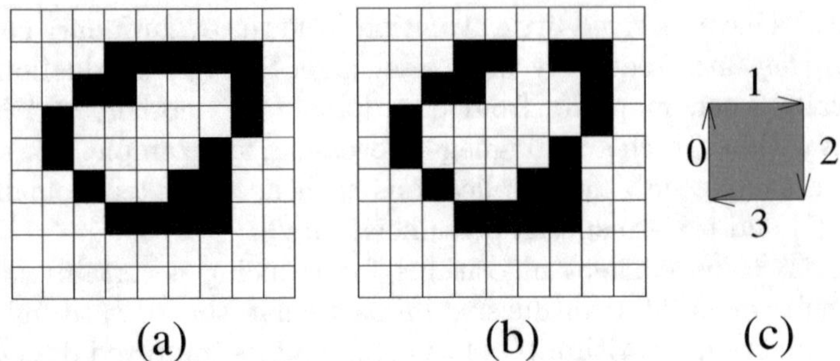

Fig. 1. Mapping an image to a chain-code. Image (a) produces two strings: (3, 1, 1111122232223333030303001010), (4, 1, 23322121101010100333); image (b) maps to the single chain code (3, 1, 01123233221211010100301122232223333030300101). The movement vectors are shown in (c).

n-tuple classifier. This operates by building statistical language models for each class of pattern, similar to conventional n-gram models, except that an ensemble of models is used with each model using different displacements between its sample points. The classification accuracy with this scheme depends on the choice of input coding. For example, 8-direction codes can significantly outperform 4-direction codes. Furthermore, in other applications of chain-coded image recognition rotation invariance can be important [14], which can be coarsely achieved by difference coding the chain-code. This then makes the code invariant to rotations of 90 degrees in the case of the 4-direction code, for example.

A raw four direction code can be transformed into an 8-direction code, or difference coded using an FST. Of course, FSTs are capable of doing much more than this, but become complex to design by hand. Furthermore, there is no clear specification of what the output strings should be in this case - other than the requirement that the transformed strings should lead to a better classification accuracy. Therefore, evolving FSTs for this task would appear to be well worth attempting.

However, the evaluation of the fitness function takes some time when applied to large image recognition datasets. We therefore began by experimenting with evolving some simple known transducers, to get a feel for how hard these would be to evolve. Note that this does not necessarily give a representative idea of the difficulty of evolving FSTs for various chain-code image recognition tasks, but is anyway interesting in its own right.

3 Finite State Transducers

A Finite State Transducer (FST) is a system for transforming strings from an input language L_I to an output language L_O. I is the alphabet of input symbols, O is the alphabet of output symbols. An FST is usually defined as a five-tuple $T = (Q, \Sigma, q_0, F, \delta)$ (e.g. Jurafsky and Martin [15]). We use a slightly modified definition that omits F, the set of final (or halting) states. We omit this because we do not wish to stop transforming the string before the end. Note however, that such a state could still evolve, as one where all transitions from that state loop back to itself while producing no output (or, alternatively stated, while producing the null symbol). Therefore, in this paper we denote an FST as a four-tuple $T = (Q, \Sigma, q_0, \delta)$ defined as follows:

- Q is the set of all states. In our case, these states will be labelled with integers from zero through to $n-1$.
- Σ is a finite set of symbols pairs. Here, each pair is denoted $i : o$ where $i \in I$ and $o \in (O \cup \epsilon)$, where ϵ is the null symbol. This specification implies that the output strings will be less than or equal to the input strings in length.
- q_0 is the start state — here $q_0 = 0$.
- $\delta(q, i : o) \rightarrow q'$ is the state transition function. Here we restrict the FST to be deterministic on the set of inputs, so that the state transition function may be rewritten as $\delta(q, i) \rightarrow q'$.

In our experiments we will pre-specify everything except for the number of states N_Q and the transition function δ, which will be evolved. For all the experiments here we have the following setup parameters:

- N_I - the number of symbols in the input alphabet: Fixed at $N_I = 4$.
- N_O - the number of symbols in the output alphabet: Fixed at $N_O = 8$.
- N_Q - the number of states (variable).

We may identify an upper bound on the size of the search space, N. We can decompose the system into a state transition function δ and an output function ω, and without loss of generality, fix the start state to be the one labelled with zero.

The state transition function is a relation S:

$$S = Q \times I \rightarrow Q \tag{1}$$

The output function is a relation:

$$Q \times I \rightarrow O' \tag{2}$$

where $O' = O \cup \{\epsilon\}$.

So:

$$N = N_Q^{(N_Q \times N_I)} + N_O^{(N_Q \times N_I)} \tag{3}$$

N is an upper bound on the size of the search space, but the true search space size is smaller than this, due to the existence of isomorphisms i.e. the number of ways of labelling a distinct FST grows combinatorially with the number of states.

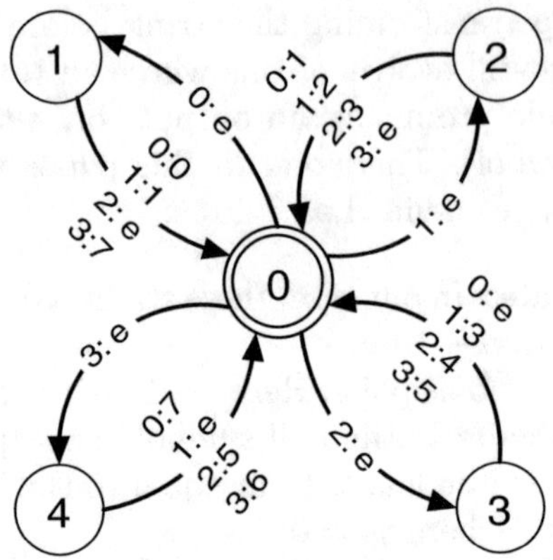

Fig. 2. A hand-coded FST for transforming 4-direction codes to 8-direction codes.

Table 1. 4-to-8 chain code FST. Each table entry is of the form $q_{i+1} : o$.

		i			
		0	1	2	3
q_t	0	1:ϵ	2:ϵ	3:ϵ	4:ϵ
	1	0:0	0:1	0:ϵ	0:7
	2	0:1	0:2	0:3	0:ϵ
	3	0:ϵ	0:3	0:4	0:5
	4	0:7	0:ϵ	0:5	0:6

3.1 Example FST

We consider the example of an FST for mapping 4-direction to 8-direction chain codes. This works by looking at the overall direction moved by each pair of 4-codes, representing it as one of 8 compass points. A hand-coded five-state FST that performs this task is shown in Figure 2. Each node (circle) in the diagrams is labelled with its state number. State zero, the start state is indicated with two concentric circles. Each arc is labelled with symbols $i : o$, where i is the input symbol to be read when moving along that arc from the source state to the destination state, and o is the output symbol produced in doing so.

Our chain-codes are defined such that they cannot directly double back on themselves, so the symbol pairs $\{02, 13, 20, 31\}$ never occur in the input. In the hand-coded model, these transitions are given default values - they lead back to the start state, and output the null symbol (ϵ). The FST can also be represented in tabular form, and this one is given in Table 1.

4 Evolutionary Algorithm

For our evolutionary algorithm we chose a random hill-climber, mainly for its simplicity. At each step a mutated copy of the current individual was created, and this replaced that individual if its fitness was greater than or equal to the current individual's fitness i.e. a (1+1) Evolutionary Strategy. The initial individual was always an FST with a single state with randomly chosen transitions (i.e. a table with a single row). We used a strict size limit of 10 states (The number of inputs and outputs are fixed to be 4 and 8 respectively, by the nature of the problem). At each stage one of three mutations could take place. If the current FST was below the maximum size, then it would grow a new randomly connected state with a probability of 0.1. Otherwise, one of two mutations could take place (with an equal chance) — either a disruption of an entire state (i.e. re-randomize all the table entries for a single row), or randomly change a single entry in the table. We have not yet analyzed which types of mutation are responsible for the greatest number of improvements. We made little effort to optimize these probabilities.

5 Fitness Functions

The choice of fitness function can play a critical part in the success of an evolutionary algorithm. In this work, we considered fitness functions based on three different string distance measures. Each distance measure is applied to the target output string s_t, and the evolved transducer output string s_e. The distance measures were strict equality (d_{strict}), normalized hamming distance (d_{Ham}), and normalized edit distance (d_{edit}). The normalization means that each string distance function has an output in the range 0.0 ... 1.0: 1.0 for two identical strings; 0.0 for two strings with nothing in common.

Each distance function was mapped to a fitness function by subtracting it from 1.0. The overall fitness on a dataset was then the average over all the fitness scores for the individual (x, y) string pairs.

$$d_{\text{strict}}(x, y) = \begin{cases} 0 & : \quad x = y \\ 1 & : \quad x \neq y \end{cases} \tag{4}$$

The normalized Hamming distance is defined in Equation 5, where Δ is zero if the symbols are equal and one otherwise. If the strings are of unequal length, then we ignore the trailing right-most symbols of the longer string. In other words, the symbol-by-symbol matching is performed with the strings left-justified. This denoted by the $\text{Min}(|x|, |y|)$ limit in the summation, where $|s|$ denotes the length of string s.

$$d_{\text{Ham}}(x, y) = \frac{\Sigma_{i=1}^{\text{Min}(|x|,|y|)} \Delta(x_i, y_i)}{\text{Max}(|x|, |y|)} \tag{5}$$

$$d_{\text{edit}}(x, y) = \frac{\text{Edits}(x, y)}{\text{MaxEdits}(x, y)} \tag{6}$$

The normalized edit distance (d_{edit}) is defined in Equation 6, as the ratio of the number edits between the two strings over the maximum number of edits possible given the string lengths. The maximum number of edits is equal to the length of the longer string, given the unweighted edit distance used here.

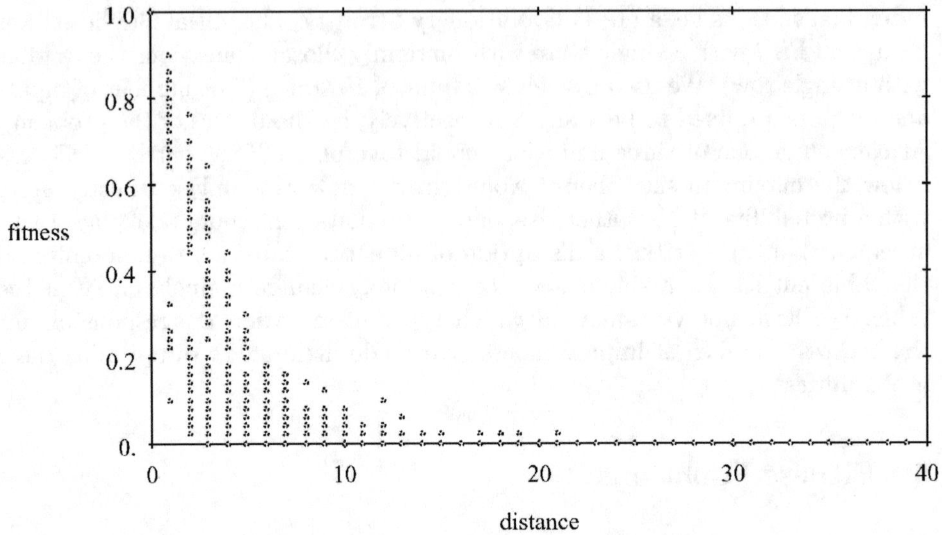

Fig. 3. Fitness distance scatter plot for hard distance. FDC=-0.57.

6 Fitness Distance Correlation Analysis

For each of the fitness functions computed the fitness distance correlations (FDCs), by taking random walks from the target 5-state automata. This type of analysis were studied by Jones [16]. FDC is a useful, but by no means fool-proof means of predicting problem difficulty for an evolutionary algorithm. A comprehensive review of problem difficulty measures is given by Naudts and Kallel [17]. The closer the FDC is to -1, the easier the problem should be for the EA. The FDC figures for *Strict*, *Hamming* and *Edit* were -0.57, -0.78 and -0.80 respectively.

In Figure 4 and Figure 5 it appears that there is a significant difference between the two measures when close to the optimum, which is masked by the similar behaviour for distances of twenty or more. To check this, we computed the FDC figures for the scatter plots of these figures when limited to a maximum distance of ten from the optimum.

When limited in this way we get FDC figures of -0.84, -0.86 and -0.91 for Hard, Hamming and Edit fitness functions respectively. Since much of the time in taken in convergence to the optimum is often spent getting the last few details correct, this may give a significant advantage to the edit distance. However, this must be balanced against the greater cost of computing it. For example, obtaining the results for these figures involved the calculation of 300,000 distances for each one, which took 0.9s for the Hamming metric and 75s for the edit metric. Hence, the simpler Hamming metric allows over eighty times more fitness evaluations in the same amount of time. Some initial experiments indicated little difference between the performance of the Edit and Hamming distance, at least when the output strings were fairly short (e.g. average length of 5), but very significant advantage for the Edit distance on long strings (length 20 or more).

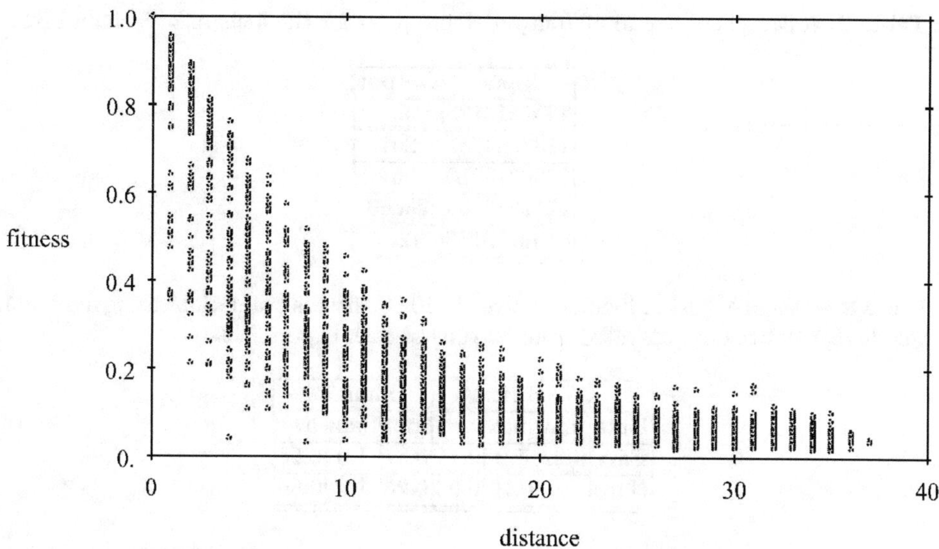

Fig. 4. Fitness distance scatter plot for hamming distance. FDC=-0.78.

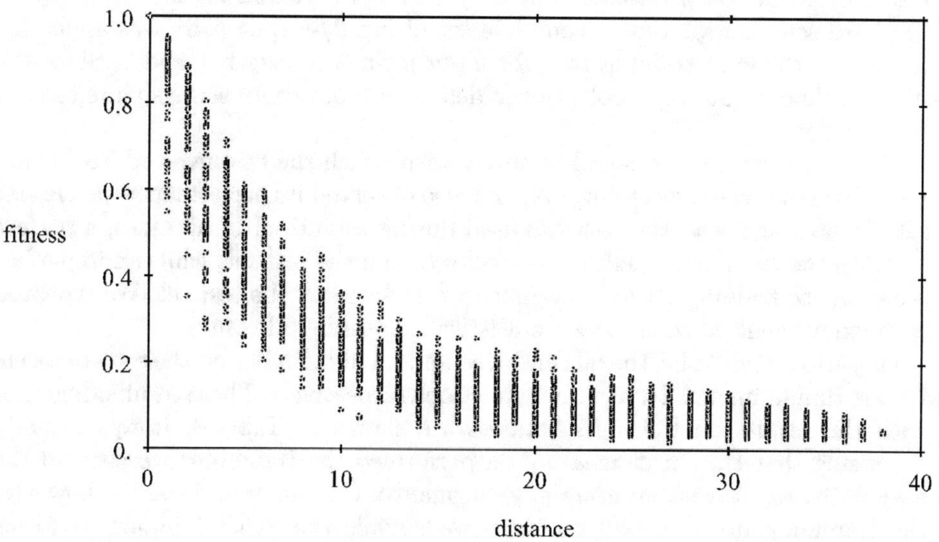

Fig. 5. Fitness distance scatter plot for normalized string edit distance. FDC=-0.80.

7 Results

To conduct initial experiments on evolving FSTs, we used the 4-chain to 8-chain FST as our target FST. For each experiment we created a training set with 50 random input strings of length 10, and a test set with random input strings of length 12. These were then passed through the target FST to produce an output string for each input string. This data we denote as the *Hard* dataset. Table 2

Table 2. A sample of five input/output string pairs for the 4-chain to 8-chain FST.

Input	Output
2331313123	55
1133203031	267
0020313210	051
1212233300	33560
0102112130	1237

Table 3. Fitness of best individual evolved in 10,000 fitness evaluations using a random hill-climber. Statistics generated from 50 runs of each experiment.

	Strict			Hamming		
Data	min	max	ave	min	max	ave
Easy	0.22	1.0	0.71	0.37	1.0	0.64
Hard	0.0	0.16	0.02	0.25	1.0	0.50

shows a sample of five such pairs. We expect it to be relatively difficult to learn an FST from input/output pairs where the strings are long. To test this, we also created an *Easy* dataset. The easy sets were created in the same way as the hard sets, except that a complete set of input/output pairs was appended to each of the easy training sets, for input strings of length 1 and 2. Since the input alphabet had 4 symbols, this added a total of twenty strings pairs to each training set.

Each experiment measured accuracy with which the best evolved FST could reproduce the training set outputs, and also observed its performance on the test set. At no stage were the test sets used during evolution. In all cases, a perfect score on the training set led to a perfect score on the test set, while an imperfect score on the training set led to a much worse score on the test set. We repeated each experiment 50 times to get statistically meaningful results.

Figures 6 and 7 plot the 50 runs of a random hill climber on the easy datasets for the Hamming and Strict fitness functions respectively. These results, together with the results on the hard datasets are shown in Table 3. It was initially surprising that the Strict measure outperformed the Hamming measure on the easy datasets, at least on average performance. On the hard datasets, however, the Hamming function still performs well, while the Strict function performs very poorly.

Table 4 shows an FST evolved using the Hamming measure on the Hard dataset. This achieved a perfect score both on the training and the test sets. On inspection it can be seen that although this FST has 10 states, 5 of them are unreachable from the start state, and when the unreachable states are pruned, we get an FST that is isomorphic to the target FST.

8 Discussion and Conclusions

This paper described some initial experiments on evolving FSTs. The results demonstrate that simple FSTs may be evolved from small samples of training

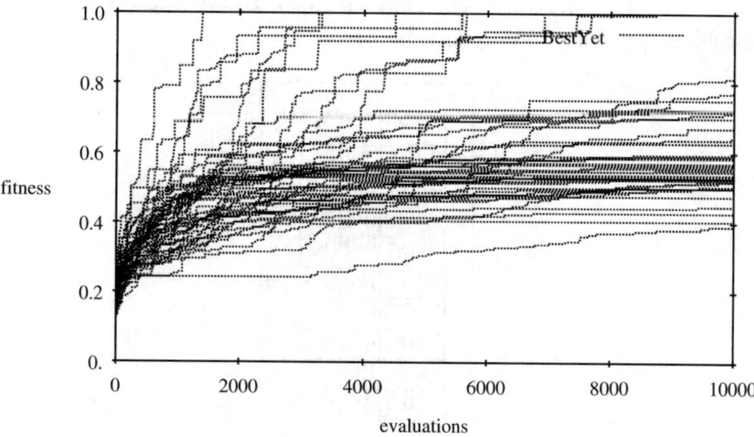

Fig. 6. 50 Runs of the random hill climber using the Hamming distance fitness function on the easy datasets.

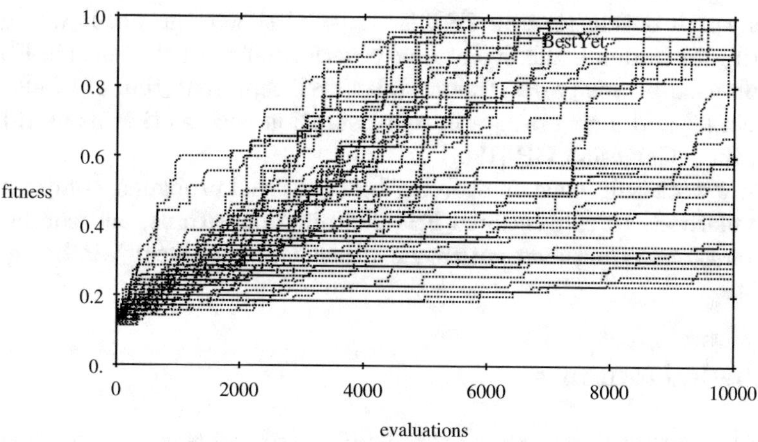

Fig. 7. As Figure 6 except for the Strict distance fitness function.

data that generalize perfectly to unseen data. Not surprisingly, the task is made much easier when the training data is augmented with a complete set of short strings - in this case the input/output pairs for input strings of length 1 and 2. This can be understood intuitively — if one is learning a foreign language, it is better to begin with single words and short phrases, rather than correspondences at longer sentence levels.

An unexpected result was that the Strict-distance fitness function outperformed the Hamming-distance fitness function on the easier augmented data. A possible reason for this could be that the Hamming function can mislead the hill-climber to false optima, whereas the Strict function creates plateaus that take longer to escape from, but when escape does come, it is less likely to be to

Table 4. An evolved 10-state FST that attained a perfect score on the 4-chain to 8-chain problem (on the training and the test data).

		i			
		0	1	2	3
q_t	0	2:ϵ	3:ϵ	6:ϵ	4:ϵ
	1	0:2	0:6	0:2	0:1
	2	0:0	0:1	0:ϵ	0:7
	3	0:1	0:2	0:3	0:ϵ
	4	0:7	0:ϵ	0:5	0:6
	5	0:2	0:3	0:7	0:ϵ
	6	0:ϵ	0:3	0:4	0:5
	7	0:ϵ	0:ϵ	0:ϵ	4:6
	8	0:1	8:5	0:ϵ	0:ϵ
	9	0:ϵ	0:6	0:1	0:1

a false optima. In the case of the hard datasets, the plateaus dominate, and the Strict version never properly escapes them.

It is worth noting that an FST is a special type of graph. It would be very interesting to evaluate the evolutionary performance of the specific FST representation used in this paper, the modular FST representation of Chellapilla and Czarnecki [2] and a general graph representation such as that as used by Miller *et al* in their Cartesian GP [18].

Future work will focus on evolving FSTs for real problems, comparing evolutionary methods to conventional FST learning algorithms, and comparing various evolutionary methods with each other - conventional GP being a prime candidate.

Acknowledgements

The author would like to thank the members of the Natural and Evolutionary Computation group at the University of Essex, UK, Thomas P. Runarsson, and the anonymous reviewers for helpful comments and discussion.

References

1. L.J. Fogel, A.J. Owens, and M.J. Walsh. Artificial intelligence through a simulation of evolution. In M. Maxfield, A. Callahan, and L.J. Fogel, editors, *Biophysics and Cybernetic Systems: Proceedings of the 2nd Cybernetic Sciences Symposium*, pages 131 – 155. Spartan Books, Washington DC, (1965).
2. Kumar Chellapilla and David Czarnecki. A preliminary investigation into evolving modular finite state machines. In *Proceedings of Congress on Evolutionary Computation*, pages 1349 – 1356. (1999).
3. D. Jefferson, R. Collins, C. Cooper, M. Dyer, M. Flowers, R. Korf, C. Taylor, and A. Wang. Evolution as a theme in artificial life: The genesys/tracker system. *Proceedings of Artificial Life II*, (1991).

4. Karl Benson. Evolving automatic target detection algorithms that logically combine decision spaces. *Proceedings of the British Machine Vision Conference*, pages 685 – 694, (2000).
5. P. Wyard. Context-free grammar induction using genetic algorithms. In R.K. Belew and L.B. Booker, editors, *Proceedings of the fourth international conference on Genetic Algorithms*, pages 514 – 518. Morgan Kaufman, San Mateo, CA, (1991).
6. S.M. Lucas. Structuring chromosomes for context-free grammar evolution. In *Proceedings of IEEE International Conference on Evolutionary Computation*, pages 130 – 135. IEEE, Orlando, (1994).
7. M. Lankhorst. A genetic algorithm for induction of nondeterministic pushdown automata. *University of Groningen, Computer Science Report CS-R 9502*, (1995).
8. J. Oncina. The data driven approach applied to the OSTIA algorithm. *Lecture Notes in Computer Science*, 1433:50–??, 1998.
9. Daniel Gildea and Daniel Jurafsky. Automatic induction of finite state transducers for simple phonological rules. In *Meeting of the Association for Computational Linguistics*, pages 9–15, 1995.
10. J. Oncina, P. Garcia, and E. Vidal. Learning subsequential transducers for pattern recognition interpretation tasks. *IEEE Transactions on Pattern Analysis and Machine Intelligence*, 13:252–264, (1991).
11. H. Freeman. Computer processing of line-drawing images. *Computing Surveys*, 6:57–97, 1974.
12. H. Bunke and U. Buhler. Applications of approximate string matching to 2d shape recognition. *Pattern Recognition*, 26:1797 – 1812, (1993).
13. S.M. Lucas and A. Amiri. Statistical syntactic methods for high performance ocr. *IEE Proceedings on Vision, Image and Signal Processing*, 143:23 – 30, (1996).
14. R.A. Mollineda, E. Vidal, and F. Casacuberta. A windowed weighted approach for approximate cyclic string matching. *International Conference on Pattern Recognition*, pages 188 –191, (2002).
15. D. Jurafsky and J.H. Martin. *Speech and Language Processing: An Introduction to Natural Language Processing, Computational Linguistics and Speech Recognition.* Prentice Hall.
16. T. Jones. *Evolutionary Algorithms, Fitness Landscapes and Search.* PhD thesis, PhD Dissertaion, The University of New Mexico, 1995.
17. B. Naudts and L. Kallel. A comparison of predictive measures of problem difficulty in evolutionary algorithms. *IEEE Transactions on Evolutionary Computation*, 4:1 – 15, (2000).
18. Julian F. Miller and Peter Thomson. Cartesian genetic programming. In Riccardo Poli, Wolfgang Banzhaf, William B. Langdon, Julian F. Miller, Peter Nordin, and Terence C. Fogarty, editors, *Genetic Programming, Proceedings of EuroGP'2000*, volume 1802 of *LNCS*, pages 121–132, Edinburgh, 15-16 April 2000. Springer-Verlag.

Reducing Population Size while Maintaining Diversity

Patrick Monsieurs and Eddy Flerackers

Expertise Center for Digital Media, Wetenschapspark 2, 3590 Diepenbeek, Belgium
{patrick.monsieurs,eddy.flerackers}@luc.ac.be

Abstract. This paper presents a technique to drastically reduce the size of a population, while still maintaining sufficient diversity for evolution. An advantage of a reduced population size is the reduced number of fitness evaluations necessary. In domains where calculation of fitness values is expensive, this results in a huge speedup of the search. Additionally, in the experiments performed, smaller populations also resulted in a faster convergence speed towards an optimal solution.

1 Introduction

Genetic programming is an optimization technique that uses a population of candidate solutions to search the solution space [7]. Because a population consists of multiple individuals, several locations in the solution space are examined in parallel. The use of a large population has several advantages. First, this allows the evolutionary algorithm to examine a large number of positions in the solution space simultaneously. Second, a large population is more resistant to the loss of diversity in the population. Diversity can be lost in a population when, due to evolutionary pressure, a large number of individuals become similar to the best individuals of the population. When this happens, the search will be restricted to the small area of the solution space containing these similar individuals. Consequently, finding new solutions becomes more difficult. When using a large population, the diversity of the population will persist longer. The disadvantage of using a large population is that more individuals have to be evaluated every generation. Often, the fitness evaluation is the most time-consuming step in genetic programming, and reducing the number of fitness evaluations can significantly speed up the search.

To reduce the size of the population while still maintaining sufficient diversity, a method can be used that detects individuals in the population that are very similar to other individuals, and remove them. As a result, the population will still cover the same areas of the solution space, but with less individuals.

This paper is structured as follows. First, existing measures to maintain diversity will be presented. Section 3 will discuss the directed acyclic graph representation of a population, originally developed by Handley [4]. This representation will be used by our similarity measure, which is discussed in section 4. Finally, the effects of this measure are tested experimentally in section 5, and conclusions are given.

2 Existing Techniques to Measure and Maintain Diversity

When a fixed-length binary string representation is used, similarity between two individuals can be measured using the Hamming distance. Hamming distance counts the

C. Ryan et al. (Eds.): EuroGP 2003, LNCS 2610, pp. 142–152, 2003.

number of bits that differ between two individuals. When such a distance measure exists, diversity in a population can be maintained by a technique called fitness sharing [3]. This technique reduced the fitness m_i of an individual i based on the distance to all other individuals. In eq. (1), p is the population size, $d(i, j)$ is the distance measure between individuals i and j, and S is a decreasing function, called the sharing function.

$$m_i = \sum_{j=1}^{p} S(d(i, j)) \tag{1}$$

When a tree representation is used, a different distance measure must be applied. Most of the existing measures compare individuals by comparing individual nodes, starting at the root node and moving down towards the leaves. For example, Mawhinney uses the Unix diff program to calculate the difference between individuals [10]. However, this is only a rough measure of the syntactic similarity between two individuals. Nienhuys-Cheng [13] define a metric between two nodes p and q with arity of n and m respectively in eq. (2). This measure was also used by De Jong in [1].

$$d(p(s_1, s_2, \ldots, s_n), q(t_1, t_2, \ldots, t_m)) = \begin{cases} 1 & \text{if } p \neq q \text{ or } n \neq m \\ \frac{1}{2n} \sum_{i=1}^{n} d(s_i, t_i) & \text{if } p = q \text{ and } n = m \end{cases} \tag{2}$$

Ekárt uses a method based on the structure of individuals to measure the difference between them [2]. The method works in three steps:

- The two individuals are placed on an identical tree structure. Empty child nodes are added where necessary.
- The distances between the types of the nodes at identical position in the identical tree structure are calculated.
- These distances are combined in a weighted sum. This sum is the distance between the two individuals.

Several other distance measures based on diversity have been developed. Keller and Banzhaf [6] and O'Reilly [14] use the "edit distance" to measure the difference between two individuals. This distance measures the number of primitive edit operations needed to transform one individual into the other. In [15], Rosca uses the fitness and "expanded structural complexity" of individuals to determine similarity between individuals. Expanded structural complexity is the size of an individual after all function calls in the individual are replaced by their function body. Because these features are computed during the evaluation of the individual without significant extra cost, there is no added time complexity for using this method. However, because structurally different individuals can still have identical fitness and/or expanded structural complexity, this method is not always accurate in detecting similar individuals. In [8], Langdon and Poli detect similar individuals by comparing their fitness values on identical test cases. A fitness penalty was added to offspring that was similar to their parents. Using this technique, the diversity of the population was increased and bloat was reduced by 50%, while performance decreased only slightly.

Keijzer [5] defines the distance between two individuals using the directed acyclic graph representation discussed in [4] and in the next section. The distance is defined as the difference between the number of different nodes in the union of the nodes of both individuals and the number of subtrees the individuals have in common, shown in eq. (3):

$$\delta_{dag}(X,Y) = |D(X) \cup D(Y)| - |D(X) \cap D(Y)| \tag{3}$$

In this equation, $D(X)$ represents the set of all different subtrees present in an individual X, and $|S|$ is the number of elements of set S. This measure can easily be calculated when using the directed acyclic graph representation in linear time relative to the number of nodes of both individuals.

In [17], Wineberg and Oppacher measure the randomness of nodes at given positions (called a locus) in an individual. Randomness of a given locus is calculated using the entropy measure in equation (4):

$$H(L) = \sum_{i \geq 1} f_i \log \frac{1}{f_i} \tag{4}$$

This measure is called the genic diversity of a locus. In this equation, L is a random variable over the range $R = \{g_1, g_2, \dots\}$, where R is the alphabet of the possible genes. $f_i = \text{prob}(L = g_i)$ is the frequency of a gene g_i occurring at the specified node, looking across the entire population. The diversity of the individual is then calculated as the average of the genic diversity across all loci of the individual. This technique could be used to remove individuals that have a low diversity.

Rosca [16] also uses entropy to measure the diversity of a population. The population is divided in a set of partitions that have similar behavior. For example, individuals that score an equal number of hits in a parity problem are placed in the same partition. The entropy of a population is calculated using equation (4), where the values f_i are the proportions of the entire population occupied by individuals in partition i.

3 Minimal Directed Acyclic Graph Representation

In genetic programming, a population is made up of many individuals that are each represented by a tree. In this population, there are typically many identical subtrees that are shared by different individuals. Normally, every instance of an identical subtree is represented by a different copy of that subtree. This can result in a large amount of duplication. If all these identical instances are represented by a single object that is shared between all individuals, the memory required to store the population can decrease considerably. This is demonstrated in Fig. 1, where the expressions (3*(2+x)) and ((2+x)-x) share their identical subtree (2+x). Also, the second expression uses the terminal x twice, and re-uses the node representing x. When the entire population is represented in this way, a directed acyclic graph (DAG) is formed. The DAG is minimal if every distinct subtree is only represented once in the DAG. This representation for a population in genetic programming was first used by Handley [4], and was later also used by Keijzer [5].

An important property of the minimal DAG representation is that identical subtrees of individuals are represented by the same object in memory. As a result, any update to a shared node of an individual will also be applied to the nodes of other individuals. In [4], Handley used this property to avoid calculation of the results of identical subtrees by caching the results of the calculation. In the next section, this property will be used to easily detect identical subtrees in a population. This will be useful to detect

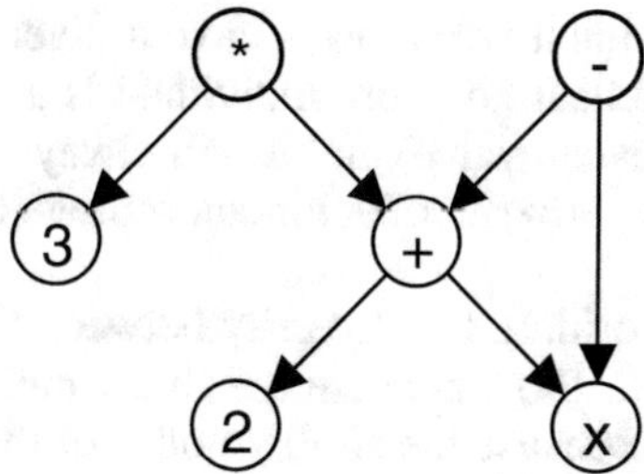

Fig. 1. Individuals share identical subtrees in a directed acyclic graph

individuals that don't contribute much to the diversity of a population, as will be explained in the next section.

4 Measuring the Added Diversity of an Individual

In our implementation, steady-state genetic programming is used. This means that a single population is used during evolution, and new individuals are added to this population. During a "generation", a number of new individuals are created and added to the population. This number is called the population increment. At the end of the generation, the population size is reduced to at most 2 times the population increment. This is done by removing the least fit individuals from the population.

To measure the diversity of individuals, the nodes of the DAG representation contain a field that indicates if that node is marked or unmarked. Nodes can be marked or unmarked by the algorithm.

After a generation has been completed, the algorithm will process the entire population to detect and remove individuals that do not add sufficient diversity to it. The algorithm is presented below:

```
* Sort the individuals of the population by fitness.
If two individuals have equal fitness, order them by
size (smaller is better).
* Unmark all nodes of the DAG representation.
* Iterate over all individuals, starting with the
fittest:
  * The added diversity of this individual =
    (number of its unmarked nodes)/(its total number of
     nodes)
  * If the individual has sufficient diversity, mark
    all nodes of the individual. Otherwise, remove it
    from the population.
```

Because the identical nodes of individuals are shared between all the population's individuals, marking one individual's nodes can also mark nodes of several other individuals in the population. It is therefore possible to efficiently compare an individual with all previously tested individuals.

The algorithm tests how much new genetic material would be added to the population by including the individual. Because all nodes are unmarked at the start of the algorithm, the fittest individual will always have a diversity of 1 (the highest value), and will always be accepted. If an entire individual is a subtree of a fitter individual, its fitness will be 0 (the lowest value) and it will always be rejected. When the entire population is processed, a garbage collector can remove all unmarked nodes from the DAG.

To demonstrate the algorithm, the diversity between the two individuals presented in Fig. 1 will be calculated. First, because the fittest individual's diversity is 1, all of its nodes will be marked. Because the similar nodes of the two individuals are shared, this means that these nodes in the other individual are marked as well (see Fig. 2). To calculate how different the second individual is from the first, the number of unmarked nodes in the second individual is counted (one). The second individual contains 5 nodes, so the diversity of the second node can be defined as the number of unmarked nodes divided by the total number of nodes (in this example 0.2).

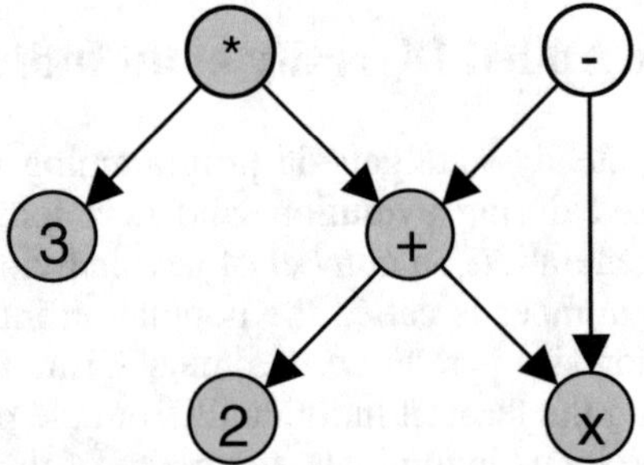

Fig. 2. Nodes are marked to determine the similarity between individuals

Note that this diversity measure is not a distance measure, since the diversity between *a* and *b* is not equal to the diversity between *b* and *a*. In the above example, if the second individual's nodes are marked first, the diversity of the first individual would be 0.4 instead of 0.2 (see Fig. 3).

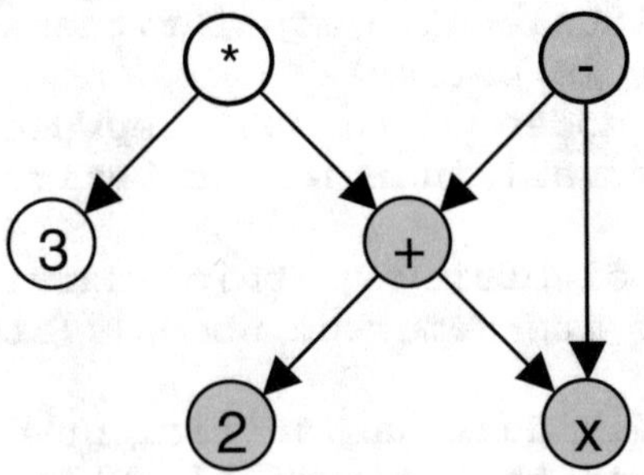

Fig. 3. Diversity measure is not symmetric

Determining when an individual will be allowed to remain in the population depends on the added diversity of the individual, and on its fitness. Very fit individual do not require much added diversity. Also, very unfit individuals that have much genetic code that does not appear anywhere else in the population can also be allowed in the population, because they introduce variety. In our current implementation, an individual is accepted in the population when eq. (5) is satisfied:

$$AddedDiversity \geq \left(\frac{i}{PopulationSize} \right)^D \tag{5}$$

In this equation, *AddedDiversity* is the diversity calculated as described above, D is a constant used to balance the effect of diversity versus fitness, and i is the rank of the individual in the population, where the fittest individual has a rank of 0. Using this criterion, the fittest individuals do not require much added diversity, while the least fit individuals are only accepted when their diversity is close to 1. In the experiments performed, the constant D was set to 1. Varying this constant between 0.5 and 2 did not seem to affect the results significantly.

5 Experimental Results

The effect of the diversity measure was tested on the problems of symbolic regression, AI planning and Robocup. The experiments also used the removal of inactive code and dynamic size limiting optimizations described in [12] to reduce the effects of bloat. Dynamic size limiting rejects newly created individuals if their size is larger than a constant C_{DSL} times the size of the best individual of the previous generation. The combination operator used in the experiments randomly selects a non-terminal root node, and uses selection, crossover or combination to create all child nodes of this root node.

5.1 Symbolic Regression

The target function used was $x^5 - 2x^3 + x$, using the function set {+, -, *, /, x}. The following parameters were used: 70% crossover, 30% combination, 1% mutation, C_{DSL} = 1.33, and a population increment of 200. A total of 100 runs were performed for a maximum of 100 generations or until a perfect solution was found. Fig. 4 lists the number of unfinished runs at a given generation with and without using the diversity measure.

When the individuals with low diversity are removed from the population, a solution is discovered faster: at generation 17, 86% of the runs have found a solution when using the diversity measure, compared to 35% otherwise. However, the overall success rate after 50 generations is similar. It should also be noted that in early generations, the diversity measure removes most of the individuals from the population and keep only between 20 and 45 individuals. This is demonstrated in Fig. 5, which shows the average reduced population size over all uncompleted runs at a given generation. Because these individuals still contain almost all the genetic material of the entire population, new combinations of genetic material will be discovered faster. This leads to the faster convergence observed in the experiment.

When a larger population increment of 1000 is used, the population converges towards a perfect solution in about 5 times less generations. This is to be expected, as 5 times more individuals are evaluated every generation. In this case, the population size is reduced to at most 130 individuals, as shown in Fig. 6. This larger size can be explained because the acceptance criterion depends on the population size. However, this reduced population size is not 5 times smaller then the experiment that used a population increment of 200.

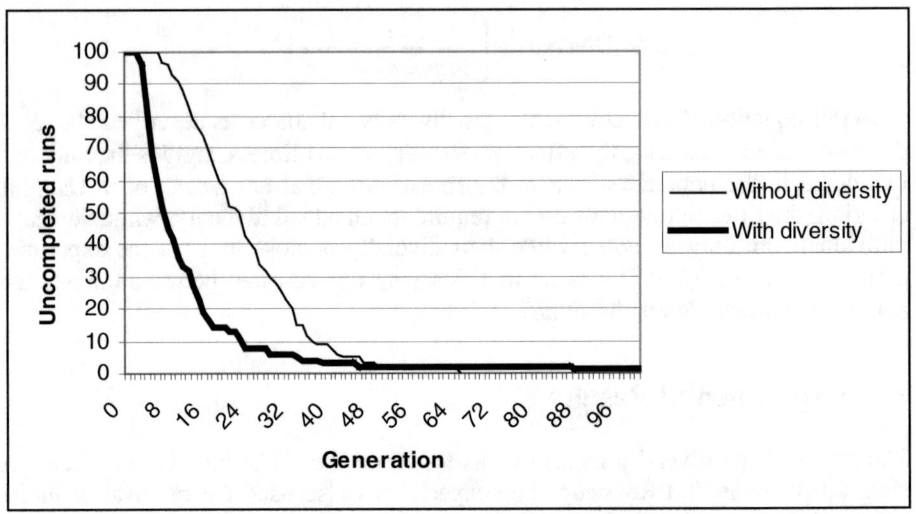

Fig. 4. Effect of diversity measure on convergence speed with the symbolic regression problem

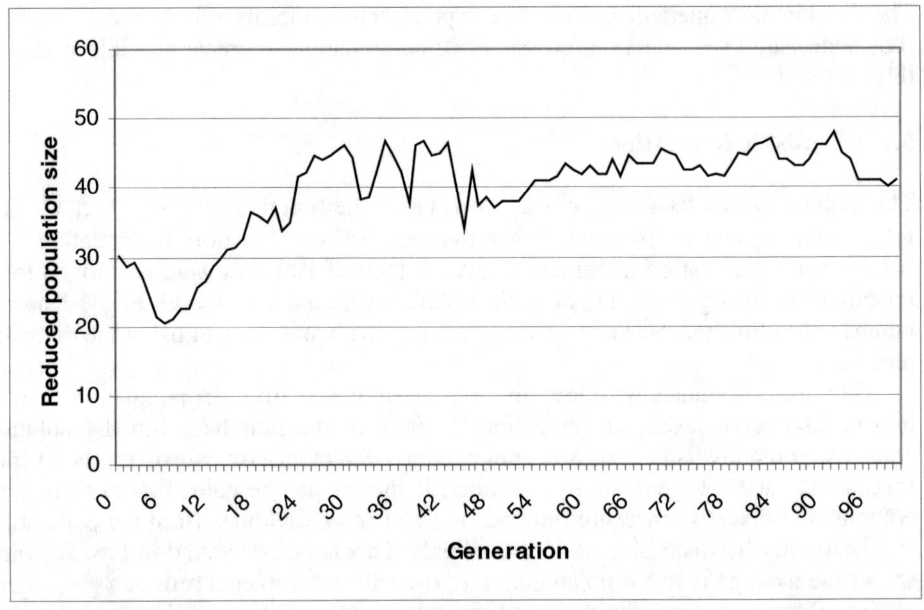

Fig. 5. Effect of diversity measure on population size with the symbolic regression problem

5.2 AI Planning

The test case used was the briefcase problem, with 5 objects, 5 briefcases, and 5 locations. In this domain, a sequence of actions must be discovered that transforms a given initial state into a specified goal state. The goal of the briefcase problem is to put the objects in a briefcase and move the briefcases to specified target locations. An

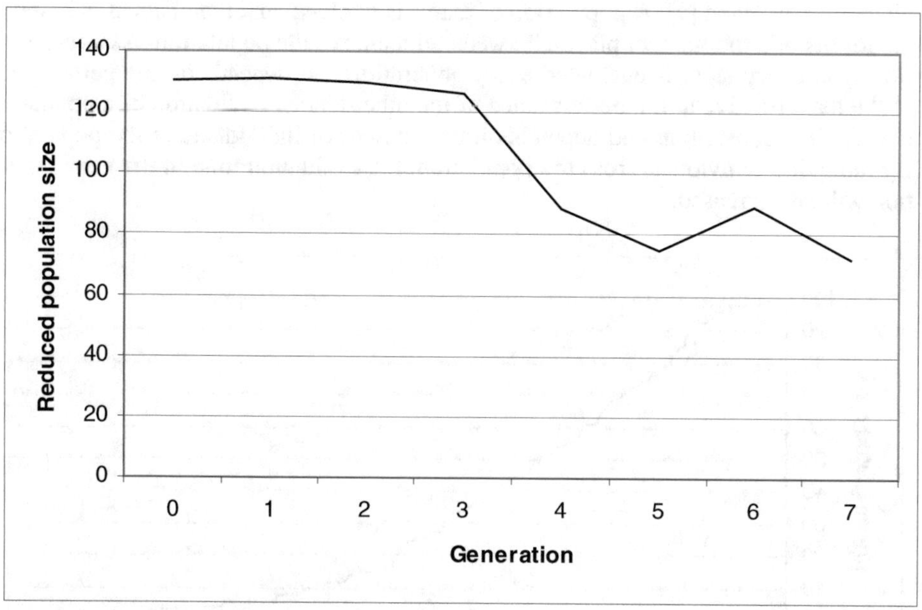

Fig. 6. Effect of diversity measure on population size when using a larger population increment

exact definition of the briefcase problem is given in [11]. The non-terminal set was {put_in, take_out, move, prog2, prog3}, and the terminal set was {0_1, ..., 0_5, L_1, ..., L_5, B_1, ..., B_5}. The settings used were 30% crossover, 30% mutation, 40% combination, C_{DSL} = 2.0, and a population increment of 200. A total of 100 runs were performed, to a maximum of 400 generations or until a perfect solution was found. Fig. 7 lists the results of using the diversity measure on this problem. When the diversity measure was used, all the runs were able to find a solution after 181 generations, while otherwise only 72% of the runs were successful after 200 generations. The convergence speed was also significantly higher in this case. It is not known whether the runs that did not use the diversity measure would eventually all find a solution.

The average reduced population size over all uncompleted runs at a given generation is shown in Fig. 8. In this case, the reduced population size varies between 25 and 35.

5.3 Robocup

The examples discussed above show that the use of the diversity measure results in a faster convergence speed and a smaller population size. Unfortunately, the evaluation time of a population is not reduced. This is because the diversity measure requires that a population is sorted by fitness, which requires a fitness evaluation of all individuals before the population size can be reduced. However, if the fitness of individuals is not static and must be re-evaluated every generation, removing individuals from the population in steady-state GP can reduce evaluation time.

Examples of problem domains where fitness is not static are domains that use co-evolution. An example is the Robocup domain, where teams of simulated soccer players are evolved [9]. A population of teams is evolved, and their fitness is based on the results of a tournament played between all teams of the population. As a result, the fitness of every team is evaluated every generation and depends on the performance of the team relative to the performance of the other teams. Evaluation of a population is very time consuming and depends on the number of individuals in the population. By removing individuals from the population, the evaluation time in the next generation will be decreased.

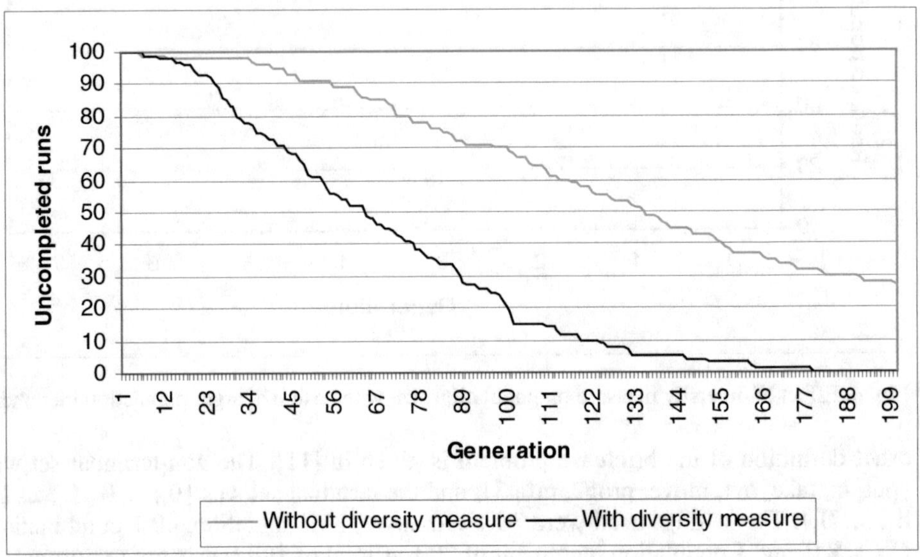

Fig. 7. Effect of diversity measure on convergence speed with the AI planning problem

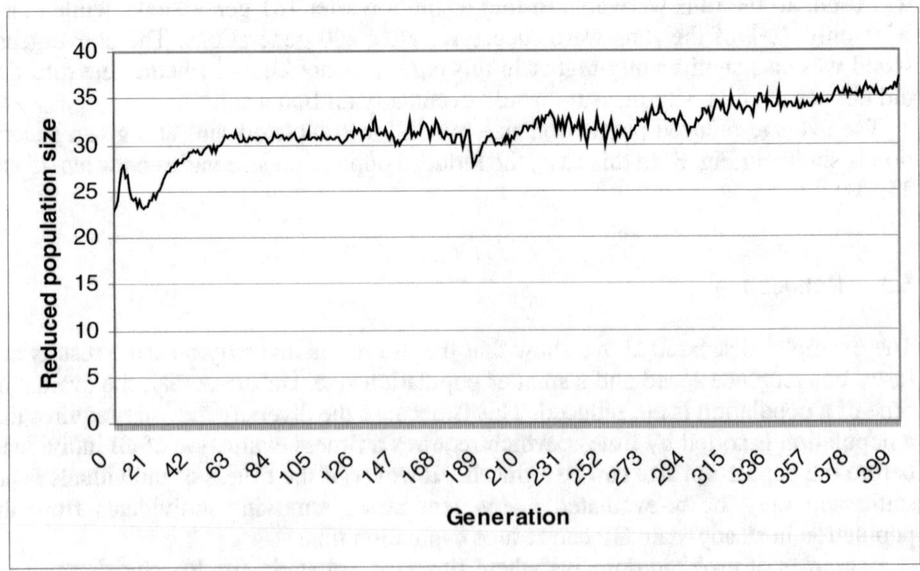

Fig. 8. Effect of diversity measure on population size with the AI planning problem

For the experiments performed in the Robocup domain, we used a primitive set similar to the one used by Luke in [9]. A detailed description of the implementation is given in [11]. A first method to reduce the evaluation time is using a small population increment. In the experiments, a size of 32 was used. Because the evaluation time was still very long (about 2 weeks for a single run of 120 generations), only 4 runs were performed. 3 of these runs used the diversity measure. The average reduced population size per generation of these 3 runs is displayed in Fig. 9. The average reduced population size over all generations is 10.58. As a result, an average of 42.58 individuals must be evaluated every generation (the reduced population size and the population increment). Without using the diversity measure, 96 individuals must be evaluated every generation. This results in a speedup of about 125%.

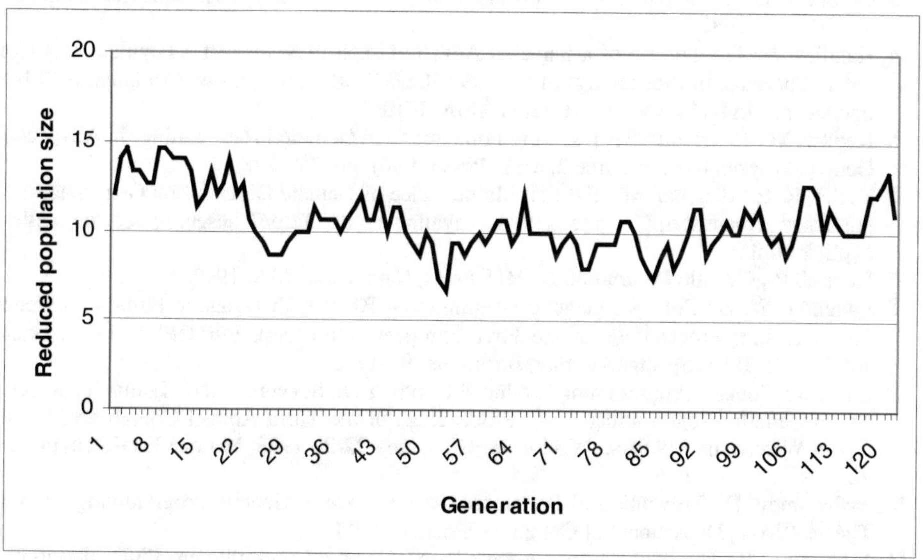

Fig. 9. Reduced population size of the Robocup domain (average over 3 runs)

6 Conclusions

This paper introduced a method to measure the diversity of individuals in a population. This measure concentrates on detecting similar subtrees in the lower parts of the tree representation of an individual. The method is based on the minimal directed acyclic graph representation of a population to efficiently determine the similarities between two individuals or between an individual and an entire population. When using the diversity measure to remove individuals that do not contribute sufficient new genetic material to the population, an increase in convergence speed was observed on the problems of symbolic regression and AI planning. This appears to indicate that the evolutionary process becomes more efficient at discovering new structures. Moreover, the use of the diversity measure to remove individuals from the population also leads to much smaller populations. These smaller populations were still able to find equally good solutions as fast or even faster as a large population. This suggests that the use of the diversity measure is a good way to reduce the population size, which is very helpful in domains where the evaluation of individuals is very time consuming, such as the Robocup domain.

References

1. De Jong, E.; Watson, R.; Pollack, J.: Reducing Bloat and Promoting Diversity using Multi-Objective Methods. In Proceedings of the Genetic and Evolutionary Computation Conference, San Fransisco, USA, July 7-11 2001, pp. 11-18.
2. Ekárt, A.; Németh, S. Z.: A Metric for Genetic Programs and Fitness Sharing. in Genetic Programming, Proceedings of EUROGP'2000, Edinburgh, 15-16 April 2000, LNCS volume 1802, pp. 259-270, ISBN 3-540-67339-3.
3. Goldberg, D. E.: Genetic Algorithms in Search, Optimization and Machine Learning. Addison-Wesley, 1989.
4. Handley, S.: On the Use of a Directed Acyclic Graph to Represent a Population of Computer Programs. in Proceedings of the 1994 IEEE World Congress on Computational Intelligence, pp. 154-159, Orlando, Florida, USA: IEEE Press.
5. Keijzer, M.: Efficiently Representing Populations in Genetic Programming. In Advances of Genetic Programming Volume 2, MIT Press (1996), pp. 259-278.
6. Keller, R. E.; Banzhaf, W.: Explicit Maintenance of Genetic Diversity on Genospaces. Unpublished manuscript, June 1994, available at http://citeseer.nj.nec.com/keller94 explicit.html .
7. Koza, J. R.: Genetic Programming. MIT Press, Cambridge, MA, 1992.
8. Langdon, W. B.; Poli, R.: Genetic Programming Bloat with Dynamic Fitness. In Genetic Programming: Proceedings of the First European Workshop, EuroGP'98, Paris, France, April 14-15 1998. Springer-Verlag, Berlin, pp. 97-112.
9. Luke, S.: Genetic Programming Produced Competitive Soccer Softbot Teams for Robocup 97. In Genetic Programming 1998: Proceedings of the Third Annual Conference, University of Wisconsin, Madison, Wisconsin, USA, July 22-25 1998, Morgan Kaufman, pp. 214-222.
10. Mahwinney, D.: Prevention of Premature Convergence in Genetic Programming. Honours Thesis, RMIT, Department of Computer Science, 2000.
11. Monsieurs, P.: Evolving Virtual Agents using Genetic Programming. Ph.D. dissertation, Department of Computer Science, Transnationale Universiteit Limburg, Belgium, 1992.
12. Monsieurs, P.; Flerackers, E.: Reducing Bloat in Genetic Programming. In Computational Intelligence, Proceedings of 7th Fuzzy Days, Dortmund, Germany, October 1-3 2001, pp. 471-478, ISBN 3-540-42732-5.
13. Nienhuys-Cheng, S.-H.: Distance Between Herbrand Interpretations: a Measure for Approximations to a Target Concept. In N. Lavraĉ, S. Dẑeroski (eds): Proceedings of the 7th International Workshop on Inductive Logic Programming, volume 1297 of LNAI, pp. 213-226. Springer-Verlag, 1997.
14. O'Reilly, U.-M.: Using a Distance Metric on Genetic Programs to Understand Genetic Operators. IEEE International Conference on Systems, Man, and Cybernetics, Computational Cybernetics and Simulation, Orlando, Florida, USA, October 12-15, 1997, pp. 4092-4097.
15. Rosca, J. P.: An Analysis of Hierarchical Genetic Programming. Technical Report 566, University of Rochester, Rochester, NY, USA, 1995. http://citeseer.nj.nec.com/ rosca95analysis.html .
16. Rosca, J. P.: Entropy-Driven Adaptive Representation. In Proceedings of the Workshop on Genetic Programming: From Theory to Real-World Applications, Tahoe City, California, USA, july 9, 1995, pp. 23-32.
17. Wineberg, M.; Oppacher, F.: The Benefits of Computing with Introns. In Genetic Programming 1996, Proceedings of the First Annual Conference, July 28-31 1996, Stanford University, MIT Press, pp. 410-415.

How Functional Dependency Adapts to Salience Hierarchy in the GAuGE System

Miguel Nicolau and Conor Ryan

Department Of Computer Science And Information Systems
University of Limerick, Ireland
{Conor.Ryan,Miguel.Nicolau}@ul.ie

Abstract. GAuGE is a position independent genetic algorithm that suffers from neither under nor over-specification, and uses a genotype to phenotype mapping process. By specifying both the position and the value of each gene, it has the potential to group important data together in the genotype string, to prevent it from being broken up and disrupted during the evolution process. To test this ability, GAuGE was applied to a set of problems with exponentially scaled salience. The results obtained demonstrate that GAuGE is indeed moving the more salient genes to the start of the genotype strings, creating robust individuals that are built in a progressive fashion from the left to the right side of the genotype.

1 Introduction

GAuGE [13], *Genetic Algorithms using Grammatical Evolution*, is a recently introduced position independent Genetic Algorithm, built using many of the principles of Grammatical Evolution [12]. GAuGE achieves position independence by encoding each gene as a pair of values, the first coding the position or *locus* of the gene, and the second its value or *allele*.

One of the interesting properties of GAuGE appears to be its ability to prioritise information finding. That is, given its position independence, it should be able to move more important genes to the start of a chromosome. This means that even if genes in the original GA representation are geographically disparate, functionally linked genes can be grouped together at the start of the chromosome.

This paper uses a set of standard benchmark problems to test this hypothesis. We take the well known BinInt [11] problem, and a variation which we call InvBinInt, and demonstrate that the system consistently places the most salient genes at the start of the chromosome, where they are less likely to be broken up.

This paper consists of seven sections. Section 2 contains an overview of the Grammatical Evolution system. Section 3 presents the GAuGE system, and includes an example of the mapping process employed, as well as a brief report of previous results obtained with the system. Section 4 presents the problems used in the experiments, while Section 5 describes the setup used with those experiments, and analyses the results obtained. Finally, Section 6 concludes the work, and Section 7 outlines some possible future lines of work.

C. Ryan et al. (Eds.): EuroGP 2003, LNCS 2610, pp. 153–163, 2003.

2 Grammatical Evolution

Grammatical Evolution (GE) is an evolutionary automatic programming type system, which evolves strings of binary values and uses a BNF (Backus-Naur Form) grammar to map those strings into programs. This mapping process involves transforming the binary individual into a string of integer values, and using those values to choose transformations from the given grammar. A given start symbol will then be mapped onto a syntactically correct program, by applying the chosen transformations.

The mapping process employed in GE is based on the idea of a genotype to phenotype mapping: an individual comprised of binary values (genotype) is evolved, which, before being evaluated for fitness, has to undergo a mapping process that will create a functional program (phenotype), which is then evaluated by the given fitness function. This process separates two distinct spaces, a search space and a solution space.

Another feature in GE is the use of degenerate genetic code [10]: by using the *mod* function to normalise each integer to a finite number of production rules from the grammar, different integer values can select the same production rule. This creates a many-to-one mapping from a genotype string to a phenotype individual, which means that the genotype can be modified without necessarily changing the phenotype, through a process known as neutral mutation [5,1].

Finally, the production rule chosen by each of the values in the integer string is dependent on the values preceding it, as those values determine which non-terminal symbols remain to be mapped in the current individual. This creates a functional dependency between each gene and those preceding it, which in turn guides each individual to be built from the leftmost genes to the rightmost ones, and helps the individual in preserving a good structure in its left-hand side during the evolution process, when it is submitted to the harsh effects of operators like crossover. This has been termed the "ripple effect" [4].

3 Genetic Algorithms Using Grammatical Evolution

GAuGE (Genetic Algorithms using Grammatical Evolution) [13] is based on many of the same ideas as GE. It uses a genotype to phenotype mapping in much the same fashion: an individual is composed of a binary sequence (genotype) that, once ready for evaluation, is mapped onto a string of integer values; these are however interpreted as a sequence of *(locus, allele)* pairs, which are then used to finally build a new binary string (the phenotype), ready to be evaluated.

Another feature of GE present in GAuGE is the functional dependency of genes within an individual, i.e. the function of each gene is dependent on those preceding it. Recent work has seen this dependency extended, and a new system, LinkGAuGE [7], was used to successfully solve a set of hard deceptive problems.

Since the position and value of each bit of the phenotype string are expressed on each gene, geographically disparate values of the phenotype can be grouped together on the genotype. This leads to the creation of tight building blocks at the start of the genome that can be gradually grown by the evolutionary process.

Work by Bean [2] with the Random Keys Genetic Algorithm (RKGA) hinted that a tight linkage between genes would result in both a smoother transition between parents and offspring when genetic operators are applied, and an error-free mapping to a sequence of ordinal numbers. More recently, Harik [3] has applied the principles of functional dependency in the Linkage Learning Genetic Algorithm (LLGA), in which a chromosome is expressed as a circular list of genes, with the functionality of a gene being dependent on a chosen interpretation point, and the genes between that point and the current gene.

3.1 Example GAuGE Mapping

To illustrate the mapping process employed in GAuGE, we will use as an example individual the following binary sequence:

`0111 0001 0001 0100 0001 1001 0010 0011`

The first step is to map it onto an integer string. For the purpose of brevity, we will use four bits to encode each integer (rather than the eight used in the actual experiments) and therefore end up with the following string:

`7 1 1 4 1 9 2 3`

This string will be evaluated as a sequence of four *(locus, allele)* pairs, and will be used to fill in a string of four bits. We start by taking the first position specified, 7, and map it onto the number of available positions in the final string (i.e., 4), by calculating the remainder of the division of 7 by 4 (7%4), giving the value 3 (i.e., the fourth position in the phenotype string). We use a similar process to map the value for that position, 1, into a binary value: $1\%2 = 1$. This is the state of the final array after the above steps are executed:

`? ? ? 1`

By taking the next pair, (1,4), we again map the position onto the number of available positions, in this case 3, which gives us $1\%3 = 1$ (second free position), and normalize the value 4 onto a binary value, which gives us $4\%2 = 0$:

`? 0 ? 1`

With the next pair, (1,9), we map the position 1 onto the number of available positions, 2, by calculating $7\%2 = 1$ (second free position, which is the third position in the string), and the value 9 onto a binary value, $9\%2 = 1$:

`? 0 1 1`

Finally, with the last pair, we map the position 2 onto the number of remaining places, in this case 1, giving the value $2\%1 = 0$, and place the value $3\%2 = 1$ in it (note that the last position will always be mapped onto value 0, since there is only one free position left in the final individual. Our phenotype, now ready for evaluation, is the string:

`1 0 1 1`

3.2 Previous Results

In previous experiments [13], GAuGE was applied to both a standard genetic algorithm problem (Onemax) and a new deceptive ordering problem. On the former, its performance was as good as that of a simple genetic algorithm, showing that its overhead processing (namely its mapping process) does not result in a loss of performance in simple problems, while on the latter, its *(locus,allele)* specification was shown to provide the flexibility of swapping elements in a solution, helping the system to avoid local optima. More recently, the functional dependency seen in the position specification was extended to the value specifications, and the resulting system was shown to have the potential to solve hard deceptive problems [7].

4 Problems

In our experiments, our aim was not to measure the performance of the system on a set of problems, but rather to understand its dynamics[1]. More specifically, the hypothesis we aimed to test is that, because of its distinct *locus* and *allele* specification, more important genes tend to be moved to the start of the genotype, whereas less important genes (or more volatile ones) tend to be pushed to the end of the genotype. In other words, the salience structure of a problem can establish a hierarchy of relevance for the genes of each individual, and GAuGE automatically models that hierarchy on its genotype string.

The following problems were therefore specifically chosen to test our hypothesis, and rather than concentrating on the success or otherwise of GAuGE on those problems, the emphasis is on the way the system handles (and possibly exploits) salience at no extra computational cost.

4.1 BinInt

The BinInt problem is an exponentially scaled problem, defined by the formula:

$$f(x) = \sum_{i=0}^{l-1} x_i 2^{l-i-1} \qquad x_i \in \{1, 0\}$$

where l is the string length, and x_i the allele at position i (with positions in a phenotype string ranging from 0 to $l-1$). This problem has the interesting characteristic that the salience of each allele is higher than the combined marginal fitness contributions of all the following alleles. This means that within an individual (phenotype), the fitness contributions decrease from left to right. Table 1 shows some examples of fitness evaluations.

This problem was first introduced by Rudnick [11], where it was used to investigate the phenomenon of *domino convergence* (the convergence speed of building blocks). Its convergence time complexity was later measured by Thierens et al. [15], to illustrate the idea of the temporal-salience structure of problems.

[1] The system does solve the problems presented, but a detailed description of the results is beyond the scope of this paper.

Table 1. Example fitness evaluations for a series of binary strings of length 8 using the BinInt problem, illustrating the salience of leftmost allele.

Binary string	Fitness value
01011111	95
01111101	125
01111111	127
10000000	128
11111111	255

4.2 InvBinInt

As a second problem we introduce the InvBinInt problem, a variation of the BinInt problem in which an individual is evaluated as an inverted binary number, i.e. encoded from right to left. It is defined by the formula:

$$f(x) = \sum_{i=0}^{l-1} x_i 2^i \qquad x_i \in \{1, 0\}$$

4.3 Onemax

This is a well known genetic algorithm problem, defined by the formula:

$$f(x) = \sum_{i=0}^{l-1} x_i \qquad x_i \in \{1, 0\}$$

In this problem, all *alleles* are equally salient, and the convergence time is uniform for all genes [15]. This means that the mutation of an *allele* will always have the same fitness impact, regardless of its *locus.*

This problem was deliberately chosen because all *alleles* are equally salient; with a uniform distribution of salience, GAuGE should not establish a hierarchy on its *locus* specifications.

5 Experiments

5.1 Experimental Setup

For all three problems, we used the same standard setup that has been used with GAuGE on previous occasions [13,7]. This is a steady-state replacement strategy with roulette-wheel selection and probabilities of one-point crossover (called *ripple crossover* [4], because of the mentioned ripple effect) and (point) mutation of 0.9 and 0.01 respectively. Each of the position and value fields were encoded using 8 bits. Several population sizes were used, of 50, 100, 200, 400, 800 and 1600 individuals, and all experiments were ran 100 times, with different random seeds. Finally, phenotype string lengths of 8, 16, 24, 32, 40, 48, 56 and 64 were used with each problem.

5.2 Results

The results for all experiments are plotted in the graphs shown in Figures 1, 2 and 3. These graphs were plotted by taking the best individual of each run, and averaging their *locus* specifications; the x-axis shows each gene in the genotype string, whereas the y-axis shows the *locus* specified in each gene, averaged over the 100 runs. For each graph, a least-squares regression equation for the data points was used to draw a line, with its label being the slope of that line.

BinInt. The results for this experiment show that GAuGE identifies the leftmost values in the phenotype to be the most salient ones, and therefore the best individuals tend on average to encode the first positions of the phenotype within the first genes of the genotype.

InvBinInt. In this problem, the opposite effect was observed, i.e. because the rightmost values of the phenotype string are the more salient ones, these tend to be encoded by the leftmost genes in the genotype string. GAuGE seems therefore to effectively build its genotype strings from the left to the right-hand side.

Onemax. In this final set of experiments, all *loci* in the phenotype string have the same salience. The results obtained show that GAuGE does not elect any particular *locus* to be encoded in the first genes of the genotype string, if there is no difference of salience for each of the values of the phenotype.

5.3 Analysis

From the results obtained, it can be seen that GAuGE effectively encodes the most salient values of the phenotype string in the left side of its genotype strings, and then builds those strings from left to right. No mechanisms were employed to prefer these individuals, other than a standard roulette wheel selection, and this phenomena spontaneously emerged from the system.

This fits nicely with the *ripple crossover* as used in GAuGE, and with the functional dependency used in the specification of *loci* in each gene. By preferring individuals that encode the more salient values on their leftmost genes, genotype strings are effectively built from left to right. As the best individuals in the population tend to encode the more salient genes on their left side, and because they will be combined with each other, the ripple effect will exchange good building blocks, as their left-hand side context will be similar (or identical).

Although the more salient *loci* tend to be stored in the left side of the genotype, GAuGE does not require this ordering at the genotype level to solve the problem, as implied by the results: in the BinInt experiments, for example, the first gene does not always code for position 0 of the phenotype; rather there is a tendency to move the more salient genes to the start of the genotype string. This suggests in turn that there is enough diversity at the genotypic level, and that GAuGE does not have to order its genes to solve problems of varying salience.

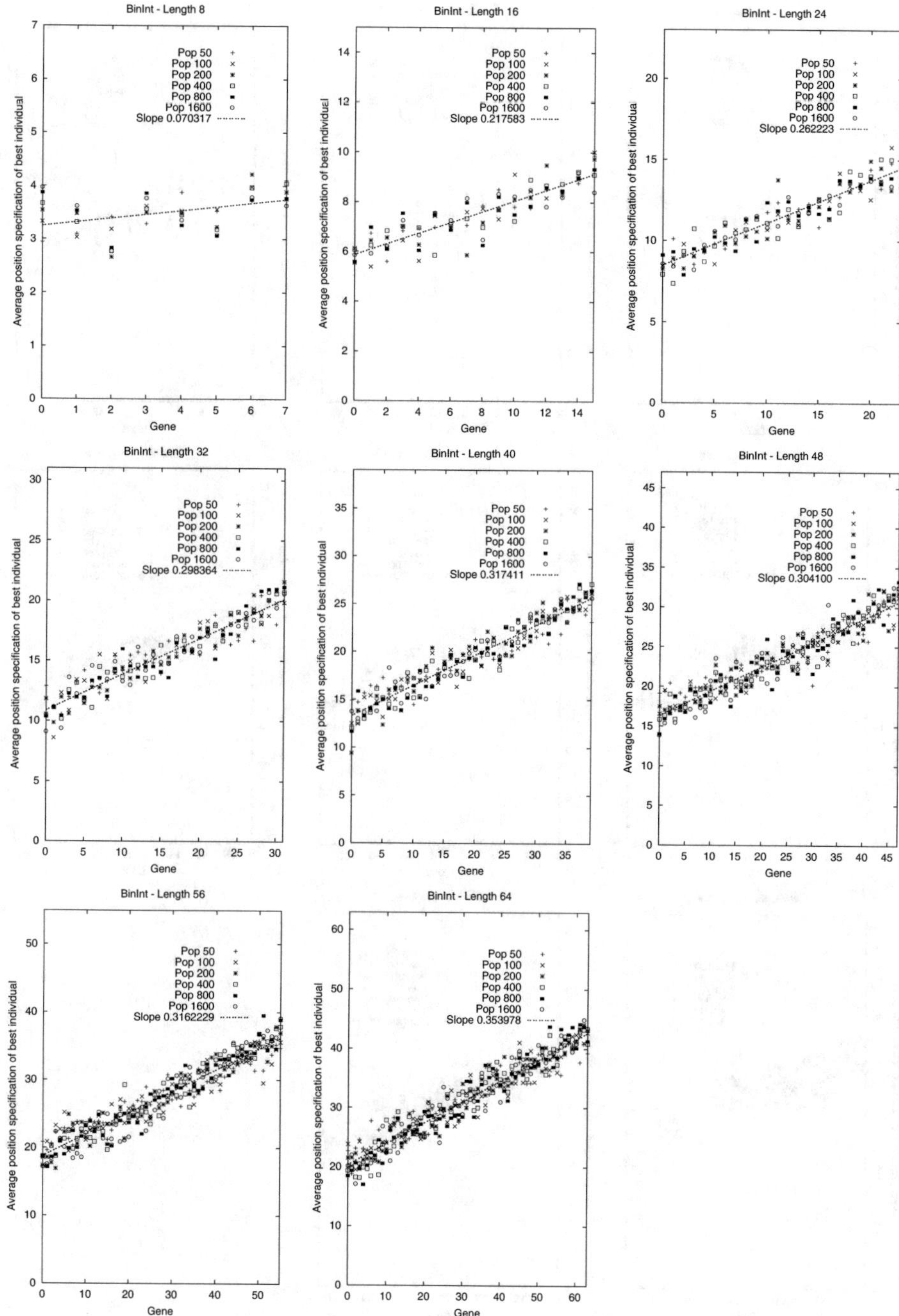

Fig. 1. Results for the BinInt problem. The graphs plot the average *locus* specification of each gene in the genotype string, averaged over 100 runs, for different problem lengths.

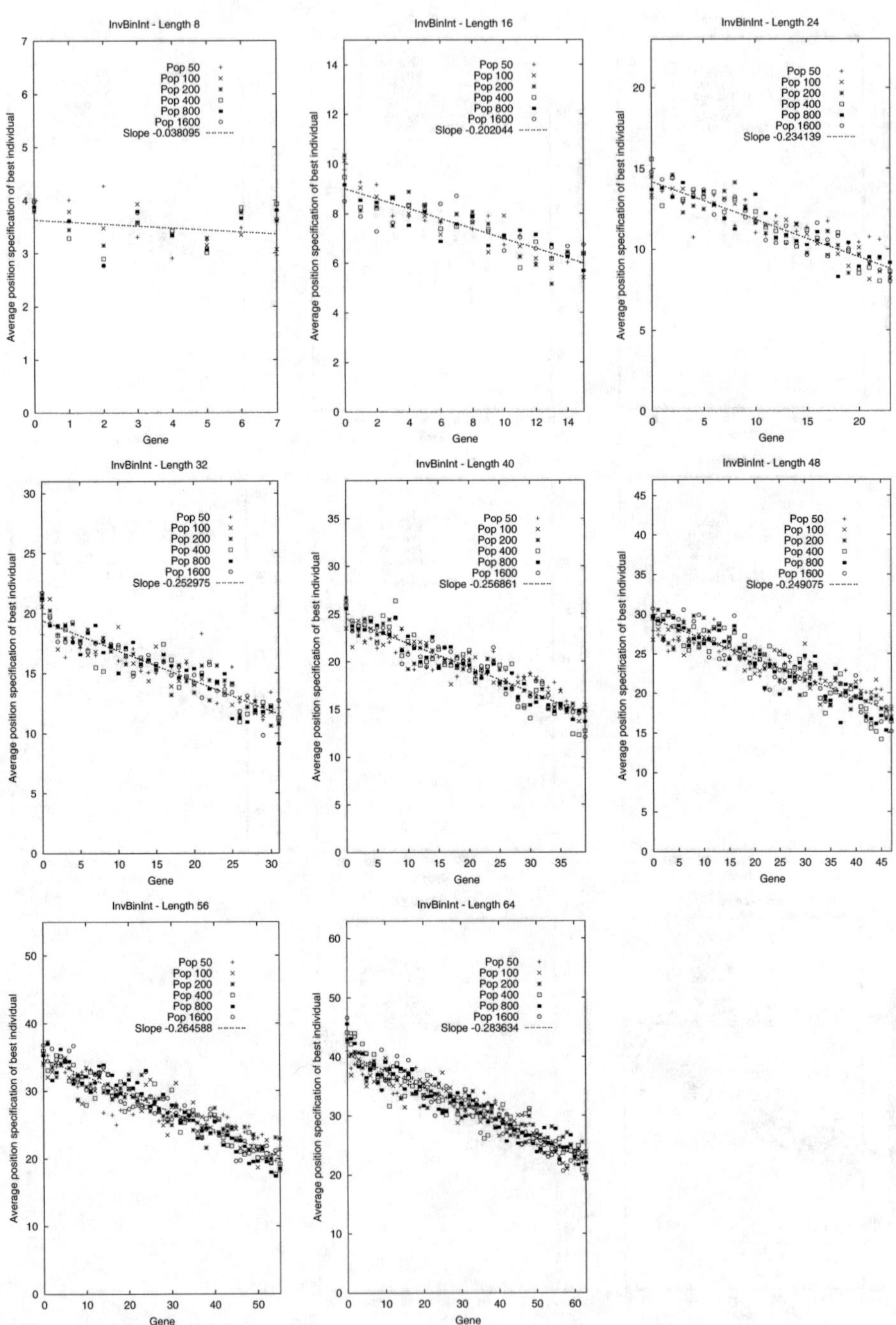

Fig. 2. Results for the InvBinInt problem. The graphs plot the average *locus* specification of each gene in the genotype string, averaged over 100 runs, for different problem lengths.

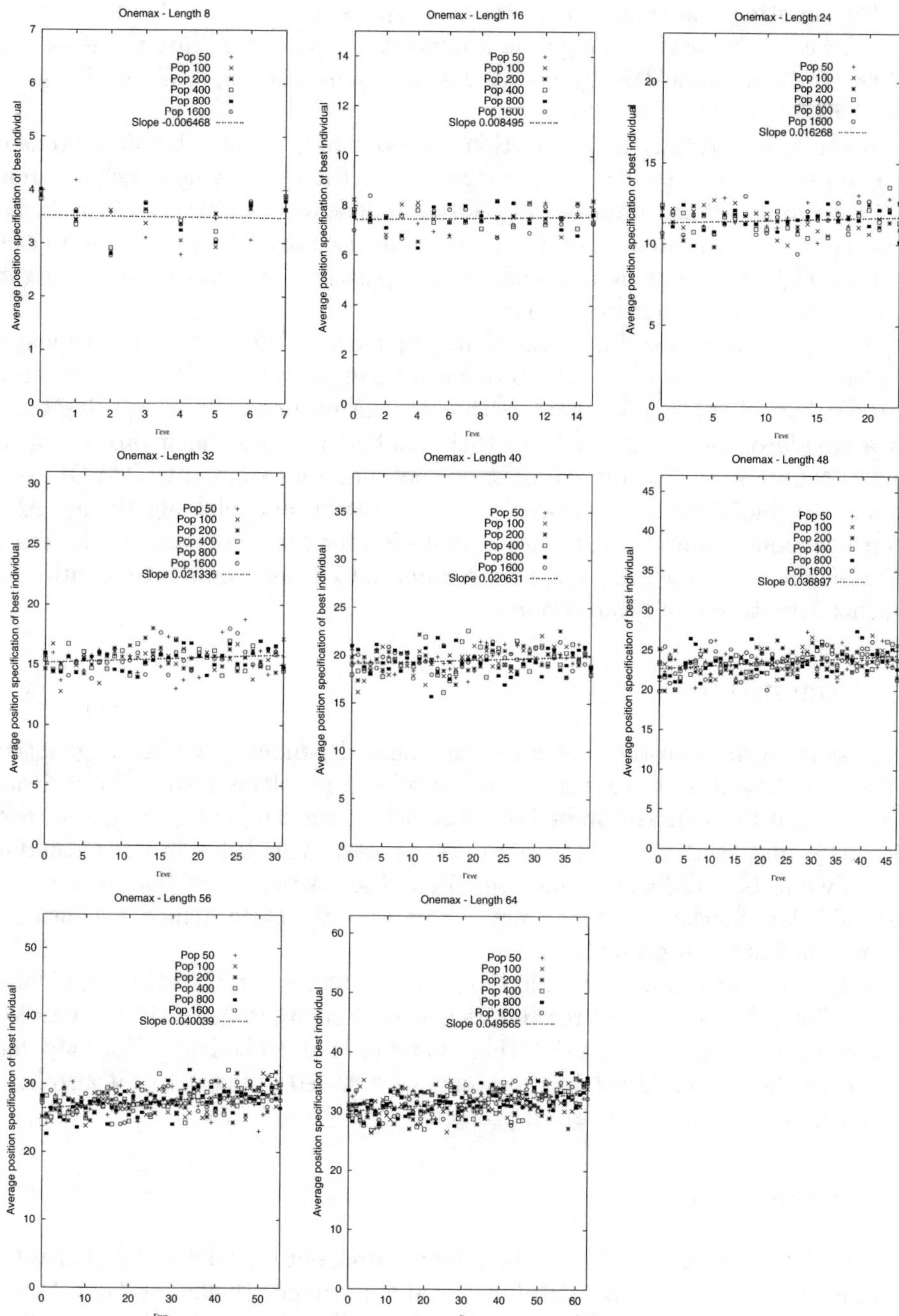

Fig. 3. Results for the Onemax problem. The graphs plot the average *locus* specification of each gene in the genotype string, averaged over 100 runs, for different problem lengths.

By adapting the structure of its genotype strings to match the problem, GAuGE can, effectively, change the fitness landscape to facilitate the search. In other words, it automatically co-evolves its representation, while evolving the solutions for the problem.

It is also interesting to observe that the slope of the regression lines tends to increase with longer strings. This suggests that the use of longer strings (more difficult problems) accentuates the position independent nature of GAuGE, but is also related to the amount of degenerate code used in each problem (as on each problem eight bits were used to encode each position, the amount of degenerate code is smaller on larger problems).

Finally, another use for GAuGE in problems of this nature is to identify the salience structure of specific problems. Stringer and Wu [14] have recently presented an effective and elegant method for this purpose. However, being based on a standard Genetic Algorithm, their method requires much processing, as counts of unique alleles and unique sub-genotypes are required; in GAuGE, only best-of-run individuals are processed, by averaging and plotting them[2]. Also, their technique requires an absence of mutation for clarity of results, whereas in GAuGE the system is ran *as is*, i.e. no changes to it are required to identify the salience structure of a given problem.

6 Conclusions

This work is an investigation into functional dependency within a genotype string, and how it improves the process of solving problems with scaled salience; it shows that individuals can be built from left to right regardless of the salience hierarchy, and sheds some light onto this process. This helps in understanding not only how GAuGE works, but also GE, and seems to suggest that, contrary to general belief, functional dependency can improve the performance of algorithms where this feature is present.

It has been shown here that, in the problems presented, GAuGE can identify their salience hierarchy, and reorder its genotype string to match it, without any specific mechanism to do so other than its functional dependency. Not only does this helps the system in solving problems with scaled salience, but it also helps in detecting salience in any given problem.

7 Future Work

This work has opened the door to broader research onto the dynamics of GAuGE systems, or even of systems with functional dependency (including GE). Future work involves a more in-depth analysis of the results obtained, such as the different features affecting the slope of the regression lines, and tackling other kinds of problems with scaled salience, such as symbolic regression problems (as used by Stringer and Wu [14]), or problems where building blocks with different salience are used, rather than single genes [6].

[2] Although this is clearly not a precise measure, but rather an estimate.

References

1. Banzhaf, W.: Genotype-Phenotype-Mapping and Neutral Variation - A case study in Genetic Programming. In: Davidor et al., (eds.): Proceedings of the third conference on Parallel Problem Solving from Nature. Lecture Notes in Computer Science, Vol. 866. Springer-Verlag. (1994) 322-332
2. Bean, J.: Genetic Algorithms and Random Keys for Sequencing and Optimization. ORSA Journal on Computing, Vol. **6**, No. 2. (1994) 154-160
3. Harik, G.: Learning Gene Linkage to Efficiently Solve Problems of Bounded Difficulty Using Genetic Algorithms. Doctoral Dissertation, University of Illinois (1997)
4. Keijzer M., Ryan C., O'Neill M., Cattolico M., and Babovic V.: Ripple Crossover in Genetic Programming. In: Miller et al., (eds.): Proceedings of the Fourth European Conference on Genetic Programming. Springer. (pp. 74-86) Lecture Notes in Computer Science, Vol. 2038. Springer-Verlag. (2001) 74-86
5. Kimura, M.: The Neutral Theory of Molecular Evolution. Cambridge University Press. (1983)
6. Lobo, F., Goldberg, D. E., and Pelikan, M.: Time complexity of genetic algorithms on exponentially scaled problems. In: Whitley et al., (eds.): Proceedings of the Genetic and Evolutionary Computation Conference GECCO-2000. Morgan Kaufmann Publishers, San Francisco (2000) 151-158
7. Nicolau, M., and Ryan, C.: LINKGAUGE: Tackling hard deceptive problems with a new linkage learning genetic algorithm. In: Langdon et al., (eds.): Proceedings of the Genetic and Evolutionary Computation Conference GECCO-2002. Morgan Kaufmann Publishers, San Francisco (2002) 488-494
8. O'Neill, M.: Automatic Programming in an Arbitrary Language: Evolving Programs with Grammatical Evolution. Doctoral Dissertation, University of Limerick (2001)
9. O'Neill, M., and Ryan, C.: Grammatical Evolution. IEEE Transactions on Evolutionary Computation, Vol. **5**, No. 4. (2001) 349-358
10. O'Neill, M., and Ryan, C.: Genetic Code Degeneracy: Implications for Grammatical Evolution and Beyond. In: Floreano et al., (eds.): Proceedings of the Fifth European Conference on Artificial Life, ECAL'99. Lecture Notes in Computer Science, Vol. 1674. Springer-Verlag. (1999)
11. Rudnick M. Genetic Algorithms and Fitness Variance with an Application to the Automated Design of Articial Neural Networks. Unpublished Doctoral Dissertation, Oregon Graduate Institute of Science and Technology (1992)
12. Ryan, C., Collins, J.J., and O'Neill, M.: Grammatical Evolution: Evolving Programs for an Arbitrary Language. In: Banzhaf et al., (eds.): Proceedings of the First European Workshop on Genetic Programming, EuroGP'98. Lecture Notes in Computer Science, Vol. 1391. Springer-Verlag. (1998) 83-95
13. Ryan, C., Nicolau, M., and O'Neill, M.: Genetic Algorithms using Grammatical Evolution. In: Foster et al, (eds.): Proceedings of EuroGP-2002. Lecture Notes in Computer Science, Vol. 2278. Springer-Verlag. (2002) 278-287
14. Stringer, H., and Wu, A. S.: A Simple Method for Detecting Domino Convergence and Identifying Salient Genes Within a Genetic Algorithm. In: Langdon et al., (eds.): Proceedings of the Genetic and Evolutionary Computation Conference GECCO-2002. Morgan Kaufmann Publishers, San Francisco (2002) 594-601
15. Thierens, D., Goldberg, D. E., and Pereira, A.G.: Domino convergence, drift, and the temporal-salience structure of problems. In: Proceedings of the 1998 IEEE World Congress on Computational Intelligence. (1998) 535-540

More on Computational Effort Statistics for Genetic Programming

Jens Niehaus and Wolfgang Banzhaf

System Analysis
Computer Science Department
University of Dortmund
D-44221 Dortmund, Germany
{jens.niehaus,wolfgang.banzhaf}@cs.uni-dortmund.de

Abstract. In this contribution we take a look at the *computational effort* statistics as described by KOZA. We transfer the notion from generational genetic programming to tournament-selection (steady-state) GP and show why, in both cases, the measured value of the *effort* often differs from its theoretical counterpart. It is discussed how systematic estimation errors are introduced by a low number of experiments. Two reasons examined are the number of unsuccessful experiments and the variation in the number of fitness evaluations necessary to find a solution among the successful experiments.

1 Introduction

Although more and more work is done examining the theory of *genetic programming* (GP) most of the publications use an empirical approach to rate new findings and modifications of traditional GP. For comparison purposes different kinds of statistics are needed. One of those used traditionally is the *computational effort* statistics as presented in [4]. Lately, however, there were several publications which took a closer look at this measure [3,2,5] and came up with several problems regarding the accuracy of the empirically measured values. In this contribution we show how *computational effort* statistics can be used in conjunction with steady-state algorithms instead of generational GP (section 3). With such an approach it is possible to reduce the difference between a theoretical *effort* value and the measured one. We show further that other inaccuracies are still remaining. They relate to the number of unsuccessful experiments (section 5) and large differences in the number of fitness evaluations needed over several experiments (section 6).

2 Measurement and Calculation of the Computational Effort

In [4] KOZA describes a method to compare the results of different evolutionary methods, e.g. different modifications of GP. The so called *computational effort*

C. Ryan et al. (Eds.): EuroGP 2003, LNCS 2610, pp. 164–172, 2003.

is calculated as the number of fitness evaluations needed to find a solution of a problem with a probability of success z of at least $z = 99\%$.

The number of fitness evaluations GP needs to solve a problem can differ a lot. Some experiments might find a solution very fast while others need many more fitness evaluations – still others won't find a solution at all in the given amount of time / evaluations. Calculating the *computational effort* for a problem is based on empirical data. We have to use relative frequencies instead of probabilities for finding the solution after a certain number of fitness evaluations. For calculating the *computational effort* $I(M, z)$ KOZA defines the following equation:

$$I(M,z) = \min_i Mi \left\lceil \frac{\ln(1-z)}{\ln(1-P(M,i))} \right\rceil \tag{1}$$

In this formula M stands for the number of individuals in the population and i is the number of generations. Thus Mi represents the number of fitness evaluations calculated in one experiment. When i generations have passed without a solution found the run has to be restarted with a different initial population. The value $P(M, i)$ represents the estimated probability for finding a solution within $M \times i$ fitness evaluations and is calculated using the results of a certain number of experiments for the examined problem. The value z represents the confidence level of finding a solution and will be set to 0.99 throughout this work.

In [2] CHRISTENSEN and OPPACHER show that values calculated using equation (1) differ up to 25% from the theoretical *computational effort*. Among other things they show the influence of the ceiling and minimum operators, which both cause deviation of the results.

3 Computational Effort for Steady-State Algorithms

After a number of *runs* experiments with KOZA's generational GP-system the probabilities $P(M, i)$ are calculated as relative frequencies $k/runs$ with k being the number of runs in which a solution was found within the first i generations. The values for $P(M, i)$ are always calculated after $M \times i$ fitness evaluations. Thus it has no influence whether the solution is always found near the beginning of a certain generation or near the end[1]. This is comparable to calculating the mean length of several lines in centimeters while each line is given in meters. The bigger a population is the more inaccurate the values of $P(M, i)$ become. Using a steady-state approach (with tournament selection) [1] the relative frequencies refer more precisely to a certain number of fitness evaluations. For the rest of this paper we use the steady-state approach with the additional option to stop an experiment after any fitness evaluation. In this way we can eliminate the ceiling operator of equation (1) and concentrate on other problems regarding the use of the *computational effort* statistics.

To calculate the number of required fitness evaluations we use the following equation:

$$1 - (1 - P(eval))^{\frac{effort}{eval}} \geq 0.99 \tag{2}$$

[1] Assuming the evaluations are executed sequentially.

The value *effort* represents the number of evaluations we are looking for. After *eval* evaluations a run is stopped and a new independent one with a new population is started with the remaining number of fitness calculations. $P(eval)$ is the probability that a solution is found after at most *eval* evaluations. As this probability is unknown we have to replace it with the estimates $\hat{P}(eval)$ that are based on empirical data collected from a number of experiments carried out previously. More on the difference between P and $\hat{P}$ can be found in [2].

Transformation of equation 2 leads to:

$$effort = \min_{eval} eval \frac{\ln 0.01}{\ln\left(1 - \hat{P}\left(eval\right)\right)} \tag{3}$$

The differences to equation (1) are (i) the transition from generational to evaluation-based calculation and (ii) the loss of the ceiling operator.

4 Experimental Framework

In [2] some inaccuracies of the *computational effort* statistics were pointed out. This section offers two more aspects that can lead to differences between the calculated *computational effort* and the theoretical value. First, the influence of the number of runs that do not find a solution is examined and second, we look at the influence of the distribution of the number of fitness evaluations needed to find a solution.

For a better illustration we use a group of hypothetical GP problems that will not find a solution with a probability of $P_{\square\square\square}$[2]. The number of fitness evaluations needed to find a solution in the remaining runs follows a $(100{,}000, sd)$-normal distribution. As we are only interested in positive integer values for the number of evaluations we use the floor operator and discard all negative values. The assumption of a normal distribution does not hold for most of the problems GP is used with, but even with this well known distribution problems appear that have a large influence on the calculated *computational effort*.

To show the influence of varying values for $P_{\square\square\square}$ and sd we chose

$$P_{\square\square\square} \in \{0.2, 0.3, 0.4, 0.5, 0.6, 0.7, 0.8\}$$

and

$$sd \in \{1{,}000, 2{,}000, 5{,}000, 10{,}000, 11{,}000, 20{,}000, 30{,}000\}.$$

For each combination we calulated the theoretical *computational effort* using equation (3) and the normal distibution's density function:

$$P(eval) = (1 - P_{\square\square\square}) \frac{1}{sd\sqrt{2\pi}} \int_0^{\square\square\square\square} \exp \frac{-(x - 100{,}000)^2}{2sd^2} dx \tag{4}$$

The results are shown in Figure 1.

[2] With *solution* we do not necessarily mean *perfect solution*. We just count the number of runs that produce a solution that we can accept as *good enough* (see [5]).

The lowest *computational effort* has the combination ($P_{fail} = 0.2, sd = 1,000$) with 295,701 evaluations, the biggest one belongs to ($P_{fail} = 0.8, sd = 30,000$) with 3,214,423 evaluations – ten times as many. The influence of P_{fail} is much higher than the one of the standard derivation. Looking at equation (3) this is quite obvious. P_{fail} directly influences the value of $(1 - \hat{P}(eval))$. For values near 1 this has a large influence on the whole fraction, while a change in *sd* in most cases only influences the linear term of *eval*. As an example we take a look at all *effort* values with $P_{fail} = 0.2$. With changing values of *sd* (between 1,000 and 30,000), the number of evaluations *eval* at which the minimum occurs changes from 103,041 to 153,192. At the same time, $\hat{P}(eval)$ remains between 0.769 and 0.799 resulting in rather similar *effort* values.

5 Influence of P_{fail} on the Computational Effort

With Figure 1 it already becomes apparent that different values of P_{fail} can have a large influence on the *computational effort*. This will result in problems when the number of independent experiments is very small, for example 50.

A small number of experiments can lead to estimated $\hat{P}_{fail}$ values differing from the original value P_{fail}. In Figure 1 this is comparable with a shift of the *computational effort* along the P_{fail}-axis.

For an empirical quantitative analysis of this behavior we used all hypothetical problems with $sd = 1,000$ and for each value of P_{fail} we created 500 experiments at random using the probability P_{fail} to decide whether an experiment finds a solution or not and for all successful experiments we randomly chose a number of evaluations needed to find the solution based on a $(100,000, sd)$-normal distribution. We used the floor operator to transform the values to integers and repeated an experiment if the picked number was negative[3].

For each value of P_{fail} we calculated the empirical *computational effort* $\widehat{effort}$ corresponding to these 500 experiments. On top of this, the $\widehat{effort}$-calculation was repeated 1,000 times with 500 different experiments. Executing 500 experiments at random means that the proportion of unsuccessful experiments $\hat{P}_{fail}$ differs from the exact value P_{fail}.

The results of these experiments are presented in Table 1. The second column contains the theoretical *computational effort*. The third column holds the mean value of the 1,000 new $\widehat{effort}$ values each calculated with 500 experiments. The percentage relative to the original *effort* value is also shown. The fourth column contains the percentage of the smallest $\widehat{effort}$ value relative to the original *effort*, the fifth column shows the highest.

As expected the mean of all new $\widehat{effort}$ values is similar to the theoretical *computational effort*. On the other hand, the last two columns indicate that some

[3] Calculating the *computational effort* with integers based on a normal distribution and the *floor*-function gives slightly smaller values than expected theoretically. In our examples these differences are always smaller than 0.001 percent and thus will be ignored throughout this document.

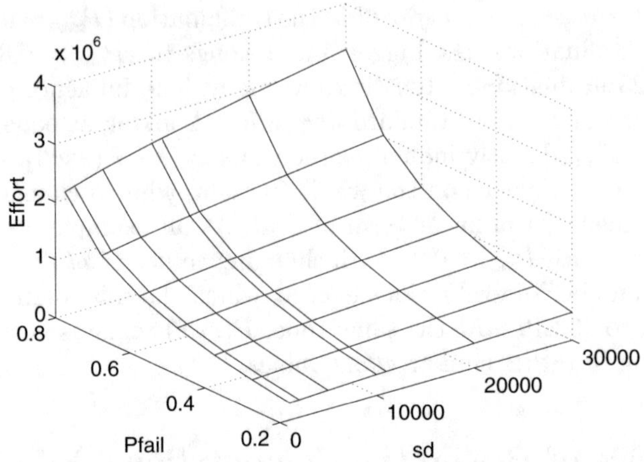

Fig. 1. The *computational effort* for the 49 hypothetical optimization problems

Table 1. Executing 500 runs with a calculated empirical *computational effort* of $\widehat{effort}$ and repeating this experiment a thousand times leads to a mean *effort* near the theoretical value with a good chance of big deviation in single cases

P_{fail}	*effort*	$\sum \widehat{effort}/1,000$	min	max
0.2	295,701	294,566 (99.6 %)	85.1 %	119.6 %
0.3	394,995	393,505 (99.6 %)	83.5 %	121.1 %
0.4	518,746	515,964 (99.5 %)	81.3 %	117.2 %
0.5	685,480	683,113 (99.7 %)	80.9 %	120.5 %
0.6	929,849	927,447 (99.7 %)	77.7 %	123.6 %
0.7	1,331,376	1,330,270 (99.9 %)	71.8 %	126.0 %
0.8	2,127,615	2,128,350 (100.0 %)	72.2 %	136.6 %

series of experiments lead to empirical *computational efforts* that underestimate the true effort by 28% or overestimate it by up to 36% (both values for P_{fail} = 0.8). The higher P_{fail} i.e. the more difficult a problem is, the larger a difference $effort - \widehat{effort}$ may result.

When decreasing the number of experiments the result becomes even more obvious. Instead of calculating an empirical *computational effort* $\widehat{effort}$ with 500 experiments we repeated the series with 200, 100 and 50 runs. Again, each of those series was repeated 1,000 times. The results are presented in Figure 2. The z-axis of the left diagram represents the differences of the percentage values of the smallest and the highest $\widehat{effort}$ in relationship to the original *effort.* For example, if the theoretical *computational effort* was 10,000 and the lowest and highest $\widehat{effort}$ values of the 1,000 series with 500 experiments were 9,000 and 10500, respectively, the percentage values (columns four and five in table 1) would be 90% and 105%. This would result in a difference of 105-90=15. Thus the higher the z value is, the larger possible mistakes in the empirically calculated *computational effort* might become.

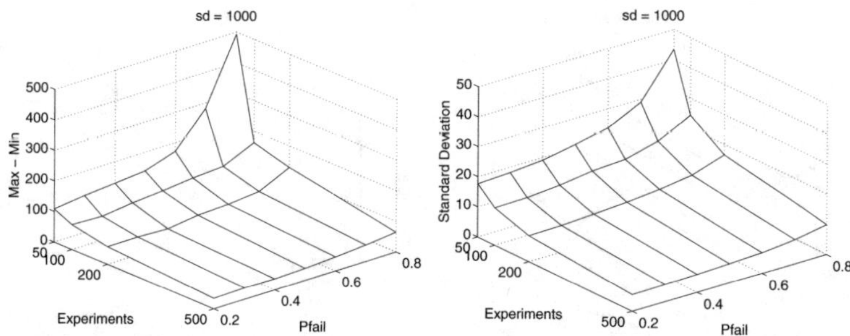

Fig. 2. Deviations (in percent compared to *effort*) between the lowest and highest $\widehat{effort}$ value

Representing 1,000 new empirical *computational effort* values $\widehat{effort}$ as percentage values in correspondence to the original *effort*, the right diagram in Figure 2 shows the standard derivations of these values.

For the series with 500 experiments the values of both diagrams are quite low. This means that a number of 500 experiments will result in an empirically calculated *computational effort* not too different from the theoretical value. The smaller the number of experiments becomes, the larger a difference we see.

Using only 50 experiments and the parameter $P_{fail} = 0.8$ one of the test series resulted in an empirical *computational effort* of 11,345,515, which is more than 500 percent of the theoretical value. $P_{fail} = 0.8$ corresponds to the fact that only 10 out of 50 runs should lead to a solution. In this special case only two of the 50 runs solved the problem, which drastically lowered the denominator of equation (3) leading to a high $\widehat{effort}$ value.

Up to now we only varied P_{fail} leaving *sd* at a constant value of 1,000. Nevertheless, all series of experiments were repeated using values of $sd =$ 2,000, 5,000, 10,000, 11,000, 20,000 and 30,000. The results show no significant difference to those for $sd = 1,000$. Again, for each number of runs 1,000 tests were performed. For some (number of runs/P_{fail}/sd) combinations there are differences in the maximum/minimum value to those shown in the left graph of Figure 2, but the differences to the standard deviation of the 1,000 newly computed $\widehat{effort}$ values for $sd = 1,000$ – as seen in the right graph of Figure 2 – is always insignificantly small. The main cause for differences between empirically calculated $\widehat{effort}$ values and theoretical values stems from the differences between P_{fail} and the empirical estimate $\widehat{P}_{fail}$ for this value.

6 Influence of *sd* on the Computational Effort

The previous section discussed the influence of the difference between the probability of success for finding a solution within one run $(1 - P_{fail})$ and its estimate $(1 - \hat{P}_{fail})$, calculated with a certain number of runs on the difference between the *computational effort* and an $\widehat{effort}$ value calculated using those runs.

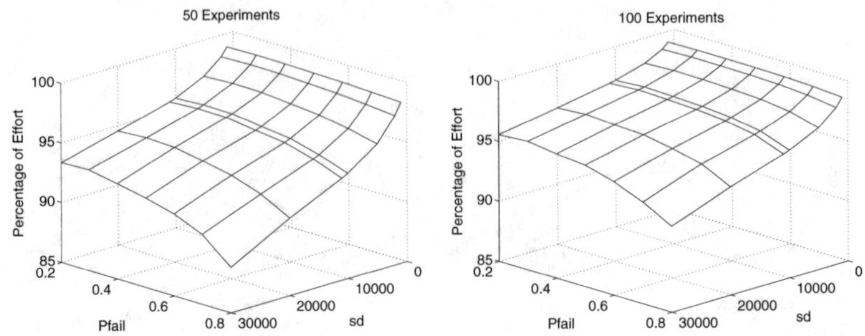

Fig. 3. The average percentage of the $\widehat{effort}$ values calculated on the base of 50 and 100 experiments in relationship to the theoretical *computational effort*

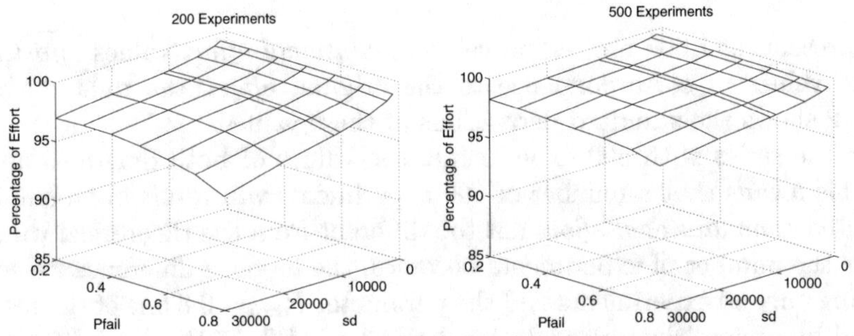

Fig. 4. The average percentage of the $\widehat{effort}$ values calculated on the base of 200 and 500 experiments in relationship to the theoretical *computational effort*

In this section we show that the values of *effort* and $\widehat{effort}$ may even vary if the estimates for P_{fail} are chosen to be identical to the theoretical probability.

We need to take a look at the distribution of the number of fitness evaluations needed to find a solution in successful runs. As written before, for each (P_{fail}/*sd*/*runs*)-combination (*runs* $\in$ {50, 100, 200, 500}) we did *runs* experiments of which now exactly $P_{fail} \times runs$ fail to find a solution. The number of fitness evaluations needed in sucessful ones is calculated as before (see section 5). This procedure guarantees that P_{fail} equals $\hat{P}_{fail}$.

For each combination (P_{fail}, *sd*, *runs*) we performed a series of 1,000 experiments, calculated $\widehat{effort}$ for each of the experiments and finally calculated the mean of all $\widehat{effort}$ values for each series.

Figure 3 and 4 show the results of these experiments. Each value of *runs* has its own graph. The x- and y-axis represent the different values of *sd* and P_{fail} while the z-axis represents the corresponding mean $\widehat{effort}$ over the 1,000 series. This value is expressed as a percentage of the theoretical *computational effort*.

In all cases the *computational effort* is slightly underestimated. For larger *sd* and P_{fail} the inaccuracy becomes more apparent. For small values of *sd* the probability of P_{fail} has only little effect on the mean $\widehat{effort}$ value. For larger *sd* the influence of P_{fail} grows. The smaller the number of runs is the more the *computational effort* is underestimated.

The reason for the underestimation is as follows: With a discrete number of experiments the minimum of equation (3) is, in most cases, associated with the highest number of fitness calculations needed within the successful runs[4]. For this valuc of *cval* the denominator of the fraction of equation (3) equals $\ln(P_{\text{[illegible]}})$. To reach the same denominator-value for the theoretical *computational effort* using equations (3) and (4) the required value of *eval* is higher in most cases and results in a higher *effort*. For smaller *eval* values the product *eval* $\times$ fraction becomes larger thus rendering this product unimportant for calculating the minimum in equation (3). The discete number of experiments means that $P(eval)$ is larger than the corresponding value of the continuous case when calculating the theoretical *computational effort*.

7 Summary

In this paper we showed how to use KOZA's *computational effort* statistics with steady-state GP-systems using tournament selection. Although the correspondence of *effort* values between theory and experiment should be higher than for generational GP-systems there were still differences between both.

We showed two different factors that have an influence on the size of errors:

1. To calculate the *computational effort* $P(eval)$ is needed. This stands for the probability a solution is found within *eval* fitness evaluations. As this value is usually unknown it has to be estimated based on empirical data. Using relative frequencies leads, on average, to a *computational effort* similar to the theoretical value but, depending on the number of runs carried out to derive the empirical value, can differ a lot in some cases.
2. The distribution of numbers of evaluations needed to find a solution plays a smaller but nevertheless important role. As an example we used a normally distributed set and demonstrated that the calculated $\widehat{effort}$ underestimates the theoretical value by up to 12 percent (Fig. 3).

While the second issue was only an example for a very specific distribution and the effect will be different for other problems and other distributions, the first issue affects all calculations of the *computational effort*.

Sections 5 and 6 showed that the differences between the theoretical value of the *computational effort* and the calculated one increases when the number of runs decreases on which the relative frequencies for $\hat{P}(eval)$ are based. We showed that calculating *effort* based on only 50 experiments may lead to values quite off the theoretical values, and that even 200 experiments often are not sufficient.

Furthermore, the more experiments fail to find a solution and the higher the differences in the number of fitness evaluations needed to find a solution in different runs are, the larger the deviation of empirical *computational effort* might become. In such cases more experiments should be carried out.

---

[4] For the series with $runs = 50$ and $sd < 30,000$ there was on average less than one *eval* value higher than the one the minimum was realized with.

References

1. W. Banzhaf, P. Nordin, R. E. Keller, F. D. Francone: Genetic Programming: An Introduction. San Francisco, CA: Morgan Kaufmann, 1998
2. S. Christensen and F. Oppacher: An Analysis of Koza's Computational Effort Statistic for Genetic In: J. A. Foster, E. Lutton, J. Miller, C. Ryan, and A. G. B. Tettamanzi,(eds.), Proceedings of the 5th European Conference on Genetic Programming, EuroGP 2002, volume 2278 of LNCS, Kinsale, Ireland, 3-5 April 2002. Springer-Verlag, pages 182–191
3. M. Keijzer, *et al*: Adaptive Logic Programming. In: Spector, L., *et al* (eds.): Proceedings of the 2001 Genetic and Evolutionary Computation Conference: GECCO 2001, Morgan Kaufmann, pages 42–49
4. J. R. Koza: Genetic Programming: On the Programming of Computers by Natural Selection. Cambridge, MA: MIT Press, 1992
5. S. Luke and L. Panait: Is the Perfect the Enemy of the Good? In: W. B. Langdon *et al.* (eds.), Proceedings of the 2002 Genetic and Evolutionary Computation Conference: GECCO 2002, Morgan Kaufman, pages 820–828

Analysis of a Digit Concatenation Approach to Constant Creation

Michael O'Neill[1], Ian Dempsey[1], Anthony Brabazon[2], and Conor Ryan[1]

[1] Dept. Of Computer Science & Information Systems
University of Limerick, Ireland
Michael.ONeill@ul.ie, Conor.Ryan@ul.ie
[2] Dept. Of Accountancy, University College Dublin, Ireland
Anthony.Brabazon@ucd.ie

Abstract. This study examines the utility of employing digit concatenation, as distinct from the traditional expression based approach, for the purpose of evolving constants in Grammatical Evolution. Digit concatenation involves creating constants (either whole or real numbers) by concatenating digits to form a single value. The two methods are compared using three different problems, which are finding a static real constant, finding dynamic real constants, and a quadratic map, which on iteration generates a chaotic time-series. The results indicate that the digit concatenation approach results in a significant improvement in the best fitness obtained across all problems analysed here.

1 Introduction

The objective of this study is to determine whether the adoption of a novel approach to constant creation by digit concatenation can outperform the more traditional expression based approach to constant creation in Grammatical Evolution, that relies on the recombination of constants using the functions and operators provided. Digit concatenation involves creating constants, which can be either whole or real numbers, by concatenating digits to form a single value.

Existing applications of digit concatenation in Grammatical Evolution adopted this approach to constant creation in the automatic generation of caching algorithms, and a financial prediction problem [10,3]. This paper extends these previous studies by conducting an analysis of the digit concatenation approach in comparison to the more traditional expression based approach using specific constant creation problem domains. The two problem domains tackled previously did not exploit constant creation to a substantial degree in successful solutions, hence the need to conduct our current investigation on different problems.

1.1 Background

Ephemeral random constants are the standard approach to constant creation in Genetic Programming (GP), having values created randomly within a prespecified range at a runs initialisation [6]. These values are then fixed throughout

C. Ryan et al. (Eds.): EuroGP 2003, LNCS 2610, pp. 173–182, 2003.

a run, and new constants can only be created through combinations of these values and other items from the function and terminal set.

Since then there have been a number of variations on the ephemeral random constant idea in tree-based GP systems, all of which have the common aim of making small changes to the initial constant values created in an individual.

Constant perturbation [14] allows GP to fine-tune floating point constants by multiplying every constant within an individual by a random number between 0.9 and 1.1, having the effect of modifying a constants value by up to 10% of their original value.

Numerical terminals and a *numerical terminal mutation* were used in [1] instead of ephemeral random constants, the difference being that the numerical terminal mutation operator selects a real valued numerical terminal in an individual and adds to it Gaussian noise with a particular variance, such that small changes are made to the constant values.

A *numeric mutation* operator, that replaces all of the numeric constants in an individual with new ones drawn at random from a uniform distribution within a specified selection range, was introduced in [4]. The selection range for each constant is specified as the old value of that constant plus or minus a temperature factor. This method was shown to produce a statistically significant improvement in performance on a number of symbolic regression problems ranging in difficulty.

1.2 Structure of Paper

This contribution is organised as follows. Section 2 provides a short introduction to Grammatical Evolution. Section 3 describes the problem domains and the experimental approach adopted in this study. Section 4 provides the results under each of the grammars. Finally, conclusions and an outline of future work are provided in Section 5.

2 Grammatical Evolution

Grammatical Evolution (GE) [12,11,9] is an evolutionary algorithm that can evolve computer programs in any language. Rather than representing the programs as parse trees, as in GP [6], a linear genome representation is used. Each individual, a variable length binary string, contains in its codons (groups of 8 bits in these experiments) the information to select production rules from a Backus Naur Form (BNF) grammar. BNF is a notation that represents a language in the form of production rules. It is comprised of a set of non-terminal symbols that can be mapped to elements from the set of terminal symbols, according to the production rules. An example excerpt from a BNF grammar is given below.

These productions state that `S` can be replaced with either one of the non-terminals `expr`, `if-stmt`, or `loop`.

```
S ::= expr      (0)
    | if-stmt   (1)
    | loop      (2)
```

The grammar is used in a generative process to construct a program by applying production rules, selected by the genome, beginning from a given start symbol (`S` in this case).

In order to select a rule in GE, the next codon value on the genome is generated and placed in the following formula:

$$Rule = Codon\ Value\ MOD\ Num.\ Rules$$

For example, if the next available codon integer value was 4, given that we have 3 rules to select from as in the above example, we get $4\ MOD\ 3 = 1$. `S` will therefore be replaced with the non-terminal `if-stmt`.

Beginning from the the left hand side of the genome codon integer values are generated and used to select rules from the BNF grammar, until one of the following situations arise: (a) a complete program is generated. This occurs when all the non-terminals in the expression being mapped are transformed into elements from the terminal set of the BNF grammar. (b) the end of the genome is reached, in which case the *wrapping* operator is invoked. This results in the return of the genome reading frame to the left hand side of the genome once again. The reading of codons will then continue unless an upper threshold representing the maximum number of wrapping events has occurred during this individuals mapping process. (c) in the event that a threshold on the number of wrapping events has occurred and the individual is still incompletely mapped, the mapping process is halted, and the individual assigned the lowest possible fitness value. A full description of GE can be found in [11].

3 Problem Domain and Experimental Approach

In this study, we compare the utility of different grammars for evolving constants by performance analysis on three different types of constant creation problems. The problems tackled are, Finding a Static Real Constant, Finding Dynamic Real Constants, and the Logistic Equation. A description of each problem follows.

3.1 Finding a Static Real Constant

The aim of this problem is to evolve a single real constant. Three target constants of increasing difficulty were selected arbitrarily, 5.67, 24.35, and 20021.11501. Fitness in this case is the absolute difference between the target and evolved values, the goal being to minimise this difference value.

3.2 Finding Dynamic Real Constants

This instance of finding dynamic real constants involves a dynamic fitness function that changes its target real constant value at regular intervals (every 10th generation). Two instances of this problem are tackled, the first sets the successive target values to be 24.35, 5.67, 5.68, 28.68, 24.35, and the second instance oscillates between the two values 24.35 and 5.67. The aim with these problems is to analyse the different constant representations in terms of their ability to adapt to a changing environment, and to investigate that behaviour in the event of both small and large changes. As in the finding static real constant problem, fitness in this case is the absolute difference between the target and evolved values, with the goal being the minimisation of this difference value.

3.3 The Logistic Equation

In systems exhibiting chaos, long-term prediction is problematic as even a small error in estimating the current state of the system leads to divergent system paths over time. Short-term prediction however, may be feasible [5]. Because chaotic systems provide a challenging environment for prediction, they have regularly been used as a test-bed for comparative studies of different predictive methodologies [8,2,13]. In this study we use time-series information drawn from a simple quadratic equation, the logistic difference equation[1]. This equation has the form:

$$x_{t+1} = \alpha x_t(1 - x_t) \qquad x \in (0.0, 1.0)$$

The behaviour of this equation is crucially driven by the parameter α. The system has a single, stable fixed point (at $x = (\alpha - 1)/\alpha$)for $\alpha < 3.0$ [13]. For $\alpha \in (3.0, \approx 3.57)$ there is successive period doubling, leading to chaotic behaviour for $\alpha \in (\approx 3.57, 4.0)$. Within this region, the time-series generated by the equation displays a variety of periodicities, ranging from short to long [7]. In this study, three time-series are generated for differing values of α. The choice of these values is guided by [7], where it was shown that the behaviour of the logistic difference equation is qualitatively different in three regions of the range (3.57 to 4.0). To avoid any bias which could otherwise arise, parameter values drawn from each of these ranges are used to test the constant evolution grammars. The goal in this problem is to rediscover the original α value. As this equation exhibits chaotic behaviour, small errors in the predicted values for α will exhibit increasingly greater errors, from the target behaviour of this equation, with each subsequent time step. Fitness in this case is the mean squared error, which is to be minimised. 100 initial values for x_t were used in fitness evaluation, and for each x_t iterating 100 times (i.e. x_t to x_{t+100}).

3.4 Constant Creation Grammars

The grammars adopted are given below. The concatenation grammar (Cat) only allows the creation of constants through the concatenation of digits, this is in contrast to the Traditional grammar (Trad) that restricts constant creation to the generation of values from expressions. The third grammar analysed here is the Traditional & Concatenation Combination grammar (Cat+Trad), which

[1] This is a special case of the general quadratic equation $y = ax^2 + bx + c$ where $c = 0$ and $a = -b$.

allows the use of both the digit concatenation and expression based constant creation approaches. The fourth grammar (Trad+Real) provides real values to the Trad grammar, giving an explicit mechanism for creating real values without relying on the arithmetic operators.

Concatenation (Cat) Grammar

```
value : real

real: int dot int | int

int: int number | number

number: 0 | 1 | 2 | 3 | 4 | 5
      | 6 | 7 | 8 | 9

dot: .
```

Traditional (Trad) Grammar

```
value: value op value
     | ( value op value )
     | number

op: + | - | / | *

number: 0 | 1 | 2 | 3 | 4 | 5
      | 6 | 7 | 8 | 9
```

Traditional & Concatenation Combination (Cat+Trad) Grammar

```
value: value op value
     | ( value op value )
     | real

op: + | - | / | *

real: int dot int | int

int: int number | number

number: 0 | 1 | 2 | 3 | 4 | 5
      | 6 | 7 | 8 | 9

dot: .
```

Traditional & Real Combination (Trad+Real) Grammar

```
value: value op value
     | ( value op value )
     | number
     | real

op: + | - | / | *

number: 0 | 1 | 2 | 3 | 4 | 5
      | 6 | 7 | 8 | 9

real : .1 | .2 | .3 | .4 | .5
     | .6 | .7 | .8 | .9
```

4 Results

For each grammar on every problem instance, 30 runs were conducted using population sizes of 500, running for 50 generations on the static and dynamic constant problems, and 100 generations for the logistic equation, adopting one-point crossover at a probability of 0.9, and bit mutation at 0.1, along with roulette selection and a replacement strategy where 25% of the population is replaced each generation. The crossover operator was allowed to select crossover points within the 8-bit codons adopted here. The results are as follows.

4.1 Finding a Static Real Constant

On all three instances of this problem, a t-test and bootstrap t-test (5% level) on the best fitness values reveal that the digit concatenation grammars (Cat & Cat+Trad) significantly outperform the standard expression based approach (Trad & Trad+Real) to constant creation through expressions. Statistics of performance for each grammar are given in Table 1, and a plot of the mean best fitness at each generation for the three grammars analysed can be seen in Fig. 1.

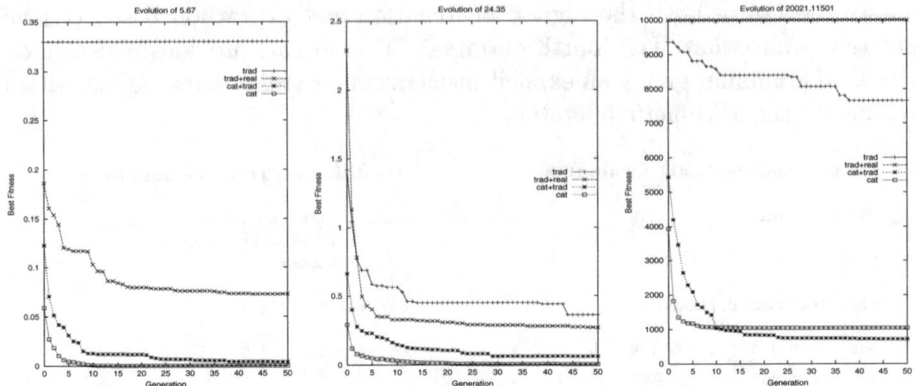

Fig. 1. Mean best fitness values (lower value is better) plotted against generations for each of the three grammars. Target values are 5.67 (left), 24.35 (center), and 20021.11501 (right).

Table 1. Statistics for best fitness values (lower value is better) at generation 50 on the Static Real Constant Problem.

Target Constant	Grammar	**Mean**	Median	*Std. Dev.*
5.67	Trad	**0.33**	0.33	*0.0*
	Trad+Real	**0.071**	0.03	*0.118*
	Cat+Trad	**0.004**	0.0	*0.017*
	Cat	**0.0**	0.0	*0.0*
24.35	Trad	**0.36**	0.35	*0.055*
	Trad+Real	**0.261**	0.35	*0.205*
	Cat+Trad	**0.057**	0.01	*0.081*
	Cat	**0.002**	0.0	*0.009*
20021.11501	Trad	**7741.35**	1.000e+04	*3828.9*
	Trad+Real	**1.000e+04**	1.000e+04	*0.0*
	Cat+Trad	**689.01**	2.117e+01	*2531.2*
	Cat	**1005.24**	9.100e-01	*3049.5*

Interestingly, the Trad+Real grammar did not perform as well as the Trad grammar on the hardest of these three problem instances, while the Cat and Cat+Trad grammars performance was statistically the same. This demonstrates that a grammar that has a concatenation approach to constant creation is significantly better at generating larger numbers[2].

4.2 Finding Dynamic Real Constants

For the first instance of this problem where the successive target constant values are 24.35, 5.67, 5.68, 28.68, 24.35 over the course of 50 generations, performance

[2] It is worth stressing that larger numbers could just as easily be large whole numbers or numbers with a high degree of precision (reals).

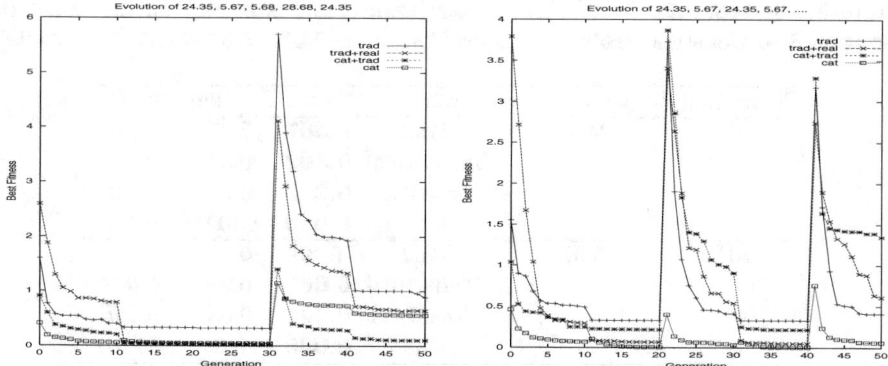

Fig. 2. Mean best fitness values (lower value is better) plotted against generations for each of the three grammars. Target values are 24.35, 5.67, 5.68, 28.68, 24.35 (left), and 24.35, 5.67,.. (right).

Table 2. Statistics for best fitness values (lower value is better) on the Dynamic Real Constant Problem (Target Constants: 24.35, 5.67, 5.68, 28.68, 24.35).

Generation	Target Constant	Grammar	**Mean**	Median	*Std. Dev.*
10	24.35	Trad	**0.4**	0.35	*0.114*
		Trad+Real	**0.766**	0.35	*1.539*
		Cat+Trad	**0.219**	0.11	*0.296*
		Cat	**0.061**	0.01	*0.133*
20	5.67	Trad	**0.33**	0.33	*0.0*
		Trad+Real	**0.05**	0.03	*0.078*
		Cat+Trad	**0.017**	0.006	*0.025*
		Cat	**0.047**	0.0	*0.17*
30	5.68	Trad	**0.32**	0.32	*1.129e-16*
		Trad+Real	**0.04**	0.02	*7.7499e-02*
		Cat+Trad	**0.009**	0.001	*2.283e-02*
		Cat	**0.046**	0.0	*1.724e-01*
40	28.68	Trad	**2.063**	1.5	*3.474*
		Trad+Real	**1.356**	0.68	*2.581*
		Cat+Trad	**0.283**	0.16	*0.347*
		Cat	**0.707**	0.007	*3.585*
50	24.35	Trad	**0.937**	0.35	*2.755*
		Trad+Real	**0.638**	0.3	*1.56*
		Cat+Trad	**0.101**	0.05	*0.244*
		Cat	**0.541**	0.002	*2.799*

statistics are given in Table 2, and a plot of mean best fitness values for each grammar can be seen in Fig. 2 (left).

Performing a t-test and bootstrap t-test on the best fitness values at generations 10, 20, 30, 40 and 50, it is shown that there is a significant (5% level) performance advantage in favour of the concatentation grammars (Cat & Cat+Trad) up to generation 30, beyond this point the advantages of one grammar over the

Table 3. Statistics for best fitness values (lower value is better) on the Oscillating Dynamic Real Constant Problem (Target Constants: 24.35, 5.67, 24.35, 5.67, 24.35).

Generation	Target Constant	Grammar	**Mean**	Median	*Std. Dev.*
10	24.35	Trad	**0.507**	0.35	*0.426*
		Trad+Real	**0.302**	0.35	*0.148*
		Cat+Trad	**0.252**	0.35	*0.143*
		Cat	**0.089**	0.011	*0.193*
20	5.67	Trad	**0.33**	0.33	*0.0*
		Trad+Real	**0.065**	0.03	*0.092*
		Cat+Trad	**0.222**	0.33	*0.156*
		Cat	**0.005**	0.0	*0.0167*
30	24.35	Trad	**0.487**	0.35	*0.426*
		Trad+Real	**0.55**	0.35	*1.113*
		Cat+Trad	**0.963**	0.35	*2.765*
		Cat	**0.046**	0.022	*0.07*
40	5.67	Trad	**0.33**	0.33	*0.0*
		Trad+Real	**0.050**	0.03	*0.077*
		Cat+Trad	**0.222**	0.33	*0.155*
		Cat	**0.004**	0.0	*0.010*
50	24.35	Trad	**0.487**	0.35	*0.426*
		Trad+Real	**0.625**	0.35	*1.53*
		Cat+Trad	**1.358**	0.35	*3.815*
		Cat	**0.061**	0.014	*0.131*

other are not as clear cut. Given the dynamic nature of this problem other issues such as loss of diversity may be coming into play, possibly obfuscating any effect of the different constant generation techniques.

In the second instance of this problem, where the target constant value oscillates, every 10 generations, between 24.35 and 5.67 over the 50 generations, again we see a similar trend. In this case, the concatenation grammar (Cat) is significantly better (based on best fitness analysis using t-tests and bootstrap t-tests at the 5% level) than all the other constant creation grammars at each of 10, 20, 30, 40 and 50 generations, however, this difference is decreasing over time. Again, loss of diversity over time is most likely playing a role here. A plot of the mean best fitness can be seen in Fig. 2 (right), and statistics are presented in Table 3.

From the results on both of these dynamic problem instances, there are clearly adaptive advantages to using the concatenation grammar over the traditional expression based approach.

4.3 The Logistic Equation

The results for all three instances of this problem can be seen in Table 4 and Fig. 3. Statistical analysis using a t-test and bootstrap t-test (5% level) reveal that the concatenation grammars (Cat & Cat+Trad) significantly outperform

Table 4. Statistics for best fitness values (lower value is better) at generation 100 on the Logistic Equation Problem.

Target Constant	Grammar	**Mean**	Median	*Std. Dev.*
3.59	Trad	**6.074e-03**	6.074e-03	*2.647e-18*
	Trad+Real	**2.203e-04**	3.613e-06	*1.108e-03*
	Cat+Trad	**1.109e-05**	8.256e-13	*5.321e-05*
	Cat	**4.818e-07**	3.902e-19	*1.249e-06*
3.80	Trad	**1.310e-03**	1.310e-03	*6.616e-19*
	Trad+Real	**5.715e-04**	1.485e-06	*0.001*
	Cat+Trad	**4.724e-19**	4.724e-19	*0.0*
	Cat	**4.724e-19**	4.724e-19	*0.0*
3.84	Trad	**7.113e-04**	7.113e-04	*2.206e-19*
	Trad+Real	**4.146e-04**	7.113e-04	*3.457e-04*
	Cat+Trad	**6.564e-05**	6.065e-19	*2.017e-04*
	Cat	**6.065e-19**	6.065e-19	*9.794e-35*

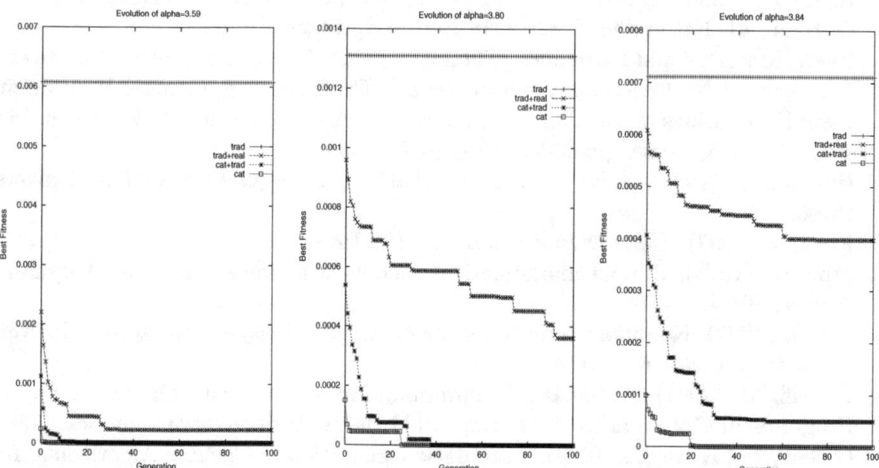

Fig. 3. Mean best fitness values (lower value is better) plotted against generations for each of the three grammars. Target α values are 3.59 (left), 3.80 (center), and 3.84 (right).

the traditional constant creation approach on each problem instance, successfully rediscovering the target α value in each case.

5 Conclusions and Future Work

An analysis of a digit concatenation approach to constant creation in Grammatical Evolution is presented. In general, the performance of concatenation grammars across the three problem domains investigated here, exhibits significantly improved fitness when compared to the more traditional expression based constant creation approach.

We now intend to extend this study by conducting a comparison of digit concatenation to an equivalent version of ephemeral random constants in Grammatical Evolution, and to look at a broader set of problem domains.

References

1. Angeline, Peter J. (1996). Two Self-Adaptive Crossover Operators for Genetic Programming. In Peter J. Angeline and K. E. Kinnear, Jr. (Eds.), Advances in Genetic Programming 2, Chapter 5, pp.89-110, MIT Press.
2. Castillo, E. and Gutierrez, J. (1998). Nonlinear time series modeling and prediction using functional networks. Extracting information masked by chaos, *Physics Letters A*, 244:71-84.
3. Dempsey, I., O'Neill, M. and Brabazon, T. (2002). Investigations into Market Index Trading Models Using Evolutionary Automatic Programming, In *Lecture Notes in Artificial Intelligence, 2464*,Proceedings of the 13th Irish Conference in Artificial Intelligence and Cognitive Science, pp. 165-170, edited by M. O'Neill, R. Sutcliffe, C. Ryan, M. Eaton and N. Griffith, Berlin: Springer-Verlag.
4. Evett, Matthew and Fernandez, Thomas. (1998). Numeric Mutation Improves the Discovery of Numeric Constants in Genetic Programming, Genetic Programming 1998: Proceedings of the Third Annual Conference, University of Wisconsin, Madison, Wisconsin, USA, pp.66-71, Morgan Kaufmann.
5. Holland, J. (1998). *Emergence from Chaos to Order*,Oxford: Oxford University Press.
6. Koza, J. (1992). *Genetic Programming.* MIT Press.
7. May, R. (1976). Simple mathematical models with very complicated dynamics, *Nature*, 261:459-467.
8. Nie, J. (1997). Nonlinear time-series forecasting: A fuzzy-neural approach, *Neurocomputing*, 16:63-76.
9. O'Neill, M. (2001). Automatic Programming in an Arbitrary Language: Evolving Programs in Grammatical Evolution. PhD thesis, University of Limerick, 2001.
10. O'Neill, M., Ryan, C. (1999). Automatic Generation of Caching Algorithms, In K. Miettinen and M.M. Mäkelä and J. Toivanen (Eds.) Proceedings of EUROGEN99, Jyväskylä, Finland, pp.127-134, University of Jyväskylä.
11. O'Neill, M., Ryan, C. (2001) Grammatical Evolution, *IEEE Trans. Evolutionary Computation*, 5(4):349-358, 2001.
12. Ryan C., Collins J.J., O'Neill M. (1998). Grammatical Evolution: Evolving Programs for an Arbitrary Language. *Lecture Notes in Computer Science 1391, Proceedings of the First European Workshop on Genetic Programming*, 83-95, Springer-Verlag.
13. Saxen, H. (1996). On the approximation of a quadratic map by a small neural network, *Neurocomputing*, 12:313-326.
14. Spencer, G. (1994). Automatic Generation of Programs for Crawling and Walking. In Kenneth E. Kinnear, Jr. (Ed), Advances in Genetic Programming, Chapter 15, pp. 335-353, MIT Press.

Genetic Programming with Boosting for Ambiguities in Regression Problems

Grégory Paris, Denis Robilliard, and Cyril Fonlupt

Université du Littoral-Côte d'Opale, LIL
BP 719, 62228 Calais Cedex, France
paris@lil.univ-littoral.fr
phone: +33-321 465 667

Abstract. Facing ambiguities in regression problems is a challenge. There exists many powerful evolutionary schemes to deal with regression, however, these techniques do not usually take into account ambiguities (*i.e.* the existence of 2 or more solutions for some or all points in the domain). Nonetheless ambiguities are present in some real world inverse problems, and it is interesting in such cases to provide the user with a choice of possible solutions. We propose in this article an approach based on *boosted* genetic programming in order to propose several solutions when ambiguities are detected.

1 Introduction

In a regression problem, the goal is to find a function that closely matches a finite set of points taken from an unknown signal or an unknown function.

Genetic Programming (GP) has been successfully applied to tackle difficult regression problems, but most of these studies make the assumption that only one function is needed to fit the sample points.

Many real world inverse problems can be seen as regression problems. Some of these are of a very important scientific or economic interest, ranging from physics, combinatorics, mathematical analysis, medicine, ecology... However these problems are often mathematically "ill-posed", meaning that the existence and the uniqueness of a solution cannot be guaranteed. For example, seeking to retrieve phytoplankton chlorophyll-a concentration in coastal waters from remote sensing spectrometer data, the so-called ocean color problem, is known to be an ambiguous problem (see [1]).

It is also possible that we are given a sample set made of points taken from several signals. In such case, we do not know how many signals there are and it is not easy to determine from which signal a given point comes.

Let us look at a simple example to illustrate the notion of ambiguity: suppose we try to invert a process modeled by $f(x) = |x|$, then what is the inverse of 3? Two values are possible, 3 and -3. So, one solution is not sufficient. Our aim in this article is to propose a way to overcome ambiguities in such cases and to be able to propose one, two or more solutions to fit the data. We will

C. Ryan et al. (Eds.): EuroGP 2003, LNCS 2610, pp. 183–193, 2003.

use the *boosting* scheme in conjunction with GP to search and propose multiple solutions on a set of ambiguous test regression problems.

Next section defines the *boosting* scheme and introduces our GP method targeted for regression problem: *GPboost*. We show then how we use it to approximate several models. In Sect. 3, we explain the dendrograms principles, hierarchical classification trees which aim at clustering some set of values. In Sect. 4, we show how to deal with the multiple hypotheses provided by the *GPboost* scheme, and then we provide results on an ambiguous regression problems in Sect. 5. Finally, we draw some conclusions and we provide ideas for further research.

2 Genetic Programming and Boosting

2.1 Principles

Boosting appeared at the beginning of the 90's, proposed by Schapire [2] and Freund [3]. It aims at improving already known methods from the machine learning field (*cf* [4]), methods which need a learning set or fitness set to provide a function which will best fit training points.

The first principle of boosting is to include a distribution on the learning set. Each point is weighted and this weight is taken into account in the learning algorithm. This distribution is changed according to the difficulty the algorithm has to learn points of the learning set.

The second principle is that the boosting algorithm offers several hypothesis. These hypothesis will finally be combined to give a final result.

To sum up, we first have an uniform distribution on the learning set. The boosted algorithm gives a function denoted f_1. Weights of the badly learned points are increased while the others are decresased. The algorithm is run a second time and provides f_2. This scheme is looped over, until we get T functions f_t (T is a parameter of the boosting method).

To determine the output value of a given point, values proposed by each function f_t are combined by a vote or another method.

Part 2.2 introduces an application of boosting to genetic programming [5] (for more details about boosting, see [6]).

There is a theoretical proof showing that error on the learning set of the final hypothesis is better than an "un-boosted" version of the algorithm, when the base algorithm is a *weak learner*, according to the PAC model [7]. Boosting may also be seen as a particular case within the family of adaptive re-weighting and combining algorithms, also called arcing algorithms, see [8], [9] and also [10].

2.2 The GPboost Algorithm

Based on the work of Drucker [11], Iba proposed in [12] a *boosting* version of GP. Our method *GPboost* [5] is dedicated to regression problems, and it differs from Iba's scheme by retaining the precision of weights for every training cases,

Require: A learning set $S = \{(x_1, y_1), \ldots, (x_m, y_m)\}$, $x_i \in \mathcal{X}, y_i \in \mathcal{R}$,
$GP(D, S)$, a genetic programming algorithm using distribution D on S.

The algorithm:
Initialize $D_1(i) = 1/m$, $D_1(i)$ is the weight of example (x_i, y_i).
For $t = 1..T$ **do**
Run GP on D_t with fitness function
$fit = \sum_{i=1}^{m} \sqrt{|f(x_i) - y_i| * D_t(i)} * m$
where f is an individual of the GP
Get the best function $f_t : \mathcal{X} \rightarrow \mathcal{R}$ given by the GP run
Calculate loss for each example:
$L_i = \frac{\sqrt{|f_t(x_i) - y_i|}}{max_{i=1..N} \sqrt{|f_t(x_i) - y_i|}}$
Calculate average loss: $\bar{L} = \sum_{i=1}^{N} L_i D_t(i)$
Let $\beta_t = \frac{\bar{L}}{1-\bar{L}}$, the confidence given to this function f_t
Update the distributions :
$D_{t+1}(i) = \frac{D_t(i)^{1-L_i}}{Z_t}$
with Z_t a normalization factor so that D_{t+1} will be a distribution
End for

Output: Final hypothesis :
$F(x) = min\{y \in \mathcal{R} : \sum_{t: f_t(x) \leq y} \log(1/\beta_t) \geq \frac{1}{2} \sum_{t=1}^{m} \log(1/\beta_t)\}$

Fig. 1. The GPboost algorithm

instead of using a discrete sampling. Although GP is not a weak learner, boosting improves GP performance, as it does with other non weak learner methods, *e.g.* C4.5 algorithm. *GPboost* algorithm is presented in Fig 1, notice the fitness function incorporating the weights values, more details being available in [5]:

2.3 Getting Several Solutions

The aim of our method is to get a model which can provide one or several output values for a given input.

To make things clear, we will use the same example through out this paper. Two signals are intertwined and points of the fitness set are randomly taken from these two signals. The two functions are $y = \frac{x^3}{10} - x^2 + x + 9$ (signal 1) and $y = 5(x^3 - 3x^2) * e^{-x} - 3$ (signal 2). Fig. 2 shows the points from the two signals. These two signals build our fitness set. Note that there is no distinction in our fitness set between points from signal 1 and points from signal 2.

As introduced before in the *boosting* scheme (*cf* 2.1), the distribution is modified in order to put emphasis on hard cases in the learning set.

In the case of ambiguous problems, the learning set will hold some cases like: (x, y) and (x, z) with $y \neq z$ (for instance, $(2, 7.8)$ and $(2, -5.707)$ for our example). It is obvious that it is impossible to find a function fitting both points with a traditional GP approach. But, as the *GPboost* method loops over several

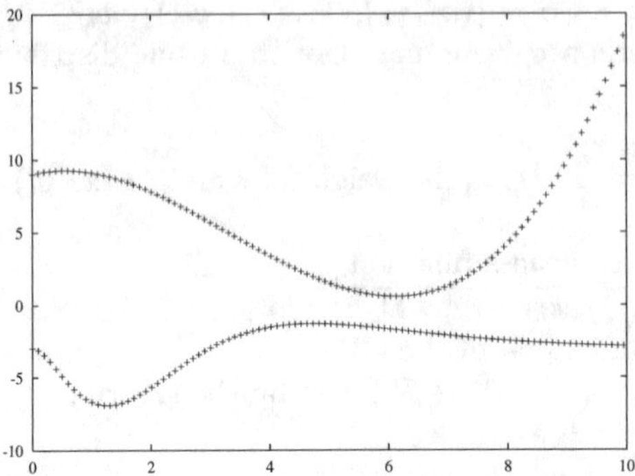

Fig. 2. Points of the fitness set

distributions, we may hope to find at a given round a function which fits (x, y) and another one at a later round which fits (x, z).

The signals we want to discover are continuous and we assume we deal with this kind of signals.

As introduced before, we do not wish to fit both points of the fitness set but only some of them in each round of boosting. Our hope is that:

1. most of the points of the same signal will be fit by the function provided by the first rounds of boosting,
2. so that the update of the distribution will increase the weight of the points coming from the other signals,
3. and the function given by the next rounds of boosting will fit many points from another signal,
4. while the remaining points of others signals will be fit at the end of the run of GPboost.

Principle of GP is that many functions are generated and that selection pressure keeps those that better respond to the problem. This selection pressure is incorporated inside the fitness function of GP and, for our problem, GP is run with the following fitness function :

$$fit = \sum_{i=1}^{m} \sqrt{|f(x_i) - y_i| * D_t(i)} * m$$

where $D_t(i)$ is the weight of example (x_i, y_i), m the size of the fitness set and t the round of boosting.

For $x = 2$, two output values are possible : 7.8 and -5.707. The fitness is higher for functions that perfectly match one of the two values than for those which provide an average value. Note that others standard fitness functions like RMS would prefer an average value between 7.8 and -5.707.

Our experiments show that when the fitness set is composed of points from many signals with slightly different input values, the fitness function correctly works.

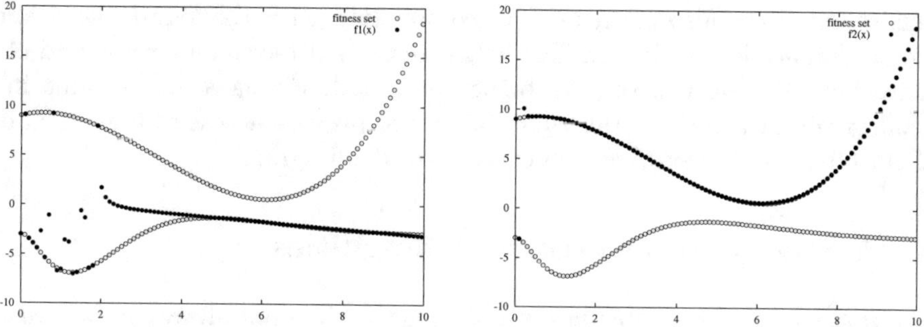

Fig. 3. Values given by f_1(left) & f_2(right) for the points of the fitness set

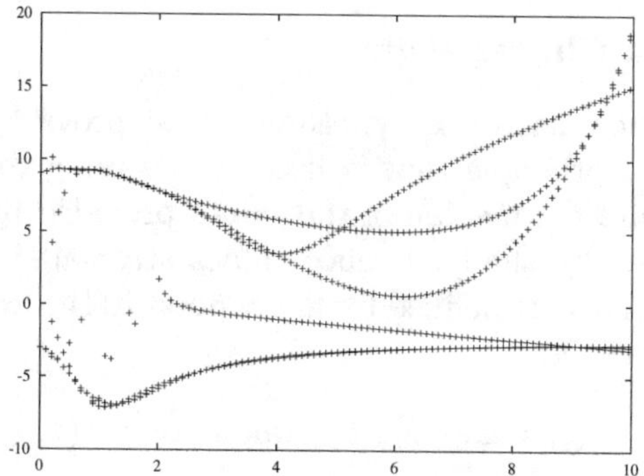

Fig. 4. Values given by all the functions f_t for the points of the fitness set

For our example, the first round of the main loop of GPboost gives the function displayed in Fig. 3. We can see that GP has somehow tried to focus on points from signal 2. As we might expect, the second round of boosting provides us with a function (Fig. 3) fitting numerous points from the other signal.

3 Dealing with Several Solutions

For each point x_0 in the learning set, T values are provided by the *GPboost* algorithm when using T rounds of boosting. Our aim is to split this set of T values into n clusters($n \leq T$), and then combine the hypotheses inside every cluster to provide n output solutions.

3.1 Dendrograms for Dealing with Ambiguities

A dendrogram can be roughly seen as a binary hierarchical cluster tree holding several partitions. For N values, the dendrogram is able to build either N clusters, $N-1$ clusters, ..., up to 1 cluster. A dendrogram consists of many upside-down, U-shaped line connecting objects in a hierarchical tree (note that dendrograms are also often used in conjunction with the Ward algorithm for factorial analysis, like PCA). The height of each U represents some kind of distance between the two objects being connected. Fixing a cutoff value in the dendrogram at some hierarchy level allows to provide access to a given number of clusters. See Annex. A for an example of dendrogram.

4 A Scheme to Overcome Ambiguities

The tricky part of an ambiguous problem is that it is not always ambiguous! For some points, several values are to be found while for some other points only one value may be needed.

4.1 Setting up a Cluster Value

In our approach, each cluster of hypotheses must provide one solution. This is done with the same principle that is used for deriving the final hypothesis in *GPboost*: we compute the median of the values provided by every hypothesis in the cluster, weighted by the confidence values associated with the hypothesis. These confidence values are defined for every point in the learning set, and stored in a confidence vector β_t:

$$\beta_t = \{\beta_t(i) = 1 - L_i : L_i \text{ evaluated over}(x_i, y_i) \in S\}$$

where L_i is the loss computed for each example during the round of boosting number t of GPboost.

When dealing with points that do not come from the learning set, a confidence value is to be computed for each function f_t. The confidence value associated to $f_t(x_0)$ when x_0 is not including in the learning set is the confidence value associated to the nearest point in the learning set. As we deal with ambiguous problem, several points can be as the same distance from x_0. In this case, the best confidence value is retained. This can be summed up in the following formula:

$$\beta_t(x_0) = max\{\beta_t(i)/\forall(x_j, y_j) \in S, d(x_0, x_i) \leq d(x_0, x_j)\}$$

4.2 Description of the Algorithm

Let $S = \{(x_1, y_1), \ldots, (x_m, y_m)\}$ be a learning set holding some ambiguous cases, with $x_i \in \mathcal{X}, y_i \in \mathcal{R}$. The *GPboost* algorithm is run on T rounds , thus at the end of the run, we get T functions $f_t(x)$. Then, instead of computing one final hypothesis, we choose a cutoff value to get one or more clusters, and so one or more final hypotheses.

The choice of cutoff value is the last difficulty of ambiguous problems and two ways are possible.

The first one is to fix the cutoff value before the execution, using some background knowledge on the problem. In the problem we deal with in this article, cutoff value can be set to 2.

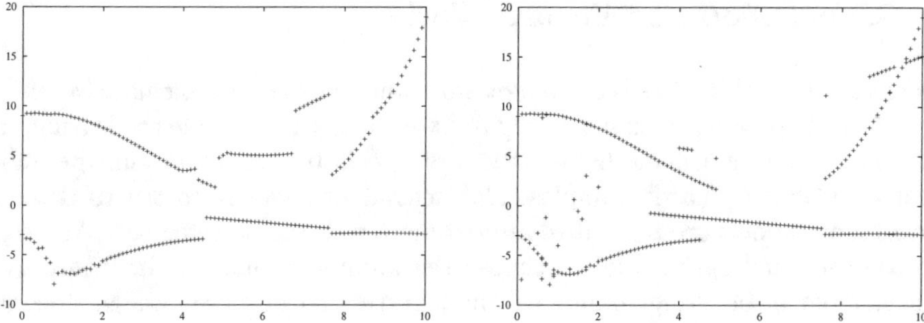

Fig. 5. Solutions obtained with fixed(left) and computed(right) cutoff value (see Fig. 2 for target result).

When no background knowledge is available to set a cutoff value, we propose to automatically choose a number of clusters such that we get the maximum error decrease over the learning set. This method is explained in details in Annex. B.

5 Experiments, Error and Results

We have applied this method to our test problem on a test set where points are different from the points of the learning set and two schemes have been tested for setting the cutoff value.

Fixing the cutoff value appears to get better result but as explained before, a knowledge of the problem is needed. However automatic determination of the cutoff value provides interesting results.

Working only with a "classic" error measure (RMS error or sum of the absolute errors) for evaluation of this method does not bring many useful information. In our opinion, we think a hit criterion based-error (based on the number of fitness cases for which the numerical value returned by the program comes within a small tolerance of the correct value, following the idea of [13]) would be more helpful.

We introduce 2 error measures:

1. the hit error which computes the ratio of hit points of the test set.
2. the miss error computes the ratio of points provided by the method which does not match anything

The two models given in both figures give these results:

model	hit error	miss error
fixed cutoff value	0.356	0.356
computed cutoff value	0.252	0.343

According to these error measures, the computed cutoff value provides better results than using the fixed cutoff value. Other experiments were also conducted and successful (*e.g.* inverting $\sin(x), x \in [0..2\pi]$,...).

6 Conclusion and Future Works

Dealing with ambiguities is a complex work and two main problems arise: the first one in the case of regression is to try to fit as closely as possible the learning data set. The *boosting* scheme helps us at doing this by providing multiple models and focusing on "hard" samples. The second problem is to try to determine how many models are needed to approximate well the learning set. We propose to use the dendrogram tool to choose the number of models. In future works, the number of boosting rounds will be investigated in more details, since more hypotheses may provide more precise clusters. It seems that our method will also work with non continuous functions, including non continuous operators in the functions set of the GP.

Comparisons should also be performed using statistical PCA analysis on the learning set in order to test alternate ways of deciding on the number of clusters solutions. The evolutionary ideas of niching [14], [15] and sharing [16] could also provide others schemes to deal with ambiguities.

References

1. Roland Doerffer and Helmut Schiller. Neural network for retrieval of concentrations of water constituents with the possibility of detecting exceptional out of scope spectra. In *proceedings of IEEE 2000 International Geoscience and Remote Sensing Symposium*, volume II, pages 714–717, 2000.
2. R. E. Schapire. The strength of weak learnability. In *Machine Learning, 5(2)*, pages 197–227, 1990.
3. Y.Freund and R.E. Schapire. Experiments with a new boosting algorithm. In *Proceedings of the International Conference on Machine Learning, ICML96*, 1996.
4. Tom Michael Mitchell. *Machine Learning.* Mc Graw-Hill, 1997.
5. Gregory Paris, Denis Robilliard, and Cyril Fonlupt. Applying boosting techniques to genetic programming. In *Proceedings of the EA01 conference (to appear in LNCS)*, 2001.
6. R.E. Schapire Y. Freund. A short introduction to boosting. *Journal of Japanese Society for Artificial Intelligence*, pages 771–780, 1999.
7. L. G. Valiant. A theory of a learnable. *Commun. ACM, 27(11)*, pages 1134–1142, November 1984.
8. L. Breiman. Bias, variance, and arcing classifiers. Technical Report Technical Report 460, Statistics Department, University of California at Berkeley, 1996.
9. L. Breiman. Arcing classifiers. *The Annals of Statistics*, 26(3):801–849, 1998.
10. A. E. Eiben and Zsofia Ruttkay. Self-adaptivity for constraint satisfaction: Learning penalty functions. In *International Conference on Evolutionary Computation*, pages 258–261, 1996.
11. H. Drucker. Improving regression unsing boosting techniques. In *Proceedings of the International Conference on Machine Learning (ICML)*, 1997.
12. Hitoshi Iba. Bagging, boosting, and bloating in genetic programming. In *[?]*, pages 1053–1060, 1999.
13. John Koza. *Genetic Programming II: Automac Discovery of Reusable Programs.* The MIT Press, 1994.

14. Brad L. Miller and Michael J. Shaw. Genetic algorithms with dynamic niche sharing for multimodal function optimization. In *International Conference on Evolutionary Computation*, pages 786–791, 1996.
15. Samir W. Mahfoud. Crossover interactions among niches. In *Proc. of the First IEEE Conf. on Evolutionary Computation*, volume 1, pages 188–193, Piscataway, NJ, 1994. IEEE Service Center.
16. D E Goldberg and J Richardson. Genetic algorithms with sharing for multi-modal function optimisation. In *Proc of the 2nd Int. Conf. on Genetic Algorithms and Their Applications*, pages 41–, 1987.

A How to Build a Dendrogram

Let's have a look at an example of how this kind of tree is built to make comprehension easier.

We have run our boosting algorithm, setting parameter T to 6. We get 6 functions f_t and have now to interpret this model.

To know the output values for $x_0 = 3$, we first have to get the 6 values $f_t(x_0)$ and then we have to cluster this set of 6 values. For this, we build the dendrogram.

Let S be the set of 6 values. $S = \{-4.34, -4.29, -0.58, 5.39, 5.69, 6.66\}$. This set can be obviously partitioned into 6 clusters, each cluster holding a single element.

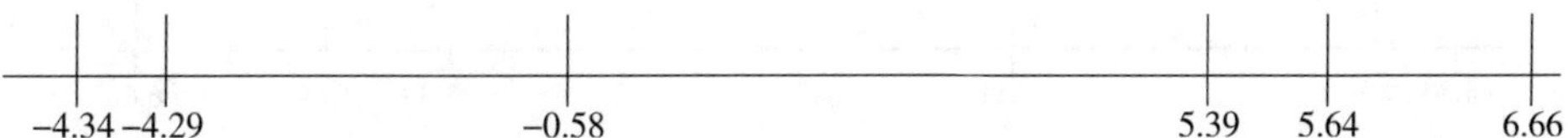

The two nearest clusters are merged, considering that the distance between any two clusters is the shortest distance between any two elements of these two clusters.

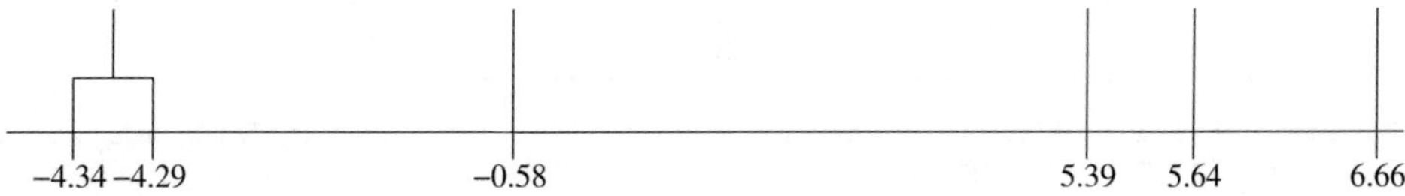

Values −4.34 and −4.29 are now in the same cluster, so we now face a new partition of 5 clusters.

The two nearest clusters are merged. The junction is made at a higher level in the hierarchy using a U-shaped line.

At each step, the two nearest clusters are iteratively merged until only one cluster remains. Height of each U represents the distance between the two clusters being connected.

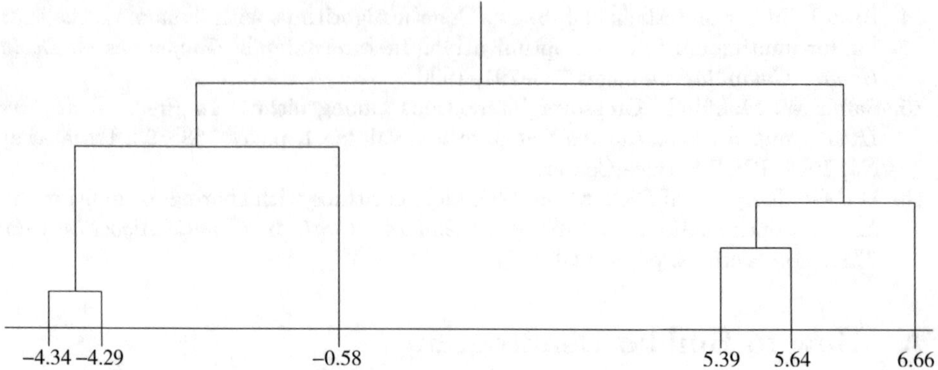

If we want to partition our set into 3 clusters, the hierarchical binary cluster tree is cut off in the following way:

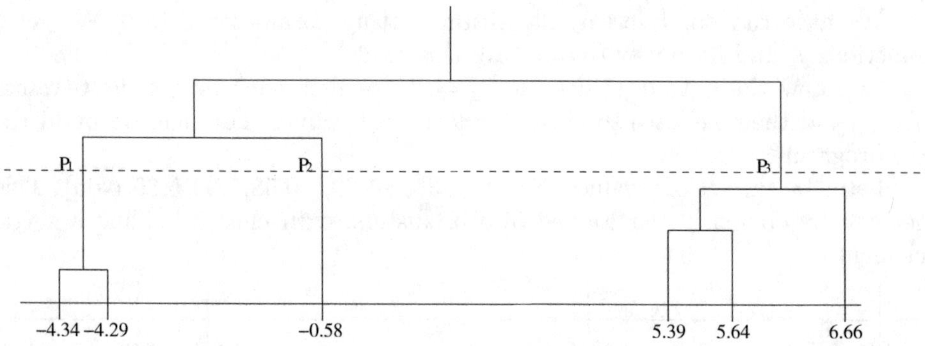

We get 3 clusters: $P_1 = \{-4.34, -4.29\}$ $P_2 = \{-0.58\}$ $P_3 = \{5.39, 5.64, 6.66\}$.

If we wish to get 2 clusters, the dendrogram should be cut off at the following height:

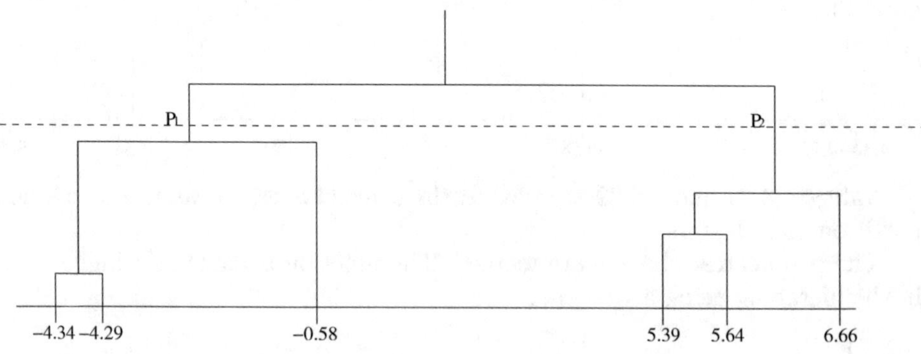

B Computing the Cutoff Value

We compute an error function on every training cases using the best fitted model among those provided by the clusters: we first consider only one cluster (*i.e.* as in standard boosting), then we lower the cutoff level and thus add new clusters one at a time until the error on the neighbouring stop decreasing. We look at the given point x_0 and at its neighbors in the training set, and then determine how many models are needed to approximate well all points belonging to this neighborhood.

More formally, we compute the following function:

$$F : \begin{array}{l} \mathcal{X} \mapsto \mathcal{R}^n \\ x \mapsto g_n(x) \end{array}$$

with:

$$g_k(x) = \{med_{/\beta}(P_1), ..., med_{/\beta}(P_k)\}$$

where P_k are the clusters of the dendrogram when the cutoff value is chosen to get k clusters, and $med_{/\beta}$ is the cluster hypothesis, that results from computing the median of the cluster functions as explained in Sect. 4.1.

The cutoff point is chosen so that we get n models and that increasing the number of models does not decrease the error anymore:

$$n = \min\{k | E(g_k, V(x, S, \rho)) \leq E(g_{k+1}, V(x, S, \rho))\}$$

where E is the cumulated error of the best model from g_k for every example in the subset $S' \subset S$:

$$E(g_k, S') = \sum_{(x_i, y_i) \in S'} (\min\{|l - y_i| : l \in g_k(x_i)\})$$

with $S' = V(x, S, \rho)$ the ρ nearest values of x in the set S, and the confidence value for x is the best confidence value in its neighborhood.

$$\beta_t(x) = \max_{x_i \in V(x,S,\rho)} \beta_t(i)$$

Maximum Homologous Crossover for Linear Genetic Programming

Michael Defoin Platel[1,2], Manuel Clergue[1], and Philippe Collard[1]

[1] Laboratoire I3S, CNRS-Université de Nice Sophia Antipolis
[2] ACRI-ST

Abstract. We introduce a new recombination operator, the Maximum Homologous Crossover for Linear Genetic Programming. In contrast to standard crossover, it attempts to preserve similar structures from parents, by aligning them according to their homology, thanks to an algorithm used in Bio-Informatics. To highlight disruptive effects of crossover operators, we introduce the Royal Road landscapes and the Homology Driven Fitness problem, for Linear Genetic Programming. Two variants of the new crossover operator are described and tested on this landscapes. Results show a reduction in the bloat phenomenon and in the frequency of deleterious crossovers.

1 Introduction

The role played by crossover in the Genetic Programming (GP) evolutionary process is a much debated question. Traditionally, individuals are encoded using a tree-based representation, and crossover consists in swapping subtrees. According to Koza [9], crossover is the central operator in the GP search process, where useful subtrees tend to spread as they are swapped. However, Banzhaf et al. [17] argue that crossover behaves more like a macro mutation operator, so GP can be viewed as a population based hill-climber. In the same way, some authors [2] have obtained worse results for crossover compared to mutation based system. Moreover, standard crossover exchanges subtrees without taking context into account; this is a brutal operation that may prevent emergence of structured solutions [6]. Altenberg [1] notes that crossover may cause the program growth phenomenon, called bloat, which arises during evolution as the population attempts to protect useful subtrees. Finally, Poli and Langdon [15] point out the fact that standard GP crossover is a local and biased operator, which can not explore search space properly.

Some new operators have been designed to overcome the drawbacks of the standard GP crossover. The main idea behind all those recombination mechanisms is *homology*. This notion comes directly from the properties of the crossover in nature which does not exchange genes randomly. Indeed, during the second stage of the prophase of meiosis (called *zygoten*), the homologous chromosomes are first aligned according to their similarity before crossover takes place. This implies that genes are swapped with others that represent similar features. We

C. Ryan et al. (Eds.): EuroGP 2003, LNCS 2610, pp. 194–203, 2003.

note several previous attempts to improve the effectiveness of crossover which, either implicitly or explicitly, try to better preserve homology, see [6][10][12][15].

The way individuals are represented in Evolutionary Computation is always crucial, this is also the case in GP. The emergence of GP in the scientific community arose with the use, *inter alia*, of a tree-based representation, in particular with the use of Lisp in the work of Koza [9]. However, GP systems manipulating linear structures exist, like in [3][14], which have shown experimental performances equivalent to Tree GP (TGP). In contrast to TGP, Linear GP (LGP) programs are sequence of instructions of an imperative language (C, machine code, ...). In this paper, we focus on LGP mainly because it allows direct access to instructions and so it provides easier way to perform recombination. Moreover, in LGP all possible sequences of instructions are valid programs, so there are no syntactical constraints on sequences swapped during recombination and classical genetic crossover operators in use could be chosen.

In Section 2, we introduce a new biologically inspired crossover for LGP, called Maximum Homologous Crossover (MHC). In order to study the way MHC works in Section 3 we introduce Royal Road Landscapes for LGP and report experimental results in Section 4.

2 Maximum Homologous Crossover

In this section, we present a new recombination mechanism mimicking natural crossover by preserving homology. In biology, homology indicates genetic relationship, i.e. the structural relatedness of genomes due to descent from common form. Indeed, reproduction in nature is a smooth process which ensures that offspring will not be so different from ancestors, allowing the structural stability that defines species.

2.1 Edit Distance

The Maximum Homologous Crossover (MHC) preserves structural and lexical homology by computing an alignment that minimises a metric of dissimilarity between parents. As a metric, we use string edit distance, like *Levenshtein distance* [11] which has been already used in GP to compute or control diversity [4], or to study the influence of genetic operators [13]. By definition, the edit distance between two programs corresponds to the minimal number of elementary operations (deletion, insertion and substitution) required to change one program into the other.

More formally, let us consider $P_x \in P_\Sigma$ a program of size m such that $P_x = x_0 x_1 \ldots x_{m-1}$, with $x_i \in \Sigma\ \forall i \in [0, m-1]$, where Σ is a finite set of available instructions[1]. Let P_x and P_y be two programs of size m and n respectively and ε be an empty instruction. An alignment $(\overline{P}_x, \overline{P}_y)$ of size p with $\overline{P}_x$ and $\overline{P}_y \in P_\Sigma \cup \{\varepsilon\}$ is:

[1] In LGP, the traditional distinction between the set of terminals and the set of functions is not relevant.

$$(\overline{P}_x, \overline{P}_y) = \begin{pmatrix} \overline{x}_0\, \overline{x}_1 \ldots\, \overline{x}_{p-1} \\ \overline{y}_0\, \overline{y}_1 \ldots\, \overline{y}_{p-1} \end{pmatrix}$$

where:

- $p \in [max(n,m), n+m]$
- $\overline{x}_i = x_j$ or $\overline{x}_i = \varepsilon$ for $i \in [0, p-1]$ and $j \in [0, m-1]$
- $\overline{y}_i = y_j$ or $\overline{y}_i = \varepsilon$ for $i \in [0, p-1]$ and $j \in [0, n-1]$
- $\nexists\, i \in [0, p-1]$ such that $\overline{x}_i = \overline{y}_i = \varepsilon$

An aligned pair of instructions $\binom{\overline{x}_i}{\overline{y}_i}$ indicates either a substitution of x_j by y_j, or a deletion of x_j (if $\overline{y}_i = \varepsilon$), or an insertion of y_j (if $\overline{x}_i = \varepsilon$). So, an alignment $(\overline{P}_x, \overline{P}_y)$ may also be viewed as a sequence of operations (insertion, deletion and substitution) that transforms P_x into P_y.

We define the cost χ of an alignment such as $\chi(\overline{P}_x, \overline{P}_y) = \sum_{i=0}^{p-1} cost(\overline{x}_i, \overline{y}_i)$ with:

$$cost(\overline{x}_i, \overline{y}_i) = \begin{cases} C_1 \text{ (insertion or deletion cost) if} & \overline{x}_i = \varepsilon \text{ or } \overline{y}_i = \varepsilon \\ C_2 \text{ (substitution cost)} & \text{else if } \overline{x}_i \neq \overline{y}_i \\ 0 & \text{else} \end{cases}$$

and $A(P_x, P_y)$ the set of all alignments of P_x and P_y, then the distance between P_x and P_y is:

$$\mathcal{D}(P_x, P_y) = min\{\chi(\overline{P}_x, \overline{P}_y) | (\overline{P}_x, \overline{P}_y) \in A(P_x, P_y)\}$$

As an example, in Figure 1, the distance between P_x and P_y is 7, i.e. 7 operations are required to transform P_x into P_y (5 insertions, 1 deletion and 1 substitution). Each column of the alignment $(\overline{P}_x, \overline{P}_y)$ refers to a program and stores a sequence of instructions with gaps inserted (corresponding to ε). Note that, during the alignment process, numerical constants of P_x and P_y are viewed as a same type of instruction.

2.2 Best Alignment and Recombination

A best alignment $(\overline{P}_x, \overline{P}_y)$ between P_x and P_y is that for which $\chi(\overline{P}_x, \overline{P}_y) = \mathcal{D}(P_x, P_y)$ holds. We denote $A^*(P_x, P_y)$ the set of all best alignments between P_x and P_y. Computation of $A^*(P_x, P_y)$ can be reasonably performed, using dynamic programming in $O(nm)$ time complexity. Such an algorithm [8] has also been used to align DNA strings in Bio-Informatics.

In order to perform MHC between P_x and P_y, only one alignment $(\overline{P}_x, \overline{P}_y)$ is randomly chosen in A^*. Recombination between $\overline{P}_x$ and $\overline{P}_y$ can then take place. Since $\overline{P}_x$ and $\overline{P}_y$ have the same length, classical crossovers existing in Genetic Algorithms (GA) can be performed (1-point, 2-point, uniform, ...). Finally, to get valid children, the ε symbols are removed.

By choosing the costs of operations, C_1 and C_2, we can define two sets A_1^*, A_2^* of best alignments:

P_x	P_y
DIV	X
SUB	COS
ADD	DIV
X	ADD
0.56	-1
MUL	SUB
	X
	-0.10
	DIV
	SIN

$\overset{1}{\Longrightarrow}$

$(\overline{P}_x, \overline{P}_y)$	
ε	X
ε	COS
DIV	DIV
ε	ADD
ε	-1
SUB	SUB
ADD	ε
X	X
0.56	-0.10
MUL	DIV
ε	SIN

$\overset{2}{\Longrightarrow}$

$Xo(\overline{P}_x, \overline{P}_y)$	
ε	X
ε	COS
DIV	DIV
ε	ADD
-1	ε
SUB	SUB
ε	ADD
X	X
-0.10	0.56
DIV	MUL
SIN	ε

$\overset{3}{\Longrightarrow}$

P'_x	P'_y
DIV	X
-1	COS
SUB	DIV
X	ADD
-0.10	SUB
DIV	ADD
SIN	X
	0.56
	MUL

Fig. 1. 1-point MHC_1 of P_x and P_y in stack based representation: Step 1, alignment and Xover site selection (here 5); Step 2, swapping sequences; Step 3, deletion of gaps.

- A_1^*, with C_2=C_1=1, where a substitution is always preferred to a pair of insertion and deletion. This setting is used to compute *Levenshtein distance.*
- A_2^*, with C_2=2 and C_1=1, where a substitution is chosen as often as a pair of insertion and deletion.

We denote MHC_1 and MHC_2, the corresponding variants of MHC.

Figure 1 gives a 1-point MHC_1 with the recombination site at position 5 between P_x and P_y in stack-based representation, producing offspring P'_x and P'_y.

2.3 Features of Maximum Homologous Crossover

We note that offspring produced with MHC could also be obtained using standard LGP crossover. Indeed, MHC only restricts the choice of possible crossover sites in both parents: for example in Figure 1, numerical constants 0.56 from P_x and -0.10 from P_y corresponds to the same crossover site in alignment $(\overline{P}_x, \overline{P}_y)$, then they could not appear together in children. Moreover, MHC modifies the probability of sites selection according to the local homology of parents. In previous example, the alignment $(\overline{P}_x, \overline{P}_y)$ gives a probability 3/11 to the sequence 'DIV, SUB' in P_x to be broken. Without alignment, this probability was only 1/6. This particular behaviour increases disruption rate of the less homologous regions (like 'DIV, SUB'), where many gaps are present, since they are more involved in sites selection. On the other hand, most homologous regions are more rarely disrupted.

An interesting property of MHC, is that the more similar the parents are to each other, the more similar the offspring are to their parents; in other words, the distance between parents and offspring are always smaller than distance between parents. We have found experimentally, by performing MHC between randomly generated programs that $\mathcal{D}(P_z, P_x) + \mathcal{D}(P_z, P_y) = \mathcal{D}(P_x, P_y)$, with P_x, $P_y \in P_\Sigma$ and $P_z \in \{MHC(P_x, P_y)\}$. Thus, we can assert that MHC performs more like GA crossover than standard LGP crossover, since it is a global search operator at the beginning of the evolutionary process, and becomes more local as the population diversity falls (decrease of distance).

3 Royal Road Landscapes for LGP

In GA, Royal Road landscapes (RR) were originally designed to describe how building blocks are combined to produce fitter and fitter solutions and to investigate how the schemata evolution actually takes place [7]. Little work is related to RR in GP; e.g. the Royal Tree Problem [16] which is an attempt to develop a benchmark for GP and which has been used in Clergue et al. [5] to study problem difficulty. Moreover there is nothing relevant for LGP.

Our aim is to examine in depth MHC's behaviour during evolution in order to quantify how it preserves homology and under what conditions. To achieve this goal, we need experiments able to highlight the destructive (or constructive) effects of crossover on building blocks. So we propose a new kind of fitness landscapes, called Royal Road landscapes for LGP, which have to be seen as preliminary steps in MHC understanding.

To define RR, we have choose a family of optimal programs and we break them into a set of small building blocks. The set of optima is:

$$O_{RR} = \{P_x \in P_\Sigma \mid \forall s \in \Sigma,\, B_K(P_x, s)\}$$

with:

$$B_K(P_x, s) = \begin{cases} true & \text{if } \exists i \in [0, m-K] \mid \forall k \in [0, K-1],\, x_{i+k} = s \\ false & \text{else} \end{cases}$$

and N the size of Σ, K the size of blocks, and x_{i+k} the $i+k$ instructions of P_x, a program of size m. The following program $P \in P_\Sigma$ is an example of RR optimum, with $N = 4$ and $K = 3$:

$$P = \mathbf{DDD}BCA\mathbf{BBB}BDD\mathbf{AAACCC}BCCC$$

with $\Sigma = \{A, B, C, D\}$. Thus, a block is a contiguous sequence of a single instruction, and only the presence of a block is taken into account in fitness evaluation (neither the position or repetition). The number of blocks corresponds to the number of instructions $s \in \Sigma$ for which the predicate $B_K(P_x, s)$ is true. In P, we only boldfaced sequences that contribute to fitness[2]. We have arbitrarily fixed the worst possible fitness[3] to F_w for programs having no blocks. In RR the contribution of each block is simply F_w/N and so, the standard fitness $\mathcal{F}(P_x)$ with P_x having n blocks is $\mathcal{F}(P_x) = F_w - n \times F_w/N$.

To efficiently reach an optimum in RR landscapes, a GP system has to create and combine blocks without breaking existing structures. RR were designed so that fitness degradation due to crossover occurs only when recombination sites are chosen inside blocks but never in case of blocks translocations or concatenations. In other words, there is no inter blocks epistasy in RR.

[2] Altough the last sequence of 'C' instruction in P is a valid block, it doesn't contribute to fitness since it is only a repetition.

[3] Actual fitness value does not matter since we use tournament selection.

4 Experimental Results

4.1 Setup

We want to compare effectiveness of two different recombination operators, the standard LGP 1-point crossover (SC) and the 1-point MHC, which have very distinct behaviours, that is why the search for the best tuning of evolutionary parameters is necessary. We have performed, on our own LGP system, 35 independent runs with various mutation and crossover rates. Let us notice that a mutation rate of 0.9 means that each program involved in reproduction has a 0.9 probability to undergo one insertion, one deletion and one substitution. The population of 1000 individuals was randomly created according to a maximum creation size of 50 and a set of N (depending on problem definition) available instructions. The evolution, with elitism, maximum program size of 100, 10-tournament selection, and steady-state replacement, took place during 400 generations. We used a T-test with 95% confidence to determine if results were significantly different.

4.2 Homology Driven Fitness Problem

We introduce the Homology Driven Fitness problem (HDF), where the fitness of a candidate program is given by its distance (homology) to a randomly chosen optimum of a given size. HDF matches the unitation problem or One-Max problem, which is known to be easier to handle using a GA than using a steepest ascent hill-climber.

We perform experiments on HDF with N=16 and size of optimum fixed to 80. Figure 2 shows that the increase of crossover rate improves the average fitness of best program found on HDF with MHC. In contrast, the use of SC decreases performance even with a small application rate. We find for both crossover operators that the best mutation rate is 0.3. Figure 3 gives evolution of the average fitness of the best program found using the best tuning of parameters found. Using MHC, the optimal program is found at generation 50 in more than 90% of runs, whereas with SC the percentage falls to 28%. This empirical results confirm that, in terms of its dynamics, MHC performs more like crossover in GA than SC.

4.3 Royal Road Landscape

Table 1 gives results on RR with N=8, 10, 16 for SC, MHC_1, and MHC_2. The average number of blocks found shows that the problem difficulty increases with N, which is to be expected, because of a smaller probability of block discovery and a stronger constraint due to size limitation (for N=16 optimum length is 80% of maximum allowed size). In this case, the best tuning of mutation rate is 0.9. For all N, MHC_2 is the best of the three crossovers, whereas MHC_1 gives surprisingly poor results even whith N=8 (convergence speed). Then, we see that using MHC_2, LGP performs better with high recombination rates, see also

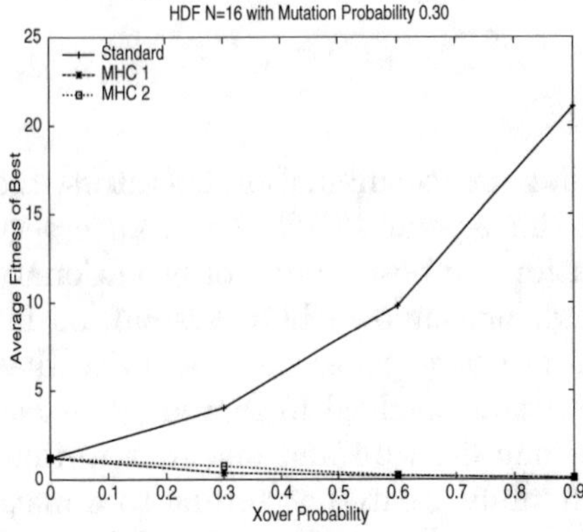

Fig. 2. Average fitness of best as a function of the crossover rate on HDF N=16 and size of optimum 80 at generation 50.

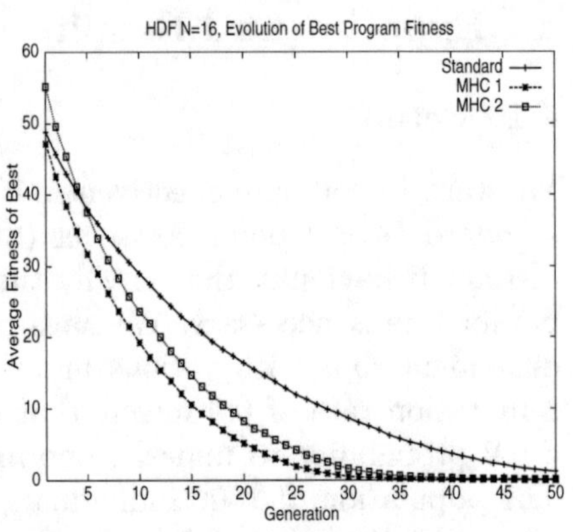

Fig. 3. Evolution of average fitness of best on HDF N=16 and size of optimum 80 with the best crossover rate found and mutation rate 0.3.

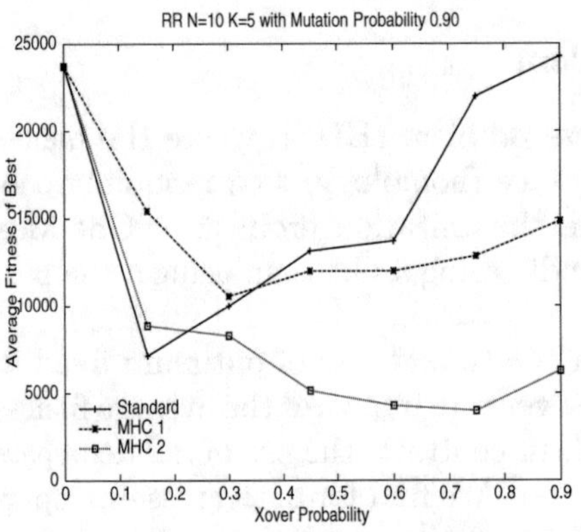

Fig. 4. Average fitness of best as a function of the crossover rate on RR N=16 and K=5.

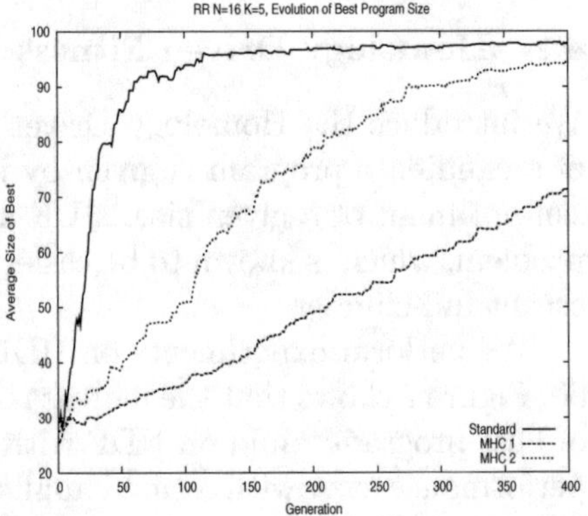

Fig. 5. Evolution of average size of best on RR N=16 and K=5 with the best crossover rate found and mutation rate 0.9.

Figure 4. Figure 5 reports evolution of average size of the best. Let us notice that the bloat phenomenon is strongly reduced with MHC. In the case of MHC_1, the size of the best increases too slowly to reach size of optimum (at least 80 instructions) in 400 generations.

In what follow, we say that a crossover event is selectively Advantageous (noted A), when at least one child outperforms both parents. We say that a crossover event is selectively Deleterious (noted D), when both parents outperforms children. Other crossover events are said selectively Neutral (noted N). Table 2 reports the frequency of such crossover events. We observe, for N=8 and N=16, that D events prevail with SC and that their frequency is dramatically reduced using MHC. Moreover, we notice a significant increase in the number of

Table 1. Best results found on RR.

Xover Type	Best Xover Rate	Best Mut. Rate	Avg. Best Fitness	Succes Rate	Avg. Generations	Avg. Number of Blocks
$N = 8$ and $K = 5$						
SC	0.45	0.9	$0_{(\sigma=0)}$	1.0	$146.6_{(\sigma=82.7)}$	8.00
MHC 1	0.75	0.9	$0_{(\sigma=0)}$	1.0	$206.0_{(\sigma=94.4)}$	8.00
MHC 2	1.0	0.9	$0_{(\sigma=0)}$	1.0	$126.2_{(\sigma=42.4)}$	8.00
$N = 10$ and $K = 5$						
SC	0.15	0.9	$7142_{(\sigma=7928)}$	0.31	$297.6_{(\sigma=73.4)}$	9.28
MHC 1	0.3	0.9	$10571_{(\sigma=7537)}$	0.22	$318.3_{(\sigma=68.4)}$	8.94
MHC 2	0.75	0.9	$4000_{(\sigma=5993)}$	0.62	$283.0_{(\sigma=71.8)}$	9.60
$N = 16$ and $K = 5$						
SC	0.15	0.9	$54462_{(\sigma=6705)}$	0	-	7.25
MHC 1	0.3	0.9	$58214_{(\sigma=6971)}$	0	-	6.68
MHC 2	0.45	0.9	$48928_{(\sigma=6423)}$	0	-	8.11

Table 2. Frequency of Deleterious, Neutral and Advantageous crossovers on RR.

	$N = 8$ and $K = 5$			$N = 16$ and $K = 5$		
Xover Type	D	N	A	D	N	A
SC	79.47	20.43	0.09	76.12	23.78	0.08
MHC 1	9.21	90.68	0.09	7.44	93.33	0.21
MHC 2	3.22	96.61	0.15	2.62	96.95	0.41

A events, when MHC is used. In Figure 6, we have plotted these frequencies as a function of the average number of blocks in parents. We see that with SC, the frequency of D events increases linearly with the number of blocks so that the SC becomes massively disruptive at the end of the evolutionary process. On the other hand, the frequency of the various events is approximately constant; it is a nearly neutral operator. The Building Blocks Hypothesis (BBH) exists in GP and states that good building blocks in individuals can be combined into even larger and better building blocks to form better individuals. However, SC works against the hypothesis since it tends to break high order blocks. As for MHC, it seems to be able to preserve and combine blocks, even when they represent the main part of the genome, as in RR with N=16 and K=5, where 80 instructions (over 100 potential) of an individual are useful.

5 Conclusion and Perspectives

A better understanding of the role of crossover, together with the improvement of its contribution to the overall performances, is a necessary search for GP. Standard crossover, that blindly swaps parts of parents, should be considered more like a macro mutation operator.

Considering the HDF problem, which should be viewed as a One-Max problem for LGP, we show that the standard crossover prevents the formation of

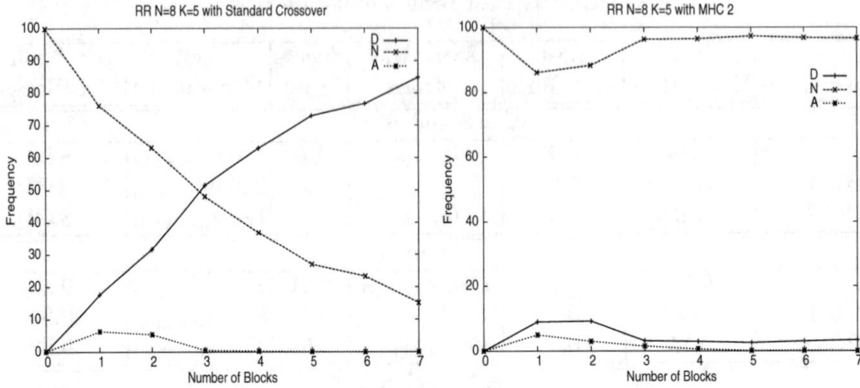

Fig. 6. RR with N=8 and K=5: Frequency of Deleterious, Neutral and Advantageous crossovers according to the number of blocks.

fitter individuals: as increasing its rate, the performances of the algorithm decrease. Blocks disruption can be studied with Royal Road landscapes. Indeed, to be efficiently treated, this problem imposes the preservation of the blocks during evolution. An insight into the disruption rate indicates that it is not the case, since children have less blocks than their worst parent in around 80% of crossover applications.

In our point of view, efficiency requires that crossover, as with GA, behaves like a recombination operator. That is the reason why we introduce the Maximum Homologous Crossover. This operator tends to keep safe similar regions of the parents, in order to favour a kind of "respect" property (the common features of the parents are present in children). MHC_2 operator gives expected results on Royal Road landscapes.

The Royal Road problem is far from real GP problems, at least for two reasons: firstly, there is no inter blocks epistasy and secondly, the relative position of blocks does not matter in the evaluation process. That is why we consider this contribution as a preliminary step to study MHC behaviour. Future work should introduce epistasy and block location, before addressing classical benchmarks and real problems, like Symbolic Regression and the Even-Parity problems.

References

1. Lee Altenberg. The evolution of evolvability in genetic programming. In *Advances in Genetic Programming*. MIT Press, 1994.
2. P. J. Angeline. Subtree crossover: Building block engine or macromutation ? In *Genetic Programming 1997: Proceedings of the Second Annual Conference*. Morgan Kaufmann, July 1997.
3. Markus Brameier and Wolfgang Banzhaf. A comparison of linear genetic programming and neural networks in medical data mining. *IEEE Transactions on Evolutionary Computation*, 5(1):17–26, 2001.

4. Markus Brameier and Wolfgang Bhanzhaf. Explicit control of diversity and effective variation distance in linear genetic programming, 2001.
5. Manuel Clergue, Philippe Collard, Marco Tomassini, and Leonardo Vanneschi. Fitness distance correlation and problem difficulty for genetic programming. In *GECCO 2002: Proceedings of the Genetic and Evolutionary Computation Conference*, pages 724–732, New York, 9-13 July 2002. Morgan Kaufmann Publishers.
6. Patrik D'haeseleer. Context preserving crossover in genetic programming. In *Proceedings of the 1994 IEEE World Congress on Computational Intelligence*, volume 1, pages 256–261, Orlando, Florida, USA, 27-29 1994. IEEE Press.
7. Stephanie Forrest and Melanie Mitchell. Relative building-block fitness and the building-block hypothesis. In *Foundation of Genetic Algorithms 2*, pages 109–126. Morgan Kaufman, 1993.
8. D. Gusfield. *Algorithms on Strings, Tree and Sequences.* Cambridge University Press, 1997.
9. J. Koza. Genetic programming - on the programming of computers by means of natural selection. Nature, 1993.
10. W. B. Langdon. Size fair and homologous tree genetic programming crossovers. In *Proceedings of the Genetic and Evolutionary Computation Conference*, volume 2, pages 1092–1097, Orlando, Florida, USA, 13-17 July 1999. Morgan Kaufmann.
11. V. I. Levenshtein. Binary codes capable of correcting deletions, insertions, and reversals. Soviet Physics-Doklady, 1966.
12. Peter Nordin, Wolfgang Banzhaf, and Frank D. Francone. Efficient evolution of machine code for CISC architectures using instruction blocks and homologous crossover. In *Advances in Genetic Programming 3*, chapter 12, pages 275–299. MIT Press, Cambridge, MA, USA, June 1999.
13. U. O'Reilly. Using a distance metric on genetic programs to understand genetic operators, 1997.
14. Tim Perkis. Stack-based genetic programming. In *Proceedings of the 1994 IEEE World Congress on Computational Intelligence*, volume 1, pages 148–153, Orlando, Florida, USA, 27-29 1994. IEEE Press.
15. Riccardo Poli and W. B. Langdon. Genetic programming with one-point crossover. In *Soft Computing in Engineering Design and Manufacturing*, pages 180–189. Springer-Verlag London, 23-27 June 1997.
16. William F. Punch, Douglas Zongker, and Erik D. Goodman. The royal tree problem, a benchmark for single and multiple population genetic programming. In *Advances in Genetic Programming 2*, chapter 15, pages 299–316. MIT Press, Cambridge, MA, USA, 1996.
17. R.E. Keller W. Banzhaf, P. Nordin and F.D. Francone. *Genetic Programming - An Introduction.* Morgan Kaufmann, 1998.

A Simple but Theoretically-Motivated Method to Control Bloat in Genetic Programming

Riccardo Poli

Department of Computer Science, University of Essex

Abstract. This paper presents a simple method to control bloat which is based on the idea of strategically and dynamically creating fitness "holes" in the fitness landscape which repel the population. In particular we create holes by zeroing the fitness of a certain proportion of the offspring that have above average length. Unlike other methods where all individuals are penalised when length constraints are violated, here we randomly penalise only a fixed proportion of all the constraint-violating offspring. The paper describes the theoretical foundation for this method and reports the results of its empirical validation with two relatively hard test problems, which has confirmed the effectiveness of the approach.

1 Introduction

The study of bloat, or code growth, has been one of the most active areas of Genetic Programming (GP) research over the last 10 years [2,18,20,31,26,17,9,13,11,16,30]. To date several theories propose to at least partially explain bloat. For the sake of brevity here we will briefly review only some of them.

The replication accuracy theory [18,2,20] is based on the idea that an important component of the success of a GP individual is its ability to reproduce accurately, i.e., have offspring that are functionally similar to the parent. This would suggest that a GP system will evolve towards representations that increase replication accuracy, all other things being equal. One way this can happen in GP is through the evolution of large blocks of inactive code.

The removal bias theory [29,17] is based on the observation that the inactive code in a GP tree tends to be in the lower parts of the tree and therefore forms smaller-than-average subtrees. Crossover events which excise one of such inactive subtrees will produce offspring with exactly the same fitness as (one of) their parents. But because, on average, the inserted subtree is bigger than the excised one, the offspring will tend to be bigger then their parents. Towards the end of a run (when producing improved individuals is difficult), when an active node is hit by crossover, the offspring will be worse than their parents more often than not. Therefore, these offspring will tend not to survive. As a result, offspring produced by neutral crossover events will make the biggest contribution to the new generation, but because they are on average bigger than their parents, this will lead to bloat.

The nature of program search spaces theory [17] is based on the experimental observation (later corroborated by strong theoretical evidence [16, Chapter 8]) that, for a variety of test problems (e.g., [15,9]), above a certain problem dependent size, the

C. Ryan et al. (Eds.): EuroGP 2003, LNCS 2610, pp. 204–217, 2003.

distribution of fitnesses does not vary a great deal with the size of the programs. Since there are more long programs, the number of long programs of a given fitness is greater than the number of short programs of the same fitness. Thus, over time GP will sample longer and longer programs simply because there are more of them.

In recent work [19], [23] a quantitative framework has been proposed within which other, more qualitative theories of bloat could be included. Because this is the starting point for the method for bloat control we propose in this paper, we will devote a later section to this theory and its implications. Before we do that, we want to summarise some of the main techniques for limiting code bloat proposed in the literature.

One of the first and most widely used methods to control bloat is to set a fixed limit on the size or depth of the programs [8]. Programs exceeding the limit are discarded and a parent is kept instead. This technique may be effective at limiting code bloat but has various drawbacks. For example, the limit can interfere with searches once the average program size approaches the size limit [4,14]. Also, this approach gives an undesirable evolutionary advantage to individuals which are likely to produce offspring violating the depth limit. Effectively programs closer to the size/depth threshold will start replicating faster than shorter programs with the same fitness. So, once programs start hitting the threshold, the threshold will start acting as an attractor for the population and will often *cause the population to bloat* until it reaches the threshold. A better alternative is to give a zero fitness to the offspring of above-threshold size. This prevents them from being used to create the next generation.

In the parsimony pressure method a term is added to the fitness function which penalises larger programs, thereby encouraging the evolution of smaller solutions. Commonly the penalty is a simple linear function of the solution size, but other approaches have also been used [6,31,1]. Some studies have shown a degradation in performance when parsimony pressure is used [7,20]. Recent research suggests that the effect of parsimony pressure depends on the magnitude of the parsimony function relative to the size-fitness distribution of the population [26,28].

Another approach to reducing code bloat has been to modify the basic operators. One can, for example, vary the rate of crossover (and mutation) to counter the evolutionary pressure towards protective code [25], vary the selection probability of crossover points by using explicitly defined introns [21], or negate destructive crossover events [27,22,5]. Each of these approaches has the goal of reducing the evolutionary importance of inactive code. Another alternative is to use the class of size-controlling operators defined in [10,12].

A recent idea to combat bloat is the use of strategies borrowed from the field of multi-objective optimisation [3,24]. The idea is to consider fitness as one objective and size as a second one. Then it is possible to modify selection to use the Pareto non-domination criterion, thereby giving a reproductive advantage to shorter programs everything else being equal.

Many of the techniques proposed to combat bloat, as noted in [17], are *ad hoc*, preceding rather than following from knowledge of the causes of bloat. In this paper we will present a very simple technique to control bloat, which is, however, a direct result of a theoretical analysis of bloat. The paper is organised as follows: in Section 2 we review the theoretical results which form the basis for this technique, in Section 3 we present our method to control bloat, in Section 4 we describe the experiments we performed to assess the performance of the method, and, finally in Section 5 we draw some conclusions.

2 Background

As reported in [23] the expected mean size of the programs at generation $t+1$, $E[\mu(t+1)]$, in a GP system *with* a symmetric subtree-swapping crossover operator in the absence of mutation can be expressed as

$$E[\mu(t+1)] = \sum_l N(G_l)p(G_l,t). \tag{1}$$

where l is an enumeration of all the possible program shapes, G_l is the set of programs with the l-th shape, $N(G_l)$ is the number of nodes in programs in G_l and $p(G_l,t)$ is the probability of selecting a program of shape G_l from the population at generation t.

This indicates that for symmetric subtree-swapping crossover operators the mean program size evolves *as if* selection only was acting on the population. This means that if there is a variation in mean size, like for example in the presence of bloat, that can only be attributed to some form of positive or negative selective pressure on some or all the shapes G_l. This can be readily seen by noting that the mean size of the individuals in the population at time t can be written as

$$\mu(t) = \sum_l N(G_l)\Phi(G_l,t) \tag{2}$$

where $\Phi(G_l,t)$ is the proportion of individuals of shape G_l in the population at time t. Direct comparison of Equations 1 and 2 tells us that there can be a change in mean program length only if

$$E[\mu(t+1) - \mu(t)] = \sum_l N(G_l)(p(G_l,t) - \Phi(G_l,t)) \neq 0.$$

Obviously, this can only happen if the selection probability $p(G_l,t)$ is different from the proportion $\Phi(G_l,t)$ for at least some l. So, because $\sum_l p(G_l,t) = 1$ and also $\sum_l \Phi(G_l,t) = 1$, for bloat to happen there will have to be some short G_l's for which $p(G_l,t) < \Phi(G_l,t)$ and also some longer G_l's for which $p(G_l,t) > \Phi(G_l,t)$ (at least on average). The condition $p(G_l,t) > \Phi(G_l,t)$, e.g., implies that there must be some members of G_l which have an above average fitness.

Starting from the results summarised above, in [19] we studied the behaviour of a linear GP system both in the absence and in the presence of fitness. Particularly relevant for this paper was the case where we can assume that the fitness function only has two values, 1 and $1+\hat{f}$. If $\{B_y\}$ is a set of linear GP programs of uniform fitness $1+\hat{f}$ (which we will call a "hole" or a "spike" depending on the sign of $\hat{f}$) , and the rest of the search space has fitness 1, then for standard crossover, no mutation, fitness proportionate selection, and for "holes", i.e., $\hat{f} < 0$, we have

$$\mu(\{B_y\},t) > \mu(t) \Longleftrightarrow E[\mu(t+1)] < \mu(t)$$
$$\mu(\{B_y\},t) < \mu(t) \Longleftrightarrow E[\mu(t+1)] > \mu(t),$$

where $\mu(\{B_y\}, t)$ is the mean length of the programs in $\{B_y\}$. (The converse is true for "spikes".) Thus if the fitness of the B_y is better than the fitness of the rest of the search space, the average size of the population will move *towards* the average size of the B_y. If, on the other hand, the fitness of the B_y is worse than the fitness of the rest of the search space, then the average size of the population will move *away from* the average size of the B_y. This observation made us suggest that the creation of artificial fitness holes might be a viable mechanisms to control bloat — a mechanism, however, which was never precisely defined nor tested.

3 The Tarpeian Method to Control Bloat

The results with the "holes" landscapes reported in the previous section suggest that if one could create artificial holes in areas of the search space which we want to avoid, like for example those containing long, bloated programs, then evolution would try to stay away from those areas. This is effectively what happens already in some methods to control bloat. For example, if one zeroes the fitness of individuals which are longer or deeper than a fixed threshold, this corresponds to creating a large fitness hole which discourages the population from getting too close to the threshold. The use of a parsimony pressure reducing the fitness of individuals proportionally to their size also corresponds to creating a hole in the fitness landscape: the only difference being that the hole has smooth, sloping edges.

Here we propose a method of controlling bloat based on the notion of creating fitness holes, but where, unlike previous methods, the holes are created dynamically and non-deterministically. We will call this the *Tarpeian method* to control bloat, from the Tarpeian Rock in Rome, which in Roman times was the infamous execution place for traitors and criminals. They would be led to its top and then hurled down. The similarity is that, in this method to control bloat, some otherwise normally fit individuals, which are, however, excessively big (and, therefore, traitors), are effectively killed by pushing them down into a fitness hole (the rock's base).

Before we introduce the method in more detail, we want to rewrite $E[\mu(t+1)-\mu(t)]$ in a form that will allow us to justify the idea of controlling bloat with fitness holes also for the case of fitness functions with more than two values. Let us start by splitting the set of all possible program shapes $\{G_l\}$ into three subsets: $G_< = \{G_l : N(G_l) < \mu(t)\}$, $G_= = \{G_l : N(G_l) = \mu(t)\}$ and $G_> = \{G_l : N(G_l) > \mu(t)\}$. Then observe that $\mu(t) = \sum_l \mu(t)p(G_l, t)$ since $\sum_l p(G_l, t) = 1$. Therefore, we have

$$E[\mu(t+1) - \mu(t)] = \sum_{g\in G_<} (N(g) - \mu(t))p(g,t) + \sum_{g\in G_=} \underbrace{(N(g) - \mu(t))}_{=0} p(g,t) + \sum_{g\in G_>} (N(g) - \mu(t))p(g,t).$$

Thus, the mean program size will be expected to grow if

$$\sum_{g\in G_>} (N(g) - \mu(t))p(g,t) > \sum_{g\in G_<} (\mu(t) - N(g))p(g,t).$$

So, clearly in order to prevent bloat, one needs to either decrease the selection probability $p(g,t)$ for the programs that are bigger than average or increase $p(g,t)$ for the programs of below-average size, or both. In this paper we will explore the former idea. (Note, however, that whenever one modifies artificially the selection probability for a part of the population, unavoidably the selection probability for the rest of the population will also be affected. This is because selection probabilities add up to 1.)

In either case, one needs to act on the selection component of the GP system. Reducing the selection probability of a set of programs with specific features does not mean, however, to reduce the selection probability of *all* the programs in the set nor to do so *deterministically*, which is exactly what most methods to reduce bloat do (with the notable exception of Ekart's Pareto-based selection [3]). All is needed is to reduce the selection probability of *some* of the individuals in the set *some of the time*. This can be done by directly changing the fitness of the those individuals, or indirectly like in [3].

In the Tarpeian method we randomly select a fixed proportion of the individuals in the population among those whose size is above the current average program size and we set their fitness to the lowest possible value available. This effectively means that those individuals will not be used to create the next generations (and therefore it is as if they had been killed), except in very pathological conditions.

All it is needed to implement the Tarpeian method is a wrapper for the fitness function like the one in the following algorithm, were n is an integer ($n \geq 2$) indicating how frequently the algorithm kills longer-than-average individuals for the purpose of creating a bloat-controlling fitness hole, $1/n$ being the proportion of individuals belonging to the hole:

```
// Tarpeian wrapper
IF size(program) > average_pop_size AND random_int MOD n = 0
THEN return( very_low_fitness ); ELSE return( fitness(program));
```

An important feature of this algorithm is that it does not require *a priori* knowledge of the size of the potential solutions to a problem. If programs need to grow in order to improve fitness, the Tarpeian method will not prevent this. It will occasionally kill some individuals that, *if evaluated*, would result in being fitter than average and this may slow down a little the progress of a run. However, because the wrapper *does not* evaluate the individuals killed, very little computation is wasted. Even at a high anti-bloat intensity (e.g., when $n = 2$) a better-than-average longer-than-average individual has still a good chance of making it into the population. If enough individuals of this kind are produced (w.r.t. the individuals which are better-than-average but also shorter-than-average), eventually the average size of the programs in the population may grow. However, this growth will still be under control because the Tarpeian method will immediately move the fitness hole so as to discourage further growth. Typically as a run progresses finding individuals with higher-than-average fitness becomes harder and harder. Then, the pressure of the last fitness hole created by the Tarpeian wrapper will make the population shrink. The effect of the parameter n is not to directly determine the maximum allowed size of the programs in the population. It determines the intensity of the repulsive force exerted by the fitness hole. Once the hole has been jumped, the algorithm recreates one of exactly the same repulsive intensity. That is, the pressure to shrink does not go up as does in the parsimony pressure method. This means that the algorithm will allow growth as long as this is associated to fitness improvements.

A good metaphor to understand the differences between the Tarpeian method and standard parsimony pressure is to imagine that height over the sea level corresponds to the average population size in a GP run and that the population is like a hot air balloon which is free to fly as high as its content of hot air will allow. Then parsimony pressure behaves like a long elastic band which connects the balloon to earth. The balloon will fly higher and higher, but eventually the force exerted by the elastic band will stop it. The Tarpeian method instead is more similar to gravity, it will not prevent the going up of the balloon. However, gravity is always there waiting for the forces which push up the balloon to weaken. When they do, and they appear to often do this in GP, it makes the balloon go down.

4 Experimental Result

To test the Tarpeian algorithm we have considered two problems: the even 10 parity function (which we will call *Even-10* in the following) and a symbolic regression problem (which we will call *Poly-10*) where the target function is the 10-variate cubic polynomial $x_1x_2+x_3x_4+x_5x_6+x_1x_7x_9+x_3x_6x_{10}$. These problems were chosen because, when attacked with small to medium size populations, they are sufficiently hard to induce a period of slow fitness improvement, which normally induces some form of bloat. The second problem was also chosen because in continuous symbolic regression problems, such as this, code growth may be in part attributed to improvements of the fit between the data and the model.

In the experiments we used a symmetric subtree swapping crossover operator in which crossover points in the two parents were chosen independently and with uniform probability. For both problems the terminal set included only the variables x_1 through to x_{10}. The function set for Even-10 included the boolean functions AND, OR, NOR, NAND, XOR, EQ and NOT. Fitness was the number of entries of the even parity 10 truth table correctly reproduced. For Poly-10 the function set included +, -, * and a form of protected division which returns the numerator if the magnitude of the denominator is smaller than 0.001. Fitness was minus the sum of the absolute values of the errors made over 50 fitness cases. These were generated by randomly assigning values to the variables x_i in the range [-1,1] and then feeding such values in the cubic polynomial mentioned above. In both cases the population was initialised with the standard GROW method with maximum depth 6. The average program sizes at generation 0 were around 10.3 and 13.1 for Even-10 and Poly-10, respectively. Tournament selection was used (with tournament sizes of 2, 5 and 10). Populations sizes of 100, 500, 1000, 5000 were used. Runs lasted 100 generations and were not stopped even if a 100% solution had been found. In the runs with Tarpeian bloat control, on average we reduced the fitness of 1 in n above-average-size individuals, with $n = 2, 3, 5, 10$ and 20. For the even parity problem the reduced fitness was 0, while for the polynomial regression this was -10^{20}. For each parameter setting we performed 30 independent runs.

One may have very different objectives when running a GP system, like for example: (a) obtaining one highly fit solution, (b) obtaining a number of highly fit solutions, (c) obtaining highly fit solutions (like in (a) or (b)) which are also very concise, (d) obtaining highly fit solutions (like in (a) or (b)) as quickly as possible, (e) obtaining highly fit solutions (like in (a) or (b)), which are as concise as possible as quickly as possible. In this paper, our objective is to achieve (a) and (d), although as a side effect of (d) we also indirectly get (c). So, in our analyses we will focus on the highest fitness individual in each generation and on the average size of the programs in the population (since this is directly related to the amount of time their evaluation will require). Instead of reporting separate plots of best-fitness vs. generation and average size vs. generation, we prefer to use average-size vs. best-fitness plots, since they represent in a more direct way the compromise between these two counteracting objectives. We will also use best-fitness vs. run and average-size vs. run plots for more detailed analyses.

We start from analysing the behaviour of runs without bloat control. As shown by Figure 1 in the absence of a mechanism GP populations tend to bloat dramatically (in this and the following figures `pop` means "population size" and `tsize` means "tournament size"). As expected smaller populations are outperformed by the larger ones. More interesting is the detrimental effect of increasing the selective pressure, with the runs with tournaments of size 2 outperforming the others.

To provide more information on what is happening in single runs, let us concentrate on the case of tournament size 2. Figure 2 shows the average-size vs. run and best-fitness vs. run diagrams for this case and for the two problems. The data are population averages taken at the last generation of each run. For the sake of visualisation clarity runs have been renumbered so as to show the fitness and size data in ascending order. As we can see from these plots, there are ample differences in performance between runs, but most runs result in bloat. When the population includes only 100 individuals, there are a small number of runs where programs grow little (in the case of Even-10) or shrink (in the case of Poly-10) with respect to their initial sizes. Inspection of the original data reveals that these are runs where fitness is also very poor, suggesting that the system got trapped by a deceptive attractor.

Let us now compare these results with what we achieve with Tarpeian bloat-control on. As shown by Figure 3 in the presence of this mechanism programs tend to grow to a much lesser extent, typically being at least one order of magnitude smaller than in the case without bloat control. Again, as expected smaller populations are outperformed by the larger ones, and, again, there is a detrimental effect of increasing the selective pressure, with the runs performed with tournaments of size 2 outperforming the others. However, here we observe a significant difference in terms of performance between populations with different numbers of individuals. When the population size is relatively small compared with the difficulty of the problem at hand, the Tarpeian method leads to a loss in terms of end-of-run best fitness. This happens for populations of 100, 500 and 1000 individuals in the case of Even-10 and for populations of 100 and 500 individuals for Poly-10. The reason for this is that the repulsive pressure exerted by the fitness hole created by the algorithm may push some populations towards a deceptive attractor. However, when populations are sufficiently large to avoid being captured by the attractor, *average performance are often increased* when Tarpeian bloat control is present (for example, see the results for populations of size 5000).

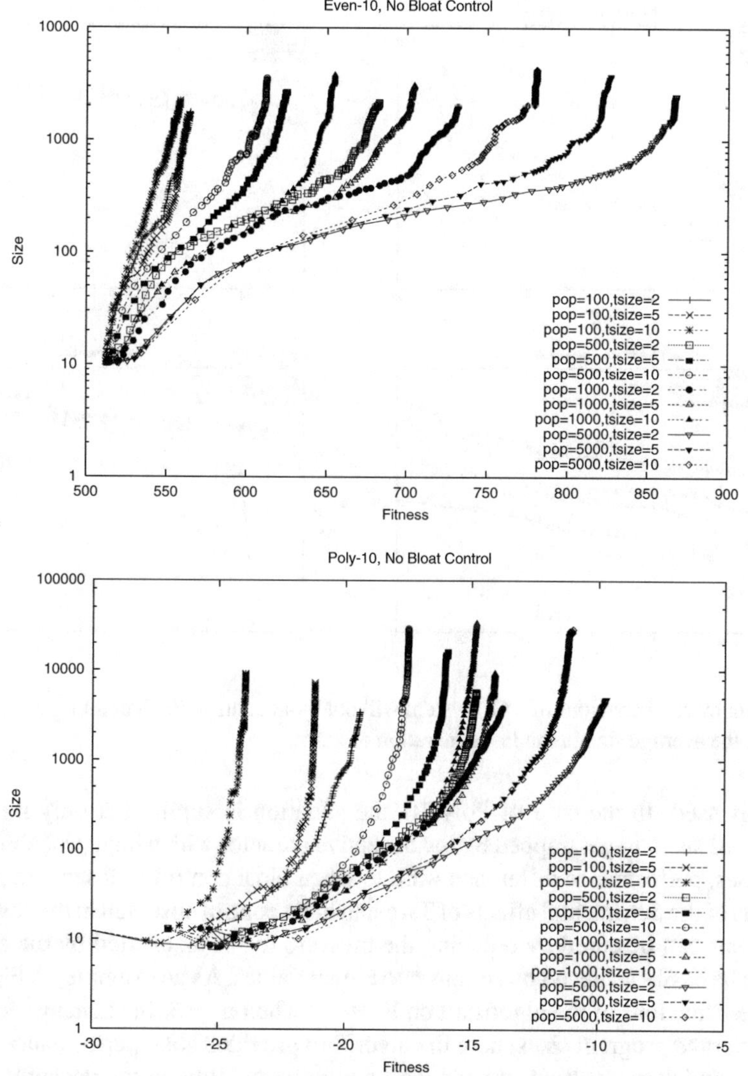

Fig. 1. Average behaviour of runs without bloat control. Each data point represents the average over 30 independent runs. Each curve contains 100 points, one per generation.

Again, to provide more information on what is happening in single runs, we concentrate on the case of tournament size 2. Figure 4 shows the average-size vs. run and best-fitness vs. run diagrams for this case. As we can see from these plots, with Tarpeian bloat control none of the runs leads to bloat. The detrimental effect of Tarpeian bloat control in the case of incorrectly sized populations is particularly evident for Even-10 with populations of 100 individuals, where most runs end up at the deceptive attractor. The problem gets progressively better as the population size is increased, and it disappears completely for populations of 5000 individuals, where the number of runs hitting a 100% fit solution is increased with respect to the case where no mechanism for bloat

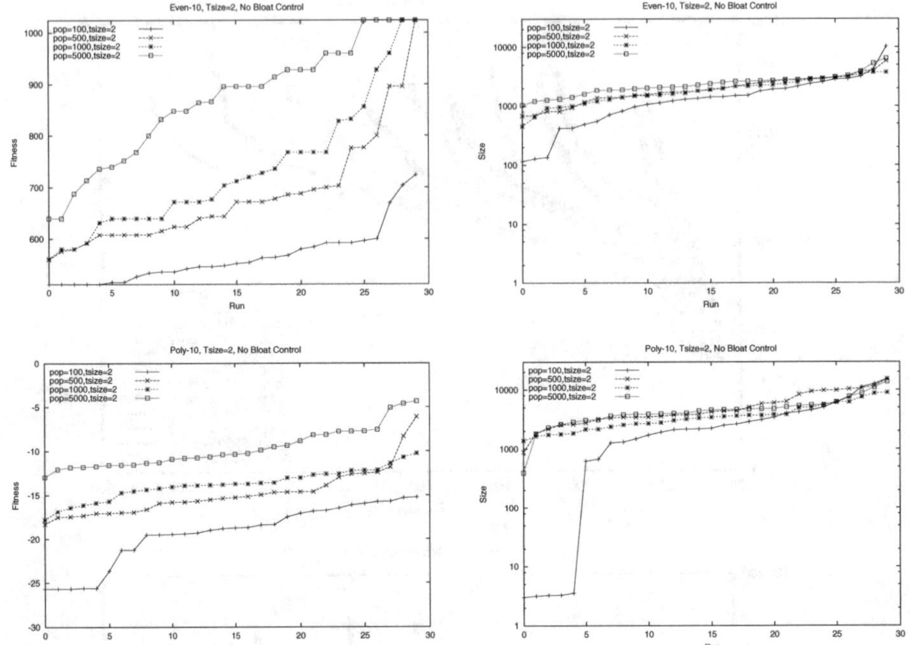

Fig. 2. Run by run behaviour of a GP system without bloat control. Each point represents the best fitness or the average size in the last generation of a run.

control is used. In the case of Poly-10, the situation is similar but only the smallest populations seem to get trapped by the deceptive attractor with a high probability. In the other cases, performance difference w.r.t. to when bloat control is absent are minor.

Some of the detrimental effects of Tarpeian bloat control observed in the case of small populations can be cured by reducing the pressure to shrink exerted by the algorithm. This can be easily achieved by setting n to bigger values. As an example, in Figure 5 we show the behaviour of the algorithm on Even-10 when $n = 3$. In exchange for slightly bigger average program sizes, here the algorithm provides good performance also with smaller populations, getting trapped with a high probability by the deceptive attractor only for the smallest population size.

The bottom line is that, although some care is needed in choosing the population size, the selective pressure and the intensity of the repulsive force exerted by the Tarpeian algorithm, when these parameters are correctly set (and this is definitely not difficult to do) the rewards provided by the Tarpeian algorithm are big in terms of best fitness achieved, execution time (runs being typically at least one order of magnitude faster) and parsimony of the evolved solutions.

5 Conclusions and Future Work

Two years ago [19] we wrote:

> "One of the most intriguing possible applications of these ideas is the possibility of using artificially created "holes" to control code growth. The two-level

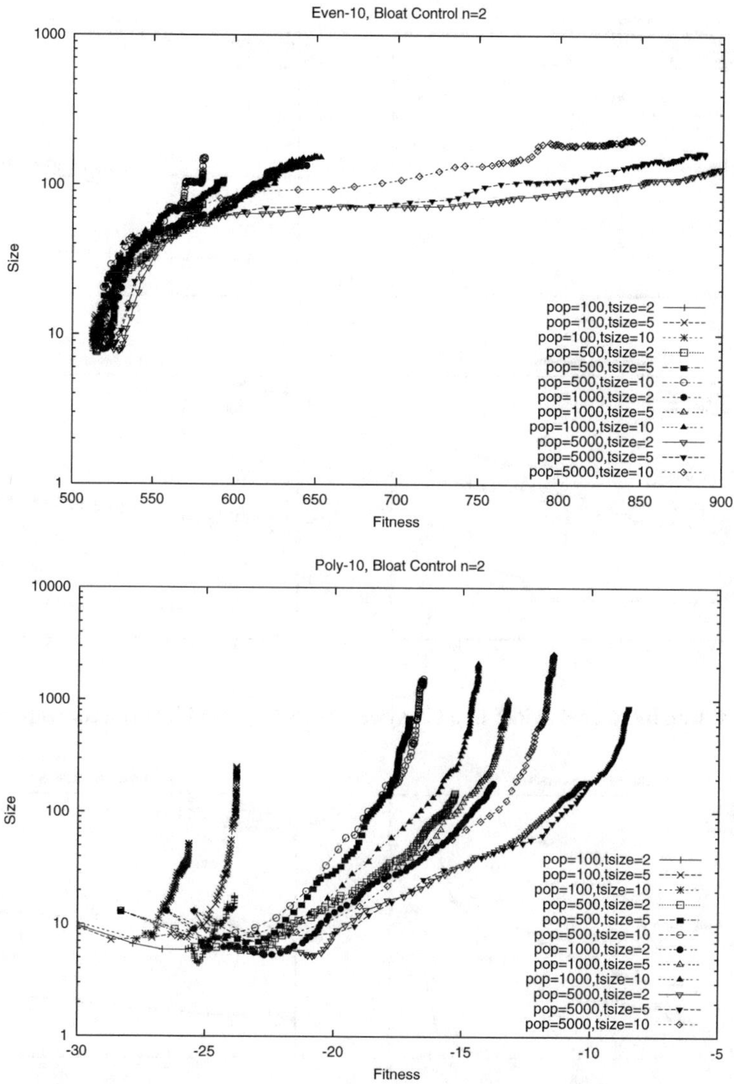

Fig. 3. Average behaviour of runs with Tarpeian bloat control with $n = 2$.

> fitness theory suggests that one might be able to slow or stop bloat either by lowering the fitness of a (possibly small) set of large individuals, or by raising the fitness of a set of small individuals. There are important issues, such as sampling errors, that would also need to be studied, but one might eventually be able to develop a method that would allow us to control code growth in a way which limits the changes made to the fitness landscape, thereby limiting the introduced bias."

In this paper we have developed a method of bloat control, the Tarpeian algorithm, which fulfills this aspiration.

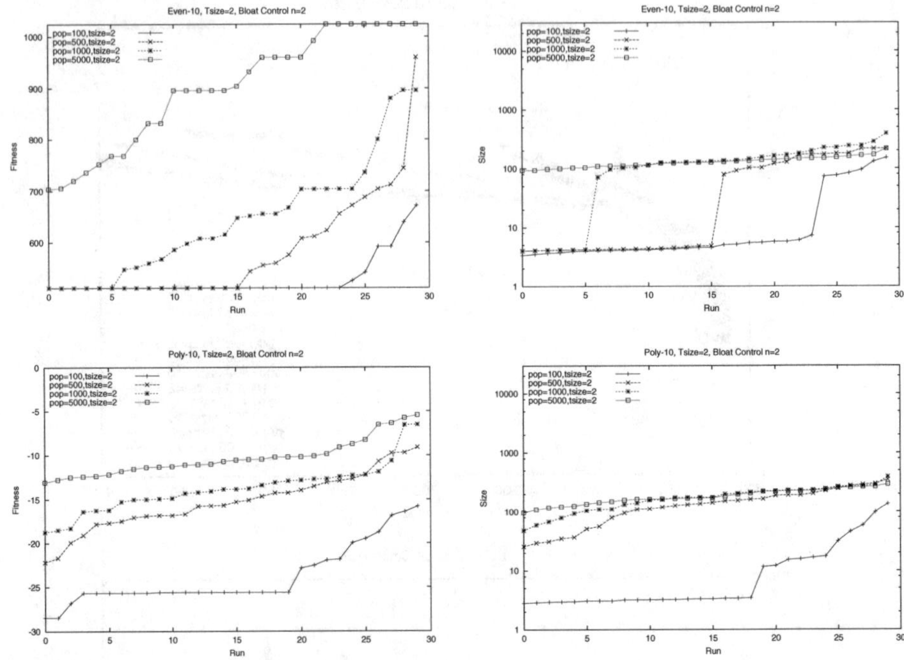

Fig. 4. Run by run behaviour of a GP system with Tarpeian bloat control with $n = 2$.

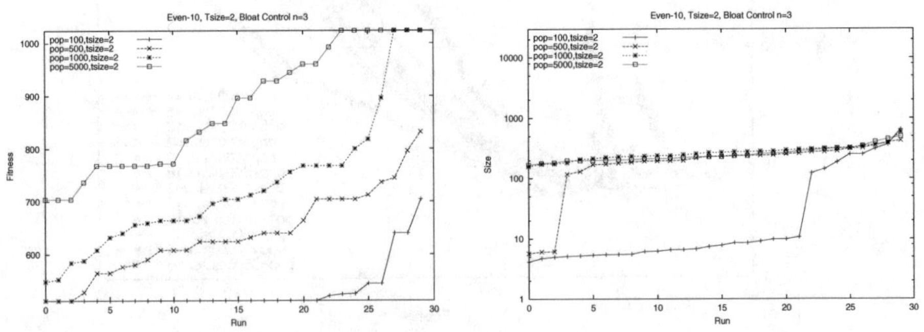

Fig. 5. Run by run behaviour of a GP system with Tarpeian bloat control with $n = 3$ on Even-10.

Unlike many other methods to control bloat, this algorithm has a strong theoretical foundation, being in fact entirely motivated by the results of theoretical investigations on the search biases induced by the genetic operators and the phenomenon of bloat. In the empirical tests on two relatively hard test problems reported in the paper, the algorithm has proved to be remarkably effective at controlling bloat. Because the individuals killed by the Tarpeian algorithm are not evaluated, the algorithm also has the advantage over other anti-bloat methods of reducing the number of fitness evaluations in addition to reducing the number of nodes to be evaluated.

In the future we intend to explore variants of this algorithm. One idea is to treat above average fitness individuals which are longer than average differently from other longer-than-average individuals, e.g. by creating fitness holes of different depths or just by excluding such individuals from the killing. An alternative approach which would definitely be worth exploring is the possibility of controlling bloat using fitness "spikes" in alternative or in addition to fitness "holes".

Acknowledgements

The author would like to thank the members of the NEC (Natural and Evolutionary Computation) group at Essex for helpful comments and discussion.

References

1. T. Blickle. Evolving compact solutions in genetic programming: A case study. In H.-M. Voigt, W. Ebeling, I. Rechenberg, and H.-P. Schwefel, editors, *Parallel Problem Solving From Nature IV. Proceedings of the International Conference on Evolutionary Computation*, volume 1141 of *LNCS*, pages 564–573, Berlin, Germany, 22-26 Sept. 1996. Springer-Verlag.
2. T. Blickle and L. Thiele. Genetic programming and redundancy. In J. Hopf, editor, *Genetic Algorithms within the Framework of Evolutionary Computation (Workshop at KI-94, Saarbrücken)*, pages 33–38, Im Stadtwald, Building 44, D-66123 Saarbrücken, Germany, 1994. Max-Planck-Institut für Informatik (MPI-I-94-241).
3. A. Ekart and S. Z. Nemeth. Selection based on the pareto nondomination criterion for controlling code growth in genetic programming. *Genetic Programming and Evolvable Machines*, 2(1):61–73, Mar. 2001.
4. C. Gathercole and P. Ross. An adverse interaction between crossover and restricted tree depth in genetic programming. In J. R. Koza, D. E. Goldberg, D. B. Fogel, and R. L. Riolo, editors, *Genetic Programming 1996: Proceedings of the First Annual Conference*, pages 291–296, Stanford University, CA, USA, 28–31 July 1996. MIT Press.
5. D. C. Hooper, N. S. Flann, and S. R. Fuller. Recombinative hill-climbing: A stronger search method for genetic programming. In J. R. Koza, K. Deb, M. Dorigo, D. B. Fogel, M. Garzon, H. Iba, and R. L. Riolo, editors, *Genetic Programming 1997: Proceedings of the Second Annual Conference*, pages 174–179, Stanford University, CA, USA, 13-16 July 1997. Morgan Kaufmann.
6. H. Iba, H. de Garis, and T. Sato. Genetic programming using a minimum description length principle. In K. E. Kinnear, Jr., editor, *Advances in Genetic Programming*, chapter 12, pages 265–284. MIT Press, 1994.
7. J. R. Koza. A genetic approach to the truck backer upper problem and the inter-twined spiral problem. In *Proceedings of IJCNN International Joint Conference on Neural Networks*, volume IV, pages 310–318. IEEE Press, 1992.
8. J. R. Koza. *Genetic Programming: On the Programming of Computers by Means of Natural Selection*. MIT Press, Cambridge, MA, USA, 1992.
9. W. B. Langdon. Scaling of program tree fitness spaces. *Evolutionary Computation*, 7(4):399–428, Winter 1999.
10. W. B. Langdon. Size fair and homologous tree genetic programming crossovers. In W. Banzhaf, J. Daida, A. E. Eiben, M. H. Garzon, V. Honavar, M. Jakiela, and R. E. Smith, editors, *Proceedings of the Genetic and Evolutionary Computation Conference*, volume 2, pages 1092–1097, Orlando, Florida, USA, 13-17 July 1999. Morgan Kaufmann.

11. W. B. Langdon. Quadratic bloat in genetic programming. In D. Whitley, D. Goldberg, E. Cantu-Paz, L. Spector, I. Parmee, and H.-G. Beyer, editors, *Proceedings of the Genetic and Evolutionary Computation Conference (GECCO-2000)*, pages 451–458, Las Vegas, Nevada, USA, 10-12 July 2000. Morgan Kaufmann.
12. W. B. Langdon. Size fair and homologous tree genetic programming crossovers. *Genetic Programming and Evolvable Machines*, 1(1/2):95–119, Apr. 2000.
13. W. B. Langdon and W. Banzhaf. Genetic programming bloat without semantics. In M. Schoenauer, K. Deb, G. Rudolph, X. Yao, E. Lutton, J. J. Merelo, and H.-P. Schwefel, editors, *Parallel Problem Solving from Nature - PPSN VI 6th International Conference*, volume 1917 of *LNCS*, pages 201–210, Paris, France, 16-20 Sept. 2000. Springer Verlag.
14. W. B. Langdon and R. Poli. An analysis of the MAX problem in genetic programming. In J. R. Koza, K. Deb, M. Dorigo, D. B. Fogel, M. Garzon, H. Iba, and R. L. Riolo, editors, *Genetic Programming 1997: Proceedings of the Second Annual Conference*, pages 222–230, Stanford University, CA, USA, 13-16 July 1997. Morgan Kaufmann.
15. W. B. Langdon and R. Poli. Why ants are hard. In J. R. Koza, W. Banzhaf, K. Chellapilla, K. Deb, M. Dorigo, D. B. Fogel, M. H. Garzon, D. E. Goldberg, H. Iba, and R. Riolo, editors, *Genetic Programming 1998: Proceedings of the Third Annual Conference*, pages 193–201, University of Wisconsin, Madison, Wisconsin, USA, 22-25 July 1998. Morgan Kaufmann.
16. W. B. Langdon and R. Poli. *Foundations of Genetic Programming*. Springer-Verlag, 2002.
17. W. B. Langdon, T. Soule, R. Poli, and J. A. Foster. The evolution of size and shape. In L. Spector, W. B. Langdon, U.-M. O'Reilly, and P. J. Angeline, editors, *Advances in Genetic Programming 3*, chapter 8, pages 163–190. MIT Press, Cambridge, MA, USA, June 1999.
18. N. F. McPhee and J. D. Miller. Accurate replication in genetic programming. In L. Eshelman, editor, *Genetic Algorithms: Proceedings of the Sixth International Conference (ICGA95)*, pages 303–309, Pittsburgh, PA, USA, 15-19 July 1995. Morgan Kaufmann.
19. N. F. McPhee and R. Poli. A schema theory analysis of the evolution of size in genetic programming with linear representations. In *Genetic Programming, Proceedings of EuroGP 2001*, LNCS, Milan, 18-20 Apr. 2001. Springer-Verlag.
20. P. Nordin and W. Banzhaf. Complexity compression and evolution. In L. Eshelman, editor, *Genetic Algorithms: Proceedings of the Sixth International Conference (ICGA95)*, pages 310–317, Pittsburgh, PA, USA, 15-19 July 1995. Morgan Kaufmann.
21. P. Nordin, F. Francone, and W. Banzhaf. Explicitly defined introns and destructive crossover in genetic programming. In P. J. Angeline and K. E. Kinnear, Jr., editors, *Advances in Genetic Programming 2*, chapter 6, pages 111–134. MIT Press, Cambridge, MA, USA, 1996.
22. U.-M. O'Reilly and F. Oppacher. Hybridized crossover-based search techniques for program discovery. In *Proceedings of the 1995 World Conference on Evolutionary Computation*, volume 2, pages 573–578, Perth, Australia, 29 Nov. - 1 Dec. 1995. IEEE Press.
23. R. Poli. General schema theory for genetic programming with subtree-swapping crossover. In J. F. Miller, M. Tomassini, P. L. Lanzi, C. Ryan, A. G. B. Tettamanzi, and W. B. Langdon, editors, *Genetic Programming, Proceedings of EuroGP'2001*, volume 2038 of *LNCS*, pages 143–159, Lake Como, Italy, 18-20 Apr. 2001. Springer-Verlag.
24. K. Rodriguez-Vazquez, C. M. Fonseca, and P. J. Fleming. Multiobjective genetic programming: A nonlinear system identification application. In J. R. Koza, editor, *Late Breaking Papers at the 1997 Genetic Programming Conference*, pages 207–212, Stanford University, CA, USA, 13–16 July 1997. Stanford Bookstore.
25. J. P. Rosca. Analysis of complexity drift in genetic programming. In J. R. Koza, K. Deb, M. Dorigo, D. B. Fogel, M. Garzon, H. Iba, and R. L. Riolo, editors, *Genetic Programming 1997: Proceedings of the Second Annual Conference*, pages 286–294, Stanford University, CA, USA, 13-16 July 1997. Morgan Kaufmann.
26. T. Soule. *Code Growth in Genetic Programming*. PhD thesis, University of Idaho, Moscow, Idaho, USA, 15 May 1998.

27. T. Soule and J. A. Foster. Code size and depth flows in genetic programming. In J. R. Koza, K. Deb, M. Dorigo, D. B. Fogel, M. Garzon, H. Iba, and R. L. Riolo, editors, *Genetic Programming 1997: Proceedings of the Second Annual Conference*, pages 313–320, Stanford University, CA, USA, 13-16 July 1997. Morgan Kaufmann.
28. T. Soule and J. A. Foster. Effects of code growth and parsimony pressure on populations in genetic programming. *Evolutionary Computation*, 6(4):293–309, Winter 1998.
29. T. Soule and J. A. Foster. Removal bias: a new cause of code growth in tree based evolutionary programming. In *1998 IEEE International Conference on Evolutionary Computation*, pages 781–186, Anchorage, Alaska, USA, 5-9 May 1998. IEEE Press.
30. T. Soule and R. B. Heckendorn. An analysis of the causes of code growth in genetic programming. *Genetic Programming and Evolvable Machines*, 3(3):283–309, Sept. 2002.
31. B.-T. Zhang and H. Mühlenbein. Balancing accuracy and parsimony in genetic programming. *Evolutionary Computation*, 3(1):17–38, 1995.

Divide and Conquer: Genetic Programming Based on Multiple Branches Encoding

Katya Rodríguez-Vázquez and Carlos Oliver-Morales

DISCA, IIMAS, National Autonomous University of Mexico, Circuito Escolar
Ciudad Universitaria, Mexico City, 04510, Mexico
katya@uxdea4.iimas.unam.mx, oliver_carlos@yahoo.com

Abstract. This paper describes an alternative genetic programming encoding, which is based on a rooted-node with fixed-content. This rooted node combines partial results of a set of multiple branches. Hence, this approach is named Multiple Branches Genetic Programming. It is tested on a symbolic regression problem and used on a Boolean domain to solve the even-*n* parity problem.

1 Introduction

The adaptive search algorithm called Genetic Programming (GP) was designed by Koza [5]. GP is an evolution-based search model which evolves populations of hierarchically structured computer programs according to their performance on a previously specified fitness criterion. GP individuals are programs which are not fixed in length or size. The maximum depth height of the parse tree of the program is specified *a priori* to constrain the search space but all solutions up to and including this maximum are considered. Because the structure of the program is not known *a priori*, different executions of the GP approach may produce correct solution programs differing in size and content. All these solutions are syntactically valid programs but some of them may possess a more complex structure. Therefore, the principle of parsimony plays an important role. This principle is founded on the fact that "things should be explained and expressed in a simple way". In the context of GP, parsimony means that a correct program is expressed in its simplest form using the shortest parse tree structure. However, since the introduction of GP by John Koza [5], controlling tree size growth (parsimony) has been a main problem. This process of evolution in program size is commonly known as *bloat*.

In his seminal book, [5] treated this factor in a simple form by a kind of penalty function. The effect of parsimony pressure is to attach a penalty to the length of programs. Thus, a longer solution will be automatically downgraded in fitness when compared with a short program. While this will prevent hierarchical individuals from growing exponentially, the strength of that penalty determines at what point in evolution hierarchical individuals become suppressed altogether. Iba *et al.* [2] proposed a method for controlling tree growth by means of a Minimum Description Length (MDL) principle. A similar approach based on the MDL principle has been proposed

C. Ryan et al. (Eds.): EuroGP 2003, LNCS 2610, pp. 218–228, 2003.

by [17]. They describe an adaptive method for fitness evaluation to dynamically guide the GP to grow and prune (restrict or cut) program trees. This MDL principle-based approach dynamically grows and prunes the program size by balancing the ratio of training accuracy to solution complexity. Further works analysed this main draw back of GP as appeard in [9], [15], [7], [12], for mention some work on this issue.

The work presented in this paper does not penalize or evaluated the parsimony of problem solutions; but, it presents a novel encoding based on a multiple branches representation. Multiple branches are defined which have a structure similar to traditional Koza-style but their maximum depth for each branch is much more smaller than Koza-style. All these branches are then combined by means of a fixed-content rooted-node whose content (function) depends on problem domain. Thus, by means of this encoding, simple functional solution can be emerged as it will be seen through this work.

Then, the aim of this paper is to present an alternative GP encoding which tends to produce simple program of good quality avoiding, in somehow, the problem of bloat. This encoding is then tested on two different problem domains: generation of math functions (symbolic regression and modeling) and Boolean circuit design. In the first case, the introduced multiple branches genetic programming is combined with a least squares parameter estimation technique. Results are compared with previous work.

Paper is then structured as follows. In section 2, a general description of multiple branches encoding is given. In section 3, this novel encoding is applied to symbolic regression and modeling comparing MBGP results with other GP approaches. Section 4 describes an application into Boolean domain. Finally, conclusions and future facts are drawn in section 5.

2 Multiple Branches Encoding: Divide and Conquer

This present work focuses on an alternative GP representation based on a branches encoding firstly used for dynamic modelling and forecasting problems [10], [11]. This approach is described in details as follows.

In this paper, genetic programming is proposed to determine the best input-output model, being the coefficients of each model term estimated by means of a least squares algorithm. In this case, individuals have the form described in Figure 1. The multiple branches are mathematical expressions represented by means of tree structures, composed of internal nodes (functions) and leaf nodes (terminals). $n+1$ constants values are obtained by means of a Least Squares parameter estimation method (a constant for each branch plus the constant term). The fixed-content rooted node, the addition function defined as *model*, has the aim of adding the response of each branch. The output is the combination of partial results from these multiple branches.

If the problem study falls into the domain of dynamic system modeling, an example of a potential MB solution is given as follows,

(***model*** T_{T-1} R_{T-1} (.* T_{T-2} R_{T-1}) R_{T-3} (.* R_{T-3} T_{T-2}) 0.95716 0.021437 -0.00087839 -0.020309 0.00090912 0.02055)

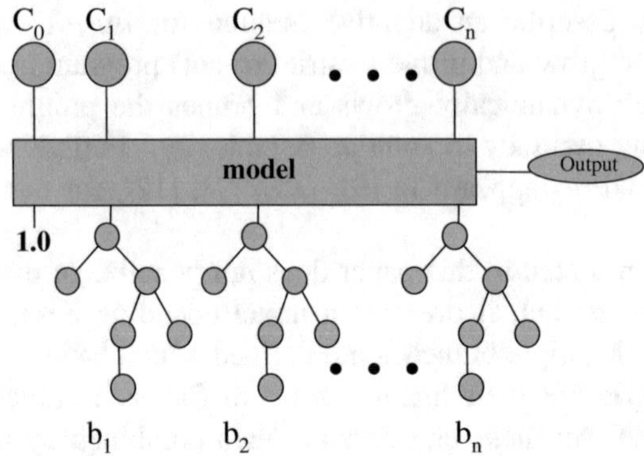

Fig. 1. Multiple branches individual structure (C_0 corresponds to constant term).

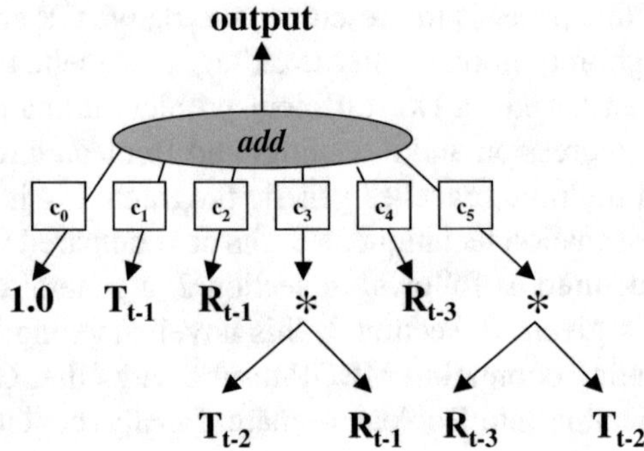

Fig. 2. Polynomial mathematical model expressed by means of MB genetic programming.

Equivalent to,

$$T(t) = 0.0255 + 0.9572T(t-1) + 0.0214R(t-1) - 0.0203R(t-3) \\ - 0.0008T(t-2)R(t-1) + 0.0009T(t-2)R(t-3) \quad (1)$$

where c_i are calculated by means of a Least Squares and whose estimated values are expressed in the equivalent model (equation (1)).

2.1 MB Individual Evaluation

Branches are evaluated as mathematical expressions. The root node (addition function) receives partial results from the evaluation of each branch, estimates the coefficients by means of a LS algorithm and finally, computes the output values.

Given the value of the independent variable i (brancjh) at data point j, the value of dependent variable at that point (y_j) is given by

$$y_j = \sum_{i=1}^{n} c_i b_{i,j} \quad (2)$$

c_i is the coefficient of branch i for i=1, ..., n and j=1, ..., m, where m is the number of data points. This can be expressed into a matrix form as follows.

$$\begin{bmatrix} b_{1,1} & b_{2,1} & \cdots & b_{n,1} \\ b_{1,2} & b_{2,2} & \cdots & b_{n,2} \\ \vdots & \vdots & \ddots & \vdots \\ b_{1,m} & b_{2,m} & \cdots & b_{n,m} \end{bmatrix} \begin{bmatrix} c_1 \\ c_2 \\ \vdots \\ c_n \end{bmatrix} = \begin{bmatrix} y_1 \\ y_2 \\ \vdots \\ y_m \end{bmatrix} \tag{3}$$

2.2 Genetic Operators

Genetic operators are defined in such a way to work on the proposed MB structures. Crossing over two MB individuals is performed by randomly selecting a single branch in each parent. Selected branches are then crossed over in the traditional GP way [5]. This MB representation is similar to Langdon's multi-tree encoding [7]. In multiple tree architecture, however, each tree describes a different operation and they are independent to each other. MBGP contents a central rooted node that combines partial results of each branch.

Note that the introduced MBGP encoding seems also similar to automatically defined function proposed by [6]. But, in this MBGP case, defining branches are only called once by the rooted-node and combined in a way defined by the content of rooted-node.

3 MBGP in Modelling

Dynamic system modelling and prediction have been one of the applications for this novel evolution-based technique. [5] describes the modelling process as a symbolic regression problem where GP is used to find a mathematical expression able to reproduce a functional relationship based on given training data. Based upon this technique, recent work by [3] describes a symbolic regression forecasting approach applied to crude oil prices. Kang et al. [4] have applied a multi-level and multi-scale evolutionary modelling system that models the macro-behaviour of the stock market by ordinary differential equations while models the micro-behaviour by natural fractals. This system has been applied for modelling and prediction of financial time series. [16] have proposed a specific hybrid technique for time series modelling which combines grammatically based GP and optimisation methods. In [8], an accelerated Genetic Programming is described which tends to generate polynomial models based on a hierarchical combination of transfer polynomials. They also have proposed a recursive Least Squares algorithm in order to accelerate parameter estimation process. These are some GP-based system for modelling amongst others.

3.1 Symbolic Regression

Based on the following non-linear multivariate function [8], the symbolic regression problem (finding a mapping from numerical data of dependent and independent variables) was tested.

$$y(\vec{x}) = 3(x_1 - 0.5) + \mathbf{sin}(x_2 * x_3) + \frac{2\,\mathbf{ln}(1 + x_4)}{x_5} \tag{4}$$

A set of 250 samples were generated (150 for training and 100 for testing), where the values for $\boldsymbol{x}_i$ were randomly taken from the interval [-1, 1]. A set of 100 runs were performed. A population of 50 programs consisting of 10 branches of maximum depth up to 4 were evolved during 200 generations. A crossover and mutation probability of 95% and 5% were used, respectively. Objective functions for modelling problems are generally based on an error measure. Here, the Mean-Square-Error (MSE) is evaluated. Function set consisted on simple arithmetic functions {+, -, *, %[1]}; where terminal set consisted on independent variables $\boldsymbol{x}_i$.

Results of these runs are then summarised in Table 1. The program that showed the best performance (accuracy) was considered in order to compare its performance with other GP techniques as shown in Table 2. Three techniques are considered: 1) Koza-style GP [5], 2) STROGANOFF proposed by [2] which is based on evolution of polynomials composed of transfer polynomials allocated in the nodes of tree structures, and 3) a STROGANOFF extended version which uses a rapid recurrent least squares for coefficient estimation, *f*GP (*fast* GP). In these three methods, an statistical fitness function was used in order to promote the survival of accurate, parsimonious and predictive polynomials. In the case of MBGP, fitness function was defined as the MSE.

The best MB program has the structure shown as follow.

```
(ADD
      V1
      (divd (.* V4 (.* V4 V4)) V5)
      (divd (divd V1 (divd V1 V4)) V5)
      (.* V1 V4)
      (divd (divd (.* V2 V2) (.* V5 V2)) V5)
      (divd V3 (divd V5 V1))
      (divd V3 V5)
      (.* (+ V1 (divd V4 V5)) V4)
      (divd V3 (divd V5 (- V3 V1)))
      3.3067 3.5036 0.87467 0.82177 0.0060857 0.70499
      -0.2266 -2.6548 0.59913 -1.6498
)
```

Its equivalent mathematical function is expressed as,

$$y(x) = 3.3067x_1 + 3.5036\frac{x_4^3}{x_5} + \frac{0.87467}{x_4 x_5} + 0.8218x_1x_4 + 0.00608\frac{x_2}{x_5^2} + 0.7050\frac{x_5}{x_1x_3} - 0.2266\frac{x_3}{x_5} - 2.6548\left(\frac{x_4^2}{x_5} + x_1x_4\right) + 0.5991\left(\frac{x_3 - x_1}{x_3x_5}\right) - 1.6498 \tag{5}$$

[1] Protected division.

Table 1. Statistics over a 100 runs of symbolic regression problem.

	Accuracy	Nodes[2]
Min	0.1565	26
Avg	0.3889	73.8
Max	0.8861	104

It is interesting to notice that MBGP tries to approximate coefficients of *constant* and x_1 terms (1.5 and 3.0 against 1.6498 and 3.3067, respectively). It is also seen that two terms involving x_4/x_5 presented in eq. (5) are related to $2ln(1+x_4)/x_5$ in eq. (4). Estimating the contribution of these terms, a partial MSE shows a value of 0.6915. Then, we can state that simple arithmetic functions are sufficient in order to generate a mathematical solution possessing a *good* approximation. Results obtained in this example have shown a less complex model improving its performance.

Table 2. Comparison of complexity and accuracy of best polynomials evolved over 100 runs on the symbolic regression problem.

System	Complexity Num. Coefficients	Accuracy (Training) MSE	Accuracy (Testing) MSE
FGP **[8]**	25	0.292	0.325
STROGANOFF [2]	22	0.338	0.404
Koza-style GP [5]	23	0.391	0.448
MBGP	10 [3]	0.156	0.133

3.2 Modelling and Prediction

In this second example, a simulated data has been considered in order to evaluate the MBGP performance. MBGP is then demonstrated on the simple Wiener process. The differential equation of the linear dynamic part of the simple Wiener process is

$$10\dot{v}(t)+v(t)=u(t) \tag{6}$$

and the static non-linear part is expressed by

$$y(k)=2+v(k)+v^2(k) \tag{7}$$

The process described above was excited by a pseudo-random ternary test signal (PRTS) with a maximum length 26, amplitude 2 and mean value 1 [1]. The sampling time was ΔT = 2s and the clock time interval of 10 seconds. Then, N = 26*5 = 130 data pairs were used for the identification. The input-output data are then shown in Figure 3.

---

[2] Complexity measured in the context of number of nodes includes also coefficient nodes and the fixed-content rooted node.

[3] Up to 10 branches were defined. This means, up to 11 coefficients (10 branches plus constant term) were estimated. This parameter showed to be enough to describe the behaviour of given data.

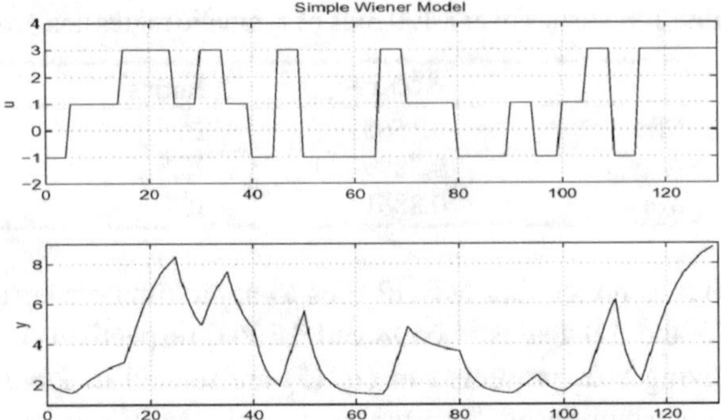

Fig. 3. Simple Wiener process input-output data.

In order to make a comparison between MBGP and previous work on Sub-Set Genetic Algorithms (SSGA) and Multi-Objective Genetic Programming (MOGP) for system identification and modelling introduced by [14] and [13], respectively, the only function in the function set was the product. A population of 50 programs of 6 branches with a maximum depth of up to 3 were defined. This population was evolved during 100 generations, using a crossover and mutation of 95% and 5%, respectively. Again, the objective function was set as the MSE, and terminal set consisted of lagged input and output values. That is, ***T*** = {u(k-1), u(k-2), u(k-3), y(k-1), y(k-2), y(k-3)}={*V1, V2, V3, V4, V5, V6*}. Results over a 50 runs are summarised in Table 3. Models generated by means of these evolutionary methods and conventional modelling techniques and their performance are summarised in Table 4. It is observed that similar results were obtained by means of MBGP and MOGP; but, MBGP showed a more diversification of solutions. Again, Orthogonal Least Squares (OLS) and Stepwise Symbolic Regression techniques, labelled here as conventional identification techniques, presented a worse results than evolutionary-based identification techniques.

4 Logic Circuits Design

In order to evaluate the MB structure encoding representation on different domains, this proposal is applied to the problem of combinatorial circuit design. As this encoding has been described, it is necessary to define the content of the root node. Based on Karnaugh Maps method, it is viable to set the rooted node as the OR Boolean function. Thus, the MBGP has to be able of generating a functional circuit of, at least, the number of gates used for the circuit produced by Karnaugh Maps. As a testing example, the even-3 parity problem has been defined. Using basic Boolean functions {AND, OR, NOT}, a population of 50 programs of 3 branches with a maximum depth up to 4 and GP parameters as defined in previous symbolic regression examples, the circuit, detailed in Table 5, was obtained.

Table 3. MBGP models for the Simple Wiener Process System.

	MSE	Generations	Nodes
Minimum	0.001655	32	18
Average	0.001919	78.3	22
Maximum	0.002752	100	24

Table 4. Model structure and performance comparison of evolutionary and conventional modelling techniques.

Method	MSE	LTPE[4]	Model
MBGP	$1.5576\text{x}10^{-3}$	$6.4279\text{x}10_{-3}$	(model V4 (.* V4 V4) (.* V1 V5) (.* V1 V1) V1 (.* V1 V2) 0.86864 -0.015674 0.061707 0.011323 0.063845 0.034129 0.31465)
MOGP	$1.5576\text{x}10^{-3}$	$6.4279\text{x}10^{-3}$	C y(k-1), u(k-1) $y(k-1)^2$, $u(k-1)^2$, y(k-2)u(k-1), u(k-1)u(k-2)
SSGA	$1.6473\text{x}10^{-3}$	$7.8151\text{x}10^{-3}$	C y(k-1), u(k-1) $y(k-1)^2$, $u(k-1)^2$, y(k-2)u(k-1), u(k-1)u(k-2)
OLS[5]	$1.6808\text{x}10^{-3}$	$7.8526\text{x}10^{-3}$	c y(k-1), y(k-2) $y(k-1)^2$, $y(k-2)^2$, y(k-1)u(k-1), $u(k-1)^2$
Stepwise Regression	$5.2243\text{x}10^{-3}$	$26.8080\text{x}10^{-3}$	c y(k-1), y(k-2) u(k-1), u(k-2) y(k-1)u(k-1), $u(k-1)^2$

Table 5. Even-3 parity circuit design.

Method	Design	Gates
Karnaugh Maps	A'B'C' + ABC' + A'BC + AB'C	12
MBGP {AND,OR,NOT}	C'(AB + (A+B)') + C(AB + (A+B)')'	9
MBGP {AND, OR, NOT, XOR}	$(A \oplus B)' \oplus C$ or $A' \oplus B \oplus C$	3

In a second experiment the function set considered also the XOR Boolean function. Again, using the even-3 parity problem as the testing example, the evolving design was defined as shown in Table 5, equivalent to the MBGP solution expressed as,

```
(OR
     0
     0
     (xor  C (not (xor  A  B)))
)
```

[4] LTPE (Long-Term Predictive Error).

[5] Results are from are from [1].

Note that up to 3 branches were defined for this Boolean problem. However, only one branch evolved and the remaining branches were empty. It is observed that including the XOR Boolean operator, an only three gates circuit is generated. The even-*4* parity problem was now introduced in the MBGP proposal. Results of this problem are shown in Table 6. Two different sets of runs were carried out. The function set, for the first case, only considered the three basic Boolean operators. In the second experiment, the XOR was also used. Again, the solution for the even-4 parity problem consisted of *(n-1)* XOR's and only one NOT. Here, diverse solutions (phenotypes) were obtained as shown in Fig 4, where three different solutions are shown.

```
(OR
    0
    0
    0
    (xor (xor (not (xor V1 V4)) V2)
     V3)
)
```

```
(OR
    (xor V2 (xor V3 (xor V4 (not
     V1))))
    (xor V2 (xor V3 (xor V4 (not
     V1))))
    (xor V2 (xor V3 (xor V4 (not
     V1))))
    (xor V2 (xor V3 (xor V4 (not
     V1))))
)
```

```
(OR
    0
    0
    0
    (not (xor (xor V2 (xor V4 V3)) V1))
)
```

Fig. 4. MBGP solutions for the even-4 parity problem.

From these results, it is possible to generalise the solution for the even-*n* parity problem by setting the root node as the XOR and evolving MBGP structures. Thus, Table 7 summarise results of even-*n* parity problem for n=3, …, 8. For each case, GP parameters are also detailed.

5 Conclusions

In this paper, a multiple branches encoding has been introduced and proposed as an alternative for modelling problems (e.g. symbolic regression, system identification, modelling and prediction). It has been tested over two different modelling problems proving that it is an alternative for generating accurate and simple solutions. Because of its representation, less nodes can be used in comparison with traditional GP encoding, without degradation in performance. This encoding keeps some similarities with [6] and the multiple trees representation used by [7] for evolving data structures. However, solutions are not excessively growing as in those works.

Table 6. Even-4 parity circuit design.

Method	Design	Gates
Karnaugh Maps	A'B'C'D' + A'B'CD + A'BC'D + A'BCD'+ AB'C'D+AB'CD'+ABC'D'+ABCD	27
MBGP {AND,OR,NOT}	AB(CD+(C+D)') + A'B'(CD+(C+D)') + A'B(CD+(C+D)')' + (AB'(CD+(C+D)')'	18
MBGP {AND, OR, NOT, XOR}	A' ⊕ B ⊕ C ⊕ D	4

Table 7. Even-n parity problem by means of MBGP and a XOR root node.

N	GP Parameters	%Correct Solutions	%Optimal	Avg. Generats.	Circuit
3	Popsize = 50 N. Branches = 3	100	23	2.45	(XOR (not A) B C)
4	Popsize = 50 N. Branches = 4	100	30	11.33	(XOR (not C) D B A)
5	Popsize = 50 N. Branches = 5	93	28	34.5	(XOR (C (xor A D) E (not B))
6	Popsize = 80 N. Branches = 6	90	20	44.39	(XOR ((xor B A) E F (not D) C)
7	Popsize = 150 N. Branches = 7	73	20	62.51	(XOR (F E C (xor (xor (not D) (xor G A)) B))
8	Popsize = 250 N. Branches = 8	61	19	61.57	(XOR B (not (xor (xor H A) C)) G E D F)

An additional point was to evaluate the flexibility of this approach on a different domain. Thus, logic circuits were designed by means of present proposal. Even-*n* parity problem was used and functional circuits were obtained for $n = 3, \ldots, 8$.

An important point that could be a drawback is the fact that this representation need setting more parameters (e.g., how many branches are required, the value of root node, etc.). But, it seems there are a compromise between simplicity of solutions and number of GP parameters to be defined.

Results presented throughout this paper are preliminary and future analysis will be need.

Acknowledgements

Authors would like to thank anonymous reviewers for their helpful comments. They also gratefully acknowledges the financial support of Consejo Nacional de Ciencia y Tecnología (CONACyT), México, under the projecto J34900-A, PAPPIT-UNAM under the project ES100201.

References

1. HABER, R. AND H. UNBENHAUEN (1990) Structure Identification of Non-Linear Dynamic Systems: A Survey of Input/Output Approaches. *Automatica*, 26 (4), pp. 651-677.
2. IBA, H., H. DE GARIS AND T. SATO. (1994) Genetic Programming Using a Minimum Description Length. In *Advances in Genetic Programming* (Kinnear, Editor) pp. 265-284. MIT Press.
3. M.A. KABOUDAN (2001) Genetically Evolved Models and Normality of Their Fitted Residuals, *Journal of Economic Dynamics & Control*, **25**, 1719-1749.
4. KANG, Z., Y. LI, H. DE GARIS AND L-S. KANG (2002) A Two Levels Evolutionary Modeling System for Financial Data. In *Proc. of the GECCO*, (W.B. Langdon et al., *editors*), pp. 1113-1118. New York City, New York, Morgan Kaufmann.
5. J.R. KOZA (1992) *Genetic Programming: On the Programming of Computers by Means of Natural Selection.* MIT Press.
6. KOZA, J.R. (1994) *Genetic Programming II: Automatic Discovery of Reusable Programs.* MIT Press.
7. LANGDON, W.B. (1998) *Genetic Programming and Data Structures*. Kluwer Academic Publishers.
8. N.I. NIKOLAEV AND H. IBA (2001) Accelerated Genetic Programming of Polinomials, *Genetic Programming and Evolvable Machines* 2(3), pp. 23-1-275.
9. NORDIN, P., F. FRANCONE AND W. BHANZAF (1996) Explicitly Defined Introns and Destructive Crossover in Genetic Programming. In: (Angeline, P.J. and Kinnear, K.E., editors) *Advances in Genetic Programming 2*, chapte 6, pp. 111-134. MIT Press.
10. OLIVER, M.C. 2002. *Programación Genética Multi-Ramas en el Modelado y Predicción de Datos Climatológicos*. Tesis de Maestría. Universidad Nacional de México, D.F., México (in spanish).
11. OLIVER-MORALES.C. AND K. RODRÍGUEZ-VÁZQUEZ (2002) MBGP in Modelling and Prediction, *Proc. of the GECCO* (E.B. Langdon, et al., *editors*), pp. 892. New York City, New York, Morgan Kaufmann.
12. POLI, R. AND W.B. LANGDON (2001) *Foundations of Genetic Programming*. Springer-Verlag.
13. RODRÍGUEZ-VÁZQUEZ, K. AND P.J. FLEMING (1998) Multiobjective Genetic Programming for Non-Linear System Identification. *Ellectronics Letters*, **34**(9), pp. 930-931.
14. RODRÍGUEZ-VÁZQUEZ, K. AND P.J. FLEMING (1999) A Genetic Algorithm for Subset Selection in System Identification. *Second Mexican International Conference on Computer Science ENC'99*, México.
15. SOULE, T. AND J.A.FOSTER (1997) Code Size and Depth Flows in Genetic Programming. *Proc. Second Annual Conf. on Genetic Programming*, (J.R.Koza, K.Deb, M.Dorigo, D.B.Fogel, M.Garzon, H.Iba, R.L.Riolo, *editors*), pp. 313-320. Morgan Kaufmann.
16. WHIGHAM, P.A. AND J. KEUKELAAR (2001) Evolving Structures – Optimising Contents. *IEEE Proc. of Congress on Evolutionary Computation*, pp. 1228-1235.
17. ZHANG, B.T. AND H. MÜHLENBEIN (1996) Adaptive Fitness Functions for Dynamic Growing/Pruning. In *Advances in Genetic Programming*, Vol. 2. (Angeline and Kinnear, Editors), MIT Press.

Feature Construction and Selection Using Genetic Programming and a Genetic Algorithm

Matthew G. Smith and Larry Bull

Faculty of Computing, Engineering & Mathematical Sciences
University of the West of England, Bristol BS16 1QY, UK
Matt-Smith@bigfoot.com, Larry.Bull@uwe.ac.uk

Abstract. The use of machine learning techniques to automatically analyse data for information is becoming increasingly widespread. In this paper we examine the use of Genetic Programming and a Genetic Algorithm to pre-process data before it is classified using the C4.5 decision tree learning algorithm. The Genetic Programming is used to construct new features from those available in the data, a potentially significant process for data mining since it gives consideration to hidden relationships between features. The Genetic Algorithm is used to determine which such features are the most predictive. Using ten well-known datasets we show that our approach, in comparison to C4.5 alone, provides marked improvement in a number of cases.

1 Introduction

Classification is one of the major tasks in data mining, involving the prediction of class value based on information about some other attributes. The process is a form of inductive learning whereby a set of pre-classified training examples are presented to an algorithm which must then generalise from those seen to correctly categorise unseen examples. One of the most commonly used forms of classification technique is the decision tree learning algorithm C4.5 [7]. In this paper we examine the use of Genetic Programming (GP) [5] and a Genetic Algorithm (GA)[3] to improve the performance of C4.5 through feature *construction* and feature *selection*. Feature construction is a process that aims to discover hidden relationships between features, inferring new composite features. In contrast, feature selection is a process that aims to refine the list of features used thereby removing potential sources of noise and ambiguity. We use GP individuals consisting of a number of separate trees / automatically defined functions (ADFs) [5] to construct features for C4.5. A GA is then used to select over the original and constructed features for a final hybrid C4.5 classifier system. Results show that the system is able to outperform standard C4.5 on a number of datasets held at the UCI repository[1].

Raymer et al. [8] have used ADFs for feature *extraction* in conjunction with the k-nearest-neighbour algorithm. Feature extraction replaces an original feature with the result from passing it through a functional mapping. In Raymer et al.'s approach each feature is altered by an ADF, evolved for that feature only, with the aim of increasing

[1] http://www.ics.uci.edu/~mlearn/MLRepository.html

C. Ryan et al. (Eds.): EuroGP 2003, LNCS 2610, pp. 229–237, 2003.

the separation of pattern classes in the feature space; for problems with n features, individuals consist of n ADFs. Ahluwalia and Bull [1] extended Raymer et al.'s approach by coevolving the ADFs for each feature and adding an extra coevolving GA population of feature selectors; extraction and selection occurred simultaneously in n+1 populations. For other (early) examples of evolutionary computation approaches to data mining see [9] for a GA-based feature selection approach using k-nearest-neighbour and [4] for a similar GA-based approach also using k-nearest-neighbour. Since undertaking the work presented here we have become aware of Vafaie and DeJong's [10] combination of GP and a GA for use with C4.5. They used the GA to perform feature selection for a face recognition dataset where feature subsets were evaluated through their use by C4.5. GP individuals were then evolved which contained a variable number of ADFs to construct new features from the selected subset, again using C4.5. Our approach is very similar to Vafaie and DeJong's but the feature operations are reversed such that feature construction occurs before selection. We find that our approach performs as well or better than Vafaie and DeJong's.

The paper is arranged as follows: the next section describes the approach; section 3 presents results from its use on a number of well-known datasets; and finally, all findings are discussed.

2 The GAP Algorithm

In this work we have used the WEKA [see 11] implementation of C4.5, known as J48, to examine the performance of our Genetic Algorithm and Programming (GAP) approach. The approach consists of two phases:

2.1 Feature Creation

A population of 101 genotypes is created at random. Each genotype consists of n trees, where n is the number of numeric valued features in the dataset, subject to a minimum of 7. This minimum is chosen to ensure that the initial population contains a significant number of compound features. A tree can be either an original feature or an ADF. That is, a genotype consists of n GP trees, each of which may contain 1 or more nodes. The chance of a node being a leaf node (a primitive attribute) is determined by:

$$P_{leaf} = 1 - \frac{1}{(depth + 1)}$$

Where *depth* is the depth of the tree at the current node. Hence a root node will have a depth of 1, and therefore a probability of 0.5 of being a leaf node. Nodes at depth 2 will have a 0.67 probability of being a leaf node, and so on. If a node is a leaf node, it takes the value of one of the original features chosen at random. Otherwise, a function is randomly chosen from the set {*, /, +, -, %} and two child nodes are generated. In this manner there is no absolute limit placed on the depth any one tree may reach but the average depth is limited. During the initial creation no two trees in a single genotype are allowed to be alike, though this restriction is not enforced in later stages. Additionally, nodes with '–', '%' or '/' for functions cannot have child nodes that are equal to each other. In order to enforce this child nodes within a function '*' or '+' are ordered alphabetically to enable comparison (e.g. [width + length] will become [length + width]).

An individual is evaluated by constructing a new dataset with one feature for each tree in the genotype. This dataset is then passed to a C4.5(J48) classifier (using default parameters), whose performance on the dataset is evaluated using 10-fold cross validation. The percentage correct is then assigned to the individual and used as the fitness score.

Once the initial population has been evaluated, several generations of selection, crossover, mutation and evaluation are performed. After each evaluation, if the fittest individual in the current generation is fitter than the fittest so far, a copy of it is set aside and the generation noted. The evolutionary process continues until the following conditions are met: at least 10 generations have passed, and the fittest individual so far is at least 6 generations old. There is no maximum generation, but in practice very rarely have more than 50 generations been necessary, and often fewer than 30 are required.

We use tournament selection here, with tournament size 8 and a 0.3 probability of the fittest individual winning (otherwise a 'winner' is selected at random from the tournament group). There is a 0.6 probability of two-point crossover occurring between the ADFs of the two selected parents (whole trees are exchanged between genotypes) and a 0.6 probability that crossover will occur between two ADFs at a randomly chosen locus (sub-trees are exchanged between trees). Mutation is used with probability 0.008 per node where a randomly created subtree replaces the subtree under the selected node. We also use a form on inversion with probability 0.2 whereby the order of the ADFs between two randomly chosen loci is reversed. Experimentation on varying these parameters has found the algorithm to be fairly robust to their setting (not shown).

Once the termination criteria have been met the fittest individual is used to seed the feature selection stage.

2.2 Feature Selection

The fittest individual from the feature creation stage (ties broken randomly) is analysed to see if any of the original features do not appear to be used. If there are any missing, sufficient trees are added to ensure that every original feature in the dataset appears at least once (the new trees are not randomly generated as in the feature creation stage, but have single nodes containing the required attribute). This extended genotype (up to twice as long as the fittest individual of the feature creation stage) replaces the initial individual and is used as the basis of the second stage.

A new dataset is constructed with one attribute for every tree in the extended genotype. In an attempt to reduce over-fitting of the data, the order of the dataset is randomised at this point. This has the effect of providing a different split of the data for 10-fold cross validation during the selection stage, giving the algorithm a chance of recognising trees that performed well only due to the particular data partition in the creation stage. As a result of the randomisation, it is usually the case that the fitness score of individuals in the selection stage is less than that of individuals in the creation stage but solutions should be more robust.

For the GA a population of 101 bit strings is randomly created. The strings have the same number of bits as the genotype has trees – there is one bit for every attribute (some composite, some primitive attributes). The last member of the population, the 101st bit string, is not randomly created but is initialised to all ones. This ensures that there are no missing alleles at the start of the selection.

Once the entire population has been created, each genotype is evaluated and assigned a fitness score that is used in selecting the parents of the next generation. A GA bit string is evaluated by taking a copy of the parent dataset and removing every attribute that has a '0' in the corresponding position in the bit string. As in the feature creation stage, this dataset is then passed to a C4.5(J48) classifier whose performance on the dataset is evaluated using 10-fold cross validation. The percentage correct is then assigned to the bit string and used as the fitness score.

If the fittest individual in the current generation has a higher fitness score than the fittest so far (from the selection stage, ignoring genotypes from the feature creation stage), or it has the same fitness score and fewer '1's, a copy of it is set aside and the generation noted. As in the feature creation stage the cycles of selection, crossover, mutation, and evaluation continue until the following conditions are met: at least 10 generations have passed, and the fittest individual so far is at least 6 generations old.

The selection scheme is the same as for the creation stage. There is a 0.6 probability of two-point crossover and a 0.005 per bit probability of mutation.

3 Experimentation

We have used ten well-known data sets from the UCI repository to examine the performance of the GAP algorithm. The UCI datasets were chosen because they consisted entirely of numeric attributes (though the algorithm can handle some nominal attributes, as long as there are two or more numeric attributes present) and had no missing values (missing values could be handled with only a minor modification to the code). Table 1 shows the details of the ten datasets used here.

Table 1. UCI dataset information.

Dataset	# Numeric features	# Nominal features	# Classes	# Instances
BUPA Liver Disorder	6	0	2	345
Glass Identification	9	0	6	214
Ionosphere	34	0	2	351
New Thyroid	5	0	3	215
Pima Indians Diabetes	8	0	2	768
Sonar	60	0	2	208
Vehicle	18	0	4	846
Wine Recognition	13	0	3	178
Wisconsin Breast Cancer (New)	30	0	2	569
Wisconsin Breast Cancer (Original)	9	0	2	699

For performance comparisons the tests were performed using ten-fold cross-validation. An additional set of ten runs using ten-fold cross validation were made (a total of twenty runs, two sets of ten-fold cross-validation) to allow a paired *t*-test to establish significant improvement over C4.5(J48).

3.1 Results

The highest classification score for each dataset is shown in Table 2 in bold underline. The first two columns show the performance of the GAP algorithm on the training data and the last column shows the results of the paired *t*-test. Results that are significant at the 95% confidence level are shown in bold.

The GAP algorithm out-performs C4.5(J48) on eight out of ten datasets, and provides a significant improvement on three (Glass Identification, New Thyroid, and Wisconsin Breast Cancer Original) – two of which are significant at the 99% confidence level. There are no datasets on which the GAP algorithm performs significantly worse than C4.5(J48) alone.

The standard deviation of the GAP algorithm's results do not seem to differ greatly from that of C4.5(J48); there are five datasets where the GAP algorithms' standard deviation is greater and five where it is smaller. This is perhaps the most surprising aspect of the results, given that the GAP algorithm is unlikely to produce the same result twice when presented with exactly the same data, whereas C4.5(J48) will always give the same result if presented with the same data.

As noted in the introduction, Vafaie and DeJong [10] have used a very similar approach to improve the performance of C4.5. They use feature selection (GA) followed by feature construction (GP). We have examined the performance of our algorithm as described above with the two processes occurring in the opposite order. Results indicate that GAP gives either equivalent (e.g. Wisconsin Breast Cancer) or better performance (e.g. New Thyroid) (Table 3). We suggest this is due to GAP's potential to construct new features in a less restricted way, i.e. its ability to use all the original features during the create stage. For instance, on the New Thyroid dataset the select stage will always remove either feature 1 or feature 2 thus preventing the create stage from being able to construct the apparently useful feature "2"/"1" (see section 3.2). That is, on a number of datasets there is a significant difference (at the 95% confidence level) in the results brought about by changing the order of the stages.

3.2 Analysis

We were interested in whether the improvement over C4.5(J48) is simply the result of the selection stage choosing an improved subset of features and discarding the new constructed features. An analysis of the attributes output by the GAP classifier algorithm, and the use made of them in C4.5's decision trees, shows this is not the case.

As noted above, the results in Table 2 were obtained from twenty runs on each of ten UCI datasets, i.e. a total of two hundred individual solutions. In those two hundred individuals there are a total of 2,425 trees: 982 ADFs and 1,443 original features - a ratio of roughly two constructed features to three original features. *All but two of the two hundred individuals contained at least one constructed feature*. Table 4 gives details of the average number of ADFs per individual for each dataset (the number of original features used is not shown).

Table 2. Comparative performance of GAP algorithm and C4.5 (J48).

Dataset	GAP Train	S.D.	GAP Test	S.D.	C4.5 (J48)	S.D.	Paired *t*-test
BUPA Liver Disorder	75.04	2.37	65.97	11.27	**66.37**	8.86	-0.22
Glass Identification	78.17	1.95	**73.74**	9.86	68.28	8.86	**3.39**
Ionosphere	95.99	0.87	89.38	4.76	**89.82**	4.79	-0.34
New Thyroid	98.22	0.68	**96.27**	4.17	92.31	4.14	**3.02**
Pima Indians Diabetes	78.15	0.96	**73.50**	4.23	73.32	5.25	0.19
Sonar	92.33	1.27	**73.98**	11.29	73.86	10.92	0.05
Vehicle	78.82	1.21	**72.46**	4.72	72.22	3.33	0.20
Wine Recognition	98.47	0.80	**94.68**	5.66	93.27	5.70	0.85
Wisconsin Breast Cancer (New)	97.86	0.47	**95.62**	2.89	93.88	4.22	1.87
Wisconsin Breast Cancer (Original)	97.65	0.38	**95.63**	1.58	94.42	3.05	**2.11**

Table 3. Comparison of ordering of Create and Select stages.

	Create then Select		Select then Create	
Dataset	Test	S.D.	Test	S.D.
BUPA Liver Disorder	65.97	11.27	**67.42**	8.23
Glass Identification	**73.74**	9.86	68.75	6.36
Ionosphere	**89.38**	4.76	89.02	4.62
New Thyroid	**96.27**	4.17	93.67	5.82
Pima Indians Diabetes	73.50	4.23	**74.09**	4.46
Sonar	**73.98**	11.29	73.16	9.05
Vehicle	72.46	4.72	72.46	3.01
Wine Recognition	94.68	5.66	**94.69**	3.80
Wisconsin Breast Cancer (New)	95.62	2.89	**95.88**	3.15
Wisconsin Breast Cancer (Original)	**95.63**	1.58	95.13	2.16

Knowing that the feature selection stage continues as long as there is a reduction in the number of attributes without reducing the fitness score, we can assume that C4.5(J48) is making good use of all the attributes in most if not all of the winning individuals. This can be demonstrated by looking in detail at the attributes in a single winner, and the decision tree created by C4.5(J48).

One of the best performers on the New Thyroid dataset had three trees, two of them ADFs and hence constructed features. The original dataset contains five features and the class:

1. T3-resin uptake test. (A percentage)
2. Total Serum thyroxin as measured by the isotopic displacement method.
3. Total serum triiodothyronine as measured by radioimmuno assay.
4. Basal thyroid-stimulating hormone (TSH) as measured by radioimmuno assay.
5. Maximal absolute difference of TSH value after injection of 200 micro grams of thyrotropin-releasing hormone as compared to the basal value.

Class attribute. (1 = normal, 2 = hyper, 3 = hypo)

Table 4. Analysis of the constructed features for each data set.

Dataset	Results			
Name	**# Features in Dataset**	**Average # Features**	**Average # ADFs**	**Minimum # ADFs**
BUPA Liver Disorder	6	4.9	2.6	1
Glass Identification	9	7.1	3.1	1
Ionosphere	34	19.7	7.6	4
New Thyroid	5	3.2	2.3	1
Pima Indians Diabetes	8	6.4	2.7	1
Sonar	60	38.0	13.6	5
Vehicle	18	16.3	5.5	2
Wine Recognition	13	5.2	2.1	0
Wisconsin Breast Cancer (New)	30	15.7	7.0	4
Wisconsin Breast Cancer (Original)	9	5.0	2.9	1

In the chosen example the newly constructed features were:

- "5" becomes `Feat0`
- (("1"/"4")*"2") becomes `Feat1`
- ("2"/"1") becomes `Feat2`

The decision tree created by C4.5 (the numbers after the class prediction indicate the count of train instances correctly / incorrectly classified) was:

```
Feat1 <= 222.352941: hypo (19.0)
Feat1 > 222.352941
|    Feat2 <= 0.113761: normal (102.0/1.0)
|    Feat2 > 0.113761
|    |    Feat0 <= 1.1: hyper (26.0)
|    |    Feat0 > 1.1: normal (3.0)
```

It is apparent that C4.5(J48) is using the constructed features to classify a large majority of the instances, and only referring to one of the original features (`Feat0`, or the fifth feature in the dataset) in 29 of 150 cases.

3.3 A Rough Comparison to Other Algorithms

Table 5 presents a number of published results we have found regarding the same ten UCI datasets using other machine learning algorithms. It should be noted that in the table are the results for C4.5 that were not obtained using J48. Cells in the table are left blank where algorithms were not tested on the dataset in question. The highest classification score for each dataset is shown in bold underline.

The results for C4.5, HIDER and XCS were obtained from [2], those for O.F. ARTMAP ('Ordered Fuzzy ARTMAP', a neural network algorithm) from [1] and LVSM (Lagrangian Support Vector Machines) from [6].

Table 5. Performance of GAP and other algorithms on the UCI datasets.

Dataset	GAP	C4.5 (J48)	C4.5	HIDER	XCS	O. F. ARTMAP	LVSM
BUPA Liver Disorder	65.97	66.37	65.27	64.29	**67.85**	57.01	68.68
Glass Identification	**73.74**	68.28	67.27	70.59	72.53	69.56	
Ionosphere	89.38	**89.82**					87.75
New Thyroid	**96.27**	92.31					
Pima Indians Diabetes	73.50	73.32	67.94	74.1	68.62	69.8	**78.12**
Sonar	73.98	73.86	69.69	56.93	53.41	**79.96**	
Vehicle	**72.46**	72.22					
Wine Recognition	94.68	93.27	93.29	96.05	92.74	**98.27**	
Wisconsin Breast Cancer (New)	**95.62**	93.88					
Wisconsin Breast Cancer (Original)	95.63	94.42	93.72	95.71	**96.27**	94.39	

The differences between the reported results for C4.5 and those for C4.5 as used in this paper (J48, the WEKA implementation of C4.5) are likely to arise from different data partitions used for the tests (the most notable being the 5.38% difference in results for Pima Indians Diabetes). This discrepancy highlights the dangers inherent in comparing results with published data – the comparison should be seen as purely informal. The only comparisons that can be relied upon are those between the GAP classifier and C4.5(J48) as these have been performed using exactly the same procedure and data partitions. The results are by no means an exhaustive list of current machine learning algorithms, nor are they guaranteed to be the best performing algorithms available, but they give some indication of the relative performance of our approach – which appears to be very good.

4 Conclusion

In this paper we have presented an approach to improve the classification performance of the well-known induction algorithm C4.5. We have shown that GP individuals consisting of multiple trees/ADFs can be used for effective feature creation and that solutions, combined with feature selection via a GA, can give significant improvements to the classification accuracy of C4.5.

Future work will apply our approach to other datasets and data mining algorithms.

References

1. Ahluwalia, M. & Bull, L. (1999) Co-Evolving Functions in Genetic Programming: Classification using k-nearest neighbour. In W. Banzhaf, J. Daida, G. Eiben, M-H. Garzon, J. Honavar, K. Jakeila, R. Smith (eds) *GECCO-99: Proceedings of the Genetic and Evolutionary Computation Conference*. Morgan Kaufmann, pp. 947–952.

2. Dixon, P. W., Corne, D. W., & Oates, M. J. (2001) A Preliminary Investigation of Modified XCS as a Generic Data Mining Tool. In P-L. Lanzi, W. Stolzmann, S. Wilson (eds) *Advances in Learning Classifier Systems*. Springer, pp.133-151.
3. Holland, J.H. (1975) *Adaptation in Natural and Artificial Systems*. Univ. Michigan.
4. Kelly, J.D. & Davis, L. (1991) Hybridizing the Genetic Algorithm and the K Nearest Neighbors Classification Algorithm. In R. Belew & L. Booker (eds) *Proceedings of the Fourth International Conference on Genetic Algorithms*. Morgan Kaufmann, pp377-383.
5. Koza, J.R. (1992) *Genetic Programming*. MIT Press.
6. Mangasarian, O. L. & Musicant, D. R. (2001) Lagrangian support vector machines. *Journal of Machine Learning Research* 1:161-177.
7. Quinlan, J.R. (1993) *C4.5: Programs for Machine Learning*. Morgan Kaufmann.
8. Raymer, M.L., Punch, W., Goodman, E.D. & Kuhn, L. (1996) Genetic Programming for Improved Data Mining - Application to the Biochemistry of Protein Interactions. In J.R. Koza, K. Deb, M. Dorigo, D.B. Fogel, M.Garzon, H. Iba & R. Riolo (eds) *Proceedings of the Second Annual Conference on Genetic Programming*, Morgan Kaufmann, pp375-380.
9. Siedlecki, W. & Sklansky, J. (1988) On Automatic Feature Selection. *International Journal of Pattern Recognition and Artificial Intelligence* 2:197-220.
10. Vafaie, H. & De Jong, K. 1995. Genetic Algorithms as a Tool for Restructuring Feature Space Representations. In *Proceedings of the International Conference on Tools with A.I.* IEEE Computer Society Press.
11. Witten, I.H. & Frank, E. (2000) *Data Mining: Practical Machine Learning Tools and Techniques with Java Implementations*. Morgan Kaufmann.

Genetic Programming Applied to Compiler Heuristic Optimization

Mark Stephenson[1], Una-May O'Reilly[2], Martin C. Martin[2], and Saman Amarasinghe[1]

[1] Laboratory for Computer Science
[2] Artificial Intelligence Laboratory
Massachusetts Inst. of Technology
Cambridge, MA, 02139
{mstephen,saman}@cag.lcs.mit.edu, {unamay,mcm}@ai.mit.edu

Abstract. Genetic programming (GP) has a natural niche in the optimization of small but high payoff software heuristics. We use GP to optimize the priority functions associated with two well known compiler heuristics: predicated hyperblock formation, and register allocation. Our system achieves impressive speedups over a standard baseline for both problems. For hyperblock selection, application-specific heuristics obtain an average speedup of 23% (up to 73%) for the applications in our suite. By evolving the compiler's heuristic over several benchmarks, the best general-purpose heuristic our system found improves the predication algorithm by an average of 25% on our training set, and 9% on a completely unrelated test set. We also improve a well-studied register allocation heuristic. On average, our system obtains a 6% speedup when it specializes the register allocation algorithm for individual applications. The general-purpose heuristic for register allocation achieves a 3% improvement.

1 Introduction

Genetic programming (GP) [11] is tantalizing because it is a method for searching a high dimensional, large space of executable expressions. GP is widely applicable because its representation, a directly *executable expression*, is so flexible. Koza [11] argues that most problems can be reformulated to accept program-style solutions.

Yet, even without reformulation, there are a vast number of problems for which a program or codelet is a *direct* solution. Consider substantially sized software systems such as compilers, schedulers, text editors, web crawlers, and intelligent tutoring systems. Current GP knowledge and practice certainly cannot generate such large scale efforts. Yet, GP can act remedially. For example, Ryan et al. [18] used GP to convert serial code to parallel. There was a sizeable payoff in updating legacy software.

When large scale software systems are developed, they inevitably acquire shortcomings. We believe that GP can address many problems associated with

C. Ryan et al. (Eds.): EuroGP 2003, LNCS 2610, pp. 238–253, 2003.

complex systems– either at development time or later. Large software systems have 'admitted' shortcomings that arise from necessity. Real world problems of complex nature often offer NP-complete sub-problems. Since these problems demand solutions to be delivered within practical time limits, the employment of heuristics is necessary. Heuristics, by definition, are supposed to be good enough, but not necessarily perfect.

The genesis of our idea for using GP came from dissatisfaction with compiler efficiency and design, combined with our realization that compiler designers are overwhelmed with countless nonlinearly complex considerations. We examined different *passes* within a compiler and their heuristics. We found a common, easily learned feature in the heuristics that we term a 'priority function'. Put simply, priority functions prioritize the options available to a compiler algorithm. Could GP generate more effective priority functions than currently exist in compilers? We use Trimaran– a freely downloadable research compiler and simulator– to answer that question [19]. This paper offers a proof of concept: we use genetic programming to optimize the priority functions associated with register allocation as well as branch removal via predication. Our contention is that priority functions are most certain to also lurk in heuristics within other similar software systems. Genetic programming is eminently suited to optimizing priority functions because they are best represented in GP terms: as directly executable expressions. Plus, GP offers the scalable means of searching through priority function space.

2 Related Work

Both GP[15] and Grammatical Evolution (GRE)[13] have been used to optimize a caching strategy. A caching strategy, in essence, has a priority function. It must determine which program memory locations to assign to cache or move to main memory in order to minimize 'misses'. A miss occurs when main memory must be accessed rather than the cache. One human designed priority function is Least Recently Used (LRU). While LRU is intuitive, results evolved via GP and GRE outperform it.

Many researchers have applied machine-learning methods to compilation, and therefore, only the most relevant works are cited here. By evolving compiler heuristics, and not the applications themselves, we need only apply our process once. This contrasts with Cooper et al. who use genetic algorithms (GA) to solve compilation phase ordering problems [7] and the COGEN(t) [10] compiler. Calder et al. use supervised learning techniques to fine-tune static branch prediction heuristics [4]. Since our performance criteria is based on execution time it requires an unsupervised technique such as the one we present in this paper.

3 Compilation, Heuristics and Priority Functions

Compiler writers have a difficult task. They are expected to create effective and inexpensive solutions to NP-hard problems such as instruction scheduling and register allocation for intractably complex computer architectures. They cope by devising clever heuristics that find good approximate solutions for a large class of applications.

A key insight in alleviating this situation is that many heuristics have a focal point. A single *priority* or *cost* function often dictates the efficacy of a heuristic. A priority function, a function of the factors that affect a given problem, measures the relative value or weight of choices that a compiler algorithm can make.

Take register allocation, for example. When a graph coloring register allocator cannot successfully color an interference graph, it 'spills' a variable from a register to memory and removes it from the graph. Choosing an appropriate variable to spill is crucial. For many allocators, this decision is handled by a single priority function. Based on an evaluation of relevant data (*e.g.*, number of references, depth in loop nest, etc.), the allocator invokes its priority function to assign a weight to each uncolored variable. Examining the relative weights, the allocator determines which variable to spill.

Compiler writers tediously fine-tune priority functions to achieve suitable performance [2]. Priority functions are widely used and tied to complicated factors. A non-exhaustive list of examples, just in compilation, includes list scheduling [9], clustered scheduling [14], hyperblock formation [12], meld scheduling [1], modulo scheduling [17] and register allocation [6]. GP's representation appears ideal for improving priority functions. We have tested this observation via two case studies: predication and register allocation.

4 Predication

Studies show that branch instructions account for nearly 20% of all instructions executed in a program [16]. The control dependences that branch instructions impose decrease execution speed and make compiler optimizations difficult. Moreover, the uncertainty surrounding branches makes it difficult (and in many cases impossible) to parallelize disjoint paths of control flow. The data and control dependences may preclude instruction level parallelism.

Unpredictable branches are also incredibly costly on modern day processors. The Pentium® 4 architecture invalidates up to 120 in-flight instructions when it mispredicts. When a branch is mispredicted, not only does the processor have to nullify incorrect operations, it may have to invalidate many unrelated instructions following the branch that are in the pipeline.

The shortcomings of branching have led architects to rejuvenate *predication*. Predication allows a processor that can execute and issue more than one instruction at a time to simultaneously execute the taken and fall-through paths of control flow. The processor nullifies all instructions in the incorrect path. A predicate operand guards the execution of every instruction to ensure only correct paths modify processor state.

Trimaran's predication algorithm identifies code *regions* that are suitable for predication. It then enumerates paths (*i.e.*, sequences of instructions that it must merge into a predicated hyperblock). Merging depends on the compiler's confidence that a path is processor efficient. The priority function assigns the confidence value of a path.

Trimaran's priority function is shown in Equation 1. In addition to considering the probability of path execution, this priority function penalizes paths that have hazards (*e.g.*, pointer dereferences), relatively large dependence height, or too many instructions.

$$priority_i = exec\_ratio_i \cdot h_i \cdot (2.1 - d\_ratio_i - o\_ratio_i) \; where \tag{1}$$

$$h_i = \begin{cases} 0.25 & : \text{ if } path_i \text{ contains a hazard.} \\ 1 & : \text{ if } path_i \text{ is hazard free.} \end{cases}$$

$$d\_ratio_i = \frac{dep\_height_i}{\max_{j=1 \to N} dep\_height_j}, \qquad o\_ratio_i = \frac{num\_ops_i}{\max_{j=1 \to N} num\_ops_j}$$

The variable *exec_ratio*, which is based on a runtime profile, is the probability that the path is executed; num_ops_i refers to the number of operations in $path_i$, and *dep_height* is the extent of control dependence.

4.1 Predication Primitives

In addition to the path properties used in Equation 1, there are other salient properties that could potentially distinguish good paths from useless paths. We created a GP terminal corresponding to each property. Tables 1 and 5 contain lists of the primitives we use.

5 Priority-Based Coloring Register Allocation

The gap between register access times and memory access times is growing. Therefore, register allocation, the process of assigning variables to fast registers, is an increasingly important compiler optimization. Many register allocation algorithms use cost functions to determine which variables to spill when spilling is required. For instance in priority-based coloring register allocation, the priority function is an estimate of the relative benefits of storing a given variable[1] in a register [6]. The algorithm then assigns variables to registers in priority order. The success of the register allocation algorithm depends on the priority function.

Priority-based coloring first associates a *live range* with every variable. This range simply denotes the portion of code in which a variable is *live*. More specifically, a live range is the composition of code segments (basic blocks), through which the associated variable's value must be preserved. The algorithm then

[1] For ease of explanation, our description of priority-based register allocation is not precisely accurate. A single variable may actually be assigned to several different registers. See [6] for details.

Table 1. GP Terminals for Predication Experiments. These properties may influence predication. Some are extracted from profile information while others do not require program execution. We also include the min, mean, max, and standard deviation of all paths to provide macroscopic information.

Property	Description
dep_height	The maximum instruction dependence height over all instructions in path.
num_ops	The total number of instructions in the path.
exec_ratio	How frequently this path is executed compared to other paths considered (from profile).
num_branches	The total number of branches in the path.
predictability	Path predictability obtained by simulating a branch predictor (from profile).
avg_ops_executed	The average number of instructions executed in the path (from profile).
unsafe_JSR	If the path contains a subroutine call that may have side-effects, it returns *true*; otherwise it returns *false*.
safe_JSR	If the path contains a side-effect free subroutine call, it returns *true*; otherwise it returns *false*.
mem_hazard	If the path contains an unresolvable memory access, it returns *true*; otherwise it returns *false*.
max_dep_height	The maximum dependence height over all paths considered for hyperblock inclusion.
total_ops	The sum of all instructions in paths considered for hyperblock inclusion.
num_paths	Number of paths considered for hyperblock inclusion.

prioritizes each live range based on the estimated execution savings of register allocating the associated variable:

$$savings_i = w_i \cdot (LDsave \cdot uses_i + STsave \cdot defs_i) \tag{2}$$

$$priority(lr) = \frac{\sum_{i \in lr} savings_i}{N} \tag{3}$$

Equation 2 is used to compute the savings of each code segment. $LDsave$ and $STsave$ are estimates of the execution time saved by keeping the associated variable in a register for references and definitions respectively. $uses_i$ and $defs_i$ represent the number of uses and definitions of a variable in code segment i. w_i is the estimated execution frequency for the segment.

Equation 3 sums the savings over the N code segments that compose the live range. Thus, this priority function represents the savings incurred by accessing a register instead of resorting to main memory.

5.1 Register Allocation Primitives

Trimaran's register allocation heuristic essentially works at the basic block level. To improve register allocation we evolved an expression to replace Equation 2.

Table 2. GP Terminals for register allocation experiments.

Property	Description
$spill\_cost$	The estimated cost of spilling this range to memory. See Equation 2.
$region\_weight$	Number of times the basic block was executed (from profile).
$live\_ops$	The number of live operations in the block.
num_calls	The number of procedure calls in a basic block.
$callee\_benefit$	The callee's 'benefit' of allocating the range.
$caller\_benefit$	The caller's 'benefit' of allocating the range.
def_num	The number of definitions in the block.
use_num	The number of uses in the block.
$STsave$	Estimate of the execution time saved by keeping a definition in a register.
$LDsave$	Estimate of the execution time saved by keeping a reference in a register.
has_single_ref	If the block has a single reference, return $true$, otherwise return $false$.
$is\_pass\_through$	If the number of live references in the block is greater than 0, return $true$, otherwise return $false$.
ref_op_count	The number of references in the block.
reg_size	The number of registers available for the register class of the live range.
$forbidden\_regs$	The number of registers that are not available to the live range (because it interferes with an allocated live range).
GPR, FPR, PR	If the live range belongs to the class GPR, FPR, or PR respectively, return $true$, otherwise return $false$.

Since Equation 3 simply sums and normalizes the priorities of the individual basic blocks, we leave it intact. Table 2 shows the quantities we used as GP terminals for the priority-based coloring register allocator.

6 Experimental Parameters

6.1 Infrastructure

Our experimental infrastructure is built upon Trimaran [19]. Trimaran is an integrated compiler and simulator for a parameterized EPIC (Explicitly Parallel Instruction Computing) architecture. Trimaran's compiler, which is called IMPACT, performs code profiling. Table 3 details the specific architecture over which we evolved. This model is similar to Intel's Itanium architecture. We enabled the following Trimaran compiler optimizations: function inlining, loop unrolling, backedge coalescing, acyclic global scheduling [5], modulo scheduling [20], hyperblock formation, register allocation, machine-specific peephole optimization, and several other classic optimizations.

We built a GP loop around Trimaran and internally modified IMPACT by replacing its predication priority function (Equation 1) with our GP expression parser and evaluator. The predication algorithm provides variable bindings for

Table 3. Characteristics of the EPIC architecture.

Feature	Description
Registers	64 general-purpose registers, 64 floating-point registers, and 256 predicate registers.
Integer units	4 fully-pipelined units with 1-cycle latencies, except for multiply instructions, which require 3 cycles, and divide instructions, which require 8.
Floating-point units	2 fully-pipelined units with 3-cycle latencies, except for divide instructions, which require 8 cycles.
Memory units	2 memory units. L1 cache accesses take 2 cycles, L2 accesses take 7 cycles, and L3 accesses require 35 cycles. Stores are buffered, and thus require 1 cycle.
Branch unit	1 branch unit.
Branch prediction	2-bit branch predictor with a 5-cycle branch misprediction penalty.

the primitives, and most of these were already available in IMPACT. We modified the compiler's profiler to extract branch predictability statistics. We added the minimum, maximum, mean, and standard deviation of all path-specific characteristics, which together encapsulate some global knowledge. In addition, we added a 2-bit dynamic branch predictor to the simulator.

Similarly, to study register allocation we modified Trimaran's Elcor register allocator by replacing its priority function (Equation 2) with another expression parser and evaluator. To more effectively stress the register allocator, we only use 32 general-purpose registers and 32 floating-point registers.

6.2 GP Run Parameters

For each run of 50 generations, the initial population consists of 399 randomly initialized expressions, as well as Trimaran's original priority function (Equation 1 for hyperblock formation, and Equation 2 for register allocation). Tournament selection with a tournament size of seven is used. We *randomly* replace 22% of the population every generation with offspring adapted by mutation and crossover. Roughly 5% of the offspring are mutated, and the remainder result from crossover. Only the *single* best expression is guaranteed survival. In addition to the specialized primitives in Table 1 and Table 2, we add the standard arithmetic and boolean logical and comparison primitives listed in Tables 4 and 5.

6.3 Evaluation

The results presented in this paper use total execution time (reported by the Trimaran system) for either one or two sets of input data to assign fitness. This approach rewards the optimization of frequently executed procedures, and therefore, it may be slow to converge upon general-purpose solutions. However, when one wants to specialize a compiler for a given program, this evaluation

Table 4. General real-valued functions included in the primitive set.

Real-Valued Function	Representation
$Real_1 + Real_2$	(add $Real_1$ $Real_2$)
$Real_1 - Real_2$	(sub $Real_1$ $Real_2$)
$Real_1 \cdot Real_2$	(mul $Real_1$ $Real_2$)
$\begin{cases} Real_1/Real_2 & : \text{if} Real_2 \neq 0 \\ 0 & : \text{if } Real_2 = 0 \end{cases}$	(div $Real_1$ $Real_2$)
$\sqrt{Real_1}$	(sqrt $Real_1$)
$\begin{cases} Real_1 & : \text{if} Bool_1 \\ Real_2 & : \text{if not} Bool_1 \end{cases}$	(tern $Bool_1$ $Real_1$ $Real_2$)
$\begin{cases} Real_1 \cdot Real_2 & : \text{if} Bool_1 \\ Real_2 & : \text{if not} Bool_1 \end{cases}$	(cmul $Bool_1$ $Real_1$ $Real_2$)
Returns real constant K	(rconst K)
Returns real value of arg from environment	(rarg arg)

Table 5. General purpose GP primitives. Both experiments use the primitives shown in this table.

Boolean-Valued Function	Representation
$Bool_1$ and $Bool_2$	(and $Bool_1$ $Bool_2$)
$Bool_1$ or $Bool_2$	(or $Bool_1$ $Bool_2$)
not $Bool_1$	(not $Bool_1$)
$Real_1 < Real_2$	(lt $Real_1$ $Real_2$)
$Real_1 > Real_2$	(gt $Real_1$ $Real_2$)
$Real_1 = Real_2$	(eq $Real_1$ $Real_2$)
Returns Boolean constant $\{true, false\}$	(bconst $\{true, false\}$)
Returns Boolean value of arg from environment	(barg arg)

of fitness works extremely well. Our system rewards *parsimony* by selecting the smaller of two otherwise equally fit expressions [11, p. 109].

Our experiments select training and testing programs from a suite of 24 benchmarks listed in Table 6. We run GP on nine benchmarks to examine specialized predication priority functions and six benchmarks for register allocation priority functions.

To find a general-purpose priority function (*i.e.*, a function that works well for multiple programs), we run GP on a set of 'training' programs, each with one set of input data. To avoid the computational expense of a large training set, we use dynamic subset selection (DSS) [8]. DSS essentially selects different subsets (size 4,5, or 6) of the benchmark training set that is used for fitness evaluation. Subset selection is based on how poorly the current best expression performs. Thus, hard to optimize training benchmarks are more likely to appear in the training set. The training set consists of twelve and eight benchmarks for predication and register allocation, respectively.

Table 6. Benchmarks used. The set includes applications from the SpecInt, SpecFP, Mediabench benchmark suites, and a few miscellaneous programs.

Benchmark	Suite	Description
codrle4 decodrle4	See [3]	RLE type 4 encoder/decoder.
huff_enc huff_dec	See [3]	A Huffman encoder/decoder.
djpeg	Mediabench	Lossy still image decompressor.
g721encode g721decode	Mediabench	CCITT voice compressor/decompressor.
mpeg2dec	Mediabench	Lossy video decompressor.
rasta	Mediabench	Speech recognition application.
rawcaudio rawdaudio	Mediabench	Adaptive differential pulse code modulation audio encoder/decoder.
toast	Mediabench	Speech transcoder.
unepic	Mediabench	Experimental image decompressor.
085.cc1	SPEC92	gcc C compiler.
052.alvinn	SPEC92	Single-precision neural network training.
179.art	SPEC2000	A neural network-based image recognition algorithm.
osdemo mipmap	Mediabench Mediabench	Part of a 3-D graphics library. similar to OpenGL.
129.compress	SPEC95	In-memory file compressor and decompressor.
023.eqntott	SPEC92	Creates a truth table from a logical representation of a Boolean equation.
132.ijpeg	SPEC95	JPEG compressor and decompressor.
130.li	SPEC95	Lisp interpreter.
124.m88ksim	SPEC95	Processor simulator.
147.vortex	SPEC95	An object oriented database.

We present the best results of all runs completed to date. This illustrates our focus on application performance. We used the recognized benchmarks in Table 6 to evaluate evolved priority functions. The set includes all of the Trimaran certified benchmarks[2] [19] and most of the Mediabench benchmarks.

7 Results

7.1 Predication: Specialized Priority Functions

Specialized heuristics are created by optimizing a priority function for a particular benchmark evaluated with one set of input data. Figure 1 shows that GP is extremely effective on this basis. The dark bar shows the speedup of each benchmark, over Trimaran's baseline heuristic, when run with the same data on which it was trained. The light bar shows the speedup when alternate input data

[2] We could not get 134.perl to execute correctly, though [19] certified it.

is used. We obtain an average speedup of 23% (up to 73%) for our evaluation suite.

As we would expect, in most cases the speedup on the training data is greater than that achieved on the test data. The alternate input data likely exercises different paths of control flow—paths which may have been unused during training.

In most runs, the *initial* population contains at least one expression that outperforms the baseline. This means that by simply creating and testing 399 random expressions, we were able to find a priority function that outperformed Trimaran's for the given benchmark and input data. In many cases, GP finds a superior priority function quickly, and finds only marginal improvements as the evolution continues. In fact, the baseline priority function is often quickly obscured by GP-generated expressions. Note, however, that human designed priority functions may have been designed for more generality than can be evaluated in our investigative setup.

Once GP has homed in on a fairly good solution, the search space and operator dynamics are such that most offspring will be worse, some will be equal and very few turn out to be better. This seems indicative of a steep hill in the solution space. In addition, multiple runs yield only minuscule differences in performance. This might indicate the search space (determined by our primitive set) has many possible solutions associated with a given fitness.

7.2 Predication: Finding General Purpose Priority Functions

We divided the benchmarks in Table 6 into two exclusive sets[3]: a 12 element training set, and a 12 element test set. We then applied the resulting priority function to all 12 benchmarks in the test set. Since the benchmarks in the test set are not related to the benchmarks in the training set, this is a measure of the priority function's generality.

Figure 2 shows the results of applying the single best priority function to the benchmarks in the training set. The dark bar associated with each benchmark is the speedup over Trimaran's base heuristic when the training input data is used. This data set yields a 44% improvement. The light bar shows results when alternate input data is used. The overall improvement for this set is 25%.

It is interesting that, on average, the general-purpose priority function outperforms the application-specific priority function for the alternate data set. The general-purpose solution is less susceptible to variations in input data precisely because it is more generally applicable.

Figure 3 shows how well the best general purpose priority function performed on the test set. The average speedup over the test set is 9%. In three cases (unepic, 023.eqntott, and 085.cc1) Trimaran's baseline heuristic marginally outperforms the GP-generated priority function. For the remaining benchmarks, the heuristic our system found is better.

[3] We chose to train mostly on Mediabench applications because they compile and run faster than the Spec benchmarks. However, we randomly chose two Spec benchmarks for added coverage.

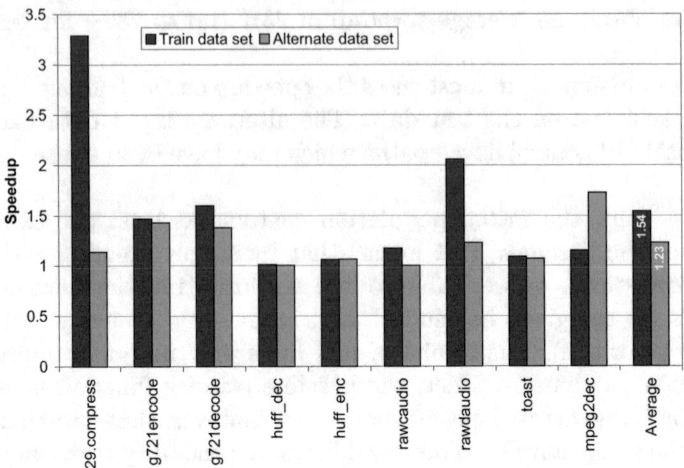

Fig. 1. GP Evolved Specialized Predication Priority Functions. Dark colored bars indicate speedup over Trimaran's baseline heuristic when using the same input data set on which the specialized priority function was trained. The light colored bars show speedup when alternate input data was tested.

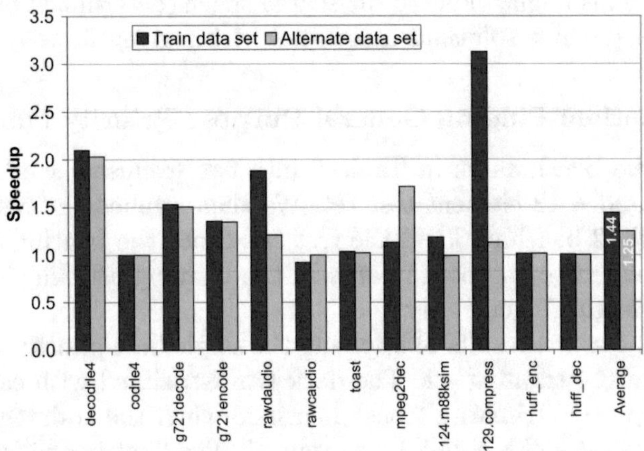

Fig. 2. GP Performance with General Purpose Predication Priority Functions. Training on multiple benchmarks. A *single* priority function was obtained by training over all the benchmarks in this graph. The dark bars represent speedups obtained by running the given benchmark on the same data that was used to train the priority function. The light bars correspond to an alternate data set.

7.3 Register Allocation: Specialized Priority Functions

Figures 4 shows speedups obtained by specializing the Trimaran register allocator's priority function for specific benchmarks. The dark bar associated with each benchmark represents the speedup obtained by using the same input data that was used to specialize the heuristic. The light bar shows the speedup when

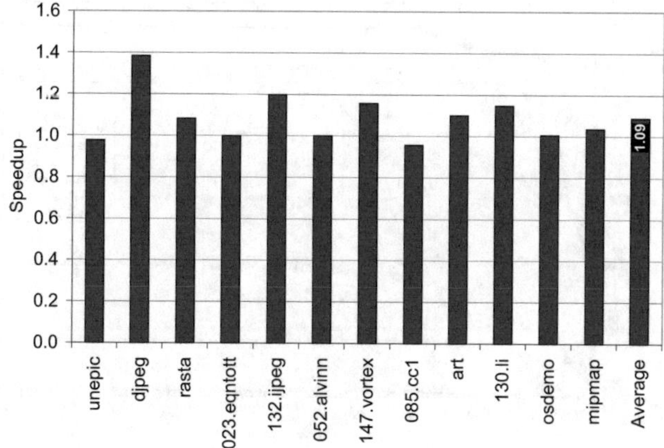

Fig. 3. GP Performance with General Purpose Predication Priority Functions. Cross validation of the general-purpose priority function. The best priority function found by training on the benchmarks in Figure 2 is applied to the benchmarks in this graph.

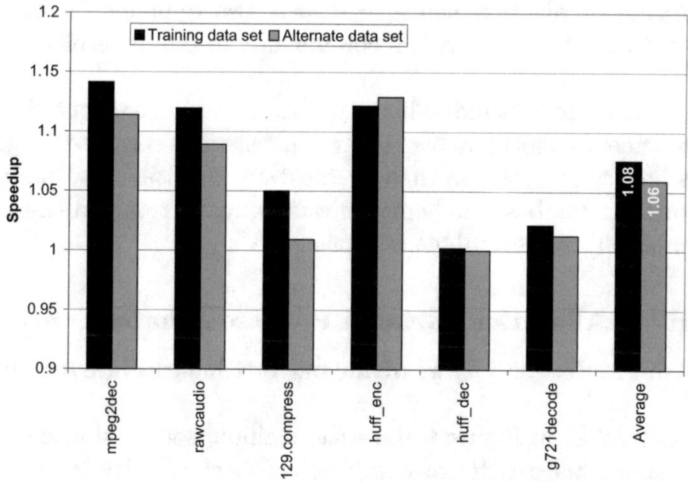

Fig. 4. GP Performance on Specialized Register Allocation Priority Functions. The dark colored bars are speedups using the same data set on which the specialized priority function was trained. The light colored bars are speedups that use an alternate data set.

an alternate input data set is used. GP evolved register allocation functions that improve the heuristic described in Section 5 by up to 13%.

Once again, it makes sense that the relative performance on training input data is better than that achieved on the alternate input data. In contrast to predication, however, with register allocation, we see that the difference between the two is less pronounced. This is likely because predication is extremely data-driven and thus vulnerable to diverse input data. An examination of the

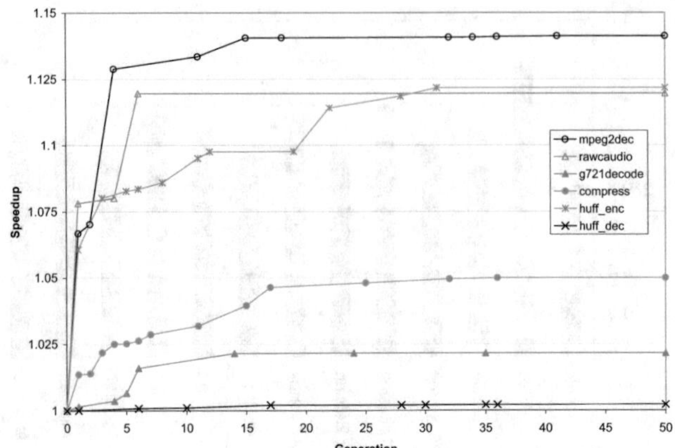

Fig. 5. GP Evolution on Specialized Register Allocation Priority Functions. This figure graphs fitness over generations. Unlike the hyperblock selection evolution, these fitnesses converge slowly.

general-purpose predication heuristic reveals two dynamic factors (*exec_ratio* and *predictability*) that are critical components in the hyperblock decision process.

Figure 5 plots the best individual's speedup over generations. The fairly constant improvement in speedup over several generations seems to suggest that this problem is harder to optimize than predication. Additionally, unlike the predication algorithm, the baseline heuristic was typically retained (*i.e.*, it remained in the population) for several generations.

7.4 Register Allocation: General Purpose Priority Functions

Just as we did in Section 7.2, we divide our benchmarks into a training set and a test set[4].

The benchmarks in Figure 6 show the training set for this experiment. The figure also shows the results of applying the best priority function (from our DSS run) to all the benchmarks in the set. The dark bar associated with each benchmark is the speedup over Trimaran's base heuristic when using the training input data. The average for this data set is 3%. The light bar shows results when alternate data is used. An average speedup of 3% is also attained with this data.

Figure 7 shows the test set for this experiment. The figure shows the speedups (over Trimaran's baseline) achieved by applying the single best priority function to all the benchmarks. Even though we trained on a 32-register machine, we also apply the priority function to a 64-register machine. It is interesting that the learned priority function is not only stable across benchmarks, it is also stable across similar platforms.

[4] This experiment uses smaller test and training sets due to preexisting bugs in Trimaran. It does not correctly compile several of our benchmarks when targeting a machine with 32 registers.

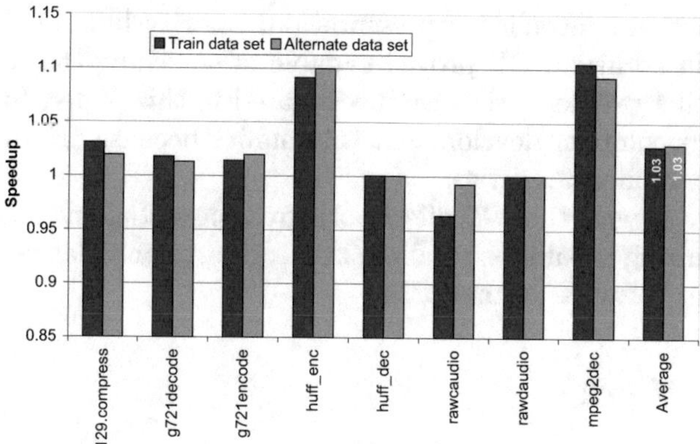

Fig. 6. GP Performance with General Purpose Register Allocation Priority Functions. Training on multiple benchmarks. Our DSS evolution trained on all the benchmarks in this figure. The single best priority function was applied to all the benchmarks. The dark bars represent speedups obtained by running the given benchmark on the same data that was used to train the priority function. The light bars correspond to an alternate data set.

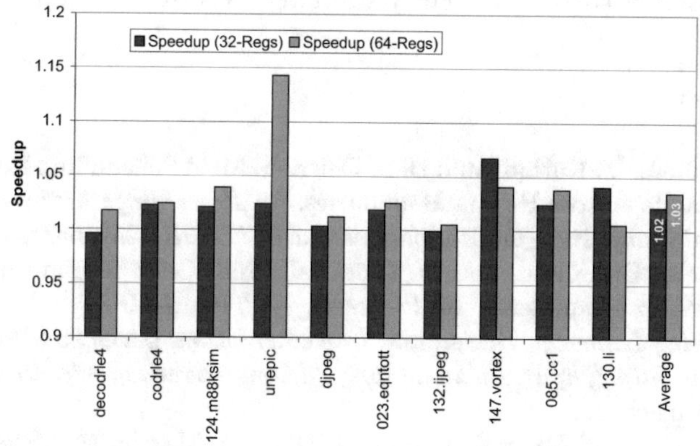

Fig. 7. GP Performance with General Purpose Register Allocation Priority Functions. Cross validation of the general-purpose priority function. The best priority function found by the DSS run is applied to the benchmarks in this graph. Results from two target architectures are shown.

8 Conclusions

We used GP in a straightforward fashion to optimize priority functions in compiler heuristics and observed impressive results that improve on existing ones. These results are valuable to the compiler development community because the speedup comes in code sections that are difficult to hand-optimize because of nonlinearities within the compiler as well as overwhelming complexity in the target processor architecture. GP is especially appropriate for this application because it offers a convenient representation; priority functions are executable expressions. In addition, GP proved capable of searching the solution space of the two compiler problems that we investigated in this paper. In general, GP is valuable to the compiler development community because priority functions are prevalent in compiler heuristics.

Our results suggest that GP offers both great potential and convenience in the niche of optimizing isolatable, smaller-sized code sections that perform heuristics within a larger software system base.

9 Future Work

We have presented our research as a proof of concept and as such, to derive general conclusions, we have used a very standard ('off the shelf') version of GP in terms of operators and the selection algorithm used. We have not added any 'bells and whistles' that might offer more improvement. In order to improve the results for a specific compiler, we must strive to better understand our system. To this end we plan to study the priority functions' fitness landscapes via hillclimbing, simplify and better understand the GP evolved expressions, and conduct additional runs with some parameter experimentation.

References

1. S. G. Abraham, V. Kathail, and B. L. Deitrich. Meld Scheduling: Relaxing Scheduling Constaints Across Region Boundaries. In *Proceedings of the 29th Annual International Symposium on Microarchitecture (MICRO-29)*, pages 308–321, 1996.
2. D. Bernstein, D. Goldin, and M. G. et. al. Spill Code Minimization Techniques for Optimizing Compilers. In *Proceedings of the SIGPLAN '89 Conference on Programming Language Design and Implementation*, pages 258–263, 1989.
3. D. Bourgin. *http://hpux.u-aizu.ac.jp/hppd/hpux/Languages/codecs-1.0/*. Losslessy compression schemes.
4. B. Calder, D. G. ad Michael Jones, D. Lindsay, J. Martin, M. Mozer, and B. Zorn. Evidence-Based Static Branch Prediction Using Machine Learning. In *ACM Transactions on Programming Languages and Systems (ToPLaS-19)*, volume 19, 1997.
5. P. Chang, D. Lavery, S. Mahlke, W. Chen, and W. Hwu. The Importance of Prepass Code Scheduling for Superscalar and Superpipelined processors. In *IEEE Transactions on Computers*, volume 44, pages 353–370, March 1995.
6. F. C. Chow and J. L. Hennessey. The Priority-Based Coloring Approch to Register Allocation. In *ACM Transactions on Programming Languages and Systems (ToPLaS-12)*, pages 501–536, 1990.
7. K. Cooper, P. Scheilke, and D. Subramanian. Optimizing for Reduced Code Space using Genetic Algorithms. In *Languages, Compilers, Tools for Embedded Systems*, pages 1–9, 1999.
8. C. Gathercole. *An Investigation of Supervised Learning in Genetic Programming.* PhD thesis, University of Edinburgh, 1998.
9. P. B. Gibbons and S. S. Muchnick. Efficient Instruction Scheduling for a Pipelined Architecture. In *Proceedings of the ACM Symposium on Compiler Construction*, volume 21, pages 11–16, 1986.

10. G. W. Grewal and C. T. Wilson. Mappping Reference Code to Irregular DSPs with the Retargetable, Optimizing Compiler COGEN(T). In *International Symposium on Microarchitecture*, volume 34, pages 192–202, 2001.
11. J. Koza. *Genetic Programming: On the Programming of Computers by Means of Natural Selection.* The MIT Press, 1992.
12. S. A. Mahlke. *Exploiting instruction level parallelism in the presence of branches.* PhD thesis, University of Illinois at Urbana-Champaign, Department of Electrical and Computer Engineering, 1996.
13. M. O'Neill and C. Ryan. Automatic generation of caching algorithms. In K. Miettinen, M. M. Mäkelä, P. Neittaanmäki, and J. Periaux, editors, *Evolutionary Algorithms in Engineering and Computer Science*, pages 127–134, Jyväskylä, Finland, 30 May - 3 June 1999. John Wiley & Sons.
14. E. Ozer, S. Banerjia, and T. Conte. Unified Assign and Schedule: A New Approach to Scheduling for Clustered Register Filee Microarchitectures.
15. N. Paterson and M. Livesey. Evolving caching algorithms in C by genetic programming. In J. R. Koza, K. Deb, M. Dorigo, D. B. Fogel, M. Garzon, H. Iba, and R. L. Riolo, editors, *Genetic Programming 1997: Proceedings of the Second Annual Conference*, pages 262–267, Stanford University, CA, USA, 13-16 July 1997. Morgan Kaufmann.
16. D. Patterson and J. Hennessy. *Computer Architecture: A Quantitative Approach.* Morgan Kaufmann, 1995.
17. B. R. Rau. Iterative Modulo Scheduling: An Algorithm for Software Pipelining Loops. In *Proceedings of the 27th Annual International Symposium on Microarchitecture (MICRO-24)*, November 1994.
18. C. Ryan and P. Walsh. Automatic conversion of programs from serial to parallel using genetic programming - the paragen system. In *Proceedings of ParCo'95.* North-Holland, 1995.
19. Trimaran. *http://www.trimaran.org.*
20. N. Warter. *Modulo Scheduling with Isomorphic Control Transformations.* PhD thesis, University of Illinois at Urbana-Champaign, Department of Electrical and Computer Engineering, 1993.

Modularity in Genetic Programming

John R. Woodward

School of Computer Science, University of Birmingham, B15 2TT, UK
J.R.Woodward@cs.bham.ac.uk

Abstract. Genetic Programming uses a tree based representation to express solutions to problems. Trees are constructed from a primitive set which consists of a function set and a terminal set. An extension to GP is the ability to define modules, which are in turn tree based representations defined in terms of the primitives. The most well known of these methods is Koza's Automatically Defined Functions. In this paper it is proved that for a given problem, the minimum number of nodes in the main tree plus the nodes in any modules is independent of the primitive set (up to an additive constant) and depends only on the function being expressed. This reduces the number of user defined parameters in the run and makes the inclusion of a hypothesis in the search space independent of the primitive set.

1 Introduction

Genetic programming (GP) [2,6] is inspired by natural evolution. Candidate solutions are generated and their performance is measured against a specific target task. The better solutions are then taken and altered typically by mutation and crossover operators and tested again. This process is repeated until terminating conditions are met. All evolutionary algorithms follow this test-and-generate approach to produce new solutions in the hope that eventually ever improving solutions will give a satisfactory solution.

GP is plagued by the number choices a user has to make at the start of a run and it is often difficult to know in advance what effect these choices may have on the success of a run. For example, trees can potentially grow without limit and this would cause the program to crash so typically the depth of tree is limited. Operators are designed that produce new trees from old ones. A suitable representation is required in which potential solutions are expressed. This is usually tree based and is expressed in terms of a set of primitives. All of these choices affect the dynamics of a genetic run. This paper is concerned with representation.

In GP, the typical representation is tree based (see Figure 1). This is for largely historical reasons due to the many of the first GP systems being coded in LISP which uses tree based representations. Other data structures have been used, namely linear and graph based structures [4,9]. Tree structures are used for illustration, as they are the most common, but the result (Theorem 2) holds for any data structure. In this paper, non-modular representations will be referred

C. Ryan et al. (Eds.): EuroGP 2003, LNCS 2610, pp. 254–263, 2003.

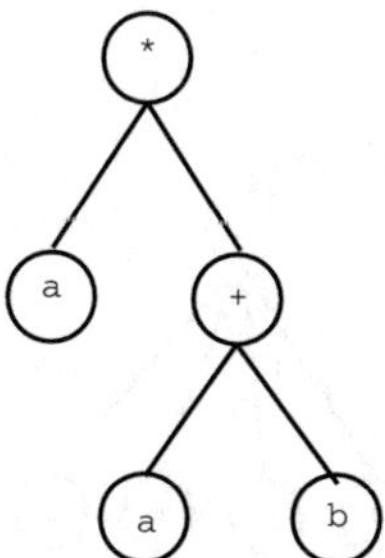

Fig. 1. A tree representation of the function a*(a+b). The function set is $\{+, *\}$ and the terminal set is $\{a, b\}$. There is no modularity within a tree, repeated subtrees have to be expressed explicitly.

to as trees (see fig 1) and modular representations will be referred to as forests (see fig 2), in order to make the distinction explicit.

Tree structures are constructed from a set of primitives. This set consists of two sets, a function set and a terminal set. The function set consists of a number of functions which can be linked together to form larger more complicated functions. Each function has an arity, which is the number of inputs, or arguments, it takes. For example each of the following arithmetic operators take two { +, -, *, / }. A typical function set for a maths problem may include { +, -, *, / } and a typical function set for a logic problem may include { and, or, xor , not } (i.e. a logically complete set). The terminal set corresponds to the input variables of the problem. The function set and terminal set together should be powerful enough to express the solution to the problem, if not then the solution lies outside the search space and GP will not be able to find the solution. Typically it is not difficult to know if the primitive set is powerful enough and is fairly obvious from the nature of the problem.

In the GP literature, the function set and terminal set are referred to as two separate sets. One reason is possibly the semantic and syntactic difference between the two sets. The function set represents what processing can be done and the terminal set represents the input data of the problem. Also, in the tree representation, terminals are always found at the leaf nodes and functions are found at the non-terminal nodes. Terminals could be considered as functions with arity zero. The function set F and terminal set T could be described as a single set called the primitive set P i.e. if $F = \{f1, f2\}$ and $T = \{t1, t2\}$ then $P = \{F, T\} = \{f1, f2, t1, t2\}$. The term primitive set will be used unless the distinction is necessary.

The outline of the paper is as follows. In section 2 modularity is defined and commented on. Section 3 looks at the current modular techniques available in GP. Definitions and proofs are laid down in section 4, followed by the implications for learning in section 5 and a discussion in section 6.

2 Modularity

Definition 1. *A module is a function that is defined in terms of a primitive set or previously defined modules.*

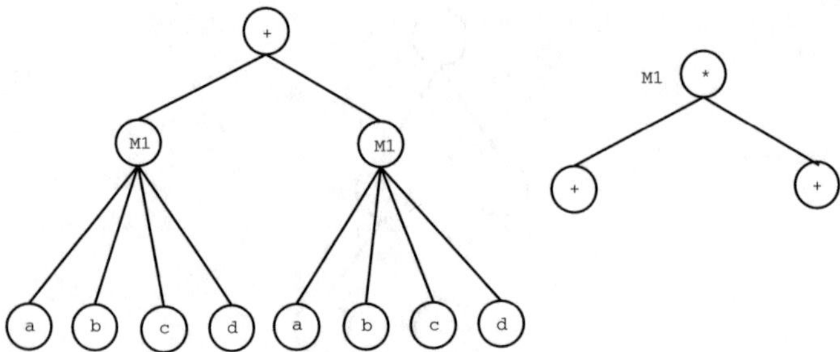

Fig. 2. A function is represented in modular form as a forest (i.e. a collection of trees). The tree on the left is the main tree and the tree on the right is a module. The function set is $\{+, *\}$ and the terminal set is $\{a, b, c, d\}$. The function represented is ((a+b)*(c+d))+((a+b)*(c+d)). This is arrived at by substituting in the module M1, defined by the right tree, at the positions of the two nodes in the left tree. There is modularity within a forest, modules are represented explicitly by the addition of trees to the forest. In this example the terminals could also be included in the module M1, obtaining further compression.

The ability of a representation to include modularity does not add expressiveness, it simply makes the expression more efficient in terms of its size. The following observations about modules are made. Firstly, they can be considered as primitives. Secondly, they interface like primitives. Finally, they can be treated as black boxs. The above definition does not permit recursion, which may be considered slightly restrictive, but this restriction does not affect the main result of the paper.

In the context of GP with an addressable memory [4] it may be more natural to talk about instructions rather than function and terminal sets. Technically functions and terminals all return a value whereas instructions do not. Also, instructions can alter the memory, whereas functions do not.

A module could be defined in terms of itself or in terms of modules that 'chain back' to the original module. While this can be allowed in some systems it is generally prohibited in GP to avoid problems of infinite recursion (see section 3).

There are a number of reasons why it is desirable to represent a solution in a compact modular form rather than in a cumbersome repetitious way. Firstly, it is well accepted the shorter solutions generalize better than longer solutions. If two solutions account for the given data, nothing can be gained by using the larger solution rather than the smaller solution. Secondly, modularity itself is a simple process to comprehend and implement. Surely, if a solution can be expressed in a neat, more elegant form this appeals to our notion of a conciseness rather than a longer solution with unnecessary repetition. Thirdly, if there is structure in the problem, then this should be exploited in the solution. Shortest solutions have no structure, if they did any repeated structure could be removed by replacing the repeated structure by appropriate modules. Later, it is argued that if there is no structure in a problem then it is effectively unlearnable in the sense that no predictions can be made about unseen inputs (see section 6). Finally, the author can see no reason for not expressing something in a modular form!

The representation defines the set of all possible solutions that a GP may explore. If, however, the GP system is allowed to modularize, it can effectively define its own primitives during evolution. In other words it can alter it representation to suit itself.

In artificial intelligence one often talks about dividing a problem into its subproblems, solving these smaller (and hopefully easier!) problems in isolation, and then combining these solutions into a solution to the original problem. Modularity is one way to attempt this, and each module could be considered as a solution to each of the subproblems. If one subproblem has been solved and occurs again later, it does not have to be solved again; the solution can simply be referred to again. Surely, the reuse of solutions to previously solved problems must appeal to our intuition of what intelligence is.

Solutions are often represented as trees and modules correspond to branches off the root node of the tree. For example, Automatically Defined Functions (see section 3) have a main result-producing branch along with one or more function-defining branches. In this paper, a non-modular representation will be represented as and referred to as a tree (see fig. 1). A modular representation will be represented as and referred to as a forest (see fig. 2). Thus a module will appear explicitly as a separate tree in the forest.

3 Related Work

Here a number of modularization methods are discussed. For each of these methods a representation is needed along with an operation which produces new candidate solutions from old ones and dynamically produces new modules. This paper is only concerned with the representation and not with the process of moving from one point to another in the search space.

Automatically Defined Functions (ADFs) [5,6] are probably the most popular of the modularization methods used in GP. Along with the main tree, additional branches are allowed to hang down from the root of the tree which define ADFs. ADFs are called just as if they belonged to the primitive set. Before starting the run, the user has to decide on the number of ADFs, the number of parameters each ADF takes and which ADFs can call which other ADFs. This final point is important to avoid infinite recursion and circular definitions. These choices all affect what structures are included in the search space.

Architecture altering operations [7] are a natural extension to ADFs which allow the structure of a solution to alter thus freeing the user from having to make these choices. ADFs can be created or deleted and new parameters added or removed from the argument lists of ADFs. Thus the number of ADFs and the parameters each one takes can change during the run. As pointed out in [2] (page 288), this has the benefit that no extra parameters are required in addition to the parameters required for standard GP run with no ADFs.

Adaptive Representation [10] creates modules on-the-fly during evolution according to population statistics. In a sense this is very similar to architecture altering operations in that the form of the representation is free to alter during the run.

Encapsulation [5] and module acquisition [1] are two similar modularization methods. With encapsulation, a point in a tree is chosen and the subtree from that point down to all the terminals in that subtree is 'encapsulated'. This encapsulated subtree is then treated as a new terminal (because it takes no arguments). With module acquisition, a point in a tree is chosen and the subtree (down to a given depth) is promoted as a module. Due to the depth restriction a module may or may not take arguments.

These two methods only allow identification of a subset of possible modules. Encapsulation forces all modules to behave like terminals as the encapsulation process captures the whole of a subtree from some point down to all the terminals in that subtree. Module acquisition is similarly limited in that a predefined depth determines what can and cannot be promoted as a module. Thus the space of potential modules is restricted.

The dynamics of how each of these methods select modules are different. The representation used with both of these methods is essentially the same; a main tree along with any modules which are also represented as trees.

If an instruction set is Turing Complete then it is implicitly capable of expressing modular solutions. There is no need to supply and additional vehicle for the purpose of modularity. Work on GP with Turing Complete instruction sets has been done, however we are not aware of any results that could be identified as having modules. Only programs with single loops have been evolved [4].

4 Definitions and Proofs

We need to be able to convert an expression in terms of one primitive set into an expression in terms of a different primitive set. This is done using a dictionary.

Definition 2. *A dictionary $D_{P_1P_2}$ is a set of trees or forests which express each member of primitive set P_2 in terms of primitive set P_1.*

The existence of $D_{P_1P_2}$ does not imply the existence of $D_{P_2P_1}$. The size of $D_{P_1P_2}$ is $|D_{P_1P_2}|$, and in general, $|D_{P_1P_2}| \neq |D_{P_1P_2}|$. The dictionary must be of finite size.

Definition 3. *Two primitive sets P_1 and P_2 are equally expressive if and only if a pair of dictionaries $D_{P_1P_2}$ and $D_{P_2P_1}$ exist.*

In terms of what can be expressed with the two sets, there is no difference, only the number of primitives in the expression will differ. There are many examples of equally expressive primitive sets. For example any pair of logically complete sets are equally expressive. Similarly, most programming languages are equally expressive as they are Turing Complete.

Definition 4. *A primitive set is a minimal primitive set if no member of the set can be expressed in terms of the other members of the set.*

Within a primitive set, one or more of the members may be expressed in terms of other members of the set. This implies that there is some redundancy in the set and these members could be removed without affecting what could be expressed with that set. An example of redundancy would be the `for` loop construct present in most programming languages. It could be removed from the language without affecting what could be expressed in the language as a `for` loop could be implemented in terms of a `do while` loop. A logically complete primitive set which is minimal is referred to as minimally logically complete. A set of instructions which are minimal and Turing Complete is referred to as minimally Turing Complete. If a primitive set is minimal it implies there is no redundancy in the set.

Definition 5. *The size $S_P(f)$ of a tree or forest, which expresses a function f, in terms of a primitive set P, is the number of nodes it contains.*

Definition 6. *The complexity $C_P(f)$ of a function f is the size of the smallest tree or forest expressing f, in terms of a primitive set P.*

A function can be expressed as different trees or forests in terms of a primitive set and each of of which may have a different size. For a given function and a given primitive set there will exist a minimum size which can express the function. This is the complexity of the function for the given primitive set.

Theorem 1. *Given two equally expressive primitive sets P_1 and P_2, the complexity $C_{P_1}(f)$ has an upper bound which is within a constant factor, $K_{P_2P_1}$, of the complexity $C_{P_2}(f)$, provided modularity is not permitted (i.e. only trees are permitted).*

$$C_{P_1}(f) \leq C_{P_2}(f) * K_{P_2P_1}$$

Proof. Given a function expressed in terms of a primitive set P_2, it can be reexpressed in terms of the primitive set P_1 by directly substituting in the definitions of each of the primitives from the dictionary. In the worst case, each node can be rewritten in terms of a tree of size $K_{P_2P_1}$. $K_{P_2P_1}$ is the complexity of the dictionary $D_{P_2P_1}$.

Theorem 2. *Given two equally expressive primitive sets P_1 and P_2, the complexity $C_{P_1}(f)$ is equal to the complexity $C_{P_2}(f)$ within an additive constant provided modularity is permitted (i.e. forests are permitted).*

$$C_{P_1}(f) \leq C_{P_2}(f) + K_{P_2P_1}$$

Proof. Given a function expressed as a forest in a primitive set P_1, it can be expressed as a forest in the primitive set P_2 by adding on the definitions of each of the primitives. Thus in the worst case all of the primitives need to be rewritten in terms of a tree of size $K_{P_2P_1}$, $K_{P_2P_1}$ is the complexity of the dictionary $D_{P_2P_1}$.

The dictionary $D_{P_1P_2}$ has complexity $K_{P_1P_2}$ and is defined to be the number of nodes in the smallest dictionary. In general $K_{P_1P_2} \neq K_{P_2P_1}$

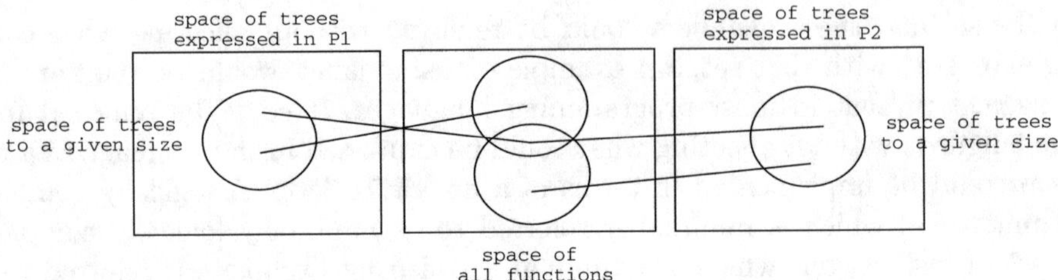

Fig. 3. In the tree representation, modularity is not permitted and the two spaces of trees of limited size map to two different spaces of functions (which overlap slightly).

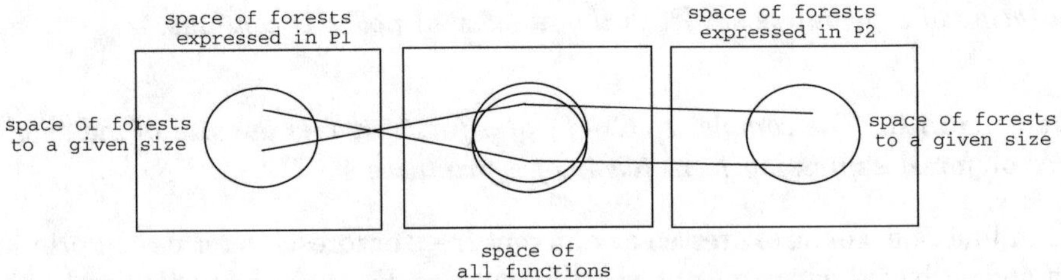

Fig. 4. In the forest representation, modularity is permitted and the two spaces of forests of a limited size map to almost the same space of functions. The smaller the complexity of the dictionaries involved the more the two spaces of functions overlap.

The definitions of size and complexity are the same as those given in Wegener (page 9 [11]), except they apply to Boolean Circuits. He also states that the complexity and depth of a Boolean Function can only increase by a constant factor if we switch from one primitive set to another.

Corollary 1. *Given two equally expressive primitive sets, the set of functions expressed by forests using either primitive set is approximately the same if the size limit on the forests is large compared to the complexity of the dictionaries.*

This follows as a consequence of Theorem 2 as the size of the dictionary can be ignored if the size limit on a forest is much bigger than the complexity of the dictionaries. This additive constant will be ignored from now on and so the set of functions defined by forests (of fixed upper size) is the same. This is realistic for most primitive sets used in GP and target functions we expect GP to find.

5 Implications for Learning

Evolution in GP can be thought of as the movement of a population of points through a search space. Each point is represented by a tree or forest and corresponds to a function. The aim is to find a point that corresponds to the target function. The terms hypothesis space and and search space are used interchangeable and a point in a search space represents a particular hypothesis. A point in the search space is the genotype and the function it represents is the phenotype.

The mapping between these two spaces is many to one as many trees represent the same function. It is interesting to note that it has been suggested that the No Free Lunch Theorem does not hold in this space [12]. The structure of the search space is defined by the representation, the operators used to move around the space and the fitness function and is often considered using the landscape metaphor [8].

Two different sets of primitives define two different search spaces. These two spaces will map to the same set of functions if the two primitive sets are equally expressive (and the size is unlimited). However, if a maximum depth or size is imposed on a tree, this will effectively cut off part of the space, and therefore limit which functions can be represented. In general, if modularity is not permitted, the set of functions defined by trees in the two spaces will be *different*. If however the representation does allow modularity, and the size of forests in the search space is limited, the set of functions will *the same*. In other words, if we do not have modularity, the functions expressed in two search spaces defined by two different primitive sets will diverge, whereas if the ability to modularize is included the sets of functions will converge as the maximum size of a tree or a forest increases.

Figure 3 shows how trees expressed in terms of two different primitive sets map to different parts of the function space. Figure 4 shows how forests (i.e. trees with the ability to modularize) expressed in terms of two different primitive sets map to the same part of the space of functions. The left and right rectangles represent the space of all trees (in fig 3) and forests (in fig 4) without a size limit, expressed in terms of P_1 and P_2 respectively. The central rectangle represents the space of all functions that can be represented. Ellipses in figure 3 on the left and right represent trees up to a fixed size. These map to two *different* subsets of functions. Note that the small overlap signifies that some functions can be represented by trees of a fixed size in either primitive set. Ellipses in figure 4 on the left and right represent forests up to a fixed size. These map to *the same* subsets of functions which is illustrated as two ellipses which largely overlap.

In summary, given two equally expressive primitive sets with a representation which permits modularity, if the size of the forests is limited then the two search spaces map to the same space of functions. If modularity is not permitted, the two search spaces will map to different spaces of functions. In general the size of the two search spaces will be different. No claims are made at this stage about the relationship between the structure of the two search spaces or appropriate operators to move around these spaces.

6 Discussion

One of the aims of GP is to synthesize a target function from a basic primitive set to express the relationship between given input and output data. Perhaps deeper aim is generalization, which is the ability to predict what should happen on unseen data (i.e. data that was not included in the training set). To express a given set of data a lookup table could be constructed recording all the inputs against all the outputs, but this says nothing about what rule, if any, there is connecting the input and output data. If we are to make predictions we need access to this rule or an approximation to it. If there is a pattern in the training data, then this pattern can be exploited and used to predict the output data, and if there is no pattern then it is impossible to make any predictions. Modularity is one vehicle which can help express regularity and patterns in data.

The Kolmogorov complexity of a bit string is the length of the shortest program, in bits, that prints out the bit string [3]. Kolmogorov complexity is thus associated with Turing Complete instruction sets, and is therefore undecidable. In a sense, Kolmogorov complexity is a special case of Theorem 2 for the case when the primitive sets are Turing Complete.

Theorem 2 is in terms of numbers of nodes in forests. Each node corresponds to either a function or a terminal in the primitive set. It may be conceptually easier to think of the complexity of a function in terms of the number of primitives required to express it rather than the number of bits.

The complexity of functions expressed in Turing Complete systems is undecidable. The complexity of, for example, a logical function expressed in terms of a logically complete primitive set and a modular representation is decidable (the space of all forests could be enumerated and searched, and each forest terminates as there is no self-referencing in the system). This may therefore be a suitable arena in which to study some aspects of complexity and modularity.

Further work includes examing learning using two equally expressive primitve sets. Comparing a minimal and non-minimal primitive set to investigate the effect of redundancy in the primitive set. Also being considered are suitable operators to move around a space of modular representations.

7 Conclusion

The main result of this paper is that the size of a solution is independent of the primitive set used provided modularity is permitted. In practice, the size of a search space is limited and the implication for the GP practioner is that the inclusion or exclusion of a target function from a search space depends only on a size parameter and not on the primitve set and hence can potentially remove any bias due to the choice of primitive set.

Modularization is important in the expression of a solution. It not only appeals to our intuition of conciseness but is also vital in expressing regularities in data and therefore the ability of solutions to make accurate predictions.

A number of modularization techniques in GP are discussed. Most of them require the user to supply parameters concerning the sizes and numbers of of modules. We prove that the minimum number of primitives needed to express a target function is independent of the primitive set if a modular representation is permitted. It should be noted that no claim is being made at this stage about the dynamics of GP, or that modularity should be enforced during a GP run.

Acknowledgements

Mark Ryan, Achim Jung, Xin Yao, Stefano Cattani.

References

1. P. J. Angeline and J. B. Pollack. The evolutionary induction of subroutines. In *Proceedings of the Fourteenth Annual Conference of the Cognitive Science Society*, Bloomington, Indiana, USA, 1992. Lawrence Erlbaum.
2. Wolfgang Banzhaf, Peter Nordin, Robert E. Keller, and Frank D. Francone. *Genetic Programming – An Introduction; On the Automatic Evolution of Computer Programs and its Applications.* Morgan Kaufmann, dpunkt.verlag, January 1998.
3. Thomas M. Cover and Joy A. Thomas. *Elements of Information Theory.* Wiley Series in Telecommunications. John Wiley & Sons, New York, NY, USA, 1991.
4. Lorenz Huelsbergen. Toward simulated evolution of machine language iteration. In John R. Koza, David E. Goldberg, David B. Fogel, and Rick L. Riolo, editors, *Genetic Programming 1996: Proceedings of the First Annual Conference*, pages 315–320, Stanford University, CA, USA, 28–31 July 1996. MIT Press.
5. John R. Koza. *Genetic Programming: On the Programming of Computers by Means of Natural Selection.* MIT Press, 1992.
6. John R. Koza. *Genetic Programming II: Automatic Discovery of Reusable Programs.* MIT Press, Cambridge Massachusetts, May 1994.
7. John R. Koza. Evolving the architecture of a multi-part program in genetic programming using architecture-altering operations. In John Robert McDonnell, Robert G. Reynolds, and David B. Fogel, editors, *Evolutionary Programming IV Proceedings of the Fourth Annual Conference on Evolutionary Programming*, pages 695–717, San Diego, CA, USA, 1-3 1995. MIT Press.
8. W. B. Langdon and Riccardo Poli. *Foundations of Genetic Programming.* Springer-Verlag, 2002.
9. Julian F. Miller and Peter Thomson. Cartesian genetic programming. In Riccardo Poli, Wolfgang Banzhaf, William B. Langdon, Julian F. Miller, Peter Nordin, and Terence C. Fogarty, editors, *Genetic Programming, Proceedings of EuroGP 2000*, volume 1802 of *LNCS*, pages 121–132, Edinburgh, 15-16 April 2000. Springer-Verlag.
10. J. P. Rosca and D. H. Ballard. Learning by adapting representations in genetic programming. In *Proceedings of the 1994 IEEE World Congress on Computational Intelligence, Orlando, Florida, USA*, Orlando, Florida, USA, 27-29 June 1994. IEEE Press.
11. I. Wegener. *The Complexity of Boolean Functions.* Wiley Teubner, 1987.
12. J. R. Woodward and J. R. Neil. No free lunch, program induction and combinatorial problems. In *Genetic Programming, Proceedings of EuroGP 2003*, Essex, UK, 14-16 April 2003. Springer-Verlag.

Decreasing the Number of Evaluations in Evolutionary Algorithms by Using a Meta-model of the Fitness Function

Jens Ziegler and Wolfgang Banzhaf

University of Dortmund, Department of Computer Science
D-44221 Dortmund, Germany
{Jens.Ziegler,Wolfgang.Banzhaf}@uni-dortmund.de
http://www.cs.uni-dortmund.de

Abstract. In this paper a method is presented that decreases the necessary number of evaluations in Evolutionary Algorithms. A classifier with confidence information is evolved to replace time consuming evaluations during tournament selection. Experimental analysis of a mathematical example and the application of the method to the problem of evolving walking patterns for quadruped robots show the potential of the presented approach.

1 Introduction

The high number of fitness evaluations in evolutionary algorithms is often expensive, time-consuming or otherwise problematic in many real-world applications. Especially in the following cases, a computationally efficient approximation of the original fitness function reducing either the number or duration of fitness evaluations is necessary: (i) if the evaluation of the fitness function is computationally expensive, (ii) if no mathematical fitness function can be defined, (iii) if additional physical devices must be used. Several approaches have been suggested to reduce the number of fitness evaluations in EA. If the fitness function is a mathematical function, approximations by interpolation between individuals in search space build a meta-model of the fitness function (see e.g. [2, 8]). In more complex cases, the fitness of an individual may be inherited from their ancestors to save evaluations (see e.g. [11]). Another approach tries to minimize the number of evaluations by clustering the individuals around "representatives" which determine the fitness of a subset of the population [9]. Statistical and information theoretical results are used in e.g. [3] to reduce the number of fitness evaluations in GP. An comprehensive collection of works in this field can be found in [7].

The article is organized as follows. The next section introduces the idea of using the result of a classifier to discriminate between better and worse individuals during tournament selection. Section 3 introduces the confidence level for classifications. Section 4 investigates the influence of the meta-model on two different problems. Section 5 describes the evolution of a classifier with GP based on data from a real world experiment and section 6 presents and discusses the results of the evolution of gait patterns for four-legged robots using the meta-model approach. Finally, section 7 gives our conclusion and hints to future works.

C. Ryan et al. (Eds.): EuroGP 2003, LNCS 2610, pp. 264–275, 2003.

2 Tournament Selection by Classification

In this section, a new method will be illustrated which replaces time consuming fitness evaluations of individuals in tournaments by classifications during evolution.

During a tournament, T individuals are compared pairwise on the basis of their fitness values and divided into two sets T_W and T_L. T_W can be considered the class of winners, T_L the class of losers. In a subsequent step, all losers will be replaced by varied copies and recombinations of winners. Whether or not an individual remains in the population can formally be seen as the result of a classification C of the comparisons V:

$$C : V \longrightarrow \{0,1\} \tag{1}$$

The comparisons $V(i,j)$ are divided into two classes, depending on which of the individuals i,j has the better fitness according to a given fitness criterion f.

$$\begin{aligned} C : V = (i,j) &\longrightarrow 0 \Leftrightarrow f(i) > f(j) \\ C : V = (i,j) &\longrightarrow 1 \Leftrightarrow f(j) \geq f(i) \end{aligned} \tag{2}$$

The fitness $f(i)$ of an individual i is usually computed by an evaluation E (see eq. (3)) that assigns a real number as a fitness value to i. A simple comparison using $<,>,\leq,\geq$, separates superior and inferior individuals afterwards. Thus, tournament selection is based on phenotypic information.

$$E : i \longrightarrow I\!R. \tag{3}$$

However, the sets T_W and T_L can be also be obtained as a result of classification (2):

$$\begin{aligned} V = (i,j) \in 0 &\Leftrightarrow i \in T_W, j \in T_L \\ V = (i,j) \in 1 &\Leftrightarrow i \in T_L, j \in T_W \end{aligned} \tag{4}$$

Any classification C that divides the tournament T in two sets T_W, T_L with $T_W \cup T_L = T$ and $|T_W| = |T_L|$ is—from a formal point of view—a valid classification. If a classification C' can be given that has the same characteristics as C, but with a reduced runtime, i.e. with a reduced need for evaluation E, the overall runtime of the algorithm will be reduced accordingly. In other words, a comparison V between two individuals, each requiring the evaluation E, can be replaced by a classification with substantially smaller runtime.

Therefore, on the one hand, C' has to operate on other criteria than C and, on the other hand, can be seen as a model of the classification C. An ideal classifier C' can now be written as

$$C' : V \longrightarrow C(V), \tag{5}$$

and is nothing else but a function that calculates the outcome of the classification $C(V)$ solely from V, i.e. from i and j. C' thus operates on genotypic information, the information coded in the genome, instead of operating on phenotypic information like C which uses E. The quality of any given classification C' on a set of comparisons V can easily be calculated as the sum of misclassifications:

$$quality(C') = \sum_V |C(V) - C'(V)|. \tag{6}$$

$quality(C')$ at the same time is the definition of a fitness function for any machine learning algorithm applied to the problem of creating an adequate substitute C' for C. The ratio of correct classifications and number of comparisons is a quality measure for C' and is known as *hit rate*.

3 Confidence Level

If a classifier C' is the result of a learning process, it is likely that the quality of C' is not optimal. This implies that there will be some misclassifications on the set V. Another observable quantity, the *confidence* k ($k \in [0,1]$) of a classification, is of particular use here. A classification with high confidence level k indicates a more reliable result than a classification with a low k-value. However, a certain error probability p_e ($p_e \in [0,1]$) will always remain. Introducing a confidence level k_V ($k_V \in [0,1]$) for C' yields

$$C' : V \longrightarrow < \{0,1\}, k_V > . \tag{7}$$

This ensures a confidence level k_V for every single classification of C'. Based on k_V a decision can be made whether to accept the result of the classification ($k_V > k$) or not ($k_V \leq k$). If the classification is rejected, two evaluations E are necessary to complete the comparison.

4 Influence on the Performance of the EA

This section is devoted to the investigation of the influence of the introduced method on the overall performance of EA. Therefore it is assumed that a classification C' exists for the two example problems used in this section.

It is difficult to quantify the influence of a certain number or percentage of misclassifications that allow individuals with inferior quality (real fitness) to persist in the population. Evolutionary algorithms are instances of beam search exploring regions of the search space that are defined by the composition of the population. The best route towards the global optimum is a priori unknown due to several reasons like e.g. the initialization of the population, application sequence of variation operators, random number effects, etc. It is therefore impossible to state that persisting individuals with worse fitness values (those misclassified as winners) have only negative influence on the EA's performance.

The following example shows experimentally the influence of certain combinations of confidence level k, error probability p_e and runtime ratio r between evaluation and classification on the performance of a Genetic Algorithm (parameters of the GA are displayed in Table 1) with two different fitness functions. The functions to be maximized are defined in (8) and (9).

$$f_1(i) = \sum_{l=0}^{9} i_l, \tag{8}$$

$$f_2(i) = \begin{cases} 100 \cdot i_9 & ,\text{if } \; i_5 + i_6 \geq 1 \\ (i_0 + 10 i_3)^2 - (i_1 + i_2 + i_4)^3 & \text{else.} \end{cases} \tag{9}$$

Table 1. Parameters of the GA used and for the computation of runtime.

Parameter	**Value**
Objective	Maximize eq.(8) (eq. (9))
Number of runs	100
Population size	100
Length of individuals	10 Bit
Prob. of mutation	70%
Prob. of crossover	30%
Initialization	random
Selection scheme	Tournament (size = 4)
Termination criterion	Av. fitness of population > 80% of max. fitness
Runtime of C (t_C)	0.1 s
Speed factor s	$[1,\dots,1000]$
Runtime of E (t_E)	$t_E = s \cdot t_C$
Minimum confidence level k	$[0.7,\dots,1.0]$
Error prob. p_e	$\{0.05, 0.1, 0.2, 0.3\}$
Duration of start phase (approx. 25% of standard runtime)	50 (eq. 8), 400 (eq. 9)
Standard runtime (t_S)	200 Tournaments (eq. 8),
	1528 Tournaments (eq. 9)
Learning time t_L for C'	10.0s

The first function just maximizes the number of ones in the genome, whereas the latter is a discontinuous nonlinear function of the elements of the individual i.

The fitness is always calculated for each individual. After a starting phase during which no classification takes place, individuals with better fitness values replace inferior ones with a probability p_r (see eq. (10)). With probability p_p (see eq. 11), inferior individuals remain in the population. It is furthermore assumed that the confidence levels k_V of C' are uniformly distributed in [0,1], resulting in a probability of $p_E = k$ that a classification has a confidence level of less than k, meaning that the evaluation E of the individual is necessary. This method simulates the outcome of a classification C' with an error probability p_e.

$$p_r = (1 - p_e)(1 - k) \tag{10}$$

$$p_p = p_e(1 - k) \tag{11}$$

Saving Runtime

To compute the overall runtime needed for the experiment, the number of evaluations and classifications during the evolution are counted. During the starting phase, only evaluations take place and their runtime is added to the total runtime. In the second phase, the runtime for a classification C is added for every comparison. If the confidence level k_V of C is less than k, the runtime for two more evaluations is added. Learning C' is assumed to need a certain time t_L. Every parameter needed for the computation of the total runtime is given in Table 1.

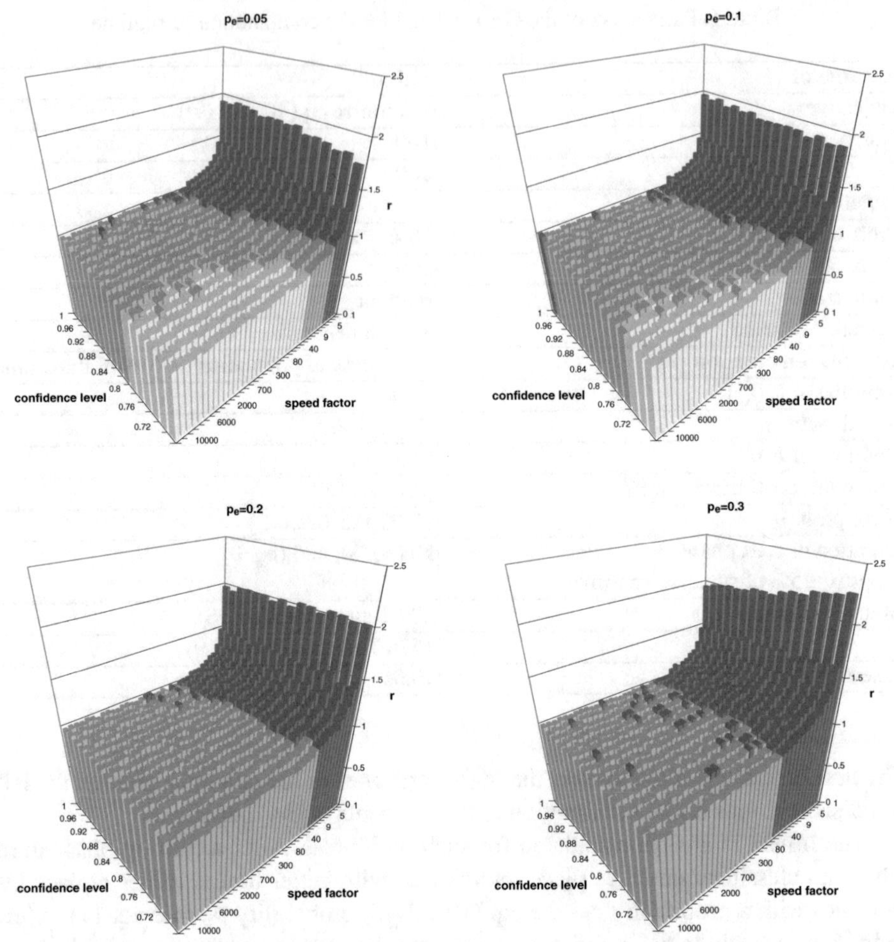

Fig. 1. Comparison of run time ratios (z-axis) of different combinations of confidence level (x-axis) and speed factor (y-axis). The lighter the colors, the smaller is the ratio. Dark regions indicate run time ratios ≥ 1, light regions indicate run time rations ≤ 0.85. Fitness function is eq. (8).

Basis for the experimental analysis is the average time of 100 identical runs (except for the random seed) until the average fitness of the whole population reaches 80% of the a priori known maximum fitness. This value is divided by the standard run time, the average runtime of 100 runs of an unmodified GA. The runtime ratio r is computed as follows:

$$r = \frac{1}{100} \sum_{i=0}^{100} \frac{n_C^i \cdot t_E + n_C^i \cdot t_C + t_L}{t_S \cdot t_E}, \tag{12}$$

with n_C^i, n_E^i the number of classifications and evaluations in run i. A ratio of one or smaller indicates that the parameter combination yields a runtime that is equal to or less than that of the standard algorithm. In Figure 1 the results are shown. It is clearly

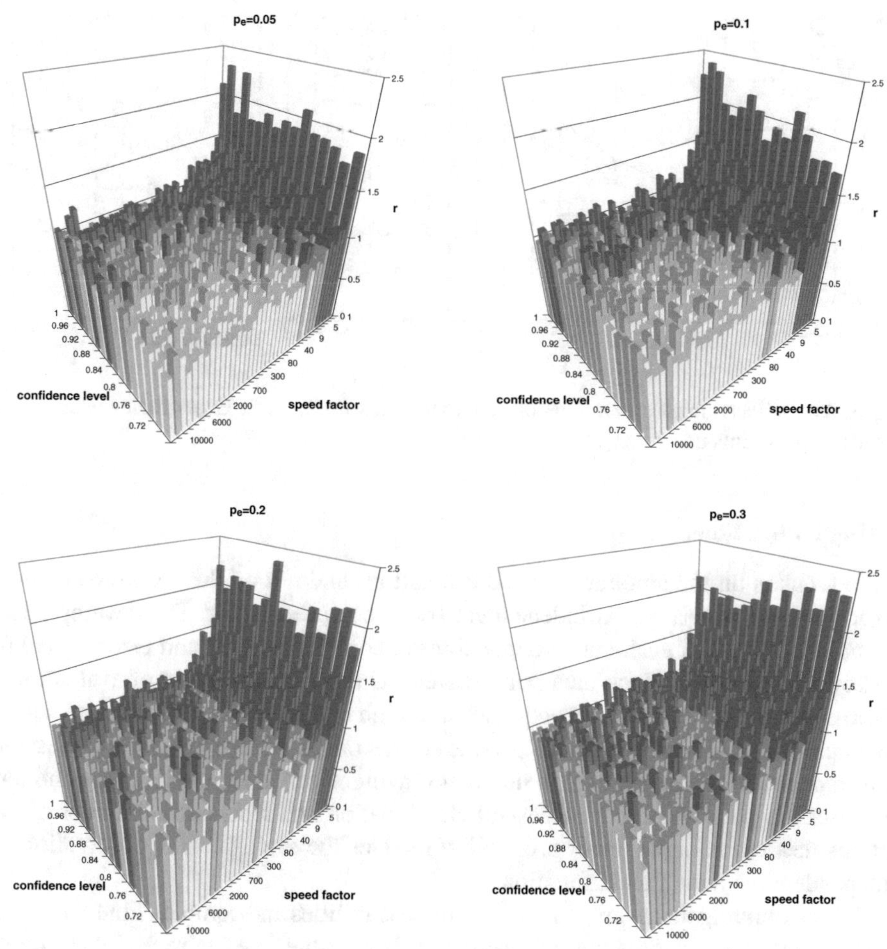

Fig. 2. Comparison of run time ratios using eq. (9).

visible that a smaller confidence level k reduces the runtime of the algorithm, whereas a smaller speed factor between classification and evaluation increases the runtime. On the other hand, increasing the speed factor to values above 300 or more does neither decrease runtime nor compensate for higher confidence levels. Contrariwise, if the speed factor falls below a certain threshold, decreasing the confidence level does not reduce the runtime any more. A common characteristic is the increasing runtime due to increasing error probability p_e. Nevertheless it is astounding that a 30% error of classification still gives run time ratios $r \leq 1$ for a significant set of parameter combinations. If the fitness function is more complex, the picture changes moderately. In Figure 2 the run time ratios are displayed according to the results using eq. (9). A more inhomogeneous behavior with different parameter combinations is visible, but the overall tendency towards lower run time ratios due to higher speed factors and lower confidence levels can be seen. Again, the run time saving reduces with increasing error probability.

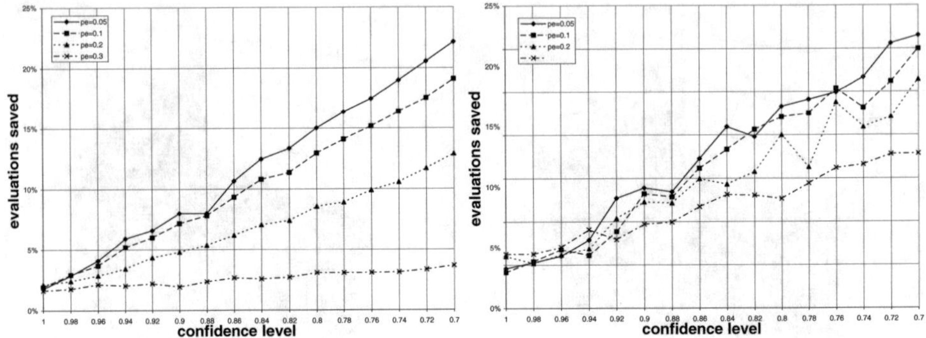

Fig. 3. Average saving of evaluations of all experiments in %. **Left:** Experiments using eq. (8). **Right:** Experiments using eq. (9).

Saving Evaluations

If the focus is on the amount of saved evaluations and not on the absolute amount of saved runtime, the saving is independent from the speed factor. The development of the number of saved evaluations depending on confidence level and error probability is shown in Figure 3. Each data point represents the average saving of evaluations of 3,700 experiments. A direct consequence of a high confidence level combined with the assumption of uniform distributed k_V values is that only a small percentage of classifications reaches this level resulting in nearly no saving. Decreasing the level of confidence increases the possibility of a successful classification and reduces the number of evaluations needed. A higher error probability reduces the savings. This observations are independent from the fitness function.

It is astounding that even with high error probabilities and complex fitness functions a 10% reduction of the number of evaluations is possible (see figure 3, right). Another interesting observation is that with a complex fitness function higher error probabilities reduce the number of evaluations more than with a simple fitness function. The reasons for this phenomenon are not yet entirely clear and need to be investigated in the future. The given example does not have enough explanatory power to justify more general conclusions.

Whether or not a classifier is able to reduce either the runtime of the algorithm or the number of evaluations can be reduced to the question if such a classifier *exists*. That the answer is positive, even for a complex genotype-phenotype-relation, will be demonstrated in the following section.

5 Evolving a Classifier with Genetic Programming

The data used for the evolution of C' have been saved during the manual evolution of control programs for a quadruped robot (see section 6). In this section a retroactive analysis of the experimental data was carried out to investigate the possibilities of online evolution of classifiers with GP [1]. The result of every comparison of every tournament was saved in the form

Table 2. Performance of classifier variants with $k = 0.65$. Lower error rates are achieved by using only data from recent generations.

		all	**last 5**	**last 2**
eq. (14)	above conf. level	63,8%	70,0%	60,0%
	variance	0.02	0.02	0.02
	misclassifications	51,7%	39,0%	32,7%
	variance	0.02	0.01	0.03
eq. (15)	above conf. level	90,3%	69,0%	78,5%
	variance	0.01	0.03	0.03
	misclassifications	54,1%	35,0%	34,7%
	variance	0.02	0.02	0.02

$$V' = < i_1, i_2, c > \tag{13}$$

with $c \in \{0, 1, 2\}$. A new class, class 2, was introduced to discriminate between clear (one individual has a significantly better fitness: class 0 or 1) and undetermined (indistinguishable fitness: class 2) comparisons. A classifier for each of the three classes was evolved using DISCIPULUS[1], a fast machine code GP system with linear representation. The three classifiers are combined using eq. (14), resulting in that class c_i which has the highest confidence level k_V.

$$C'(V') = < c, k_V > \text{ with } c = c_i | k_V = max(k_V(c_i)), i = 0, 1, 2 \tag{14}$$

Taking into consideration that a low confidence level k_V in favor of a certain class at the same time stands for a high confidence level $1 - k_V$ in favor of the other classes we use eq. (15) to combine the results alternatively.

$$C'(V') = < c, p > \text{ with } c = c_i | k'_V(c_i) = max\left(k'_V(c_i)\right), i = 0, 1, 2 \tag{15}$$

$$k'_V(c_i) = max\left(k_V(c_i), \frac{\sum\limits_{c_j \neq c_i} (1 - k_V(c_j))}{2} \right), i, j = 0, 1, 2 \tag{16}$$

Training and validation set are composed in three different variants. (i) All data are used, 50% training, 50% validation. (ii) Data from the last five generations are used (50%-50%) (iii) Only data of the last two generations are used (50%-50%). The evolved classifiers are then used to predict the outcome of the comparisons in the actual generation.

In Table 2, the results of a series of experiments are shown. The three variants of training/validation set formation are each evaluated with both versions of result combination. If the overall classification result follows eq. (14), the average saving of evaluations is slightly higher with simultaneously similar classification rates. Obviously, using only the results of recent generations for the evolution of classifiers leads to better classification results. It seems that ignoring earlier data sharpens the classification

[1] DISCIPULUS is a trademark of AIM Learning Inc. The free academic version was used with standard GP settings for classification problems, no changes were made by the authors [5].

Fig. 4. The four-legged Sony Aibo robot used in the experiments. The robot has 20 degrees of freedom.

results. This might might be caused by the fact that the fitness of a classifier is based on a uniform classification rate on all elements of the training set, a fact that neglects the changing structure of the population during an evolutionary process.

This example demonstrates that it is possible to generate classifiers with GP based on genotypic information alone that are able to replace the time consuming evaluations normally necessary for tournament selection in Evolutionary Algorithms. The next section shows an online application of this technique.

6 Application

The method introduced above is now tested with a real world problem, the evolution of gaits for walking robots. The used robot is a Sony Aibo, a four-legged robot (figure 4) which has successfully been used for similar experiments before [4]. Here, a set of 16 parameters of an inverse kinematic transformation [10] has to be evolved describing gait patterns for four-legged walking robots (Sony Aibo robots). The parameters of the GA can be found in Table 3.

The evaluation of the individual is done manually due to reasons inherent in the problem of evolving control programs for real walking robots: it is on the one hand difficult to mathematically formulate a sufficiently precise fitness function, on the other hand, once you have such a function, it is difficult to set up all necessary measuring devices to get detailed information about the actual state of the experiment. Using a simulated robot here reduces the wear out but entails other problems instead [13, 6]. Therefore, a interactive evolution[2] with tournament selection was started, during which the experimenter just had to decide which of two individuals had better fitness (this

[2] Interactive evolution embedds human intuition, preference, subjectivity, cognition, perception, and sensation into an EA. An introduction into the field of interactive evolution can be found e.g. in [12].

Table 3. Parameter setting of the GA for the Evolution of gait patterns.

Parameter	Value
Objective	maximize forward walking speed
Population size	26
individual size	16
Terminal set	$\mathbb{R}$
Prob. of crossover	0.5
Prob of mutations	0.2
Prob. of reproduction	0.3
Selection scheme	Tournament (size = 4)
Initialization	Standard parameter set (GT2002) with added noise

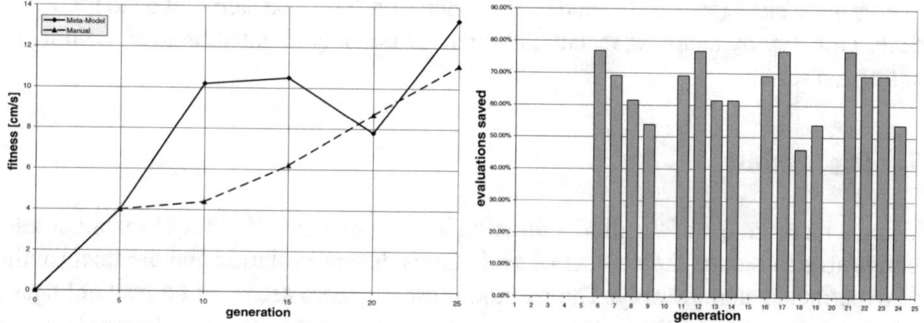

Fig. 5. Left: The fitness of the best individual of the population with manual and meta-model evolution. **Right:** Percentage of classifications per generations. The meta-model evolution reaches a similar fitness with only approx. 53% of evaluations needed in the manual evolution. The whole population is evaluated manually every five generations to extract reliable information about convergence (therefore $p_{1,2,3,4,5,10,15,20,25} = 0$.)

is, in fact, a realization of eq. (2) with subsequent mapping (4)). In order to get an unbiased overview over the performance of the individuals, the whole population is evaluated manually every five generations and the forward speed of each individual is measured. This first experiment was carried out to have a basis to compare the results of the meta-model evolution with.

To evolve 25 generations takes 650 manual evaluations and yields the results shown in Figure 5. The best-of-run individual, when executed on the robot, reaches a speed of 11 cm/s (see Figure 5).

In a second evolutionary experiment, starting from generation five of the manual evolution, a meta-model for every generation was created by evolving classifiers with DISCIPULUS as presented in section 5. The manually evaluated tournaments of the past five generations together formed the training and validation set (75%-25% here, because of the small amount of reliable fitness cases, i.e. manually evaluated ones) for the evolution. The evolved three classifiers (for every class 0,1, and 2) were used to compute the outcome of each of the 13 comparisons V (using eq. (15)) to combinate the particular results. If the confidence level k_V of the overall classification C' was smaller than the minimal value k, which was set to 0.65 here, both individuals of the comparison were executed on the real robot and the result was manually determined. This comparison was afterwards added to the training set for the next generation. The better individuals, either determined by classification or manually, formed the set T_W. After the variation step, Individuals of T_W replace the worse individuals in T_L.

In Figure 5, the best-of-generation individuals are displayed, showing a better performance (the best-of-run individual reaches a maximum speed of approx. 13 cm/s). It is remarkable that the evolution just uses 306 manual evaluations, summing up to a total saving of **approx. 53%**. The number of classifications per generation are shown in Figure 5, too.

Carrying out the manual evolution took about 8 hours, the meta-model evolution took about twice the time, due to the time consuming 48 evolutions of classifiers for every single class (see eq. 14) and every generation. The next step will be to reduce this time, probably by adapting recent classifiers to the only slightly changed training and validation sets.

7 Discussion

Using a meta-model of the fitness function in form of a classifier for tournament selection is able to reduce the number of evaluations during evolution and the total runtime of experiments significantly. The method presented here seems to be resilient against misclassifications permitting worse individuals to persist in the population. However, the classifiers have to be generated by another machine learning algorithm, raising another computationally intensive problem to be solved. The number and nature of experiments shown here do not give sufficient background for more general statements, but the method seems to be powerful enough to be investigated further in the future.

Acknowledgements

This project is supported by the Deutsche Forschungsgemeinschaft (DFG), under grant Ba 1042/6-2. The authors wish to thank Walter Nowak and Philipp Limbourg for their technical support.

References

1. W. Banzhaf, P. Nordin, R Keller, and F. Francone. *Genetic Programming — An Introduction*. dpunkt/Morgan Kaufmann, Heidelberg/San Francisco, 1998.
2. M. Emmerich, A. Giotis, M. Özdenir, T. Bäck, and K. Giannakoglou. Metamodel-assisted evolution strategies. In J.J. Merelo Guervos, P. Adamidis, H.-G. Beyer, J.-L. Fernandez-Villacanas, and H.-P. Schwefel, editors, *Parallel Problem Solving from Nature VII (PPSN)*, Lecture Notes in Computer Science, pages 361–370. Springer, Berlin, 2002.
3. M. Giacobini, M. Tomassini, and L. Vanneschi. Limiting the number fitness cases in genetic programming using statistics. In J.J. Merelo et al., editor, *Proccedings of the Seventh International Conference on Parallel Problem Solving from Nature (PPSN)*, Lecture Notes in Computer Science, LNCS 2439, pages 371–380. Springer Verlag, 2002.

4. G. S. Hornby, M. Fujita, S. Takamura, T. Yamamoto, and O. Hanagata. Autonomous evolution of gaits with the sony quadruped robot. In W. Banzhaf et al., editor, *Proceedings of the Genetic and Evolutionary Computation Conference*, pages 1297–1304. Morgan Kaufmann, 1999.
5. AIM Learning Inc. *Discipulus Owner's Manual.* http://www.aimlearning.com/Technology Overview.htm. WWW-Document.
6. N. Jakobi, P. Husbands, and I. Harvey. Noise and the reality gap: The use of simulation in evolutionary robotics. In F. Moran et al., editor, *Proceedings of the 3rd European Conference on Artificial Life*, Lecture Notes in Artificial Intelligence, pages 704–720. Springer New York, Berlin, Heidelberg, 1995.
7. Y. Jin. *Fitness Approximation in Evolutionary Computation - Bibliography.* http://www.soft-computing.de/amec.html. WWW-Document.
8. Y. Jin, M. Olhofer, and B. Sendhoff. A framework for evolutionary optimization with approximate fitness functions. *IEEE Transactions on Evolutionary Computation*, 6(5):481–494, 2002.
9. H.-S. Kim and S.-B. Cho. An efficient genetic algorithms with less fitness evaluation by clustering. In *Proceedings of the IEEE Congress on Evolutionary Computation*, pages 887–894. IEEE Press, 2001.
10. M. Risler. *InvKinWalkingEngine - Kurze Beschreibung der Parameter.* Technische Universität Darmstadt, GermanTeam 2002, 2002.
11. K. Sastry, D.E. Goldberg, and M. Pelikan. Don't evaluate, inherit. In L. Spector et al., editor, *Proceedings of the Genetic and Evolutionary Computation Conference (GECCO)*, pages 551–558. Morgan Kaufmann, 2001.
12. H. Tagaki. Interactive evolutionary computation: System optimization based on human subjective evaluation. In *IEEE International Conference on Intelligent Engineering Systems (INES)*, pages 1–6. IEEE Press, 1998.
13. J. Ziegler, J. Barnholt, J. Busch, and W. Banzhaf. Automatic evolution of control programs for a small humanoid walking robot. In P. Bidaud and F. Ben Amar, editors, *Proceedings of the 5th International Conference on Climbing and Walking Robots (CLAWAR)*, pages 109–116. Professional Engineering Publishing, 2002.

Assembling Strategies in Extrinsic Evolvable Hardware with Bidirectional Incremental Evolution

Igor Baradavka and Tatiana Kalganova

Department of Electronic and Computer Engineering,
Brunel University, Uxbridge, UB8 3PH, UK
{igor.baradavka,tatiana.kalganova}@brunel.ac.uk
http://www.brunel.ac.uk/~eesttk/

Abstract. Bidirectional incremental evolution (BIE) has been proposed as a technique to overcome the "stalling" effect in evolvable hardware applications. However preliminary results show perceptible dependence of performance of BIE and quality of evaluated circuit on assembling strategy applied during reverse stage of incremental evolution. The purpose of this paper is to develop assembling strategy that will assist BIE to produce relatively optimal solution with minimal computational effort (e.g. the minimal number of generations).

1 Introduction

For almost a decade evolvable hardware (EHW) has been limited to evolution of relatively small logic circuits [1], [2], [3]. The solution of scalability problem will open the possibility to use evolvable hardware technique for real-world applications.

Recently a number of techniques have been developed to overcome this problem. Some of them are focused on speeding up the genetic algorithm computations using principles of parallelism [4], [5], [6]. Other approaches to the problem have used variable length chromosomes [7], function-level evolution [8], [9], automatically defined functions [10]. Further, a divide-and-conquer approach (known also as an increased complexity evolution) has been introduced [11], [12], [13], [14]. The basic idea of this approach is to split problems into sub-problems and evolve each sub-problem separately. The principle of this approach is very similar to incremental evolution introduced to solve complex tasks using evolutionary processes [15], [16], [17]. In incremental evolution approach the complexity of evolved tasks increases with evolution. This allows to reduce the computational effort to solve the task and overcome the "stalling" effect in evolution [18], [16]. The approach can successfully evolve relatively large circuits if there is human participation at the decomposition stage. The final solution is unlikely optimal because it is assembled from separately evolved logic circuits. Bidirectional Incremental Evolution (BIE) allows to eliminate these two drawbacks [19]. In BIE approach the EHW-oriented decomposition has been introduced to provide automatic decomposition of circuits and perform direct incremental evolution (DIE).

C. Ryan et al. (Eds.): EuroGP 2003, LNCS 2610, pp. 276–285, 2003.

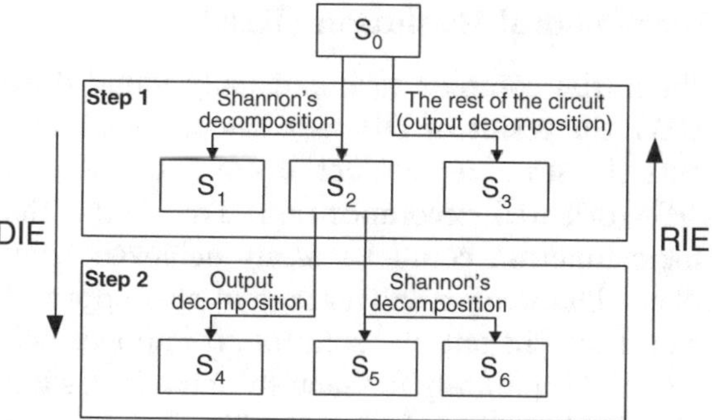

Fig. 1. An example of evolutionary process that may take place during DIE.

The optimization of obtained solution has been also carried out during reverse incremental evolution (RIE), where the sub-tasks are step-by-step assembled and further optimized using evolutionary process. Although larger circuits have been evolved using BIE with significant reduction in the evolution duration, the assemble strategies during RIE have not been considered in detail. The use of correct assembling technique is very important because it can significantly influence on both duration of evolution and quality of evolved circuits. This paper is devoted to analysis of assembling strategies during RIE.

2 Bidirectional Incremental Evolution

The bidirectional incremental evolution contains 2 main evolutionary processes: (1) Direct Incremental Evolution (DIE); (2) Reverse Incremental Evolution (RIE).

2.1 Direct Incremental Evolution (DIE)

The main purpose of DIE is to obtain a fully functional solution of given task. This is achieved by decomposition of complex task to certain set of sub-tasks of reduced complexity when the stalling effect takes place [19]. Thus BIE approach *guaranties* that at the end of DIE stage of evolutionary process the fully functional solution is found.

An example of BIE is given in Fig. 1. In this example DIE has been completed in two main decomposition steps. The DIE always starts with evolution of initial complex circuit S_0. Once the stalling effect has appeared, this circuit is decomposed into three smaller sub-circuits (see Step 1, Fig. 1). The sub-circuits S_1 and S_2 are obtained as a result of Shannon's decomposition and sub-circuit S_3 is the left part of the circuit S_0. The evolution of the sub-circuits S_1 and S_3 has been completed but another EHW-oriented decomposition (Step 2 in Fig. 1) is required to finish evolution of the sub-circuit S_2. During this step the sub-circuit S_2 is decomposed into another three sub-circuits using both output and Shannon's decompositions.

2.2 Reverse Incremental Evolution (RIE)

The solution of the initial complex task is usually found during the DIE. With relation to the EHW the result of DIE is a set of combinational logic circuits. This set implements the set of logic functions or sub-tasks. These sub-tasks are defined during EHW-oriented decomposition. The design that implements the initial complex logic function could be easily achieved by joining all evolved sub-circuits together. The main disadvantage of this approach is that obtained complex circuit is far from the optimal solution. It happens because the evolution during DIE is performed separately for each sub-circuit. Usually there exist some common parts between different sub-circuits. To overcome this problem further reverse incremental evolution of assembled circuits can be performed.

During RIE the evolution towards optimized circuit is carried out and the most important role during this stage is played by assembling process. At this stage the logic circuits are assembled back and further optimized using evolutionary process. This process consists of three assembling sub-processes:

1. Assembling process at RIE level;
2. Assembling process at decomposition level;
3. Assembling process at chromosome level.

Assembling strategy at RIE level defines how many logic circuits can be assembled at once in order to produce successful and fast evolution. For example, sub-circuits S_1, S_2 and S_3 can be assembled together at once (Fig. 2.B). From another point of view the evolution of sub-circuits S_1 and S_2 can be carried out as first step and only then the combined evolution of S_1, S_2 and S_3 can be considered.

The type of the decomposition used during DIE determines the way how the sub-circuits are linked together into a larger circuit during RIE. Such decomposition dependent circuit linkage is performed during the second assembling sub-process. For example, sub-circuits S_5 and S_6 shown in Fig. 1 can be merged using a set of multiplexors because they has been created during DIE as the result of Shannon's decomposition of S_2. Next, S_4 and S_{5-6} can be linked together. No additional sub-circuits are necessary at this step because the output decomposition has been used.

The way how the logic gates of sub-circuits are assembled together into one chromosome is considered during third assembling sub-process. This defines the positions of logic gates in the assembled chromosome. Since the new chromosome is built from several separate circuits the result of this linkage must be the combinational logic circuit.

This paper concentrates on the extrinsic EHW proposed in [9], [20]. The chromosome representation of circuit is shown in Fig. 3. The circuit is described by set of logic gates and the circuit output genes. Each logic gate is defined by the following genes: cell type, number of inputs, inputs (e.g. connectivity with other logic gates and circuit inputs).

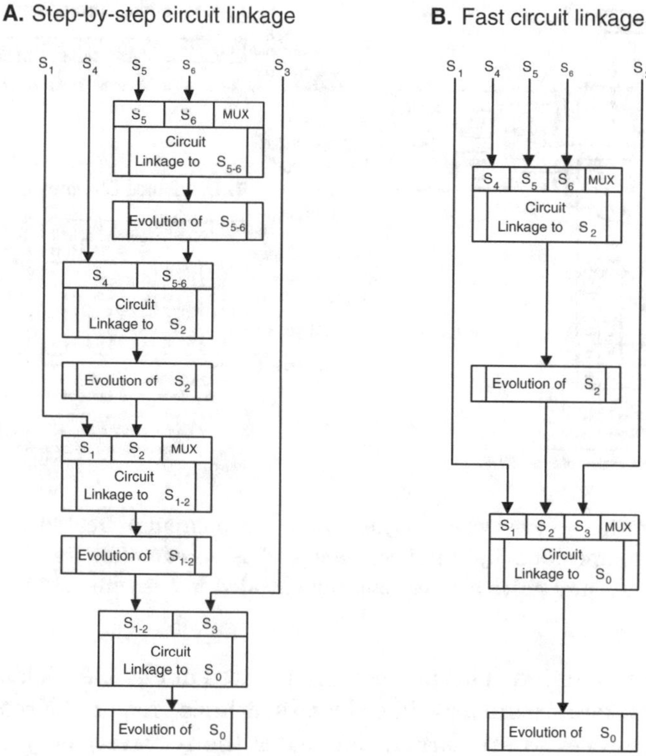

Fig. 2. Assembling strategies in RIE. There are two possible schemes of the evolutionary process RIE according to the decompositions shown in Fig. 1, where MUX is the set of multiplexors.

3 Assembling Processes

In this section we will consider in detail specific futures of all assembling processes mentioned in previous section.

3.1 Assembling Strategies at RIE Level

The success of evolutionary process is entirely depends on how the evolutionary process towards optimized system can be carried out. From this point of view it is important to consider how the circuits are linked to each other during RIE. We define two basic linkage strategies:

1. Step-by-step circuit linkage.
2. Fast circuit linkage.

The idea of step-by-step linkage is to assemble only two sub-circuits at once and perform evolutionary process under assembled circuit. Step-by-step linkage allows gradually increase the complexity of the circuit and optimize it at the

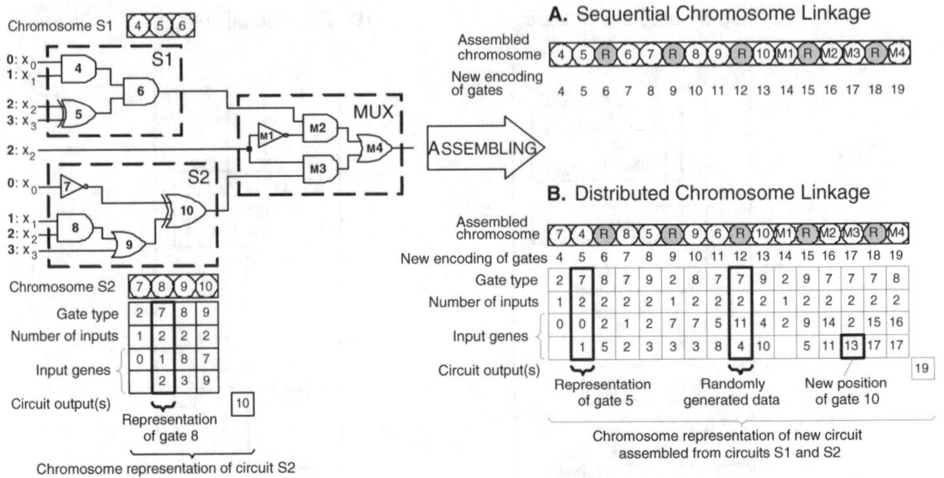

Fig. 3. Generation of new chromosome from 2 sub-circuits created as the result of Shannon's decomposition by input x_2, where R is a redundant randomly generated logic gate. Inputs and gates are sequentially encoded in the same numeric space.

early stages of evolution. This process is illustrated in Fig. 2.A. A large number of evolutionary processes are used in order to synthesize required circuit. But these evolutionary processes are carried out under the relatively easy tasks. As the result relatively small number of generations is required to successfully complete their evolution. Therefore, they require less computational efforts. For example, let us consider BIE shown in Fig. 1. There are 3 sub-circuits that have been generated during Step 2. The step-by-step circuit linkage at Step 2 involves two evolutionary processes. First, the circuit S_{5-6} assembled from sub-circuits S_5 and S_6 is evolved. Then the sub-circuit S_4 is added to already optimized S_{5-6} and evolutionary process is carried out again for S_2 circuit. Next optimized circuit S_2 is assembled with S_1 and optimization of result circuit S_{1-2} is carried out. The linkage of S_{1-2} and S_3 to S_0 finalizes the Step 1 (see Fig. 1) and final evolution of entire circuit S_0 is performed.

The idea of the fast circuit linkage is to evolve the assembled circuit without intermediate steps. For instance, the optimization process shown in Fig. 2.B is performed just in two steps. In this case the number of optimization sub-tasks is two times less, but the evolution will be undertaken under more complex tasks in comparison with step-by-step circuit linkage and require more computational effort to optimize every task.

3.2 Circuit Linkage at the Decomposition Level

There is one global difference between output and Shannon's decompositions. The circuits evolved using output decomposition are independent from each other. This means that they do not require any additional "linkage" sub-circuit in order to obtain a fully functional solution of assembled circuit (Fig. 4.A).

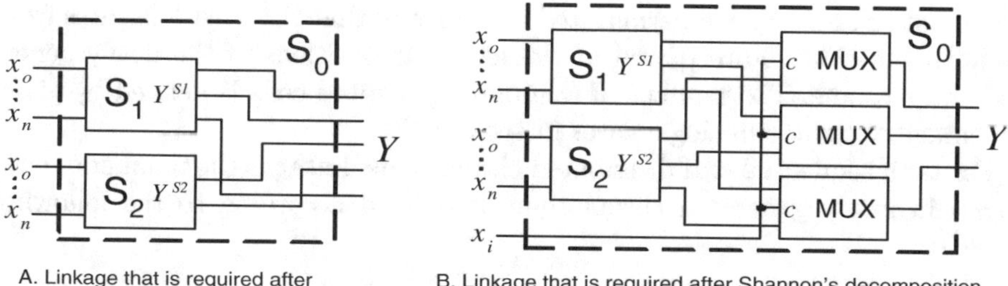

A. Linkage that is required after output decomposition

B. Linkage that is required after Shannon's decomposition by input x_i provided the functional set contains multiplexers

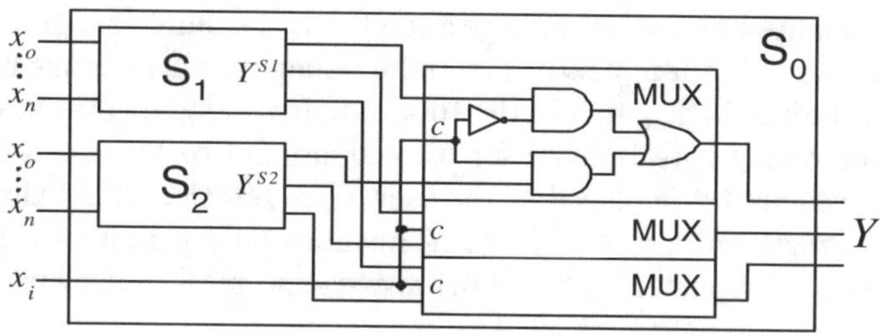

C. Linkage that is required after Shannon's decomposition by input x_i with replacement of multiplexers by primitive active gates

Fig. 4. Circuit linkage at the decomposition level, where Y, Y^{S_1} and Y^{S_2} are the outputs of the sub-circuits S_0, S_1 and S_2 respectively.

Shannon's decomposition always produces a pair of logic circuits. Each of these circuits is fully functional only for particular part of input-output combination matrix of initial circuit. As the result, a set of multiplexors is required to join the outputs of these circuits (Fig. 4.B). The number of multiplexors is equal to the number of outputs in the circuits to be linked. For example, the logic circuit shown in Fig. 4.B is generated using 3 multiplexors because each sub-circuit has 3 outputs. The implementation of the linkage circuit depends on the chosen functional set of logic gates. Thus, if the multiplexer is included into the functional set, the "linkage" circuit can be represented using multiplexors only. Otherwise multiplexer could be replaced by 4 primitive active logic gates. A set of multiplexors could share one NOT-gate as it is shown in Fig. 4.C. Thus, in this example only 10 primitive active gates are needed to represent 3 multiplexors.

3.3 Assembling Strategies at the Chromosome Level

Logic gates can be assembled differently inside chromosome. For example, in [19] the sequential chromosome linkage has been considered. In this case all logic gates of the sub-circuit S_1 are placed at the most left position of the newly generated chromosome. Then all logic gates of the sub-circuit S_2 are placed just next to the logic gates of the sub-circuit S_1 and so on. The additional linkage circuit is placed at the most right position of the chromosome (see Fig. 3.A).

The process of assembling one chromosome from 2 sub-circuits using distributed chromosome linkage is shown in Fig. 3.B. The logic gates from the sub-circuits S_1 and S_2 are permutated in such way that the least left gates from the both sub-circuits are placed at the least left positions of the newly generated chromosome. The number of randomly generated cells is defined by given percentage of redundant logic gates in the circuit.

For both sequential and distributed chromosome linkages the number of cells C_{NEW} in newly generated chromosome is defined according to the following formula:

$$C_{NEW} = \frac{\sum_1^k C_i + C_{MUX}}{r},$$

where C_i is the number of active logic gates in i-th circuit, C_{MUX} is the number of logic gates required for special linkage circuit, k is the number of sub-circuits to be linked, r is the redundancy rate. The redundancy rate defines the ratio of the number of redundant logic gates to the total number of logic gates in the circuit [21]. The redundancy rate is fixed for all sub-circuits to be assembled. If the multiplexer is required it is placed at the least right position of the chromosome. If the chosen functional set of logic gates includes only primitive active gates, every multiplexer is replaced by 3 or 4 primitive logic gates as shown in Fig. 4.C.

4 Experimental Results

The purpose of our experiments is to investigate how the assembling strategy can influence on the algorithm performance. In order to do so 3 functions from standard benchmark library have been used: mult3.pla, m1.pla and squar5.pla. The functions have been chosen in a such way that the same experiments were performed under circuits with relatively various complexity and structure. The complexity of circuits has been considered in terms of the number of inputs and outputs. Thus, 3-bit multiplier (mult3.pla) has 6 inputs and 6 outputs. At the same time, m1 function (m1.pla) has 5 inputs and 12 outputs and squar5 function (squar5.pla) has 5 inputs and 8 outputs.

The initial data for the experiments are given in Table 1. The rudimentary $(1+\lambda)$ evolutionary strategy has been used [9]. Any type of genes in chromosome genotype allowed to be changed with constant gene mutation probability. The functional set of logic gates contains {AND, OR, EXOR, NOT}. Each function has been successfully evolved at least 100 times. One of the noticeable features of the BIE is that it *guaranties* to evolve fully functional solution. Therefore, after each run of evolutionary algorithm the fully functional solution has been obtained. The obtained experimental results are summarized in Table 2. The analysis of results shows that it is more difficult to evolve m1 function rather then mult3 and squar5. It can be seen that the slowest strategy is A (combination of Sequential and Step-by-step assembling strategies) for all 3 circuits.

Let us consider the average number of active logic gates in final circuits that have been evolved. Best results were achieved by strategies A and C and the worst - by strategy B (Table 2). However strategy A performed slower then strategy C although the quality of optimization was the same.

Therefore, based on the experimental results one may conclude that combination of the step-by-step circuit linkage and distributed chromosome linkage

Table 1. Initial data, where η_{fc} is the limitation of number of generations after last change of fitness function, # is "the number of ...".

Circuit	mult3	m1	squar5
Max # rows	1	1	1
Max # columns for DIE	40	50	40
Levels back for DIE	40	50	40
Max # of inputs in the logic gate	2	2	2
Population size	5	5	5
# generations for DIE	100000	100000	100000
# generations for RIE	500000	500000	500000
η_{fc} for initial system evolution	14000	14000	14000
η_{fc} for DIE with $\gamma(F_1)$ [20]	22000	22000	22000
η_{fc} for DIE with $\gamma(F_1 + F_2)$ [20]	7000	7000	7000
η_{fc} for RIE	45000	45000	45000
# successful runs of BIE	100	100	100
Cell mutation rate	5%	5%	5%

Table 2. Experimental results, where Avg. No. is the average number, Min. No. is the minimal number, n is the number of inputs, m is the number of outputs, *s-b-s* and *fast* is the step-by-step and the fast circuit linkage respectively.

Circuit	Strategy	A	B	C	D
Circuit	Assembling at chromosome level	Sequential		Distributed	
(n, m)	Assembling at RIE level	*s-b-s*	*fast*	*s-b-s*	*fast*
mult3 (6, 6)	Avg. No. of generations (BIE)	487000	361000	545000	368000
	Avg. No. of generations during RIE	329000	197000	346000	173000
	Avg. No. of gates in evolved circuit	46	52	46	51
	Min. No. of gates found	37	35	34	35
m1 (5, 12)	Avg. No. of generations (BIE)	788000	403000	766000	460000
	Avg. No. of generations during RIE	577000	196000	511000	207000
	Avg. No. of gates in evolved circuit	67	77	64	81
	Min. No. of gates found	61	68	49	69
squar5 (5, 8)	Avg. No. of generations (BIE)	530000	282000	484000	295000
	Avg. No. of generations during RIE	407000	148000	328000	141000
	Avg. No. of gates in evolved circuit	39	50	39	48
	Min. No. of gates found	34	34	29	32

allows to obtain the most optimal solution with minimal computational effort in terms of the number of generations used.

5 Conclusions and Future Work

This paper describes the evolutionary design of combinational logic circuits in terms of use of different assembling strategies in bidirectional incremental evolution. The distinctive feature of the algorithm is that it *guaranties* the evolution of fully functional circuit. We have introduced distributed assembling strategy, which allows us not only to assemble logic circuits with random genes into one chromosome but to make sure that the logic gates from *all* sub-circuits participate equally in evolution. We have also proposed step-by-step assembling strategy at decomposition level that allow us to optimize small sub-circuits on early stages of evolution when the performance of BIE does not seriously degrade because of complexity of the circuit. These two aspects allow us to significantly improve the quality of evolved circuits with minimal amount of computational efforts.

We have investigated several assembling strategies at both RIE and chromosome levels. Analysis of experimental results allow us to make following conclusions:

1. Different logic functions behave similarly for different linkage strategies.
2. The sequential chromosome linkage reduces the quality of optimization when the fast circuit linkage is used. When the step-by-step circuit linkage is used, it also reduces performance of RIE.
3. The step-by-step circuit linkage and distributed chromosome linkage provides the best synthesis and optimization of combinational logic functions. However, if the better performance is required, the fast circuit linkage and and distributed chromosome linkage can be recommended as the most cost-effective technique.

So we can conclude that the use of correct assembling strategy is very important in implementation of BIE.

A great deal of further work could be done in the area. Automatic control of duration of evolutionary process could be introduced in order to improve further the computational effort of BIE algorithm.

References

1. Coello C. A., Christiansen A. D., and Hernández A. A. Towards automated evolutionary design of combinational circuits. *Computers and Electrical Engineering*, 2000.
2. Higuchi T., Murakawa M., Iwata M., Kajitani I., Liu W., and Salami M. Evolvable hardware at function level. In *Proc. of IEEE 4th Int. Conference on Evolutionary Computation, CEC'97.* IEEE Press, NJ, 1997.
3. Thompson A. *Hardware Evolution: Automatic Design of Electronic Circuits in Reconfigurable Hardware by Artificial Evolution.* PhD thesis, University of Sussex, School of Cognitive and Computing Sciences., 1996.
4. Birge J.R. Stochastic programming, computation and applications. *INFORMS, Journal on Computing*, pages 111–133, 1997.
5. Zenious S.A. Vladiviriou H. Parallel algorithms for large-scale stochastic programming in parallel computing and optimisation. pages 413–469, 1997.
6. Poli R. Evolution of graph-like programs with parallel distributed genetic programming. In Bäck T., editor, *Genetic Algorithms: Proc. of the Seventh International Conference.*, pages 346–353. Morgan Kaufmann, San Francisco, CA, 1997.

7. Iwata M., Kajitani I., Yamada H., Iba H., and Higuchi T. A pattern recognition system using evolvable hardware. In *Proc. of the Fifth International Conference on Parallel Problem Solving from Nature (PPSNIV)*, volume LNCS 1141 of *Lecture Notes in Computer Science*. Springer-Verlag, Heidelberg, 1996.
8. Murakawa M., Yoshizawa S., Kajitani I., Furuya T., Iwata M., and Higuchi T. Hardware evolution at function level. In *Proc. of the Fifth International Conference on Parallel Problem Solving from Nature (PPSNIV)*, Lecture Notes in Computer Science. Springer-Verlag, Heidelberg, 1996.
9. Kalganova T. An extrinsic function-level evolvable hardware approach. In Poli R., Banzhaf W., Langdon W.B., Miller J., Nordin P., and Fogarty T.C., editors, *Proc. of the Third European Conference on Genetic Programming, EuroGP2000*, volume 1802 of *Lecture Notes in Computer Science*, pages 60–75, Edinburgh, UK, 2000. Springer-Verlag.
10. Koza J. R. *Genetic Programming II: Automatic Discovery of Reusable Programs.* MIT Press, 1994.
11. Torresen J. A divide-and-conquer approach to evolvable hardware. In Sipper M., Mange D., and Perez-Uribe A., editors, *Proc. Of the 2nd Int. Conf. on Evolvable Systems: From Biology to Hardware (ICES'98)*, volume 1478 of *Lecture Notes in Computer Science*, pages 57–65, Lausanne, Switzerland, 1998. Springer-Verlag, Heidelberg.
12. Torresen J. Increased complexity evolution applied to evovable hardware. In *Smart Engineering System Design, ANNIE'99.* St. Louis, USA, 1999.
13. Torresen J. Two-step incremental evolution of a prosthetic hand controller based on digital logic gates. In *Proc. of the 4th Int. Conference on Evolvable Systems, ICES.*, Lecture Notes in Computer Science. Springer-Verlag, 2001.
14. Torresen J. A scalable approach to evolvable hardware. *Genetic Programming and evolvable machines*, 3(3), 2002.
15. Gomez F. and Miikkulainen R. Incremental evolution of complex general behaviour. *Adaptive Behaviour.*, 5:317–342, 1997.
16. Gomez F. and Miikkulainen R. Solving non-markovian control tasks with neurevolution. In *Proc. of the International Joint Conference on Artificial Intelligence (IJCAI'99)*, Stockholm, Sweden, 1999. Denver: Morgan Kaufmann.
17. Filliat D., Kodjabachian J., and Meyer J.A. Incremental evolution of neural controllers for navigation in a 6-legged robot. In Sugisaka and Tanaka, editors, *Proc. of the Fourth International Symposium on Artificial Life and Robotics.* Oita Univ. Press, 1999.
18. Harvey I. Artificial evolution for real problems. In Gomi T., editor, *Proc. of the 5th Intl. Symposium on Evolutionary Robotics, Evolutionary Robotics: From Intelligent Robots to Artificial Life (ER'97)*, Tokyo, Japan, 1997. AAI Books.
19. Kalganova T. Bidirectional incremental evolution in ehw. In *Proc. of the Second NASA/DoD Workshop on Evolvable Hardware.* IEEE Computer Society, July 2000.
20. Kalganova T. and Miller J. Evolving more efficient digital circuits by allowing circuit layout evolution and multi-objective fitness. In Stoica A., Keymeulen D., and Lohn J., editors, *Proc. of the First NASA/DoD Workshop on Evolvable Hardware*, pages 54–63. IEEE Computer Society, July 1999.
21. Kalganova T. and Miller J. Circuit layout evolution: An evolvable hardware approach. In *Coloquium on Evolutionary hardware systems. IEE Colloquium Digest.*, London, UK, 1999.

Neutral Variations Cause Bloat in Linear GP

Markus Brameier and Wolfgang Banzhaf

Department of Computer Science, University of Dortmund
44221 Dortmund, Germany
{markus.brameier,wolfgang.banzhaf}@cs.uni-dortmund.de

Abstract. In this contribution we investigate the influence of different variation effects on the growth of code. A mutation-based variant of linear GP is applied that operates with minimum structural step sizes. Results show that neutral variations are a direct cause for (and not only a result of) the emergence and the growth of intron code. The influence of non-neutral variations has been found to be considerably smaller. Neutral variations turned out to be beneficial by solving two classification problems more successfully.

1 Introduction

One characteristic of genetic programming (GP) is that variable-length individuals grow in size. To a certain extent this growth is necessary to direct the evolutionary search into regions of the search space where sufficiently complex solutions with a high fitness are found. It is not recommended, in general, to initiate the evolutionary algorithm already with programs of a very large or even maximum size.

However, by the influence of variation operators and other reasons discussed in this paper genetic programs may grow too fast and too large such that the minimum size of programs required to solve the problem is exceeded significantly. As a result, finding a solution may become more difficult. This negative effect of code growth, i.e., that programs emerge larger than necessary without corresponding fitness improvements became known as the *bloat effect.* Code growth has been widely investigated in the GP literature [9,5,12,10,13,11,14,2] (see below). In general, a high complexity of GP programs causes an increase of evaluation time and reduces the flexibility of evolutionary manipulations. Moreover, it is argued to lead to a worse generalization performance.

Most evolutionary computation (EC) approaches model the Darwinian process of natural selection and adaptation. Contrary to this theory, Kimura's [8] neutral theory considers the random genetic drift of neutral mutations as the main force of evolution. In EC such variations are argued to explore flat regions of the fitness landscape more widely while non-neutral variations exploit regions with (positive or negative) gradient information. Banzhaf [1] first emphasized the relevance of neutral variations in genetic programming. Yu and Miller [16] demonstrated that neutral variations are advantageous after extra neutral code

C. Ryan et al. (Eds.): EuroGP 2003, LNCS 2610, pp. 286–296, 2003.

has been explicitly included into a graph representation of programs. Better performance was found for a Boolean problem with neutral mutations than without.

It is well-known, that a high proportion of neutral code (also referred to as introns) in genetic programs may increase the probability for variations to become neutral. But which type of variation creates the intron code in the first place? In our linear GP approach we apply minimum mutations. We demonstrate experimentally that neutral variations almost exclusively represent a *direct cause* for the growth of intron code. The influence of different variation effects on code growth and on prediction quality is verified for two approximation and two classification problems. Our observations differ from results reported for crossover-based GP which identify destructive variations as a direct [13] or indirect [12] cause of code growth.

2 Basics on Linear GP

In linear genetic programming (LGP) [3,6] the program representation consists of variable-length sequences of instructions from an imperative programming language. *Operations* manipulate variables (*registers*) and constants and assign the result to a destination register, e.g., $r_i := r_j + 1$. Single operations may be skipped by preceding *conditional branches*, e.g., $if(r_j > r_k)$.

The imperative program code is divided into *effective* and *non-effective* instructions. Such a separation of instructions already results from the linear program structure – prior to execution – and can be computed efficiently in linear runtime $O(n)$ where n is the program length [6]. Only the effective code may influence program behavior. Non-effective instructions manipulate registers not impacting the program output at the current position and are, thus, not connected to the data flow generated by effective instructions. Non-effective instructions are also referred to as *structural introns* for a better distinction from *semantic introns* that may still occur within the (structurally) effective part of code [6]. For instance, all instructions preceding $r_0 := r_1 - r_1$ that only influence the content of register r_1 are semantic introns. Note that structural introns do not exist in tree-based GP, because in a tree structure, by definition, all program components are connected to the root. Hence, intron code in tree programs is semantic.

The length of a linear genetic program is measured as the number of instructions it holds. In linear GP the *absolute program length* and the *effective program length* are discerned. While the first simply includes all instructions of a program, the latter counts effective instructions only.

2.1 Variation Effects

Basically, two different effects of a variation operator can be discerned in EC. These are its effect on the genotype representation and its effect on the phenotype (fitness). In the current study, we focus on the proportion of constructive, destructive, and neutral operations per generation as semantic measurements of variation effects. If we assume that a better fitness always means a smaller fitness value the following definitions are valid: A variation is *constructive* if the difference in fitness between the parent individual $\mathcal{F}_p$ and the its offspring $\mathcal{F}_o$ is positive, i.e., $\mathcal{F}_p - \mathcal{F}_o > 0$. In case of a negative difference we refer to a *destructive* variation, i.e., $\mathcal{F}_p - \mathcal{F}_o < 0$. Finally, a genetic operation is *neutral* if it does not change the fitness, i.e., $\mathcal{F}_p = \mathcal{F}_o$.

On the structural level we measure the proportion of effective and non-effective variations. According to the distinction between effective code and non-effective code, as defined above, let an *effective variation* denote a genetic operation that modifies the effective code of a linear genetic program. Otherwise, a variation is called *non-effective*. Note that there is no change of program behavior (fitness) guaranteed by such (structurally) effective variations.

The notion of *variation step size* refers to the *amount* of structural change between parent and offspring that is induced by the variation operator. In this paper we apply a pure mutation-based variant of linear GP that induces minimum variation steps on the imperative program structure. We distinguish macro-mutations from micro-mutations. Programs grow by *macro-mutations* which include insertions or deletions of single random instructions. *Micro-mutations* exchange the smallest program components that comprise a single operator, a register or a constant.

3 Code Growth in GP

Several theories have been proposed to explain the phenomenon of code bloat in genetic programming. Basically, three different causes of code growth have been distinguished up to now that do not contradict each other while each being capable of causing code growth for itself. In general, the minimally required complexity of a solution may be exceeded by incorporating intron code (may be removed without changing the program behavior) or by mathematically equivalent extensions. All causes require the existence of fitness information, i.e., may not hold on (completely) flat fitness landscapes. The (effective) program size develops depending on how strongly it is correlated to the fitness. In this way, fitness may be regarded as a necessary precondition for code growth.

One theory (*protection theory*) [12,5,2,14] argues that code growth occurs as a protection against the destructive effects of crossover. The destructive influence on the program structure strongly depends on the absolute variation step size. If the maximum amount of code that may be exchanged in one variation step is large, e.g., restricted only by the program size, evolution may reduce the strength of variation on the effective code by developing a higher proportion of introns within the replaced subprograms. This phenomenon may occur when using crossover as well as subprogram mutations.

Another theory (*drift theory*) [10,11] claims that code growth results from the structure of the search space or, more precisely, from the distribution of semantically identical solutions. For many problems more larger program solutions exist with a certain fitness than smaller ones. Therefore, larger solutions are created and selected for a higher probability.

Finally, the third theory (*bias theory*) [15,11,14] of code growth is based on the hypothesis of a removal bias in tree-based GP. The potential destruction caused by removing a subtree depends on the subtree size. The effect of the replacing subtree on the fitness, instead, is independent from its size. As a results, the growing offspring from which the smaller subtree is removed (and in which the longer is inserted) will survive for a higher probability than the shrinking offspring.

Soule *et al.* [13] demonstrated for tree-based GP that significantly less code growth (especially of introns) emerges if only those offsprings are incorporated into the population that perform better than their parents. The authors hold the missing destructive crossover results responsible for this behavior. While a direct influence of destructive variations on the growth of (intron) code is not doubted here, it has to be noted that not only destructive but also neutral variations are excluded from evolutionary progress in [13]. Moreover, the proportion of (the remaining) constructive variations is usually rather low in GP.

If we want to clearly identify a reason for code growth it is important to design the experiment in such a way that the other mechanisms (if existent) are disabled as much as possible. In linear GP, the protection theory may not be valid if the step size of the variation operator is reduced to a minimum and code is not exchanged, but only added *or* removed. Both may be achieved easily for the imperative program structure by single instruction mutation as described above.

With a mutation step size of one instruction only, intron instructions cannot be inserted or deleted directly along with a *non*-neutral variation. In particular, this allows destructive variations to be analyzed with only a minimum influence on the size of intron code. Structural introns may only emerge with such operations by deactivation of other depending instructions (apart from the mutation point). The same is true for the creation of introns on the semantic level. In general, linear GP allows structural variation steps to be permanently minimum at each position of the genom. On reason for this is that the data flow in linear genetic programs is graph-based [4]. Due to stronger constraints of the tree representation, small variation step sizes are especially difficult in upper tree regions. If single tree nodes are tried to be deleted only one of its subtrees may be reconnected while the others get lost.

The influence of the second cause is reduced, too, because the difference between parent and offspring is only one instruction. At least, using such minimum variation steps exclusively will make the evolutionary process drift less quickly towards more complex regions of the search space. In general, the maximum step size of a variation operator decides on the potential maximum speed of code growth but does not represent a explicit force (if the variation operator is not length-biased).

4 Conditional Variation

We use a steady state evolutionary algorithm that applies tournament selection with a minimum of two participants per tournament. Variations happen on copies of the parent individuals (tournament winners) that replace the tournament losers. The integration of newly created individuals into the population is restricted so that offsprings are accepted only if they result from certain types of variation (see Section 2.1). Such a *conditional acceptance* of a variation implies automatically that the reproduction of parents is omitted, too, since the population remains unchanged.

5 Benchmark Problems

The different experiments documented in this contribution are conducted with four benchmark problems – including two symbolic regressions and two classification tasks. The first problem is represented by the two-dimensional *mexican hat* function as given by Equation 1. The function constitutes a surface in three-dimensional space that resembles a mexican hat.

$$f_{mexicanhat}(x, y) = \left(1 - \frac{x^2}{4} - \frac{y^2}{4}\right) \times e^{\left(-\frac{x^2}{8} - \frac{y^2}{8}\right)} \tag{1}$$

The second regression problem, called *distance*, requires the Euclidean distance between two points (vectors) $\boldsymbol{x}$ and $\boldsymbol{y}$ in n-dimensional space to be computed by the genetic programs (see Equation 2). The higher the dimension is chosen ($n = 3$ here) the more difficult the problem becomes.

$$f_{distance}(x_1, y_1, .., y_n, y_n) = \sqrt{(x_1 - y_1)^2 + .. + (x_n - y_n)^2} \tag{2}$$

The third problem is the well-known *spiral* classification [9] where two intertwined spirals have to be distinguished in two-dimensional data space. Finally, the *three chains* problem concatenates three rings of points that each represent a different data class. Actually, one "ring" denotes a circle of 100 points in three-dimensional space whose positions are slightly noisy. The rings approach each other at five regions without leading to intersection. The problem difficulty may be scaled up or down depending on both the angle of the rings to one another and on the number of rings.

6 Experimental Setup

Table 1 summarizes attributes of the data sets that have been created for each test problem. Furthermore, problem-specific configurations of our linear GP system are given that comprise the compositions of the function set, the fitness function, and the number of registers.

It is important for the performance of linear GP to provide enough registers for calculation, especially if the input dimension is low. Thus, the total number of available registers – including the minimum number that is required for the input data – is an important parameter. In general, the number of registers decides on the number of program paths that can be calculated in parallel. If it

Table 1. Problem-specific parameter settings.

Problem	*mexican hat*	*distance*	*spiral*	*three chains*
Problem type	Regression	Regression	Classification	Classification
#Inputs	2	6	2	3
Input range	$[-4.0, 4.0]$	$[0, 1]$	$[-2\pi, 2\pi]$	$[0, 5]$
Output range	$[-1, 1]$	$[0, 1]$	$\{0, 1\}$	$\{0, 1, 2\}$
#Output classes	–	–	2	3
#Registers	6	12	6	6
#Fitness cases	400	300	194	300
Fitness function	SSE	SSE	CE	CE
Instruction set $\cup \{+, -, \times, /\}$	$\{x^y\}$	$\{\sqrt{x}, x^2\}$	$\{sin, cos, if >\}$	$\{x^y, if >\}$

Table 2. General parameter settings.

Parameter	Setting	Parameter	Setting
Number of generations	1000	Initial program lengths	5-15
Population size	1000	Macro-mutations	75%
Tournament size	2	Micro-mutations	25%
Maximum program length	200	Set of constants	$\{1, .., 9\}$

is not sufficient there may be too many conflicts by overwriting register content within programs.

For the approximation problems the fitness is defined as the continuous *sum of square errors* (SSE) between the predicted outputs and the example outputs. For the two classification tasks specified in Table 1 the fitness function is discrete and equals the *classification error* (CE) here, i.e., the number of wrongly classified inputs.

The *spiral* problem applies an *interval classification* method, i.e., if the output is smaller than 0.5 it is interpreted as class 0, otherwise it is class 1. For the *three chains* problem we use an *error classification* method, instead. That is the distance between the problem output and one of the given output classes (0, 1, or 2) must be smaller than 0.5 to be accepted as correct. General configurations of our linear GP system are summarized in Table 2 and are valid for all experiments and test problems.

7 Experimental Results

The experiments documented in Tables 3 to 6 investigate the influence of different variation effects on both, the complexity of (effective) programs and the prediction performance. The average prediction error is calculated by the best solutions of 100 independent runs together with the statistical standard error.

Table 3. *Mexican hat* problem: Conditional acceptance of mutation effects and conditional reproduction. Average results over 100 runs.

Experiment ID	SSE		Length			Variations (%)		
	mean	*std.err.*	*abs.*	*eff.*	%	*constr.*	*neutral*	*noneff.*
std	3.5	0.5	140	60	43	0.8	54	52
nodestr	3.3	0.5	139	61	44	0.2	53	52
noneutr	1.6	0.1	**38**	**28**	72	7.5	37	34
nononeff	1.5	0.1	**41**	**30**	74	4.8	41	32

Table 4. *Distance* problem: Conditional acceptance of mutation effects and conditional reproduction. Average results over 100 runs.

Experiment ID	SSE		Length			Variations (%)		
	mean	*std.err.*	*abs.*	*eff.*	%	*constr.*	*neutral*	*noneff.*
std	6.5	0.3	78	32	41	0.5	63	63
nodestr	8.0	0.3	78	32	41	0.1	64	63
noneutr	6.0	0.3	**24**	**15**	63	6.3	48	47
nononeff	6.5	0.2	**25**	**16**	62	4.7	52	48

The absolute and the effective program length are averaged over all programs that are created during runs. (Figure 1 shows exemplarily the generational development of the average program length in the population.) Due to the small step size of mutations used here, the average length of best individuals develops almost identically (not documented). The proportion of effective code is given in percent while the remaining proportion comprises the structural introns. Additionally, we calculate the average proportions of constructive, neutral and non-effective variations among all variations during a run (see Section 2.1). The rates of destructive and effective variations are obvious then.

In the no∗ experiments of Tables 3 to 6 offsprings are not inserted into the population if they result from a certain type of variation. Additionally, the reproduction of the parent individuals is skipped. Simply put, the variation is canceled completely without affecting the state of the population. Nevertheless, with all configurations the same number of variations (and evaluations) happens, i.e., the same number of new individuals (1000) defines a generation. Thus, unaccepted variations are still included in the calculation of the prediction error, the program lengths and the variation rates.

The standard mutation approach std is characterized by a balanced ratio of neutral operations and non-neutral operations, on the one hand, and effective operations and non-effective operations, on the other hand.

Destructive variations hardly contribute to the evolutionary progress here. The average prediction error changes only slightly with both the two continuous test problems, *mexican hat* and *distance*, and the two discrete test problems, *spiral* and *three chains*, if offsprings from destructive variations are not accepted

Table 5. *Spiral* problem: Conditional acceptance of mutation effects and conditional reproduction. Average results over 100 runs.

Experiment ID	CE		Length			Variations (%)		
	mean	*std.err.*	*abs.*	*eff.*	%	*constr.*	*neutral*	*noneff.*
std	13.6	0.6	128	64	50	0.3	50	42
nodestr	12.4	0.5	117	64	55	0.02	46	39
noneutr	20.0	0.6	**37**	**31**	82	5.0	32	20
nononeff	13.1	0.5	69	62	89	1.5	32	13

Table 6. *Three chains* problem: Conditional acceptance of mutation effects and conditional reproduction. Average results over 100 runs.

Experiment ID	CE		Length			Variations (%)		
	mean	*std.err.*	*abs.*	*eff.*	%	*constr.*	*neutral*	*noneff.*
std	15.5	0.6	132	57	43	0.2	62	49
nodestr	16.4	0.7	124	53	43	0.03	62	49
noneutr	24.6	0.8	**34**	**28**	82	5.3	38	20
nononeff	12.9	0.7	80	71	88	1.0	45	13

(nodestr). This is true even though about 50 percent of all variations are rejected and even if the rate of constructive variations decreases significantly, especially with the classification problems (in Tables 5 and 6). Hence, almost only neutral variations are responsible for evolution here. Obviously, the probability for selecting an individual, that performs worse than its parent, seems to be so low, on average, that it hardly makes any difference if this individual is copied into the population or not. Due to the low survival rate of these offsprings and due to the small mutation step size (see below), destructive mutations almost do not have any influence on code growth here.

The influence of neutral variations is in clear contrast to the influence of destructive variations. Obviously, the survival probability of offsprings is higher after a neutral (or a constructive) variation. This facilitates both a continuous further development of solutions and the growth of programs. An important result is that both the absolute size and the effective size of programs are reduced most if we skip neutral variations (noneutr).

Non-effective neutral variations, as defined in Section 2.1, create or modify non-effective instructions, i.e., structural introns. Accordingly, we may assume that mostly *effective neutral* variations are responsible for the emergence of semantic introns – within the (structurally) effective part of program. Effective neutral variations (and semantic introns) are harder to induce if the fitness function is continuous and, thus, occur less frequently. This is reflected here with the two regression problems by similar rates of non-effective operations and neutral operations. For the discrete classification problems, instead, the proportion of neutral variations has been found significantly larger than the proportion of non-effective variations which means a higher rate of effective neutral variations. Additionally, the frequency of neutral variations on the effective code depends on the function set. Especially, branches create semantic introns easily while the resulting larger effective code indirectly increases the probability for effective (neutral) variations.

In the nononeff experiments non-effective variations are rejected, i.e., only effective variations are accepted. This includes effective neutral variations in contrast to the noneutr experiment. Semantic introns created by those variations may be responsible for the larger effective code that occurs with both classifications in nononeff runs. With the two regressions the effective size is half-reduced for both noneutr and nononeff because most neutral variations are non-effective here.

We may conclude that neutral variations – in contrast to destructive variations – dominate code growth almost exclusively. Since mutation step sizes are small, constructive variations may only play a minor role for code growth already because of their low frequency. This is true even if the rate of constructions increases (together with the rate of destructions) when not accepting the result of neutral variations in the population (noneutr). One reason for this is the lower rate of structural and semantic introns. Moreover, non-neutral variations may hardly be responsible for an (unnecessarily) growth of code here because the variation step size is minimum. Then intron code cannot be directly created by such operations and *all* changes of a program are exposed to fitness selection.

As noted in Section 3, the possibility to induce small structural mutations at each position of the linear representation is important for our results. Indirect creation of intron instruction by deactivations seems to play a minor role only. Note that due to changing register dependencies non-effective (effective) instructions may be reactivated (deactivated) in a linear genetic program above the mutated instruction. Besides, an increasing robustness of the effective code lets deactivation of instructions occur less frequently in the course of a run [7].

When step sizes are larger, i.e., more than one instruction may be inserted per variation, as this occurs with crossover, programs may grow faster and by a smaller total number of variations. In particular, introns may be directly inserted by variations, too, that are not neutral as a whole.

Concerning the prediction quality the noneutr experiment has a small positive or no effect with the two approximation problems but a clear negative effect with the two classification problems. Contrary to this, the performance never drops in the nononeff experiment (compared to the baseline result). Consequently, effective neutral variations may be supposed to be more relevant than non-effective neutral variations, in general. This is not obvious, because all neutral changes may be reactivated later in (non-neutral) variations.

We may not automatically conclude here that neutral variations are more essential for solving classifications only because those problems are discrete. It has to be noted, that a better performance may also result from the fact that programs grow larger by neutral variations. Depending on the problem definition, the configuration of the instruction set, and the observed number of generations,

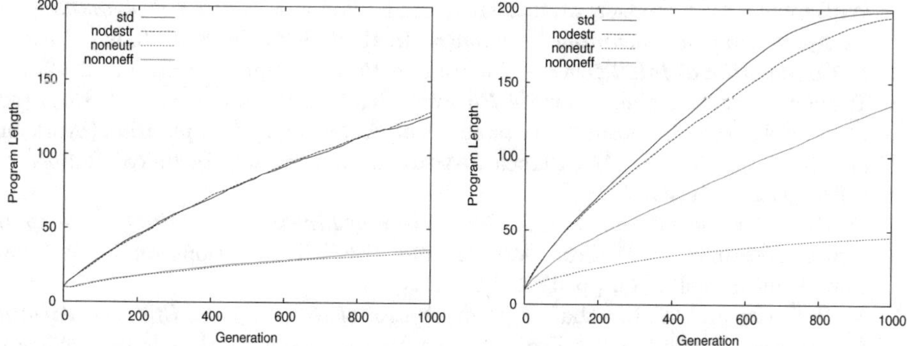

Fig. 1. Development of absolute program length for *distance* (left) and *three chains* (right) (similar for *mexican hat* and *spiral*). Code growth significantly reduced without neutral variation effects. Average figures over 100 runs.

the optimum speed of code growth may be quite different. By making use of branches, that allow many special cases to be considered in a program, both classification problems profit less from a lower complexity of solutions than the two symbolic regressions.

8 Conclusion

We have analyzed the influence of different variation effects on the development of program size for a mutation-based LGP approach. In all test cases neutral variations have been identified as a major reason for code growth. Almost no bloat effect occurred if (1) neutral variations are not accepted and (2) the variation step size is reduced to a minimum. Especially, the linear (imperative) representation of programs allows structural variation steps to be constantly small.

Acknowledgements

This research was supported by the German Research Community (DFG), Collaborative Research Center (SFB) 531, project B2.

References

1. W. Banzhaf, *Genotype-Phenotype-Mapping and Neutral Variation: A Case Study in genetic programming.* In *Proceedings of the Conference on Parallel Problem Solving from Nature III*, pp. 322–332, Springer-Verlag, Berlin, 1994.
2. W. Banzhaf and W.B. Langdon, *Some considerations on the reason for bloat.* Genetic Programming and Evolvable Machines, vol. 3(1), 81–91, 2002.
3. W. Banzhaf, P. Nordin, R. Keller, and F. Francone, *Genetic Programming – An Introduction. On the Automatic Evolution of Computer Programs and its Application.* dpunkt/Morgan Kaufmann, Heidelberg/San Francisco, 1998.

4. W. Banzhaf, M. Brameier, M. Stautner, and K. Weinert. *Genetic Programming and its Application in Machining Technology.* In H.-P. Schwefel *et al.* (eds.) *Advances in Computational Intelligence – Theory and Practice*, Springer, Berlin, 2002.
5. T. Blickle and L. Thiele, *Genetic Programming and Redundancy.* In J. Hopf (ed.) *Genetic Algorithms within the Framework of Evolutionary Computation* (Workshop at KI-94), pp. 33–38, Max-Planck-Institut für Informatik, Technical Report No. MPI-I-94-241, 1994.
6. M. Brameier and W. Banzhaf, *A Comparison of Linear Genetic Programming and Neural Networks in Medical Data Mining.* IEEE Transactions on Evolutionary Computation, vol. 5(1), pp. 17–26, 2001.
7. M. Brameier and W. Banzhaf, *Explicit Control of Diversity and Effective Variation Distance in Linear Genetic Programming.* In J.A. Foster *et al.* (eds.) *Genetic Programming, Proceedings of the 5th European Conference (EuroGP 2002)*, pp. 37–49, Springer-Verlag, LNCS, Berlin, 2002.
8. M. Kimura, *The Neutral Theory of Molecular Evolution.* Cambridge University Press, 1983.
9. J.R. Koza, *Genetic Programming.* MIT Press, Cambridge, MA, 1992.
10. W.B. Langdon and R. Poli, *Fitness Causes Bloat.* In P.K. Chawdhry *et al.* (eds.) *Soft Computing in Engineering Design and Manufacturing*, pp. 13–22, Springer-Verlag, Berlin, 1997.
11. W.B. Langdon, T. Soule, R. Poli, and J.A. Foster, *The Evolution of Size and Shape.* In L. Spector *et al.* (eds.) *Advances in Genetic Programming III*, pp. 163–190, MIT Press, Cambridge, MA, 1999.
12. P. Nordin and W. Banzhaf, *Complexity Compression and Evolution.* In L.J. Eshelman (ed.) *Proceedings of the Sixth International Conference on Genetic Algorithms (ICGA'95)*, pp. 310–317, Morgan Kaufmann, San Francisco, CA, 1995.
13. T. Soule and J.A. Foster, *Code Size and Depth Flows in Genetic Programming.* In J.R. Koza *et al.* (eds.) *Genetic Programming 1997: Proceedings of the Second Annual Conference (GP'97)*, pp. 313–320, Morgan Kaufmann, San Francisco, CA, 1997.
14. T. Soule and R.B. Heckendorn, *An Analysis od the Causes of Code Growth in Genetic Programming.* Genetic Programming and Evolvable Machines, vol. 3(3), pp. 283–309, 2002
15. T. Soule and J.A. Foster, *Removal Bias: A new Cause of Code Growth in Tree-based Evolutionary Programming.* In *Proceedings of the International Conference on Evolutionary Computation (ICEC'98)*, pp. 781–786, IEEE Press, 1998.
16. T. Yu and J. Miller, *Neutrality and the Evolvability of Boolean Function Landscapes.* In J.F. Miller *et al.* (eds.) *Genetic Programming, Proceedings of the 4th European Conference (EuroGP 2001)*, pp. 204–217, Springer-Verlag, LNCS, Berlin, 2001.

Experimental Design Based Multi-parent Crossover Operator

Kit Yan Chan and Terence C. Fogarty

Faculty of Engineering, Science and Technology
South Bank University, 103 Borough Road
London, SE1 0AA
{chankf,fogarttc}@sbu.ac.uk

Abstract. Recently, the methodologies of multi-parent crossover have been developed by performing the crossover operation with multi-parent. Some studies have indicated the high performance of multi-parent crossover on some numerical optimization problems. Here a new crossover operator has been proposed by integrating multi-parent crossover with the approach of experimental design. It is based on experimental design method in exploring the solution space that compensates the random search as in traditional genetic algorithm. By replacing the inbuilt randomness of crossover operator with a more systematical method, the proposed method outperforms the classical GA strategy on several GA benchmark problems.

1 Introduction

In the genetic algorithm, the most commonly used crossover operator uses two parents to produce offspring. A few attempts to study the effect of using multi-parent crossover in genetic algorithms have been reported in the literature [4] [5] [11]. The rationale is to provide crossover with more parents to improve the performance. In evolution strategies, a crossover operator was first proposed to produce new offspring that may inherit genes from more than two parents. In that approach, the number of parents is not fixed.

Eiben [4] has proposed diagonal crossover for producing new offspring with allele inherited from multiple parents. Experimental result show that it can improve the performance of the genetic algorithm on some numerical optimization problems. Similar to multi-point crossover [10], it generalizes crossover point in N parents and composing N children by taking the resulting in N chromosome segments from the parent "along the diagonals".

In traditional quality engineering, experimental design techniques are extremely effective for robust product and process design to improve product quality while keeping the cost of product or manufacturing processes low [2]. In particular, sample points are under a systematic control mechanism to explore the search space. Our main idea is based on the observation that the diagonal crossover operator [4] can be considered as an experiment. If a sophisticated

C. Ryan et al. (Eds.): EuroGP 2003, LNCS 2610, pp. 297–306, 2003.

	O_1	O_2	O_3	O_4
S_1	Y_1	Y_4	Y_2	Y_3
S_2	Y_4	Y_3	Y_1	Y_2
S_3	Y_3	Y_2	Y_4	Y_1
S_4	Y_2	Y_1	Y_3	Y_4

S_i - the ith loom
O_i - the ith operator
Y_i - the ith type of treated yarn

Fig. 1. Arrangement of experiment with a L_4.

experimental design technique is applied to strengthen this operator, the resulting operator can be statistically sound and have a better performance. Here a new multi-parent crossover operator is proposed by integrating crossover with an experimental design method. By compensating for the random searching in the traditional genetic algorithm, it has the characteristic of experimental design method in exploring the solution space effectively.

We tested the proposed algorithm on a set of GA benchmark problems including four De Jong's functions (function one to four) [7], one multi-local optimum function (function five) [9] and a Fletcher-Powell function (function six) [1], and compared with the performance of classical genetic algorithm and Eiben's multi-parent genetic algorithm [4]. It showed that the proposed method has a better performance in terms of quality of solution and computational efficiency comparing with the other two approaches.

2 Experimental Design Methods (Preliminary)

For the combinatorial problem, because of limited time, we do not insist that every combination be represented with all possible operand values. It is required that for any given ordered pair of contents-factor levels there exists an ordered pair of index-factor levels and is tested in the context provided by the pair of index-factor levels. Thus, every combination of contents-factor levels has been tested in exactly one context. From the variety of experiment-design methods used in statistics, Latin square design and Orthogonal Latin square design is useful [8]. It might be applied to test the application of four different treatments of yarn (i.e.: Y_1, Y_2, Y_3 and Y_4) to four different operators (i.e.: O_1, O_2, O_3 and O_4) and different looms (i.e.: S_1, S_2, S_3 and S_4) [2]. In this scheme, each of the four treatment levels Y_1, Y_2, Y_3, Y_4 appears precisely once in each row/column of the Latin square L_4 as shown in Figure 1.

In this way, each treatment of yarn gets the advantages or disadvantages of being span in each of the four looms and the four operators respectively. 4^2=16 experiments is carried out in the Latin square design while testing all possible combinations require 4^3=64 experiments. The generalization from "4 looms, 4 operators, and 4 treatments of yarn" to "n looms, n operators, and n treatment of yarn" is immediate. Exhaustive testing in this situation would require n^3 tests, whereas Latin-squares testing requires only n^2 tests.

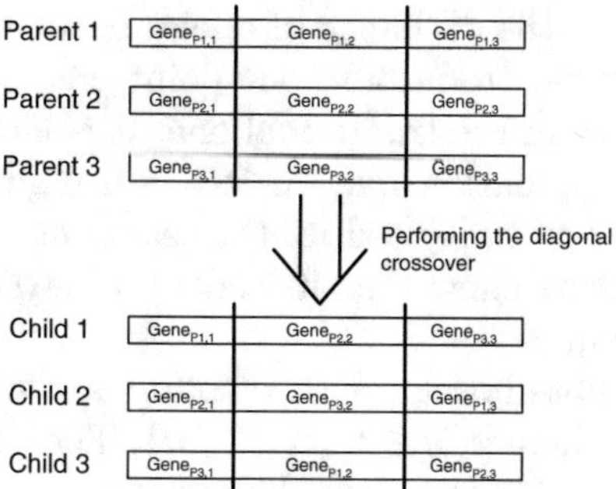

Fig. 2. Multi-parent diagonal crossover.

3 Multi-parent Diagonal Crossover

In genetic algorithm, the most commonly used crossover operator involves two parents to produce offspring. The effect of using multi-parent crossover in genetic algorithm have been reported in the literatures [5]. The rationale is to bias the crossover with more parents to improve the performance. Multi-parent diagonal crossover (MPDC) has been introduced in [4]. The results show that it outperforms the classical two-parents crossover on some parametrical problems. It creates r offspring from r parents by selecting (r-1) crossover points in the parents and composing the offspring by taking the resulting in r chromosome segments from the parents "along the diagonal". The resulting operator has the number of parents, and therefore is tunable on the extent of sexuality. This tunability is a new feature as compared to global crossover and gene pool crossover, where the multi-parent option can only be switched on or off, but it is not scalable.

Similar to multi-point crossover, it uses $n \geq 1$ crossover points and creates $n+1$ children by taking the resulting in $n+1$ chromosome segments from the parents "along the diagonals". For instance, Figure 2 illustrates the idea of MPDC with three parents. Child 1 is composed by taking $\text{Gene}_{P1,1}$ from Parent 1, $\text{Gene}_{P2,2}$ from Parent 2, and $\text{Gene}_{P3,3}$ from Parent 3. Child 2 has $\text{Gene}_{P2,1}$ from Parent 2, $\text{Gene}_{P3,2}$ from Parent 3 and $\text{Gene}_{P1,3}$ from Parent 1.

The study has shown that using more than two parents in the crossover mechanism can increase GA performance in many parametrical problems [4]. The use of more parents in MPDC leads to an improvement of GA performance; the search becomes more explorative without hindering exploitation. From the experimental design point of view, the allocation of each gene is based on the Latin square design [8]. It has the advantages and disadvantages of being sampled in each child. Hence, it has more information exchanging than the one using the two parents crossover. The combination of parts are based on the Latin square:

$$\begin{matrix} 1 & 2 & 3 \\ 2 & 3 & 1 \\ 3 & 1 & 2 \end{matrix}$$

The operator increases the exchange of alleles between members of the population, w.r.t., for example, traditional one-point crossover. The resulting offspring are more diverse than the traditional one. It is more energetic in mixing, which means that the population may in fact converge more rapidly towards linkage equilibrium. Thus it can speed up the searching process of genetic algorithm. Experimental results show that it lead to a better performance in some parametrical problems [4].

A Latin square is denoted as L_n with n columns/rows. Its element is represented as $a(x, y) \in L_n$, where $x, y \in \{1, 2, \ldots\ldots, n\}$. The detailed implementation of MPDC[4] is shown in Algorithm 1 in the appendix.

4 Multi-parent Crossover with Orthogonal Latin Square Design

In multi-parent diagonal crossover, Latin square design is a scheme with a total of three variables (i.e. the first, second and third variable are represented by the row (parent), column (gene) and element (exchanging the information of the gene) respectively). To investigate the impact of the fourth variable, one could perform two separate experiments, each described by a Latin square as above: however, this scheme would yield no information about any effect of the simultaneous presence of the two substances: the substance represented by the first Latin square and the substance represented by the second Latin square. An economical design for studying the combined effects would consist of a orthogonal Latin square [8]:

$$\begin{matrix} 1\,2\,3 & 1\,2\,3 \\ 2\,3\,1 & 3\,1\,2 \\ 3\,1\,2 & 2\,3\,1 \end{matrix}$$

where each of the 9 combinations of the elements inside the first and second Latin square occurs precisely once. It can be defined to be orthogonal Latin square, if they are combined entry by entry and each pair of symbols occurs precisely once in the combined square [3].

Based on this observation, we incorporate the orthogonal Latin square design [8] into MPDC by considering the fourth variable (we define it as parameter). The resulting operator is called Orthogonal Latin Multi-Parent Crossover (OMPC). To explain the idea, we consider the example of a parametric optimization problem with two parameters in which we use the orthogonal Latin square of order 3 to sample the genes from three parents for crossover. Since each parent contains the information of the two parameters (A, B), we divide each parent into two parameter genes, which contain the information of each individual parameter (A, B), and then divide each parameter gene into three parts as shown in P_1, P_2 and P_3 as in Figure 3.

In P_1, the first, second and third part of the parameter gene A are named as $A_{P1,1}$, $A_{P1,2}$ and $A_{P1,3}$. We do the same in the rest of the parameter genes. Then, based on the combination of orthogonal Latin square of order 3, three parents are reproduced into three offspring as shown in Figure 3.

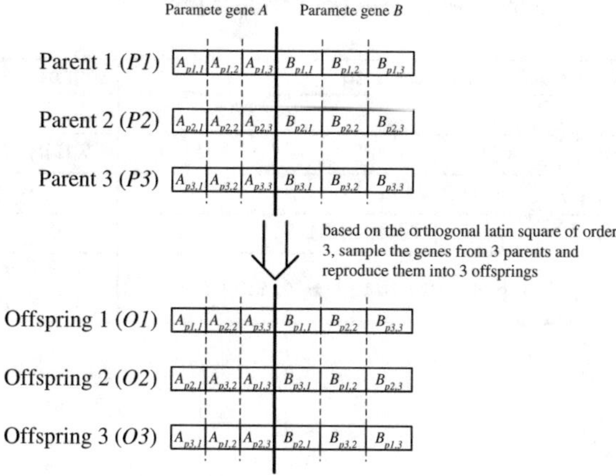

Fig. 3. Orthogonal Latin Multi-Parent crossover.

According to the orthogonality of the orthogonal Latin square, each parameter gene A_{ij} and each parameter gene B_{ij} are superimposed on each other in the reproduced offspring, where $1 \leq i \leq 3$ and $1 \leq j \leq 3$. The combination of parameter genes are defined to be completely orthogonal and the selected combinations are good representatives for all the possible combinations of the parameter genes. In particular, the combinations are under a systematic control mechanism to explore the search space. It is effective for evaluating the experiment that involves a large number of treatment combinations. It is suitable for a large number of decision variables with a small number of searching steps that can be taken into account the combinatorial problem.

In general, an orthogonal Latin square is denoted as L_n^m with n columns/rows and m Latin squares. Its element is represented as $a(x, y, z) \in L_n^m$, where $x, y \in \{1, 2, \ldots\ldots, n\}$ and $z \in \{1, 2, \ldots\ldots, m\}$. The detailed algorithm for a m-parametric problem is given in Algorithm 2 in the appendix.

5 Algorithm Comparison

To examine the applicability of the proposed crossover operator, we employed a set of six GA benchmark problems, including four De Jong's functions (F_1-F_4) [7], one multi-local optimum function (F_5) [9] and a Fletcher-Powell function (F_6) [1]. We have chosen these functions because they represent the common difficulties in optimization problems in an isolated manner. These benchmark functions, including unimodal and multi-modal as well as continuous and discontinuous functions, are executed in the experimental studies described below. By running the comparison on these functions, we can make judgements about the strengths and weaknesses of particular algorithms. Also, these functions are quite popular in genetic algorithms literature, so it is possible to make direct comparison. The details of F_1 to F_5 can be found in Table 1. Function six (F_6) is the Fletcher-Powell function, which is retrieved from [1].

Table 1. GA benchmark problems.

Problem	GA benchmark problem	Testing domain
F_1	$\min\left(\sum_{i=1}^{30} x_i^2\right)$	$-5.12 \leq x_i \leq 5.12$
F_2	$\min \sum_{i=2}^{30} \left(100\left(x_i - x_{i-1}^2\right) + \left(x_i - 1\right)^2\right)$	$-2.048 \leq x_i \leq 2.048$
F_3	$\min\left(\sum_{i=1}^{30} \text{integer}\left(x_i\right)\right)$	$-5.12 \leq x_i \leq 5.12$
F_4	$\min\left(\sum_{i=1}^{30} i x_i^4 + Gauss\left(0, 1\right)\right)$	$-1.28 \leq x_i \leq 1.28$
F_5	$\max(21.5 + x_1 \sin\left(4\pi x_1\right) + x_2 \sin\left(20\pi x_2\right))$	$-3.0 \leq x_1 \leq 12.1$, $4.1 \leq x_2 \leq 5.8$

Function F_6:

$$F_6\left(\vec{x}\right) = \min \sum_{i=1}^{30} \left(A_i + B_i\right)^2 ,$$

$$A_i = \sum_{j=1}^{30} \left(a_{ij} \sin \alpha_j + b_{ij} \cos \alpha_j\right) ,$$

$$B_i = \sum_{j=1}^{30} \left(a_{ij} \sin x_j + b_{ij} \cos x_j\right) ,$$

$$\text{where } -\pi \leq x_i \leq \pi .$$

The $a_{ij}, b_{ij} \in$ {-100, ...,100} are random integers, and $\alpha_j \in [-\pi, \pi]$ is the randomly chosen global optimum position. In Eiben's paper [4], experimental result shows that there is no significant difference between the multi-parent diagonal crossover and two-parent crossover.

The test functions were tested using the following algorithms:

1. Pure genetic algorithm (PGA): The basic process of PGA is same as the one of the classical genetic algorithm [6]. Initially, a population is coded as a set of chromosomes in binary string. Reproduction is performed by using the traditional bit-by-bit mutation and two-parent crossover. After the initial population is formed, reproduction begins and a new generation evolves based on the relative fitness of every chromosome. Then, the probability of its reproduction and the survivors for the next generation can be determined. The evolutionary process of PGA stops until it approaches the pre-defined number of generations.
2. Multi-parent genetic algorithm (MPGA): The basic process of MPGA is similar to the PGA except crossover utilizes the multi-parent diagonal crossover (MPDC) [4] as illustrated in Algorithm 1 in the appendix.
3. Orthogonal Latin genetic algorithm (OLGA): The basic process of OLGA is similar to the classical genetic algorithm except crossover utilizes the orthogonal Latin multi-parent crossover as illustrated in Algorithm 2 in the appendix.

Simulation conditions are described as follows:

1. Simulation has been done 20 times on each function.
2. Four-parent crossover has been performed in OLGA and MPGA.
3. All parameters x_i are coded binary into chromosomes.
4. Population size is 50.
5. Probability of crossover and the initial probability of mutation are set to be P_c=0.50 and P_m=0.02 respectively.

In each generation, the algorithms only evaluate the fitness of individuals in population and no function evaluation is carried out in the crossover operator. Thus, the computational cost of all algorithms are the same. In Figure 4 to Figure 9, the functions and the best fitness values (elite in the generation) found until that generation is plotted against the number of generations. The figures show the average (over 20 runs) of the best individuals in each generation seen so far in each run. For F_1 to F_4, the maximum number of generations is set to be 500 and for F_5, it is set to be 2000. For F_6, it is set to be 500. In the figures, the results of pure genetic algorithm, multi-parent genetic algorithm and orthogonal Latin genetic algorithm are labelled as PGA, MPGA and OLGA respectively. The elite strategy is presented from Figure 4 to figure 9.

We can see from figures 4 to 9 that the proposed OLGA strategy could reach relatively better solution quality and smaller computational effort than PGA and MPGA. The proposed OLGA converged to the global optimum faster than PGA and MPGA when applied to function F_1, F_2, and F_3 (Figure 4, 5 and 6). With function F_4 (Figure 7), while the proposed OLGA found a solution with a cost near 0.3 within 200 generations, MPGA and PGA converged to a solution around 0.5 and 0.6 after 200 generations. In function F_5 (Figure 8), OLGA is able to search the better solution than PGA and MPGA in the pre-defined number of generations. For solving F_6, the result of [4] shows that there is no significant difference between MPGA and PGA. Here we use the proposed OLGA to simulate the function F_6 and can see what is the difference. In function F_6 (Figure 9), the performance of OLGA is better than both MPGA and PGA, even the result of [4] shows that there is no significant difference between the PGA and MPGA. We can conclude that OLGA is more efficiency and more promising than MPGA and PGA.

6 Conclusion

In this paper, a new multi-parent crossover operator, that aids to searching the optimal solution and accelerating the searching process, is proposed here based on the approach of orthogonal Latin square design. The results show that the proposed method is more efficient than the traditional methods. This paper mainly focus on whether applying the orthogonal Latin square design method in multi-parent crossover results in better performance. However, the number of parents involved in the crossover mechanism has many limitations such as the population size. The question is whether increasing the number of parents always improves the performance of the genetic algorithm. In some cases, [4] shows that increasing the number of parents improves the performance, but the degree of improvement becomes smaller and smaller.

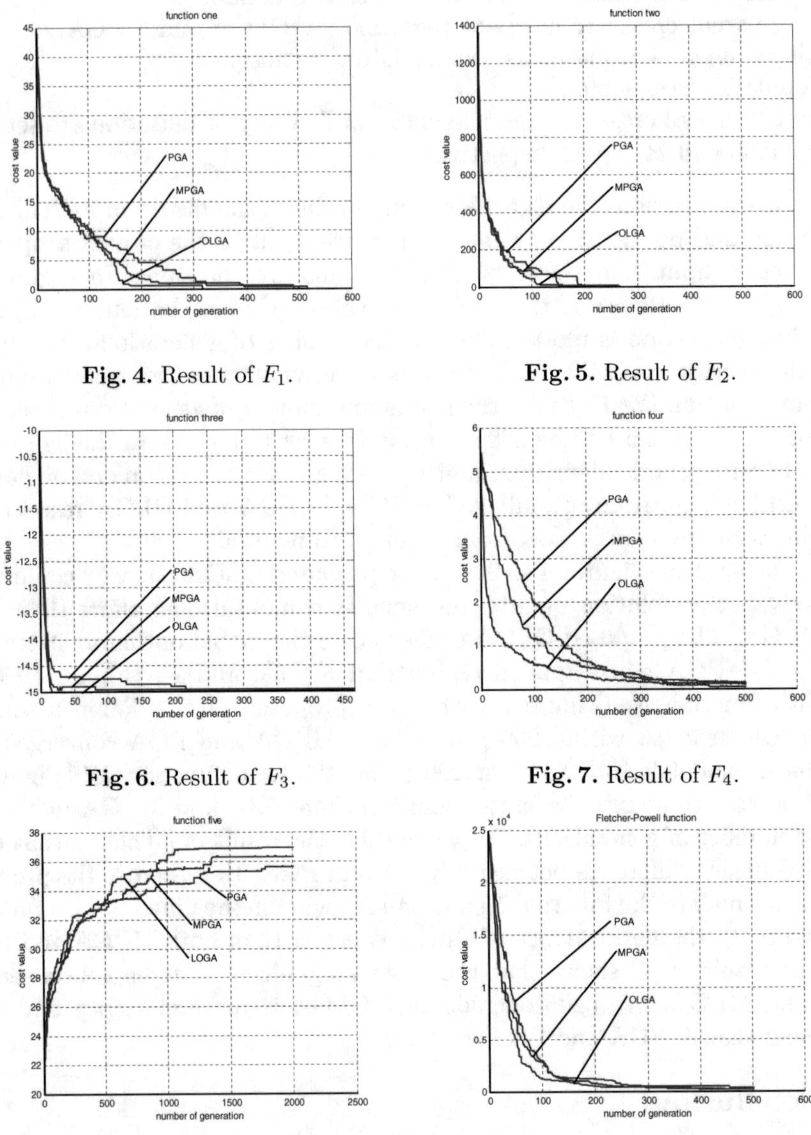

Fig. 4. Result of F_1.

Fig. 5. Result of F_2.

Fig. 6. Result of F_3.

Fig. 7. Result of F_4.

Fig. 8. Result of F_5.

Fig. 9. Result of F_6.

A further investigation could aim at deciding the optimal size of the orthogonal Latin square in the case of obtaining the optimal values for each test-function. We will investigate the optimal number of parents and the optimal number of genomes split. Looking at the performance of the proposed operator, we will compare different numerical versions of mutation and crossover operators. To get a better understanding of this study, we will study the behavior of our proposed operator. This can be obtained by monitoring the diversity of the population along the evolution.

Acknowledgement

Most of all, the authors are grateful to express our sincere thanks to James Werner and Emin Aydin for many useful discussions and valuable suggestions.

References

1. T. Back, *Evolutionary algorithms in theory and practice.* Oxford University Press, New York, 1996.
2. W.G. Cochran, G.M. Cox, *Experimental designs*, John Wiley and Sons, 1957.
3. J. Denes, A.D. Keedwell, *Latin squares and their application*, Academic Press, 1974.
4. A.E. Eiben, H.M. Kemenade, Diagonal crossover in genetic algorithms for numerical optimization, *Journal of Control and Cybernetics*, pp. 447-465, vol. 26, no. 3, 1997.
5. A.E. Eiben, P.E. Raue, Zs. Ruttkay, Genetic algorithms with multi-parent recombination, *Proceedings of the third Conference on Parallel Problem Solving from Nature*, Springer-Verlay, pp. 78-87, 1994.
6. D. Goldberg, *Genetic algorithms in search, optimization and machine learning*, Addison-Wesley, 1989.
7. K.A. De Jong, *An analysis of the behavior of a class of genetic adaptive systems*, Ph.D. Thesis, University of Michigan, Ann Arbor, MI., 1975.
8. C.F. Laywine, G. L. Mullen, *Discrete mathematics using Latin squares*, A Wiley Interscience Publication, 1998.
9. Z. Michalewicz, *Genetic algorithms+Data structures=Evolution programs*, Springer-Verlag, 1992.
10. M.W. Spears, K. DeJong, An analysis of multi-point crossover, *Foundations of Genetic Algorithms*, pp. 301-315, 1991.
11. S. Tsutsui, A. Ghosh, A study on the effect of multi-parent recombination in real coded genetic algorithms, *Proceedings of the Second International Conference on Knowledge-Based Intelligent Electronic Systems*, vol. 3, pp. 155-160, 1998.

Appendix

Algorithm 1: Multi-parent Diagonal Crossover (MPDC)
Input n parent strings P_i for all $1 \leq i \leq n$.
Output n offspring strings $\overline{O}_i$ for all $1 \leq i \leq n$.
Begin
Step 1: Divide each parent string into n parts as
$P_i = [P_i(1), P_i(2), \ldots, P_i(m)]$ for all $1 \leq i \leq n$.
Step 2: Based on the ith combination in the Latin square
$(a(1,i), a(2,i), \ldots, a(n,i))$, produce the binary string
$O_i(j) = \left[P_{a(1,i),1}(j), P_{a(2,i),2}(j), \ldots, P_{a(n,i),n}(j)\right]$, for all $1 \leq i \leq n$.
Step 3: Each O_i undergoes mutation with a small probability and produce the resulting offspring $\overline{O}_i$ for $1 \leq i \leq n$.
End

Algorithm 2: Orthogonal Latin Multi-parent Crossover (OMPC)

Input n parent strings P_i for all $1 \leq i \leq n$.

Output n offspring strings $\overline{O}_i$ for all $1 \leq i \leq n$.

Begin

Step 1: Divide each parent string into m parameter genes as $P_i = [P_i(1), P_i(2), ..., P_i(m)]$ for all $1 \leq i \leq n$.

Step 2: Divide each parameter gene into n parts as $P_i(j) = [P_{i,1}(j), P_{i,2}(j), ..., P_{i,n}(j)]$ for all $1 \leq i \leq n$. and $1 \leq j \leq m$.

Step 3: Based on the ith combination in the kth Latin square $(a(1,i,k), a(2,i,k), ..., a(n,i,k))$, produce the binary string $O_i(j) = \left[P_{a(1,i,k),1}(j), P_{a(2,i,k),2}(j), ..., P_{a(n,i,k),n}(j)\right]$, for all $1 \leq i \leq n$ and $1 \leq j, k \leq m$.

Step 4: Each O_i undergoes mutation with a small probability and produce the resulting offspring $\overline{O}_i$ for $1 \leq i \leq n$.

End

An Enhanced Framework for Microprocessor Test-Program Generation

F. Corno and G. Squillero

Politecnico di Torino
Dipartimento di Automatica e Informatica
Corso Duca degli Abruzzi 24 I-10129, Torino, Italy
http://www.cad.polito.it/

Abstract. Test programs are fragment of code, but, unlike ordinary application programs, they are not intended to *solve* a problem, nor to *calculate* a function. Instead, they are supposed to give information about the machine that actually executes them. Today, the need for effective test programs is increasing, and, due to the inexorable increase in the number of transistor that can be integrated onto a single silicon die, devising effective test programs is getting more problematical. This paper presents μGP, an efficient and versatile approach to test-program generation based on an evolutionary algorithm. The proposed methodology is highly versatile and improves previous approaches, allowing the test-program generator generating complex assembly programs that include subroutines calls.

1 Introduction

Test programs are fragments of code, but, unlike ordinary application programs, they are not intended to *solve* a problem, nor to *calculate* a function. Instead, they are supposed to give information about the machine that actually executes them. For instance, during the design phase of a new microprocessor, engineers may exploit test programs to uncover errors and blunders. Such a process is sometimes called *hardware debugging*. Test programs are required to check all possible functionalities of the design and excite interactions between the different blocks. Conversely, after production, test programs may be exploited to check the correct functionality of the devices. Such test programs detect faulty microprocessors or microcontrollers by exposing internal defects to accessible outputs trough suitable sequences of operations.

Devising effective test programs is a challenging task even for relatively-simple microprocessors, and it is getting more demanding at an always-increasing pace. Moore's law, first postulated in 1965, forecasted a doubling of transistor density every 18-24 months. Despite numerous predictions that the end is in sight, the law has held true for the last 35 years. This has resulted in an increase in the number of transistor on a chip from 2,300 on Intel 4004 to 5.5 million on the Pentium® Pro® processor in 1995 to 42 million on the Pentium® 4 processor in 2000, and computer architects continue to find ways to use all these transistors to design even more complex and elaborated devices.

C. Ryan et al. (Eds.): EuroGP 2003, LNCS 2610, pp. 307–316, 2003.

Roughly speaking, it may be maintained that the number of bugs in a new design is linearly proportional to the number of lines in its structural Register-Transfer Level (RTL) description [1]; on the other hand, the number of modeled physical defects (faults) is linearly proportional to the number of transistors [2].

As a general consideration, it may be stated that the behavior of modern microprocessor is not determined by the single instruction being executed, but it is determined by a *set of instructions* and *all their operands*. For instance, to represent the state of a pipeline it is necessary to consider the whole sequence of instructions inside it and the dependencies between their operands.

The need for effective test programs is increasing, and, concurrently, devising effective test programs is getting more problematical. Pseudo-random test-program generators cannot be used since only syntactically correct and semantically meaningful programs may be effectively exploited and may be able to successfully check corner cases. However, automatic and semi-automatic approaches usually require big efforts from expert engineers to be exploited and it is common for designers to rely on test programs meticulously written by hand.

This paper presents a new framework based on an evolutionary algorithm for generating a test programs for a microprocessor, where the test case is an assembly program able to maximize a predefined verification metric.

2 Related Work

Creating, in an automated way, computer programs able to solve problems is one of the more desired goals of computer science. Pioneering ideas of automatically-evolved programs date back to [3], but, more recently, the exploitation of the methodology called *Genetic Programming* (GP) managed achieving interesting success. Koza defines GP as "a domain-independent problem-solving approach in which computer programs are evolved to solve, or approximately solve, problems. Genetic programming is based on the Darwinian principle of reproduction and survival of the fittest and analogs of naturally occurring genetic operations such as *crossover* (*sexual recombination*) and *mutation*" [4].

However, despite the general definition, common GP-based approaches are unable to evolve programs with the possibilities and complexity of hand-written ones. Programs are usually represented as trees [5], i.e., as directed acyclic graph where there is only one path between any two nodes. Tree representations have been traditionally implemented in the *LISP* language as *S-expressions*. Several different representations have also been proposed in the past: in [6] the whole population was stored as a single directed acyclic graph, rather than as a forest of trees, leading to considerable savings of memory (structurally identical sub-trees are not duplicated) and computation (the value computed by each sub-tree for each fitness case can be cached). In [7] a significant speed-up was achieved extending the representation from trees to generic graphs and parallelizing the evolution process. [8] suggested to represent each individual as a linear graph, for matching closely had-written program.

For the purpose of this work, however, it is interesting to examine techniques based on the idea of *compiling* GP programs either into some lower level, more efficient, virtual-machine code or even into machine code. [9] suggested to evolve programs in machine-code form for completely removing the inefficiency in interpreting trees. More recently, a genome compiler has been proposed in [10], which transforms standard GP trees into machine code before evaluation. The possibilities offered by the Java virtual machine are also currently being explored [11], [12].

[13] presented *μGP*, an evolutionary approach devised specifically for generating assembly-level test programs. Program generation exploits a single directed acyclic graph for representing the flow of a program, and an instruction library for describing the assembly syntax. Generated assembly programs are fragments of code that may contain all arithmetic and logic operations, unconditional forward jumps and conditional forward branches. The loose coupling between the instruction library and the generator enables exploiting the approach with different instruction sets, formalisms and conventions. μGP also relies on an external function able to evaluate the fitness of individuals, i.e., to evaluate how close programs in the population are to the final goal.

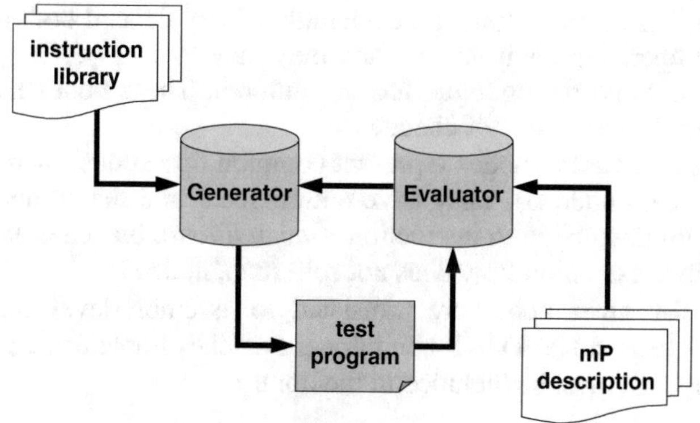

Fig. 1. *μGP System Architecture*

Afterward, the original idea has been enhanced with an auto-adaptation mechanism, tuned and improved several times. The methodology has been exploited to tackle different problems. μGP has been exploited against the Intel microcontroller i8051 for both verification [14] and test [15]. On more complex microprocessors, in [16] the μGP is shown attaining promising results on the DLX/pII (a 5-stage pipelined implementation of the DLX microprocessor [17]).

Despite several advantages, the main drawback of μGP is that the adopted representation prevents the exploitation of subroutines and this may strongly reduce the efficacy of the generated programs.

This paper proposes a further evolution to the μGP framework. The underlying idea of exploiting three loosely interconnected blocks is not modified, while the evolutionary core has been completely rewritten. A new internal representation has been devised, improving the syntactic power and allowing full support to subroutine calls. A prototype of the proposed approach has been evaluated on a complex SPARC microprocessor and has been shown able to tackle the complexity of the design.

3 Proposed Approach

The *test-program generator* cultivates a population of test programs, exploiting the description of the syntax of the microprocessor assembly language stored in an external *instruction library*. Induced test programs are evaluated by an external *test-program evaluator* that provides feedback to the *test-program generator*.

Individuals are represented as special directed acyclic graph (DAG). Such a DAG can be considered as a collection of disconnected sub-DAGs, each one belonging to a defined *frame*.

3.1 Sub-DAG

A single sub-DAG (Figure 2, left) corresponds to a distinct *fragment* in the test program and it is built with four kinds of nodes:

- **Prologue** and **epilogue** nodes are always present and represent required operations, such as initializations of function declaration. They depend both on the processor and on the operating environment, and they may be empty. The prologue has no parent node, while the epilogue has no children. These nodes may never be removed from the program, nor changed.
- **Sequential-instruction** nodes represent common operations, such as arithmetic or logic ones (e.g., node **B**). They have out-degree 1 and the number of parameters changes from instruction to instruction. *Unconditional* branches are considered sequential, since execution flow does not split (e.g., node **D**).
- **Conditional-branch** nodes are translated to assembly-level conditional-branch instructions (e.g., node **A**). All conditional branches implemented in the target assembly language must be included in the library.

3.2 Frames

Each sub-DAG describes a fragment of code and, ideally, belongs to a *frame*. Frames define the *type* of fragment and its syntactical property. The current implementation of µGP supports two types of frames: *ample* and *scant*. A scant frame may contain only one DAG (frame *S2* in Figure 2, left), while an ample one is allowed to contain several DAGs (frame *A1* in Figure 2, left).

When a new individual is created, a single DAG is generated inside a scant frame called *MAIN*.

Different sub-DAGs are united by special edges that connect an internal node to the prologue of a different graph. Frames have been implemented to describe subroutines, interrupt service routines and other fragment of code distinct from the main body. The prologue may contain standard operations, such as setting the frame pointer, while the epilogue usually contains the code for returning to the caller. Indeed, there is no explicit edge from the epilogue to the caller node since this link is not explicit in the assembly program.

An ample frame is well suited to describe subroutines, or other fragment of codes that can appear several times in a program. Scant sections are designed to describe more critical fragments. For instance, the MAIN section is defined as scant since its prologue usually contains initialization code that need to be executed only once.

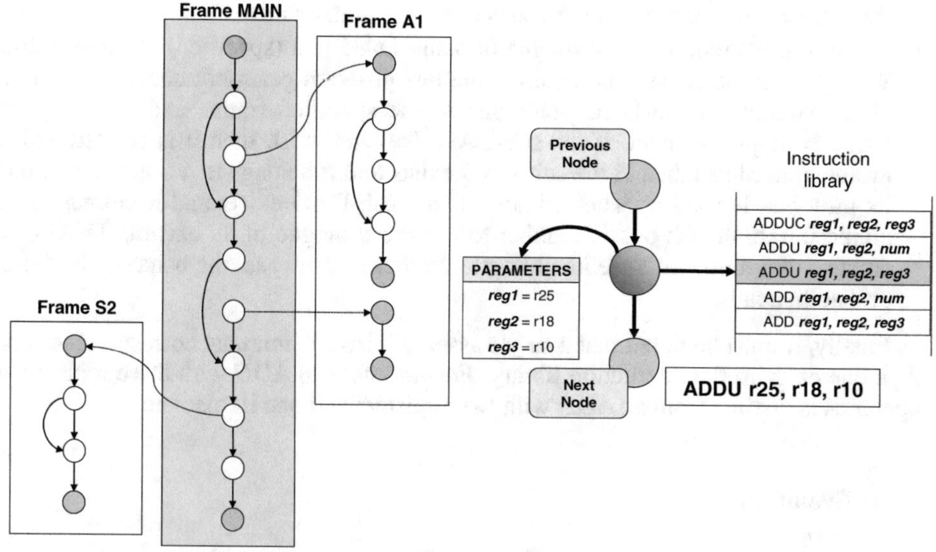

Fig. 2. Individual Representation (left), a Sequential Instruction (right)

3.3 Instruction Library and Nodes

The instruction library for describes the assembly syntax, listing each possible instructions with the syntactically correct operands. More exactly, instruction library contains a collection of macros, but, with the exception of prologue and epilogue, all these macros correspond to individual assembly instructions.

The instruction library also contains the specification of all frames and the list of instructions possible in each frame.

Each node is identified by a unique name; the test-program generator inserts labels corresponding to node names when it maps the individual to an assembly program, if the node is the target of one or more branches. The format of the label is fully customizable to fit different assembly language formalisms. Each node also contains a pointer inside the instruction library and, when needed, its parameters. Five types of parameters are currently supported:

- **Integer constant** represents a numeric value and may be used as immediate value, offset or any other numeric data supported by the assembly language. The instruction library specifies the valid range.
- **String constant** represents a string inside a predefined set. They are usually used for specifying a register together with a specific addressing mode (e.g., "@R1"). For instance, Figure 2 (right) shows a sequential node that will be translated into an "ADDU r25, r18, r10", i.e., store in *r25* the unsigned sum of *r18* and *r10*.
- **Inner Forward Labels** are the only kind of labels supported by [13] and represent a generic subsequent node inside the same sub-DAG.
- **Inner Generic Labels** represent a generic node inside the current sub-DAG. Such labels may produce endless loops and non-terminating programs. Thus, although

already supported by the test-program generator, they have not been included in the instruction library and their use is currently under study.

- **Outer Labels** represent a prologue of a sub-DAG in a (specified) different frame. Whenever an outer label is required, the test-program generator checks if the individual contains a sub-DAG belonging to the specified frame, and whenever the frame is ample or scant. If the sub-DAG does not exist, then it is created and its prologue used as label. If the sub-DAG exists and it belongs to a scant frame, then its prologue is used as label. Finally, if the sub-DAG exists and it belongs to an ample frame, then it possible either to use the prologue of an existing DAG or to create a new DAG and use its prologue. In these latter case, the behavior is chosen probabilistically.

Finally, it must be noted that a single assembly instruction may correspond to more than one entry in the instruction library. For instance, an *ADD* with three registers as operands is distinct from an *ADD* with two registers and one immediate.

3.4 Evolution

Test programs are induced by modifying a DAG topology and by mutating parameters inside a DAG node. No recombination has been implemented yet. All modifications are embedded in an evolutionary algorithm implementing a $(\mu+\lambda)$ strategy.

In more details, a population of μ individuals is cultivated, each individual representing a test program. In each step, an offspring of λ new individuals are generated. Parents are selected using tournament selection with tournament size τ (i.e., τ individuals are randomly selected and the best one is picked). Each new individual is generated by applying one or more genetic operators. The probability to apply two consecutive operators to the same individual is denoted with p_c, the cumulative probability of applying at least n consecutive operators is equal to p_c^n.

After creating new λ individuals, the best μ programs in the population of $(\mu+\lambda)$ are selected for surviving.

The initial population is generated creating μ empty programs (only prologue and epilogue) and then applying i_m consecutive random mutations to each.

The evolution process iterates until the population reaches a *steady state* condition, i.e., no improvements are recorded for S_g generations.

Three mutation and one crossover operators are implemented and activated with probability p_{add}, p_{del}, p_{mod} and p_{xover} respectively.

- **Add node:** a new node is inserted into the DAG in a random position. The new node can be either a sequential instruction or a conditional branch. In both cases, the instruction referred by the node is randomly chosen. If the inserted node is a branch, either unconditional or conditional, one of the subsequent nodes is randomly chosen as the destination. When an unconditional branch is inserted, some nodes in the DAG may become unreachable.
- **Remove node:** an existing internal node (except prologue or epilogue) is removed from the DAG. If the removed node was the target of one or more branch, parents' edges are updated.
- **Modify node:** all parameters of an existing internal node are randomly changed.

3.5 Auto Adaptation

The proposed approach is able to internally tune both the number of consecutive random mutations and the activation probabilities of all operators. Modifying these parameters, the algorithm is able to shape the search process, significantly improving its performance.

The number of consecutive random mutations is controlled by parameter p_c, which, intuitively, molds the mutation strength in the optimization process. Generally, in the beginning it is better to adopt a high value, allowing offspring to strongly differ from parents. On the other hand, toward the end of the search process, it is preferable to reduce diversity around the local optimum, allowing small mutations only. Initially, the maximum value is adopted ($p_c = 0.9$). Then, the μGP monitors improvements: let I_H be the number of newly created individuals attaining a fitness value higher than their parents over the last H generations. At the end of each generation, the new p_c value is calculated as $p_c^{new} = \alpha \cdot p_c + (1-\alpha) \cdot \frac{I_H}{H \cdot \lambda}$. Then p_c is saturated to 0.9. The coefficient α introduces inertia to unexpected abrupt changes.

Regarding activation probabilities, initially they are set to the same value $p_{add} = p_{del} = p_{mod} = p_{xover} = 0.25$. During evolution, probability values are updated similarly to mutation strength: let O_1^{OP} be the number of successful invocation of genetic operator *OP* in the last generation, i.e., the number of invocations of *OP* where the resulting individual attained a fitness value higher than its parents; and let O_1 be the total number of operators invoked in the last generation. At the end of each generation, the new values are calculated as $p_{OP}^{new} = \alpha \cdot p_{OP} + (1-\alpha) \cdot \frac{O_1^{OP}}{O_1}$. Since it is possible that $p_c > 0$, O_1 may be significantly larger than λ. Activation probabilities are forced to avoid values below .01 and over 0.9, then normalized to $p_{add} + p_{del} + p_{mod} + p_{xover} = 1$. If $O_1 = 0$, then all activation probabilities are pushed towards initial values.

4 Experimental Evaluation

A prototypical implementation of the test-program generator has been implemented and tested against a *LEON P1754* microprocessor. The microprocessor design is in RT-level VHDL, i.e., as a set of interconnected blocks in the hardware description language called VHDL. The prototype was exploited to maximize the *statement coverage* metric. To avoid confusion, in the following the term "instruction" denotes an *instruction* in an assembly program, and the term "statement" refers to a *statement* in a hardware description. The term "execute" is commonly used in both domains: instructions in a program are executed when the processor fetches them and operates accordingly; statements in a VHDL description are executed when the simulator evaluates them to infer design behavior. The verification metric exploited in this paper measures the percentage of executed (evaluated) RT-level statements when the execution (run) of a given test program is simulated.

Statement coverage can be considered as a required starting point for any design verification process. Such analysis ensures that no part of the design missed functional test during simulation, as well as reducing simulation effort from "over-verification" or redundant testing. Moreover, use of coverage analysis provides an easy and objective way of measuring simulation effectiveness to ensure that all bugs would be exposed with the minimum amount of effort. Indeed, most CAD vendors have recently added code-coverage features to their simulators.

LEON P1754 is the commercial name of a synthesizable VHDL model of the 32-bit SPARC-V8 microprocessor [18]. It was initially developed by the European Space Agency (ESA). The LEON P1754 implements 90 instructions: 20 arithmetic or logic ones, 6 branch, 18 special, 25 load/store and 21 floating point. Only two addressing modes are supported: addresses can be specified either as "register plus register" or "register plus immediate". The adopted LEON contains a 5-stage pipeline, an internal floating-point unit, and two separate, direct-mapped caches of 2KBytes each for instructions and data. The description of the microprocessor is about 3K statement long.

The instruction library for the LEON P1754 consists in 230 entries: prologue, epilogue, 118 sequential operations and 110 conditional branches. Listing instructions and their syntax was a trivial task.

Table 1. LEON Statement Coverage summary

Program	INST	CLK	SC[%]
TB	4,964	102,888	73.56
fib100	28	30,072	67.86
Random	571	1,264	65.90
μGP	54	575	72.68

Table 1 reports 4 programs in terms of: number of instructions (INST), clock cycles required for execution (CLK), and attained RT-level statement coverage (SC). Considered programs include a functional test bench provided by LEON designers (*TB*), a routine for calculating the first 100 numbers in the Fibonacci series (*fib100*), and a test program induced with the proposed approach (*μGP*). For devising the test program, the μGP requires the simulation of about 5,000 programs, corresponding to about two days on a Sun Enterprise 250 with an UltraSPARC-II CPU at 400MHz, and 2GB of RAM. For the sake of comparison, 5,000 random programs were generated and evaluated; the result attained by the best one is reported in row (*random*). Since computation effort devoted to evolutionary mechanisms is negligible compared to simulation, also the random test required two days on the same Sun Enterprise 250.

The striking fact is that the induced test program is able to attain a statement coverage comparable to the one achieved by the test bench using 10% of the instructions and 0.5% of the execution time.

The induced program shows a lower efficacy than *TB*. This can be easily explained, since interrupts can not be induced by the actual version of the test-program generator. Indeed, induced test-program efficacy on interrupt-control modules is equal to *fib100* and *random*. On the other hand, the induced test program attains the best results testing the cache interface, the integer unit, and the external memory controller, showing its capability to handle complex interactions inside pipeline stages.

5 Conclusions

This paper presented μGP, an efficient and versatile approach to test-program generation based on an evolutionary algorithm. The proposed methodology is able to tackle complex designs and different assembly languages. The methodology exploits a loose interconnection between a *test-program generator*, an *instruction library* and a *test-program evaluator*, and can be used to induce test programs with different goals, e.g., maximizing diverse verification metric.

The proposed methodology is highly versatile and improves previous approaches, allowing the test-program generator the capability to generate complex assembly programs that include subroutines calls.

The algorithm is able to tune internal parameters to optimize search process. New auto-adaptive mechanisms dramatically enhance both performances and quality of the results.

A prototype of the proposed approach has been developed in ANSI C language, and exploited to generate test programs against a LEON P1754 (a 5-stage pipelined, synthesizable, 32-bit SPARC-V8 processor). While experimental results are still preliminary, it may be maintained that exploiting the approach engineers could get high-quality test programs with acceptable computation effort.

Current work is targeted to apply the proposed approach to analyze more complex microprocessors.

Acknowledgement

This work has been partially supported by Intel Corporation through the research project *GP Based Test Program Generation.*

References

1. Bob Bentley, “High Level Validation of Next-Generation Microprocessor”, *Proceedings 7th International High-Level Design Validation test Workshop*, 2002, pp. 31-35
2. M. L. Bushnell, V. D. Agrawall, *Essentials of Electronic Testing for Digital, Memory & Mixed Signals VLSI Circuits*, Kluwer Academic Publishing, 2000
3. R. M. Friedberg, “A Learning Machine: Part I”, *IBM Journal of Research and Development*, 1958, vol. 2, n. 1, pp 2-13
4. J. R. Koza, “Genetic programming”, *Encyclopedia of Computer Science and Technology*, vol. 39, Marcel-Dekker, 1998, pp. 29-43
5. J. R. Koza, *Genetic Programming*, MIT Press, Cambridge, MA, 1992
6. S. Handley, “On the use of a directed acyclic graph to represent a population of computer programs”, *Proceedings of the 1994 IEEE World Congress on Computational Intelligence*, 1994, pp 154-159
7. R. Poli, “Evolution of graph-like programs with parallel distributed genetic programming”, *Genetic Algorithms: Proceedings of the 7th International Conference*, 1997, pp 346-353
8. W. Kantschik, W. Banzhaf , “Linear-Graph GP — A new GP Structure”, *Proceedings of the 4th European Conference on Genetic Programming*, 2002, pp. 83-92
9. P. Nordin, “A compiling genetic programming system that directly manipulates the machine code,” *Advances in Genetic Programming*, 1994, pp. 311-331
10. A. Fukunaga, A. Stechert, D. Mutz, “A genome compiler for high performance genetic programming”, *Genetic Programming 1998: Proceedings of the 3rd Annual Conference*, 1998, pp. 86-94

11. S. Klahold, S. Frank, R. E. Keller, W. Banzhaf, "Exploring the possibilites and restrictions of genetic programming in Java bytecode", *Late Breaking Papers at the Genetic Programming 1998 Conference*, 1998
12. E. Lukschandl, M. Holmlund, E. Moden, "Automatic evolution of Java bytecode: First experience with the Java virtual machine," *Late Breaking Papers at EuroGP'98: the First European Workshop on Genetic Programming*, 1998, pp. 14-16
13. F. Corno, G. Cumani, M. Sonza Reorda, G. Squillero, "Efficient Machine-Code Test-Program Induction", *Congress on Evolutionary Computation*, 2002, pp. 1486-1491
14. F. Corno, G. Cumani, M. Sonza Reorda, G. Squillero, "Evolutionary Test Program Induction for Microprocessor Design Verification", *Asian Test Symposium*, 2002, pp. 368-373
15. F. Corno, G. Cumani, M. Sonza Reorda, G. Squillero, "Fully Automatic Test Program Generation for Microprocessor Cores", to appear in: *DATE: IEEE Design, Automation & Test in Europe*, March 2003
16. F. Corno, G. Cumani, M. Sonza Reorda, G. Squillero, "Automatic Test Program Generation for Pipelined Processors," to appear in: *SAC: 18th ACM Symposium on Applied Computing*, March 2003
17. D. A. Patterson and J. L. Hennessy, *Computer Architecture - A Quantitative Approach, (second edition)*, Morgan Kaufmann, 1996
18. SPARC International, *The SPARC Architecture Manual*

The Effect of Plagues in Genetic Programming: A Study of Variable-Size Populations

Francisco Fernandez[1], Leonardo Vanneschi[2], and Marco Tomassini[2]

[1] University of Extremadura, Computer Science Department
Centro Universitario de Merida
C/ Sta Teresa de Jornet, 38. 06800 Merida, Spain
fcofdez@unex.es
http://atc.unex.es/pacof

[2] Computer Science Institute
University of Lausanne
1015 Lausanne, Switzerland
{Leonardo.Vanneschi,Marco.Tomassini}@iis.unil.ch

Abstract. A study on the effect of variable size populations in genetic programming is presented in this work. We apply the idea of plague (high desease of individuals). We show that although plagues are generally considered as negative events, they can help populations to save computing time and at the same time surviving individuals can reach high peaks in the fitness landscape.

1 Introduction

Population size is recognized to have a large impact on the dynamics of evolutionary algorithms (EAs). A number of researchers have focused on the study of this important parameter during the last few years. For example, Goldberg studied the relationship between the size of populations in genetic algorithms (GAs) and the number of building blocks that can be generated and developed during evolution [1]. In Genetic Programming (GP), researchers have been even more concerned with the problem of deciding the size of populations [3,4] because of the well known problem of bloat [6], which characterizes any EA with variable size chromosomes. Bloat means that the size of individuals composing a population, and thus the computational effort required to evaluate their fitness, tend to grow as generations are computed. For example, in [6] it is suggested that the size of the individuals grows subquadratically with time. The importance of the population size is thus twofold: on the one hand it establishes a lower bound for the computational effort required to evaluate individuals fitness, and on the other it is related to the quality of the solutions found, since it has been shown that difficult problems usually require large populations, while easy problems can be solved employing smaller ones [1,4]. The decision about the size of populations is thus usually based on an “a priori” knowledge of the difficulty of the problem or determined by means of a series of experiments. Once the population size has been decided, it is usually kept constant during experiments. The

C. Ryan et al. (Eds.): EuroGP 2003, LNCS 2610, pp. 317–326, 2003.

idea of changing the size of the population during the evolutionary process has not been widely addressed until now: only a small number of studies have been performed [5], but those studies have only dealt with fixed size chromosomes. Thus more research is required in order to understand the behavior of variable size populations in GP. The paper is structured as follows: section 2 describes our performance measure, the computational effort, in section 3 we present some simulated results on varying population sizes in GP, section 4 shows experimental results on the even parity problem, and finally we offer our conclusions in section 5.

2 Computational Effort

In EAs studies, results are usually presented by showing fitness values obtained at each computed generation, or the number of fitness evaluations spent to reach a certain fitness value. But, as described in [7], this is misleading in GP, since individuals change their size dynamically. We thus prefer to use a measure that takes into account the complexity of individuals: the *computational effort*. It is calculated by computing the average number of nodes at generation g (we indicate it as avg_length_g) and then by computing the partial effort at that generation (that we indicate as PE_g) defined as:

$$PE_g = n \times avg\_length_g \tag{1}$$

where n is the number of individuals in the population. Finally, we calculate the effort of computation E_g, at generation g, as

$$E_g = PE_g + PE_{g-1} + PE_{g-2} + \ldots + PE_0 \tag{2}$$

We present our results by showing curves representing the relationship between fitness and computational effort. This curves usually present a rapid fitness improvement at the beginning, when a relatively small computational cost has been produced, and a slow improvement later in the run, when large amounts of computational effort are spent (see for instance the black curve in figure 1). In other words, it is easy to make large improvements on solutions, when they are bad ones, but it is difficult to improve a good solution. Moreover, due to the bloat, the size of individuals and thus the computational effort required to evaluate their fitness, grow as generations are computed, thus decreasing performances. In synthesis, after a certain number of generations, a large amount of computational effort is usually spent for a small gain in the fitness quality. The technique presented here, consisting in removing a fixed number of individuals (the ones with the worst fitness values) from the population at each generation, is aimed at limiting the computational effort spent as generations are computed, even in presence of bloat, thus hopefully reducing its effects on performances.

3 A Model of Plagues

The black and continuous curve in figure 1 has been experimentally obtained by averaging effort and best fitness on 50 runs of GP using one population of

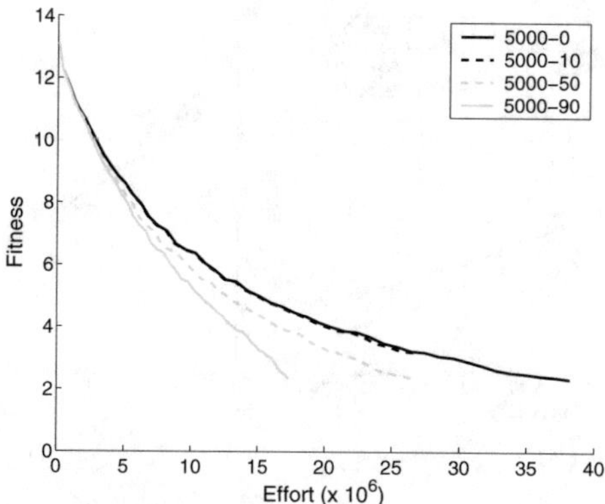

Fig. 1. Fitness Vs. effort for the even parity 5 problem using 5000 individuals. Thick curve: an actual experiment. Dotted and gray curves: simulation results calculated on the data of the actual experiment, where the effort is calculated by removing 10, 50 or 90 individuals per generation and the fitness is maintained unchanged.

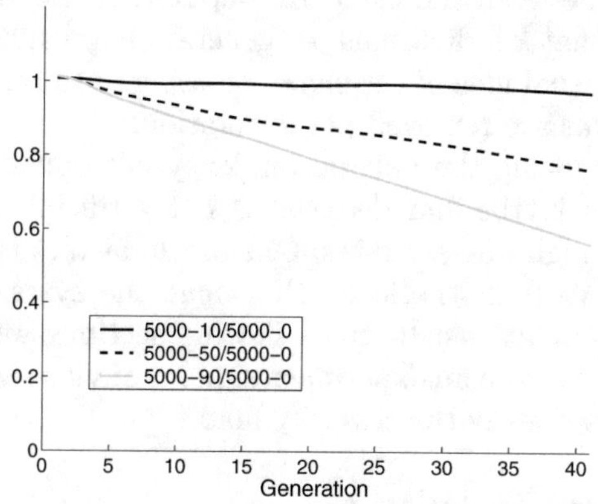

Fig. 2. Curves of the ratio of the effort between fixed size and shrinking populations (y-axis) with respect to generation number (x-axis).

constant size (equal to 5000 individuals) on the even parity 5 problem (see [8] for a detailed description of this standard problem). Starting from the data of this curve, it is easy to calculate the analogous curves for a theoretical GP process in which a fixed number k of individuals is suppressed from the population at each generation. It is sufficient to replace the constant n in definition (1) with a constant n_g that represents the size of the population at generation g. n_1 is considered to be equal to 5000 and, at a generic generation g, the value of n_g is equal to $n_{g-1} - k$. As a first approximation, we are considering best fitness values not to be affected by the process of suppression of the individuals. Under these assumptions, the other curves of figure 1 can be drawn, in which we have considered $k = 10$, $k = 50$ and $k = 90$. As figure 1 shows, the reduction of the computational effort due to the suppression of k individuals from the population offers a marked performance improvement. In figure 2 we present

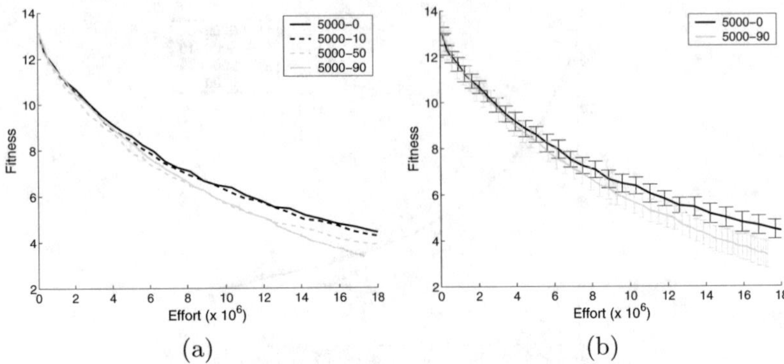

Fig. 3. (a) Best fitness against effort for a fixed size population of size 5000 (thick curve) and various shrinking populations. Data obtained averaging over 50 runs. (b) Error bars for the same graphs shown in (a) for the fixed population and the best shrinking population. Error bars represent the standard deviation over the 50 runs.

effort relationships between the fixed size population and the theoretical values obtained assuming that k individuals per generation are systematically removed. This figure gives a visual idea of the slope incresing in the effort ratio as a higher number of individuals are removed per generation.

The idea of destroying the natural tendency of populations to maintain an equilibrium between births and deseases is not artificial. Natural populations sometimes undergo high desease rates. One of the factors that can produce this effect is a plague. We will therfore call *plague* the systematic elimination of individuals along generations. In the following sections we study the effect of plagues in populations from an experimental point of view, where the assumption of unchanged fitness does not necessarily hold.

4 Experimental Results

In this section we present an experimental study of plagues on the even parity 5 problem. All experiments have been performed using generational GP, tournament selection (10 individuals), 1% mutation probability, 95% crossover probability, a maximum depth of 17 for the individuals and elitism.

4.1 Fitness vs. Effort

Figure 3 presents results on the even parity 5 problem, with an initial population of 5000 individuals, and removing sistematically 10, 50 and 90 individuals per generation. Each of the experiments has been performed for 50 generations, and each of the curves is an average of 50 different runs. First of all we see that the relationships among the different curves are similar to those observed in figure 1: none of the plagues achieve worse results than the fixed size population. Moreover, as in figure 1, when we supress 90 individuals we obtain the best results. The reason of this behavior is that the effort for obtaining a certain fitness value with the plague is smaller than that required by the fixed size population.

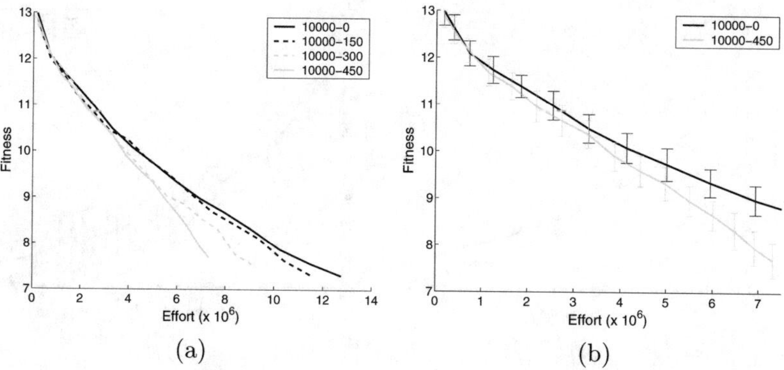

Fig. 4. (a) Best fitness against effort for a fixed size population of size 10000 (thick curve) and various shrinking populations. Data obtained averaging over 50 runs. (b) Error bars for the same graphs shown in (a) for the fixed population and the best shrinking population. Error bars represent the standard deviation over the 50 runs.

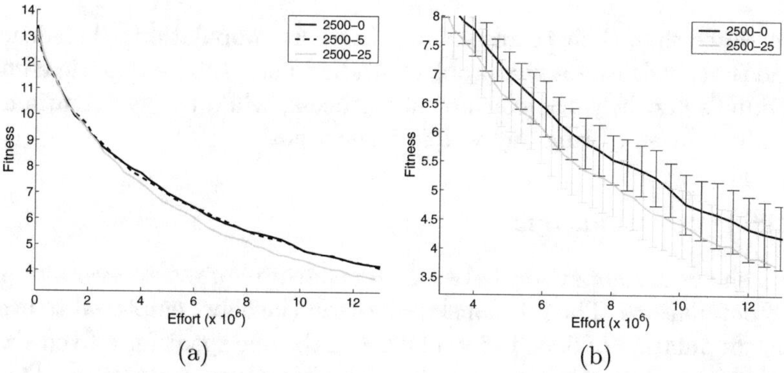

Fig. 5. (a) Best fitness against effort for a fixed size population of size 2500 (thick curve) and various shrinking populations. Data obtained averaging over 50 runs. (b) Error bars for the same graphs shown in (a) for the fixed population and the best shrinking population. Error bars represent the standard deviation over the 50 runs.

Similar experiments were performed with other population sizes (10000, 2500 and 1000) and eliminating different numbers of individuals. Results are always consistent (see figures 4, 5, and 6), thus confirming the suitability of using plagues as a strategy for reducing the computational effort and maintaining a good quality in the solutions. As the graphics of standard deviations clearly show (see (b) parts of figures 3, 4, 5, 6), the advantage of employing plagues is more evident (differences are more statistically significant) when using larger populations.

Experiments increasing the size of populations as they evolve have also been performed. This time a fixed number of new randomly generated individuals are added in the population at each generation. Figure 7 shows results obtained with populations of initial sizes of 5000 and 2500 individuals. For both cases variable size populations, in which an amount of new random individuals equal to the 1% of the initial population size is added to the populations at each iteration,

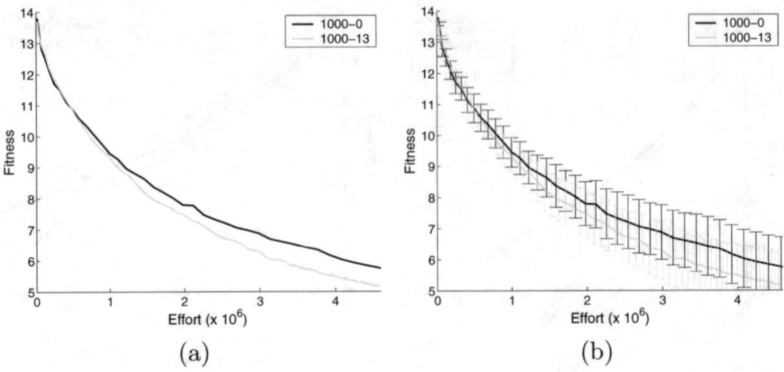

Fig. 6. (a) Best fitness against effort for a fixed size population of size 1000 (thick curve) and various shrinking populations. Data obtained averaging over 50 runs. (b) Error bars for the same graphs shown in (a) for the fixed population and the best shrinking population. Error bars represent the standard deviation over the 50 runs.

perform worse than their corresponding fixed size populations. This leads us to conclude that, at least for the problem studied here, the systematic elimination of individuals can help the convergence process, while the systematic addition of individual doesn't bring any visible advantage.

4.2 Effort Relationships

Figure 8 shows a comparison between the efforts required to evaluate different kinds of populations. The relationship between the effort employed to evaluate a fixed size population of 5000 individuals, and the one spent for a fixed size population of 2500 individuals is more or less constant along generations. The largest population, containing a double number of individuals, requires about twice the computational effort. This means that, since both populations are undergoing bloat, both are bloating at a proportional rate, i.e. the average growth in the size of individuals is more or less the same independently from the population size. Figure 8 also shows the relationship among the effort to evaluate the fixed size population of 5000 individuals at each generation and those undergoing plagues. We see that the value of that relationship at the first generation is 1, and this value decreases as we remove individuals, thus confirming that plagues can limit the computational effort.

4.3 Diversity

Curves in figure 9 show two measures of diversity of the evolving populations: one genotypic and the other phenotypic. Phenotypic diversity of a population P is defined as the entropy $H_p(P)$ of fitness values partitions. Formally:

$$H_p(P) = -\sum_{j=1}^{N} f_j \log(f_j)$$

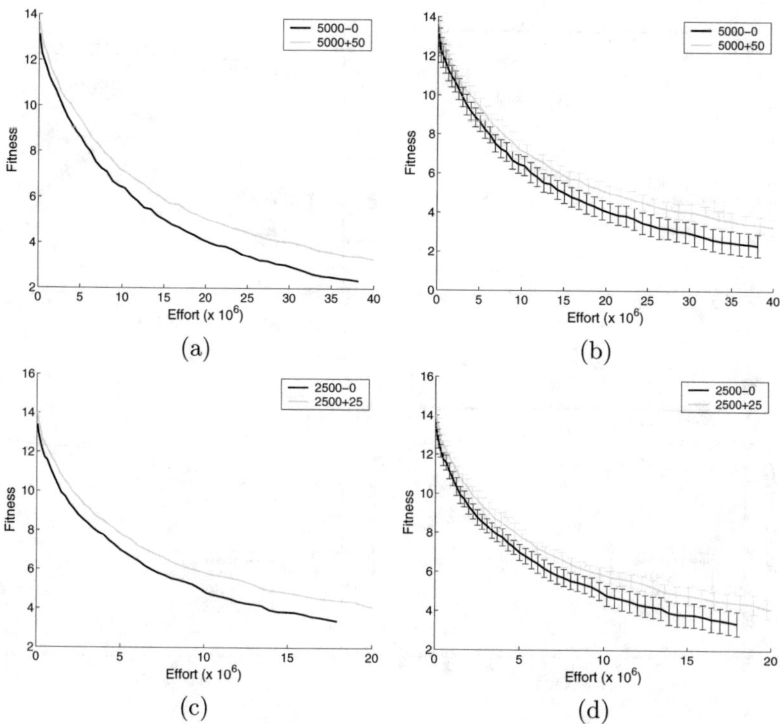

Fig. 7. (a) and (b): fitness against effort for the even parity 5 problem with a fixed population of 5000 individuals and a growing population and their standard deviations. (c) and (d): fitness against effort for a fixed population of 2500 individuals and a growing population and their standard deviations.

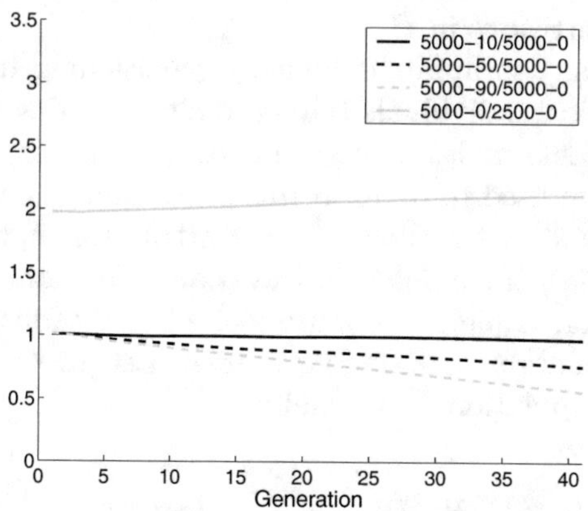

Fig. 8. Effort ratios (y-axis) against generation number (x-axis). Gray curve: ratio with a fixed population of size 5000 and a fixed population of size 2500. The other curves represent the ratio of shrinking populations with respect to a fixed population size of 5000 with three different rates of individual suppression.

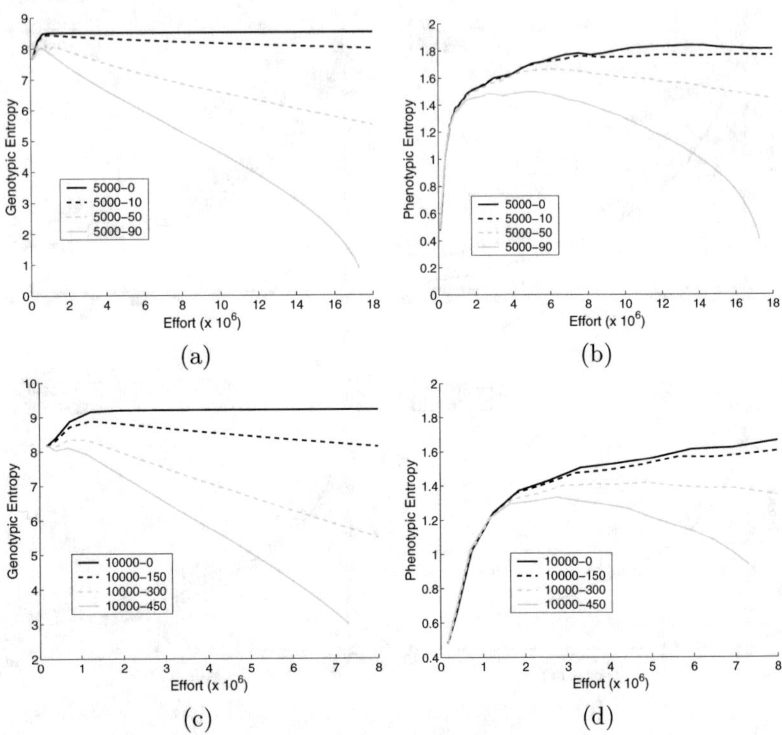

Fig. 9. Genotypic diversity (a) and (c) and phenotypic diversity (b) and (d) for two population sizes (5000 and 10000) for fixed and variable size populations.

where f_j is the number of individuals in P having a certain fitness and N is the number of fitness partitions in P.

Genotypic diversity is approximated by partitioning individuals in such a way that only identical individuals (i.e. individuals having the same syntactical structure and the same nodes at corresponding positions) belong to the same group. The algorithm used to perform this partitioning is efficient, because it is based on previously stored triplets of trees attributes. A triplet comprises the total number of nodes, the number of leaves and the number of internal nodes. Only in case of equal triplets, trees are visited to establish if they are indeed identical. This population partitioning is then used to calculate the genotypic entropy $H_g(P)$ of population P. Formally:

$$H_g(P) = -\sum_{j=1}^{N} g_j \log(g_j)$$

where g_j is the number of individuals in the population P belonging to partition j and N is the number of genotype partitions in P.

A number of similar diversity measures for GP are described in detail in [2], where Burke *et al.* observe that phenotypic diversity in fixed populations, after an initial increase, normally tends to decrease as generations are computed, while genotypic diversity tends to increase at the beginning of the evolution and to stay constant later in the run. However, when the population sizes decrease steadily, one sees from figure 9 that phenotypic and genotypic population diversities are more correlated (i.e. both are decreasing more or less at the same rate). This seems to indicate that for the most part, the high genotypic diversity still present at the end of the run in fixed size populations does not help much in finding better solutions. This can be due to bloat and, in general, to the presence of neutral networks of solutions. On the other hand, the loss of phenotypic and genotypic diversity for populations undergoing plagues doesn't seem to have a negative influence on performance. However, it must be noticed that only one test case is considered in this paper (even parity 5) and this is not enough to uncover a general trend. Thus, it might well be that, for other problems, the loss of diversity provoked by the plagues might actually reduce too much the exploration, thus causing a decrease in performances.

5 Conclusions and Future Work

A new technique for reducing the computational effort required to evaluate GP populations has been presented in this paper. This technique has been called plague and has been defined as the systematic elimination of a fixed number of individuals (the ones with the worst fitness) from a population at each generation. In this way populations size is progressively reduced during evolution. Experimental results showing performances of populations undergoing different kinds of plagues clearly show that solutions of similar qualities to those obtained employing fixed size populations can be obtained reducing the population size at each generation, thus saving important amounts of computational effort. The opposite can be said when we add new (randomly generated) individuals to populations at each generation: our experiments show that with this technique the computational effort to evaluate the population increases considerably as generations are computed. It is important to note that our results are based on the even parity problem only and thus they only represent an encouraging first step in this new direction. In order to assess the generality of the results shown here, we plan to extend this study to other known GP benchmarks (such as the artificial ant on the Santa Fe trail, various kinds of symbolic regressions, etc.). Furthermore, we plan to investigate which of the individuals contained in the population are the most suitable to be removed in order to have the larger gain in terms of performances and/or to save the larger amount of computational effort. Results on genotypic and phenotypic diversity show that diversity is not maintained during evolution if we delete the individuals with the worst fitness. New techniques can be employed to maintain diversity, for instance deleting duplicates from a genotypic or phenotypic point of view. On the other hand, removing individuals with the larger sizes would obviously allow a larger gain in computational effort. Finally, we plan to investigate the effect of plagues on parallel and distributed GP.

References

1. D. E. Goldberg. Sizing Populations for serial and parallel genetic algorithms. In Schaffer, J. D. (Ed.), *Proceedings of the Third International Conference on Genetic Algorithms*, pages 70-79. San Mateo, CA: Morgan Kaufmann, 1989.
2. E. Burke, S. Gustafson, G. Kendall, and N. Krasnogor. Advanced population diversity measures in genetic programming. In J. J. Merelo, P. Adamidis, H. G. Beyer, J.-L. Fernández-Villacanas, and H.-P. Schwefel, editors, *Parallel Problem Solving from Nature - PPSN VII*, volume 2439 of *Lecture Notes in Computer Science*, pages 341–350. Springer-Verlag, Heidelberg, 2002.
3. C. Gathercole and P. Ross. Small populations over many generations can beat large populations over few generations in genetic programming. In J. Koza, K. Deb, M. Dorigo, D. B. Fogel, M. Garzon, H. Iba, and R. L. Riolo, editors, *Genetic Programming, Proceedings of the Second Annual Conference*, pages 111–118, Morgan Kaufmann, San Francisco, CA, USA, 1997.
4. M. Fuchs. Large populations are not always the best choice in genetic programming. In W. Banzhaf, J. Daida, A. E. Eiben, M. Garzon, V. Honavar, M. Jakiela, and R. Smith, editors, *Proceedings of the genetic and evolutionary computation conference GECCO'99*, pages 1033–1038, Morgan Kaufmann, San Francisco, CA, 1999.
5. Tan, K.C., Lee, T.H., and E. F. Khor. Evolutionary Algorithms With Dynamic Population Size and Local Exploration for Multiobjective Optimization. IEEE Transactions on Evolutionary Computation, Vol. 5, Num. 6, pages 565-588, 2001.
6. W. B. Langdon and R. Poli. Foundations of Genetic Programming. Springer-Verlag, Heidelberg, 2001.
7. F. Fernandez, M. Tomassini and L. Vanneschi. An Empirical Study of Multipopulation Genetic Programming, in Genetic Programming and Evolvable Machines, Kluwer Academic Publishers. To appear, 2002.
8. J. R. Koza. Genetic Programming. On the Programming of Computers by Means of Natural Selection, The MIT Press, Cambridge, MA, 1992.

Multi Niche Parallel GP with a Junk-Code Migration Model

Santi Garcia[1], John Levine[2], and Fermin Gonzalez[3]

[1] Computer Science Department, University of Oviedo, Spain
carbajal@lsi.uniovi.es
[2] University of Edinburgh. School of Informatics
johnl@inf.ed.ac.uk
[3] INDRA. Alcala de Henares. Madrid. Spain
fgmartinez@indra.es

Abstract. We describe in this paper a parallel implementation of Multi Niche Genetic Programming that we use to test the performance of a modified migration model. Evolutive introns is a technique developed to accelerate the convergence of GP in classification and symbolic regression problems. Here, we will copy into a differentiated subpopulation the individuals that due to the evolution process contain longer Evolutive Introns. Additionally, the multi island model is parallelised in order to speed up convergence. These results are also analysed.
Our results prove that the multi island model achieves faster convergence in the three different symbolic regression problems tested, and that the junk-coded subpopulation is not significantly worse than the others, which reinforces our belief in that the important thing is not only fitness but keeping good genetic diversity along all the evolution process. The overhead introduced in the process by the existence of various island, and the migration model is reduced using a multi-thread approach.

1 Introduction. Background

In this section we present the background knowledge about junk code growth, and multi niche Genetic Programming, that is the starting point to this study.

1.1 Junk Code

The benefits and disadvantages of existing non coding segments inserted in the genotype of the individuals of a population have been a theme of discussion in the GP community during the last years. Some of these studies show that introns can grow up excessively and exhaust the memory of the system, [2]. In other studies, introns seem to be useful as they appear as the evolution process goes on, protecting good building blocks from the destructive effect of the crossover operator [15], [10], [7], [12], [3]. In these studies, introns seem to be non random code which, given an appropriate crossover, can increase the fitness of the coding sections.

C. Ryan et al. (Eds.): EuroGP 2003, LNCS 2610, pp. 327–334, 2003.

In [6], a strategy to promote the automatic growth and shrinking of non coding segments in the individuals of a GP population is proposed. The method consists of adapting the probability of selection of every node in the tree after each application of the crossover operator. Artificially generated introns are called Evolutive Introns since as the process goes on they usually grow, and shrink in different phases of the learning process.

In [14], the three hypothesised causes of code growth are examined. Removal Bias and Protective hypotheses come reinforced after this study, while drift hypothesis is not supported by this experiments.

1.2 Multi Niche Genetic Programming

The use of multiple populations, or niches, is called *distributed genetic algorithm*, or *island model.* In [8], two different Multi niche Genetic Programming techniques are tested. In the first one, (MP ring architecture), each subpopulation chooses its five best individuals and sends it to the next subpopulation in the ring. Each subpopulation takes the individuals sent to it, and uses them to replace its five worst members. The second, (injection architecture) is a hierarchical arrangement. For example, in a 3 subpopulation model, two subpopulations would send their best five individuals to the third one, that would use this ten individuals to replace its worst ten [13]. The most important thing when setting up a multi niche system is the migration model, and its parameters, as stated in [4].

2 Multi Niche Parallel GP

In[1], D. Andre and John Koza studied the effects of parallelisation on GP comparing the results obtained using different migration rates with the ones obtained using only one panmictic population. The study of these performance variations is absolutely out of the scope of this work.

We will study the behaviour of a multi island model of four different islands (POP0, POP1, POP2, and POP3), and a panmictic isolated population of size POP1 + POP2 + POP3.

The system works as follows: upon completion of a pre-defined number of generations (a parameter of the system), a certain number of individuals in POP1, POP2 and POP3 will be probabilistically selected for migration to each one of the other two subpopulations (see figure 1). Each one of these populations will contribute to the migration process with the same number of individuals. The amount of migration will be another parameter of the system. Each time this migration process occurs, the same number of individuals will be selected from the three island model, and copied into the population named POP0, using the value of the longest intron contained in each individual as selection criterion. We will not make an exhaustive study of the results obtained with different migration rates, because of the extension of the paper, and we will focus our study in the behaviour of the panmictic model, the enriched population, and the classic 3 island model. From now on, we will refer to these as Panmictic, POP0,

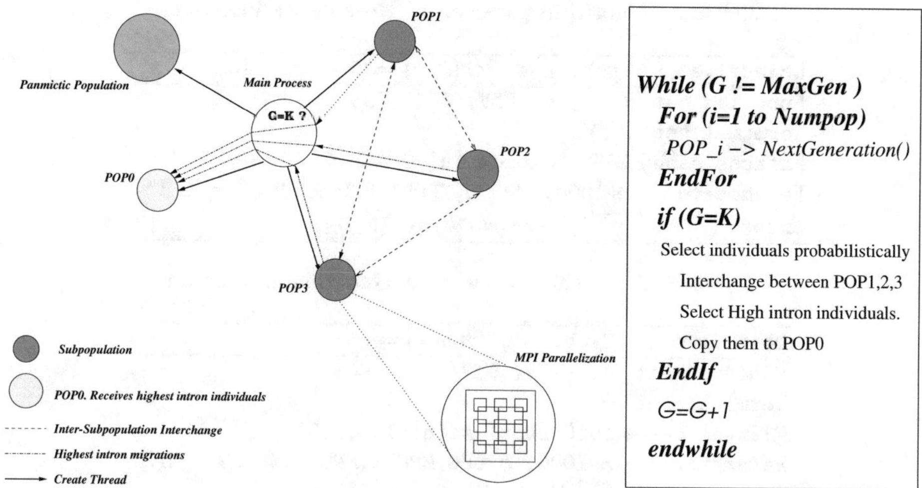

Fig. 1. Two-level parallelisation. The main process is responsible of the creation and synchronisation of the on going different evolution processes.

POP1, POP2,and POP3 subpopulations, respectively, where POP0 is the one where we will copy the individuals with longer introns.

Our Hypothesis is that POP0 will converge as well as PO1, POP2, POP3 because the individuals with high value introns represent useful genetic material in the population.

2.1 Parallelisation Strategy

We used a two-level parallelisation approach. With the help of standard POSIX threads we can create a separate thread of execution for each population. For the parallelisation of the process of passing from one generation the the next, inside each population we tried to use MPI library [5], [11] but mixed code using POSIX threads and MPI was not reliable at all, so we decided to keep the multithtread POSIX based model, and use MPI only for parallelising the repetition of experiments. The main process is responsible for creating a process for each subpopulation (three subpopulations, the one breeded with higher value introns, and the panmictic one), and synchronise the evolution of each one, directing the migration process when the adequate number of generations have passed. Each one of these secondary processes is responsible for carrying on the evolution on each subpopulation, (see figure 1). In this work we will use the migration model proposed by J. Koza and D. Andre, and will introduce one more population where we will copy the individuals with larger Evolutive Introns [6]. We will carry on evolution simultaneously in a panmictic population whose size will be three times the niches. This way, we will try to analyse the behaviour of an Evolutive Intron based migration model.

Table 1. Algorithm parameters. Rosenbrock Function.

Objective	Symb. Reg $Ros(x,y) = (x-1)^2 + 10(x^2 - y^2)$
Function set	+, -, *, DIV, SIN, COS
Terminal set	X, Y
Fitness cases	2500 samples in[-2.4,2.4]
Parameters	M=1000, MPOP0,MPOP1,MPOP2,MPOP3 = M/3
Error	$\sum_{i=1}^{2500} \lvert Ros(x_i, y_i) - f(x_i, y_i) \rvert$

Table 2. Algorithm parameters. Gudermann function.

Objective	Symb. Reg $Gud(x) =$
Function set	+, -, *, DIV, SIN, COS
Terminal set	X
Fitness cases	1000 samples in[-1.5,1.5]
Parameters	M=1000, MPOP0,MPOP1,MPOP2,MPOP3 = M/3
Error	$\sum_{i=1}^{1000} \lvert Gud(x_i) - f(x_i) \rvert$

2.2 Experimental Setup

In this section we describe the three problems we chose to test the performance of the multi niche model.

Rosenbrock's Function. Rosenbrock's valley [2], also known as Banana function, is a classic optimisation problem. The global optimum is inside along, narrow, parabolic shaped flat valley(see figure 2). To find the valley is trivial, however convergence to the global optimum is difficult and hence this problem has been repeatedly used in assess the performance of optimisation algorithms.

$$f(x,y) = (x-1)^2 + 10(x^2 - y^2) \tag{1}$$

We will take the value of the function in 2500 points along the XY plane between -2.4 and 2.4, to compute the value of the fitness function.

Gudermann's Function. The Gudermannian function gd(x) is a relative of the circular and hyperbolic functions, namely, the inverse tangent of sinh(x). It is shown that the motion of a simple pendulum released from its equilibrium position with just enough kinetic energy to reach the inverted position is naturally described by this function. This non-periodic solution of the pendulum equation can be viewed as completing the family of periodic solutions classically expressed by elliptic functions. See figure 2.

$$f(x) = \ln \frac{1}{\cos x + \tan x} \tag{2}$$

Koza's Symbolic Regression Problem. The third problem is the symbolic regression on

$$Koz(x) = x^4 + x^3 + x^2 + x \tag{3}$$

as stated [9].

Table 3. Algorithm parameters. Koza's symbolic Regression Problem.

Objective	Symb. Reg $Koz(x) = x^4 + x^3 + x^2 + x$
Function set	+, -, *, DIV,SIN, COS
Terminal set	X
Fitness cases	20 samples in[-1,+1]
Parameters	M=500, MPOP0,MPOP1,MPOP2,MPOP3 = M/3
Error	$\sum_{i=1}^{20} \lvert Koz(x_i) - f(x_i) \rvert$

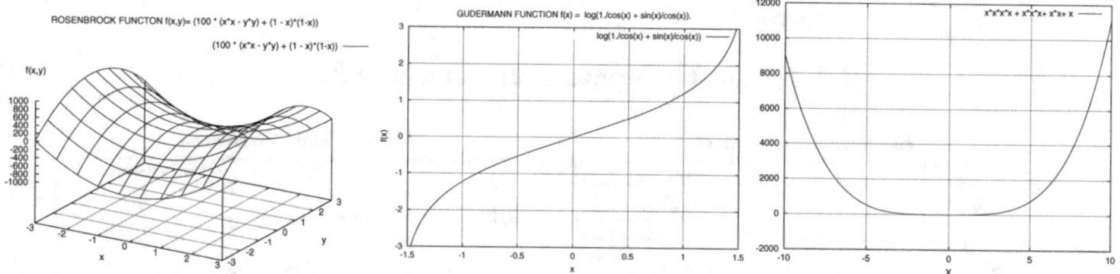

Fig. 2. Rosenbrock function(left). Gudermann function (center). Koza's symbolic regression problem (right).

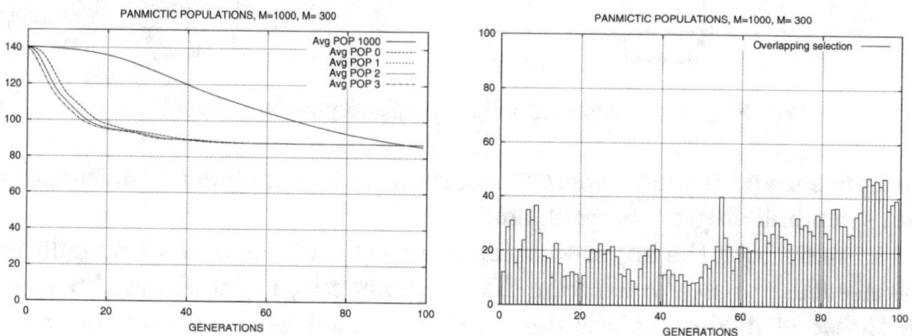

Fig. 3. Rosenbrock function. Results.

2.3 Results

This section summarises the results obtained when applying this multi niche approach on the problems described in section 2.2.

Figure 3 (left) shows the medium error in panmictic populations were size M= 1000, and 1000/3 for POP0, POP1, POP2,and POP3, when applying the approach to Rosenbrock's function. It is clear that, in this problem, the panmictic approach was clearly inferior to the multi niche island model. The same figure (right) shows the averaged percentage of individuals that would have been selected for migration using both methods (standar fitness, or Evolutive Introns length). This study was made in order to determine if the population named POP0 was really receiving different migrated individuals than the selected if the migration criterion was only fitness. Figures 4(center) and 5(center) show the same behaviour in the other two benchmark problems. The percentage of coincidence between fitness and introns-length criteria is rarely over 40%.

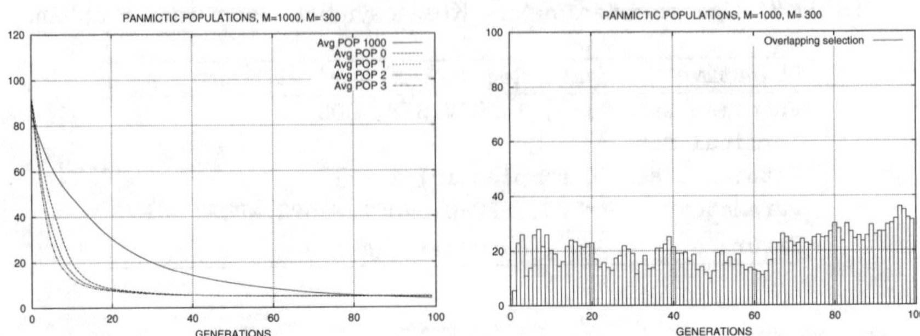

Fig. 4. Gudermann function. Results.

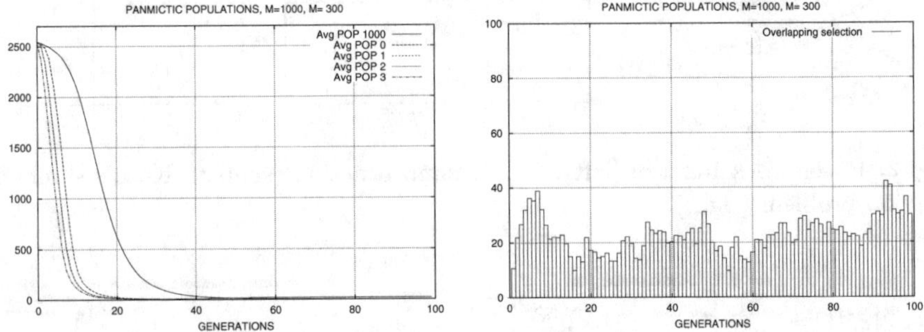

Fig. 5. Koza's symbolic regression problem. Results.

Figures 4 and 5 show coherent results when using Gudermann function and Koza's symbolic regression problem.

Figure 6 shows the important difference between the average cumulative cpu time needed to reach generation 100 in panmictic, multi island threaded, and non threaded model. This is due to the overload generated by the process of looking for the longest intron individuals. The difference between panmictic and multipopulation models is stretched when threads are enabled.

Finally, as the experiments on Rosenbrock's function with only 100 generations did not show clearly if the evolution was finished or not (see figure 3), we repeated this runs over 200 generations with the results shown in figure 7. In this figure, it can be seen that panmictic population is still decreasing medium error in generation 200. Multi niche model is stuck after a very fast initial error decreasing. This is probably due to a insufficient population size of the islands.

3 Conclusions

We have obtained coherent results in the three selected symbolic regression experiments. Based on our results, our conclusions can be summarised in

1. As we stated in our hypothesis, a subpopulation breeded with selected individuals according to a different selection criterion, as intron length, can converge as fast the ones in which the selection criterion was fitness function.

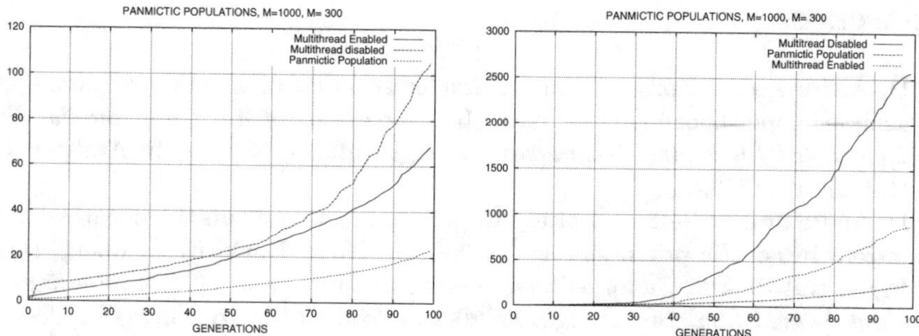

Fig. 6. Accumulated cpu time needed to reach generation 100.

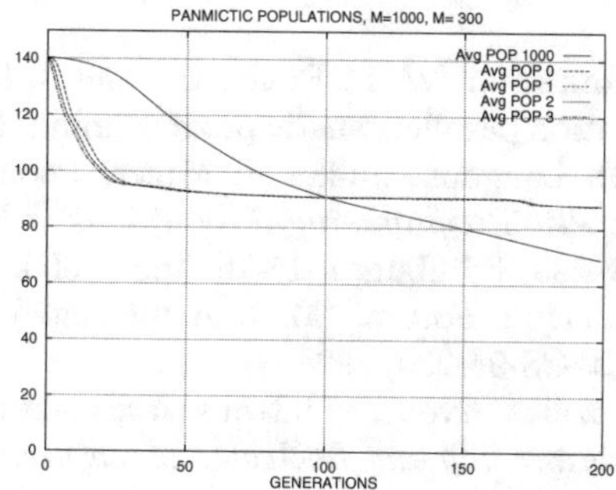

Fig. 7. Rosenbrock function. Results over 200 generations. Panmictic population reaches better results due to a bad selection of the sub populations size.

2. Multi Niche Genetic Programming can improve the convergence in Symbolic Regression problems, even if sometimes some kind of genetic drift could appear. This problem is probably due to a bad selection of population size.
3. The use of a multithreaded model reduces time performance degradation caused by the extra processing work needed to carry on evolution in a multi-niche system.

Acknowledgements

The set of experiments described in this work were conducted using the machines of the EPCC, in the University of Edinburgh. Mainly, the runs were executed in a Sun HPC cluster. It comprises an eight processor 400 MHz UltraSPARC-II system , with 8 Gbyte of shared memory and 276 Gbyte of disc space. This machine acts as front-end to three Sunfire 6800 systems two of which have twenty four 750 MHz UltraSPARC-III processors and 48 Gbyte of shared memory, and the third of which has sixteen such processors.

The authors would like to acknowledge the support of the European Community Access to Research Infrastructure action of the Improving Human Potential Programme (contract No HPRI-CT-1999-00026), and the people from EPCC at Edinburgh University.

References

1. D. Andre and J. Koza. A parallel implementation of genetic programming that achieves super-linear performance. In *Proceedings of int. Conf. on Parallel and Distributed Processing Techniques and Applications*, pages –. In Arabnia, Hamid R. (editor), 1996.
2. D. Andre and A. Teller. A study in program response and the negative effects of introns in genetic programming. In John R. Koza, David E. Goldberg, David B. Fogel, and Rick L. Riolo, editors, *Genetic Programming 1996: Proceedings of the First Annual Conference*, pages 12–20, Stanford University, CA, USA, 28–31 July 1996. MIT Press.
3. P. J. Angeline. Genetic programming and emergent intelligence. In Kenneth E. Kinnear, Jr., editor, *Advances in Genetic Programming*, chapter 4, pages 75–98. MIT Press, 1994.
4. F. Fernandez, M. Tomassini, W. F. Punch III, and J. M. Sanchez. Experimental study of multipopulation parallel genetic programming. In Riccardo Poli, Wolfgang Banzhaf, William B. Langdon, Julian F. Miller, Peter Nordin, and Terence C. Fogarty, editors, *Genetic Programming, Proceedings of EuroGP'2000*, volume 1802 of *LNCS*, pages 283–293, Edinburgh, 15-16 April 2000. Springer-Verlag.
5. Message Passing Interface Forum. MPI: A message-passing interface standard. Technical Report UT-CS-94-230, 1994.
6. S. García and F. González. Evolutive introns: A non-costly method of using introns in GP. *Genetic Programming and Evolvable Machines*, 2(2):111–122, June 2001.
7. T. Haynes. Duplication of coding segments in genetic programming. In *Proceedings of the Thirteenth National Conference on Artificial Intelligence*, pages 344–349, Portland, OR, 1996.
8. I. M. A. Kirkwood, S. H. Shami, and M. C. Sinclair. Discovering simple fault-tolerant routing rules using genetic programming. In *ICANNGA97*, University of East Anglia, Norwich, UK, 1997.
9. J. R. Koza. *Genetic Programming: On the Programming of Computers by Means of Natural Selection.* MIT Press, Cambridge, MA, USA, 1992.
10. J.R. Levenick. Inserting introns improves genetic algorithm success rate: Taking a cue from biology. *Proceedings of the Fourth International Conference on Genetic algorithms*, 1:123–127, 1991.
11. Message Passing Interface Forum MPIF. MPI-2: Extensions to the Message-Passing Interface. Technical Report, University of Tennessee, Knoxville, 1996.
12. P.Nordin, F. Francone, and W. Banzhaf. Explicitly defined introns and destructive crossover in genetic programming. In Justinian P. Rosca, editor, *Proceedings of the Workshop on Genetic Programming: From Theory to Real-World Applications*, pages 6–22, Tahoe City, California, USA, July 1995.
13. B. Punch. Royal trees as a benchmark problem for genetic programming: A parallel processing example. In Peter J. Angeline and K. E. Kinnear, Jr., editors, *Advances in Genetic Programming 2*, pages –. MIT Press, Cambridge, MA, USA, 1996.
14. Terence Soule and Robert B. Heckendorn. An analysis of the causes of code growth in genetic programming. *Genetic Programming and Evolvable Machines*, 3(3):283–309, September 2002.
15. M. Wineberg and F. Oppacher. The benefits of computing with introns. In John R. Koza, David E. Goldberg, David B. Fogel, and Rick L. Riolo, editors, *Genetic Programming 1996: Proceedings of the First Annual Conference*, pages 410–415, Stanford University, CA, USA, 28–31 1996. MIT Press.

Tree Adjoining Grammars, Language Bias, and Genetic Programming

Nguyen Xuan Hoai, R.I. McKay, and H.A. Abbass

School of Computer Science, Australian Defence Force Academy, ACT 2600, Australia
x.nguyen@student.adfa.edu.au, {rim,abbass}@cs.adfa.edu.au

Abstract. In this paper, we introduce a new grammar guided genetic programming system called tree-adjoining grammar guided genetic programming (TAG3P+), where tree-adjoining grammars (TAGs) are used as means to set language bias for genetic programming. We show that the capability of TAGs in handling context-sensitive information and categories can be useful to set a language bias that cannot be specified in grammar guided genetic programming. Moreover, we bias the genetic operators to preserve the language bias during the evolutionary process. The results pace the way towards a better understanding of the importance of bias in genetic programming.

1 Introduction

The use of bias has been a key subject in inductive learning for many years [13]. Theoretical arguments for its necessity were presented in [20, 23]. Bias is the set of factors that influence the selection of a particular hypothesis; therefore, some hypotheses are preferred over others [18].

Three main forms of bias can be distinguished [21]: selection, language and search bias. In selection bias, the criteria for selecting a hypothesis create a preference ordering over the set of hypothesis in the hypothesis space. A language bias is a set of language-based restrictions to represent the hypothesis space. A search bias is the control mechanism for reaching one hypothesis from another in the hypothesis space.

A bias can be either exclusive or preferential. An exclusive bias eliminates certain hypotheses during the learning process, whereas a preferential bias weights each hypothesis according to some criteria. An inductive bias is said to be correct when it allows the learning system to elect the correct target concept(s) whereas an incorrect bias prevents the learning system from doing so. An inductive bias is said to be strong when it focuses the search on a relatively small portion of the space; and weak when it focuses the search on a large portion of the hypothesis space.

A declarative bias in an inductive learning system is one specified explicitly in a language designed for the purpose; if the bias is simply encoded implicitly in the search mechanism, it is said to be procedural. An inductive bias is static if it does not change during the learning process; otherwise it is dynamic.

A genetic programming (GP) system [1, 11] can be seen as an inductive learning system. In a GP system, fitness-based selection, the bias towards programs that perform well on the problem, is a selection bias. The language bias is implemented through the selection of the function and terminal sets, and the search bias is imple-

C. Ryan et al. (Eds.): EuroGP 2003, LNCS 2610, pp. 335–344, 2003.

mented with genetic operators (mainly crossover and mutation). The language bias of a traditional GP system [11] is fixed, while GP with automatic-defined functions (ADF) [12] has a dynamic language bias.

Whigham [21, 22] introduced grammar guided genetic programming (GGGP), where context-free grammars (CFGs) are used to declaratively set the language bias. He also proposed genetic operators to implement search bias and overcome the closure requirement, and showed that GGGP generalizes GP [22, page 129]. However, GGGP cannot handle context-sensitive language biases, and preserving a preferential language bias during the evolutionary process is difficult. Geyer-Schulz [5] independently proposed another GGGP system. His use of a complicated counting procedure on the derivation tree set of the CFG resulted in a better initialization scheme. With no restriction on the chromosome's (derivation tree) size or depth, the similar work of Gruau [4] quickly resulted in code bloat during the evolutionary process. Wong and Leung [24] used logic grammars that allow the handling of context-sensitive information and encoding problem-dependent knowledge. Ryan and O'Neil [16, 17] proposed grammatical evolution (GE), where a genotype-to phenotype mapping is employed.

Hoai et al. [6, 7] introduced tree adjunct grammar guided GP (TAG3P), but the approach had some limitations. It used a restricted form of derivation, which has not been shown to subsume context-free languages (though [6] gives a range of context-sensitive problems covered by this form). Importantly, the method often generates large numbers of elementary trees, especially when the number of terminals is large. In computational linguistics, this issue led to a shift from tree adjunct grammars (adjunction only) to tree adjoining grammars (adjunction and substitution) [9]. Furthermore, their work did not discuss bias.

The objective of this paper is to propose tree adjoining grammars (TAGs) for evolving computer programs and study the effect of bias. In Section 2, the concepts of tree adjoining grammars and its advantages over context-free grammars are presented. All the components of TAG3P+, and an example using bias on the 6-multiplexer problem, are discussed in Sections 3 and 4. Section 5 draws conclusions.

2 Tree Adjoining Grammars

Joshi and his colleagues in [10] proposed tree-adjunct grammars, the original form of tree adjoining grammars (TAG). Adjunction was the only tree-rewriting operation. Later, the substitution operation was added and the new formalism became known as TAG. Although the addition of substitution did not change the strong and weak generative power of tree adjunct grammars (their tree and string sets), it compacted the formalism with fewer elementary trees [9]. TAGs have gradually replaced tree adjunct grammars in the field of computational linguistics.

TAGs are tree-rewriting systems, defined in [9] as a 5-tuple (T, V, I, A, S), where T is a finite set of terminal symbols; V is a finite set of non-terminal symbols ($T \cap V = \emptyset$); $S \in V$ is a distinguished symbol called the start symbol; and $E = I \cup A$ is a set of elementary trees (initial and auxiliary respectively). In an elementary tree, all interior nodes are labeled by non-terminal symbols, while the nodes on the frontier are labeled either by terminal or non-terminal symbols. The frontier of an auxiliary tree must contain a distinguished node, the foot node, labeled by the same non-terminal as the root. The convention in [9] of marking the foot node with an asterisk (*) is followed here. With the exception of the foot node, all non-terminal symbols on the frontier of an elementary tree are marked as $\downarrow$ (i.e. substitution).

Initial and auxiliary trees are denoted α and β respectively. A tree whose root is labeled by X is called an X-type tree. A derivation tree in TAG [17, 19] is a tree-structure which encodes the history of derivation (substitutions and adjunctions) to produce the derived tree. Each node is labelled by an elementary tree, the root with an α tree, and other nodes with either an α or β tree. Links from a node to its offspring are marked by addresses for adjunction or substitution.

Adjunction builds a new (derived) tree γ from an A-type auxiliary tree β, and a tree α (elementary or derived) with an interior node labeled A. Sub-tree α_1 rooted at A is disconnected from α, and β is attached to α to replace it. Finally, α_1 is attached back to the foot node of β (which by definition, also has label A), to produce γ.

In substitution, we replace a non-terminal node on the frontier of an elementary tree by an initial tree whose root has the same label.

The set of languages generated by TAGs is a superset of the context-free language, and is properly included in indexed languages [9]. Lexicalized TAGs (LTAGs) [16], require each elementary tree to have at least one terminal node. [16] presents an algorithm which, for any context-free grammar G, produces an LTAG G_{lex} which generates the same language and tree set as G (G_{lex} is said to strongly lexicalize G). The derivation trees in G are the derived trees of G_{lex}.

TAGs have a number of advantages for GP. The separation between derivation and derived trees provides a natural genotype-to-phenotype map. Derivation trees in TAGs are more fine-grained structures than those of CFG. They are compact (since each node is an elementary tree, equivalent to a number of nodes in CFG derivation trees) and they are closer to a semantic representation [2]. Finally, in growing a derivation tree from the root, one can stop at anytime and still have a valid derivation tree and a valid derived tree. We call this property "feasibility". Feasibility helps TAG3P+ (described in Section 3) to control the exact size of its chromosomes, and also to implement a wide range of genetic operators, a number of them bio-inspired, which cannot be implemented either in GP or in GGGP.

3 Tree Adjoining Grammar Guided Genetic Programming

In this section, we propose a new GGGP system, tree adjoining grammar guided GP (TAG3P+ to distinguish it from TAG3P [6, 7]). To relate this work to previous systems in the context-free domain, we frame the discussion in terms of a context-free grammar G and corresponding LTAG, G_{lex}. However G is strictly unnecessary, and of course, for context-sensitive problems, would not exist. TAG3P+ evolves the derivation trees in G_{lex} (genotype) instead of the derived trees (the derivation trees in G – phenotype). It thus creates a genotype-phenotype map, potentially many-one. As in canonical GP [11], TAG3P+ has the following five main components:

Program representation: the derivation trees in LTAG G_{lex}. As usual, programs are restricted to a bounded size. Each node also contains a list of lexemes for substitution within the elementary tree at that node (Figure 1). The main operation is adjunction.

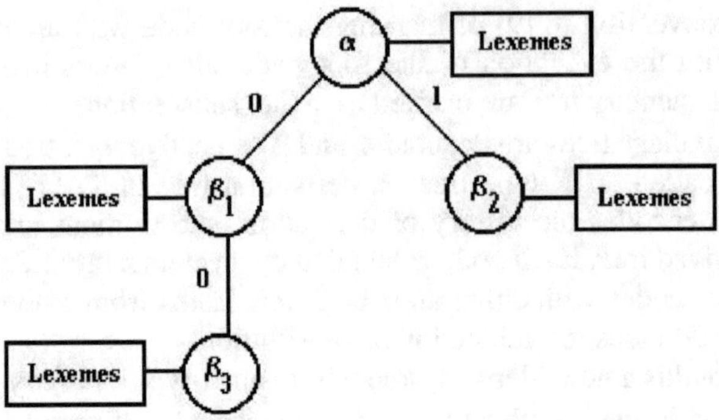

Fig. 1. Example of an individual (derivation tree) in TAG3P+.

Parameters: minimum size of genomes (MIN_SIZE), maximum size of genomes (MAX_SIZE), size of population (POP_SIZE), maximum number of generations (MAX_GEN) and probabilities for genetic operators.

Initialization procedure: Each individual is generated by randomly growing a derivation tree in G_{lex} to a size randomly chosen between MIN_ and MAX_SIZE (unlike most GP systems, which use depth bounds). Thanks to the TAG feasibility property, the procedure always generates valid individuals of the exact size. Another initialization scheme (corresponding to ramped half-and-half initialization) generates a portion of the derivation trees – usually 50% – randomly but in a full shape.

Fitness Evaluation: an individual (a derivation tree in G_{lex}) is first mapped to a derived tree (a derivation tree in G) through the sequence of adjunctions and substitutions encoded in its genotype. The expression defined by the derived tree is then semantically evaluated as in GGGP.

Genetic operators: sub-tree crossover and sub-tree mutation.

In sub-tree crossover, two individuals are selected based on their fitness. A randomly chosen point in each of the two derivation trees is chosen, subject to the constraint that each sub-tree can be adjoined to the other parent tree. If this point can be found, the exchange of the two sub-trees is then undertaken; otherwise the two individuals are discarded. This process is repeated until a valid crossover point is found or a bound is exceeded.

In sub-tree mutation, a point in the derivation tree is chosen at random, then the sub-tree rooted at that point is replaced by a newly generated sub-derivation tree.

Two further constraints may optionally be imposed on the operators. Adjunction context preservation requires the adjunction addresses of the replacing sub-trees to be the same as the adjunction addresses of the replaced sub-trees. Due to the feasibility property, it is simple to implement fair-size operators: the randomly generated sub-tree in mutation, or the sub-tree from the other parent in crossover, must have size within a pre-specified tolerance of the size of the original sub-tree.

4 An Example of TAG3P+ with Language Bias

In this section, we show how TAG3P+ can be used to preserve context-sensitive language bias in the evolutionary process. Because of limited space, we restrict our discussion to preferential language bias, but the argument extends to exclusive bias. Unless we state otherwise, the word "bias" will refer to "preferential bias".

We use the 6-multiplexer problem, a standard Boolean function problem in GP [11]. A 6-multiplexer uses two address lines to output one of four data lines. The task is to learn this function from its 64 possible fitness cases.

Following [11], the non-terminals and terminals are {IF, AND, OR, NOT} and {a0,a1,d0,d1,d2,d3}, respectively. The corresponding CFG [22, page 51], is:

G={N={B}, T={a0, a1, d0, d1, d2, d3, d4, and, or, not, if}, P, {B}}, where the rule set P is defined as follows:

B →a0| a1| d0| d1| d2| d3. (lexical rules)
B →B and B| B or B | not B | if B B B (structure rules)

Applying the algorithm in [16], we obtain the LTAG G_{lex} that strongly lexicalizes G as follows. G_{lex}={N={B, TL}, T={a0, a1, d0, d1, d2, d3, and, or, not, if}, I, A}, where I ∪ A is depicted in Figure 2. TL is a lexicon (or category) that can be substituted by one lexeme in {a0, a1, d0, d1, d2, d3}.

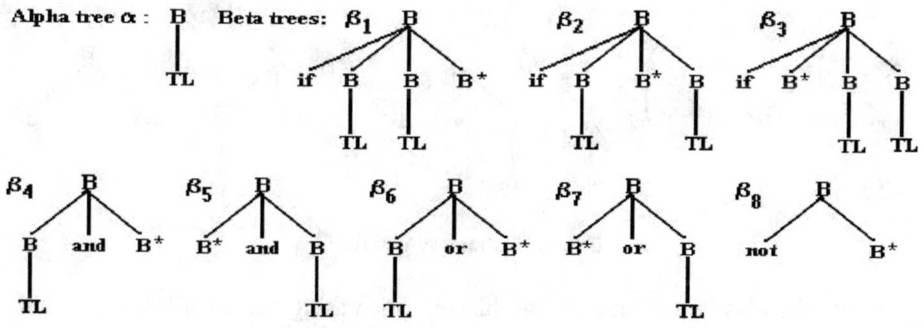

Fig. 2. Elementary trees for G_{lex}.

In [22], the bias was implemented by attaching a selection merit to each rule in the rule set of G, which acts as a probability for choosing which rule to re-write. In effect, the grammar G becomes a stochastic CFG.

In TAG3P+, the bias is implemented by using adjunction and substitution probabilities. The former – structure bias – is the probability of choosing a β tree to adjoin into a given tree. The latter – lexicon bias – is the likelihood of choosing a lexeme to substitute into a lexicon (category) positioned in an elementary tree.

We firstly examine the performance of TAG3P+ using the pairs of grammars G and G_{lex}, without any initial bias. Consequently, the probability distributions for adjunctions and substitutions are uniform. The parameter setting is as follows: Terminal operands are a0, a1, d0, d1, d2, d3; Terminal operators are and, or, if, not; 64 fitness cases of the 6-multipler; the raw fitness is the total number of hits; the standardized fitness is number of misses (= 64 – number of hits); tournament selection size is 3; sub-tree crossover (unfair and adjunction-context-preserving) and sub-tree mutation (fair with a tolerance of 5 and adjunction-context-preserving); ramped Initialization; MIN_SIZE is 2; MAX_SIZE is 40; POP_SIZE is 500; MAX_GEN is 50; crossover probability is 0.9; mutation probability is 0.1.

50 independent runs (**UB**) were conducted, 23 of them (46%) succeeded in finding perfect solutions. The proportion of success in GP [11, page 195] and GGGP [22, page 54] with similar setting were 28% and 34%, respectively. In the next three experiments, we show how to improve the performance of TAG3P+ with lexical bias.

Each elementary tree in Figure 2 has only one lexicon (category) for substitution, so there is no obvious advantage for TAG over CFG in implementing lexical bias. Once we allow different lexicons the lexicons used for substitutions might be context-sensitive. For the 6-multiplexer we know that there are two main categories of terminals: data and addresses. Can this information provide a useful bias to the learner? An LTAG G_{lex2} equivalent to G_{lex1} is defined; G_{lex2} is the same as G_{lex1} but has three additional lexicons T1, T2 and T3. Each can be substituted by any lexeme in {a0, a1, d0, d1, d2, d3}. The elementary trees for G_{lex2} are given in Figure 3.

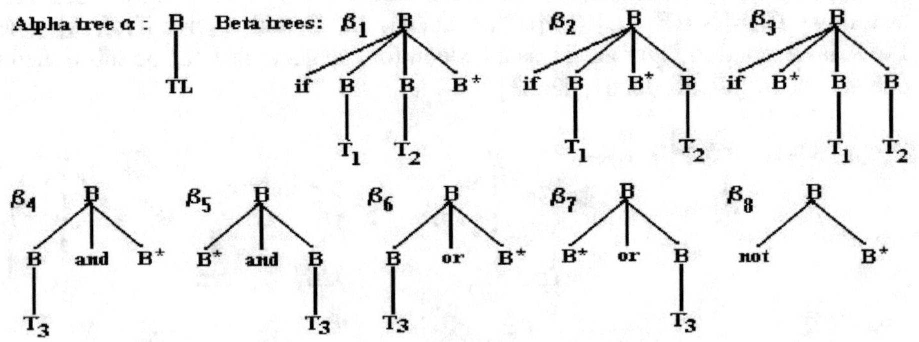

Fig. 3. Elementary tree for G_{lex2}.

A lexicon bias is implemented by biasing (increasing the substitution probability) T1 and T2 towards the address (a0-a1) and data (d0-d3) lines respectively.

Note that GGGP cannot represent this bias because CFGs cannot handle context-sensitive information (the location–dependent probabilities). TAGs can represent these probabilities and handle the context-sensitive information and categories.

For example, consider the elementary tree β_1 in Figure 3 (also Figure 4-left). To construct a similar structure with β_1 in CFG G, it requires three separate rewriting steps. In Figure 4, we use B---B to stress that there are two different and independent Bs in re-writing steps in the CFG G. Since these two Bs use the same re-writing probability distribution for symbol B (as in stochastic context-free grammars), it is impossible for the two Bs to have different and location-dependent probabilities. Moreover, not all context-free grammars are lexicalized, and it is not always possible to strongly lexicalize a CFG by a CFG [16], so that lexical bias cannot be imposed in GGGP using CFGs. In addition, since CFGs are not lexicalized, biasing the selection towards particular re-writing rules can result in unexpected side effects. For instance, in [22, page 55] Whigham set a bias towards the if structure, by setting the probability of the rule B→ if B B B four times higher than other rules. While this means the IF structure will appear more frequently, the non-lexicalization of the rule creates a side effect of generating bushier derivation trees (not the aim of the bias).

The lexical bias may be useful in applications where we know that solutions must have particular types of lexicons. The question then becomes, how to bias these lexi-

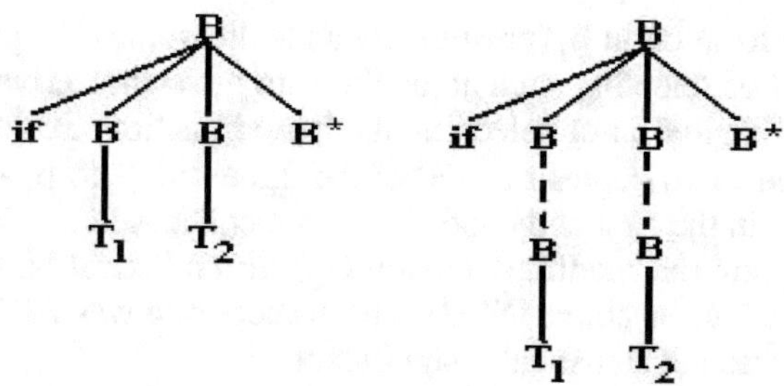

Fig. 4. An elementary tree in G_{lex2} (left) and re-writing steps in the corresponding CFG G.

cons towards the appropriate lexemes. For the 6-multiplexer problem, we experimented with TAG3P+ using G_{lex2} and three different strengths of lexical bias. In separate experiments, we biased T_1 to be substituted by address lines a0, a1, and T_2 to be substituted by data lines d0-d3 to 2, 4, and 8 times higher than the other lexemes. T_3 was uniformly likely to be substituted by either address or data lines (Table 1-3).

Table 1. Substitution likelihood for lexical bias with strength 2 (**B2**).

Lexicon/lexemes	A0	a1	d0	d1	d2	d3
T_1	4	4	1	1	1	1
T_2	1	1	1	1	1	1
T_3	2	2	1	1	1	1

Table 2. Substitution likelihood for lexical bias with strength 4 (**B4**).

Lexicon/lexemes	a0	a1	d0	d1	d2	d3
T_1	8	8	1	1	1	1
T_2	1	1	2	2	2	2
T_3	2	2	1	1	1	1

Table 3. Substitution likelihood for lexical bias with strength 8 (**B8**).

Lexicon/lexemes	a0	a1	d0	d1	d2	d3
T_1	16	16	1	1	1	1
T_2	1	1	4	4	4	4
T_3	2	2	1	1	1	1

Each set of three experiments was run 50 times using TAG3P+. The proportion of success was 62%, 72%, and 74% for **B2**, **B4**, and **B8** respectively. All results were statistically significantly different from unbiased TAG3P (α=0.05). Further increases in the bias did not improve the performance.

Although the lexical bias can alter the likelihood of particular lexemes being substituted into particular lexicons within an elementary tree, it does not guarantee to maintain this after adjunctions of elementary trees, because substitution happens only within the elementary tree level. To prevent the bias from being destroyed by adjunction, structure bias (adjunction bias) is needed. It operates on the interaction between elementary trees by biasing the likelihood of one tree to adjoin to another.

In the 6-multiplexer problem above, if β_3 in Figure 3 is adjoined into address B (which is connected to T2), the biased lexeme for T_2 (presumably a data line) may be placed in a wrong location in β_3 (presumably an address line). To prevent this happening, the likelihood of selecting such adjunctions to grow the derivation trees in G_{lex2} is set at 10% of the likelihood of selecting another adjunction. To fully implement this initial structure bias, two copies of each of the three sets β_4 to β_8 were created and T_3 was renamed to T_1 in the first copy and T_2 in the second. Another 50 independent runs were conducted using the modified version G_{lex2} with a lexical bias strength of 8 plus the initial structure bias as above (**SLB**). The success rate was 78%. Compared to **B8**, the improvement was not statistically significant.

In trying to understand why the impact of a lexical and structure bias was less than expected, we found that crossover occasionally destroyed this bias. In the final experiment (**FB**), we used a biased crossover (search bias) to preserve the trend of the lexical and structure biases. Here, whenever two points are chosen for crossing-over, we calculate the joint probability for adjunctions at the two corresponding addresses. If this probability decreases after crossing over (i.e. we are moving from more likely adjunctions to less likely adjunctions), we use a low crossover probability of 10%. We conducted 50 more independent runs with TAG3P+, using lexical bias strength 8 plus initial structure bias plus bias-preserving crossover. The proportion of success was 88%. This improvement over **B8** is statistically significant (α=0.05). The cumulative frequency of success for all 6 experiments is given in Figure 5.

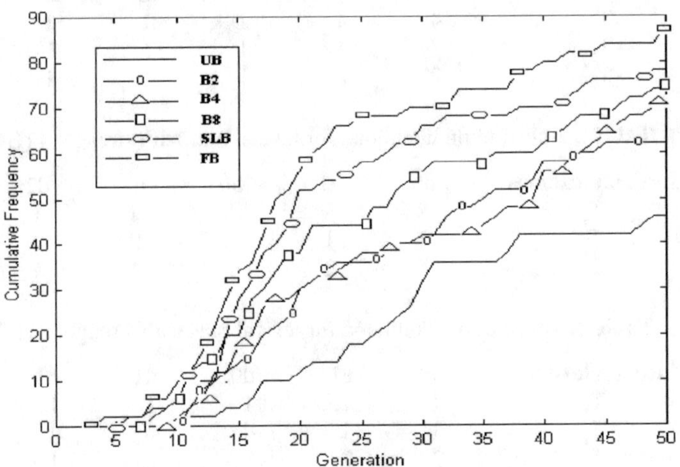

Fig. 5. The cumulative frequencies of success in 6 experiments.

As with lexical bias, GGGP using CFGs cannot implement structure bias because a structure bias needs to consider the inter-relation between different elementary trees in LTAG: it involves several rewriting steps in the corresponding CFG. It is impossible for CFGs to represent this context-sensitive information. The lexical and structure biases used here are declarative biases; the crossover bias is procedural.

5 Conclusions and Future Work

We have proposed a new GGGP system, TAG3P+, using tree-adjoining grammars. By experiments on a standard GP problem, we showed that TAG permits context-sensitive language bias on the lexicon and structure levels that cannot be specified in CFG-based GGGP.

Although we considered preferential bias in this paper, the same arguments hold for exclusive biases, viewed as a limiting case in which some probabilities are set to zero.

In this paper, we assumed the correctness of the biases provided by the user. Currently, we are studying mechanisms to help TAG3P+ to automatically shift biases. We are also investigating a more general bias-preserving crossover using probabilistic models for adjunctions. Lastly, we are also investigating bio-inspired operators within TAG3P+ such as transposition, translocation and replication, which can be implemented thanks to the feasibility feature of TAGs.

References

1. Banzhaf W., Nordin P., Keller R.E., and Francone F.D.: *Genetic Programming: An Introduction*. Morgan Kaufmann Pub (1998).
2. Candito M. H. and Kahane S.: Can the TAG Derivation Tree Represent a Semantic Graph? An Answer in the Light of Meaning-Text Theory. In: *Proceedings of TAG+4*, Philadelphia, (1999) 25-28.
3. Cohen, W. W.: Grammatically Biased Learning: Learning Logic Programs Using an Explicit Antecedent Description Language. *Technical Report*, AT and Bell Laboratories, Murray Hill, NJ, (1993).
4. Gruau F.: On Using Syntactic Constraints with Genetic Programming. In: *Advances in Genetic Programming* II, The MIT Press, (1996) 377-394.
5. Geyer-Schulz A.: Fuzzy Rule-Based Expert Systems and Genetic Machine Learning. Physica-Verlag, Germany, (1995).
6. Hoai N. X.: Solving the Symbolic Regression Problem with Tree Adjunct Grammar Guided Genetic Programming: The Preliminary Result. In: the *Proceedings of 5th Australasia-Japan Workshop in Evolutionary and Intelligent Systems*, (2001) 52-61.
7. Hoai N. X., Mac Kay R. I., and Essam D.: Solving the Symbolic Regression Problem with Tree Adjunct Grammar Guided Genetic Programming. *Australian Journal of Intelligent Information Processing Systems*, 7(3), (2002) 114-121.
8. Hoai N.X., Y. Shan, and R. I. MacKay: Is Ambiguity is Useful or Problematic for Genetic Programming? A Case Study. To appear in: The Proceedings of 4th Asia-Pacific Conference on Evolutionary Computation and Simulated Learning (SEAL'02), (2002).
9. Joshi, A. K. and Schabes, Y.: Tree Adjoining Grammars. In: *Handbook of Formal Languages*, Rozenberg G. and Saloma A. (eds) Springer-Verlag, (1997) 69-123.
10. Joshi, A. K.. Levy, L. S., and Takahashi, M.: Tree Adjunct Grammars. *Journal of Computer and System Sciences*, 10 (1), (1975) 136-163.
11. Koza, J. : *Genetic Programming*, The MIT Press (1992).
12. Koza, J. : *Genetic Programming* II, The MIT Press (1994).
13. Mitchell T. M.: *Machine Learning*. McGraw-Hill, (1997).
14. Micthell T. M., Utgoff P., and BanerJi R.: Learning by Experimentation: Acquiring and Refining Problem-Solving Heuristics. In: *Machine Learning: An Artificial Intelligence Approach*. Springer-Verlag, (1984) 163-190.
15. O'Neil M. and Ryan C.: Grammatical Evolution. *IEEE Trans on Evolutionary Computation*, 4 (4), (2000) 349-357.
16. Schabes Y.: *Mathemantical and Computational Aspects of Lexicalized Grammars*, Ph.D. Thesis, University of Pennsylvania, USA, (1990).
17. Shanker V.: *A Study of Tree Adjoining Grammars*. PhD. Thesis, University of Pennsylvania, USA, 1987.

18. Utgoff P.: *Machine Learning of Inductive Bias*. Kluwer Academic Publisher, (1986).
19. Weir D. J.: *Characterizing Mildly Context-Sensitive Grammar Formalisms.* PhD. Thesis, University of Pennsylvania, USA, 1988.
20. Valiant L.: A Theory of the Learnable. *ACM*, 27(11), (1984) 1134-1142.
21. Whigham P. A.: Search Bias, Language Bias and Genetic Programming. In: *Genetic Programming* 1996, The MIT Press, USA, (1996) 230-237.
22. Whigham P. A.: *Grammatical Bias for Evolutionary Learning*. Ph.D Thesis, University of New South Wales, Australia, (1996).
23. Wolpert D. and Macready W.: No Free Lunch Theorems for Search. *Technical Report* SFI-TR-95-02-010, Santa Fem, NM, 87501.
24. Wong M. L. and Leung K. S.: Evolutionary Program Induction Directed by Logic Grammars. *Evolutionary Computation*, 5 (1997) 143-180.

Artificial Immune System Programming for Symbolic Regression

Colin G. Johnson

Computing Laboratory, University of Kent, Canterbury, Kent, CT2 7NF, England
C.G.Johnson@ukc.ac.uk

Abstract. *Artificial Immune Systems* are computational algorithms which take their inspiration from the way in which natural immune systems learn to respond to attacks on an organism. This paper discusses how such a system can be used as an alternative to genetic algorithms as a way of exploring program-space in a system similar to genetic programming. Some experimental results are given for a symbolic regression problem. The paper ends with a discussion of future directions for the use of artificial immune systems in program induction.

1 Introduction

One way to view genetic programming is that it is the combination of a *representation* of potential solutions and a *search algorithm* which looks through that solution-space in search of an effective solution to the problem at hand.

The early GP work of Koza [15,16], Cramer [4] and others uses a tree-based representation. In recent years several other representations have been created, for example *grammatical evolution* which uses a bitstring representation which is converted into a program by means of a grammar [18], and *cartesian GP* [17] where a graph of functions and connections is described in a linear chromosome. Several other representations have also been used.

However less interest has been payed to the use of alternative *search* strategies within a GP-like system. A small amount of work has been carried out on the use of simulated annealing rather than genetic algorithms as a search strategy [3,19,20], but there appears to be little work beyond this.

Biological systems have proven to be a powerful source of inspiration for the creation of new search algorithms [21]. In recent years algorithms inspired by the adaptive immune system have proven successful on a number of problems. This paper investigates the application of such learning algorithms to systems similar to genetic programming.

2 Artificial Immune Systems

Organisms such as humans need to resist *antigens* (harmful bacteria, viruses et cetera) in order to survive in the world. This resistance is achieved via a multi-layered *immune system*. Initially physical barriers prevent antigens from getting inside the body, then an *innate* immune system destroys antigens which

C. Ryan et al. (Eds.): EuroGP 2003, LNCS 2610, pp. 345–353, 2003.

present certain molecular certain patterns to the body, and finally an *adaptive* immune system destroys antigens which are recognized from previous attacks on the body and through a process of maturation where the immune system learns to distinguish between self and non-self.

The learning systems by which organisms learn to identify antigens and distinguish between harmful, non-self cells and those cells which are part of the body or which live commensally within it can be abstracted and implemented as computational learning algorithms. Systems based on such techniques are known as *Artificial Immune Systems* (AIS) [7].

The natural application for such systems is clearly in computer security, and indeed such applications were amongst the earliest applications of AIS [9,13]. However the learning algorithms at the heart of AIS have proven to be applicable to a wide variety of problems, e.g. data mining, robot control, optimization, control, and scheduling. Surveys are given in [5,7].

At the core of any immune system is some kind of *pattern recognition*. In the natural immune system this is carried out by a molecular "lock and key" system. Molecules on the surface of antigens (*epitopes*) match up with molecules known as *antibodies* which are found on the surface of *lymphocytes* which are the main cells in the immune system. This recognition then triggers a stream of chemical signals which trigger other components of the immune system to destroy the antigen.

A number of learning and memory mechanisms are important within the immune system. One mechanism is *clonal selection*, which combines the matching system above with a hypermutation mechanism to discover antibodies which accurately match antigens. This both allows rapid learning at the infection site and provides some basic material to feed into immune memories. This mechanism is applied below (section 3) and is described in more detail there.

Another learning mechanism which is important in the immune system is distinguishing between *self* (i.e. the cells in the body) and *non-self* (i.e. cells which are invading the body). This distinction is important for avoiding auto-immune reactions. One important mechanism for this is *negative selection* [2]. Once lymphocytes have been generated they go through a process of *maturation* in the protected environment of the thymus gland. Within the thymus lymphocytes are presented to a variety of self-cells, and those which match are eliminated. As a result the mature cells which are finally released into the main immune system from the thymus are capable of identifying non-self.

Another computationally important aspect of the immune system is *immunological memory*, where the immune system "remembers" previous infections and can therefore attack reinfections or related infections quicker than unknown infections.

There are two main reasons why we may be interested in the application of AIS in GP-like systems. Firstly the search algorithm may work more efficiently than the GA-like algorithms traditionally used, or find more accurate solutions. Secondly there may be additional features of the immune-inspired algorithms which expand the scope of the GP system.

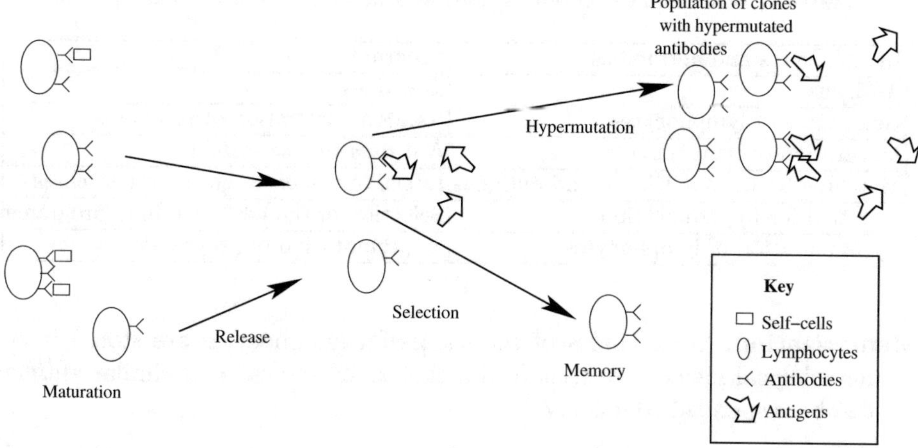

Fig. 1. A summary of clonal selection (after [7]).

3 A Clonal Selection Algorithm

This section describes the application of a simple AIS-based system to a GP-like problem. This is based on the *clonal selection* concept. The AIS algorithm used is similar to the CLONALG algorithm by DeCastro et al. [6,8]. The basic idea of clonal selection is summarized in figure 1.

The core function of the clonal selection process is to create lymphocytes which are able to recognize antigens whilst not attacking self cells. There are a number of key stages in this.

Generation. The antibodies on the lymphocyte surface are generated via a process of gene assortment which assembles a random fragment of gene segments drawn from a *gene library* and expresses the protein defined by the resultant DNA sequence.

Maturation. The lymphocytes undergo a process such as *negative selection* which removes those which react against self-cells.

Release. The lymphocytes are released into the body (via the lymphatic system) and diffuse around the body.

Selection. If an antigen invades the body the antibodies on the surface of the lymphocytes will attempt to match against the epitopes on the surface of the antigens. Those which match (within a certain tolerance) will continue to the next two stages (in parallel).

Hypermutation. The lymphocytes which match will undergo a hypermutation process whereby many copies are generated with random changes in the lymphocytes. Some of these may match the antigens better than the originals. There is some degree of cycling between this stage and the previous stage as successful products of one hypermutation stage are themselves copied and hypermutated.

Table 1. How clonal selection is used as a metaphor in a GP-like system.

Lymphocytes and antibodies	Programs
Antigens	Test data
Generation of lymphocytes	Random generation of programs
Maturation of lymphocytes	*Not used in this system*
Matching between antibody and antigens	Effectiveness of program on test cases
Selection for hypermutation	Selection of the best-matching programs
Hypermutation of lymphocytes	Hypermutation of programs

Memorization. Some copies of the successful lymphocytes are stored in immunological memory so that future attacks by the same or similar antigens can be responded to quickly.

This can be abstracted into a *clonal selection algorithm*. In the context of a GP-like system the various components of the problem are translated into the immune metaphor using the scheme given in table 1.

Here is the pseudocode for the algorithm:

```
Generate a set of test data
Generate a random population of lymphocytes
LOOP: Loop a fixed number of timesteps
   Calculate a match between each lymphocyte in the population
      and the test data
   Select the strongest nth of the lymphocytes for hypermutation
   LOOP: through the selected lymphocytes
      Make popSize/n copies of the lymphocyte
      First copy: Replace in the population
      Remaining copies: Apply hypermutation then
         place in the population
   END OF LOOP
END OF LOOP
```

where n is a parameter which controls the proportion of lymphocytes which are selected to form the basis of the next population.

There are similarities between this algorithm and a standard genetic algorithm. Perhaps the most important reason for placing this work in this framework is that it suggests new directions for future work. Asserting that something "is" a genetic algorithm suggests certain ways in which it might be developed; suggesting that it "is" an AIS provokes different avenues for development. The process of reframing existing algorithms in terms of alternative forms of inspiration could be argued to be a valuable activity because of this.

4 Applying the Algorithm to Symbolic Regression

The above algorithm has been applied to a simple symbolic regression problem (after the problems in [15]).

The programs are represented as lisp parse-trees in the standard manner given in [15]. The function set is $+$, $-$, $\times$, $\div$ (protected for divide by zero), EXP, RLOG (defined in [15]), COS, SIN. The only terminal is a single real variable x, defined on $[-1.0, 1.0]$.

The problem being used in the test below is to find a function to match $x^4 + x^3 + x^2 + x$ on the interval $[-1.0, 1.0]$. The test cases are 100 data points generated randomly in this interval. The match between the lymphocyte and test data is defined as

$$\max\left(0.0, 250.0 - \sum_{\text{test cases}} |f_t(x) - f_p(x)|\right)$$

where f_t is the true function defined on the test data, and f_p is the value of the function given by the program at that point. This turns the error into something which can be used by a maximization procedure.

The initial population is calculated via a standard ramped half-and-half procedure. During each round of the algorithm the top 20% of the population is chosen for hypermutation; one copy of the program is retained and four mutated copies are made and returned to the population. The population size is 1000.

The hypermutation stage is carried out as follows. A random node in the program-tree is chosen and replaced by a randomly generated tree. This new tree is generated by the grow method, and the maximum depth is equal to the depth of the current tree at that position +1 (the +1 is to allow the trees to grow in depth; otherwise the trees are fixed with a depth at most their initial depth). This has similarities with *headless chicken crossover* [1,12,23].

A comparison of the effectiveness of the two search algorithms is given in figures 2 and 3. This gives comparisons between the AIS-based algorithm described above with a standard GP system (similar to the system used for the standard experiments in [15], except that elitism is used). The graphs show the mean results over 20 rounds. The AIS algorithm typically converges to a good solution quicker than the standard GP algorithm. Both algorithms find perfect solutions around half the time (AIS 9/20 trials, GP 12/20 trials). Figure 4 shows the size of trees evolved (where size is measured by counting nodes), both as a per-generation average and as an average of the sizes of the best-performing individuals.

5 Future Work

Clearly the application of these ideas to other test problems is the most immediate piece of future work.

The *immune memory* concept has potential for application in this area. In the natural immune system a proportion of the lymphocytes generated by the hypermutation/selection stages of the algorithm are not used to match with antigens, but are instead added to an immune memory structure. One of the

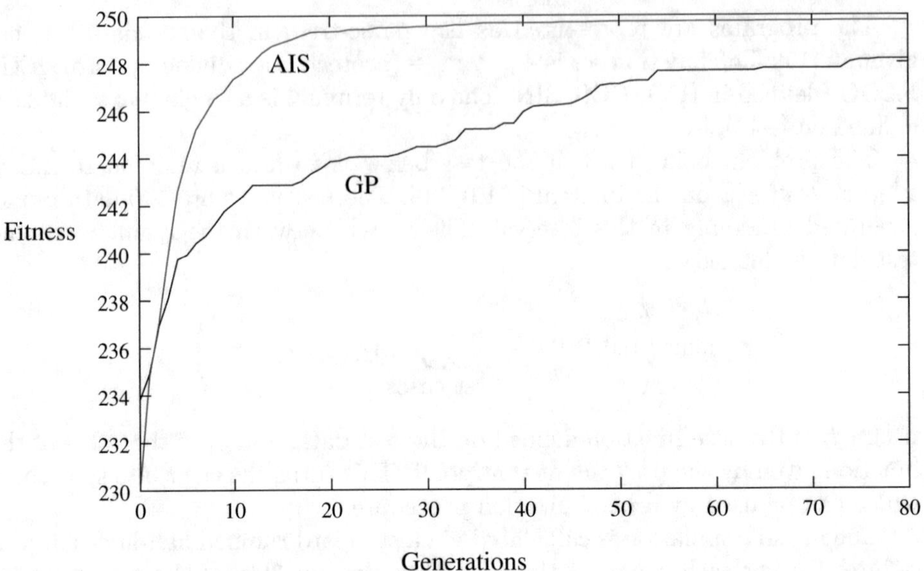

Fig. 2. Comparative fitness curves for AIS and standard GP search algorithms. Best fitness achieved in each generation.

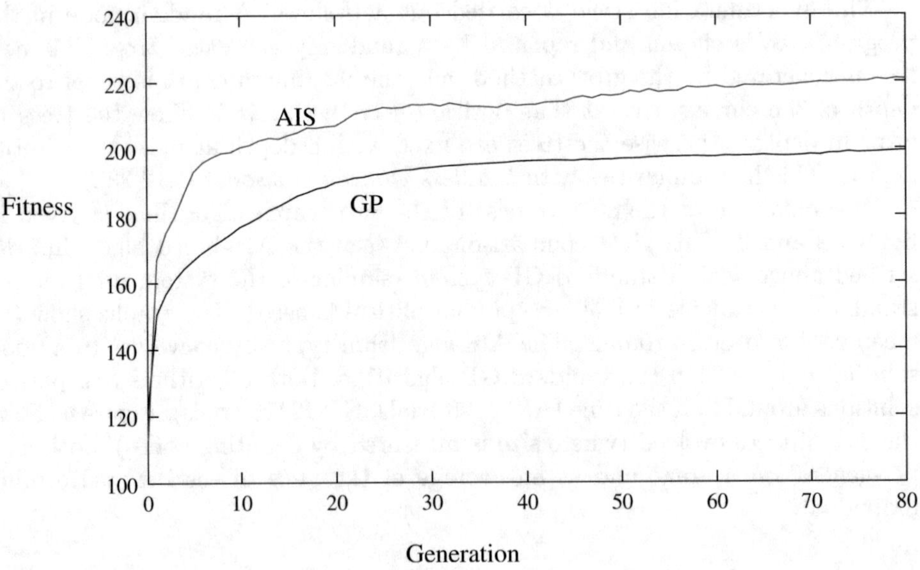

Fig. 3. Comparative fitness curves for AIS and standard GP search algorithms. Average fitness achieved in each generation. Mean over 20 runs.

most interesting areas of immunology is concerned with this memory structure, because the immune system can maintain a memory of which lymphocytes have been effective for many years, many times the lifespan of a single lymphocyte. A number of theories exist to explain this, one of which is the *idiotypic network*

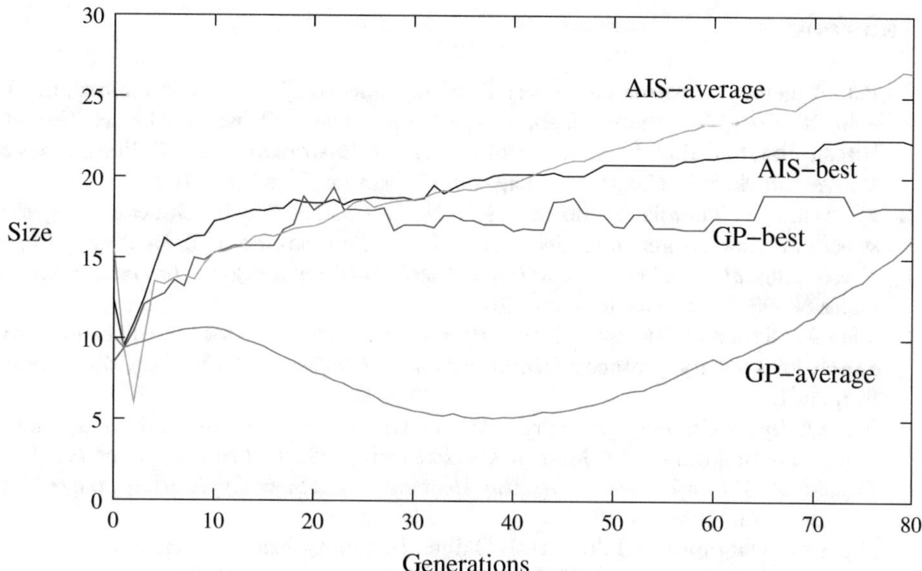

Fig. 4. Comparative tree size for AIS and GP search algorithms.

theory of Jerne [11], which suggests that immune memory is maintained by chains of mutually-stimulating lymphocytes, which select matching replacements for gaps in the network as lymphocytes decay. This theory has proved to be an powerful model in AIS applications [14].

Such memory concepts have potential for being applied to program induction by the accumulation of knowledge about a related set of problems. Instead of each new problem being tackled by a randomly-generated set of lymphocytes, some of the lymphocytes are taken from a memory-network which contains lymphocytes from successful related problems.

Another important mechanism is the evolution of the *gene libraries* from which lymphocytes are created in the first place. In recent work on the application of AIS in scheduling systems, Hart and Ross [10] discuss the learning of libraries of antibody patterns which match sub-schedules in a number of different scheduling problems. This is used to build up a repertoire of “useful patterns” for solving a certain class of scheduling problems.

A final idea is to exploit the way in which the immune system works in a distributed fashion. Real lymphocytes do not always recognize whole antigens at once; different antibodies will recognize different epitopes on the surface of a single antigen, so several lymphocytes may attack a single antigen. Can this be exploited to produce a system where several coordinated mini-programs tackle different aspects of a large problem?

Acknowledgements

Many thanks to Jon Timmis for many discussions on Artificial Immune Systems.

References

1. P.J. Angeline. Subtree crossover: Building block engine or macromutation? In John R. Koza, Kalyanmoy Deb, Marco Dorigo, David B. Fogel, Max H. Garzon, Hitoshi Iba, and Rick L. Riolo, editors, *Genetic Programming 1997: Proceedings of the Second Annual Conference*, pages 9–17. Morgan Kaufman, 1997.
2. M. Ayara, J. Timmis, R. de Lemos, L.N. de Castro, and R. Duncan. Negative selection: How to generate detectors. In J. Timmis and P.J. Bentley, editors, *Proceedings of the First International Conference on Artificial Immune Systems*, pages 89–98. University of Kent, 2002.
3. John A. Clark and Jeremy L. Jacob. Protocols are programs too: the meta-heuristic search for security protocols. *Information and Software Technology*, 43(14):891–904, 2001.
4. Nichael Lynn Cramer. A representation for the adaptive generation of simple sequential programs. In John J. Greffenstette, editor, *Proceedings of the First International Conference on Genetic Algorithms and their Applications*, pages 183–187. Erlbaum, 1985.
5. Dipankar Dasgupta and Nii Attoh-Okine. Immunity-based systems: a survey. In *Proceedings of the 1997 IEEE International Conference on Systems, Man and Cybernetics.* IEEE Press, 1997.
6. Leandro N. de Castro and Jon Timmis. An artificial immune network for multimodal function optimization. In *Proceedings of the 2002 Congress on Evolutionary Computation*, pages 699–704. IEEE Press, 2002.
7. Leandro N. de Castro and Jon Timmis. *Artificial Immune Systems: A New Computational Intelligence Approach.* Springer, 2002.
8. L.N. de Castro and F.J. Von Zuben. Learning and optimization using the clonal selection principle. *IEEE Transactions on Evolutionary Comptuation*, 6(3):239–251, 2002.
9. Patrik D'haeseleer, Stephanie Forrest, and Paul Helman. An immunological approach to change detection: Algorithms, analysis and implications. In *IEEE Symposium on Security and Privacy.* IEEE Press, 1996.
10. Emma Hart and Peter Ross. The evolution and analysis of a potential antibody library for use in job-shop scheduling. In David Corne, Marco Dorigo, and Fred Glover, editors, *New Ideas in Optimization*, pages 185–202. McGraw-Hill, 1999.
11. Niels K. Jerne. Towards a network theory of the immune system. *Annals of Immunology (Institute Pasteur)*, 125C:373–389, 1974.
12. Terry Jones. Crossover, macromutation and population-based search. In L. Eshelman, editor, *Proceedings of the Sixth International Conference on Genetic Algorithms*, pages 73–80. Morgan Kaufmann, 1995.
13. J.O. Kephart, G.B. Sorkin, and M. Swimmer. An immune system for cyberspace. In *Proceedings of the 1999 IEEE International Conference on Systems, Man and Cybernetics*, pages 879–884, 1997.
14. T. Knight and J. Timmis. AINE: An immunological approach to data mining. In N. Cencone, T. Lin, and X. Wu, editors, *Proceedings of the 2001 IEEE International Conference on Data Mining*, pages 297–304. IEEE Press, 2001.
15. John R. Koza. *Genetic Programming : On the Programming of Computers by means of Natural Selection.* Series in Complex Adaptive Systems. MIT Press, 1992.
16. John R. Koza. *Genetic Programming II.* Series in Complex Adaptive Systems. MIT Press, 1994.

17. Julian F. Miller and Peter Thomson. Cartesian genetic programming. In Poli et al. [22], pages 121–132. LNCS 1802.
18. Michael O'Neill and Conor Ryan. Grammatical evolution. *IEEE Transactions on Evolutionary Computation*, 5(4):349–358, August 2001.
19. Una-May O'Reilly and Franz Oppacher. Program search with a hierarchical variable length representation: Genetic programming, simulated annealing and hill climbing. In *Parallel Problem Solving from Nature III, Jerusalem*, pages 397–406. Springer, 1994.
20. John O'Sullivan and Conor Ryan. An investigation into the use of different search strategies with grammatical evolution. In Poli et al. [22], pages 268–277. LNCS 1802.
21. R.C. Paton, H.S. Nwana, M.J.R. Shave, and T.J.M. Bench-Capon. An examination of some metaphorical contexts for biologically motivated computing. *British Journal for the Philosophy of Science*, 45:505–525, 1994.
22. Riccardo Poli, Wolfgang Banzhaf, William B. Langdon, Julian Miller, Peter Nordin, and Terence C. Fogarty, editors. *Proceedings of the 2000 European Conference on Genetic Programming.* Springer, 2000. LNCS 1802.
23. Riccardo Poli and Nicholas Freitag McPhee. Exact GP schema theory for headless chicken crossover and subtree mutation. In *Proceedings of the 2001 Congress on Evolutionary Computation.* IEEE Press, 2001.

Grammatical Evolution with Bidirectional Representation

Jiří Kubalík[1], Jan Koutník[2], and Léon J.M. Rothkrantz[3]

[1] Department of Cybernetics, CTU Prague, Technicka 2
166 27 Prague, Czech Republic
kubalik@labe.felk.cvut.cz

[2] Department of Computers, CTU Prague, Technicka 2
166 27 Prague, Czech Republic
koutnij@cs.felk.cvut.cz

[3] KBS Group, Department of Mediamatics, TU Delft
P.O. Box 356, 2600 AJ Delft, The Netherlands
L.J.M.Rothkrantz@its.tudelft.nl

Abstract. Grammatical evolution is an evolutionary algorithm designed to evolve programs in any language. Grammatical evolution operates on binary strings and the mapping of the genotype onto the phenotype (the tree representation of the programs) is provided through the grammar described in the form of production rules. The program trees are constructed in a pre-order fashion, which means that as the genome is traversed first the left most branch of the tree is completed then the second from the left one etc. Once two individuals are crossed over by means of simple one-point crossover the tail parts of the chromosomes (originally encoding the structures on the right side of the program tree) may map on different program structures within the new context. Here we present a *bidirectional representation* which helps to equalize the survival rate of both the program structures appearing on the left and right side of the program parse tree.

1 Introduction

Grammatical evolution (GE) is an evolutionary algorithm designed to evolve programs in any language, which can be described by a context free grammar [6], [9]. Unlike standard genetic programming (GP) [4], GE does not operate directly on the tree representation of the programs. It adopts an idea of phenotype-genotype encoding instead. The programs are represented as linear bit-string genomes and the correspondence between the phenotype and genotype is provided through the grammar described in the form of production rules.

The genotype is read piece by piece from left to right, generating integer values that are used to determine the production rules to be used. In standard GE the parse tree of the program is constructed in a depth-first manner, which means that as the genome is traversed first the left most branch of the phenotype is completed then the second from the left one etc. Once two individuals are crossed

C. Ryan et al. (Eds.): EuroGP 2003, LNCS 2610, pp. 354–363, 2003.

over by means of simple one-point crossover, the head parts of the chromosomes pass on the offspring with exactly the same meaning as they had in parents whilst the tail parts may map on different phenotype since their context changed. The consequence of this fact is that the "deeper" the program structures (partial solutions) are coded in the tail of the chromosome the less chance they will survive the crossover operation they have.

In this paper we present an enhancement of the standard GE that lies in so-called *bidirectional representation* which equalizes the survival rate of both the program structures appearing on the left and right side of the program parse tree. The paper starts with a brief description of GE. We focus on the aspect of the pre-order phenotype generation. Then the bidirectional representation is introduced and first experiments are presented. The paper concludes with discussion on the effect of the bidirectional representation.

2 Grammatical Evolution

GE is designed to evolve programs in any language, which can be described by a context free grammar. A commonly used notation for context free grammar is Backus Naur Form (BNF). BNF describes the grammar in the form of production rules that use terminals, which are the non-expandable items that are used in the language, i.e. +, − etc. and non-terminals, which can be expanded into one or more terminals and non-terminals. A grammar can be represented by the tuple $\{N, T, P, S\}$, where N is set of non-terminals, T is set of terminals, P is a set of production rules that maps the elements of N to $N \cup T$, and S is a start symbol, which is a member of N. As an example let us take the BNF below with $\{N, T, P, S\}$ defined as follows

$$N = \{expr, op, pre - op, var\}$$

$$T = \{+, -, *, /, sin, cos, exp, log, X\}$$

$$S = expr$$

P :

<expr> ::= *<expr> <op> <expr>*
| *<pre-op> <expr>*
| *<var>*

<op> ::= +
| −
| *
| /

<pre-op> ::= *sin*
| *cos*
| *exp*
| *log*

<var> ::= *X*

The key to success and efficiency of GE lies in the method for generating and preservation of valid programs. GE does not work with a natural tree representation of the programs; instead it runs the evolution on binary strings. The genotype-phenotype mapping works so that the binary string is translated into a sequence of integers, called codons, each specifying the number of the production rule to be applied for currently expanded non-terminal. Thus the sequence of codons determines a sequence of choices to be made in the process of derivation of the program.

As the codon's value is typically larger than the number of available rules for the expanded non-terminal (codons are usually coded using 8 bits), the modulo of the codon's value to the number of rules is taken as the final rule choice:

$$choice = codon\ MOD\ number\_of\_rules$$

As a consequence of the use of the rule we can observe that multiple codon values can select the same rule. The role of such a redundancy in genetic code was studied in [5] and it turned out to be useful for proper functioning of GE.

Note it is possible for an individual to have more codons than needed for generating the complete program. In such a case the left over codons can be deleted. It is also possible that all codons have been read, but the generated tree still contains non-terminals to be expanded. If this happens the technique called wrapping can be used, which consists in the repeated reuse of the individual's codons. Obviously, using the described mapping mechanism only syntactically correct programs can be generated from any binary string.

The evolutionary algorithm of GE itself is quite simple. Standard genetic operators for binary representation are employed in GE. Namely the one-point crossover, called the *ripple crossover* in the context of GE [3], exhibits very good characteristics in terms of the generative and explorative capabilities. It can use a duplication operator, which randomly selects a number of codons that are placed at the end of the chromosome. For more detailed description of GE we refer the reader to [6].

The mapping process finishes as all of the nonterminal symbols have been replaced by terminals. In standard GE the left-most nonterminal out of the nonterminals to be processed is selected for substitution. Thus the program tree is constructed in a pre-order fashion, which means that as the genome is traversed first the left most branch of the phenotype is completed then the second from the left one etc. This becomes an important issue when looking closer at how new programs are generated by crossover operation.

3 Information Loss during Crossover in GE

Likewise other evolutionary algorithms, e.g. genetic algorithms (GA) and GP, GE searches for the optimal solution through the process of identifying some promising parts of the solution (partial solutions, in GA and GP called building blocks, [1], [2], [8]), which are grouped together in bigger and bigger parts finally assembled in the optimal solution. In order to work so the algorithm should be able to sample those good partial solutions with higher frequency than the useless ones when choosing the material for creating the candidate solutions. It should further be ensured that those important parts have high chance not to be disrupted through a recombination operation. This is called the exploitation ability of the algorithm. On the other hand the algorithm must be resistant against early stagnation of the population, which requires the algorithm to have enough exploration ability to effectively sample the solution space. Thus the best performance of any evolutionary algorithm is achieved when the optimal trade-off between its exploitation and exploration is found. The major impact on the generative or explorative power of the algorithm has the recombination operator. In standard GP crossover operators based on the single sub-tree swapping are used usually. It turns out that such operators cannot provide a sufficient information exchange in later stages of the run. Simply because the trees are already too large, usually containing a lot of meaningless code so just a single sub-tree exchange is not very likely to bring much new.

In GE a simple one-point crossover is used. An application of the operator on the linear chromosomes results generally in, what is called a rippling effect in [3], multiple sub-tree exchange between the involved parental individuals. Briefly said, the head part of the chromosome, i.e. that one before the crossover point, of each parent constitutes a spine of the program tree expression while the tail part represents number of sub-trees removed from the original tree. The offspring are then completed so that vacated sites of the spine of one mate are filled by sub-trees removed from the other mate and vice versa, see [3]. Moreover, the head parts of the chromosomes pass on the offspring with exactly the same meaning as they had in parents whilst the tail parts may map on different phenotype. This may happen if the sub-tree is grafted onto a site that is expecting a different symbol than that in the root of the sub-tree. The consequence of such a context dependent codon's interpretation, called *intrinsic polymorphism* of GE [3], is that the likelihood of transfer of a sub-tree from the parent to the offspring with a constant interpretation changes with its position within the original tree. The "left-most and shallow" structures (partial solutions) are less likely to be changed than the "right-most and deep" ones coded in the tail of the chromosome.

From this point of view, the crossover operation in GE should not be seen as the information exchange between two solutions as usually observed in standard GA and GP. It is rather partial re-initialisation of one solution with the code taken from the other one (that is likely to be re-interpreted at the new place).

The effect of one-point crossover is schematically depicted in Fig. 1. On average, a half of the tree is changed during the crossover. The offspring is given half of the code from the first and half of the code from the second parent. The black and white parts of the parental trees go unchanged to the offspring while the grey parts represent the probably wasted information, the structures which are likely to change their interpretation.

Apparently the amount of information damaged in each application of the crossover has a severe impact on the performance of the whole algorithm. As the evolution goes on only the left-most sub-tree structures (represented by the

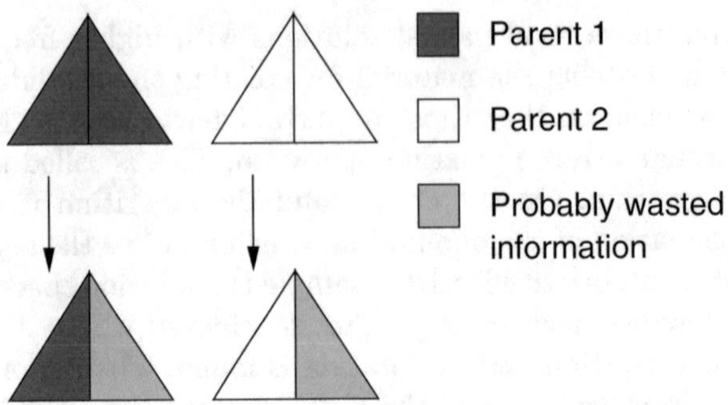

Fig. 1. One-point crossover with prefix encoding only

head-parts of chromosomes) are easily propagated to the successive populations. The sub-trees which are deep and in the right part of the tree have reduced chance to survive to the next population. This effect would become even more pronounced when the tree representation has strictly defined placement of the solution traits within the tree. Then the shallow and left structures would be formed, correctly identified and proliferated in the population prior to the deep and right ones. Thus the exploration of the whole search space would be biased by those "first-coming" partial solutions. Instead of a parallel exploration of the solution space the algorithm would seek the optimal solution in a partially sequential way - step by step. Clearly the risk of such an evolution become trapped in some sub-optimal solution increases.

In order to remedy this problem of preferring certain parts of the tree to the others and possible discarding the information during the crossover operation we introduce an extension of the standard GE representation as described in the following section.

4 Bidirectional Representation

In standard GE the programs are generated from a linear chromosome in a pre-order fashion as described above. So the linear encoding can be considered as a prefix expression of the program. In the extended GE so called bidirectional representation of the programs is employed. Each particular solution is encoded by two *paired chromosomes*: one expresses the program parse tree in a prefix notation and the other one in a postfix notation.

Now, when a pair of parental individuals is chosen to generate the offspring the crossover is applied twice (*i*) on the pair of their prefix chromosomes and (*ii*) on the pair of their postfix chromosomes. This results in four new chromosomes - two of them describing a couple of new programs in the prefix notation and two of them describing another couple of new programs in the postfix notation.

Finally the paired chromosome, representing the same program in the opposite way, must be constructed for each newly created chromosome (i.e. the prefix chromosome for the postfix one and vice versa). This is done in order to keep the

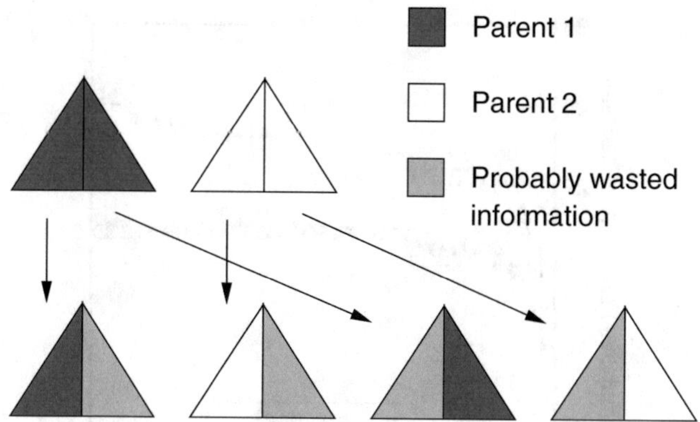

Fig. 2. One-point crossover with prefix and postfix encoding

prefix and postfix expressions for each individual consistent. However an issue arises as how to treat the newly generated under-specified individuals i.e. those with fewer codons in the chromosome than needed for complete generation of the program. In the current version a wrapping operator is invoked in such a way that the reused codons are appended at the end of the chromosome. Thus the paired chromosome describing the same tree must have the same number of codons.

The schema of the crossover performed on the enhanced representation is shown in Fig. 2. It illustrates the idea that using the bidirectional representation should better balance the exploitation of the information of the head and tail structures of the parental trees and so to reduce the losses of the information encoded in the tails of the "one-directional" chromosomes in original GE.

5 Setup of the Experiments

In order to test effect of the bidirectional representation in GE the concept was tested and compared to the standard GE. We have carried out series of experiments on the problem of symbolic regression as the test problem commonly used by the GP and GE community for evaluating the algorithms. We have used the following two target functions $X^4 + X^3 + X^2 + X$ and $X^5 - 2X^3 + X$. For both the fitness cases were taken from the interval [-1, 1]; 20 cases for the former function and 50 cases for the later one. Fifty runs were carried out with each algorithm on both problems. Both the standard GE and the bidirectional GE used the grammar from Sect. 2 and the configuration as follows:

- Raw fitness: the sum of the error taken over 20 respectively 50 fitness cases,
- Hits: the number of fitness cases for which the error is less than 0.01,
- *Populationsize*: 500,
- *Generations*: 200,
- *pmut*: 0.01,
- *pcross*: 1.0.

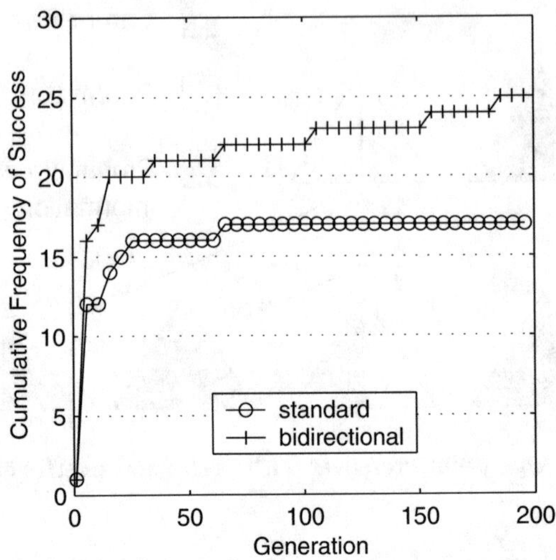

Fig. 3. Cumulative frequency of success obtained with standard GE and GE with bidirectional representation on $X^4 + X^3 + X^2 + X$

A commonly used condition under which different evolutionary algorithms are compared is the same number of fitness function evaluations. Note that in GE with bidirectional representation each crossover generates four new individuals instead of two as in standard GE. For the sake of simplicity a generational replacement strategy was used in the experiments where one generation means a replacement of a population by the completely new one. So the number of crossover operations needed for generating of the new population in bidirectional GE is of one half of the number of crossovers in standard GE while the number of performed evaluations is equal.

6 Results

First experiments clearly demonstrate the effect of bidirectional representation in GE. Figures 3 and 4 show a significant improvement in cumulative frequency of success obtained with bidirectional GE, which outperforms the standard GE in ratio 25/17 on the problem $X^4 + X^3 + X^2 + X$ and 12/4 on $X^5 - 2X^3 + X$. Steep beginnings of the plots in Fig. 3 may seem a bit surprising as there are quite some successes encountered already in $4^{th} - 5^{th}$ generation. This might be caused by rather robust initialization of the first population where the chromosomes up to 100-codon length are generated. Nevertheless, the difference in the explorative or generative power of the two approaches is distinct. Bidirectional GE exhibits a continuous progress in improving of the cumulative frequency of success whilst the standard GE does not yield anything new after $60^{th} - 70^{th}$ generation.

An interesting observation is that considering the formulas found by the GE. While on the first test problem the success formula almost always represented the target expression $X^4 + X^3 + X^2 + X$ on the later problem quite diverse

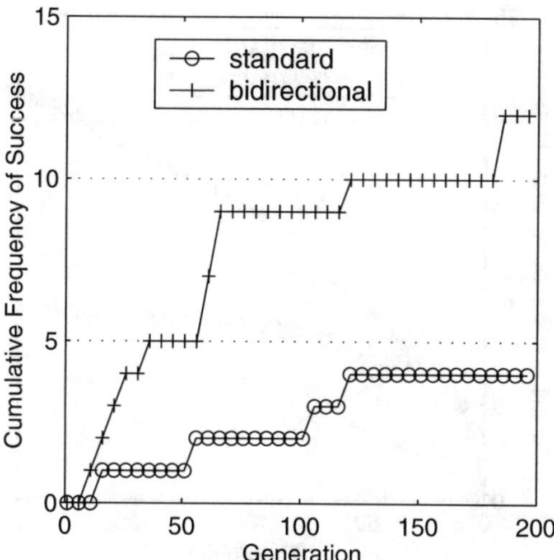

Fig. 4. Cumulative frequency of success obtained with standard GE and GE with bidirectional representation on $X^5 - 2X^3 + X$

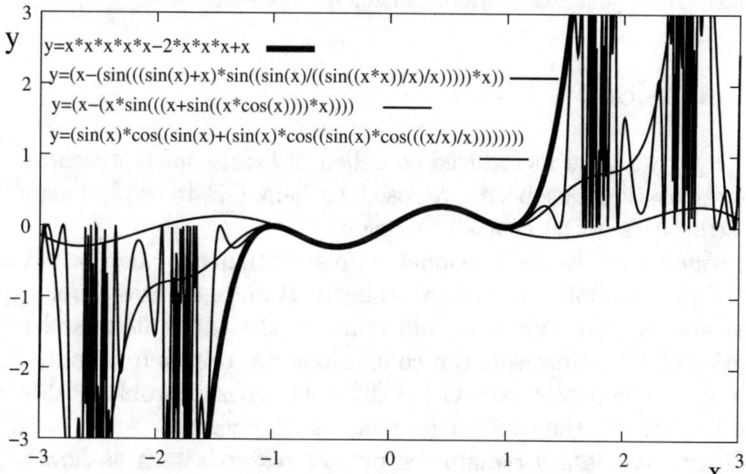

Fig. 5. Examples of functions that best approximate function $X^5 - 2X^3 + X$ within the interval [-1, 1] obtained with the GE with bidirectional representation

success formulas were produced. Some examples are given in Fig. 5. Note that all of them perfectly approximate the target function within the interval [-1, 1] while the error drastically grows up outside the interval.

The last figure shows cumulative numbers of improvements of the *best-so-far* observed between two successive populations. It illustrates the explorative power of bidirectional GE which exhibits sustained improvement of the *best-so-far* solution during the whole run.

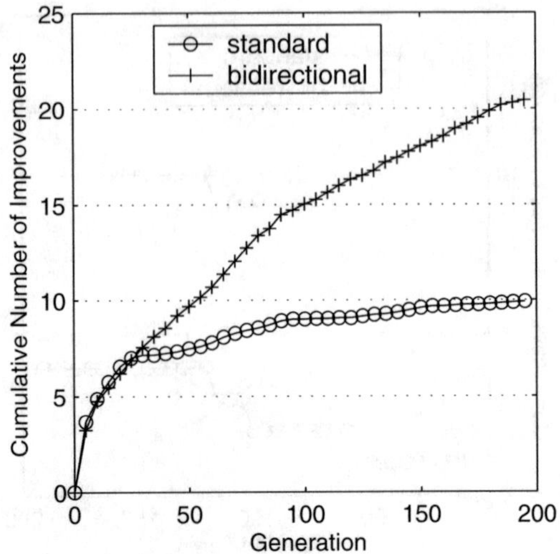

Fig. 6. Cumulative number of improvements of the *best-so-far* solution obtained with standard GE respectively GE with bidirectional representation on the problem $X^4 + X^3 + X^2 + X$. Only improvements observed between two successive populations are counted. Intra-generation improvements are not considered

7 Conclusions

In this paper we have introduced so-called *bidirectional representation* for GE. The representation has been proposed to help GE to exploit equally all the partial structures of the evolved programs.

The concept of the bidirectional representation has been tested on two instances of the symbolic regression problem. Results approved our expectations that the new representation should enhance the exploration and exploitation capabilities of GE. However, the conclusions are drawn from only two experiments in symbolic regressions. Other different types of problems should be tried in order to evaluate the concept to a satisfactory extent.

However some issues remain for further research such as how to treat the under-specified chromosome when building its equivalent paired chromosome. The version of the wrapping operator used in this work meet a requirement on consistent and equal paired chromosomes. On the other hand, this technique clearly causes the chromosomes to grow long leading likely to superfluous complex structures.

Acknowledgments

This research work is supported by the Grant Agency of the Czech Republic within the project No. 102/02/0132.

References

1. Angeline, P. J.: Subtree Crossover: Building Block Engine or Macromutation? Genctic Programming 1997: Proceedings of the Second Annual Conference, pp. 9-17, Morgan Kaufmann, 13-16 July 1997.
2. Goldberg D. E.: *Genetic Algorithms in Search, Optimization and Machine Learning.* Addison-Wesley, Reading, MA, 1989.
3. Keijzer M., Ryan C., O'Neill M., Cattolico M., and Babovic V.: Ripple Crossover in Genetic Programming. *Proceedings of EuroGP'2001*, LNCS, Vol. 2038, pp. 74-86, Springer-Verlag, 2001.
4. Koza, J.: *Genetic Programming.* MIT Press. 1992.
5. O'Neill, M., Ryan, C.: Genetic Code Degeneracy: Implications for Grammatical Evolution and Beyond, *Advances in Artificial Life*, LNAI, Vol. 1674, p. 149, Springer Verlag, 1999.
6. O'Neill, M., Ryan, C.: Grammatical Evolution. *IEEE Transactions on Evolutionary Computation*, Vol. 5 No.4, August 2001.
7. Poli, R., Langdon, W. B.: A Review of Theoretical and Experimental Results on Schemata in Genetic Programming, *Proceedings of the First European Workshop on Genetic Programming*, LNCS, Vol. 1391, pp. 1-15, Springer-Verlag, 14-15 April 1998.
8. Poli, R.: Hyperschema Theory for GP with One-Point Crossover Building Blocks, and Some New Results in GA Theory, Genetic Programming, *Proceedings of EuroGP'2000*, LNCS, Vol. 1802, pp. 163-180, Springer-Verlag, 15-16, 2000.
9. Ryan C., Collins J.J., O'Neill M.: Grammatical Evolution: Evolving Programs for an Arbitrary Language. *Proceedings of the First European Workshop on Genetic Programming* , LNCS 1391. pp. 83-95. 1998.

Introducing a Perl Genetic Programming System – and Can Meta-evolution Solve the Bloat Problem?

Robert M. MacCallum

Stockholm Bioinformatics Center, Stockholm University
106 91 Stockholm, Sweden
maccallr@sbc.su.se

Abstract. An open source Perl package for genetic programming, called PerlGP, is presented. The supplied algorithm is strongly typed tree-based GP with homologous crossover. User-defined grammars allow any valid Perl to be evolved, including object oriented code and parameters of the PerlGP system itself. Time trials indicate that PerlGP is around 10 times slower than a C based system on a numerical problem, but this is compensated by the speed and ease of implementing new problems, particularly string-based ones. The effect of per-node, fixed and self-adapting crossover and mutation rates on code growth and fitness is studied. On a pi estimation problem, self-adapting rates give both optimal and compact solutions. The source code and manual can be found at `http://perlgp.org`.

1 Introduction

Many packages for genetic programming (GP) are now freely available on the Internet. For example, the C package lilgp[10], the ECJ[5] Java system, and the Open BEAGLE framework[2] in C++. Many other languages are also represented but Perl is conspicuously absent, except for two proof-of-concept implementations [6,9] which are not intended for general use. Perl is seen by many as just a quick-and-dirty tool for hacking together web interfaces or backup scripts. It has its origins in these areas but is now a mature language, with modularisation and object orientation. Speed of execution is not Perl's strong point since it is (usually) interpreted, however when intensive numerical computation is needed, C-coded extensions often exist to take care of it (such as the PDL extension [http://pdl.perl.org]). Perl allows fast project development and prototyping and it has a number of built-in features which make it easy to implement tree-based GP. These include hash tables, powerful string manipulation and run-time evaluation. Here I introduce perhaps the first major open source GP system written in Perl, called PerlGP. This paper intends to give a full introduction to the system, explain some of the design decisions and show examples of use as part of some brief analyses of execution speed, bloat and meta-evolution.

C. Ryan et al. (Eds.): EuroGP 2003, LNCS 2610, pp. 364–373, 2003.

2 Implementation

The following sections describe how the PerlGP system is put together. Many features of the system are inspired from Nature or the literature. Unfortunately space limitations prevent proper attribution for all of them here.

2.1 Object-Oriented Design

There are three main object types: `Individual`, `Population` and `Algorithm`. The user provides the implementation for a few key methods (for example the fitness function, data input/output) in these classes and specifies the base classes from which they should inherit. The base classes, such as `TournamentGP` (`Algorithm`) and `GeneticProgram` (`Individual`) take care of the rest. Other search strategies and representations can be added to the package, and it should be trivial to swap them in and out as required using inheritance.

The `Individual` is the most important object, it *is* the genetic program. Each instance has a tree-represented genome and can convert it into Perl code for evaluation. The object also knows how to perform mutations, crossovers and saving to disk. `Population` is a container class for individuals, and does little except provide a method for picking random individuals, and methods for migration between populations, via disk. The `Algorithm` class is concerned with manipulating a population; selecting individuals, feeding them input data, collecting the output, and calculating fitnesses.

2.2 Tree-as-Hash-Table Genotype Representation

Hash tables, also known as associative arrays, can be hijacked to encode string-based tree structures as explained in Figure 1. The keys in the genome hash-tree follow the syntax: `nodeTYPExx`, where `TYPE` is replaced by an all-capitals string describing the type of the node (see Section 2.3), and `xx` is a unique identifier (for there may be many nodes of the same type).

2.3 Grammar Specification

PerlGP is a strongly typed system. In fact, all evolved code must be syntactically correct to be awarded fitness. When random individuals or subtrees are generated, PerlGP follows a grammar (defined by the user). The format of this grammar is analogous to the tree-as-hash encoding described above, and is explained in Figure 2.

2.4 Random Initialisation of Programs

A random tree is generated simply by starting with a new node of type `ROOT`, picking a random element from the array stored in `$F{ROOT}`, creating new nodes wherever `{TYPE}` is seen. This is illustrated in Figure 3.

```
$tree{nodeS0} = 'One day in {nodeS1}.';
$tree{nodeS1} = '{nodeS2} {nodeS3}';
$tree{nodeS2} = 'late';
$tree{nodeS3} = 'August';
$string = $tree{nodeS0};
do { print "$string\n" } while ($string =~ s/{(\w+)}/$tree{$1}/);

# outputs the following:
  One day in {nodeS1}.
  One day in {nodeS2} {nodeS3}.
  One day in late {nodeS3}.
  One day in late August.
```

Fig. 1. Tree-as-hash-table explanation. In Perl, the syntax `$one{two} = 'three'` means that in a hash table named 'one', the value 'three' is stored for the key 'two'. The iterated search-and-replace (`s/patt/repl/`) looks for hash keys contained within curly braces and replaces them with the contents of the hash.

Tree termination and size control can be achieved in three ways. The author prefers to construct the Grammar with biased frequencies of branching and non-branching functions so that trees terminate naturally.

Whereas the following grammar definition tends to produce very deep trees:

`$F{STRING} = ['{STRING}, {STRING}','{WORD}'];`,

this modification produces more reasonably sized trees:

`$F{STRING} = ['{STRING}, {STRING}','{WORD}','{WORD}','{WORD}'];`

because the `WORD` type is non-branching and only terminals are defined for it.

Alternatively or additionally, maximum and minimum tree sizes (number of nodes) can be imposed, along with an early termination probability and a maximum tree depth limit.

2.5 Persistence of GP Individuals

The standard library for Perl contains many useful things, including the "DBM" modules. These provide a simple interface for storing key-value pairs on disk with fast indexed access. Their use is extremely simple: using `tie()`, a normal Perl hash-table is linked to a file, and every change made to the hash is also made to the file. Using `tie()`, the genome hash of every individual is transparently mirrored on disk. This is useful if the user wants to use populations that are too large to fit into RAM. It also provides continuous checkpointing, allows the population to be sampled/examined by another program during the run.

2.6 Code/Fitness Evaluation

Every object of type `Individual` has to implement the method `evaluateOutput()`. This method takes as input the training data and produces

```
$F{ROOT} = [ '{STATEMENT}' ];
$T{ROOT} = [ '# nothing' ];
$F{STATEMENT} = [ 'print "{STRING}!\n";',
                  '$s = "{WORD}"',
                  '{STATEMENT} {STATEMENT}' ];
$T{STATEMENT} = [ '# just a comment',
                  'chomp($s);',];
$F{STRING} = [ '{STRING}, {STRING}',
               '{WORD}' ];
$T{STRING} = $T{WORD} = [ 'donuts',
                          'mmm',
                          '$s' ];
```

Fig. 2. Grammar specification as a pair of hashes, %F for functions and %T for terminals. The keys in the hashes are the user-defined node types (i.e. data types). Node types must be in capital letters only. The values are anonymous arrays containing the possible expansions for that type. When another function or terminal is needed, it is signalled by a node type in curly braces. The ROOT node type must always be defined. Function definitions are optional (in this example there is no function of type WORD) but terminals must be defined for every type.

```
1  $genome{nodeROOT0}       = '{nodeSTATEMENT0}';
2  $genome{nodeSTATEMENT0} = '{nodeSTATEMENT1} {nodeSTATEMENT2}';
3  $genome{nodeSTATEMENT1} = '$s = "{nodeWORD0}";';
4  $genome{nodeSTATEMENT2} = 'print "{nodeSTRING0}!\n";';
5  $genome{nodeSTRING0}    = '{nodeSTRING1}, {nodeSTRING2}';
6  $genome{nodeSTRING1}    = '{nodeWORD1}';
7  $genome{nodeSTRING2}    = '{nodeWORD2}';
8  $genome{nodeWORD0}      = 'donuts';
9  $genome{nodeWORD1}      = 'mmm';
10 $genome{nodeWORD2}      = '$s';
```

Fig. 3. To make a new tree: start with a ROOT node, assign a new genome key nodeROOT0 and pick one of the available ROOT type functions from the grammar (see Figure 2). In this case there is only one choice (line 1). The contents of the new node require a new STATEMENT type node to be created, and a random function of that type is chosen (line 2). Now there are two child nodes to be expanded (lines 3 and 4). The process continues recursively along all branches and when a function can not be found, a terminal node is used instead.

some kind of output data structure that the fitness function (in Algorithm) can understand. The user can either provide an evolved evaluateOutput() method (the definition for this method is usually in the ROOT node of the tree), or some function or method which is called from a non-evolved evaluateOutput().

When the fitness of an individual is required (and is not cached in memory), the genome is expanded into code which is evaluated with Perl's eval() function. This redefines `evaluateOutput()` and/or other methods - overwriting any previously defined methods (from the last individual's fitness evaluation, for example). Normally Perl would emit warnings about this, but these are suppressed. Then, `evaluateOutput()` is called and the fitness is calculated from the return value. The fitness is stored both in memory and on disk (in the genome hash), to avoid unnecessary recalculation and allow faster restarts.

3 Genetic Algorithm Design

3.1 The Genetic Algorithm

The first release of this software provides an `Algorithm` superclass implementing tournament-based GP, which is a good starting point for developing biologically realistic algorithms (at least with respect to higher organisms). Each tournament involves the random selection of a group of individuals which are sorted by decreasing fitness. Individuals which have participated in more than a certain number of tournaments are automatically given the worst possible fitness, to simulate the natural ageing process. Then, the first parent is taken from the top of the list, and a mate is selected either from the next in line, or a random selection biased towards the top of the list (the user decides which strategy). Crossover (see Section 3.2) is performed on these two parents to create two offspring which replace individuals at the bottom of the sorted list. Each offspring is subjected to mutation (see Section 3.3) before being placed back in the population. Mutation is only applied after reproduction because in biology, the only relevant mutations are those that occur in the germ-line. If desired, more pairs of parents are chosen from the same sorted list and are crossed over as before. As a somewhat crude anti-stagnation measure, two parents may only produce offspring if their fitnesses are not identical, otherwise the second parent is mutated.

3.2 "Homologous" Crossover

When trying to draw inspiration from biology, the crossover mechanism should perhaps deserve the most attention. In PerlGP, by default, the number of crossovers per reproduction event is variable and depends on the number of nodes in the tree (this is called a uniform, or per-node crossover rate). When no crossover is performed, parents are simply copied into the offspring. This design decision is discussed in more detail in Section 4.2.

Another biology-based decision was to attempt "homologous" crossover: where crossover points are biased to give subtrees of similar size and contents. This is achieved, crudely, by randomly sampling two subtrees, A and B, from each parent respectively, until a pair is accepted as a crossover point with the probability:

$$\left(1-\left(\frac{|N_A - N_B|}{\max(N_A, N_B)}\right)^s\right)\cdot\left(\frac{I_{A,B}}{\min(N_A, N_B)}\right)^h ,$$

where N is the number of nodes in a subtree, and I is simply the number of identical nodes seen during the parallel descent of two subtrees (stopping at non-identical nodes and not allowing for insertions or deletions). This contrasts with Langdon's approach[4] which looks towards the root of the tree for similar contexts. The exponents s and h (which default to 1) can be changed to give more or less emphasis on size and "homology" respectively.

Crossover is only allowed between nodes of the same type and the subtree sampling may be biased to give larger subtrees than random sampling would normally give. When multiple crossover points are required, subsequent points are not allowed to lie within in the subtrees of previous crossover points.

3.3 Mutation Operators

As with crossover, the default behaviour of PerlGP is to apply a random number of mutations proportional to the number of nodes in the tree. The two main types of mutation are *point mutation* and *macromutation*, and the choice between them is random (with a user-defined bias). Point mutations involve picking a random node (internal or terminal) and picking a new function (of the same arity) or terminal from the grammar. In some cases, the replacement function or terminal will be identical to the original, so there is an option to repeat the process until some change is made (switched off by default). Numeric terminal nodes can be treated specially so that point mutations make a random adjustment to the number instead of replacing it - this is called *numeric mutation*.

Macromutation is a little more complex. Nodes are (optionally) biased towards internal nodes, and the following operations are chosen from at random:

Replace subtree. Subtree replaced with a random subtree.

Copy subtree. Two independent nodes (subtrees not containing each other) are selected and one subtree is copied, replacing the other.

Swap subtrees. As above, but subtrees are swapped.

Insert internal. A node is chosen, (e.g. a terminal node: `2`) and is replaced with a non-terminal node (e.g. `{NUM} + {NUM}`). One of branches is linked back to the original node, and any remaining branches are expanded with new subtrees (e.g. result: `1 + 2`).

Delete internal. Two nodes are chosen, the second belongs to the subtree of the first and is of the same type. The nodes are reconnected, and any intervening nodes are removed from the tree.

4 Benchmarking

4.1 Speed Comparison with lilgp

A popular open source GP package is lilgp[10] which, being quite minimal and written in C, is presumably one of of the fastest GP systems available (excluding machine-code systems of course). To get a feeling for how much slower a Perl-based system executes compared to a system in a "proper" language, both

Table 1. Summary of settings for lilgp and PerlGP systems in the time trials.

	lilgp	**PerlGP**
target function	$y = \sin(3x)$ for $-1 < x < 1$	
training data	100 points	
fitness function	$1/(1 + \sum \lvert y_{correct} - y_{gp} \rvert)$	
success criteria	fitness >= 0.4 (fit looks good) within 4 hours	
functions	$+ \quad - \quad *$ pdiv(a, b) (returns a if $b = 0$)	
terminals	ephemeral random constants $0 \rightarrow 1$	1000 random numbers $0 \rightarrow 1$
tree limits	init.method = half-and-half init.depth = 2-6 max_depth = 8 max_nodes = unlimited	naturally terminating trees max_depth = 20 (safety) max_nodes = 1000 (safety) rebuild trees < 20 nodes
population size	4000	2000
max. generations	5000	no limit
genetic algorithm	generational, fitness based selection, 90% crossover, 5% reproduction, 5% “keep trying” mutation	tournaments of 50 individuals, reproduce top 20, age limit: 4 tournaments

Table 2. Speed comparison of PerlGP and lilgp. The mean time and tree sizes are calculated for successful runs only (achieving fitness of 0.4 in less than 4h).

GP system	total runs	successful runs in 4h	mean time (min)	mean tree size (nodes)
lilgp	100	70	24	120
PerlGP	100	55	82	83

PerlGP and lilgp were challenged with symbolic regression of a sine curve. The aim was to use identical training data, function sets, and fitness functions, but allow each each system to use its “default” algorithm to reach a certain fitness in a fixed time. The main reason behind this decision was to avoid a major of overhaul of PerlGP to make carbon-copy lilgp emulation possible, when we know the Perl system is going to be slower anyway. The experimental setup is outlined in Table 1, and a summary of the results is given in Table 2.

The main conclusion is that lilgp manages to complete more runs within a fixed time period than PerlGP. When considering only the runs which reach the desired fitness, PerlGP takes about 3.5 times longer. It would be desirable to let all runs terminate naturally, but this was not feasible for a number of reasons; one being that an optimal solution cannot be guaranteed, another being that 17 if the lilgp runs behaved strangely and converged to a population of small unfit individuals. However, one can guestimate that PerlGP would be around 10 times slower than lilgp if all runs did terminate (this often quoted as a Perl-to-C speed differential).

PerlGP gives more compact solutions (more on this in Section 4.2). For the interested reader, one such solution is given here (slightly simplified from the evolved code):

$$sin(3x) \approx \frac{1.42291(0.57915 - x^2)}{0.38103/x + 0.32766x} + x \quad \text{for} \quad -1 < x < 1 \quad .$$

4.2 Mutation and Crossover Strategies

In biology, mutations result from uncorrected replication errors or by the action of mutagens such as radiation, chemicals, free radicals, viruses and transposable elements[1]. The number of mutation events occurring depends on the amount of DNA for most types of mutation. And while crossover points appear to be non-uniformly distributed in eukaryotic chromosomes, their numbers too are correlated with chromosome size[3]. Therefore PerlGP, which tries to be biologically inspired, applies mutations and crossovers with probabilities depending on the genome size (as default behaviour). Others have studied this approach and found that it (in contrast to the standard approach with fixed numbers of mutation and crossover) is an effective measure to protect against bloat[7,8]. Bloat is the rapid increase in size of GP individuals without a corresponding increase in fitness. It is thought that larger GP individuals can "soak up" mutations and destructive crossovers and therefore are more likely to produce viable offspring. The counter argument is that uniform mutation and crossover are simply another form of parsimony pressure, penalising larger individuals. Here I ask the question, can a regime of uniform mutation and crossover allow code growth when the solution to the problem demands it?

The problem is a simple one: to find an integer arithmetic approximation of pi. The functions and terminals are `+ - * pdiv 1 2 3 5 7`, and the fitness function is the absolute error. Clearly, a more accurate solution will contain more terms, so the code tree will have to be bigger. Initially, two types of run were performed: one with per-node mutation/crossover rates of 1/102 and 1/34 respectively, and one with a single fixed mutation and crossover occurring with 3/10 and 9/10 probability (recall that mutation is applied to each offspring after crossover). The ratio of crossover to mutation in both cases is 3:1 and the rates were chosen to give similar amounts of actual mutation and crossover in the first few hundred tournaments of a run. Runs were terminated after 90 minutes and the final fitness *vs.* solution size from 50 runs of each type is shown in Figure 4. It was not surprising to see that the fixed-mutation runs produced larger solutions, however the increased size was also accompanied by increased fitness. In this case, the size increase did not seem to be detrimental to learning (by slowing down evaluations or tree manipulation, for example). Indeed, many of the runs were well on their way to the best possible fitness (1e-15). In the other experiment, the high per-node mutation rate is slowing down learning by limiting code growth, but these runs would eventually find optimal solutions (data not shown).

Out of curiosity, a third type of run was performed using self-adapting mutation and crossover probabilities. Meta-evolution is simple to implement in PerlGP - the user simply creates evolved code for the `evolvedInit()` method, which is called before fitness evaluation, mutation and crossover. In this function, the per-node mutation and crossover probabilities are redefined, and these values

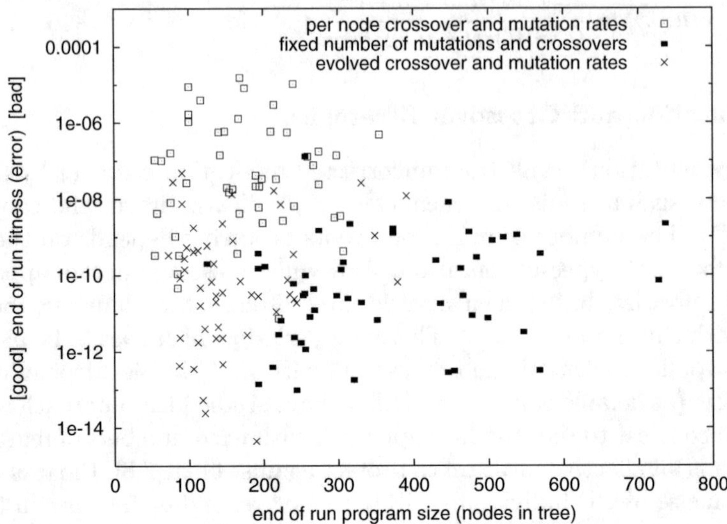

Fig. 4. End-of-run fitness on the pi approximation problem with different mutation and crossover regimes.

are allowed to change by numeric mutation only. The results on the pi problem (also shown in Figure 4) were surprising. The distribution of fitnesses in these runs was indistinguishable from the fixed-mutation/crossover runs (two-sample t-test on logged or unlogged errors gives $d < 1.96$), but the solution trees were significantly smaller ($d = 8.7$).

Meta-evolution of parameters has not yet been fully explored in the PerlGP system. The pi problem has a fitness landscape where improvements are always possible. In flatter or more complex fitness landscapes, self-adapting mutation and crossover rates may converge towards zero because increases in fitness are so rare that conservatism is the most rewarding strategy, in terms of survival.

5 Conclusion

PerlGP is a robust and flexible tool which has already been applied in my group to a variety of string and number based projects, including protein secondary structure prediction and time-series modelling of medical data. New projects can be started quickly without the need to provide code for the functions and terminals that Perl already has. Object oriented code can also be evolved, along with self-adapting parameters and genetic operators. Results suggest that self-adapting uniform mutation and crossover rates may be the answer to the bloat problem. Open source status will ensure that the project evolves in response to the demands of the community. The project's homepage is `http://perlgp.org`.

References

1. J. S. Bertram. The molecular biology of cancer. *Mol Aspects Med*, 21(6):167–223, Dec 2000.
2. Christian Gagné and Marc Parizeau. Open BEAGLE: A new C++ evolutionary computation framework. In W. B. Langdon and *et al*, editors, *GECCO 2002: Proceedings of the Genetic and Evolutionary Computation Conference*, page 888, New York, 9-13 July 2002. Morgan Kaufmann Publishers.
3. J. L. Gerton, J. DeRisi, R. Shroff, M. Lichten, P. O. Brown, and T. D. Petes. Inaugural article: global mapping of meiotic recombination hotspots and coldspots in the yeast Saccharomyces cerevisiae. *Proc. Natl. Acad. Sci. USA*, 97(21):11383–11390, Oct 2000.
4. W. B. Langdon. Size fair and homologous tree genetic programming crossovers. In Wolfgang Banzhaf, Jason Daida, Agoston E. Eiben, Max H. Garzon, Vasant Honavar, Mark Jakiela, and Robert E. Smith, editors, *Proceedings of the Genetic and Evolutionary Computation Conference*, volume 2, pages 1092–1097, Orlando, Florida, USA, 13-17 July 1999. Morgan Kaufmann.
5. Sean Luke. A java-based evolutionary computation and genetic programming research system. Technical report, George Mason University, USA, Nov 2002.
6. Brad Murray and Ken Williams. Genetic algorithms with Perl. The Perl Journal (online), Issue 15 Vol. 5 No.3 http://www.samag.com/tpj, 1999.
7. J. Page, R. Poli, and W. B. Langdon. Smooth uniform crossover with smooth point mutation in genetic programming: A preliminary study. In Riccardo Poli, Peter Nordin, William B. Langdon, and Terence C. Fogarty, editors, *Genetic Programming, Proceedings of EuroGP'99*, volume 1598 of *LNCS*, pages 39–49, Goteborg, Sweden, 26-27 May 1999. Springer-Verlag.
8. Terry Van Belle and David H. Ackley. Uniform subtree mutation. In James A. Foster, Evelyne Lutton, Julian Miller, Conor Ryan, and Andrea G. B. Tettamanzi, editors, *Genetic Programming, Proceedings of the 5th European Conference, EuroGP 2002*, volume 2278 of *LNCS*, pages 152–161, Kinsale, Ireland, 3-5 April 2002. Springer-Verlag.
9. Mark S. Withall, Chris J. Hinde, and Roger G. Stone. Evolving perl. In Erick Cantú-Paz, editor, *Late Breaking Papers at the Genetic and Evolutionary Computation Conference (GECCO-2002)*, pages 474–481, New York, NY, July 2002. AAAI.
10. Douglas Zongker and Bill Punch. lilgp 1.01 user's manual. Technical report, Michigan State University, USA, 26 March 1996.

Evolutionary Optimized Mold Temperature Control Strategies Using a Multi-polyline Approach

Jörn Mehnen, Thomas Michelitsch, and Klaus Weinert

University of Dortmund, Department for Machining Technology (ISF)
44227 Dortmund, Baroper Str. 301, Germany
{mehnen,michelitsch,weinert}@isf.mb.uni-dortmund.de
http://www.isf.de

Abstract. During the machining process the tools for pressure and injection molding have to keep an optimal working temperature. This temperature depends on the workpiece material and allows a safe, efficient and precise machining process. The compact and very expensive steel molds are penetrated with deep hole drilling bores that are combined to form mold temperature control circuits. Today the structure of these circuits are designed manually. Here, a new automatic layout system for mold temperature control strategies is introduced which uses a multiobjective fitness function. The circuits are encoded via a polyline approach. The complex optimization problem is solved using a variation of the evolution strategy. The evolutionary approach as well as first results of the system will be discussed.

1 Introduction

Expert know-how approaches are typical for the design of die casting and injection molding tools [4]. Molds belong to the most expensive tools in industry and have to meet high demands on accuracy and endurance [13]. Hence, an optimal design is decisive for an efficient application of these precious tools. A combination of expert knowledge and objective technological quality measures is needed for further improvement of the efficiency of molds.

Beside the structural and mechanical construction of a mold, especially the thermal design of casting tools is an important factor for high production rates and optimal workpiece qualities. The temperature of a molding tool is controlled by deep hole drillings that are combined to form mold temperature control circuits which penetrate the complete tool. The entire net of bores works as a heat exchanger. Depending on the temperature of the fluid which is lead through the bores, the mold temperature control circuits can have a cooling or a heating effect [5].

The thermal design of injection molds can be calculated by the thermal balance strategy, the difference method or the automatic finite element method (FEM) [8]. These methods yield results about the thermal effect of the the layout of the net of bores but they do not generate optimal designs for mold

C. Ryan et al. (Eds.): EuroGP 2003, LNCS 2610, pp. 374–383, 2003.

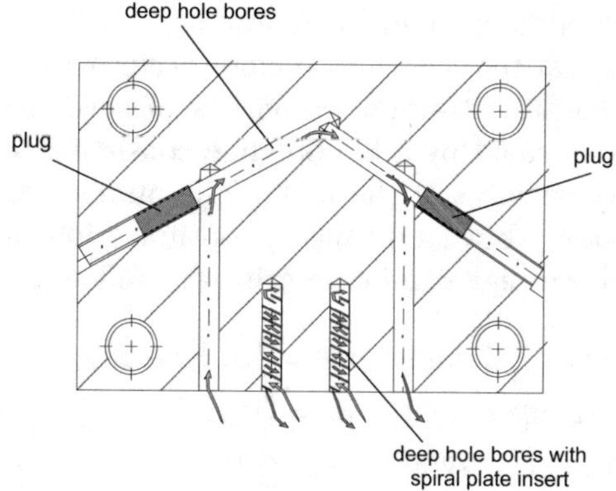

Fig. 1. Different types of mold temperature control strategies.

temperature control circuits. A fast and realistic estimation of the effects of a control circuit for die casting and injection molding tools combined with an automatic optimization system for the layout of the circuits will be presented next. The encoding of a mold temperature control circuit using a multi-polyline approach is discussed. A multiobjective quality function for the estimation of the cooling effect of the control circuits is introduced. The structure of a multi-population evolutionary algorithm is described and first results of its application to artificial and real world geometries are discussed.

2 Encoding

2.1 Mold Temperature Control Circuits

Mold temperature control circuits are combinations of one or more bores. Single bores with a spiral plate inside or double threaded mandrels are used in the case of strong geometric restrictions due to the structural composition of the tool. These bores have only a local temperature control effect on the mold surface. The designer is anxious to use temperature control circuits that approximate the cavities uniformly and as near as possible – a minimum safety clearance to the mold surface of about two times the diameter of a bore should be kept [2].

Single bores are surely not the best solution. Temperature control circuits consisting of several bores which may be arranged in 3D-space have better heat exchange abilities. These circuits are combinations of single bores that are interconnected to form polylines. In current practical applications the flow direction of the fluid must always be unique,i. e. a circuit must not intersect with itself nor with other circuits. This simplifies the construction, because i.e. the problems of flow resistance must not be taken into account. Plugs help to control the flow direction of the fluid and prevent leakages. Plugs make it possible to combine several bores to a complex net structure and allow to use single bores more than once. A mold is often penetrated by several independent mold control circuits which can be used for cooling or heating separately.

In order to have enough room for inflow and outflow connectors, a circuit always starts and ends at the accessible boundary surfaces of the tool. A complete mold temperature control strategy Φ consists of several independent circuits ϕ_i. Each circuit is described by a 3D-polyline consisting of vertices ν_{j_i} that lie within the boundary surfaces of the mold. The number $n_{\phi_i} \in \mathbb{N}$ of vertices of each polyline is arbitrary but fix during the optimization run. Therefore, a mold temperature control strategy can be described as follows:

$$\text{complete set of circuits} \quad \Phi = \{\phi_i \mid i \in \mathbb{N}\} \tag{1}$$

$$\text{polyline describing one circuit} \quad \phi_i = (\nu_1, \ldots, \nu_{n_{\phi_i}})_i^T \in \mathbb{R}^{3\, n_{\phi_i}}, \quad \nu_j \in \mathbb{R}^3 \tag{2}$$

$$\text{number of vertices per circuit} \quad n_{\phi_i} \in \mathbb{N} \tag{3}$$

2.2 The Mold

The mold is modeled as a rectangular solid cuboid. The cavity of the mold is a free form surface. All surfaces are described by triangulations which are the most general interface to typical CAD systems. Triangulations also simplify the calculations of the bore to surface interactions. Geometric restrictions such as sleeves or nozzles are introduced by cylinders or cuboids. The resolution of the triangulation of the free form surface can be reduced strongly because the heat exchange itself is blurred by the integrative character of the interaction between the bores and the free form surface.

3 Fitness

The practical layout problem for mold temperature control strategies is multi-objective. An optimal design has to meet demands such as [10][3]:

- a given average tool surface temperature has to be reached,
- in order to prevent distortions in the workpiece, the temperature of the mold surface should be regionally uniform,
- the cooling time – and hence the cycle time – should be as short as possible to reach high production rates.
- the number of bores should be as low as possible,
- the heat exchange should be as high as possible,
- the bores should not intersect with functional parts of the tool, such as sliders, sleeves or injection bores,
- the mold temperature control circuits must not intersect with themself nor with other circuits,
- due to technological reasons of the deep hole drilling process, the angle between the bores must not become to small,
- etc.

The temperature of the mold surface has a decisive impact on the flow characteristics of the workpiece material. A too low mold temperature may yield an incomplete filling of the tool or insufficient surface properties of the workpiece. A mold that is too hot has also disadvantageous effects on the workpiece surface quality and increases the cycle times of the machine. The adjustment of the mold temperature depends on the characteristic working temperature of the workpiece material. E.g. for *Durethan AKV* plastic, the mold temperature lies between $80°C$ and $120°C$, the melt temperature is $280°C$ to $300°C$ and the demoulding temperature is $140°C$ [13].

In practice for all thermal balance calculations a quasi-stationary average tool surface temperature is used. In a quasi-stationary state, exactly that amount of energy is emitted into the cooling fluid and the environment that has been introduced into the system by the hot workpiece material. In the following calculation this practical assumption has been adopted. Although the variation of the tool temperature from the average can be quite large, the fluctuations of the average tool temperature must not change more than a few Kelvin (about $10K$). This stabilization of the average tool surface temperature is one of the main tasks of mold temperature control systems.

Additionally to the temporal constant average tool temperature, the spacial temperature distribution within the tool should be as homogeneous as possible. Generally, any local heat accumulation at the free form surface should avoided. Therefore, the layout of the control circuits can be transformed to a minimization of the number of hot spots. Algorithmically, the distribution of the local heat exchange values at each triangle has to be optimized.

A good thermal heat exchange can be realized by good local approximations of the free form surface by the system of bores. Therefore, the layout of the bores also includes an approximation problem. Technically, the sum of the local heat exchange values has to be maximized.

In this work several different models, which describe the heat exchange effect between a bore and the triangles of the mold surface, have been compared. The first and very efficient approach was motivated by computer graphics. Each pipe is modeled as a hot wire or a neon tube which radiates heat or light. The power density of a point light source decreases with the reciprocal squared distance. The heat effect on the center point of a triangle is integrated over the length of each bore. All bores of Φ within optical reach contribute to the local heat exchange value of a triangle. The exchange value $T_{triangle}$ of one triangle is

$$T_{triangle} = \sum_{i} \sum_{j=1}^{n_{\phi_i}} \int_{\phi_j} \frac{1}{r(u)^2} \, du \tag{4}$$

The second approach is motivated by the FEM. The effect of a heat point to a surface decreases according to Fourier's rule of heat conduction

$$\dot{q} = -\lambda \frac{dT}{dx} \tag{5}$$

The heat effect between a long heated line to a triangle can be calculated by numerical integration. Here, a FEM calculation using the commercial software system *ANSYS* was used.

A comparison of the results of both approaches show only slight differences for small pipe to surface distances. Furthermore, the calculations using the radiation model take only few milliseconds, while the FEM system takes about a minute for an average geometry. Therefore, the light emission model was used for all further calculations. In order to be able to find an optimal layout for geometries with deep cavities or for exact verification purposes, *ANSYS* has still been integrated into the mold temperature control optimization tool.

A difficult problem of the design of mold temperature control strategies are geometric restrictions. Some areas such as slides or other circuits must not be penetrated by any bore. Any intersection with the free form surface should also be avoided. Sometimes collisions of a bore and the surface are unavoidable to generate good surface heat exchange probabilities. Although these damages can be repaired, the mending process can be very cost-intensive. Accordingly, the intersection of a bore and the surface is modeled by a strong penalty function. In order to introduce a direction out of forbidden regions, the penalty value is – in the case of a bore to free form surface intersection – indirectly proportional to the distance of the bore to the center point of the mold. The introduction of a search direction into the penalty is important to improve the speed of the optimization process. Any circuit to circuit interaction is strictly not legal because in many practical constructions the flow direction of the fluid is unique. Again a strong continuous penalty function is used to allow short term interpenetration of the bores.

The pipes of the mold temperature control channels are produced with deep hole drilling machines. Technological problems requires angles between crossing bores that are not less than 20°. The best technological case are T-shaped crossings. Therefore, an additional fitness criterion for the minimization of the intersectional volume of the cylindric bores was introduced.

The multiobjective fitness function is designed as an arbitrary linear or nonlinear combination of single quality and penalty criteria. A graphical user interface (GUI) allows to build the global fitness function according to the actual complexity of the optimization problem. A Pareto approach is matter of current research activities.

4 The Evolutionary Algorithm

The basis of the optimization algorithm is a variation of the classic evolution strategy (ES) of Schwefel and Rechenberg [6]. Due to the fact, that already quite simple mold surface geometries show several suboptimal mold temperature control strategy layouts, conventional deterministic optimization strategies may not seem applicable. Especially the multimodal, high dimensional and multiobjective fitness function with restrictions requires high-performance optimization algorithm. Evolutionary algorithms and their variants have already proven their abilities in a lot of complex real world applications [7].

The evolution strategy (ES) uses a set of μ real valued vectors from $\mathbb{R}^{2n}$ as initial solutions. This set is called the parent population. Each individual is composed of objective variables and strategy variables. The n objective variables x_i are the input parameters for the n-dimensional fitness function. The n strategy variables σ_i are used for the genetic variation operators that adjust the objective variables. I.e., each of individual I_i shows the following structure:

$$I_i = \{x_1, \ldots, x_n, \sigma_1, \ldots, \sigma_n\} \in \mathbb{R}^{2n} \tag{6}$$

From this parent population an offspring population is generated by application of the nondeterministic genetic operators recombination and mutation. The number of offspring individuals is λ. The ratio λ/μ is called the selection pressure and lies usually in the range of 5 to 7. This surplus of offspring is important for the optimization speed. The recombination operator selects two or more individuals for the mating process and combines a new individual from the parents. Typically, the new objective variables are calculated by intermediate recombination of the objective vector components of the parents. The strategy variables of the offspring are typically generated by discrete recombination.

$$x'_{o_{m\,i}} = (x_{p_{j\,i}} + x_{p_{k\,i}})/2 \tag{7}$$

$$\sigma'_{o_{m\,i}} = \text{either } \sigma_{p_{j\,i}} \text{ or } \sigma_{p_{k\,i}}, \tag{8}$$

where j, k are randomly chosen from $\{1, \ldots, \mu\}$ and i runs from $1, \ldots, n$ and m from $1, \ldots, \lambda$. The objective variables for parent and offspring are denoted by x'_p, x'_o and the strategy variables for parent and offspring by σ'_p and σ'_o, respectively.

After recombination the mutation operator changes the new offspring objective variables via the following two step approach. First the newly recombined strategy variables (also called step sizes) are varied by a standard log-norm distribution. Then the objective variables are changed via a standard normal distribution which uses the new sigma as variance values.

$$\sigma_{o_{m\,i}} = \sigma'_{o_{m\,i}} \cdot exp(\tau' \cdot N(0,1) + \tau \cdot N_i(0,1)) \tag{9}$$

$$x_{o_{m\,i}} = x'_{o_{m\,i}} + \sigma_{o_{m\,i}} \cdot N_i(0,1), \tag{10}$$

where i runs from 1 to n and m from 1 to λ. $\tau \propto (\sqrt{2\sqrt{n}})^{-1}$ and $\tau' \propto (\sqrt{2n})^{-1}$ are external fix parameters of the algorithm. The advantage of that two step approach is that the evolution strategy is able to adapt its strategy variables automatically. An external function to find the correct (function depending) step sizes is not necessary.

After the application of the genetic operators, a selection scheme chooses these μ individuals from the population of λ offspring that seem to be most promising. Alternatively the offspring together with the parent population is used. In ES the truncation selection is used, i.e. the individuals to be selected are ordered according to their fitness and the μ best replace the old parent individuals for the next run [1].

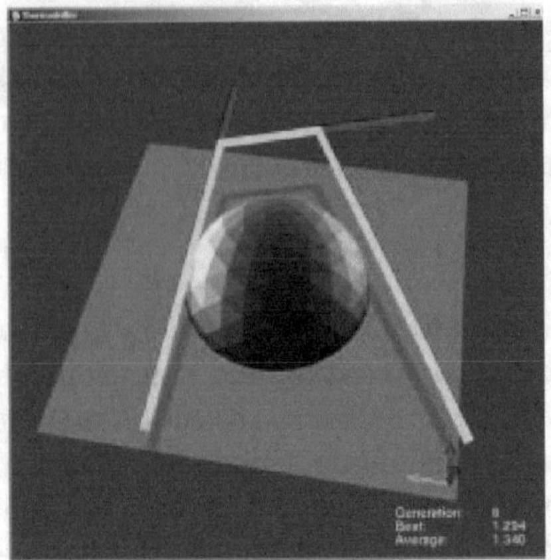

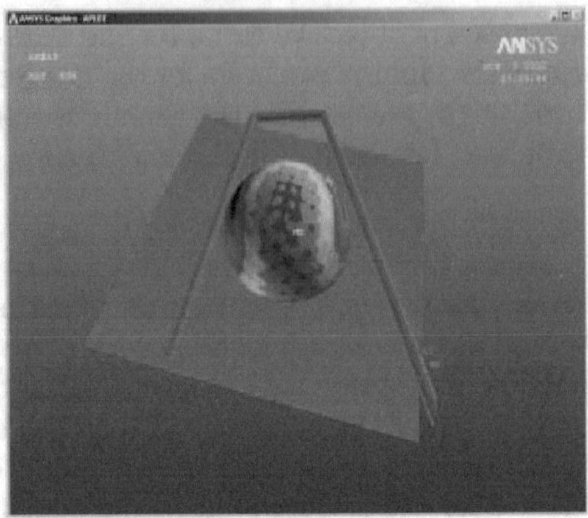

Fig. 2. Optimized mold temperature control circuit for a spheric cavity. Visualization using the light emitting approach (left) and FEM (right).

5 Results

5.1 Basic Analyzes

In order to analyze the behavior of the algorithm, simple geometries such as spheres, cylinders and cuboids have been used to describe the basic structure of a mold surface. In Figure 2 the cooling strategy for a sphere after 8 generations is shown. The evolutionary algorithm starts with a population of $\mu = 10$ and $\lambda = 100$ individuals. The initial population consists of a set of open polylines with arbitrarily chosen vertex coordinate values. The vertices are always mapped into the box shaped space of the tool that surrounds the mold surface.

Each mold temperature control circuit always starts and ends on one of the surrounding tool borders. Often the holes do not penetrate the whole tool from one end to the other. In fact each pipe can be divided into a section that is used for heat exchange (with fluid) and a passive section. The passive part has no heat exchange capability and should be avoided or kept as short as possible. In practice, the active and the passive parts are separated by plugs. In Figure 2 the active section is highlighted while the passive section is drawn with dark colors. The plugs are not displayed.

The light intensity of the triangles in the visualization is proportional to the calculated heat exchange effect. The stronger the exchange the brighter the triangle. A comparison with the FEM using the same structure of bores shows the similarity of the heat exchange effect in this example (see Figure 2).

Typically a lot of individuals of the initial population intersect the mold surface. The penalty function "pushes" the bores after only few generations away from the mold surface center. After that period the first general structures of the circuits appear. Depending on the mold geometry and the number of bores, a solution is found after typically 200 generations, i.e. after about 2 minutes. Because the fitness calculation lasts only a few milliseconds, in this case the progress of the evolutionary process can be watched in nearly real time.

Due to the fact that there exist several local optima, a parallel approach with distributed populations is used [12]. An island model [11] was implemented. Typically 20 populations run in parallel. For a given number of steps, e.g. 30, each population discovers its local optimum of the solution. The best and average solution of each population are selected to become the start population for the next parallel runs. For complex geometries this approach significantly reduces the chance to get stuck in local optima.

The correct adjustment of the multiobjective fitness function is crucial for the structure of the resulting mold temperature control circuit. A higher focus on an equally strong temperature distribution yields long bores that try to cover as much space as possible. A focus on a more local heat exchange yields bores that approximate the object surface by small active sections of the bores.

The number of bores is also decisive for the structure of the circuit. Especially the spherical geometry yields interesting geometric properties for good mold control circuits. Often the circuits seem to approximate the sphere in triangular loops that subdivide into smaller triangular loops.

5.2 Practical Application

Real world injection molds often have a quite complex structure. An example of a typical injection-molded part – an indicator holder – is shown in Figure 3. The original object is made of plastic and has a global wall thickness of $2mm$. The object is composed of a triangular plate, a large protruding cylinder, some small holes and a slot. The surface was scanned and reconstructed via a triangulation. The high number of $239,560$ original sampling points was reduced to $11,235$ points by a point reduction scheme that originally had been designed for smooth surface reconstructions [9].

Figure 3 shows a solution of a mold temperature control system after 361 generations. The evolution of one generation of the $(20,100)$-ES took about 10 seconds for the given triangulation, i.e. the complete evolutionary run took about an hour. An increase in speed of about 10 times is surely possible for triangulations that are better adapted to the calculation of the heat exchange. These triangulations should have vertices that are equally distributed over the scanned surface to allow the modeling of a uniform tempered surface.

One can see from Figure 3 that the evolutionary computed temperature mold control circuit of eight bores covers the different areas of the holder uniformly. This structure is typical and has been discovered in several other runs for the same holder geometry. The cylindric dome is surrounded by a star shaped structure while the planar triangular plane area is cooled by a triangular bore structure with a median line. The global structure of the bores mirror the triangular shape of the holder. The circuit exploits the full three dimensionality of phenotypic search space to yield a good result. These 3D-structures can be generated for tools that are used for the production of small parts like the holder in Figure 3. Due to manufacturing problems of deep holes for large and heavy die casting tools these bores may lie in a planar sections of the 3D space. The

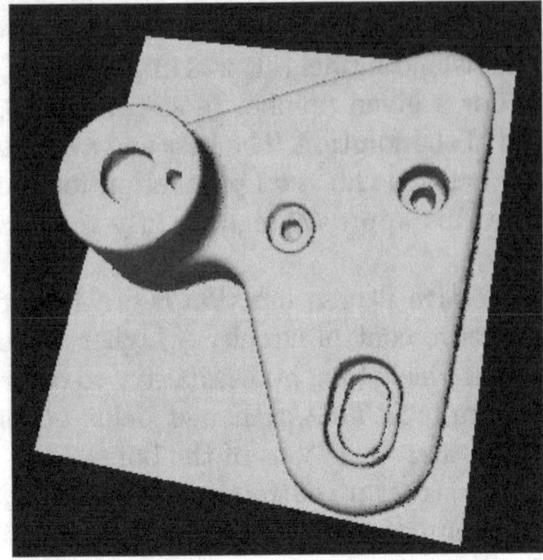

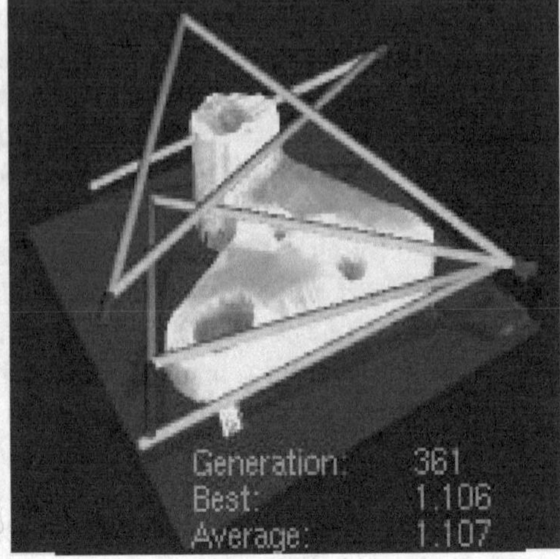

Fig. 3. Triangulation (239, 560 points) of a plastic indicator holder (left) and mold temperature control strategy (right).

algorithm is able to cope with these restrictions and can also find an optimal planar section through the tool.

5.3 Experimental Setup

All experiments have been run on a standard PC with a 1.2 MHz processor and 512 MB RAM. The evolutionary algorithm and all components such as the evaluator of the fitness criteria, the GUI and the visualization system are implemented in C++. The PC runs the operating system Windows2000. The visualization tool uses a standard OpenGL library for PC. The parallel approach was tested on five equally equipped PCs.

6 Conclusions and Outlook

The layout of mold temperature control strategies is a complex task that can be solved well with evolutionary algorithms. A new and efficient multiobjective fitness function with restrictions to calculate the heat exchange effect has been introduced. The results that are generated with the this new fitness function have been compared with FEM results. The models show good similarities. The multimodal problem requires a parallel setup of the populations of the evolutionary algorithm. The parallel approach increased the convergence probabiblity siginifantly. The algorithm has been tested successfully for real world objects. The mathematical model for these objects has to be improved to increase the efficiency of the calculations even more. Future research tasks will focus on alternative encodings of the mold temperature control strategies and on multiobjective Pareto EA. Analyzes of the efficiency of branched circuits and the effect of the heating up of the fluid are matter of future work.

Acknowledgments

This research was supported by the Deutsche Forschungsgemeinschaft as part of the Collaborative Research Center "Computational Intelligence" (SFB 531).

References

1. Bäck, T.: Evolutionary Algorithms in Theory and Practice. Oxford University Press, NY, USA, 1996.
2. Beck, R.: Hinweise zur Auslegung von Temperierkanälen in Druckgießformen. In: Gorbach, P. (ed.): Handbuch der Temperierung mittels flüssiger Medien, volume 11 of Plast Praxis. Hüthig GmbH, St. Gallen, Switzerland, 5 edition, 1997, p. 116–118.
3. Bichler, M.: Kunststoffteile fehlerfrei spritzgießen, volume 16 of Plast Praxis. Hüthig GmbH, St. Gallen, Switzerland, 1999.
4. Gastrow, H., Lindner, E., and Unger, P. (eds.): Injection Molds: 130 Proven Designs. Hanser Gardner Pubns, 3rd edition, 2002.
5. Gorbach, P. (ed.): Handbuch der Temperierung mittels flüssiger Medien, volume 11 of Plast Praxis. Hüthig GmbH, St. Gallen, Switzerland, 5 edition, 1997.
6. Schwefel, H.-P.: Evolution and Optimum Seeking. Wiley-Interscience, New York, 1995.
7. Schwefel, H.-P., Weinert, K., and Wegener, I. (eds.): Advances in Computational Intelligence. Springer, New York, 2002. (in print).
8. Thienel, P.: Rechnereinsatz in der Spritzgiesstechnik – thermische Auslegung von Spritzgiesswerkzeugen. In: Gorbach, P. (ed.): Handbuch der Temperierung mittels flüssiger Medien, volume 11 of Plast Praxis. Hüthig GmbH, St. Gallen, Switzerland, 5 edition, 1997, p. 100–106.
9. Weinert, K. and Mehnen, J.: Comparison of Selection Schemes for Discrete Point Data for Evolutionary Optimized Triangulations and NURBS Surface Reconstructions. In: Nagdy, F. and Kurfess, F. (eds.): ISA 2000, Intelligent Systems & Applications, CI'2000, p. 104–110, University of Wollongong, Australia, 2000.
10. Weinert, K., Mehnen, J., and Meyer, H.-W.: Evolutionary Optimization of Deep Drilling Strategies for Mold Temperature Control. In: Teti, R. (ed.): 3rd CIRP International Seminar on Intelligent Computation in Manufacturing Engineering, ICME 2002, p. 291–296, Ischia, July 3-5 2002. University of Naples.
11. Weinert, K., Mehnen, J., and Rudolph, G.: In: Complex Systems, volume 13/3, chapter Dynamic Neighborhood Structures in Parallel Evolution Strategies, p. 227–244. S. Wolfram, Sadorus, IL, USA, 2002.
12. Weinert, K., Surmann, T., and Mehnen, J.: Parallel Surface Reconstruction. In: EuroGP 2002, Lecture Notes in Computer Science LNCS 2278. Springer, 2002, p. 113–122.
13. Zöllner, O.: Optimierte Werkzeugtemperierung / Optimized Mold Temperature Control (German and English). Technical report, Informationsschrift, Bayer AG, Leverkusen, Germany, 1997.
http://bayerplastics.com/AG/AE/technology/part/00363/index.jsp.

Genetic Programming for Attribute Construction in Data Mining

Fernando E. B. Otero[1], Monique M. S. Silva[1],
Alex A. Freitas[2], and Julio C. Nievola[1]

[1] Pontificia Universidade Catolica do Parana (PUC-PR), Postgraduate Program in Applied Computer Science, Rua Imaculada Conceicao 1155, Curitiba – PR. 80215-901, Brazil
{fbo,mmonique,nievola}@ppgia.pucpr.br

[2] Computing Laboratory, University of Kent
Canterbury, Kent, CT2 7NF, UK
A.A.Freitas@ukc.ac.uk
http://www.cs.ukc.ac.uk/people/staff/aaf

Abstract. For a given data set, its set of attributes defines its data space representation. The quality of a data space representation is one of the most important factors influencing the performance of a data mining algorithm. The attributes defining the data space can be inadequate, making it difficult to discover high-quality knowledge. In order to solve this problem, this paper proposes a Genetic Programming algorithm developed for attribute construction. This algorithm constructs new attributes out of the original attributes of the data set, performing an important preprocessing step for the subsequent application of a data mining algorithm.

1 Introduction

This paper addresses the classification task of data mining [3]. In this task the goal of a data mining algorithm is to predictive the class of an example (a record, or data instance), given the values of a set of attributes for that example.

For a given data set, its set of attributes defines its data space representation. The quality of a data space representation is one of the most important factors influencing the performance of a data mining algorithm. The attributes defining the data space can be inadequate, making it difficult to discover high-quality knowledge. However, when the original attributes are individually inadequate, it is often possible to combine them in order to construct new attributes with greater predictive power than the original attributes, facilitating the discovery of knowledge with a high predictive accuracy.

This paper proposes a Genetic Programming (GP) algorithm developed for attribute construction (also called constructive induction). This algorithm constructs new attributes out of the original attributes of the data set, performing an important preprocessing step for the subsequent application of a data mining algorithm.

The main motivation for developing a GP algorithm for this task is that it performs a global search in the space of candidate solutions (new constructed attributes, in our

C. Ryan et al. (Eds.): EuroGP 2003, LNCS 2610, pp. 384–393, 2003.

case). In data mining, this has the advantage of coping better with attribute interaction, being less likely to get trapped into local maxima in the search space, by comparison with greedy, local search-based data mining algorithms [2], [4].

The remainder of this paper is organized as follows. Section 2 reviews attribute construction. Section 3 proposes our new GP algorithm for attribute construction. Section 4 reports computational results. Finally, section 5 concludes the paper.

2 A Review of Attribute Construction

The majority of inductive learning algorithms for the classification task discover rules (or another kind of knowledge representation) involving only the original attributes of the data being mined. In addition, the majority of rule induction methods analyze the data on a one-attribute-at-a-time basis. Hence, the performance of these methods is considerably limited by the predictive power of individual attributes, so that these methods do not cope very well with the problem of attribute interaction.

The goal of an attribute construction method is to construct new attributes out of the original ones, transforming the original data representation into a new one where regularities in the data are more easily detected by the classification algorithm, which tends to improve the predictive accuracy of the latter.

Attribute construction methods can be roughly divided into two groups, with respect to the construction strategy: hypothesis-driven methods and data-driven methods [6].

Hypothesis-driven methods construct new attributes out of previously-generated hypotheses (discovered rules or another kind of knowledge representation). In general they start by constructing a hypothesis, for instance a decision tree, and then examine that hypothesis to construct new attributes [13]. These new attributes are then added to the set of original attributes, and a new hypothesis is constructed out of this extended set of attributes. The new hypothesis is used to generate new attributes, and so on. This process is repeated until a given stopping criterion is satisfied, such as a satisfactory extended set of attributes has been found. Note that the performance of this strategy is strongly dependent on the quality of the previously-discovered hypotheses.

By contrast, data-driven methods do not suffer from the problem of depending on the quality of previous hypotheses. They construct new attributes by directly detecting relationships in the data. Two examples of data-driven attribute construction methods are GALA and GPCI.

GALA [8] constructs new attributes using two logical operators, AND and OR. First, all original attributes are transformed into boolean attributes. Then it generates new attributes by using the AND and OR operators to produce combinations of the boolean attributes. Although GALA does not use any evolutionary algorithm to construct attributes, it is interesting to note that apparently it was the "parent" of GPCI [7], a GP algorithm for attribute construction.

Like GALA, GPCI starts by transforming all original attributes into boolean attributes, and then it generates new attributes by using AND and OR operators to produce combinations of the boolean attributes. The difference is that is searches for new attributes by using a GP algorithm. In essence, each individual of GPCI represents a new attribute. The terminal set consists of the booleanized original attributes, whereas the function set consists of the AND and OR operators.

The process of attribute construction can also be roughly divided into two approaches, namely the interleaving approach and the preprocessing approach.

In the preprocessing approach the process of attribute construction is independent of the inductive learning algorithm that will be used to extract knowledge from the data. In other words, the quality of a candidate new attribute is evaluated by directly accessing the data, without running any inductive learning algorithm. In this approach the attribute construction method performs a preprocessing of the data, and the new constructed attributes can be given to different kinds of inductive learning methods.

By contrast, in the interleaving approach the process of attribute construction is intertwined with the inductive learning algorithm. The quality of a candidate new attribute is evaluated by running the inductive learning algorithm used to extract knowledge from the data, so that in principle the constructed attributes' usefulness tends to be limited to that inductive learning algorithm. An example of an attribute construction method following the interleaving approach can be found in [15].

In this paper we follow the data-driven strategy and the preprocessing approach, mainly for two reasons. First, using this combination of strategy/approach the constructed attributes have a more generic usefulness, since they can help to improve the predictive accuracy of any kind of inductive learning algorithm. Second, an attribute-construction method following the preprocessing approach tends to be more efficient than its interleaving counterpart, since the latter requires many executions of an inductive learning algorithm.

It should be noted that both GALA and GPCI also follow the data-driven strategy and the preprocessing approach. However, both these algorithms have the limitation that all attributes have to be booleanized in a preprocessing step, before the attribute construction method starts to run. Intuitively, this booleanization can lead to a significant loss of relevant information. Our proposed GP for attribute construction (described in the next section) does not have this disadvantage, since it does not require any booleanization of the original attributes.

3 A New GP for Attribute Construction

3.1 Individual Representation

We use a standard tree-structure representation for each individual [9], [1]. The GP constructs new attributes out of the continuous (real-valued) attributes of the data set being mined. Each individual corresponds to a candidate new attribute. The terminal set consists of all the continuous attributes in the data being mined. The function set consists of four arithmetic operators, namely "+", "–", "*", "%" (where the latter is protected division [9]), and two relational comparison operators, namely "≤", "≥".

The use of these operators in the tree associated with an individual must satisfy some constraints about the data types of these operators, as shown in Table 1. As can be seen in the table, the arithmetic operators require two continuous input arguments and produce a continuous output. The relational comparison operators also require two continuous input arguments, but they produce a boolean output.

Table 1. Data types restrictions for the function set

Operator	Input arguments	Output
+,–,*,%	(continuous, continuous)	(continuous)
≥, ≤	(continuous, continuous)	(boolean)

As a result of the data type restrictions shown in Table 1, there are some restrictions on the hierarchy of nodes in a tree. These restrictions are shown in Table 2. Each cell of this table indicates whether or not (Y or N, respectively) the corresponding combination of parent node and child node is allowed. Note that the relational comparison operators ("≥", "≤") cannot be used as child nodes. I.e., these operators can be used only in the root node of a tree.

Table 2. Restrictions on the hierarchy of nodes in the tree

		parent node					
		+	–	*	%	≥	≤
child node	+	Y	Y	Y	Y	Y	Y
	–	Y	Y	Y	Y	Y	Y
	*	Y	Y	Y	Y	Y	Y
	%	Y	Y	Y	Y	Y	Y
	≥	N	N	N	N	N	N
	≤	N	N	N	N	N	N
	terminal	Y	Y	Y	Y	Y	Y

We have also used a restriction on the size of the tree associated with an individual. This restriction consists of specifying a parameter representing the maximum tree size (number of nodes) of a tree. As will be seen later, we have done experiments with different values of this parameter, to determine how robust our GP is to variations in the setting of this parameter.

This size restriction is important for at least two reasons. First, from a predictive data mining view point, avoiding the generation of very large trees helps to combat overfitting and so potentially improves the predictive power of the candidate attribute. Second, from a GP viewpoint, this size restriction helps to avoid the effects of code bloat [12], [10] – i.e., the tendency of GP trees to grow in an uncontrolled manner.

It should be mentioned that some GP algorithms specify a predefined maximum depth for an individual's tree. There is no such maximum tree depth in our GP. Rather, we have preferred to specify a maximum tree size in terms of the number of nodes. The rationale for this choice is that, if a maximum tree depth is specified, the GP will probably be somewhat biased to produce balanced trees, growing the trees in width after the maximum tree depth has been reached. Such bias seems unnatural, limiting the flexibility of the GP to search for solutions (trees) of different shapes.

Actually, there is some evidence that predefining a maximum tree depth has some negative effects in GP [5], [11]. A size restriction based on the total number of nodes, rather than tree depth, helps to avoid this kind of problem.

Note that the function set of our GP is inclusive enough to allow the GP to construct either a continuous attribute or a boolean attribute, depending on the kind of operator used in the root node of the individual's tree. If the root node contains an arithmetic operator ("+","–","*", or "%") the constructed attribute will be continuous, whereas if the root node contains a relational comparison operator ("≥" or "≤") the constructed attribute will be boolean.

3.2 Selection Method and Genetic Operators

We use tournament selection. In essence, this method works as follows. First, k individuals are randomly chosen from the population. Then the individual with the best fitness is selected. This method has an important parameter, the tournament size, k. This parameter determines the selective pressure of the method. Larger values of k correspond to larger selective pressures, favouring individuals with the best values of fitness. As will be seen later, we have done experiments with different values of this parameter, to determine how robust our GP is to variations in the setting of this parameter.

In order to create a new population from the current population we use three operators, namely reproduction, crossover and mutation. Reproduction and crossover are conventional GP operators – we use standard tree crossover [9].

The mutation operator works as follows. First, it randomly chooses a tree node. Then the current symbol in this node is replaced by a randomly chosen symbol of the same kind which is different from the current symbol. More precisely, a terminal symbol is replaced by another terminal symbol, an arithmetic operator is replaced by another arithmetic operator, and a relational comparison operator is replaced by another relational comparison operator.

3.3 Fitness Function

The fitness function used in this work is information gain ratio [14], which is a well-known attribute-quality measure in the data mining and machine learning literature. It should be noted that the use of this measure constitutes a data-driven strategy. As mentioned above, an important advantage of this kind of strategy is that it is relatively fast, since it avoids the need for running a data mining algorithm when evaluating an attribute (individual). In particular, the information gain ratio for a given attribute can be computed in a single scan of the training set.

The Information Gain Ratio of an attribute A, denoted by IGR(A), is computed by dividing the Information Gain of A, denoted by IG(A), by the amount of Information of the attribute A, denoted I(A), i.e.:

$$\mathrm{IGR}(A) = \mathrm{IG}(A)\ /\ \mathrm{I}(A)\ . \quad (1)$$

The Information Gain of an attribute A, denoted IG(A), represents the difference between the amount of Information of the goal (class) attribute G, denoted I(G), and that amount given the knowledge of the values of an attribute A, denoted I($G|A$). IG(A) is given by:

$$\mathrm{IG}(A) = \mathrm{I}(G) - \mathrm{I}(G|A), \tag{2}$$

where

$$\mathrm{I}(G) = - \sum_{j=1}^{n} \mathrm{p}(G_j) \,.\, \log_2 \mathrm{p}(G_j), \tag{3}$$

and

$$\mathrm{I}(G|A) = \sum_{i=1}^{m} \mathrm{p}(A_i) \left(- \sum_{j=1}^{n} \mathrm{p}(G_j|A_i) \,.\, \log_2 \mathrm{p}(G_j|A_i) \right), \tag{4}$$

where $\mathrm{p}(G_j)$ is the estimated probability (computed in the training set) of observing the j-th class (i.e., the j-th value of the goal attribute G), n is the number of classes, $\mathrm{p}(A_i)$ is the estimated probability of observing the i-th value of the attribute A, m is the number of values of the attribute A, and $\mathrm{p}(G_j|A_i)$ is the empirical probability of observing the j-th class conditional on having observed the i-th value of the attribute A. Finally, I(A) is given by:

$$\mathrm{I}(A) = - \sum_{i=1}^{m} \mathrm{p}(A_i) \,.\, \log_2 \mathrm{p}(A_i) \,. \tag{5}$$

Recall that the attribute constructed by the GP can be either continuous or boolean (see the last paragraph of section 3.1). When the constructed attribute is boolean, the above formulas are used in a straightforward manner to compute the IGR of the attribute. When the constructed attribute is continuous the GP computes the IGR associated with each possible cut point (attribute value) defining a candidate booleanization of the attribute, and it chooses the largest value of IGR, among all those IGR values, as the value to be assigned to IGR(A). For more details about this procedure and the information gain ratio measure in general, see [14].

4 Computational Results

In this section we report the results of computational experiments performed to evaluate our proposed GP for attribute construction. The experiments were performed with four public-domain data sets from the UCI (*University of California at Irvine*) data set repository, available at: http://www.ics.uci.edu/~mlearn/MLRepository.html.

Table 3 shows the main characteristics of the data sets used in our experiments. In the third column, the number before the slash ("/") is the number of continuous attributes, whereas the number after the slash is the total number of attributes in the data set. As can be seen in the table, for these experiments we have chosen data sets where all or almost all attributes were continuous. Future work will involve data sets with mixed kinds of attributes (both continuous and categorical ones).

In all our experiments the probabilities of reproduction, crossover and mutation were 10%, 80% and 10%, respectively. The initial population was created by using the well-known ramped half-and-half method [9]. The population size was 600, and the GP evolved for 100 generations. We made no attempt to optimize the parameters mentioned in this paragraph. However, we did experiments with different values of two other parameters, the tournament size and the maximum tree size, as will be discussed below.

Table 3. Data sets used in the experiments

Data set	No. of records	No. of Cont. Attrib. / Total No. of Attrib.	No. of classes
Abalone	4177	7 / 8	28
Balance-scale	625	4 / 4	3
Waveform	5000	21 / 21	3
Wine	178	13 / 13	3

The evaluation of the quality of the attributes constructed by our GP was performed by using C4.5 [Quinlan, 1993], a very well-known classification algorithm that builds a decision tree. Hence, in the experiments we compare the classification error rate of C4.5 using only the original attributes with the error rate of C4.5 using not only the original attributes but also the new attribute constructed by the GP.

The error rate was computed by a well-known 10-fold cross-validation procedure, which essentially works as follows. First, the data set is divided into 10 mutually exclusive and exhaustive partitions. Then the algorithm is run 10 times. In the i-th run, i=1,...,10, the i-th partition is used as the test set and the remaining 9 partitions are grouped and used as the training set. Finally, the reported result is the average error rate (in the test set) over the 10 runs.

In addition to the goal of evaluating the quality of the attributes constructed by the GP, our experiments also had the goal of determining how robust the GP is to variations in the setting of two important parameters, namely the tournament size k and the maximum tree size (number of nodes). Hence, we did experiments with three different values for the tournament size k (2, 4, 8) and three different values for the maximum tree size (31, 63, 127). The experiments involved all the 9 possible combinations (3 x 3) of values of these two parameters.

For each of those 9 combinations of parameter values we have run a 10-fold cross-validation procedure, as explained above. Note that each run of an entire cross-validation procedure involved running GP 10 times and running C4.5 20 times (10 times using only the original attributes and 10 times using both the original attributes and the new attribute constructed by the GP).

The results are reported in Tables 4, 5, 6, and 7, for the Abalone, Balance-Scale, Waveform and Wine data sets, respectively. In these tables, each cell contains the error rate obtained by C4.5 using the attribute constructed by GP, with the combination of parameter values corresponding to that cell. In the second line of the title of each table, between brackets, we report the error rate obtained by C4.5 using only the original attributes. In these tables, the value of a cell is shown in bold if the error rate obtained using the new attribute constructed by the GP is smaller than the error rate obtained using only the original attributes. Therefore, cells in bold represent cases where the attribute constructed by the GP was useful to reduce the error rate associated with the original attributes, being evidence of the good quality of the constructed attribute. The numbers after the "±" symbol denote standard deviations.

In the Abalone data set (Table 4) the use of the new attribute constructed by the GP has led to a slight increase in error rate in 6 out of the 9 cases (combinations of parameter values), and has led to a slight reduction in the error rate in only 3 cases. However, in general the differences in error rates are not significant, since the corresponding error rate intervals (considering the standard deviations) overlap. (The very high error rates obtained by C4.5, with and without the attribute constructed by the GP, show that this data set represents a very difficult classification problem. This seems to be at least in part due to the relatively large number of classes, 28.)

In the Balance-Scale data set (Table 5) the use of the new attribute constructed by the GP has clearly led to a very significant reduction in the error rate in all the 9 combinations of parameter values.

In the Waveform data set (Table 6) the use of the new attribute constructed by the GP has led to a reduction in the error rate in 8 of the 9 combinations of parameter values. These reductions in error rate are significant – the corresponding error rate intervals (considering the standard deviations) do not overlap.

In the Wine data set (Table 7) the use of the new attribute constructed by the GP has led to a reduction in the error rate in all the 9 combinations of parameter values. However, these reductions in error rate are not significant.

With respect to the ability of the attributes constructed by the GP in reducing the error rate associated with the original attributes, one can summarize the above results as follows. In one data set (Abalone) the attribute constructed by GP has led to a slight increase in error rate, but this increase was not significant. In another data set (Wine) the attribute constructed by GP has lead to some reduction in error rate, but again this reduction was not significant. In the other two data sets (Balance-Scale and Waveform) the attribute constructed by GP has led to a reduction in error rate which was significant, since the corresponding error rate intervals, considering the standard deviations, do not overlap. The reduction in error rate was particularly strong in the Balance-Scale data set. Overall, we consider these results quite promising.

Recall that another goal of our experiments was to determine how robust the GP is to variations in the setting of two important parameters, namely the tournament size k and the maximum tree size (number of nodes).

First of all, as expected, there is no combination of parameters values that turned out to be the "best" one for all data sets. This is a common result in data mining and machine learning, where the best parameter setting is strongly dependent on the data being mined. In any case, the GP turned out to be quite robust to variations in the parameters k and maximum tree size. There are, of course, a few exceptions. In particular, in the Waveform data set (Table 6) the combination of $k = 8$ and maximum number of nodes = 127 led to an error rate significantly larger than the other combinations of parameter values. But this result is clearly an exception. In general, in all the four data sets the differences in error rates associated with different combinations of parameter values was not significant, which is evidence of a reasonable robustness of GP to variations in these two parameters.

Table 4. Error rate (%) of C4.5 using both original attributes and attribute constructed by the GP in Abalone data set (Error rate (%) of C4.5 using only the original attributes: 79.2 ± 0.37)

		Maximum tree size (number of nodes)		
		31	63	127
Tournament size	2	79.31 ± 0.36	**79.18 ± 0.35**	79.21 ± 0.41
	4	79.21 ± 0.33	79.21 ± 0.33	**79.16 ± 0.36**
	8	79.21 ± 0.33	79.21 ± 0.33	**79.16 ± 0.36**

Table 5. Error rate (%) of C4.5 using both original attributes and attribute constructed by the GP GP in Balance-Scale data set (Error rate (%) of C4.5 using only the original attributes: 22.42 ± 1.34)

		Maximum tree size (number of nodes)		
		31	63	127
Tournament size	2	**11.47 ± 2.13**	**7.78 ± 0.66**	**8.58 ± 0.58**
	4	**9.06 ± 0.42**	**8.26 ± 0.65**	**8.26 ± 0.44**
	8	**8.58 ± 0.67**	**8.74 ± 0.68**	**8.10 ± 0.63**

Table 6. Error rate (%) of C4.5 using both original attributes and attribute constructed by the GP in Waveform data set (Error rate (%) of C4.5 using only the original attributes: 25.06 ± 0.66)

		Maximum tree size (number of nodes)		
		31	63	127
Tournament size	2	**23.04 ± 0.40**	**22.48 ± 0.45**	**22.68 ± 0.57**
	4	**22.44 ± 0.59**	**22.86 ± 0.50**	**22.56 ± 0.57**
	8	**22.22 ± 0.49**	**22.60 ± 0.42**	28.86 ± 2.74

Table 7. Error rate (%) of C4.5 using both original attributes and attribute constructed by the GP in Wine data set (Error rate (%) of C4.5 using only the original attributes: 6.48 ± 2.05)

		Maximum tree size (number of nodes)		
		31	63	127
Tournament size	2	**5.31 ± 1.38**	**4.72 ± 1.47**	**4.72 ± 1.47**
	4	**3.54 ± 1.30**	**5.31 ± 1.63**	**3.54 ± 1.30**
	8	**3.54 ± 1.30**	**4.72 ± 1.47**	**5.30 ± 1.62**

5 Conclusions and Future Research

We have proposed a new GP for attribute construction. It constructs new attributes out of the original continuous (real-valued) attributes of the data being mined. We have also evaluated the ability of the attributes constructed by the GP in reducing the error rate associated with the original attributes. This was done by comparing the error rate obtained by C4.5 using only the original attributes with the error rate obtained by C4.5 using both the original attributes and the new attribute constructed by the GP.

Experiments were performed with four public-domain data sets. In two of those data sets there was no significant difference in the error rate of C4.5 with and without the attribute constructed by the GP. However, in the other two data sets the difference was significant, and in both of these cases the error rate of C4.5 with the constructed attribute was smaller than the error rate of C4.5 without the constructed attribute. Hence, these can be considered promising results.

In addition, GP turned out to be quite robust to variations in the settings of two important parameters, namely the tournament size and the maximum tree size (number of nodes). Experiments with 9 different combinations for the values of these two parameters showed that, in general (with a few exceptions), the differences in error rates associated with different combinations of these parameter values was not significant.

References

1. Banzhaf, W.; Nordin, P.; Keller, R.E.; Francone, F.D. Genetic Programming ~ an Introduction: On the Automatic Evolution of Computer Programs and Its Applications. Morgan Kaufmann, 1998.
2. Dhar, V.; Chou, D. and Provost, F. Discovering Interesting Patterns for Investment Decision Making with GLOWER – A Genetic Learner Overlaid With Entropy Reduction. Data Mining and Knowledge Discovery 4(4), 251-280. Oct. 2000.
3. Fayyad, U. M.; Piatetsky-Shapiro, G; Smith, P.; Uthurusamy, R. (Eds) Advances in Knowledge Discovery and Data Mining, 1-34. AAAI/MIT Press, 1996.
4. Freitas, A.A. Understanding the crucial role of attribute interaction in data mining. Artificial Intelligence Review 16(3), Nov. 2001, pp. 177-199.
5. C. Gathercole and P. Ross. An adverse interaction between crossover and restricted tree depth in genetic programming. Genetic Programming 1996: Proc. 1st Annual Conf., 291-296. MIT Press, 1996.
6. Hu, Y-J. A Genetic Programming Approach to Constructive Induction . In Proceeding of 3rd Anual Genetic Programming Conference, pp. 146–151, 1998.
7. Hu, Y–J. Constructive Induction: Covering Attribute Spectrum. In: H. Liu & H. Motoda (Eds) Feature Extraction Construction and Selection, pp. 257–272. Kluwer, 1998.
8. Hu, Y-J & Kibler, D. Generation of Attributes for Learning Algorithms. In Proceeding of the 13th National Conference on Artificial Intelligence, pp. 806–811, 1996
9. Koza, J. Genetic Programming: On the Programming of Computers by Means of Natural Selection. MIT Press, 1992.
10. W.B. Langdon. Quadratic bloat in genetic programming. Proc. 2000 Genetic and Evolutionary Computation Conf. (GECCO-2000), 451-458. Morgan Kaufmann, 2000.
11. Langdon, W.B. & Poli, R. An analysis of the MAX problem in genetic programming. Genetic Programming 1997: Proc. 2nd Annual Conf., 222-230. Morgan Kaufmann, 1997.
12. Langdon, W.B.; Soule, T.; Poli, R. and Foster, J.A.. The evolution of size and shape. In: L. Spector, W.B. Langdon, U-M. O'Reilly and P.J. Angeline. (Eds.) Advances in Genetic Programming Volume 3, 163-190. MIT Press, 1999.
13. Pagallo, G. & Haussler, D. Boolean Feature Discovery in Empirical Learning. In Machine Learning 5, pp. 71–99. 1990.
14. Quinlan, J.R. C4.5: Programs for Machine Learning. Morgan Kaufmann, 1993.
15. Zheng, Z. Constructing X-of-N attributes for decision tree learning. Machine Learning 40 (2000), 1-43.

Sensible Initialisation in Chorus

Conor Ryan and R. Muhammad Atif Azad

Department Of Computer Science And Information Systems
University of Limerick, Ireland
{Conor.Ryan,Atif.Azad}@ul.ie

Abstract. One of the key characteristics of Evolutionary Algorithms is the manner in which solutions are evolved from a primordial soup. The way this soup, or initial generation, is created can have major implications for the eventual quality of the search, as, if there is not enough diversity, the population may become stuck on a local optimum.
This paper reports an initial investigation using a position independent evolutionary algorithm, *Chorus*, where the usual random initialisation has been compared to an approach modelled on the GP ramped half and half method. Three standard benchmark problems have been chosen from the GP literature for this study.
It is shown that the new initialisation method, termed *sensible* initialisation maintains populations with higher average fitness especially earlier on in evolution than with random initialisation. Only one of the benchmarks fails to show an improvement in a probability of success measure, and we demonstrate that this is more likely a symptom of issues with that benchmark than with the idea of sensible initialisation.
Performance seems to be unaffected by the different derivation tree depths used, and having a wider pool of individuals, regardless of their average size, seems enough to improve the performance of the system.

1 Introduction

The first step in performing a run in an evolutionary algorithm is to initialise the population. The purpose is to give the algorithm a starting point by creating a diverse array of structures with, where appropriate, a variety of shapes and sizes. These structures are then manipulated by different genetic operators as the evolution progresses.

Some of these methods are *smart*, in that they try to incorporate some useful information into the population, such as previous solutions [10], or domain specific knowledge [2]. Other methods, on the other hand, are merely what we term *sensible*, in that they only attempt to make the initial population as general as possible.

This paper is concerned with initialisation in the *Chorus* [8] system. Chorus is a Genetic Programming type system that uses a genotype-phenotype mapping to produce programs from linear genomes using a Backus Naur Form(BNF) grammar. Due to the unique manner in which Chorus maps individuals, there is a large degree of position independence in the genomes. In particular, while the order of certain genes can be important, their absolute location never matters. Chorus has been shown to be successful in domains such as automatic programming [8] and, in particular, Control Theory [1], in which it was used to discover a flaw in a common GP benchmark. The paper compares a

C. Ryan et al. (Eds.): EuroGP 2003, LNCS 2610, pp. 394–403, 2003.

version of ramped half and half [3] to random initialisation on three benchmark problems from GP literature [3], the symbolic regression of a quartic polynomial, the Santa Fe ant trail problem and the boolean 6 multiplexer problem.

The results suggest that, while the ramped half and half method does perform better in the earlier generations, random initialisation shows improved performance towrads later generations especially in the artificial ant problem.

The paper first gives a brief description of the Chorus System. We then move on to discuss some of the existing approaches to population initialisation and describe the technique that has been followed in this approach along with random initialisation. Section 4 describes the experimental setup and discusses the results obtained from the experiments. It is followed by a few conclusions that we derive from this exercise.

2 Chorus

Chorus is a grammar based EA that recognizes a distinction between genotype and phenotype. The genome consists of a binary string composed of 8 bit codons, where each codon represents a particular rule from the grammar. This differs from Grammatical Evolution (GE) [9], where the meaning of every codon is dependent upon its predecessors. A mapping process translates the binary strings into expressions from a high level language which is described using a context free grammar in Backus Naur Form(BNF). The 8 bit codon is **mod**ed with the total number of rules in the grammar so as to point to a rule from the grammar. This behaviour deviates from GE, where the interpretation of a codon depends upon the state of the mapping process. GE makes sure that the codon being read produces a rule for the non-terminal under consideration. This is achieved by **mod**ing the codon with the number of rules for the non-terminal that needs to be resolved. Depending upon the state of the mapping process, the same codon can be read in corresponding to different non-terminals. This means that the behaviour of a codon depends upon its situation in the chromosome. As total number of rules remains fixed in the grammar regardless of the state of the mapping process, meaning of a codon remains fixed in Chorus regardless of its situation in the chromosome.

When the mapping begins, the genome is read from left to right, to pick the rules from the grammar so as to arrive at a legal sentence comprising of all terminals. However, fixed valued codons may not necessarily be in the order the mapping process may demand. We keep track of all the rules that we come across in a *concentration table*. The concentration table has an entry for every rule in the grammar and is initialised to all zeros when the mapping begins. The table is divided into different sections, each pertaining to a particular non-terminal. Every time a codon is read, concentration of the corresponding rules is incremented in the table.

When we have to find a rule corresponding to a non-terminal, we consult the *relevant* section from the table. The rule with the highest concentration at that time is chosen. In case of a tie (e.g at the beginning of the mapping) we read the genome left to right. The reading stops when only one of the rules from the relevant section claims the highest concentration. The stopping position in the chromosome is noted to allow the subsequent scanning of the genome to continue from there.

The mechanics of the sytem are so that a codon may not be immediately consumed as it is read in. This delay in the expression of a codon, combined with the requirement to be in the majority to make a claim brings the position independence in the system. The important thing is the presence or otherwise of a codon and its location is less so. For more information, consult [8][1].

2.1 Chorus Initialisation

The initial population in Chorus has so far been generated by choosing random 8 bit numbers for each codon. Even though the genome lengths are pre-specified by the user at the beginning of the run, this does not mean that the phenotypes will necessarily have identical or even similar lengths. Also, as is the nature of the mapping process, an individual may run out of the codons and may still be unable to map completely. A way to tackle this situation may be to re-use the genetic material using *wrapping* operator as described by Ryan *et al.* [9]. Wrapping around the genome may allow the re-use of the existing terminal symbols, but may introduce further non-terminals thus aggravating the situation.

The current version of Chorus punishes the individuals that fail to map by assigning a fitness value of exactly zero. Roulette wheel selection makes sure that such individuals get no chance to indulge in any reproductive activity, terminating their role in the generation of future population. An initial investigation revealed that about 56% of the individuals fail to map completely in the initial generation for the symbolic regression problem, even when allowed to wrap for about 30 times. The figure is about 43% for the Santa Fe Trail problem and 61% for the multiplexer problem with a similar number of wrappings. Considering these facts, it is reasonable to assume that a more sensible method of intialisation, something on the lines of ramped half and half approach may bless the system with a much bigger pool of feasible and structurally diverse individuals to begin with, which may be conducive towards the later evolution.

3 Initialisation

Amongst the *smart* initialisation methods are those examined by such as Grefenstette [2], who discussed methods and showed the value of incorporating problem specific knowledge into the genetic algorithms(GAs) including seeding the population. Another approach, described by Whitley *et al.* [10] iteratively uses previous best solution as a basis for altering the representation used during a restart. The individuals in the subsequent runs are represented by a string of *delta* values. A delta value represents the difference with the best solution found in the previous run at a particular gene location. It is argued that this avoids the need to maintain diversity and leads to smaller search space. However, comparing every individual with a pre-specified individual limits the use of this approach for GAs involving individuals with variable lengths.

3.1 Initialisation in Genetic Programming

Koza [3] describes methods to initialise a population for tree based Genetic Programming(GP). The *grow* method chooses elements from the functions set and the terminals set with equal probability until a certain depth of the tree has been reached. The restriction is that the root node is always chosen from the functions set and the trees can not grow beyond a certain maximum depth which is specified by the user. Grow produces trees of irregular shapes and sizes because of random selection from the functions and the terminals set. A branch stops extending upon containing a terminal even if the maximum depth has not been reached. The *full* method, on the other hand, only chooses functions until the maximum depth has been reached and then only picks from the terminal sets. This results in trees with all the branches extending to the maximum depth.

To encourage structural diversity in GP populations, Koza uses a mix of the two approaches mentioned before. This hybrid approach is termed *ramped half and half*. It generates the initial population in groups of different maximum depths. Each group is then divided into two halves. One half is initialised using full, while grow is used for the other half.

Ratel and Sebag [7] have employed an approach for producing derivation trees of suitable depths for Grammar-Guided Genetic Programming(G_3P). A grammar specified in Backus Naur form involves production rules that map non terminals to terminals in one or more steps. Every step taken in this attempt increments the depth of the derivation tree. A pre-defined maximum depth parameter is used to pick only those productions, which allow mapping to the terminal symbols with a derivation tree of a depth less than or equal to the maximum depth. This can be seen as an approach similar to grow method for Koza's GP.

This paper employs an approach similar to ramped half and half for Chorus. The abstract syntax trees used by Koza are replaced here by derivation trees, showing the sequence of derivations leading from the start symbol to a legal sentence of the grammar (a collection of only terminal symbols). As a derivation tree is grown, the index is noted down for every production rule that is used to expand the tree. When all the leaves of the tree contain terminal symbols, the expansion is stopped. The list of the indices noted down thus far in the sequence of expression, represents the genome for this tree and is stored in the population.

3.2 Sensible Initialisation in Chorus

As described above, sensible initialisation in Chorus has been inspired by the ramped half and half method described by Koza. In Koza's GP, functions are responsible for the growth of a tree. As Chorus uses grammars, this role is taken over by the *recursive* production rules. We define a rule to be recursive due to three reasons.

- The right hand side of the production rule may contain the non-terminal on the left hand side.
- The right hand side of a rule may contain a non-terminal which points to a rule that is recursive due to any of the other two reasons.
- The right hand side of a rule may contain a non-terminal that leads back to the same production rule. Consider the mutually recursiverules given below.

```
<line>      ::= <condition>
<condition> ::= if(trail.food_ahead())
                  { <line> } else { <line> }
```

`<line>` leads to the non-terminal `<condition>`, which in turn takes us back to `<line>`. This labels both the rules as recursive. We also calculate the minimum depth required by a production rule to lead to all terminal symbols. Consider the grammar given below where S is the start symbol.

```
S=<expr>
<expr>     ::=  <expr> <op> <expr>     (0)
              | <var>                  (1)
<op>       ::= +                       (2)
<var>      ::= X                       (3)
```

Consider rule 0 from the grammar. Non-terminal <op> maps directly to terminals, thus its minimum depth is 2. <expr> on the other hand first maps to rule 1, which in turn takes one more step to map to the terminal symbol employing rule 3, thus requiring a minimum depth of 3. As rule 0 involves both <op> and <expr>, the maximum of the minimum depths of the two non-terminals, i.e 3, is the minimum depth for rule 0.

Once these two parameters have been noted for every rule, i.e its recursive nature and the minimum depth, we can generate derivation trees in the manner similar to ramped half and half for Koza's GP. Whenever the tree has to be grown, only those productions are chosen from, whose minimum depth is less than or equal to the remaining allowed depth. This is calculated by subtracting the tree's current depth from the maximum allowed depth. If we are using the full method, if possible, we only choose recursive rules. In case of grow, recursive and non-recursive rules are chosen with equal probability.

This is a very inexpensive way to generate trees, as no effort is made to encode any kind of problem specific information in them, and no test is done to determine if two trees are functionally identical which, given that trees of different shapes can be functionally identical could be a very expensive exercise. A simple clone check can be carried out by comparing the linear chromosomes, however, to determine if two individuals have made exactly the same choices. Again, this is a very cheap operation, as comparisons only have to be made against individuals of identical length.

4 Experimental Setup

To test the effectiveness of sensible initialisation in Chorus, three standard benchmark problems from GP literature are used for this investigation, i.e. Symbolic Regression of a quartic polynomial, Artificial Ant problem using Santa Fe trail and the boolean 6 multiplexer problem (see [3] for details). All the experiments involve 100 independent runs with a population size of 500 spanning 250 generations. Crossover probability is set to 0.9, while mutation flips 1% of the bits in the binary string. The grammars used for the experiments have the same terminal symbols as the GP functions and GP terminals used by Koza. In case of regression problem, absolute errors are summed up for all the 20 test cases in the range $[-1, 1]$.

The reciprocal of the sum represents the fitness of an individual. In the case of the Santa Fe Ant trail fitness is the number of pieces of food eaten by the ant, while the correct number of outputs mark the fitness in the multiplexer problem. Experiments compare the performance of random initialisation against ramped half and half method.

Random initialisation uses a modified form of wrapping in the initial generation in which, after wrapping occurs, the individual is unrolled. This means that the genetic material is copied to the end of the genome the number of times the genome wrapped. Ramped half and half experiments have been conducted with three different derivation tree depths, i.e., 5, 10 and 15. The use of different depths helps us average out the effects of this method. A variant of random initialisation has also been tried where an individual is allowed into the population only if it has a positive fitness. It is marked with the legend 'No Zero Fitness' in the graphics. A similar strategy has also been tried for sensible initialisation with depth 5 in the artificial ant problem only. It isn't necessary for the other problems because, as described later on, sensible initialisation filters out almost all zero fitness individuals in the other two problems. Hence, this test is not needed for the other two problems. The legend title is 'No Zero - Depth 5'.

All the experiments use roulette wheel selection with steady state replacement. An offspring can only get into the population if it scores better then the worst fit of the existing population.

4.1 Results

Figure 1 shows the cumulative success frequency in the problems. In case of Symbolic Regression, the ramped half and half approach is faster to begin with, but random initialisation appears to be catching up towards the later part of evolution, especially after the 200th generation. The Santa Fe trail problem shows a different situation. Random initialisation, with and without zero fitness values, clearly seems to be the winner throughout the evolution.

The multiplexer problem shows just 3% success in the random initialisation, a figure dropping to 0% for 'No Zero Fitness' case. Sensible method doesn't boost the performance much except for depth 5 where it shows a 15% success rate, but this does not give a conclusive picture.

Figure 2 shows the *average fitness* comparison for the problems. If we consider the first 50 generations, the regression and the multiplexer graphs are consistent with the figure showing the cumulative frequency, in the sense that sensible initialisation performs better than the random method. The Santa Fe ant trail results, however, show a different picture altogether, with random initialisation seeming to be lagging behind the others.

Cumulative success frequency has already been challenged as a valid measure for performance of a run [5] and this seems to be another case to support that argument. In the case of the Santa Fe trail, despite having a lower average fitness in first 50 generations, those runs using random initialisation still have enough diversity to make a dramatic leap to perfect fitness. Whether this is a symptom of the fact that the Santa Fe trail has been demonstrated to have a large number of solutions [4] to the extent that it can even be solved by random search [6], or a symptom of there being greater diversity in the random population remains to be tested.

If we look at later generations, up to 250, we see that while regression problem hints at convergence in performance of the initilisation methods, the random initilisation overtakes the sensible method in Santa Fe ant trail problem around 80th generation. The multiplexer problem remains consistent with the previous figure, maintaining a difference[1] in performance.

[1] Claims of performance difference have been tested with Mann-Whitney-Wilcoxon test, a non parametric test that makes no assumptions about the normal distribution of the samples.

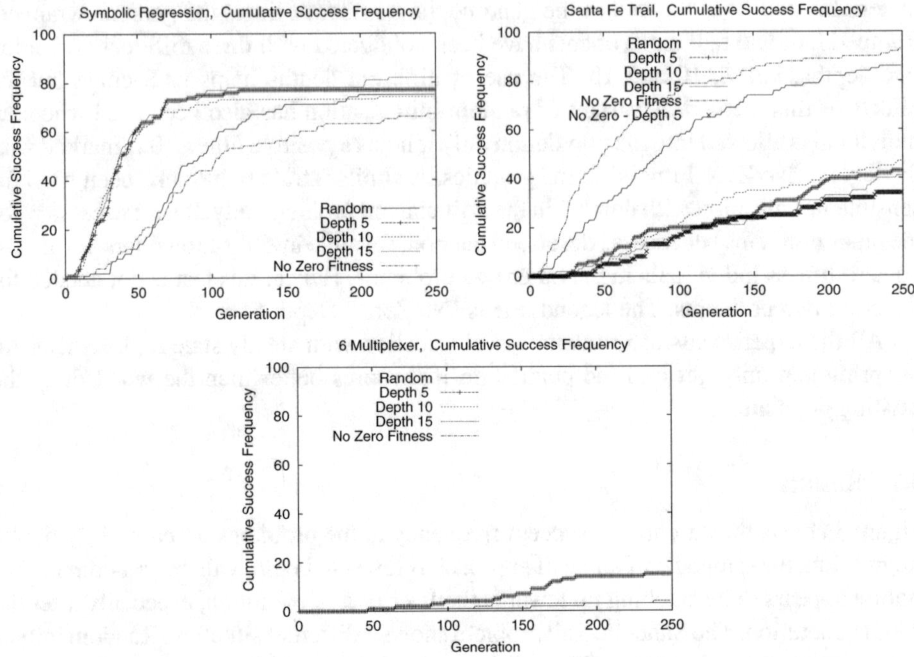

Fig. 1. The cumulative frequency of success over the problems.

We also note the number of times a crossover event led to introduction of new individuals in the population and take their ratio with the total number of individuals produced by crossovers(see figure3). As crossover probability is set to 0.9, on average 450 crossover events take place in every generation. All the problems show that earlier on sensible initialisation has a high turn out. The situation changes from generation 19 to 50, where methods involving random initialisation show superior performance, except for the Santa Fe Trail problem, which shows convergence. No significant difference is found between performances of different depths for sensible initialisation. These findings, however, do not involve the amount of increases in fitness associated with the incoming individuals. Together with the earlier figures, they maintain that difference in perforance is more prominant in the earlier generations.

4.2 Discussion

The figures described in the previous section suggest that, while sensible initialisation has made an impression in the regression and multiplexer problems, Santa Fe Ant Trail does well with the random initialisation method. Before reaching a conclusion, however, we have to consider what it is that sensible initialisation brings into the system. As suggested earlier, part of its effect is that it is a remedy for losing out a significant portion of the population to incomplete mappings. Incomplete mappings are assigned a fitness value of exactly zero and hence play no part in further evolution. An investigation into random initialisation reveals that other than incomplete mappings, only 0.1% individuals that

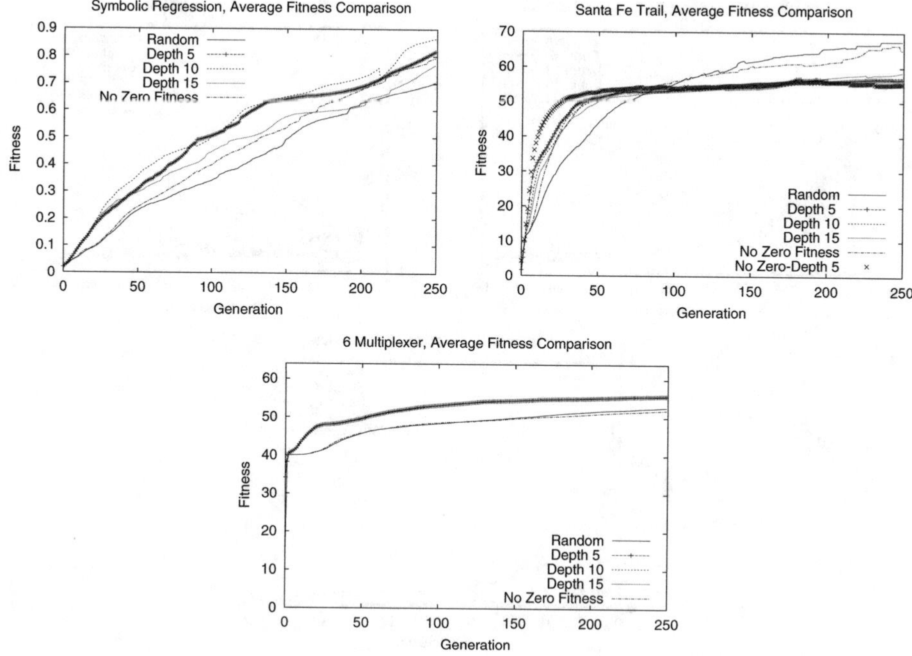

Fig. 2. Average fitness across 250 Generations.

manage to map completely, get a zero fitness value in the regression problem. In case of multiplexer problem, this figure is exactly 0.0%.

Section 2.1 mentions that regression problem loses almost half the population to incomplete mappings. The figure is even higher for the multiplexer problem. This means that, if this void is filled with individuals with positive fitnesses, we can have a larger pool to evolve from thus being one of the reasons for the boost in performance. The regression problem reports only 0.2% of the population to have a fitness value of 0.0 with sensible initialisation. The figure drops to exactly zero percent for the multiplexer problem.

The figures for the 'No Zero Fitness', however, depict that this is not the only reason for better performance. Average fitness increases compared to purely random initialisation in regression problem but remains unaffected in the multiplexer problem. Paradoxically, cumulative success frequency drops in both the problems. Sensible initialisation still maintains a perfromance superior to random initialisation, with or without zero fitness values in both the problems. This gives a hint that the structural diversity brought in by the sensible method also has a part to play.

While the Santa Fe Trail problem seems to be easier for random initialisation, it was thought that it could be so due to the reduced effect of sensible initialisation to induce individuals with positive fitness. Section 2.1 reports that even though 43% individuals suffer from incomplete mappings, about 79% individuals still have zero fitness in case of random initialisation. This is because many solutions fail to pick even a single piece of food. In case of sensible initialisation, the number of incomplete mapping falls to

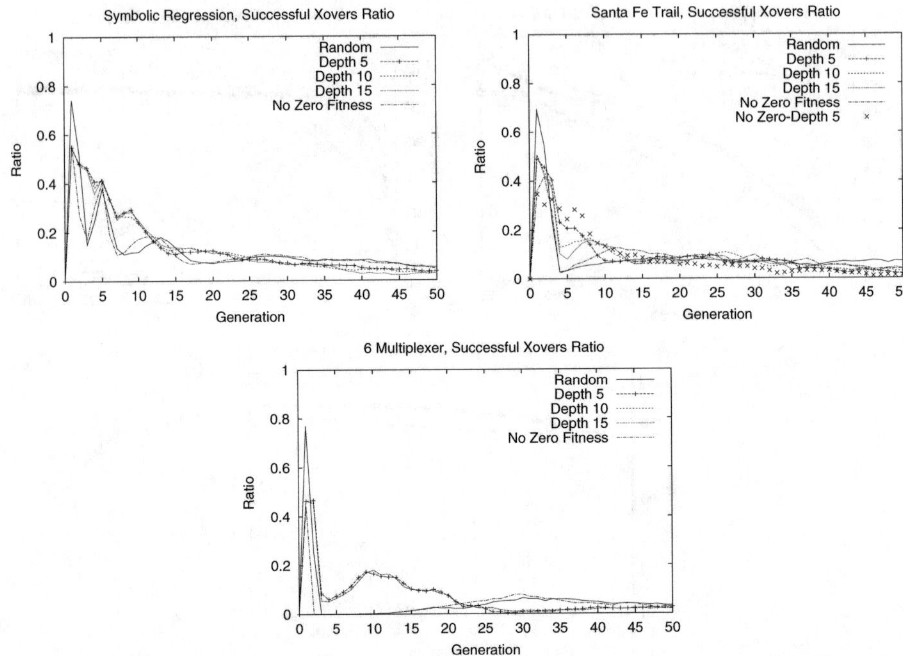

Fig. 3. Ratio of the number of individuals that successfully propagated to the next generation and the total number of crossovers.

zero, but number of individuals with zero fitness values only falls to 56% on average, as compared to very low percentages in case of the other two problems. However, filtering out zero fitness individuals in both the initialisation approaches reveals that even though earlier generations show better performance with sensible method, in the long term, this problem does seem to suit random initialisation.

5 Conclusions

We have described a method for initialisation in the *Chorus* system which is modelled on the popular *ramped half-and-half* approach often employed in GP. We describe a simple implementation, which can be applied with very little overhead.

In the three problems examined here, Sensible Initialisation always maintains populations with higher average fitnesses than random initialisation, especially so in the earlier generations. In all but the Santa Fe trail, there is also an increase in cumulative probability of success, but we further question the use of this problem as a benchmark, and the use of its cumulative probability of success measures in comparisons.

Significantly, the most profound difference is apparent in the multiplexer, the most difficult of all the problems. Furthermore, in general, performance seems to be unaffected by the actual depths used, in that simply having a good spread of individuals, regardless of their average depth, is enough to improve the system.

References

1. R.M.A. Azad, C. Ryan, M.E. Burke and A.R. Ansari, A Re-examination Of The Cart Centering Problem Using The Chorus System. In the proceedings of *Genetic and Evolutionary Computation Conference (GECCO), 2002* (pp 707-715), Morgan Koffman, NYC, NY, 2002.
2. J.J. Grefenstette, Incorporating Problem Specific Knowledge into Genetic Algorithms. *Genetic Algorithms and Simulated Annealing* (pp 42-60), L. Davis(ed.),Morgan Koffman, Los Altos, CA, 1987.
3. J.R. Koza, Genetic Programming: On the Programming of Computers by Means of Natural Evolution, MIT Press, Cambridge, MA, 1992.
4. W. B. Langdon and R. Poli, Why Ants are Hard. In the proceedings of *Genetic Programming 1998: The Third Annual Conference*, 1998.
5. S. Luke and L. Paniat, Is Perfect the enemy of the Good? In the proceedings of *Genetic and Evolutionary Computation Conference(GECCO) 2002* (pp 820-828), Morgan Koffman, NYC, NY, 2002.
6. J. O'Sullivan and C. Ryan, An Investigation into the Use of Different Search Strategies with Grammatical Evolution. In the proceedings of *European Conference on Genetic Programming (EuroGP2002)* (pp268-277), Springer, 2002.
7. A. Ratle and M. Sebag, Genetic Programming and Domain Knowledge: Beyond the Limitations of Grammar-Guided Machine Discovery. In the proceedings of *Parallel Problem Solving from Nature(PPSN VI)*(pp 211-220), Springer, 2000.
8. C. Ryan, A. Azad, A. Sheahan and M. O'Neill, No Coercion and No Prohibition, A Position Independent Encoding Scheme for Evolutionary Algorithms - The Chorus System. In the Proceedings of *European Conference on Genetic Programming (EuroGP 2002)* (pp131-141), Springer, 2002.
9. C. Ryan, J.J. Collins and M. O'Neill, Grammatical Evolution: Evolving Programs for an Arbitrary Language, in *EuroGP'98: Proc. of the First European Workshop on Genetic Programming* (Lecture Notes in Computer Science 1391, pp 83-95), Springer, Paris, France, 1998.
10. D. Whitley, K. Mathias and P. Fotzhorn, Delta Coding: An Iterative Search Strategy for Genetic Algorithms. Proceedings of *Fourth International Conference on Genetic Algorithms* (pp 77-84), Morgan Koffman, San Diego, CA, 1991.

An Analysis of Diversity of Constants of Genetic Programming

Conor Ryan[1] and Maarten Keijzer[2]

[1] CSIS Dept., University of Limerick, Ireland
Conor.Ryan@ul.ie
[2] CS Dept., Free University, Amsterdam
mkeijzer@cs.vu.nl

Abstract. This paper conducts an investigation into the manner in which constants evolve during the course of GP run. It starts by describing an intuitive Gaussian type mutation for constants and showing that its ability to produce small changes in individuals leads to a high performance. It then demonstrates the surprising result that, in a selection of real world problems, simple random mutation performs better. The paper then finishes with an analysis of the diversity of constants in the population, and the manner in which this changes over time.

1 Introduction

When applying Genetic Programming to Symbolic Regression problems, one often employs the ephemeral random constant $\Re$, in the hope that it will be used to synthesise (or at least approximate) constants that appear in the target function. Typically, no mutation is performed on these constants, so individuals must structurally adapt to whatever constants were present in the initial generation.

This paper examines the effects of different types of mutation on constants, including *creep* mutation, a stepwise mutation that only permits small changes, and it is demonstrated that the ability to make these smaller changes appears to improve the search power of a system. We examine their performances and, inspired by [5], the paper then investigates the manner in which the diversity of constants declines in a GP run.

We then examine a number of increasingly more difficult problems which give the surprising result that, despite performing so poorly on the benchmark problem, *uniform* (random) mutation performs quite considerably better.

Finally, the paper then investigates some of the evolutionary dynamics of constant mutation. In particular, the temporal qualities of mutation are examined, demonstrating that there is a dramatic drop off in the number of mutations that make it into the best of run individual as a run progresses. This section also investigates the number of constants in use, and shows that the number present in the final generation, and, in particular, in the best of run, is heavily dependent on the type of mutation used. It also investigates the appearance of an *Eve* individual[5], and demonstrate that, although the constants can appear anywhere in an individual, in most runs all constants in the final population come from a handful of ancestors.

Section 2 decribes the traditional approach to evolving constants in GP, and outlines the approach to constant evolution (which is conducive to mutation) used in the

C. Ryan et al. (Eds.): EuroGP 2003, LNCS 2610, pp. 404–413, 2003.

paper. The *Eve* phenomenon and its relevance to this work is outline in section 3, while section 4 describes the experimental set up and initial results. Section 5 is concerned with an investigation into some of the temporal elements of constant evolution, and conducts a number of experiments designed to shed some light on the manner in which constant diversity diminishes throughout a run. Finally, section 6 finishes up with some observations and conclusions on the work presented here.

2 Constants in Genetic Programming

When running a GP experiment that is likely to require one or more constants in the final individual, it is common practice to introduce a terminal known as $\Re$, the ephemeral random constant. Whenever this is terminal is chosen in the initial generation of individuals, a random constant in some predetermined range is created.

As acknowledged by Koza [4], it is extremely unlikely that any of the initial constants will appear unmodified in the final individual. Instead, constants are combined together by arithmetic functions to produce more useful ones. In fact, he noted that the *best-of-run* individuals produced in many of his experiments had a tendency to reuse a small number of the original constants many times.

2.1 Implementation and Optimization of Constants

Many approaches have been considered to efficiently implement constants in a genetic programming system. The easiest method is to simply allow the occurance of doubles in the parse tree. This is particularly easy to achieve in a language like LISP. For C and C++ however, Keith and Martin showed that an approach using a prefix jumptable is a most flexible and efficient [3] one. To accomodate constants, a seperate array of floating point values is maintained and the genome consists simply of a linear array of indices. In the case of constants, the indices point to a floating point value. Because the indices are of finite size (usually one or two bytes), a limited number of constants can be accomodated, however, Keith and Martin note that this is not a problem as a genetic programming system will use only a few constants.

Howard and D'Angelo introduced a hybrid method for optimizing constants called GA-P[1]. This system uses genetic programming for finding a model structure, and a genetic algorithm for finding the values for constants. To achieve this, constants in the tree are indices into an array of values, only here each individual has its private (small) array of values. Search and optimization of constant values can then be performed on this seperate array.

Although the above gives an overview of implementations, many more approaches exist for finding the optimal constant value. Apart from hybridizing a genetic algorithm and genetic programming as in [1], the most popular methods are the use of uniform range or gaussian mutations (for instance [6]), and nonlinear optimization using gradient descent [7] or quadratic approximations [8].

The idea behind most of these constant optimization techniques is that of strong causality: small changes in a floating point terminal will lead to small changes in the overall fitness. The numerically expensive techniques of gradient descent and hybridization with a genetic algorithm or evolution strategy that run a seperate optimization loop inside the main genetic programming loop have to find a careful balance between the effort that is used to optimize the constants in the individual and the probability that this effort goes to waste by the individual getting deleted instantly. The less expensive techniques of making small changes have to either fix adaptation rates before the run, or adapt these rates themselves during the run. In contrast with static optimization problems, the functions that need to be optimized (i.e. the errors a parse tree makes) is dynamic. Due to subtree crossover and node mutations, the structures will change radically during the run.

2.2 Sorted Table Method

This paper employs a method similar to [3]. Prior to generating initial population, a random list of constants is produced, and then sorted. When an individual selects $\Re$ they are simply given an index with which to look up the table. The advantage of this method is that small changes in the index value will lead to small changes in the actual value used. Similarly, larger changes in the index value will have larger changes in the actual value associated with them. This method thus mimics the use of small step changes with a finite set while at the same type having a very efficient implementation.

This system has two different types of mutation, namely *uniform* and *creep*. With uniform mutation, a new value for the index can be anything within the range of the list. This is a discrete variant of simply choosing a new random value uniformly from some specified range. *Creep*, on the other hand will only ever choose a value directly above or below the current value, thus ensuring that any change will be relatively small. For pre-mutation values at the extreme of the list, *creep* will only ever mutate them in such a way that the value will still only change by one.

The motivation behind creep mutation is that smaller changes are likely to be less disruptive than larger ones, particularly later on in a run. In Koza's original GP, the individual structures were forced to adapt to the initial set of constants, while with this system, both structures and constants can adapt. The use of discrete steps on a finite set of constants makes it easier to analyze the usage of constants. All experiments below are performed with a set of 245 constants that are spread regularly in the range [0,1].

3 The Eve Phenomenon

The so-called *Eve* phenomenon was noted in GP populations by McPhee and Hopper [5]. They performed an analysis of the ancestors of the final population in a run, to determine, firstly, how many different individuals from the *initial* generation managed to produce a descendent that made it to the final population. Their results showed that, in the vast majority of runs (72 out of 80) there was but a single root ancestor for *every* individual in the final population.

Further analysis demonstrated that it wasn't only the root nodes that individuals in the final population shared, but that substantial portions of the population shared several of their top levels with a common ancestor.

Clearly, when a run employs the ephemeral real constant, it is reasonable to expect that a relatively small number of individuals will contribute to the number of constants present in the final generation. This raises the question of what is the impact of this loss of diversity? Typically, loss of diversity is associated with premature convergence and other negative phenomena, but it is also possible that such lack of diversity of constants could be a positive thing, as some element of convergence is necessary if a population is to produce a solution.

Recall that Koza acknowledged that it is highly improbable that the actual desired constants will appear in the initial generation, so one can expect GP to synthesise constants based on those present in the initial population. Evolutionary dynamics would suggest that, rather than maintain a diverse balance of constants, the same constants would be reused many times. Indeed, Koza's [4] experience suggests this is the case.

Furthermore, if these constants are in a state of flux, for example, through mutation, it is possible that the power of the search will be damaged, as individuals will have to keep modifying structurally to adapt to changing constants even to *maintain* their original fitness. This leads to a key question: can we design a mutation operator that permits exploration of different constants, without causing catastrophic changes to individuals' fitness?

4 Experimental Setup

Initial experiments were designed to examine the effects of adding constant mutation. Four different setups were considered; no mutation, creep mutation only, 50% creep and 50% uniform (known as *mix*), and *uniform* only. The problem was to evolve a target constant, 1234.567, using only standard arithmetic operators and ephemeral constants. The constants are initialized between zero and one in a regular, uniform pattern. Constants thus need to be synthesized in order to reach the target value.

To vary the difficulty, a number of different population sizes were examined, that is, 50, 100, 250, 500 and 1000 individuals. Similarly, three different maximum node counts were permitted, 32, 64 and 128. Runs that had all significant digits of the target right were considered to be successful, and higher scores in the table below indicate greater proportions of successful runs. All experiments were repeated on 1800 different initial populations, and all results were treated to a student t-test for statistical significance. The algorithm was steady-state, with tournament selection of size 5, both for parents and replacements.

4.1 Results

Clearly, experiments with a relatively small population size and/or a relatively small maximum number of nodes present a more difficult problem for GP. In general, however, increasing the population size appears to compensate for having small individuals.

The best performers across the experiments were *creep* and *mix*, with *creep* only performing worse than *mix* on two settings, both of which occured at maximum depth. However, a t-test indicates that there is no statistical significance across the results of those two methods.

When comparing *uniform* to *creep*, on the other hand, the same test indicates a statistically significant difference in all cases but those involving the maximum size

Table 1. Percentage of successful runs when trying to evolve a constant.

None	32	64	128
50	0.05	2.5	9.0
100	0.3	9.8	35.7
250	3.6	40.6	79.7
500	15.9	76.5	96.3
1000	42.4	94.1	99.2

Uniform	32	64	128
50	1.4	5.9	16.2
100	2.8	21.3	47.6
250	20.0	60.2	88.8
500	47.8	85.5	97.7
1000	78.5	98.3	99.3

Creep	32	64	128
50	2.7	10.6	22.0
100	9.5	33.4	51.5
250	32.7	73.9	89.7
500	63.5	94.2	97.6
1000	90.6	99.3	99.6

Mix	32	64	128
50	2.5	10.6	20.0
100	8.7	28.0	50.1
250	31.7	72.4	90.2
500	63.7	93.4	98.8
1000	90.4	99.2	99.6

with a population size of 100 and above. Similarly, the only case in which the *creep* wasn't statistically signficantly better than no mutation was at the maximum size for populations of 500 and above.

This would seem to suggest that the ability to make small changes to the constants stimulates the adaptability of the system. If this is indeed the case, then either of the mutation operators that perform in a localized manner, i.e. *creep* and *mix* would be an good addition to a GP system. However, the problem that was studied here is relatively easy, where the change in a single constant is in many evolving structures likely to have a small effect on the error. The acid test, of course, is to determine if these small changes are actually useful to GP when evolving towards a more realistic structure, that is, a function that involves several terms, including trignometric and logarithmic functions. The next section applies all four mutation strategies to a family of such functions.

4.2 Application to Real Symbolic Regression Problems

The problem chosen is adapted from [2], and the function target is $0.3 * x * \sin(x * 2\pi)$. Four different versions of the problem were examined, with input ranges of [-0.5,.5], [- 1,1], [-2,2] and [-3,3]. The greater the range, the more unpredictable the funtion is. The population size was set at 500 individuals, the maximum size at 256 nodes, and the function set consisted of arithmetic, exponentiation, logarithm, square root, sine and cosine. A run was considered a success when the best-of-run individual had a normalized root mean squared error smaller than 0.5. The results are based on 500 independent runs for each setting and each problem.

4.3 Results

Rather surprisingly, as shown in table 2 these results overturned those in the previous section, with *uniform* performing better than the others across all problems. Even more surprising was the fact that *creep* was the worst performer in all but one instance of the problem. The next best performer was *mix*, although its performance never exceeded

Table 2. Percentage of successful runs for each the four mutation methods on $0.3 * x * \sin(x * 2\pi)$

Problem range	None	Creep	Mix	Uniform
[-0.5,.5]	21	19.8	28.2	44.4
[-1,1]	60.2	59.6	65.8	76.2
[-2,2]	32.8	33.6	34	41
[-3,3]	16.6	15.8	20.2	22.0

that of *uniform*. Only for the last problem the difference between *mix* and *uniform* was not significant.

These results suggest that *uniform* appears to be doing a better job than the more intuitive *creep*. As mentioned above, part of the motivation behind using a stepwise type mutation operator like *creep* is that the changes it makes tend to be smaller, thus giving a greater causality between parent and offspring. One could reasonably expect that being permitted to make these smaller changes would allow a smoother adaptation of the structures, i.e. trees.

However, this doesn't appear to be the case. The following section examines some of the characteristics of each strategy, and offers some suggestions as to why the simple *uniform* strategy appears to be best.

5 Temporal Properties of Mutation

Another set of experiments were conducted using the same problem set as in the previous section, to identify some of the characteristics of populations undergoing evolution under the various strategies. There are three characteristics that we analyse, i) the lineage of constants in the *best-of-run* individuals, ii) the number of distinct constants in a population over time, and iii) the temporal traits of successful mutation events. A succesful mutation is defined by taking the lineage of the constants appearing in the *best-of-run* individual and examining the generations at which the value changed for each constant.

5.1 Lineage of Constants

For each of the four problems, we encoded extra information about each constant, in a similar way to [5]. This information included what individual from generation 0 contained *this* constant (notice that it is possible for more than one individual in generation 0 to have the same constant), when the constant was mutated, what value it took on each of these mutations, and what the final value of the constant was.

Table 3 below indicates the average number of original constants present in the *best-of-run* individuals, and the ratio of the number of final distinct constants to the number of original distinct constants.

In this table, a score of 1 indicates that none of the constants underwent mutation during the evolution of the population. Higher numbers indicate that at least some of the (distinct) constants present in the final population underwent mutation. The fact that all of the strategies bar *no mutation* have a measure of greater than one indicates that there is some element of loss and rediscovery in the process of evolution. That is, rather than

Table 3. Left: The average number of original contants in the best of run individual for each of the problems. Right: The average ratio of total constants in the best of run individual to the number of original constants.

Problem	None	Creep	Mix	Uniform
[-0.5,.5]	3.479	2.8878	3.4900	4.6413
[-1,1]	4.0695	3.6970	4.3110	4.7762
[-2,2]	4.2323	4.0382	4.3481	5.2121
[-3,3]	4.1697	3.7520	4.0966	5.0284

Problem	None	Creep	Mix	Uniform
[-0.5,.5]	1	1.6529	2.1143	2.4031
[-1,1]	1	1.9558	2.2649	2.2914
[-2,2]	1	1.9964	2.4764	2.4159
[-3,3]	1	2.0691	2.5651	2.4874

maintain a diverse pool of constants which can be called upon as required, the system rather mutates existing constants. A score of 2 indicates that half of the final constants in the population are derived by mutating other constants *also present in this individual.* A score of 3 would indicate that only a third of the constants are original.

Uniform routinely generates around 66% of final constants from mutations of about 33% of constants that appeared in the initial, random generation.

5.2 Distinct Constants

The next characteristic examined was the number of distinct constants present in the population over time, as plotted in figure 1. In this case there is a dramatic drop in the number present in the population in the first few generations, before the number settles down. Across all experiments, *uniform* always maintained the most diverse array of constants, while *no mutation* always had the least number. In effect, it seems that the number of constants in use after the second generation for a large part determines the number of constants used during the rest of the run. In the first few generations, competition is fiercest between randomly generated individuals, where the focus of search is highly in favour of individuals that achieve reasonable performance quickly. Because no structure is determined yet, the strong causality assumption behind the use of small changes does not hold, and the more wildly varying behaviour of *uniform* mutation is able to find useful contants for new structures more often. Interestingly enough, only with *uniform* mutation, a small increase in the number of distinct constants in use is observed for the first two problems in a few generations after this initial phase. It is hypothesized that uniform mutation is adapting constants to the structures that survived the initial struggle. The *creep* mutation does not show this, indicating that small changes are not helpful in this respect.

This would suggest that populations employing the *no mutation* strategy are forced to resort to synthesis of other constants, and could go some way to explaining the disparity in quality of performance between it and the other strategies.

5.3 Successful Mutations

The final characteristic we examine in this paper is *when* successful mutations happened. Space only permits us to report on one version of our problem, although the shapes of all the graphs are very similar. This graph is in figures 2.

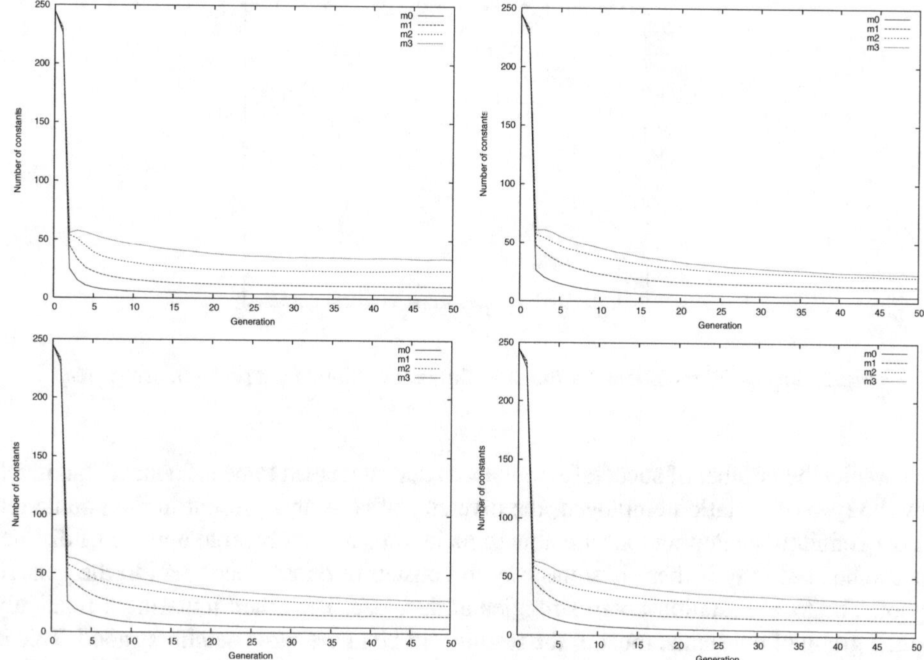

Fig. 1. Average number of distinct constants in the population. The maximum is 245. A distinct constant is counted only when it appears at least three times in the population.

In virtually all runs, the number of successful mutations drops off dramatically until about generation 15-20, at which stage they settle down. Interestingly, in all cases, successful mutations keep occurring right up until the final generation, indicating that making only small tweaks at the later stages of evolution isn't necessarily the best strategy.

Notice that the number of successful mutations tends to level out shortly after the loss of diversity of distinct constants through selection.

6 Conclusions

Clearly, without mutation, a very small number of constants survive to the final generation, while *uniform* mutation routinely maintains the largest number. Our hypothesis is that having too few constants present in the population results in the system being forced to synthesise the required constants at a cost of performance, while those with a sufficient number of constants enjoy greater success.

While [5] discovered that the top nodes of a population tend to come from a common ancestor, our results indicate that this is also true of constants, which is somewhat surprising, as constants are always on leaf nodes. Further, the number of constants that contribute to those present in the *best-of-run* individual is directly related to the type of mutation used. The more disruptive the operator, the greater the diversity, and the greater the number of constants contributing is.

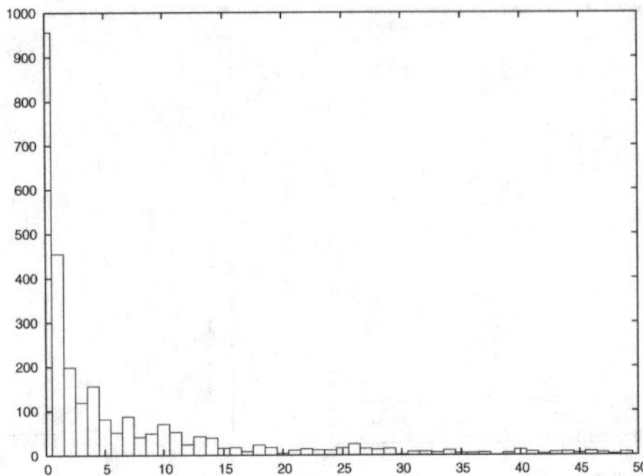

Fig. 2. Successful mutations for the most difficult version of the problem using *creep*.

While the number of successful mutations does not seem to be influenced that much by the type of mutation employed, the diversity of constants present in the population most definitely is. Populations are able to maintain a relatively large number of distinct constants, but only if there is some way to constantly reintroduce them to the genetic pool. The local mutation *creep* struggles at this, because, when mutating a relatively small group of constants, most of the results will be in the same neighbourhood. This is not the case for *uniform*, which selects new values without respect to the original ones.

Traces of the number of distinct constants in a population during runs indicates that there is a sharp fall off initially, which soon tapers into an altogether more gentle decline after around ten generations. This coincides roughly with a decline in the number of successful mutations, which tends to level out a few generations later.

The original motivation behind *creep*, which appeared to be validated by the initial experiments, was that the ability to make small perturbations to constants would facilitate the further adaptation of the structures (trees) in a GP run. Our results indicate, however, that the opposite can be the case. Not only does *uniform* maintain a more diverse array of constants, its trees appear to be able to adapt to this larger array.

In section 3 we posed the question *can we design a mutation operator that encourages exploration?* It appears that the answer is that we already have such an operator, simple random mutation.

References

1. Les M. Howard and Donna J. D'Angelo, *The GA–P: A genetic algorithm and genetic programming hybrid*, IEEE Expert **10** (1995), no. 3, 11–15.
2. Maarten Keijzer and Vladan Babovic, *Genetic programming, ensemble methods and the bias/variance tradeoff - introductory investigations*, Genetic Programming, Proceedings of EuroGP'2000 (Edinburgh) (Riccardo Poli, Wolfgang Banzhaf, William B. Langdon, Julian F. Miller, Peter Nordin, and Terence C. Fogarty, eds.), LNCS, vol. 1802, Springer-Verlag, 15-16 April 2000, pp. 76–90.
3. Mike J. Keith and Martin C. Martin, *Genetic programming in C++: Implementation issues*, Advances in Genetic Programming (Kenneth E. Kinnear, Jr., ed.), MIT Press, 1994, pp. 285–310.

4. John R. Koza, *Genetic programming: On the programming of computers by means of natural selection*, MIT Press, Cambridge, MA, USA, 1992.
5. Nicholas Freitag McPhee and Nicholas J. Hopper, *Analysis of genetic diversity through population history*, Proceedings of the Genetic and Evolutionary Computation Conference (Orlando, Florida, USA) (Wolfgang Banzhaf, Jason Daida, Agoston E. Eiben, Max H. Garzon, Vasant Honavar, Mark Jakiela, and Robert E. Smith, eds.), vol. 2, Morgan Kaufmann, 13-17 July 1999, pp. 1112–1120.
6. Marc Schoenauer, Michele Sebag, Francois Jouve, Bertrand Lamy, and Habibou Maitournam, *Evolutionary identification of macro-mechanical models*, Advances in Genetic Programming 2 (Peter J. Angeline and K. E. Kinnear, Jr., eds.), MIT Press, Cambridge, MA, USA, 1996, pp. 467–488.
7. Alexander Topchy and W. F. Punch, *Faster genetic programming based on local gradient search of numeric leaf values*, Proceedings of the Genetic and Evolutionary Computation Conference (GECCO-2001) (San Francisco, California, USA) (Lee Spector, Erik D. Goodman, Annie Wu, W. B. Langdon, Hans-Michael Voigt, Mitsuo Gen, Sandip Sen, Marco Dorigo, Shahram Pezeshk, Max H. Garzon, and Edmund Burke, eds.), Morgan Kaufmann, 7-11 July 2001, pp. 155–162.
8. Vassili V. Toropov and Luis F. Alvarez, *Application of genetic programming to the choice of a structure of multipoint approximations*, 1st ISSMO/NASA Internet Conf. on Approximations and Fast Reanalysis in Engineering Optimization, June 14-27 1998, Published on a CD ROM.

Research of a Cellular Automaton Simulating Logic Gates by Evolutionary Algorithms

Emmanuel Sapin, Olivier Bailleux, and Jean-Jacques Chabrier

Université de Bourgogne, LERSIA
9 avenue A. Savary, B.P. 47870, 21078 Dijon Cedex, France
{olivier.bailleux,jean-jacques.chabrier}@u-bourgogne.fr
emmanuelsapin@hotmail.com

Abstract. This paper presents a method of using genetic programming to seek new cellular automata that perform computational tasks. Two genetic algorithms are used : the first one discovers a rule supporting gliders and the second one modifies this rule in such a way that some components appear allowing it to simulate logic gates. The results show that the genetic programming is a promising tool for the search of cellular automata with specific behaviors, and thus can prove to be decisive for discovering new automata supporting universal computation.

1 Introduction

Cellular automata are discrete systems in which a population of cells evolves from generation to generation on the basis of local transitions rules. They can simulate simplified forms of life [8][9] or physical systems with discrete time and space and local interactions [5][6][7].

Wolfram showed that one-dimensional cellular automata can present a large spectrum of dynamic behaviours. In "Universality and Complexity in Cellular Automata" [11], he introduces a classification of cellular automata, comparing their behaviour with that of some continuous dynamic systems. He specifies four classes of cellular automata on the basis of qualitative criteria. For all initial configurations, Class 1 automata evolve after a finite time to a homogeneous state where each cell has the same value. Class 2 automata generate simple structures where some stable or periodic forms survive. Class 3 automata's evolution leads, for most initial states, to chaotic forms. All other automata belong to Class 4. According to Wolfram, automata of Class 4 are good candidates for universal computation.

The only binary automaton currently identified as supporting universal computation is Life, which is in Class 4. Its ability to simulate a Turing machine is proved in [2], using gliders (periodic patterns which, when evolving alone, are reproduced identically after some shift in space), glider guns, and eaters. The glider gun emits a glider stream that carries information and creates logic gates through collisions. The eaters permit, in absorbing gliders, the creation of logic circuits using any combination of logic gates.

The identification of new automata able to simulate logic circuits is consequently a promising lead in the search for new automata supporting universal computation. In

C. Ryan et al. (Eds.): EuroGP 2003, LNCS 2610, pp. 414–423, 2003.

this paper, we show how evolutionary algorithms can be used for the research of automata simulating logic gates and we set out an example.

Section 2 describes in detail the creation of logic gates by Life using gliders, glider guns, and eaters as shown in [2]. The framework of our study is then presented in Section 3. Section 4 describes how evolutionary algorithms can be used for seeking new automata supporting gliders and periodic patterns. Using the proposed approach, we found several rules, such as the one described in Section 5, that support a glider gun. Section 6 describes the use of an evolutionary algorithm for modifying the rule in such a way that it supports an eater. Section 7 presents a discussion about some related works. Finally, in the last section we summarize our results and discuss directions for future research.

2 Simulation of a Logic Gate

In [2], sufficient components allowing Life to simulate logic gates are laid out. Data streams are encoded by gliders streams (i.e. the absence of gliders represents the value 0 and the presence of gliders represents the value 1). Figure 1 shows the simulation of an AND gate with 2 inputs streams A and B. A pattern called *glider gun,* which emits a new glider every 30 generations, is used by this simulation. The glider gun creates a glider stream that "crashes" stream A. If a glider is present in stream A, the two gliders are destroyed by this collision, else the glider emitted by the gun continues its run. The stream resulting from this first collision, at a right angle to stream A, is not(A). This stream crashes stream B producing two streams:

- The first, which is aligned with the stream B, is the result of the operation "A and B".
- The second one is destroyed by a pattern called eater. When a glider crash a eater, the eater survives and the glider dies.

The synchronization and the position of the different components are critical to the proper function of the simulation.

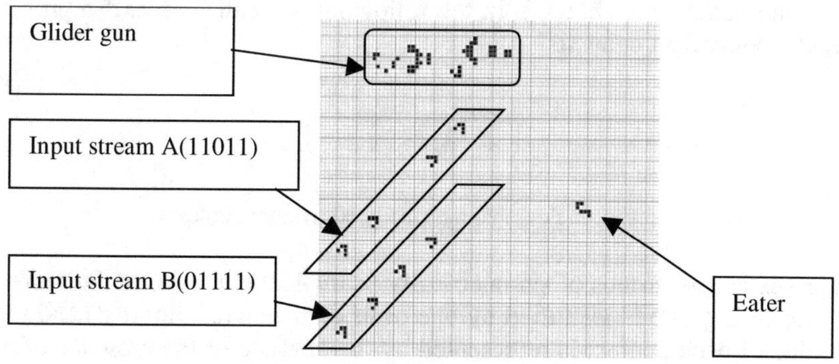

Fig. 1. An AND gate simulated by Life

In the following, we call *motif* a configuration of cells and its evolution. Then, the simulation of a logic gate by Life is possible with four motifs:

- A glider.
- A glider gun.
- A eater.
- A collision, called *vanishing*, of two streams at right angles, with the following result:
    - The destruction of the two gliders if a glider is present in each stream.
    - The survival of a glider, if a glider is present in one stream and absent in the other.

The presence of these motifs in a cellular automaton is sufficient for the possibility of a simulation of an AND gate and a NOT gate by this automaton.

3 Framework

3.1 Cellular Automata

Concerning this study, we explore only cellular automata with the following specifications:

- Cells have 2 possible values, 0 and 1.
- They evolve in a 2D matrix, called *universe*.
- Transition rules only take into account the eight direct neighbours of a cell for the current generation, so as to determine its states for the next generation.

We call *context of a cell* the states of the cell and its 8 neighbours. A cell thus can have 512 different contexts. A transition rule is defined as a boolean function that maps each of the 512 possible contexts to the value which will be taken by the concerned cell at the next generation. Therefore the underlying space of automata includes 2^{512} rules.

The simulation of logic circuits by Life uses a glider moving in any direction so, we choose to consider only isotropic rules. An isotropic rule is a rule in which symmetrically equivalent contexts have the same associated value (cf. Figure 2 where 4 symmetric contexts are shown). In the following, we call "context" a group of symmetrically equivalent contexts.

Fig. 2. Four symmetrically equivalent contexts

There exist 102 groups of symmetrically equivalent contexts. In the representation of a rule, each group is identified by one of its elements (cf. figure 3) and the associated value of each context is represented by the absence or the presence of a point at its right. This representation is used in the following.

We call *critical context of a motif* every context to which all the transition rules supporting this motif map the same value. For example, if a rule t supports a glider then all rules mapping the same values as t to the critical context of the glider support this glider.

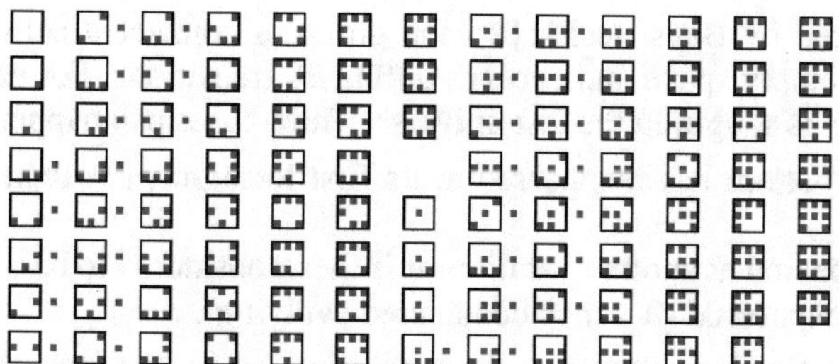

Fig. 3. Representation of a rule

3.2 Evolutionary Algorithms

The evolutionary algorithm is a stochastic tool that tries to maximize a fitness function on a set of individuals called search space. A subset of the search space, population, evolves during several generations. At each generation, taking into account the fitness value of the individuals, the selection, crossover, and mutation operators produce a new population from the old one. In the two evolutionary algorithms that we present in this paper, we tried several crossover and mutation operators, several fitness functions, and several initializations of the population. For clarity, we set out only the versions of the operators and the values of the parameters which gave us the expected results.

4 A New Rule

This section describes the utilization of an evolutionary algorithm for the search of new rules accepting gliders and periodic patterns.

4.1 Starting Rules

Rules have been encoded by 512-bit strings in which all the bits of symmetrically equivalent contexts have the same value. The algorithm manages 50 rules produced in the following way: for each value n between 1 and 50, a string of 512 zeros is generated. In each string, n randomly chosen bits are then modified, and likewise the bits of symmetrically equivalent contexts.

4.2 Crossover and Mutation

A mutation consists of modifying a randomly chosen bit, with the same weight for each of the 512 bits of a rule and likewise the bits of symmetrically equivalent contexts. Then, the isotropy of rules is kept.

We implemented a simple crossover operator at a median point.

4.3 Fitness Function

The computation of the fitness function is based on the evolution, during thirty transitions, of a "primordial soup", randomly generated in a square of 40*40 centered in a 200*200 space. During this evolution the primordial soup is the object of the following test, inspired by Bays' test [1] : each group of connected cells (see figure 4) is isolated in an empty space and evolves during 20 transitions. For each transition, the original pattern is sought in the test universe. Three cases can happen:

- The initial pattern has reappeared at its first location (it is then considered to be periodic).
- It has reappeared at another location (it is then considered to be a glider).
- It has not reappeared (it's then considered evolving).

The fitness function is evaluated as the multiplication of the number of appearances of gliders by the number of appearances of periodic patterns.

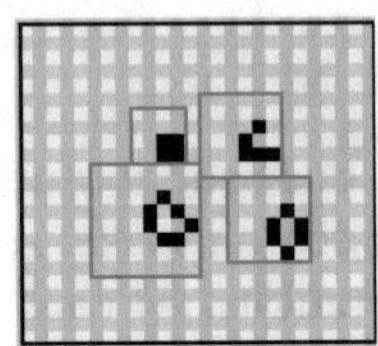

Fig. 4. Group of isolated cells

4.4 Evolutionary Algorithm

After the initialization of the 50 rules, the following cycle is iterated:

- The fitness function evaluates the rules.
- The 20 rules with the highest fitness function are kept.
- From each kept rule, a new rule is created by mutation.
- The 20 kept rules are dispatched randomly into ten couples, and from each couple a rule is created by crossover.
- A new population is created with the kept rule, the ones created by crossovers, and the ones created by mutations.

4.5 Result

This evolutionary algorithm allow us to discover rules accepting gliders. When the algorithms discovers a new rule supporting gliders, we observe a quick convergence to a population of this rule and some variants of this rule accepting the same gliders. For reasons explained in the next section, we are interested in a rule, called R (cf. figure 5), obtained by the evolutionary algorithm.

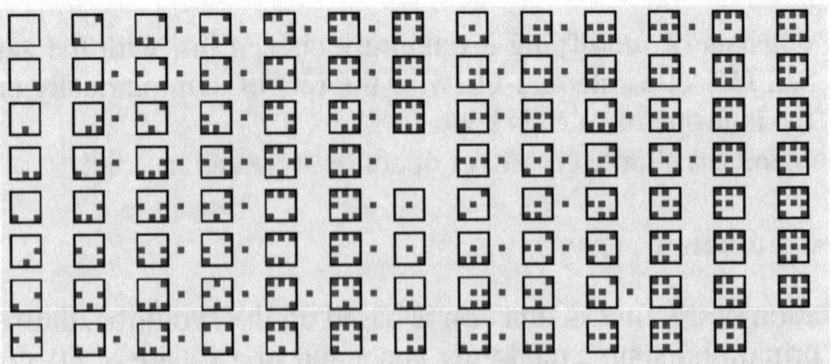

Fig. 5. Representation of rule R

5 Rule R

5.1 The Glider of R

The figure 6 shows the evolution of a primordial soup under R after 100 generations of the automaton.

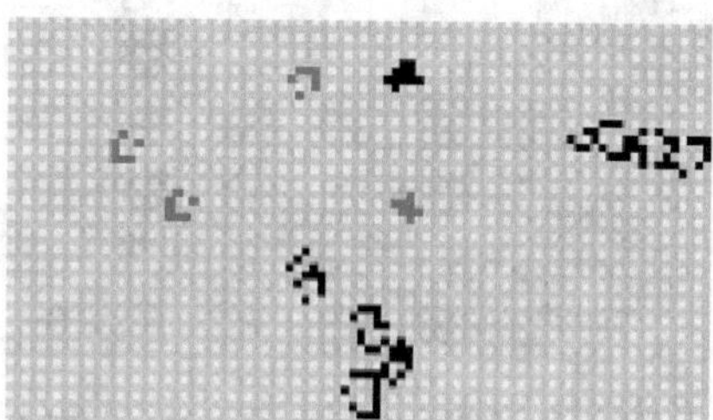

Fig. 6. Evolution of a primordial soup under R after 100 generations of the automaton (in light: a glider)

We notice the presence, in this evolution, of a glider (figure 7).

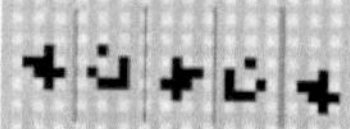

Fig. 7. Evolution of the glider of R

This glider has a period of 4 and a speed of 0,5 cells per generation.

5.2 The Glider Gun of R

The figure 8 shows the evolution of a primordial soup under R after 100 generations of the automaton. We are interested in this rule because we notice the presence, in this evolution, of a glider gun, shown Figure 8.

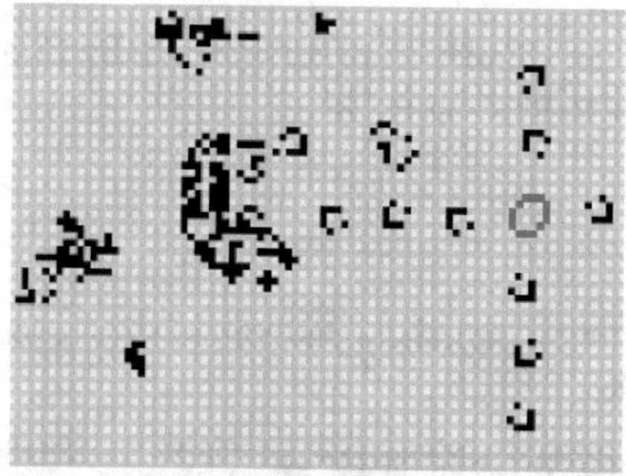

Fig. 8. Evolution of a primordial soup under R after 100 generations of the automaton (in light: a glider gun)

This glider gun emits 4 gliders in all cardinal directions every 18 generations. We wanted to know how many rules support the gun. In order to do that, we recorded the critical contexts of the gun. These are shown in black Figure 9.

Fig. 9. R (in black : the critical contexts of the glider gun)

The gun has 81 critical contexts among the 102 existing ones, thus 2^{21} rules support the gun (and the corresponding glider) of R.

5.3 Collisions

The simulation of a logic gate by Life uses a collision of two streams of gliders. This collision must have the *vanishing* property, as described in Section 2. The critical contexts of the vanishing collision used, shown Figure 10, are critical for the glider gun, too.

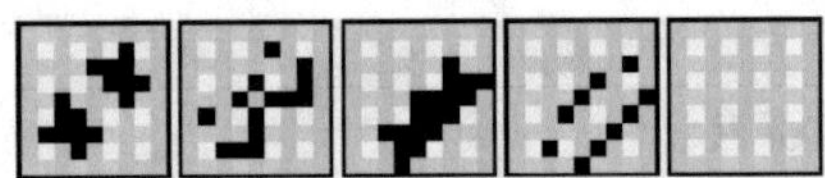

Fig. 10. Vanishing collision used of two streams of gliders

6 Eater

Inspired by [2], where the simulation of a logic gate by Life use an eater, we search, by evolutionary algorithm, an eater in R.

6.1 Population

We chose the most common periodical patterns in R to be candidate for the search of an eater (cf. Figure 11).

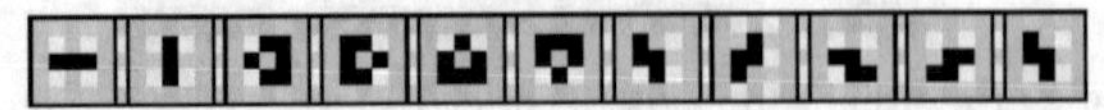

Fig. 11. The ten candidate patterns for the search of a eater

Figure 12 shows the position of the candidate pattern along with the stream of gliders. In this figure, the different candidate patterns for the search of a eater are in the filled square of 5*5 and this square can move in the black rectangle.

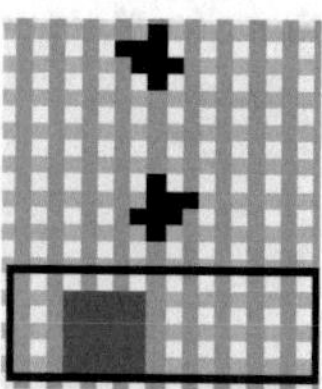

Fig. 12. Position of the candidate eater pattern along with the glider stream

An individual is defined by a triplet:

- Pattern : number, from 1 to 10, of the candidate pattern.
- Position : coordinates of the pattern compared with the glider stream.
- Rule: one of the 2^{19} rules supporting the glider gun.

The algorithm manages 50 individuals. For each individual, the pattern and the position are randomly chosen with the same weight for each of the possible choices and the rule is initialised as R.

6.2 Offspring

A mutation can have 4 variants:

- A pattern from the possible ones replaces the old one.
- The position is modified by incrementing or decrementing the ordinate.
- The position is modified by incrementing or decrementing the abscissa.
- The value mapped to a randomly chosen context, among the non-critical ones for the glider gun, is modified in the rule.

We do not use crossover in this algorithm.

6.3 Fitness Function

The fitness function's goal is to evaluate the capacity of an individual to stop a glider stream. The fitness value of an individual is determined by the collision of the glider and the candidate pattern. It is equal to the number of gliders stopped by the pattern (a pattern can, for example, stop a glider but be destroyed, thus not stopping following gliders).

6.4 Evolutionary Algorithm

After the initialisation of each individual, the following cycle is iterated:

- The fitness function evaluates each individual.
- The 25 rules with the highest fitness function are kept.
- From each kept rule, a new individual is created by mutation.
- A new population is created with the kept rules and the ones created by mutation.

After about ten tries of 1000 generations, we obtained a eater shown Figure 13.

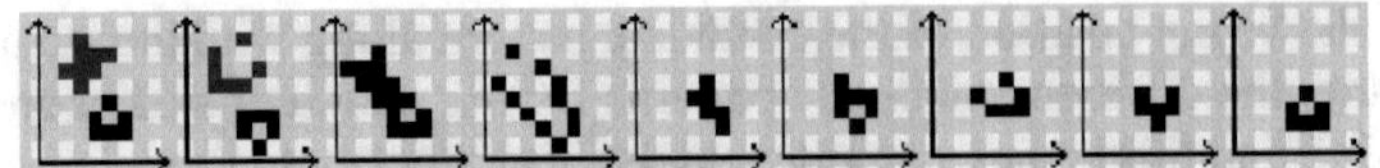

Fig. 13. Collision of a glider stream and a eater

7 Related Works

Another type of evolutionary programming, based on cellular automata, is set out in [3][4], where R. Das, M. Mitchell, and J. P. Crutchfield used genetic algorithms to evolve 1D cellular automata in order to perform computational tasks that require global information processing. In [10], genetic programming is also applied to evolve CA for random number generation.

In a previously submitted work, we discovered, by evolutionary algorithm, new 2D automata with 2 states supporting gliders. Contrary to the ones shown here, those automata are not isotropic. Still, that result contributed to demonstrating that an evolutionary algorithm can be promising for the research of automata presenting specific behaviors.

8 Synthesis and Perspectives

Based on the Conway's approach for the simulation of logic gate by Life, and using evolutionary algorithms, we identified a new automaton that is able to simulate logic gates AND and NOT. It follows from this result that genetic programming proves to be very promising for the research of 2D complex automata presenting specific behaviors.

We plan to use genetic programming for the search of the missing components for the simulation of any logic circuit, e.g. motifs allowing us to duplicate glider streams and to change their direction. Later on, our aim will be the utilization of genetic programming for the search of new universal automata.

References

1. Bays C.: Candidates for the game of life in three dimensions. In Complex Systems, 1 (1987), 373-400.
2. Berlekamp E.,. Conway J.H, Guy R.: Winning Ways for your mathematical plays. Academic press, New York
3. Das R., Mitchell M., Crutchfield J. P. : Evolving Cellular Automata with Genetic Algorithms: A Review of Recent Work. In *Proceedings of the First International Conference on Evolutionary Computation and Its Applications (EvCA'96)*, Russian Academy of Sciences, 1996.
4. Das R., Mitchell M., Crutchfield J. P.: The Evolutionary Design of Collective Computation in Cellular Automata. SFI Working Paper 98-09-080.
5. Dytham C., Shorrocks B.: Selection, Patches and Genetic Variation: A Cellular Automata Modeling Drosophila Populations. In Evolutionary Ecology, 6 (1992) 342-351

6. Epstein I. R.: Spiral Waves in Chemistry and Biology. In Science,252 (1991) 67.
7. Ermentrout, G. Lotti, and l. Margara ,"Cellular Automata Approaches to Biological Modeling," Journal of Theoretical Biology, 60 (1993) 97-133
8. Gardner M.: The fantastic combinaisons of John Conway's new solitaire game « Life », In Scientific American, (1970)
9. Gardner M.: On Cellular Automata, Self-reproduction, the Garden of Eden, and the Game of Life. In Scientific American, 224 (1971) 112-118
10. Hordijk W., Crutchfield J. P. , Mitchell M.: Mechanisms of Emergent Computation in Cellular Automata., *Parallel Problem Solving from Nature-V*, 613-622, Springer-Verlag, 1998.
11. Wolfram S.: Universality and complexity in cellular automata. In Physica D, 10 (1984) 1-35.

From Implementations to a General Concept of Evolvable Machines

Lukáš Sekanina

Faculty of Information Technology, Brno University of Technology
Božetěchova 2, 612 66 Brno, Czech Republic
sekanina@fit.vutbr.cz
phone: +420 541141215

Abstract. This paper introduces a little bit different view on evolvable computational machines than it is usually presented. Evolvable machines are considered as mathematical machines. Traditional tools of theoretical computer science are then employed in order to obtain qualitatively new understanding the evolvable machines. In particular the questions related to formal definition and computational power are discussed. The concept is proposed in framework of traditional software and hardware implementations of evolvable machines.

1 Introduction

From a machine learning perspective, *genetic programming* is very often considered as a technique allowing the automatic design of *computational machines* [8,1]. In the most popular approach, a *program* is evolved. In order to create the computational machine, the evolved program is uploaded into a universally programmable computer and the program is executed. In another approach, referred to as *Cartesian genetic programming* (CGP) [12], digital circuits are evolved directly. The resulting circuits can be considered as computational machines too.

It could theoretically be possible to evolve using genetic programming whatever computational machine based on an arbitrary model of computation. However only relatively simple computational machines (such as small programs [8], circuits [11], cellular automata [15] or Turing machines [20]) were designed successfully because of scalability problems.

Genetic programming also enables the design of *adaptive computational machines.* In this case, opposite to the evolutionary computational machines design, the evolutionary algorithm is inherent part of a target (e.g. embedded) system. The evolutionary algorithm has to autonomously produce computational machines according to requirements represented via dynamic fitness function which reflects a changing environment. Adaptive computational machines, which utilize the evolutionary approach, are known as *evolvable (computational) machines.*

Computer engineering concerns itself with implementation of a given computational machine in reality (in software, hardware etc.). On the other hand computer science usually defines theoretical models of computation for these

C. Ryan et al. (Eds.): EuroGP 2003, LNCS 2610, pp. 424–433, 2003.

computational machines. It is advantageous to have such models because then various methods might be applied to investigate machines' properties, limits and classes. Furthermore, computer engineers can prepare an effective design strategy easily if suitable theoretical models exist.

This paper compares three viewpoints on computational machines designed using evolutionary methods: a software implementation viewpoint, a hardware implementation viewpoint and a formal approach viewpoint. While software implementations are well developed in the genetic programming community and hardware implementations are realized in the *evolvable hardware* community, a formal approach seems to be quite overlooked. Hence this paper introduces some formal definitions as a potential way in which software as well as hardware implementations of evolvable machines can systematically be integrated, studied and understood. In particular we emphasize a *computational scenario* of evolvable machines that differs from conventional computational scenarios.

The approach used in this paper represents a high-level insight to the problem. The method can show what we really do in the evolutionary machine design and how evolvable machines perform the computation. In particular it becomes important for (semi)automatic design tools in which we are looking for a universal description suitable for specification of evolvable systems.

The paper is organized as follows. Section 2 deals with software, hardware and formal viewpoints related to the evolutionary computational machines design. A formal definition of a dynamic environment and computational power in dynamic environment are discussed in Section 3. Section 4 provides summary of the obtained results. Finally conclusions are given in Section 5.

2 Evolutionary Computational Machines Design

In case of the evolutionary computational machine design, genetic programming is only to assist (or "replace") the designer and thus a genetic programming system is utilized only in the design phase. Only a single fitness function is usually constructed. We are interested in *innovative* designs. The resulting machine is much more important than the design method applied since only the resulting machine is interesting for potential customers.

2.1 A Software Viewpoint

Let us recall a programmer's perspective. In genetic programming, (variable length) chromosomes represent either trees or machine language instructions. All candidate programs are executed in order to obtain their fitness values. Every new population is formed using genetic operators working over the chromosomes. The algorithm is terminated when a perfect solution is produced or a pre-defined number of populations are generated.

From a theoretical computer science viewpoint, tree representation can be modeled using expressions of λ-calculus. Machine language instructions directly represent programs of the RAM (Random Access Machine) computer model [7].

Hence a target computational machine looks like a *universal computer*; the evolutionary algorithm is only to supply a program which is uploaded into a memory of the computer and which is executed.

In another approach, genetic programming was employed to construct cellular automata rules. (Non-uniform) *cellular automaton* is a d-dimensional grid of finite automata (known as *cells*) that operate according to their *local transition functions* (also known as *rules*). The cells work synchronously—a new state of every cell is calculated from its previous state and the previous states of cell's "neighbors" in each time step. Local transition functions can also be defined as syntactic trees. These trees can be evolved using genetic programming. Koza [8], Ferreira [6], Sipper [15] and others evolved a number of high-quality rules in tasks where human approach has led to poor results.

The previous paragraph has demonstrated that genetic programming can be applied to design not only a program for a universal computer, but also to design a *component* of computational machine definition (i.e. cellular automata rules in our example). Note that such a computer model (i.e. cellular automaton) differs from traditional universally programmable computers (e.g. von Neumann's computer organization) substantially. However the cellular automaton is typically simulated on a machine of traditional organization.

Finally, genetic programming in cooperation with a software simulator of practically whatever behavior might be able to discover innovative designs. That is clearly demonstrated, for instance, on the automatic design of analog circuits using genetic programming and an analog circuit simulator [16].

2.2 A Hardware Viewpoint

In case of hardware we have to distinguish hardware implementations of genetic programming and evolvable hardware.

In order to speed up the evolution, parallel genetic programming implementations (employing hundreds processors like in [16]) or hardware implementations are constructed. As an example of conventional hardware approach, Martin implemented a simple variant of parallel genetic programming in an FPGA (Field Programmable Gate Array) [10]. The programs, which can be evolved directly in an FPGA, consisted of a few types of instructions and were evaluated in p small "processors" constructed and distributed inside the FPGA. We would like to mention that Martin's approach couldn't be classified as evolvable hardware because no circuits were actually evolved.

In case of evolvable hardware [23], chromosomes are considered as circuit configuration bitstreams which are used to configure a *reconfigurable circuit.* Every candidate configuration is evaluated either in a circuit simulator (i.e. *extrinsic evolution*) or in a physical hardware (i.e. *intrinsic evolution*). It is crucial to distinguish these approaches. In case of so-called *unconstrained evolution* discovered by A. Thompson [19] (it is intrinsic evolution too), the evolution is free to exploit physical properties of a chip as well as other environmental characteristics (like temperature during experiment) for building the resulting circuit. Because of the "side effects" of the unconstrained evolution, it is possible to obtain two

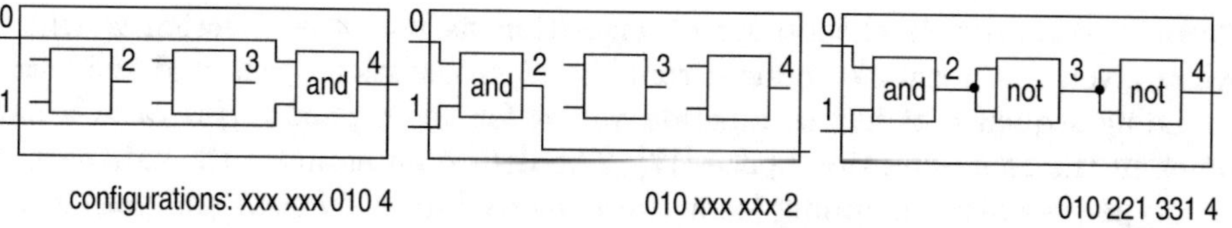

Fig. 1. Three different phenotypes with identical behavior. Parameters of CGP: $n_c = 3, n_r = 1, n_i = 2, n_o = 1, n_n = 2, n_f = 2, F = \{\text{and, not}\}$.

different fitness values (related to the same configuration) when formally the same fitness calculation process is carried out in a software circuit simulator and then in a physical reconfigurable circuit. Note that the software simulator and the constrained evolution in hardware always yield the same fitness value for the same configuration. Although unconstrained evolution causes a number of problems in practice, it is a tool how to discover really innovative circuits [19].

Miller's CGP is probably one of the most developed models of FPGA-based genetic programming [12]. In CGP a reconfigurable circuit is modeled as an array of n_c (columns) $\times$ n_r (rows) programmable nodes (see Fig. 1). The number of circuit inputs n_i and outputs n_o are fixed. A node's input can be connected to the output of some element in the previous columns or to some of circuit inputs. A node has up to n_n inputs and a single output. Every node is programmed to implement one of n_f functions defined in set F. Finally, circuit interconnectivity is defined by *levels back parameter* L, which determines how many previous columns of nodes may have their outputs connected to a node in the current column. For example, if $L = 1$, only neighboring columns may be connected; if $L = n_c$, the full connectivity is enabled. Nodes in the same column are not allowed to be connected to each other, and any node may be either connected or disconnected. Circuit outputs can be taken from any node output. A configuration of every node is represented in a chromosome using $n_n + 1$ integer values, which define connection of node's inputs, and a function realized in the node. While chromosomes are of fixed length, phenotypes are of variable length.

From a theoretical computer science viewpoint, Boolean circuits represent a model of computation too. While Turing machine and RAM are examples of uniform and infinite computer models (in sense that each particular computer can process inputs of an arbitrary size), a single Boolean circuit computes only a single Boolean function. In order to make a universal computer model of the same power as Turing machines out of Boolean circuits, uniformly designed families of Boolean circuits have to be considered [7].

2.3 A Formal Viewpoint

Up to now we mentioned various models of computational process in this paper. These models are formally defined in many textbooks, e.g. [7]. Genetic programming was employed in order to design computational machines based on the discussed models. Let us try to formalize this well-known concept.

Any evolutionary algorithm E (and thus genetic programming too) can be considered as a stochastic population-based search algorithm. For instance, Surry formally defines a stochastic search algorithm as recursive function Ψ which, when given a sequence of points from the representation space and the corresponding sequence of fitness function values for those points, generates a new point in the representation space [17]. The definition assumes the existence of genotype-phenotype mapping (sometimes referred to as a *growth function*) which is important from (our) machine design viewpoint.

Classical evolutionary algorithms utilize fitness function of the form $\Phi : \mathcal{C} \rightarrow \mathbb{R}$ where $\mathcal{C}$ denotes a set of chromosomes (representation space). Conceptually, chromosomes are not evaluated. Only machines (more precisely, behaviors of these machines) are and can be evaluated. Hence it is reasonable to define a set of machines $\mathcal{M}$ which can be constructed from chromosomes for a given problem domain using *growth function* $g : \mathcal{C} \rightarrow \mathcal{M}$. It is supposed that g is surjective. The machines are then evaluated using "machine" fitness function $f : \mathcal{M} \rightarrow \mathbb{R}$. Finally, Φ is expressed as composition $\Phi = f \circ g$.

In order to illustrate the proposed formal approach, assume that a definition of cellular automaton A consists of four components $A = (c_1, c_2, c_3, R)$, where $R = \{0, 1\}^n$ denotes cellular automaton rules encoded as n-bit string. Then a set of all machines that can be evolved corresponds to a 2^n-element set of cellular automata of the form

$$\mathcal{M} = \{(c_1, c_2, c_3, R) \mid c_1 = k_1, c_2 = k_2, c_3 = k_3\}$$

where k_1, k_2, and k_3 are invariable objects. Genotype-phenotype mapping is constructed as $g : \{0, 1\}^n \rightarrow \mathcal{M}$. Cellular automata are then evaluated using f.

According to the previous analysis, we can summarize that any evolutionary design of computational machines is fully defined in terms:
E – evolutionary algorithm employed (with fitness function $\Phi : \mathcal{C} \rightarrow \mathbb{R}$);
$\mathcal{M}$ – a set of possible machines which can be created;
g – a surjective growth function of the form $g : \mathcal{C} \rightarrow \mathcal{M}$;
f – a "machine" fitness function of the form $f : \mathcal{M} \rightarrow \mathbb{R}$;
$\Phi = f \circ g$

We can see that only four mathematical components $(E, \mathcal{M}, g, f)$ are needed in the definition. Note that f is a problem specific function, g can cover any type of constructional process (e.g. such as a development of phenotypes from genotypes described and implemented initially in Dawkins's biomorphs [5]) and $\mathcal{M}$ is defined implicitly or explicitly before the evolution is executed. Looking via the proposed definition all evolvable machines operate in the *same way*. We could perhaps say that they are (iso)morphic each other in some sense. Some other properties have been investigated in [13].

2.4 Relation of the Approaches

When software, hardware and theoretical views (together with underlying models) are formulated, we can investigate their relations and mutual translatability. However, if we accept the proposed definition as a general paradigm, we could easily get into troubles.

Theoretically, $\mathcal{M}$ is infinite but enumerable set. Practically, $\mathcal{M}$ is always finite because of finite resources of any implementable universal computer or any electronic circuit. If we accept that $\mathcal{M}$ is a finite set then software implementations can always correspond to the proposed formal model. Furthermore, all Martin's style hardware implementations of genetic programming always correspond with the proposed formal model too.

However it is *not* case of evolvable hardware. There is not any problem in the constrained evolution: the number of possible distinguishable phenotypes (circuits) is given by the number of possible different circuit configurations. For instance, we derived using a simple combinatorial analysis that CGP enables

$$P = n_f^{n_c n_r}(n_i + n_c n_r)^{n_o}(n_i + L n_r)^{n_n n_r (n_c - L)} \prod_{j=0}^{L-1} (n_i + j n_r)^{n_r n_n}$$

different configurations and so circuits to emerge, i.e. $|\mathcal{M}| = P$. Note that the circuits, which perform the same logical behavior, are treated as different phenotypes because they are not placed in physically identical nodes as seen in Fig. 1.

Although the unconstrained approach supports P configurations too, the number of different circuit behaviors which can appear is P', but P' is greater than P. It is due "analog" nature of the evolved circuits and various side effects (like variability of material characteristics of "the same" chips or changing temperature during evolution). Hence it is practically impossible to specify $\mathcal{M}$ in this case. Hypothetically, if one would like to specify $\mathcal{M}$, (s)he has to create a detailed model for a given piece of silicon (chip), to explore all possible configurations and to take in account all working conditions (so-called *operational envelope* in [18]).

This problem can also be interpreted in the following way: f is not a function, but f is a relation. Hence two (or more) different fitness values might be assigned to a single machine in the formally same fitness calculation process (see Fig. 2CD). The situation traditionally leads in theoretical computer science to definition of *non-deterministic* variant of the computational model. In our case, we can speak about *non-deterministic evolvable machines*.

In practical designs of evolvable hardware, growth function g has always been a bijection. This means that a single configuration bitstream encodes a single physical circuit. In case of software, redundancy of encoding is sometimes introduced as shown in Fig. 2BD. It yields genotype *neutrality*. Note that the mappings in Fig. 2A exactly correspond with the circuits depicted in Fig. 1.

3 Evolvable Machines

Evolvable machines operating in a dynamic environment (e.g. with a changing fitness function in scheduling tasks [2] or in dynamic hashing [4]) introduce in embedded systems the following situation: Problem representation and genetic operators (and architecture of a reconfigurable circuit in case of evolvable hardware) remain unchanged and cannot be altered when a new fitness function is

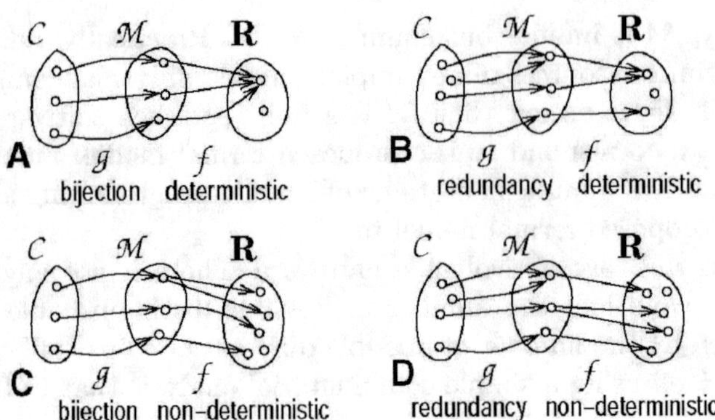

Fig. 2. Properties of g and f in four different types of evolvable machines.

specified. Formally, $E, \mathcal{M}$, and g are *invariable*. This is unpleasant from a performance (No Free Lunch theorem [22]) point of view. Hence it is important to define a problem domain carefully in order to outperform random search for a reasonable class of fitness functions.

3.1 Formal Approach

In order to provide a simple formal framework for machine evolution in a dynamic environment, the following specification of *machine context* (environment) is proposed. The machine context is considered as a set of fitness functions (we can call them *context functions*) together with a mechanism of transition between them. Context functions are changed in discrete time points modeled as natural numbers $\mathbb{N} = \{1, 2, \ldots\}$. A set of all mappings from $\mathcal{M}$ into $\mathbb{R}$ will be denoted $\mathbb{R}^{\mathcal{M}}$. Formally, machine context is defined in terms:
$\Gamma \subseteq \mathbb{R}^{\mathcal{M}}$ – a set of context functions ($\varphi_i \in \Gamma$ specifies fitness function in environment i).
$\varphi_0 \in \Gamma$ – an initial context function.
$\varepsilon : \Gamma \times \mathbb{N} \to \Gamma$ – a relation that determines successive context function.

The following example illustrates the proposed formal definitions: Consider a real-time adaptive image filtration realized using an evolvable computational machine. The evolutionary algorithm is applied to automatically design image filters. The filters should suppress a noise presented in images taken from a camera. The evolvable machine in fact produces a (potentially endless) sequence of filters (i.e. machines from $\mathcal{M}$), each for more recent type of noise. Assume, for instance, that the machine is a part of a traffic control system. Type of noise is reflected in context function φ_i and hence φ_i depends on daytime, weather and other factors. A change of type of noise (i.e. a change of context function described by ε) is unpredictable as weather is.

3.2 Computational Power

The example has demonstrated that if we put together the definition from Section 2.3 with the definition of machine context (i.e. $f = \varphi_i$), we obtain a formal definition of an arbitrary evolvable machine working in a dynamic environment.

It was shown in an emerging field—hypercomputation (or super-Turing computation) [3,9,21]—that some theoretical models and modern computational systems do not share the computational scenario of a standard Turing machine and hence they can not be simulated on Turing machines. Let us note that a standard Turing machine supposes that input data are available before a computation is started (no interaction is enabled later) and that a uniform algorithm (which is invariable and never changed during execution) processes them.

Nevertheless van Leeuwen and Wiedermann have shown that such computations may be realized by an *interactive Turing machines with advice* [9]. Interactive Turing machine with advice is a classical Turing machine endowed with three important features: advice function (it is a weaker type of oracle [7]), interaction and infinity of operation. The same authors have proposed the following extension of the Church-Turing thesis [9]: *Any (non-uniform interactive) computation can be described in terms of interactive Turing machines with advice.*

For example, a model of Internet possesses the same computational power as an interactive Turing machine with advice. However, only in the case that its life-span is *infinite*. Otherwise, the computation is finite and remains in the scope of standard Turing machine and the standard Church-Turing thesis [9].

We can observe that evolvable computational machines operating in a dynamic environment show simultaneous non-uniformity of computation, interaction with an environment, and infinity of operations. Furthermore, relation ε is in general *uncomputable*. It was proven that computational power of an evolvable computational machine operating in a dynamic environment is equivalent with the computational power of an interactive Turing machine with advice, however, only in the case that evolutionary algorithm is tuned to the problem [14].

Also physical implementations of evolvable machines (for instance, the evolvable image filter mentioned in the previous subsection), Internet and other similar devices are very interesting from a computational viewpoint. At each time point they have *finite* description. However, when one observe their computation in time, they represent *infinite* sequences of reactive devices computing non-uniformly. The "evolution" of machine's behavior is supposed to be endless. In fact it means that they offer an example of real devices (physical implementations!) that can perform computation that no single Turing machine (without oracle) can. Nevertheless they can be modeled *a posteriori* by interactive Turing machine with advice [9].

4 Summary

We can now summarize the most important results of the paper.

- It is reasonable and useful to support various approaches in order to describe and understand the evolvable machines.
- General formal definition of an evolvable machine can be introduced.
- One-to-one mapping exists between the formal definition, software and "conventional" hardware implementations of any evolvable machine.

- If a hardware implementation of an evolvable machine is realized using the unconstrained evolution then it is practically impossible to define set of machines $\mathcal{M}$.
- The unconstrained evolution can be modeled using a non-deterministic evolvable machine.
- Evolvable machines operating in a dynamic environment exhibit a super-Turing computational power.

Some open problems for future research are as follows:

- How (iso)morphism of evolvable machines should be defined.
- How classes of evolvable machines (comprising machines of the same computational power) should be defined.
- How to reflect all the proposed ideas in practical design tools.

5 Conclusions

The paper presents an original contribution to the theory of evolvable machines. We showed that theoretical computer science has methods for effective description of evolvable machines. Application of these methods allowed interesting results to appear. We are going to go on in the proposed approach in future research. The ultimate goal is (1) to establish a widely acceptable mathematical theory of evolvable computational machines and (2) to apply the results in practical designs.

Acknowledgments

The research was performed with the financial support of the Grant Agency of the Czech Republic under No. 102/03/P004 and 102/01/1531, and from the Research Intention No. CEZ: J22/98:262200012.

References

1. Banzhaf, W., Nordin, P., Keller R., E., Francone, F., D.: Genetic Programming – An Introduction. Morgan Kaufmann Publishers, 1998
2. Branke, J.: Evolutionary Approaches to Dynamic Optimization Problems – Updated Survey. In: Proc. of the GECCO Workshop on Evolutionary Algorithms for Dynamic Optimization Problems, 2001, p. 27–30
3. Copeland, B., J., Sylvan, R.: Beyond the Universal Turing Machine. Australasian Journal of Philosophy. 77, 1999, p. 46–66
4. Damiani, E., Liberali, V., Tettamanzi, A.: Dynamic Optimisation of Non-linear Feed-Forward Circuits. In: Proc. of the 3rd Conference on Evolvable Systems: From Biology to Hardware ICES'00, LNCS 1801, Springer-Verlag, 2000, p. 41–50
5. Dawkins, R.: The Blind Watchmaker. Penquin Books, London, 1991
6. Ferreira, C.: Discovery of the Boolean Functions to the Best Density-Classification Rules Using Gene Expression Programming. In: Proc. of the 5th European Conference on Genetic Programming EuroGP2002, LNCS 2278, Springer, 2002, p. 50–59

7. Gruska, J.: Foundations of Computing. International Thomson Publishing Computer Press, 1997
8. Koza, J., R., Bennett III., F., H., Andre, D., Keane, M., A.: Genetic Programming III: Darwinian Invention and Problem Solving. Morgan Kaufmann, 1999
9. van Leeuwen, J., Wiedermann, J.: The Turing Machine Paradigm in Contemporary Computing. In: Mathematics Unlimited – 2001 and Beyond, Springer-Verlag, 2001, p. 1139–1155
10. Martin, P.: A Hardware Implementation of a Genetic Programming System Using FPGAs and Handel-C. Genetic Programming and Evolvable Machines, Vol. 2(4), 2001, p. 317–343
11. Miller, J., Job, D., Vassilev, V.: Principles in the Evolutionary Design of Digital Circuits – Part I. Genetic Programming and Evolvable Machines, Vol. 1(1), Kluwer Academic Publisher, 2000, p. 8–35
12. Miller, J., Thomson, P.: Cartesian Genetic Programming. In: Proc. of the 3rd European Conference on Genetic Programming EuroGP2000, LNCS 1802, Springer-Verlag, 2000, p. 121–132
13. Sekanina, L.: Evolvable Computational Machines: Formal Approach. In: Intelligent Technologies – Theory and Applications, 2nd Euro-International Symposium on Computational Intelligence, 2002, IOS Press Amsterodam 2002, p. 166–172
14. Sekanina, L.: Component Approach to Evolvable Systems. PhD thesis, Brno University of Technology, 2002, p. 132
15. Sipper, M.: Evolution of Parallel Cellular Machines – The Cellular Programming Approach. Springer-Verlag Berlin, 1997
16. Streeter, M., J., Keane, M., A., Koza, J. R.: Routine Duplication of Post-2000 Patented Inventions by Means of Genetic Programming. In: Proc. of the 5th European Conference on Genetic Programming EuroGP2002, LNCS 2278, Springer-Verlag, 2002, p. 26–36
17. Surry, P., D.: A Prescriptive Formalism for Constructing Domain-specific Evolutionary Algorithms. PhD thesis, University of Edinburgh, 1998
18. Thompson, A.: On the Automatic Design of Robust Electronics Through Artificial Evolution. In: Proc. of the 2nd Conference on Evolvable Systems: From Biology to Hardware ICES'98, LNCS 1478, Springer-Verlag, 1998, p. 13–35
19. Thompson, A., Layzell, P., Zebulum, S.: Explorations in Design Space: Unconventional Electronics Design Through Artificial Evolution. IEEE Transactions on Evolutionary Computation, Vol. 3(3), 1999, p. 167–196
20. Vallejo, E., E., Ramos, F.: Evolving Turing Machines for Biosequence Recognition and Analysis. In: Proc. of the 4th European Conference on Genetic Programming EuroGP2001, LNCS 2038, Springer-Verlag, 2001, pp. 192–203
21. Wegner, P., Goldin, D.: Computation Beyond Turing Machines. Communications of the ACM. Accepted (2002) `http://www.cs.brown.edu/people/pw/home.html`
22. Wolpert, D., H., Macready, W., G.: No Free Lunch Theorems for Optimization. IEEE Transactions on Evolutionary Computation, Vol. 1(1), 1997, p. 67–82
23. Yao, X., Higuchi, T.: Promises and Challenges of Evolvable Hardware. In: Proc. of the 1st International Conference on Evolvable Systems: From Biology to Hardware ICES'96, LNCS 1259, Springer-Verlag, Berlin, 1997, p. 55–78

Cooperative Evolution on the Intertwined Spirals Problem*

Terence Soule

Department of Computer Science
University of Idaho
Moscow, Idaho 83844-1010
tsoule@cs.uidaho.edu

Abstract. This paper examines the evolution cooperation on the intertwined spirals problem. Multiple cooperation mechanisms are tested. Cooperation evolves fairly easily for each of the cooperation mechanisms, producing compact, successful team based solutions. Importantly, the team members' fitness is relatively poor.

1 Introduction

Genetic programming (GP) and evolutionary computation (EC) in general have been very successful at solving a wide variety of problems. However, there are still concerns regarding how well it scales to larger problems. The standard solution for human programmers faced with a large complex problem is to use divide and conquer strategies to break the problem into more manageable sub-problems. Giving GP access to similar techniques may significantly improve its scalability.

One divide and conquer approach appropriate to GP is to create teams of individuals that can cooperate. Each team member can specialize to solve a subproblem that is smaller and simpler than the complete problem. However, this approach requires GP to successfully evolve cooperative solutions.

In this paper we examine the evolution of cooperation on the intertwined spirals problems using a variety of different cooperation mechanisms. The results show that strong cooperation does evolve in all cases, demonstrating that cooperation is relatively easy to evolve. In addition, the results with teams are comparable to or slightly better than the results with individuals.

2 Background

Early team research focused on evolving teams of programs for problems that require team solutions, such as simplified versions of team sports and pack based

* This research supported by a University of Idaho Seed Grant and an NIH Grant NCRR P20 RR16448. The experiments were performed on a Beowulf cluster built with funds from NSF grant EPS80935 and a generous hardware donation from Micron Technologies.

C. Ryan et al. (Eds.): EuroGP 2003, LNCS 2610, pp. 434–442, 2003.

predator-prey problems (see for example [1,2,3,4,5]). This research demonstrated that GP can evolve cooperative behavior. However, because this work focused on problems that require teams and that include implicit cooperation mechanisms it does not directly address the issue of scalability.

More recently team approaches have been applied to problems that do not inherently require a team to solve, such as parity problems, the intertwined spirals problem and symbolic regression [6,7,8,9]. Cooperation is achieved through an explicit cooperation mechanism, such as voting. Overall, these experiments demonstrated the evolution of cooperation and performance improved with the use of teams. In several cases the evolved teams had the unexpected benefit of producing more compact code [6,8].

Iba evolved individuals in separate populations [5]. The evolved individuals were then combined into teams to control a robot. Individual moves were chosen by the team via voting and showed an improvement over evolved individuals. Imamura et al. also used individuals drawn from isolated populations to create teams [10]. The goal was to find promoter regions in E. coli DNA. His work focused on finding team members with non-correlated faults to reduce the variation on test data, rather than specifically on improving average performance. However, performance improvements were observed with the teams.

Potter and DeJong successfully used isolated populations that represented separate 'species' to evolve solutions to the intertwined spirals problem [7]. An individual's fitness was measured by combining the individual with individuals from other species to create a team. This approach encourages the evolution of cooperation because cooperation is tested in each generation. However, it can limit the evolution of specialization because each individual gets teamed with different individuals for every evaluation.

Other researchers have used a single population in which each 'individual' is actually a team. This approach was used by Haynes on a predator-prey problem [2,4], by Soule on parity and symbolic regression problems [6,8] and by Brameier and Banzhaf on several classification and regression problems [9]. In each of these experiments the use of teams lead to strong specialization, cooperation and improved performance. Treating each team as an individual emphasizes specialization and cooperation, but not the individual team members' fitness.

Because the goal of these experiments is the study of cooperation, the third method, in which each individual is actually a team of (three) members, is used. This emphasizes cooperative solutions over individual performance. To encourage heterogeneity crossover was applied between the equivalent team member (chosen randomly) in the two parent individuals. A number of different cooperation mechanisms are tested to determine how the cooperation mechanism effects the evolution of cooperation.

3 Cooperative Mechanisms

For the intertwined spirals problem two spirals coil around the origin of the x-y plane. Each spiral is defined by 97 points along its length. The goal is to find a function that classifies the points as belonging to spiral 1 or spiral 2 based on

the x,y value of the point (see for example [11]). An evolved program returns a real value that is mapped to a binary value representing spiral 1 or spiral 2. In these experiments the mapping function is:
Spiral 1 if $f(x, y) \leq 0.0$
Spiral 2 otherwise
This mapping function allows for many different types of cooperation mechanisms. We studied five cooperation mechanisms: voting, averaged voting, median voting, the use of a leader and the use of sub-functions. Each of these cooperation mechanisms is described below.

To simplify the following discussion we will assume that each team has exactly three members. Each member represents an evolved function: $f_1(x, y)$, $f_2(x, y)$ and $f_3(x, y)$ respectively.

Majority Voting: For the majority voting cooperation mechanism the mapped values (i.e. spiral 1 and spiral 2) are used in a simple vote. If a majority of the team members favors spiral 1 then spiral 1 is the team's answer. The fitness of the team is the percentage of incorrect votes on the 196 test points.

This type of voting does not allow the team members to weight their votes. Each vote is of equal value in determining the teams answer. A perfect team solution requires that at least two third of the outputs are correct.

Average Voting: The average voting approach averages the outputs of the team members. This is effectively a weighted vote with each team member determining the weight of its own vote. For example, an output of 20 is a fairly string vote for spiral 2, whereas an output of -0.2 is a weak vote for spiral 1.

Median Voting: In median voting the real values returned by the team members are compared. The median value of the member's output is taken as the team's output and is used as input to the mapping function. I.e. for each test point the output is the mapping of $median(f_1(x, y), f_2(x, y), f_3(x, y))$.

Leader: The leader cooperation mechanism uses the first team member as a 'leader' that decides for each test point which of the other team members has the task of classifying the point. The leader's decision is based on the input values. Thus, the leader is a function whose inputs are the x,y value of the current training point and whose output $f(x, y)$ is mapped as follows:
Use member 2 if $f(x, y) \leq 0.0$; use member 3 otherwise.
Thus, the team's accuracy can be equal to the sum of member 2 and member 3's accuracy if the leader function picks the correct member function for each input.

Functions: The function cooperation mechanism uses the third team member as a type of leader. The input values to the team leader, instead of being the raw x and y values are the outputs of the other two team members. Thus, the output is the normal mapping of the function $f_3(f_1(x, y), f_2(x, y))$.

Clearly, there exists a single function $f(x, y) = f_3(f_1(x, y), f_2(x, y))$. However, evolutionarily it may be simpler to evolve the functions f_1, f_2 and f_3 in parallel rather than trying to evolve the equivalent single function. In fact this approach is quite similar to ADFs, which have been shown to improve performance on a wide range of problems [12].

Table 1. Summary of the Genetic Program parameters.

Function Set	+, -, *, /, iflte, sin, cos
Terminal Set	x, y, random constants
Population Size	800
Crossover Probability	0.9 (0.1 are copied without crossover)
Mutations Probability	0.001
Selection	3 member tournament
Generations	100
Maximum Tree Size	None
Elitism	2 copies of the best individual are preserved
Initial Population	Ramped, half-and-half
Number of trials	50

4 The Genetic Program

These experiments used a simple generational GP with a single population. Each individual in the population represented a team of 3 members. Each team member is a separate function tree.

Crossover was applied between the same team member (chosen randomly) in the two parent individuals. E.g. once two parent individuals are chosen a random team member i (from 1 to N) is picked and crossover is applied to the two member trees i. This is sometimes referred to as heterogeneous crossover [4]. The combination of single population in which each 'individual' is actually a team and heterogeneous crossover has been shown to produce strong specialization and cooperation [6,8].

The other details of the GP are presented in Table 1. The constants are initially randomly generated in the range -5.0 to 5.0. Mutation changes a single node to another node of the same arity. Constant nodes are mutated by changing their values by -0.5 to 0.5.

5 Results – Fitness

Figure 1 shows the fitness of the best individuals averaged across 50 trials. Interestingly, all of the cooperation mechanisms appear to perform equivalently, with the exception of functions, which performs slightly worse.

Figure 2 shows the average fitness of all individuals averaged across all 50 trials. For average fitness the individuals perform slightly better. Again all of the cooperation mechanisms are roughly equivalent, except for functions. Our results with the program sizes suggest that this difference occurs because the team programs are smaller (see section 7).

Table 2 shows the average best fitness and the standard deviation in the final generation. Student's two-tailed t-test was performed between the individuals and each of the team approaches for the best program fitnesses. The function and averaging cooperation mechanisms were not significantly different (at the 1% level) from the individuals ($t = 0.294$ and 1.715 respectively). The poor performance with the function mechanism is particularly interesting because

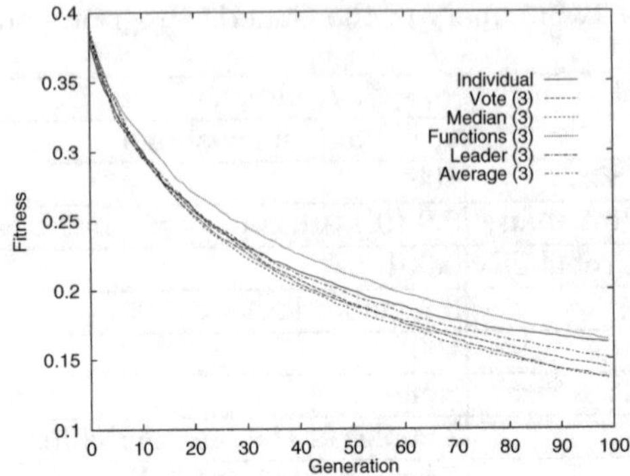

Fig. 1. Maximum fitness for each of the cooperation mechanisms. Performance is equivalent for all mechanisms except functions.

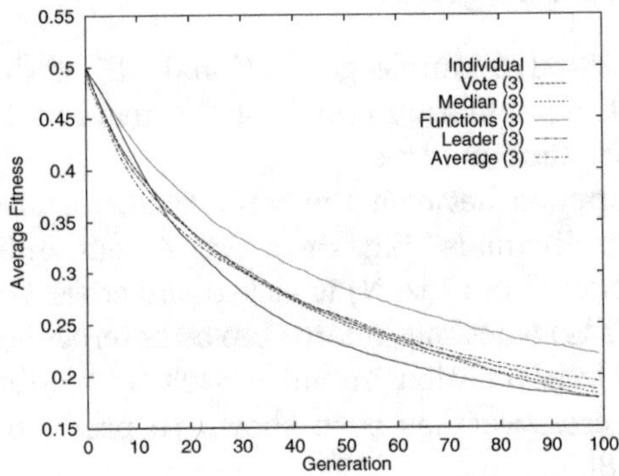

Fig. 2. Average fitness for each of the cooperation mechanisms

this mechanism is fairly similar to ADFs, suggesting that further comparisons with ADFs need to be made. The voting, median voting and leader cooperation mechanisms were all significantly better when measured at the 1% level (t = 2.946, 4.469 and 4.008 respectively).

The nearly equivalent performance results raises an important question: is cooperation evolving? For each of these cooperation mechanisms there is a non-cooperative solution. For example, with the averaging approach two of the three team members could consistently return 0. The actual output would be determined solely by the remaining team member. Similar non-cooperative scenarios can occur with the other cooperation mechanisms.

6 Results – Cooperation

To test whether cooperative behavior is being evolved we examine the behavior of the individual team members for each of the cooperation mechanisms.

Figure 4 shows the behavior of the average team and the average team members for each of the cooperation mechanisms. These results clearly show that cooperation is evolving with each of the cooperation mechanisms.

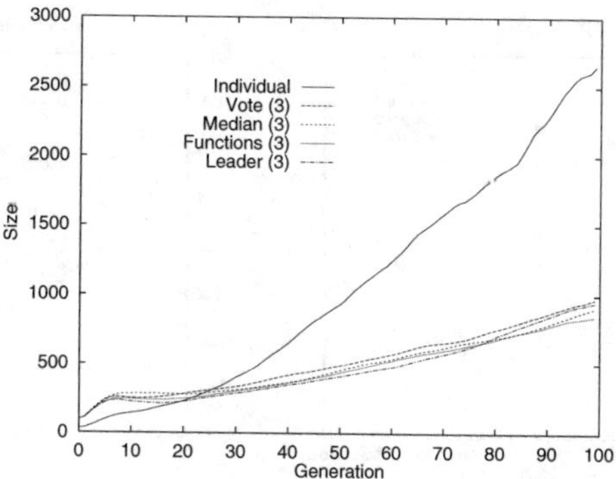

Fig. 3. Average size of the evolved individuals and teams. The teams are initially three times as large as the individuals, but the individuals grow much more rapidly due to the higher effective crossover rate.

Table 2. Best fitness results in the final generation.

Mechanism	Average	Standard Deviation
Individual	0.162	0.0347
Vote	0.143	0.0296
Median	0.136	0.0221
Functions	0.164	0.0332
Leader	0.136	0.0300
Average	0.151	0.0292

With all three voting mechanisms the error rates of the team members are relatively high, whereas the error rate of the team is considerably lower. Furthermore, the team fitness is improving in the later generations significantly faster than the member fitnesses. This can only occur if the team members are 'arranging' their votes to maximize success, which is a form of cooperative behavior.

Under the leader based cooperation mechanisms the leader performs extremely poorly (equivalent to random guessing) because that program is not trained to solve the problem, rather the leader is trained to pick which team members' answer is correct for each training case. Each of the other two team members has relatively poor performance, much worse than the team as a whole. Thus, the relatively high team performance implies that the leader is correctly picking which member should handle each training case, which represents (a form of) cooperation.

Similarly, with function based cooperation in isolation each of the team members performs very poorly, equivalent to random guessing. In this case members 1 and 2 are not evolved to solve the problem, rather they return new values which are the inputs to the team leader. Thus, when they attempt to solve the problem directly they perform no better than random guessing. Team member 3 is evolved to classify the test cases based on the outputs of members 1 and 2. Figure 4 shows that when required to solve the problem based on the raw inputs x,y member 3 performs no better than random guessing. This demonstrates

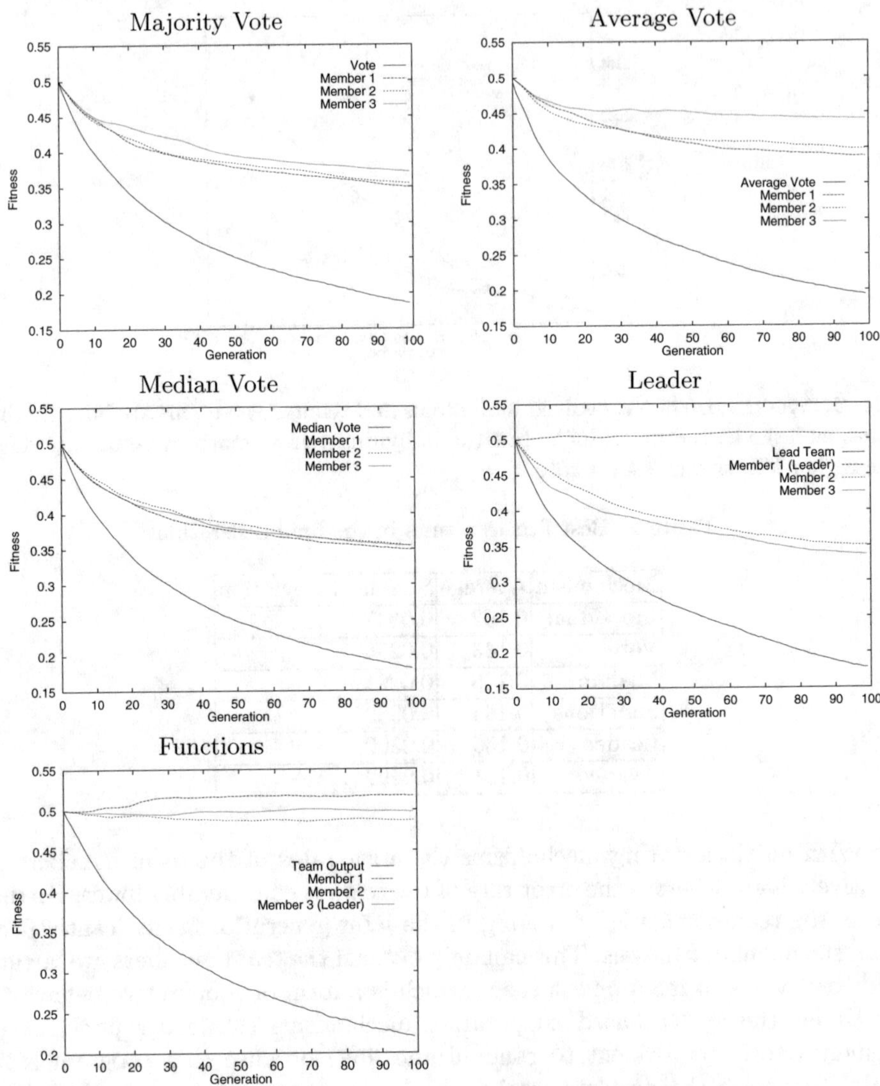

Fig. 4. Fitness for each of the team members and the team as a whole for each of the cooperation mechanisms. The high performance of the team relative to the team members implies that cooperation is taking place.

that cooperation has evolved; reasonable performance is only achieved when the member programs act as a team. Thus, for each of the cooperation mechanisms the evolved behaviors are cooperative; the teams' performances depends upon the proper combination of the team members.

7 Results – Size

Figure 3 shows the size (the number of nodes) of all individuals averaged across all 50 trials. The team size is defined as the number of nodes in all of the team members. Thus, initially the teams are exactly three times as large as the individuals because the teams consist of three members. However, the size of the teams increases much less rapidly and by generation 30 the individual programs are clearly considerably larger than even three team members combined.

There is a simple explanation for the decreased growth rate for the teams. Larger programs are created by crossover. With the team approach individual trees are only crossed once in every three generations, rather than in every generation (actually the crossover rates are slightly less because crossover is only applied 90% of the time, but the idea holds). Growth appears to be compounding process; the average program size in generation i is some function of the average size in generation i-1. With teams this compounding process is reduced to every third generation, leading to much slower growth. We performed separate experiments in which all three team members were crossed in every generation (not show). The increased number of crossovers did result in much higher growth rates for the teams.

The slow growth may also explain the poorer average fitness observed with the teams. It is generally believed that growth has a protective effect, reducing the usually negative impact of crossover. Because the team members are small they are more likely to be damaged by crossover. Because fitness is recorded after crossover this results in the lower average fitness that is seen in Figure 2.

8 Conclusions and Future Work

This research has several important results. First, the best solutions produced by the team approach are significantly better than those produced with individuals for three of the cooperation mechanisms. Second, the teams are considerably smaller than the individuals. This difference in size represents a considerable advantage for the teams in terms of both space and execution time. Third, cooperative solutions evolved for each of the cooperation mechanisms, even though non-cooperative solutions were possible. This demonstrates that cooperation is a fairly easy/likely feature to evolve.

The spirals problem was chosen because it makes it easy to use multiple cooperation mechanisms. However, it is not a problem that naturally lends itself to cooperation as it is not easily sub-divided into distinct, simpler sub-problems. Thus, cooperative may perform even better on problems that do have natural sub-problems.

In these experiments the average member fitness was quite low compared to the fitness of evolved individuals (compare the average member performance in Figure 4 to the average performance of individuals in Figure 2). However, the team fitnesses are equivalent to (or better than) the individual fitnesses, despite the low member fitness. This demonstrates that cooperation is evolving to improve performance in these experiments. The combination of easily evolved cooperation, smaller team solutions and high team performance despite low member performance suggests that cooperation is a very promising technique for evolutionary systems. Also significant, it appears likely that the team performances could be significantly improved by improving the team members' performance. This could be achieved by including the members' fitnesses in the selection criteria and will be the subject of future research.

References

1. Simon Raik and Bohdan Durnota. The evolution of sporting strategies. In Russel J. Stonier and Xing Huo Yu, editors, *Complex Systems: Mechanisms of Adaption*, pages 85–92. IOS Press, 1994.
2. Thomas Haynes, Sandip Sen, Dale Schoenefeld, and Roger Wainwright. Evolving a team. In Eric V. Siegel and John Koza, editors, *Working Notes of the AAAI-95 Fall Symposium on GP*, pages 23–30. AAAI Press, 1995.
3. Sean Luke and Lee Spector. Evolving teamwork and coordination with genetic programming. In John R. Koza, David E. Goldberg, David B. Fogel, and Rick R. Riolo, editors, *Genetic Programming 1996: Proceedings of the First Annual Conference on Genetic Programming*, pages 150–156. Cambridge, MA: MIT Press, 1996.
4. Kim Harries and Peter Smith. Exploring alternative operators and search strategies in genetic programming. In John R. Koza, Kalyanmoy Deb, Marco Dorigo, David B. Fogel, Max Garzon, Hitoshi Iba, and Rick R. Riolo, editors, *Genetic Programming 1997: Proceedings of the Second Annual Conference*, pages 147–155. San Francisco, CA: Morgan Kaufmann, 1997.
5. Hitoshi Iba. Multiple-agent learning for a robot navigation task by genetic programming. In John R. Koza, Kalyanmoy Deb, Marco Dorigo, David B. Fogel, Max Garzon, Hitoshi Iba, and Rick R. Riolo, editors, *Genetic Programming 1997: Proceedings of the Second Annual Conference*, pages 195–200. San Francisco, CA: Morgan Kaufmann, 1997.
6. Terence Soule. Voting teams: A cooperative approach to non-typical problems. In Wolfgang Banzhaf, Jason Daida, Agoston E. Eiben, Max H. Garzon, Vasant Honavar, Mark Jakiela, and Robert E. Smith, editors, *Proceedings of the Genetic and Evolutionary Computation Conference*, pages 916–922, Orlando, Florida, USA, 13-17 July 1999. Morgan Kaufmann.
7. Mitchell A. Potter and Kenneth A. DeJong. Cooperative coevolution: An architecture for evolving coadapted subcomponenets. *Evolutionary Computation*, 8(1):1–30, 2000.
8. Terence Soule. Heterogeneity and specialization in evolving teams. In *Proceedings of the Genetic and Evolutionary Computation Conference (GECCO-2000)*, pages 778–785, Las Vegas, Nevada, USA, 2000. Morgan Kaufmann.
9. Markus Brameier and Wolfgang Banzhaf. Evolving teams of predictors with linear genetic programming. *Genetic Programming and Evolvable Machines*, 2(4):381–408, 2001.
10. K. Imamura, Robert B. Heckendorn, Terence Soule, and James A. Foster. N-version genetic programming via fault masking. In James A. Foster, Evelyne Lutton, Julian F. Miller, Conor Ryan, and Andrea Tettamanzi, editors, *Genetic Programming, 5th European Conference, EuroGP 2002*, 2002.
11. John Koza. A genetic approach to the truck backer upper problem and the intertwined spiral problem. In *Proceedings of IJCNN International Joint Conference on Neural Networks*, pages 310–318. IEEE Press, 1992.
12. John R. Koza. *Genetic Programming II: Automatic Discovery of Reusable Programs*. Cambridge, MA: The MIT Press, 1994.

The Root Causes of Code Growth in Genetic Programming

Matthew J. Streeter

Genetic Programming, Inc.
mjs@tmolp.com

Abstract. This paper discusses the underlying pressures responsible for code growth in genetic programming, and shows how an understanding of these pressures can be used to use to eliminate code growth while simultaneously improving performance. We begin with a discussion of two distinct components of code growth and the extent to which each component is relevant in practice. We then define the concept of resilience in GP trees, and show that the buildup of resilience is essential for code growth. We present simple modifications to the selection procedures used by GP that eliminate bloat without hurting performance. Finally, we show that eliminating bloat can improve the performance of genetic programming by a factor that increases as the problem is scaled in difficulty.

1 Introduction

The problem of code growth in genetic programming is well documented [2,6-7, 11-13]. In addition to making successive generations take longer and making the solutions produced by GP be larger than is necessary, it has been speculated that this growth essentially prevents long runs from being effective and limits the scalability of genetic programming [6]. For these reasons, there has been much research in the GP community both on theoretical explanations of code growth and on practical measures to prevent it. This paper seeks to provide a starting point for addressing both of these concerns. We provide evidence that code growth is indeed a protective mechanism, but that the means by which this protection may be achieved are more complex than those that have previously been hypothesized. We also show that simple changes to the selection scheme that are motivated by our investigation can actually eliminate code growth. Further, we show that eliminating code growth in this way leads to an improvement in performance by a factor that increases as the problem is scaled up.

Section 1.1 defines the terms used in this paper. Section 1.2 reviews existing theories of code growth. Section 1.3 discusses the problems and methodology. Section 2 describes two distinct components of code growth. Section 3 introduces the concept of resilience of program trees and presents an empirical study of resilience. Section 4 shows that the phenomenon of code growth requires phenotypically near-neutral crossovers. Section 5 discusses the effects of removing code growth on scalability. Section 6 is the conclusion.

C. Ryan et al. (Eds.): EuroGP 2003, LNCS 2610, pp. 443–454, 2003.

1.1 Terminology and Background

In this paper we will define an *intron* as a subtree that can be deleted (i.e. replaced with a constant terminal) without changing the behavior of the overall program. For example, in the tree (+ (* X X) (- X X)), the subtree (- X X) would be an intron. *Inviable* code is code belonging to a subtree that can be replaced by any other subtree without changing the behavior of the overall program, e.g. (* (- X X) <*inviable*>). A *neutral crossover* is a crossover that produces a child whose behavior is identical to that of the receiving parent, while a crossover is *disruptive* to the extent that it produces a large change in behavior. We will use the terms code growth and bloat interchangeably.

In analyzing code growth it will also be useful to define several distinct populations. The child population $c(n)$ is just the set of individuals that are members of generation n (i.e. what is usually called the "population"). The parent population $p(n)$ consists of N copies of each individual that participates N times as a parent of a member of $c(n)$. The grandparent population $g(n)$ consists of N copies of each individual that participates N times as a parent of a member of $c(n)$ who wins at least one tournament. We define $p_r(n)$ and $g_r(n)$ to be the subsets of $p(n)$ and $g(n)$ containing only those individuals that participated as receiving parents in a crossover, and $p_d(n)$ and $g_d(n)$ to be the subsets containing only donor parents. We will use absolute value bars to denote the average size of the individuals in a population, e.g. $|c(0)|$ indicates the average size of the individuals in generation 0.

Most explanations of code growth make the assumption that a child which is the result of a neutral or near-neutral crossover will in general be more likely to be fit than a child that results from a more disruptive crossover. The reason for this assumption is that it has been empirically shown that, once an evolutionary run has progressed beyond the first few generations, the vast majority of crossovers will produce offspring that are less fit than their parents [10]. Thus, children that are similar to their parents (who must be relatively fit in order to become parents) will be at advantage relative the majority of the offspring population.

1.2 Existing Theories of Code Growth

At the time of this writing there are four major theories of code growth, which we summarize in roughly the order they were originally proposed.

The Intron Theory: Perhaps the earliest theory of code growth concerns what in this paper is termed inviable code [1,8,9]. This theory is motivated by the idea that, since the majority of crossovers are destructive, individuals structured in such a way that they are likely to undergo neutral crossovers will be at an advantage relative to equally fit individuals which are not similarly structured. Trees with large amounts of inviable code are more likely to undergo a neutral crossover when selected as receiving parents, since any subtree inserted into the inviable code will have no affect on the program's behavior. Thus, the accumulation of larger and larger amounts of inviable code as a defense against crossover and mutation is a possible cause of code growth.

The Diffusion Theory: Langdon [3-5] has observed that for many problems the proportion of trees having a given fitness is constant as a function of size so long as the size exceeds some critical threshold. It follows that the absolute number of trees having a given fitness increases as a function of size in the same way as the total number of trees (i.e. exponentially in general). Based on this he has proposed a general explanation of bloat, which is that "any stochastic search technique ... will tend to find the most common programs in the search space of the current best fitness" [4] and due to the properties mentioned above these most common programs are large.

The Theory of Removal Bias: Building on the observation that the children of an inviable node are always inviable, while the parents are not necessarily so, Soule has proven that inviable nodes on average occur deeper in trees than do nodes as a whole [11]. Thus, a crossover that is neutral due to removal of an inviable subtree will tend to remove a relatively small tree, but will insert in its place a tree of average size, so that children produced through neutral crossovers (which due to the generally destructive nature of crossover will tend to be relatively fit) will tend to be larger than their parents, leading to an overall pattern of growth.

The Depth-Correlation Theory: Luke [6,7] has presented a two-part theory involving the relationship between the depth at which crossover occurs and the change in behavior that crossover produces in the offspring. Across a variety of problem domains, Luke has shown that there is a correlation between the depth at which the subtree removed by crossover occurs in the larger overall tree and the degree to which the child program's behavior is different from that of the receiving parent, with deeper removed subtrees corresponding to smaller changes in behavior. This suggests two mechanisms that may contribute to code growth. First, since fit children tend to be the result of crossovers that are relatively non-disruptive, they will tend to be the offspring of receiving parents in whom a deep crossover point was selected, but there will be no corresponding bias toward deep crossover points in the donor parent, thus tending to make fit children larger than their parents. Note that this part of the theory predicts the same phenomenon as removal bias, but assigns it a more general cause. The second part of the theory simply notes that, as receiving parents, larger trees will on average have subtrees removed at deeper points (and due to the correlation will therefore typically produce offspring less different from themselves), thus making size *in itself* a defense against genetic operators such as crossover and mutation.

1.3 Problems and Methodology

The problems studied in this paper lie in the symbolic regression domain, and use target functions that are polynomials of the form $x+x^2+...+x^n$. Such problems have previously been studied in connection with code growth by Langdon [4]. Fitness cases consist of 101 points uniformly spaced over the interval [0,1]. The function set is {+,-,%,*}, where % is a protected division operator that returns 1.0 upon division by zero, and the terminal set is {X, $\Re$}, where $\Re$ denotes the random numeric terminal. Tournament selection is used with a tournament size of 3. Population size is 1000. Unless otherwise noted, we use 100% crossover, a depth limit of 17, and a size limit of 500 points.

2 Components of Code Growth

Code growth occurs when the children in successive generations are consistently larger than the children in previous generations, i.e. $|c(n+1)|>|c(n)|$. It is known that crossover alone cannot increase the expected size of individuals in a population, so that on average $|p(n)|=|c(n)|$. It is also true on average that $|p(n)|=|p_r(n)|=|p_d(n)|$, since receiving and donor parents are selected in the same way. This means that the growth $|c(n+1)|-|c(n)|$ that occurs at generation n is on average equal to $|p_r(n+1)|-|p_r(n)|$.

Recalling that $g_r(n)$ is the subset of the receiving parents $p_r(n)$ whose children win at least one tournament ("the grandparent population"), we can write the difference $|p_r(n+1)|-|p_r(n)|$, as the sum of two terms: $|p_r(n+1)|-|g_r(n)|$ and $|g_r(n)|-|p_r(n)|$. The first term measures the extent to which the fit children (i.e. those who win tournaments) are larger than their parents, while the second term measures the extent to which the parents of fit children are larger than parents as a whole. By arguing that fit children will tend to be larger than their parents, both the theory of removal bias and the first part of the depth-correlation theory predict that the first term will be positive. By arguing that larger parents will be more likely to produce fit children, both the intron theory and the second part of the depth-correlation theory predict that the second term will be positive. Thus, by explicitly tracking the values of these two terms in an actual run, we can determine to what extent each of these two types of theories has the potential to explain code growth.

We tracked the values of these two terms over two sets of 20 runs of the degree 9 polynomial problem. The first set of runs used no size or depth limits and a run length of 50 generations, while the second set used a depth limit of 17 and run length of 300 generations. When running with depth limits, we use one-offspring crossover and retry the selection of both crossover points when the depth limits would be violated (in this case $|c(n)|<|p(n)|$ on average). Figures 1 and 2 show the average sizes of $c(n)$, $p_r(n)$, and $g_r(n)$ for 5 typical generations from each set of runs. For the runs with no depth limits, the average value of the term $|p(n+1)|-|g(n)|$ was 7.60 and the average value of the term $|g(n)|-|p(n)|$ was 12.5. Thus, for this problem it is reasonable to say that 37.9% of the growth was attributable to fit children being larger than their parents, while 62.1% was attributable to the parents of fit children being larger than parents as a whole. In the runs with depth limits, however, only the second term is positive on average, with the average values of the two terms being -1.47 and 2.24, respectively. It must be noted that Luke [6] has found that in symbolic regression problems there is a statistical bias toward fit children being the result of crossovers in which small subtrees were inserted (in addition to the bias toward small subtrees being removed), so that the relationships between these two terms observed in this problem are not necessarily reflective of the relationships that are typical for problems as a whole. Nevertheless, it appears that at least for the problems studied here the dominant cause of code growth is the second term, i.e. that the parents of fit children are larger than parents as a whole.

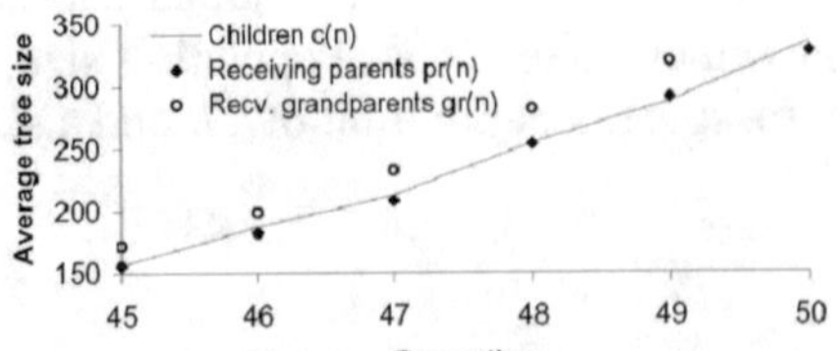

Fig. 1. CPG graph, no size/depth limits.

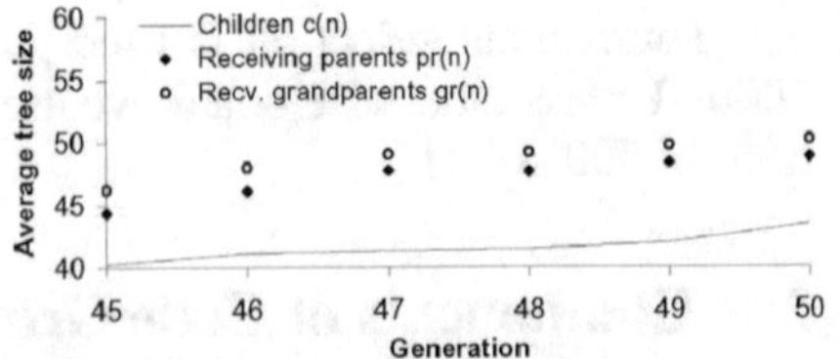

Fig. 2. CPG graph, depth limit of 17.

3 Resilience in GP Trees

The key idea behind both the intron theory and the second part of the depth-correlation theory is that the receiving parents who produce offspring more similar to themselves will tend to be large, i.e. that it is large trees which will be most *resilient* in the face of crossover. In this section we present an empirical measure of resilience and investigate the relationship between size and resilience by applying our empirical measure to randomly generated trees.

Conceptually, the resilience of an individual is determined by the probability distribution over all possible values of the behavioral difference between parent and child (quantified in some application-specific way) that is associated with the application of a genetic operator to that individual. In empirically sampling this distribution, we have found that its mean value is often arbitrarily large, since there is in general no limit on the maximum value of behavioral change. For this reason, we instead characterize this distribution by its median value, using the resilience measure described below.

3.1 Our Measurement of Resilience

We measure the resilience of an individual by performing a large number of mutations on separate copies of the individual, and recording for each mutation the difference in behavior between the parent and the child. For the symbolic regression problems we are studying, we define the behavioral difference between two individuals as the average absolute difference between corresponding points on the curves produced by the two individuals. We define *vulnerability* as the median of the behavioral differences associated with the mutations, and *resilience* as -1 times vulnerability. For all experiments reported here, we will use 101 subtree mutations to estimate resilience. Subtree mutations are performed using a 90% internal, 10% leaf weighted choice of subtree insertion points, and the inserted subtrees are created using the grow algorithm with a minimum depth of 1 and maximum depth of 5. Note that we define resilience in terms of mutation rather than crossover since using crossover would introduce a population-dependence that would make experiments on random trees considerably more complicated.

3.2 The Resilience of Randomly Generated Trees

Our first experiment with resilience was to measure the resilience of arbitrary random trees of various sizes. However, it soon became apparent that many of these trees would be very unlikely to appear in any later generation GP population. For example, the most resilient randomly generated trees had the form (* *<always-zero>* *<always-zero>*), and thus could only be meaningfully changed by a mutation that replaced the entire tree. At the other extreme, some trees performed computations involving final and intermediate values on the order of 10^{15}, which made them extremely non-resilient. Since neither of these two types of trees are likely to be fit with respect to any reasonable fitness function, we chose to narrow our sampling of randomly generated trees using a specific target curve — in this case the quartic polynomial f(x) = $x+x^2+x^3+x^4$. Specifically, any tree whose average difference over the interval [0,1] from this function was less than or equal to 0.5 was considered "fit", while any tree with more than this level of error was discarded as unfit.

1000 relatively fit trees of each size (3 through 31, odd sizes only) were generated, and their resiliences calculated as described in section 2.1 (note that there are no binary trees containing an even number of nodes). All trees were generated using the grow initialization method. Since the use of the grow algorithm introduces a certain shape bias to the trees which are generated, this experiment could admittedly be improved by using a ramped uniform initialization method [4].

Figure 3 shows the average and median vulnerability (-1 times resilience) of randomly generated trees as a function of their size. With the exception of one point on the curve for average resilience, both average and median vulnerability decrease monotonically as the tree size increases. Random trees of size 31, for example, on average had 61% of the vulnerability value of random trees of size 9. Figure 3 establishes that with respect to the given domain (symbolic regression), the given genetic operator (subtree mutation), and the given subset of all randomly generated trees which were actually used in the experiment (those which had an average difference of 0.5 or less from the quartic polynomial), large trees are on average less vulnerable (more resilient) than small trees.

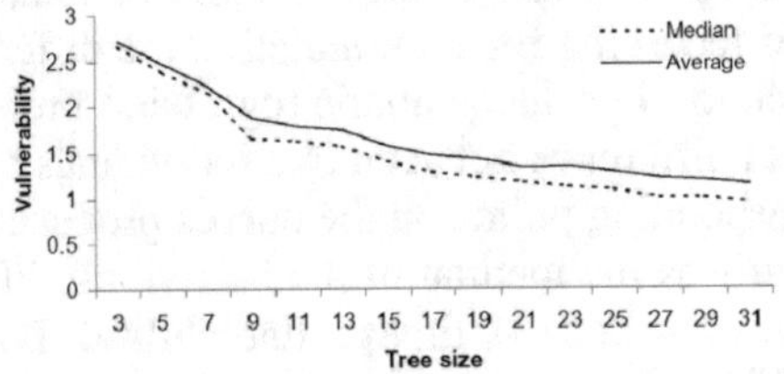

Fig. 3. Vulnerability as a function of tree size. Larger trees are typically more resilient.

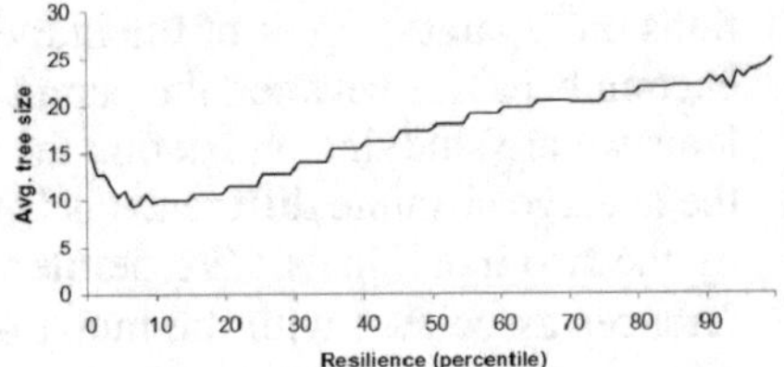

Fig. 4. Average tree size by resilience percentile. Resilient trees are large.

It is also possible to study tree size as a function of resilience. Based on the same experiment described above, figure 4 shows average tree size as a function of resilience, where resilience is given as a percentile, i.e. the point above the label 90 on the horizontal axis denotes the average size of trees that were in the 90-91st percentile with respect to resilience. Figure 4 makes clear that in addition to large trees being on average more resilient than small trees, the most resilient trees are large on average.

3.3 Resilience in Actual GP Runs

A quantity that is closely related to the average vulnerability of trees in a GP population is the median of the difference between offspring and receiving parent behavior for all offspring created at a particular generation. For all problems discussed in this paper, two relationships concerning this quantity consistently hold: median behavioral change decreases during the lifetime of the run, and the median behavioral change for fit children is always lower than that for the child population as a whole. As an example, figure 5 illustrates the median behavioral change from the receiving parent for children $c(n)$ and for fit children $p(n+1)$ for a typical run against the 9th degree polynomial target function. Though the run described by figure 5 used 100% crossover, these two relationships also hold if subtree mutation is used as the sole genetic operator (though in this casc bchavioral change decreases considerably more slowly). Since the genetic operators do not change during the course of the run, this can only be the result of the population in one way or another becoming more resilient with respect to the genetic operators.

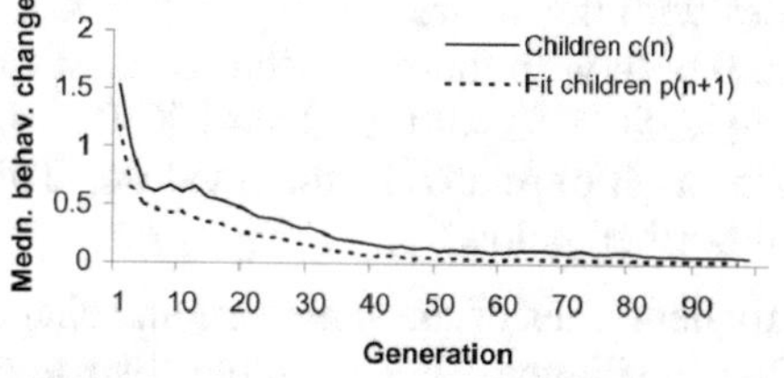

Fig. 5. Median behavioral change in a typical run of degree 9 polynomial.

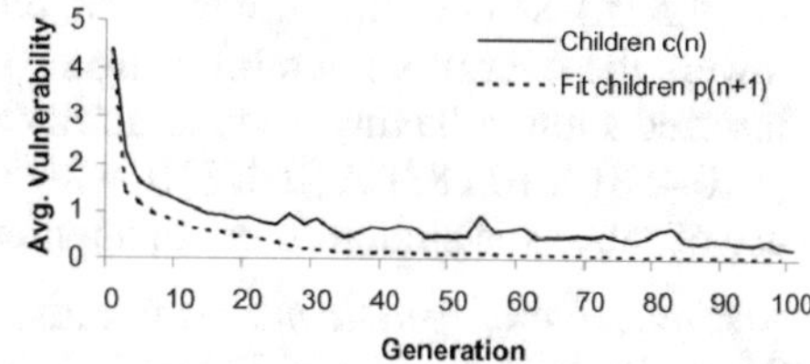

Fig. 6. Average vulnerability in the run described by figure 5.

Figure 6 tracks the average vulnerability of individuals in the same run described by figure 5, as measured by explicitly applying our resilience measure to every individual in the population history. As shown in the figure, individuals become more resilient over time, and selected individuals are consistently more resilient on average than individuals as a whole. It is significant that individuals bred only through crossover also become more resilient with respect to subtree mutation. The fact that the children who are selected are consistently more resilient than children as a whole indicates that evolution is preferentially selecting resilient individuals (though it does not necessarily establish that the children's resilience is the cause of this preference). However, if we accept that evolution is in a sense seeking out the more resilient individuals, it follows from our analysis in section 2.2 that doing so would require it to generate larger and larger trees.

3.4 What Makes Trees Resilient

The above sections have quantified resilience on a per-individual basis; however, to understand the mechanisms by which resilience may be achieved it will be necessary to quantify it on a per-node basis. To do this, we define a per-node measure of vulnerability that is identical to the measure given above, except that in measuring the vulnerability of a node N we will only perform mutations where N is the insertion point for the randomly generated subtree. We refer to the set of per-node vulnerability values for a tree as its *vulnerability map*. As an example, the S-expression (* (- X X) (+ X X)) has a vulnerability map (* [2.15] (- [1.70] X [1.44] X [1.58]) (+ [0] X [0] X [0])), where each value in brackets is the vulnerability of the node whose identity is given by the symbol to the left of the brackets. Note that inviable nodes are indicated by zeroes in the vulnerability map. Through experiments both with individuals from actual GP runs and with hand-created trees, we have found that there are at least 4 distinct means by which low vulnerability can be achieved, which we summarize below. In all cases where examples are given, more dramatic examples could be created using larger trees. Additionally, some examples depend on X being restricted to the interval [0,1], but examples exist that do not have this dependency.

Inviable code: Inviable code has an obvious affect on both the vulnerability map and on vulnerability. As illustrated above, inviable code is indicated by zero values in the vulnerability map. Since each per-node vulnerability can never be less than zero, the presence of inviable code can only make individuals more resilient.

Introns: Introns can be used to make trees more resilient. For example, in the tree (+ (+ (* X X) X) (- 0 0)), replacing the two zeroes with the subtree (* (* X X) (* X X)) lowers the overall vulnerability from 0.823 to 0.666, with the first occurrence of the inserted subtree having a vulnerability map (* [1.55] (* [0.408] X [0.444] X [0.314]) (* [0.458] X [0.283] X [0.478])), which contains a set of relatively small values. This use of introns is similar to depth attenuation (described below).

Arrangement of genetic material: Among equivalent trees of the same size and shape, the arrangement of specific symbols can affect resilience. For example, two trees which code for the expression x^2+x are (* (+ X 1) X) and (+ (* X X) X). The former expression has a vulnerability map of (* [2.35] (+ [1.04] X [.718] 1 [.754]) X [2.47]) and vulnerability of 1.04, while the latter has a vulnerability map of (+ [2.35] (* [1.64] X [0.718] X [0.788]) X [1.52]) and vulnerability of 0.865. In this case, the placement of * at the root of the former tree gives its rightmost leaf node a high vulnerability which accounts for most of the overall difference.

Depth-attenuation: It is relatively easy to create trees whose per-node vulnerability values decrease monotonically with depth. For example, the tree (* (* X X) (* X X)) has a vulnerability map (* [2.34] (* [0.567] X [0.39] X [0.418]) (* [0.467] X [0.323] X [0.242])) which has this property. This, in combination with cancelling or near-cancelling terms such as those in the example in the "Introns" section above, provides a simple way to create large trees that are highly resilient.

In actual GP runs that we have studied, the predominant way in which trees achieve resilience appears to be depth-attenuation. In looking at the vulnerability maps for later-generation trees, we consistently find that the vulnerability of deeper nodes tends to be lower than that of nodes near the root (though this is not consistently true for randomly generated trees). As an example, the following data is from an individual from generation 50 of a run against the degree 9 polynomial. The individual had a depth of 17, and its per-node vulnerability values averaged over depths 0 through 16 respectively were 2.89, 1.91, 2.71, 1.7, 0.649, 0.566, 0.257, 0.420, 0.309, 0.232, 0.203, 0.0501, 0.0488, 0.0368, 0.0329, 0.0299, and 0.0369. The individual's overall vulnerability was 0.335. Notice that the per-node vulnerabilities for depths 13 through 16 are approximately 1/10 this value.

4 A Selection Scheme that Eliminates Bloat

Our preceding analysis has suggested that code growth is a result of the tendency of GP to seek out trees that are more resilient. If this is the case, it should follow that preventing GP from evolving a population of more and more resilient individuals should eliminate bloat. One certain way to prevent the average behavioral change from falling to an arbitrarily low value is simply to introduce a certain *minimum behavioral change* (MBC) that individuals must undergo as a result of crossover or mutation in order to be eligible for selection. For example, if we specify an MBC of 0.05 and heavily penalize (i.e. assign infinite fitness to) any child which differs from its receiving parent by an value lower than this, then we would not expect the average behavioral change to drop much below 0.05. Note this often penalizes children that are *better* than their parents.

We want to emphasize that we do not necessarily think this is a good idea for a selection scheme. For one thing, it is extremely heavy-handed, imposing a strict penalty on individuals whose genetic material may be of value to the population. It may even penalize what would otherwise be the best-of-generation individual. It also eliminates the possibility of neutral walks, which are considered an important aspect of artificial evolution [14]. Nevertheless, the fact that this selection method limits the buildup of resilience means that using it will tell us something about our explanation of code growth.

We conducted experiments using 4 levels of MBC: 0.2, 0.1, 0.05, and 10^{-5}, in addition to a control experiment with no MBC. No size or depth limits were used in these experiments. Each experiment involved 20 separate runs against the degree 10 target polynomial, each lasting 300 generations, with the exception that the experiment with MBC of 10^{-5} and the control experiment were run for only 50 generations due to the extreme increase in tree size. The degree 10 polynomial was used to allow most or all of the growth to occur before the run solved. In practice we found for MBC values of 0.05, 0.1 and 0.2 that between 5% and 15% of the individuals were penalized in each generation.

As shown in figure 7, tree growth was lower for each successively higher value of MBC. Moreover, for MBC values of 0.1 and 0.2 the average tree size plateaus rather than continuing to increase. For these MBC values, we have continued individuals runs for up to 10,000 generations and have never seen any deviation from this plateau. Note that eliminating only neutral crossovers (MBC of 10^{-5}) did not dramatically reduce code growth, which is consistent with the results of Luke [6-7]. However, eliminating (phenotypically) near-neutral crossovers did eliminate code growth. Furthermore, as will be shown in section 5, eliminating code growth in this way actually improves performance independent of the obvious savings in execution time per generation.

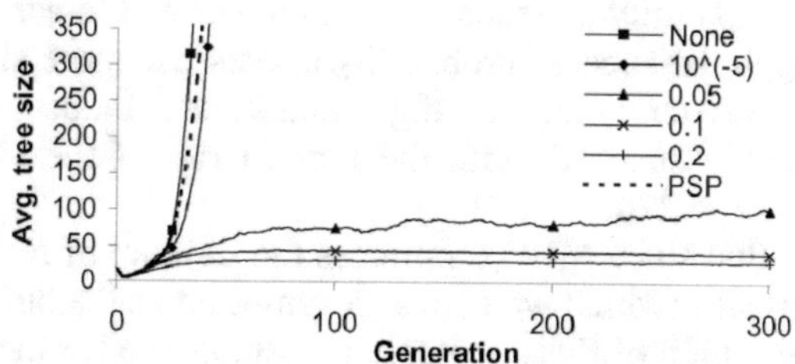

Fig. 7. Average tree sizes for various levels of minimum behavioral change (MBC).

4.1 The Possibility of MBC as a Probabilistic Size Penalty

Since we have shown in section 2.2 that the more resilient trees are typically large, and since MBC tends to penalize resilient trees, the possibility exists that the effect of MBC on code growth is due to its penalizing of some critical fraction of the larger trees, rather than to any connection with the underlying causes of code growth. To test this possibility we recorded, for all 50 runs of the degree 9 polynomial using an MBC of 0.1, the average fraction of individuals of each size S that were penalized in each generation N. We then performed 20 additional runs in which, for every S and N, this same fraction of individuals were penalized, but the individuals to be penalized were selected at random from among individuals of the given size (rather than being selected based on behavioral change). The curve labeled PSP in Figure 7 shows the average tree size for these additional runs. As shown in the figure, the probabilistic size penalty used in these additional runs has only a very slight affect on code growth. Thus, that an MBC of 0.1 did eliminate code growth depended critically on the fact that it was the *resilient* individuals that were specifically penalized.

5 Effects on Scalability

As mentioned in section 3, there are a number of reasons not to use MBC as a selection scheme, including its heavy-handedness, its ability to penalize good individuals, and its elimination of neutral walks. Nevertheless, it is worth studying the affect of this approach on performance for two reasons. First, doing so will give us at least a rough idea of the affect on performance of eliminating bloat. Second, the performance of this approach can act as a benchmark for any more sophisticated measures that are devised to eliminate bloat. We tested the performance of this approach using 6 symbolic regression problems with target functions of the form $x+x^2+x^3 + \ldots + x^n$ for $4 \leq n \leq 9$, using 50 runs for each problem. Figures 8 and 9 give the success probability curves associated with MBC and with standard GP selection, respectively. Table 1 summarizes the computational effort associated with each selection method, where I_A, G_A, and R_A denote the computational effort, optimum number of generations, and optimum number of runs, respectively for standard GP selection, and I_B, G_B, and R_B denote the corresponding quantities for MBC selection.

The affect of MBC on scalability in these problems is dramatic. With standard GP selection, the probability of finding a perfect solution increases rapidly up to a certain generation, and then plateaus. As the problem is scaled up in difficulty, the value at which the success probability plateaus becomes lower and lower. In contrast, with an MBC of 0.1, although the success probability curves rise more slowly as the problem is scaled up, they consistently attain a high final value. Indeed, with an MBC of 0.1 all 300 runs eventually succeed, with the longest run of the 9th degree polynomial succeeding at generation 276.

It must be noted that since MBC eliminates the buildup of resilience in addition to eliminating code growth (which we take as a symptom of the buildup of resilience), it is not entirely clear which of these features is responsible for the performance difference we observe. In other words, although we believe code growth happens because creating larger trees is a natural and easy way to build up resilience, it may still be possible to eliminate code growth while allowing the buildup of resilience to occur in other ways. At the moment, we do not have a way to know what the affect on performance of eliminating code growth without eliminating the buildup of resilience would be in these problems. But in any case, it appears there is untapped potential to increase the scalability of GP by taking the issues of resilience and code growth into account.

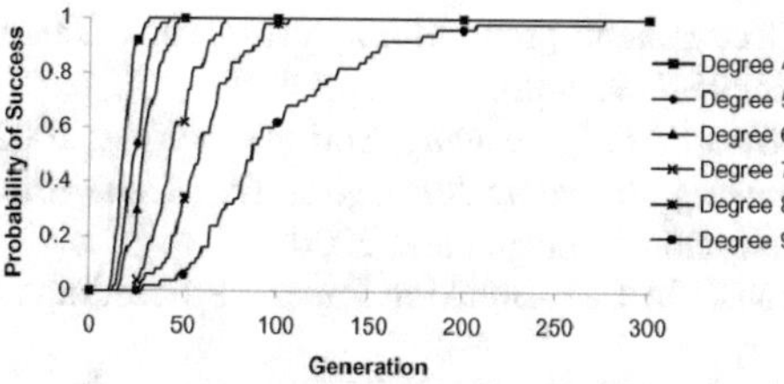

Fig. 8. Success probabilities using MBC of 0.1. Probability of success continues to improve even late in the run.

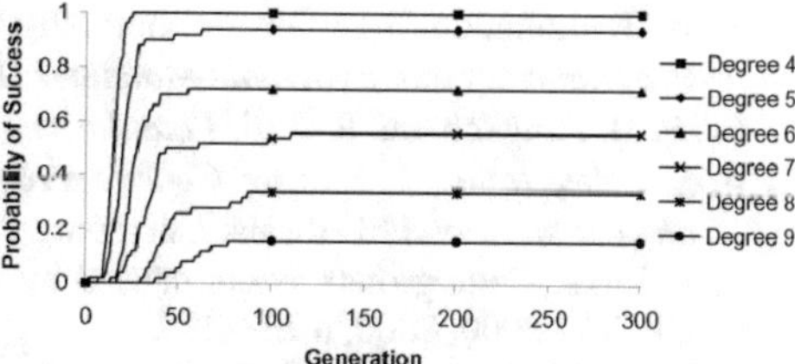

Fig. 9. Success probabilities using standard GP selection. Probability of success plateaus at different levels as problem is scaled up.

Table 1. Comparison of computational effort for standard GP selection (A) and for MBC of 0.1 (B).

Degree	$I_A(M,i,z)$	G_A	R_A	$I_B(M,i,z)$	G_B	R_B	I_A/I_B
4	26,000	25	1	32,000	31	1	0.81
5	64,000	31	2	43,000	42	1	1.5
6	164,000	40	4	48,000	47	1	3.4
7	308,000	43	7	73,000	72	1	4.2
8	784,000	48	16	107,000	106	1	7.3
9	2,106,000	77	27	277,000	276	1	7.6

6 Conclusions

We have proposed an explanation of code growth based on the concept of resilience, and have shown that preventing the buildup of resilience also prevents code growth. Through random sampling of equal numbers of individuals of 15 different sizes, we have found that the most resilient individuals are larger than average. By monitoring resilience in actual runs, we have found that trees become more resilient over time and that selected individuals are consistently more resilient than individuals as a whole. We have also shown that by using a selection method that prevents the population from becoming resilient, we can eliminate code growth. All of this strongly suggests that code growth occurs as a side effect of the seeking out by evolution of resilient trees. Finally, we have shown that eliminating code growth in this way yields an improvement in performance that increases as the problem is scaled in difficulty.

References

1. T. Blickle and L. Thiele. Genetic programming and redundancy. In J. Hopf (ed.), *Genetic Algorithms Within the Framework of Evolutionary Computation*, Max-Planck-Institut fur Informatik: Saarbrucken, Germany, 1994, p 33-38.
2. J. R. Koza. *Genetic Programming: On the Programming of Computers by Means of Natural Selection.* Cambridge, MA: The MIT Press; 1992.
3. W. B. Langdon, T. Soule, R. Poli, and J. A. Foster. The evolution of size and shape. In *Advances in Genetic Programming III*, Cambridge, MA: The MIT Press, 1999, p 163-190.

4. W. B. Langdon. Size-fair and homologous tree genetic programming crossovers. *Genetic Programming and Evolvable Machines*, 1(1/2):95-119, 2000.
5. W. B. Langdon and R. Poli. *Foundations of Genetic Programming*. Springer-Verlag; 2002.
6. S. Luke. *Issues in Scaling Genetic Programming: Breeding Strategies, Tree Generation, and Code Bloat*. PhD thesis, University of Maryland, College Park, 2000.
7. S. Luke. Code growth is not caused by introns. In Late-Breaking Papers, Proceedings of GECCO 2000, 2000, p 228-235.
8. N. F. McPhee and J. D. Miller. Accurate replication in genetic programming. In L. J. Eshelman (ed.), *Proc. Sixth Int. Conf. Genetic Algorithms*, Morgan Kaufmann, 1995, p 303-309.
9. P. Nordin and W. Banzhaf. Complexity compression and evolution. In L. J. Eshelman (ed.), *Prof. Sixth Int. Conf. Genetic Algorithms*, Morgan Kaufmann, 1995, p 310-317.
10. P. Nordin and F. Francone. Explicitly defined introns and destructive crossover in genetic programming. In P. Angeline and K.E. Kinnear Jr (eds.), *Advances in Genetic Programming II*, Cambridge, MA: The MIT Press, 1996, p 111-134.
11. T. Soule. *Code Growth in Genetic Programming*, PhD thesis, University of Idaho, 1998.
12. T. Soule and J. A. Foster. Removal bias: a new cause of code growth in tree-based evolutionary programming. In *ICEC 98: IEEE International Conf. on Evolutionary Computation*, IEEE Press, 1998, p 781-786.
13. T. Soule and R. B. Heckendorn. An analysis of the causes of code growth in genetic programming. *Genetic Programming and Evolvable Machines*, 3(3):283-309, 2002.
14. T. Yu and J. Miller. Finding needles in haystacks is not hard with neutrality. In Foster et al. (eds.), *Proceedings of EuroGP'2002*, Springer-Verlag, 2002, p 13-25.

Fitness Distance Correlation in Structural Mutation Genetic Programming

Leonardo Vanneschi[1], Marco Tomassini[1], Philippe Collard[2], and Manuel Clergue[2]

[1] Computer Science Institute, University of Lausanne, Lausanne, Switzerland
{Leonardo.Vanneschi,Marco.Tomassini}@iis.unil.ch
[2] I3S Laboratory, University of Nice, Sophia Antipolis, France
{pc,clerguem}@i3s.unice.fr

Abstract. A new kind of mutation for genetic programming based on the structural distance operators for trees is presented in this paper. We firstly describe a new genetic programming process based on these operators (we call it structural mutation genetic programming). Then we use structural distance to calculate the fitness distance correlation coefficient and we show that this coefficient is a reasonable measure to express problem difficulty for structural mutation genetic programming for the considered set of problems, i.e. unimodal trap functions, royal trees and MAX problem.

1 Introduction

Studies of fitness distance correlation (*fdc*) as a tool for measuring problem difficulty in genetic algorithms (GAs) and genetic programming (GP) have lead to controversial results: even though some counterexamples has been found for GAs ([1], [17]), *fdc* has been proven an useful measure on a large number of GA (see for example [7] or [11]) and GP functions (see [5], [18]). In particular, Clergue *et al.* ([5]) have shown *fdc* to be a reasonable way of quantifying problem difficulty for GP for a set of functions. To calculate *fdc* they defined a genotypic distance for trees based on recursion. No particular relationship between this distance and the genetic operator they used (standard GP crossover) was evident (as is the case in GAs with Hamming distance and standard crossover). The distance metric should instead be defined with regard to the actual neighborhood produced by the genetic operators, so to assure the conservation of the genetic material between neighbors. In this paper we want to overcome this limitation, establishing a strong relationship between distance and genetic operators. Thus, we use structural distance (see [9,12]) to calculate *fdc* and we use the tranformations on which structural distance is based to define two new genetic operators. The new resulting evolutionary process will be called *structural mutation genetic programming* (SMGP), to distinguish it from GP based on the standard Koza's crossover (that will be referred to as standard GP).

So, this paper deeply differs from [5] for the following main reasons: a different distance measure is used, for the first time here, to calculate *fdc*; an original

C. Ryan et al. (Eds.): EuroGP 2003, LNCS 2610, pp. 455–464, 2003.

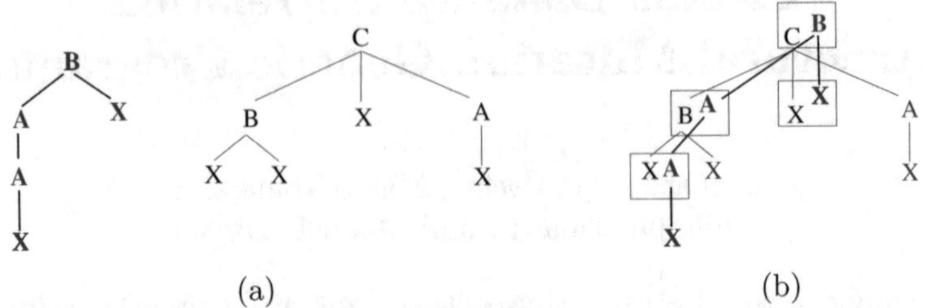

Fig. 1. (a): Two trees T_1 and T_2 (b): The trees T_1 and T_2 overlapped at the root node. Overlapped nodes are included inside a rectangle.

evolutionary process with new genetic operators is used; the coherence between these operators and the distance used is not only hint, but it is formally proven. Finally, a larger set of test functions is used to validate our hypothesis, including two MAX problems, in which fitness is also a function of the semantics of the programs and not only of their syntactical structure, thus overcoming a critic that had been moved to [5].

This paper is structured as follows: in section 2 we describe one version of the structural distance. In section 3 we define two new mutations based on the structural operators and we describe SMGP. In section 4, *fdc* is tested as a measure of problem difficulty for SMGP on trap functions, royal trees and two MAX problems. Finally, in section 5 we offer our conclusions.

2 Distance Measure for Genetic Programs

In genetic algorithms (GAs) individuals are represented as strings of digits and typical distance measures are Hamming distance or alternation (see for instance [6]). Defining a distance between genotypes in GP is much more difficult, given the tree structure of the individuals. In [9] a version of the structural distance for trees has been proposed. According to this measure, given the sets $\mathcal{F}$ and $\mathcal{T}$ of functions and terminals, a coding function c must be defined such that $c : \{\mathcal{T} \cup \mathcal{F}\} \rightarrow \mathbb{N}$. One can think of many guidelines for the specification of c, for example the "complexity" of the functions or their arity. The distance between two trees T_1 and T_2 is calculated in three steps: (1) T_1 and T_2 are overlapped at the root node and the process is applied recursively starting from the leftmost subtrees (see [3] for a description of the overlapping algorithm and figure 1 for a visual intuition of it). (2) For each pair of nodes at matching positions, the difference of their codes (eventually elevated to an exponent) is computed. (3) The differences computed in the previous step are combined in a weighted sum. Formally, the distance of two trees T_1 and T_2 with roots R_1 and R_2 is defined as follows:

$$dist(T_1, T_2) = d(R_1, R_2) + k \sum_{i=1}^{m} dist(child_i(R_1), child_i(R_2)) \tag{1}$$

where: $d(R_1, R_2) = (|c(R_1) - c(R_2)|)^z$, $child_i(Y)$ is the ith of the m possible children of a generical node Y, if $i \leq m$, or the empty tree otherwise, and c evaluated on the root of an empty tree is 0. Constant k is used to give different weights to nodes belonging to different levels and z is a constant usually chosen in such a way that $z \in \mathbb{N}$.

In most of this paper, except the MAX function, individuals will be coded using the same syntax as in [5] and [16], i.e. considering a set of functions A, B, C, etc. with increasing arity (i.e. $arity(A) = 1$, $arity(B) = 2$, and so on) and a single terminal X (i.e. $arity(X) = 0$) as follows: $\mathcal{F} = \{A, B, C, D, \ldots\}, \mathcal{T} = \{X\}$ and the c function will be defined as follows: $\forall x \in \{\mathcal{F} \cup \mathcal{T}\} \quad c(x) = arity(x) + 1$. In our experiments we will always set $k = \frac{1}{2}$ and $z = 2$. By keeping $0 < k < 1$, the differences near the root have higher weight. This is convenient for GP as it has been noted that programs converge quickly to a fixed root portion [14].

3 Structural Mutation Operators

Given the sets $\mathcal{F}$ and $\mathcal{T}$ and the coding function c defined in section 2, we define c_{max} (respectively, c_{min}) as the maximum (respectively, the minimum) value assumed by c on the domain $\{\mathcal{F} \cup \mathcal{T}\}$. Moreover, given a symbol n such that $n \in \{\mathcal{F} \cup \mathcal{T}\}$ and $c(n) < c_{max}$ and a symbol m such that $m \in \{\mathcal{F} \cup \mathcal{T}\}$ and $c(m) > c_{min}$, we define: $succ(n)$ as a node such that $c(succ(n)) = c(n) + 1$ and $pred(m)$ as a node such that $c(pred(m)) = c(m) - 1$. Then we can define the following operators on a generic tree T:

- **grow mutation**. A node labelled with a symbol n such that $c(n) < c_{max}$ is selected in T and replaced by $succ(n)$. A new random terminal node is added to this new node in a random position (i.e. the new terminal becomes the ith son of $succ(n)$, where i is comprised between 0 and $arity(n)$).
- **shrink mutation**. A node labelled with a symbol m such that $c(m) > c_{min}$, and such that at least one of his sons is a leaf, is selected in T and replaced by $pred(m)$. A random leaf, between the sons of this node, is deleted from T.

The *grow* and *shrink* mutations defined above should not be confused with the well known homonimous mutation operators that have already been proposed in GP. Figure 2 gives an example of the application of the above new operators. Given these definitions, we can prove the following property:

Property 1. Distance/Operator Consistency.
Let's consider the sets $\mathcal{F}$ and $\mathcal{T}$ and the coding function c defined in section 2. Let T_1 and T_2 be two trees composed by symbols belonging to $\{\mathcal{F} \cup \mathcal{T}\}$ and let's consider the k and z constants of definition (1) to be both equal to 1. If $dist(T_1, T_2) = D$, then T_2 can be obtained from T_1 by a sequence of $\frac{D}{2}$ structural operations, where a structural operation can be a grow mutation or a shrink mutation.

The proof of this property can be found in appendix A (note that, given the sets $\mathcal{F}$ and $\mathcal{T}$ and the coding function c defined in section 2, and having set

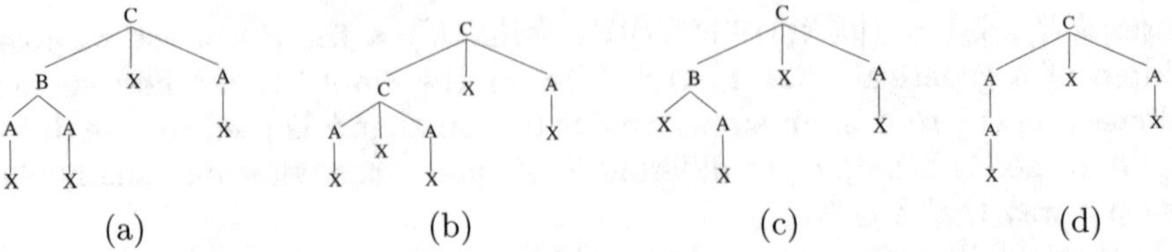

Fig. 2. The tree in (b) can be obtained from the tree in (a) in one step with the grow mutation. The tree in (d) can be obtained from the tree in (c) in one step with the shrink mutation.

$k = z = 1$ in definition (1), $dist(T_1, T_2)$ is an even natural number for every couple of trees T_1 and T_2. The proof of this property can be done by recursion on the depths of T_1 and T_2 and is omitted for reasons of space). From property 1 we deduce that, at least for the language used to code trees in most of this paper (except the MAX function), the operators of grow mutation and shrink mutation are completely coherent with the notion of structural distance defined in section 2: an application of these operators allow us to move on the research space from a tree to its neighbors according to the structural distance. Thus we are interested in defining a new GP process based on these operators. We call this process structural mutation genetic programming (SMGP).

4 Experimental Results

4.1 Fitness Distance Correlation

An approach proposed for GAs [11] states that an indication of problem hardness is given by the relationship between fitness and distance of the genotypes from known optima. Given a sample $F = \{f_1, f_2, ..., f_n\}$ of n individual fitnesses and a corresponding sample $D = \{d_1, d_2, ..., d_n\}$ of the n distances to the nearest global optimum, *fdc* is defined as:

$$fdc = \frac{C_{FD}}{\sigma_F \sigma_D}$$

where:

$$C_{FD} = \frac{1}{n} \sum_{i=1}^{n} (f_i - \overline{f})(d_i - \overline{d})$$

is the covariance of F and D and σ_F, σ_D, $\overline{f}$ and $\overline{d}$ are the standard deviations and means of F and D. As shown in [11], GA problems can be classified in three classes, depending on the value of the *fdc* coefficient: **misleading** ($fdc \geq 0.15$), in which fitness increases with distance, **difficult** ($-0.15 < fdc < 0.15$) in which there is virtually no correlation between fitness and distance and **straightforward** ($fdc \leq -0.15$) in which fitness increases as the global optimum approaches. The second class corresponds to problems for which the difficulty can't be estimated, because *fdc* doesn't bring any information. In this case, examination of the fitness-distance scatterplot may give information on problem difficulty (see [11]).

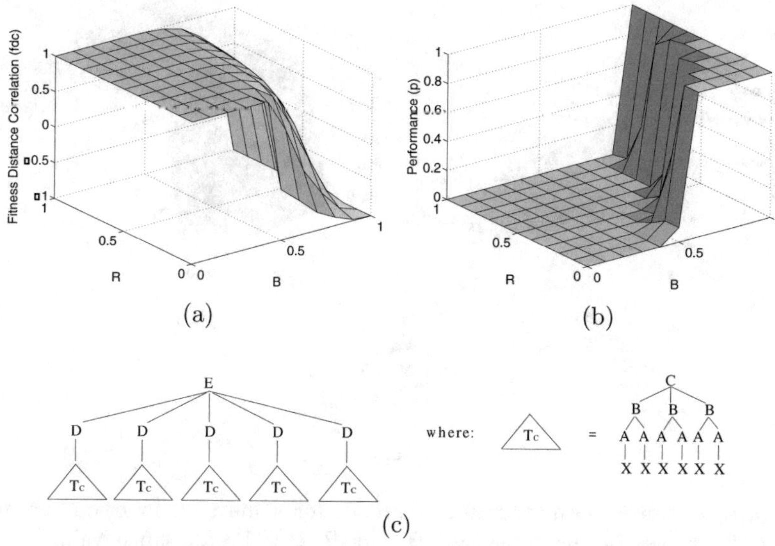

Fig. 3. (a): *fdc* values with structural distance for some trap functions obtained by changing the values of the constants B and R. (b): Performance values of SMGP with structural distance for traps. (c): Stucture of the tree used as optimum in the experiments reported in (a) and (b).

4.2 Trap Functions

Trap functions [8] allow to define the fitness of the individuals as a function of their distance from the optimum. A function $f : distance \rightarrow fitness$ is an unimodal trap function if it is defined in the following way:

$$f(d) = \begin{cases} 1 - \dfrac{d}{B} & \text{if } d \leq B \\ \\ \dfrac{R \cdot (d - B)}{1 - B} & \text{elsewhere} \end{cases}$$

These functions have a number of different optima and d is the distance of the current individual from the unique global one, while B and R are constants $\in [0, 1]$. B allows to set the width of the attractive basin for each of the two optima and R sets their relative importance. By construction, the difficulty of trap functions decreases as the value of B increases, while it increases as the value of R increases.

Figures 3 and 4 show values of the performance p (defined as the number of executions for which the global optimum has been found in less than 500 generations divided by the total number of executions, i.e. 100 in our experiments) and of *fdc* for various trap functions obtained by changing the values of the constants B and R.

Two trees of different shapes are considered as optimum in the different experiments (see (c) parts of the figures). In all cases *fdc* is confirmed to be a

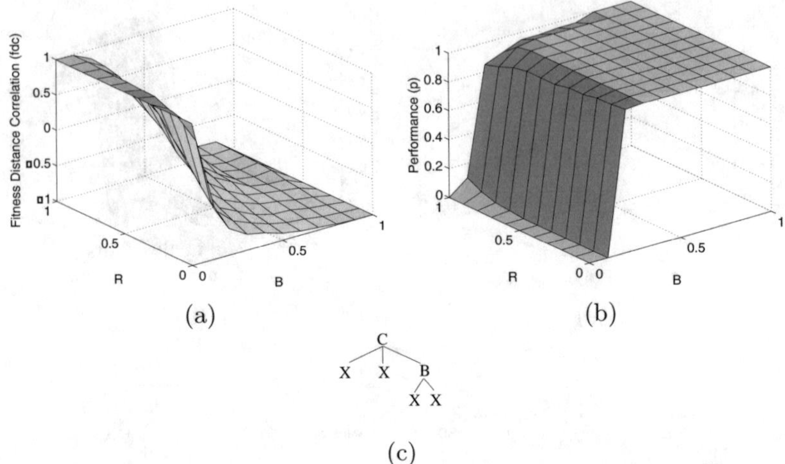

Fig. 4. (a): *fdc* values with structural distance for some trap functions obtained by changing the values of the constants B and R. (b): Performance values of SMGP with structural distance for traps. (c): Stucture of the tree used as optimum in the experiments reported in (a) and (b).

reasonable measure to quantify problem difficulty. The same experiments have been repeated using two other differently shaped trees as global optimum and the results (not shown here to save space) are qualitatively analogous to the ones shown in figures 3 and 4. In all experiments *fdc* has been calculated via a sample of 40000 randomly chosen individuals. All the experiments have been done with generational SMGP, a total population size of 100 individuals, tournament selection of size 10 and E as the node with maximum arity allowed.

4.3 Royal Trees

The next functions we take into account are the royal trees proposed by Punch *et al.* [16]. The language used is the same as in section 2, and the fitness of a tree (or any subtree) is defined as the score of its root. Each function calculates its score by summing the weighted scores of its direct children. If the child is a perfect tree of the appropriate level (for instance, a complete level-C tree beneath a D node), then the score of that subtree, times a *FullBonus* weight, is added to the score of the root. If the child has a correct root but is not a perfect tree, then the weight is *PartialBonus*. If the child's root is incorrect, then the weight is *Penalty*. After scoring the root, if the function is itself the root of a perfect tree, the final sum is multiplied by *CompleteBonus* (see [16] for a more detailed explanation). Values used here are as in [16] i.e. *FullBonus* = 2, *PartialBonus* = 1, *Penalty* = $\frac{1}{3}$, *CompleteBonus* = 2. Results on the study of *fdc* are shown in table 1.

Fdc correctly classifies the difficulty of level-B, level-C and level-D functions. Level-E function is "difficult" to be predicted by the *fdc* (i.e. no correlation be-

Table 1. Results of *fdc* for the Royal Trees using SMGP.

Root	*fdc*	*fdc* prediction	*p* (SMGP)
B	-0.31	straightf.	1
C	-0.25	straightf.	1
D	-0.20	straightf.	0.76
E	0.059	difficult	0
F	0.44	misleading	0
G	0.73	misleading	0

Table 2. Results of *fdc* for the MAX problem using SMGP with structural distance. The first column shows the sets of functions and terminals used in the experiments.

MAX problem	*fdc*	*fdc* prediction	*p* (SMGP)
{+} {1}	-0.87	straightf.	1
{+} {1,2}	-0.86	straightf.	1

tween fitness and distance is observed). Finally, level-F and level-G functions are predicted to be "misleading" (in accord with [16]) and they really are, since the global optimum is never found before generation 500. In conclusion, it appears that royal trees problem spans all the classes of difficulty as described by the *fdc*.

4.4 MAX Problem

The task of the MAX problem for GP, defined in [10] and [13], is "to find the program which returns the largest value for a given terminal and function set with a depth limit d, where the root node counts as depth 0". We set d equal to 8 and we use the set of functions $\mathcal{F} = \{+\}$ and the set of terminals $\mathcal{T}_1 = \{1\}$ or $\mathcal{T}_2 = \{1, 2\}$. When using $\mathcal{T}_1$, we specify the coding function c as: $c(1) = 1$, $c(+) = 2$, when using $\mathcal{T}_2$, we pose: $c(1) = 1$, $c(2) = 2, c(+) = 3$. The grow and shrink mutations, this time, are defined in such a way that, when using $\mathcal{T}_1$, a terminal symbol 1 can be transformed in the subtree $T_1 = +(1, 1)$ by one step of grow mutation and the vice-versa can be done by the shrink mutation. When using $\mathcal{T}_2$, the grow mutation can transform a 1 node into a 2 node and a 2 node into the subtrees $T_2 = +(2, 1)$ or $T_3 = +(1, 2)$ (with a uniform probability). On the other hand, the shrink mutation can tranform T_1 or T_2 into a leaf labelled by 2, and a 2 node into a 1 node. Table 2 shows the *fdc* and p values for these test cases.

5 Conclusions and Future Work

Two new tree mutations corresponding to the structural distance operators are defined in this paper. Fitness distance correlation (*fdc*) calculated using a version of the structural distance is shown to be a reasonable measure to quantify the difficulty of trap functions, royal trees and two MAX functions for GP using these mutations as genetic operators (SMGP). Experiments using GP based on standard crossover (and no mutation) have also been performed on all the test cases considered here. Results (not shown for reasons of space) confirm *fdc* as a reasonable measure of problem difficulty also for GP with standard crossover. This seems to point in the same direction as in [2], [4] and [15], where the standard GP crossover is defined as a "macro-mutation". In view of some counterexamples that have been mentioned in the text, it remains to be checked whether the use of *fdc* extends to other classes of functions, such as typical GP benchmarks. In the future we also plan to investigate the use of *fdc* in cases of fitness landscapes containing multiple optima and to look for a measure for GP difficulty that can be calculated without prior knowledge of the global optima, thus eliminating the strongest limitations of *fdc*. Moreover, we plan to build a counterexample for *fdc* in GP. Another open problem consists in taking into account in the distance definition the phenomenon of introns (whereby two different genotypes can lead to the same phenotypic behavior). Finally, we intend to look for a better measure than performance to identify the success rate of functions, possibly independent from the maximum number of generations chosen.

A Proof of the Distance/Operator Consistency Property

Let's prove property 1 (see section 3) by recursion on the depths of T_1 and T_2. Let p_1 and p_2 be the respective depths of T_1 and T_2. If $p_1, p_2 \leq 0$ (i.e. $p_1, p_2 = 0$), then T_1 and T_2 are both composed of a single node X. In this case, their distance is equal to zero and the number of structural mutations to transform T_1 into T_2 is obviously equal to zero. So the property holds. Let's now suppose the property true $\forall p_1, p_2 \leq p$ (with $p \geq 0$) and, starting from this hypothesis, let's prove it $\forall p_1, p_2 \leq p+1$. Let's consider two trees T_1 and T_2 of depths p_1 and p_2 with $p_1, p_2 \leq p+1$. Let R_1 be the root of T_1 and R_2 be the root of T_2. Let the difference between the codes of R_1 and R_2 be equal to y (i.e. $d(R_1, R_2) = y$) and, without lost of generality, let's consider $c(R_1) \leq c(R_2)$. Now, to transform R_1 into R_2, we have to perform y grow mutations on R_1, which lead to y increments of R_1's label cost and to the creation of y new X nodes. Let's call T_1' the tree generated from T_1 after these y operations. Then, we have: $dist(T_1, T_2) = 2y + dist(T_1', T_2)$, since T_1's root has been incremented y times and y new X nodes have been created. Moreover, since T_1' and T_2 have the same root, we can write:

$$dist(T_1, T_2) = 2y + \sum_{i=1}^{m} dist(child_i(R_1), child_i(R_2)) \tag{2}$$

where m is T_2's arity. On the other hand, it is clearly possible to transform T_1 into T_2 with the same number of operations that can be used to transform T_1' into T_2, plus y operations (used to transform T_1 into T_1'). Let's express this property with the notation: $op(T_1, T_2) = y + op(T_1', T_2)$ and, since T_1' and T_2 have the same root:

$$op(T_1, T_2) = y + \sum_{i=1}^{m} op(child_i(R_1), child_i(R_2)) \tag{3}$$

Now, $child_i(R_1)$ and $child_i(R_2)$ have respective depths p_1^i and p_2^i where $p_1^i, p_2^i \leq p$ and so, by recursive hypothesis, if we call D_i the distance between $child_i(R_1)$ and $child_i(R_2)$, it is possible to tranform $child_i(R_1)$ into $child_i(R_2)$ with $\frac{D_i}{2}$ structural operations. We can express it with the following notation:

$$dist(child_i(R_1), child_i(R_2)) = D_i \tag{4}$$

and

$$op(child_i(R_1), child_i(R_2)) = \frac{D_i}{2} \tag{5}$$

As a consequence, by replacing (4) in (2), we obtain: $dist(T_1, T_2) = 2y + \sum_{i=1}^{m} D_i$ and by replacing (5) in (3) we obtain: $op(T_1, T_2) = y + \sum_{i=1}^{m} \frac{D_i}{2} = \frac{1}{2} dist(T_1, T_2)$, i.e. it is possible to transform T_1 into T_2 with a number of structural operations equal to the distance between T_1 and T_2 divided by 2. This proves the property. □

Acknowledgment

We would like to thank Leslie Luthi for his help with the proof of property 1.

References

1. L. Altenberg. Fitness distance correlation analysis: an instructive counterexample. In T. Back, editor, *Seventh International Conference on Genetic Algorithms*, pages 57–64. Morgan Kaufmann, 1997.
2. P. J. Angeline. Subtree crossover: Building block engine or macromutation? In J. R. Koza, K. Deb, M. Dorigo, D. B. Fogel, M. Garzon, H. Iba, and R. L. Riolo, editors, *Genetic Programming 1997: Proceedings of the Second Annual Conference*, pages 9–17, Stanford University, CA, USA, 1997. Morgan Kaufmann.
3. E. Burke, S. Gustafson, G. Kendall, and N. Krasnogor. Advanced population diversity measures in genetic programming. In J. J. Merelo, P. Adamidis, H. G. Beyer, J.-L. Fernández-Villacanas, and H.-P. Schwefel, editors, *Parallel Problem Solving from Nature - PPSN VII*, volume 2439 of *Lecture Notes in Computer Science*, pages 341–350. Springer-Verlag, Heidelberg, 2002.
4. K. Chellapilla. Evolutionary programming with tree mutations: Evolving computer programs without crossover. In J. R. Koza, K. Deb, M. Dorigo, D. B. Fogel, M. Garzon, H. Iba, and R. L. Riolo, editors, *Genetic Programming 1997: Proceedings of the Second Annual Conference*, pages 431–438, Stanford University, CA, USA, 1997. Morgan Kaufmann.
5. M. Clergue, P. Collard, M. Tomassini, and L. Vanneschi. Fitness distance correlation and problem difficulty for genetic programming. In *Proceedings of the genetic and evolutionary computation conference GECCO'02*, pages 724–732, San Francisco, CA, 2002. Morgan Kaufmann.
6. P. Collard, M. Clergue, and F. Bonnin. Misleading functions designed from alternation. In *Congress on Evolutionary Computation (CEC'2000)*, pages 1056–1063. IEEE Press, Piscataway, NJ, 2000.
7. P. Collard, A. Gaspar, M. Clergue, and C. Escazut. Fitness distance correlation as statistical measure of genetic algorithms difficulty, revisited. In *European Conference on Artificial Intelligence (ECAI'98)*, pages 650–654, Brighton, 1998. John Witley & Sons, Ltd.

8. K. Deb and D. E. Goldberg. Analyzing deception in trap functions. In D. Whitley, editor, *Foundations of Genetic Algorithms, 2*, pages 93–108. Morgan Kaufmann, 1993.
9. A. Ekárt and S. Z. Németh. Maintaining the diversity of genetic programs. In J. A. Foster, E. Lutton, J. Miller, C. Ryan, and A. G. B. Tettamanzi, editors, *Genetic Programming, Proceedings of the 5th European Conference, EuroGP 2002*, volume 2278 of *LNCS*, pages 162–171, Kinsale, Ireland, 3-5 April 2002. Springer-Verlag.
10. C. Gathercole and P. Ross. An adverse interaction between crossover and restricted tree depth in genetic programming. In J. R. Koza, D. E. Goldberg, D. B. Fogel, and R. L. Riolo, editors, *Genetic Programming 1996: Proceedings of the First Annual Conference*, pages 291–296, Stanford University, CA, USA, 28–31 July 1996. MIT Press.
11. T. Jones. *Evolutionary Algorithms, Fitness Landscapes and Search.* PhD thesis, University of New Mexico, Albuquerque, 1995.
12. R. Keller and W. Banzhaf. Explicit maintenance of genotypic diversity on genospaces. Unpublished, 1994. http://ls11-www.informatik.uni-dortmund.de/people/banzhaf/gp.html.
13. W. B. Langdon and R. Poli. An analysis of the max problem in genetic programming. In J. R. Koza, K. Deb, M. Dorigo, D. B. Fogel, M. Garzon, H. Iba, and R. L. Riolo, editors, *Genetic Programming 1997: Proceedings of the Second Annual Conference on Genetic Programming*, pages 222–230, San Francisco, CA, 1997. Morgan Kaufmann.
14. N.F. McPhee and N.J. Hopper. Analysis of genetic diversity through population history. In W. Banzhaf, J. Daida, A. E. Eiben, M. H. Garzon, V. Honavar, M. Jakiela, and R. E. Smith, editors, *Proceedings of the Genetic and Evolutionary Computation Conference*, volume 2, pages 1112–1120, Orlando, Florida, USA, 13-17 July 1999. Morgan Kaufmann.
15. U.-M. O'Reilly. *An Analysis of Genetic Programming.* PhD thesis, Carleton University, Ottawa, Ontario, Canada, 1995.
16. B. Punch, D. Zongker, and E. Goodman. The royal tree problem, a benchmark for single and multiple population genetic programming. In P. Angeline and K. Kinnear, editors, *Advances in Genetic Programming 2*, pages 299–316, Cambridge, MA, 1996. The MIT Press.
17. R.J. Quick, V.J. Rayward-Smith, and G.D. Smith. Fitness distance correlation and ridge functions. In *Fifth Conference on Parallel Problems Solving from Nature (PPSN'98)*, pages 77–86. Springer-Verlag, Heidelberg, 1998.
18. V. Slavov and N. I. Nikolaev. Fitness landscapes and inductive genetic programming. In *Proceedings of International Conference on Artificial Neural Networks and Genetic Algorithms (ICANNGA97)*, University of East Anglia, Norwich, UK, 1997. Springer-Verlag KG, Vienna.

Disease Modeling Using Evolved Discriminate Function

James Cunha Werner and Tatiana Kalganova

Department of Electronic & Computer Engineering, Brunel University
Uxbridge, Middlesex, UB8 3PH
jamwer2000@hotmail.com, Tatiana.Kalganova@brunel.ac.uk

Abstract. Precocious diagnosis increases the survival time and patient quality of life. It is a binary classification, exhaustively studied in the literature. This paper innovates proposing the application of genetic programming to obtain a discriminate function. This function contains the disease dynamics used to classify the patients with as little false negative diagnosis as possible. If its value is greater than zero then it means that the patient is ill, otherwise healthy. A graphical representation is proposed to show the influence of each dataset attribute in the discriminate function. The experiment deals with Breast Cancer and Thrombosis & Collagen diseases diagnosis. The main conclusion is that the discriminate function is able to classify the patient using numerical clinical data, and the graphical representation displays patterns that allow understanding of the model.

1 Introduction

Britain has the worst survival rates for cancer of any nation in the western world. The five-year survival rate for breast cancer, if diagnosed early, is 78% in the UK, compared with 97% in America and 93% in the rest of the Europe [1]. The study found many British patients were diagnosed only when their cancer was at an advanced stage and that was more difficult to treat. Early diagnosis increases the survival chances.

One way to improve early diagnosis is to develop modeling techniques able to identify imperceptible patterns from datasets and support decision making. In practice, what has to be done is to input the patient records into the model and obtain a forecast of the diagnosis.

Extensive work has already been carried out in this area (see Table 1). The adopted paradigms adapt parameters and threshold values in a pre defined fixed mathematical structure.

Analysis of existing approaches (Table 1) show two main drawbacks: (1) the created model of the knowledge does not take into account false negative events. (2) the adaptation of a previous defined model structure (such as If-then-else, or Neural Network with back propagation, etc) to the problem. The first drawback is that false negative and false positives have the same weight in the obtainment of the model. While false positive is a safe condition to the patient because new clinical analysis will be carried on, false negative is a dangerous postponing of the diagnosis and decreases survival chances. The consequence of a second bottleneck is that some problems will not have the best model, e.g. they will have an approximate solution using the structure. This approximation masks the dynamics of the disease.

C. Ryan et al. (Eds.): EuroGP 2003, LNCS 2610, pp. 465–474, 2003.

Table 1. Knowledge representation for medical diagnosis(KR – knowledge representation, NN – Neural Network, SVM - Support Vector Machines, EA – Evolutionary algorithm, DT – Decision Trees, FZ – Fuzzy, GP – Genetic Programming).

Author	Algorithm	Description
Kononenko 2001 [2]	naïve Bayesian classifier, NN and DT	*KR: statistical parameters, parameter adaptation, and rules* Only decision tree builders are able to select the appropriate characteristics (performance, transparency, explanation, reduction, and missing data handling).
West 2000 [3]	NN	*KR: parameter adaptation* Several different neural networks were applied and will be used as reference to compare with our approach
Setiono 1996 [4], 2000 [5]	rules from NN	*KR: rules to represent the parametric model* Extraction of rules from a trained NN to overcome its black box concept
Flach 2001 [6] Joachins[7]	SVM	*KR: Geometrical approach.* Optimum margin classifier + kernel. Training examples are linearly separable and try to obtain a hyper plane with maximum margin from positive and negative points
Land Jr 2002 [8]	EA to configure SVM	*KR: optimal hyper planes geometry* Improvement of the specificity by 45.3% at 100% (missing no cancer) when compared with iterative method
Pendharkar 1999 [9]	machine learning	*KR: rules* Rules and the observation of patterns and knowledge acquisition for various knowledge base systems. The application in breast cancer diagnosis shows that the method is a viable tool
Nauck 1999 [10]	FZ	*KR: linguistic rules* Fuzzy rule based classifier with simple linguistically interpretable rules
Freitas 2002 [11]	EA	*KR: rules coded in the chromosome.* Chromosome codes rules If-Then-Else with the attributes and the classification can be understood
Pena-Reyes 1999 [12]	EA + FZ	*KR: rules with optimal transition values.* Breast cancer diagnosis with high performance
Proposed method	EA(GP)	*KR: mathematical model of the disease.* Obtain the discriminate function for the disease to classify the patients.

Our approach differs from all previous approaches because it generates a mathematical algebraic model (discriminate function) used to classify the patient data. We define the operators that should be used in the model assembly, which results in an enormous degree of freedom. Any type of model can be obtained by Genetic Programming (GP).

Discriminate function maps the original multi dimensional space in a one-dimensional real number image. The output space has a threshold with separate diagnostic classes. In this paper the origin was adopted as a threshold: positive values mean an ill patient and negative values a healthy patient.

A multiplicative weight (termed punishment) is introduced to give more priority to false negatives. It guarantees minimal false negatives, which costs accuracy in true negative values. Again, this is a safe condition for the patient.

The experimental results prove the reliability of the proposed approach. However, more than 95% accuracy is not enough if the user is not able to understand how the algorithm works and what they have learned. To overcome this difficulty, a new graphical representation is proposed to analyze the discriminate function and show the contribution of each attribute in the fitness function.

The experimental results used two datasets to evaluate the method: one is the Wisconsin Breast Cancer dataset and the other is the Collagen Disease and Thrombosis dataset.

2 Genetic Programming

GP is an optimization algorithm which mimics the evolution and improvement of life through reproduction. Each individual contributes with its own genetic information to the building of new ones (offspring) adapted to the environment with higher chances of surviving. This is the basis of genetic algorithms and programming [13], [14], [15], [16]. Specialized Markov Chains underline the theoretical bases of this algorithm, changes of states and searching procedures.

The software we have developed is an adaptation of LilGP [17], where GP is structured in a pre-compiled library, with other artificial intelligence procedures, such as NN, FZ, adaptive algorithms, etc. Outputs are written in Excel XLS format direct from the program, to generate an accessible and functional Human-Computer Interface (HCI).

Chromosome Representation. The chromosome represents the model of the problem solution using trees. A tree is a model representation that contains nodes and leaves.

Nodes are mathematical operators. We have used multiplication, addition, subtraction, and division. Leaves are terminals (the attributes of the dataset and numbers). The discriminate function in a GP context is a tree using operators (or so called Functions) and leaves (or so called Terminals). Let us consider the following discriminate function:

$$X_1+3.14 \cdot X_2+5.3 / X_3$$

In the tree representation it can be rewritten as following:

$$(+\ X_1\ (+\ (\cdot\ 3.14\ \ X_2)\ (/\ 5.3\ \ X_3)))$$

where X_1, X_2, and X_3 are the attributes of the clinical data, and multiplication(·), addition(+), subtraction (-), and division(/) are the operators. Replacing the values of the clinical data in the equation results in a number which should be positive (the patient is ill) or negative (the patient is healthy).

Genetic Operators. Trees are manipulated through genetic operators. The crossover operator points a tree branch and exchanges it with another branch and obtains new trees. The mutation operator changes the branch for a random new branch. The length of the chromosome is variable.

The probability of crossover is 60% and the probability of mutation is 20%. We adopt a high value of the mutation probability to spread the population over all solution space.

Fitness Function. Fitness function defines the quality of chromosome as a solution to the problem. It is a numerical positive value. The dataset is divided in two parts: one is for training and the second is for validation. The training dataset is used to obtain the model and the validation dataset is used to measure the accuracy of the model with data that was not used in training.

The fitness function evaluates how good the diagnostic model coded in chromosome is, over all training dataset using Receiver Operating Characteristics (ROC) [18].

ROC criterion value is sliding in the output projection and the number of true negative (N_{TN}), true positive (N_{TP}), false negative (N_{FN}), and false positive (N_{FP}):

$$\alpha = \frac{N_{TP}}{N_{TP} + N_{FN}} \qquad \beta = \frac{N_{TN}}{N_{TN} + N_{FP}} \tag{1}$$

where α is the *Sensitivity*, and β is the *Specificity*. Sensitivity is the probability that a test result will be positive when the disease is present (true positive rate, expressed as a percentage). *Specificity* is the probability that a test result will be negative when the disease is not present (true negative rate, expressed as a percentage).

The fitness function F used in the disease diagnostic is the accuracy of the model, with a weight over false negatives predictions:

$$F = \frac{N_{ok}}{N_{ok} + N_{FP} + \sigma * N_{FN}} \tag{2}$$

where σ is the overprice for false negative (high risk condition), or punishment weight, N_{ok} is the number of correct forecast, N_{FP} is the number of false positives and N_{FN} is the number of false negatives.

3 Diagnosis of Severe Diseases Using Discriminate Function

To analyze the knowledge represented in the discriminate function, the separation between positive and negative cases and the influence of each variable, we introduced a graph of the partial derivative with respect to a variable by the difference in the discriminate function if this variable is set to zero. Each axis of the function is defined as:

$$XAxis : \delta = 0.01x; \frac{\partial z}{\partial x} = \frac{z(x+\delta, y, ...) - z(x-\delta, y, ...)}{2\delta} \tag{3}$$

$$YAxis : \Delta = \frac{z(x, y, ...) - z(x=0, y, ...)}{z(x, y, ...)}$$

where 2·δ is the step of the numerical derivative in axis X; x,y,… are attributes of the dataset and z is the discriminate function. On the Y axis, the value of the attribute less itself set to null is used to evaluate its effects in the total value of the discriminate function.

The X axis shows the behavior of the patient, if he is better (negative values) or worse (positive values). The Y axis shows the contribution of the variable to the improvement of the patient condition (negative value) or to aggravate their condition (positive values). The ideal conditions are both negative values, and the sickly conditions are both positive values.

We termed this graphic as *Disease Pathway Graphic - DPG*, because it reproduces the pathway the patients follow during their recovery in the plane defined by the transformation in Eq. 3.

4 Experimental Results

The following subsections present the experimental results for breast cancer from Wisconsin University [19], [20] and Collagen Disease and Thrombosis from Chiba Hospital [21], [22]. In both cases, GP was applied to obtain the discriminate function with the training dataset and the test is done applying a validation dataset to evaluate its effectiveness.

Breast-cancer testing is an important application because it is crucial to develop a reliable but inexpensive test to identify women with high risk for a more expensive and accurate clinical procedure.

Collagen diseases are auto-immune diseases. Patients generate antibodies attacking their own bodies. For example, if a patient generates antibodies in lungs, he/she will chronically lose the respiratory function and finally lose life. The disease mechanisms are only partially known and their classification is still fuzzy. Some patients may generate many kinds of antibodies and their manifestations may include all the characteristics of collagen diseases.

Experiment 1: Breast Cancer Diagnostic. The Wisconsin Diagnostic Breast Cancer [19], [20] contains 679 events (236 ill and 443 healthy records) without any missing values. The dataset contains the following attributes: Clump Thickness (clth), Uniformity of Cell Size(uncz), Uniformity of Cell Shape (uncs), Marginal Adhesion (mara), Single Epithelial Cell Size (sepc), Bare Nuclei (barn), Bland Chromatin (blac), Normal Nucleoli (norn), Mitoses (mito), Class (2 benign 4 malignant). Each attribute is an integer between 1 and 10.

An input routine reads the data and stores it in memory and fitness function evaluates the accuracy of the discriminate function of each individual. The discriminate function is checked against the type of tumor (benign or malign) to find the fitness function (Eq. 2).

The first study was the effect of punishment factor in the sensitivity. The complete dataset is modeled using GP to obtain the discriminate function with different values of punishment in the fitness function (Eq. 2). The results shown in Table 2 present the effect of different values of punishment weight in sensitivity and specificity.

The highest value of sensitivity (with lower false negative) is obtained when punishment is equal to 10 (see bold values in Table 1). The occurrence of false negatives decays for values greater than or equal to 5, and oscillates around 4 false negative values, without vanishing for 500 generations of 100 individuals.

Table 2. Study of punishment value (column Punishment) for breast cancer modelling. Bold value point to the highest sensitivity value ($\boldsymbol{\alpha}$ is the sensitivity and $\boldsymbol{\beta}$ is the specificity).

Punishment	N_{TN}	N_{FP}	N_{TP}	N_{FN}	α	β
1	425	18	226	10	95.7	95.9
3	417	26	227	9	96.1	94.1
5	412	31	231	5	97.8	93.0
10	**420**	**23**	**234**	**2**	**99.1**	**94.8**
15	402	41	231	5	97.8	90.7
20	406	37	233	3	98.7	91.6

Punishment equal to 10 is used in a run to obtain the model where the number of false negatives is null. This experiment will be used to generate the Disease Pathway Graphic. The maximum number of generations was 2000, and the best solution was obtained after 543 generations. The discriminate function was:

$$\text{(barn + uncs) (-34.72 + barn + clth + barn clth - barn sepc + norn / uncs + clth * clth / ((85.53/ blac - 2 blac + mara - mito + blac sepc) (sepc + uncs)) + blac (sepc + uncs) + barn uncz + (mara - uncs)/ (sepc/norn + uncz))} \quad (4)$$

The number of true negatives is 426, false positives is 17, and true positives is 236. The accuracy is 97.5%.

Breast cancer was studied by many authors and is a benchmark. We will follow the same methodology of West [3] to compare the results and accuracy. To obtain the discriminate function for diagnostics proposes the original data is divided into 10 blocks, using each block to test while the rest are used to train the algorithms. The 10 test blocks form all original databases used in the test stage.

Table 3. Different approaches to cancer diagnosis [3]

Method	OK (%)	% False negative	% False positive
Multilayer perceptron	0.957206	0.087448	0.018594
General regression	0.967647	0.054393	0.020408
Radial basis function	0.970441	0.030126	0.029252
Mixture of experts	0.962941	0.062762	0.023129
Logistic regression	0.9633968	0.0711297	0.018018
Logistic	0.972182	0.029289	0.027027
K search neighbor	0.967789	0.033473	0.031532
Kernel	0.95022	0.117155	0.013514
GP (proposed)	**0.963235**	**0.008368**	**0.05180**

The software should run until a model is found without false negative. However, it is not a guarantee that new data will be modeled without false negatives. In this experiment we used the same parameters of the study of punishment weight (100 individuals, 500 generations, 60% crossover probability and 20% mutation probability). This will give an idea of the usual level of false negatives.

The comparison with several techniques from [3] shows that all these techniques have more false negatives than the discriminate function using GP. Table 3 shows the different results for different data mining techniques.

The occurrence of false negative is the least value of available approaches without compromise of the total accuracy, paying the price of a greater false positive than the other approaches. For example, the average false negative of the other methods is 0.60%. If the method were applied in London (9 million people) there were 543,000 patients false negative against "only" 74,700 using our method. Let us consider that the algorithm can be improved for a null false negative model.

This experiment shows a good level of accuracy with low false negatives. The algorithm can model the disease with an algebraic equation which reproduces the dynamics of the disease. However, the model (Eq. 4) does not allow the user to understand the importance of each attribute in the diagnostic, and the effect it causes in the model.

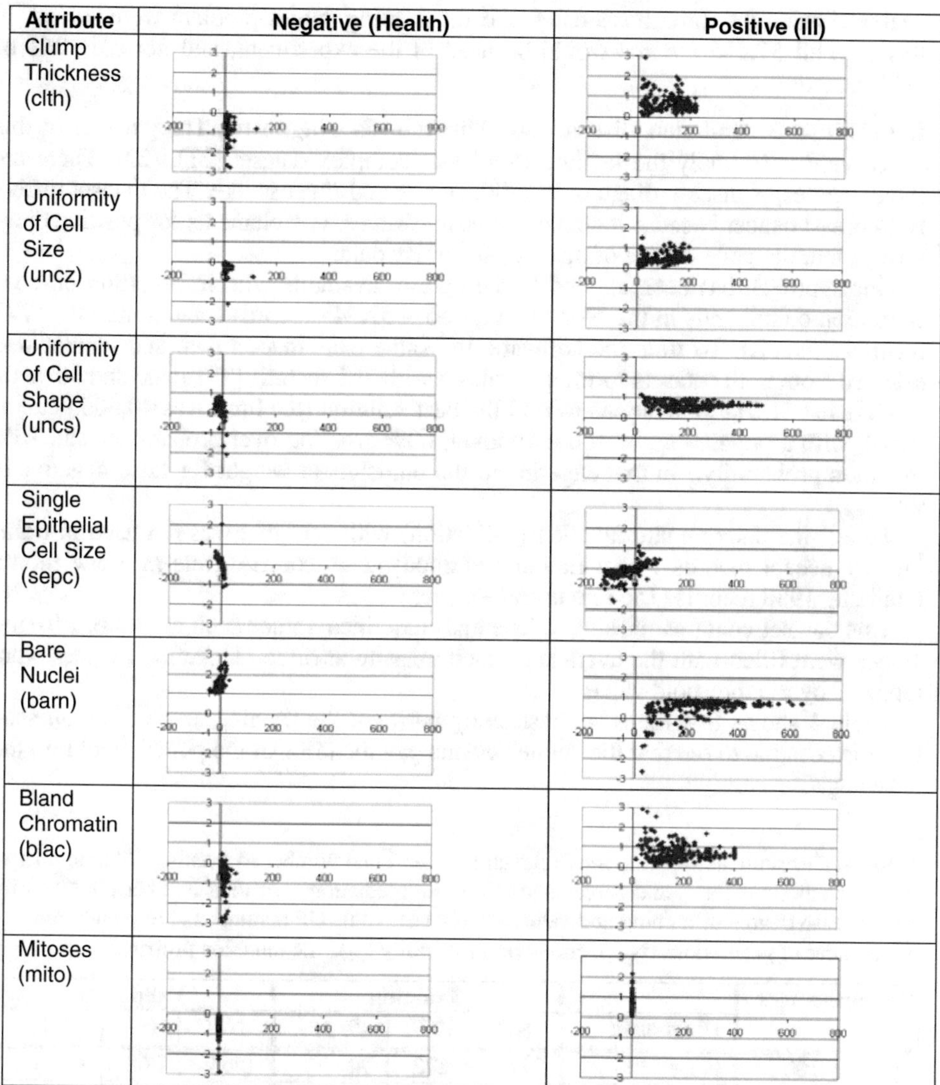

Fig. 1. Different behavior of the variables in the disease pathway graphics.

Analysis of the Disease Model. To study the disease dynamics model of breast cancer, we use all true negative events and all true positive events to draw the graphics of disease pathway (transformed with Eq. 3) in Fig. 3 obtained with Eq. 4. There is a different pattern for ill and health patients.

Healthy patients are clustered close to the origin, while ill patients are spread under a pattern over the first quadrant. The end of the scale is fixed to the same value to all variables to show the comparative behavior.

The attributes “Marginal Adhesion (mara)” and “Normal Nucleoli (norn)” are distributed around the origin and do not influence the diagnosis at all. The dataset fail to provide a history of each patient, to plot its temporal evolution. However, this can be analyzed using the thrombosis dataset, if the missing values problem were solved. In this case all 57,545 records would be used in the experiment, and not only 261 or 1988 records.

Experiment 2: Collagen Disease and Thrombosis Diagnostic. The purpose of this experiment is to apply the method to a more complex dataset [21], [22]. There are three degrees of disease diagnostic: mild, severe and most severe. The dataset differs from breast cancer because it contains missing values, few elements for positive diagnosis, more than one degree of disease, and noisy data.

Our approach has been applied to the dataset available with information on concentration compounds in the blood exam (lab – 57,545 records - and antibody – 773 records - exams). To train the software, the same examination date and patient was selected from both datasets forming a dataset with 261 records (231 none and 30 yes).

GP used 11,072 generations to find the best solution (the limit was 40,000 generations), with a population of 100 individual, 60% crossing over probability, and 20% mutation probability. In this experiment the punishment weight for false negative is 20.

To test the discriminate function (validation) with data that was not used in training, we accept records where Lab and antibody date exams differs into one month totalizing 1988 records (1564 none and 424 yes).

This dataset contains missing values and undefined values such as < 3.0. Missing values were filled with the average of each missing attribute. Undefined values were replaced by the threshold value.

Table 4 shows that there is consistency between the training and validation sets, but it is possible to see that the "none" events pay the price of the punishment into the false negative case.

Table 4. Discriminate function for Collagen Disease.Total number of events (N^{Tot}), number of correct predictions (N^{CP}) and percentage of correct prediction over total number (% N^{CP}) for each disease degree in training and validation datasets runs. GP parameters are population size (λ), number of generations (N_{gen}), crossover probability (p_c), and mutation probability (p_m).

GP parameters			**Training**			**Validation**		
		Diagnostic	N^{Tot}	N^{CP}	% N^{CP}	N^{Tot}	N^{CP}	% N^{CP}
λ	100	None	231	172	**74**	1564	968	**61**
N_{gen}	3924	Mild	1	1	**100**	1	1	**100**
p_c	60 %	Severe	11	10	**90**	250	231	**92**
p_m	20 %	Most severe	18	18	**100**	173	168	**97**

In validation results, the number of false negative is 24 (1.2%), with represent risk for the patient. The accuracy of the method is 76% for training and 68% for validation.

There are two possible explanations for these results: the effect of missing values and the use of average values; the low number of diseases in the training dataset (only 11% of the cases are ill patients) and the low number in the training dataset (261 records).

However, the method was able to obtain a model for the disease with low false negative.

5 Summary and Conclusion

This paper presents an approach for classification using a mathematical discriminate function. To reduce false negative, different punishment values were tested. It shows that its value is critical below a threshold and does not affect the result accuracy after this point.

With the punishment value, we obtained the discriminate function for breast cancer and collagen disease with good accuracy, showing that the method can be applied to model diseases using an algebraic equation of the attributes. To extract information from the model, we proposed a graphical representation of the discriminate function that allows visualization of each attribute and its effects in the discriminate function. The graphical presentation of each variable gave a better understanding of each attribute contribution and would help to clarify the knowledge acquire by the model. Due to the capability to predict the disease, the model contains the dynamics of the disease under study and this approach can contribute to the improvement of diseases treatment. Thanks to Susan McCracken and Owen Parry for proof reading in this paper.

References

1. Newman,M.; "UK's cancer death rate is worst in the world"; Metro News, Tuesday, July 2, 2002.
2. Kononenko,I.; "Machine learning for medical diagnosis: history, state of the art and perspective"; Artificial Intelligence in medicine 23:89-109, 2001.
3. West,D; West,V; "Model selection for a medical diagnostic decision support system: a breast cancer detection case" Artificial Intelligence in medicine 20(2000)183-204.
4. Setiono,R.; "Extracting rules from pruned neural networks for breast cancer diagnosis" Artificial Intelligence in Medicine 8(1):37-51, 1996.
5. Setiono,R.; "Generating concise and accurate classification rules for breast cancer diagnosis"; Artificial Intelligence in medicine 18:205-219, 2000
6. Flach,P.A.; "On the state of art in machine learning: a personal review"; Artificial Intelligence 131:199-222, 2001.
7. Joachins, T.; "Tutorial Support Vector Machines" In Internet http://www.afia.polytechnique.fr/CAFE/ECML01/SVM.html
8. Land Jr., W.H.; Lo,J.Y.; Velazquez,R.; "Using evolutionary programming to configure support vector machine for the diagnosis of breast cancer". In Dagli,C.H. et al (Eds) Intelligent engineering systems through artificial neural networks ANNIE'2002, Volume 12, Smart engineering system design, ASME Press, New York, 2002.
9. Pendharkar,P.C.; et al; "Association, statistical, mathematical and neural approaches for mining breast cancer patterns"; Expert Systems with Applications 17:223-232, 1999.
10. Nauck,D.; Kruse,R.; "Obtaining interpretable fuzzy classification rules from medical data"; Artificial intelligence in medicine 16:149-169, 1999
11. Freitas,A.A.; "Data mining and knowledge discovery with Evolutionary Algorithms"; Springer 2002.
12. Pena-Reyes,C.A.; Sipper,M.; "A fuzzy-genetic approach to breast cancer diagnosis"; Artificial intelligence in medicine 17:131-155, 1999.
13. HOLLAND,J.H. "Adaptation in natural and artificial systems: na introductory analysis with applications to biology, control and artificial intelligence." Cambridge: Cambridge press 1992.

14. GOLDBERG,D.E. "Genetic Algorithms in Search, Optimisation, and Machine Learning." Reading, Mass.: Addison-Whesley, 1989.
15. CHAMBERS,L.; "The practical handbook of Genetic Algorithms" Chapman & Hall/CRC, 2000.
16. KOZA,J.R. "Genetic programming: On the programming of computers by means of natural selection." Cambridge,Mass.: MIT Press, 1992.
17. LilGP "Genetic Algorithms Research and Applications Group (GARAGe)", Michigan State University; http://garage.cps.msu.edu/software/lil-gp/lilgp-index.html
18. Bradley, A.P.; "The use of the area under the ROC curve in the evaluation of machine learning algorithms"; Pattern Recognition, 30(7):1145-1159, 1997.
19. WDBC Dr. William H. Wolberg, General Surgery Dept.,; W. Nick Street, Computer Sciences Dept.; Olvi L. Mangasarian, Computer Sciences Dept.; University of Wisconsin http://www.ics.uci.edu/~mlearn/MLRepository.html
20. Werner,J.C.; Fogarty,T.C.; "Severe diseases diagnostics using Genetic Programming." Intelligent Data Analysis in medicine and pharmacology – IDAMAP2001; September 4th, 2001 London http://magix.fri.uni-lj.si/idamap2001/scientific.asp
21. 5th European Conference on Principles and Practice of Knowledge Discovery in Databases (PKDD'01) Challenge on Thrombosis data – Germany/ Freiburg September 3-7, 2001
22. Werner,J.C.; Fogarty,T.C.; "Genetic programming applied to Collagen disease & thrombosis." in PKDD 2001 Challenge on Thrombosis data – Germany/ Freiburg September 3-7, 2001.

No Free Lunch, Program Induction and Combinatorial Problems

John R. Woodward and James R. Neil

School of Computer Science, University of Birmingham, B15 2TT, UK
{J.R.Woodward,J.R.Neil}@cs.bham.ac.uk

Abstract. This paper has three aims. Firstly, to clarify the poorly understood No Free Lunch Theorem (NFL) which states all search algorithms perform equally. Secondly, search algorithms are often applied to program induction and it is suggested that NFL does not hold due to the universal nature of the mapping between program space and functionality space. Finally, NFL and combinatorial problems are examined. When evaluating a candidate solution, it can be discarded without being fully examined. A stronger version of NFL is established for this class of problems where the goal is to minimize a quantity.

1 Introduction

For every problem that an optimizer does well on, there is a corresponding problem on which it does poorly. Over all possible problems the performance of all optimizers are equivalent. There are many ways of stating NFL and a number of papers have been published [1,2,3,4,5]. NFL may seem counter intuitive, but this is because the conditions under which NFL hold are not usually stated. Firstly, no point in the search space is revisited. Secondly, all functions are considered. Finally, the overhead of determining the next point to visit is ignored. These points are discussed and illustrated in section 3.

Program induction involves generating a program and testing it against a serise of test cases [6]. This process is repeated until terminating conditions are met. The method of generation of the program is not of concern in this paper. An error score is assigned to a program depending on its performance on the set of test cases. A number of test cases are needed to reflect the behaviour of the desired program beyond 'reasonable doubt'. The practitioner is faced with the job of providing a set of test cases in the hope that if a program that passes the test cases, it will generalize well. In general, the optimum set of test cases will be highly problem dependent. In this paper, program induction will be taken to mean over a space of programs defined by a Turing Complete instruction set. Often, program induction uses a function set that is specific to the problem and in most cases is not Turing Complete.

Imagine the following typical situation in program induction. A search algorithm produces a series of programs as candidate solutions. As each program is tested on the series of test cases, if at any point the error score of program

C. Ryan et al. (Eds.): EuroGP 2003, LNCS 2610, pp. 475–484, 2003.

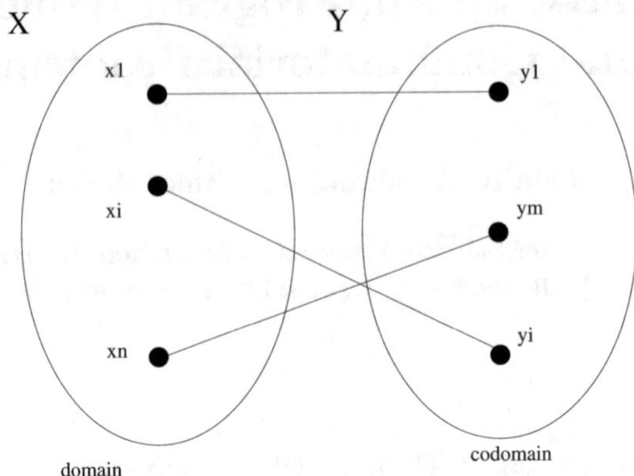

Fig. 1. A function is a mapping from X to Y. Points in the set X map to points in the set Y. In general point x_i maps to point y_i and $|X| \geq |Y|$.

exceeds that of the best program so far testing can be halted. Search algorithms that halt testing in this case are called *terminating* search algorithms.

The original motivation of this work was to establish a terminating version of NFL for program evolution which states all terminating search algorithms perform equally. However, due to the nature of the mapping between programs and their functionality, it is found NFL does not hold.

The original motivation can still be applied to combinatorial problems where the goal is to minimize a quantity. A combinatorial problem is one which involves selecting a subset from a set in order to minimize or maximize a certain quantity subject to certain constraints (the ordering may be important for some problems).

Possibly the best know example of a combinatorial problem is the travelling salesman problem, where the goal is to minimize the total distance travelled between a set of cities. If a route is being examined, and after only a few cities it has exceeded the total distance of the best route so far, it can be discarded and hence does not need to be fully evaluated.

Section 2 repeats a number of definitions from [3] which are biult upon on in section 6 in order to prove a terminating version of NFL for combinatorial problems. In section 3 the three reasons why NFL is misunderstood are discussed. NFL and program induction are considered together in section 4 and the claim is made that there is a potential free lunch. In section 5 , combinatorial problems are considered in the context of search algorithms that can terminate. In section 6 a terminating version of NFL is proved.

2 Search Algorithm Framework

This section repeats a framework presented in Schumacher [3] that allows a simple analysis of search algorithms. This framework is perhaps simpler that the one presented by Wolpert and Macready[4,5].

Functions. Let X and Y be finite sets and $f : X \rightarrow Y$ be a function where $y_i \equiv f(x_i)$. The size of X is $|X|$ and the size of Y is $|Y|$. Each value in X maps to a single value in Y. For a given X and Y there are $|Y|^{|X|}$ possible functions.

Search Operators and Search Vectors. A search operator and a search algorithm are taken to be the same and represent any algorithm that produces a search vector. A search vector V is an ordered sequence of points in X (this is equivalent to the concept of a walk in English [2])$V \equiv \langle x_1, x_2, \ldots, x_m \rangle$. It is assumed that no point is revisited. The *ith* element in this vector corresponds to the *ith* point visited. A complete search vector is any vector that lists all points in X once and only once and has length $|X|$. There are $|X|!$ distinct complete search vectors. We are not concerned with how the search vectors are generated.

A search vector corresponds to a path in X. Given search vector and function will produce a corresponding path in Y. Let us call this sequence of points in Y a performance vector. A search vector of length l corresponds to a performance vector of length l, given a specific function.

Define an overall performance measure to be a function that maps the set of performance vectors generated by a given search vector A and a set of functions F to a real number. A NFL result over a set of functions F is defined to exist when two algorithms have the same overall performance measure. In [3] four equivalent statements of NFL are discussed, the third is stated here;

Theorem 1. *NFL: Every search algorithm generates precisely the same collection of performance vectors when all functions are considered.*

3 Discussion of NFL

Revisiting Points. NFL only considers unique points visited in X, if a point is visited again it is not counted. Let us look at the issue of revisiting points. Consider two search algorithms, random search and exhaustive search, and a search space of n points. Random search visits points and also has a chance of revisiting points. Exhaustive search moves systematically from point to point visiting each point only once. Exhaustive search is guaranteed to find the target point within n evaluations, while we can only make probabilistic statements about random search. Exhaustive search will do better than random search over all problems due to the fact that random search will revisit points. NFL only considers novel evaluations, so in the above case both algorithms are considered to behave the same (random search can only make n novel evaluations). One might argue that we could supplement the random search algorithm with a memory so it avoids revisiting points, however this will require some computational overhead (see subsection Overheads). Over all functions, exhaustive search is better than random search if revisiting points *is counted.*

All Functions. A value in the domain maps to a value in the codomain under one function, but under another function could map to a different value. If we consider all functions, one value in the domain maps to *every* value in the codomain. If we only consider one function then the best algorithm visits the optimal point first. This means other points will be visited later. Therefore there exists a function where the target point is visited last in the search. For every function a search algorithm does well on, there is a corresponding function on which it does badly.

Overheads. The overhead of calculating the next point to visit is not taken into account. If two search algorithms produce the same search vectors, they appear to behave the same in terms of the points they visit, but one may involved a more expensive computation than the other. In terms of wall clock time they will appear to perform differently. Real search algorithms do revisit points but this could be avoided by keeping a record of points visited. However, for any reasonable sized problem space this overhead becomes considerable and cannot be ignored.

When evolutionary algorithms are compared, they are run for a certain number of generations, and so the overheads are ignored. As in the case above comparing exhaustive search with random search, the overhead of maintaining a list of points visited is much more computationally expensive than the overhead associated with a typical exhaustive search algorithm.

4 Program Induction and NFL

Program induction involves searching the space of computer programs to find a target function represented by a set of test cases [6]. In practice, limits are placed on the length of programs, the amount of memory the program can access and the length of time a program can run. Often these limits are imposed by the user, but could be self adapted.

The mapping between the program space and the space of functionality is very specific and is related to the universal distribution and Kolmogorov complexity[7]. Kolmogorov complexity is the length of the shortest program that produces a given functionality. In essence, the universal distribution says there are lots of programs with simple functionality and few with complex functionality and this is independent of the computer language used to express the programs. There is a many to one mapping between the space of programs and the space of functionality. In the terminology of Evolutionary Computation there are many genotypes for a given phenotype [6]. In the more tradional tree based genetic programming.

It is interesting to note that a similar universal distribution exists in the more tradional tree based genetic programming provided modularity is permitted in the representation [8].

Langdon [9] has investigated the distribution of functionality of programs with varying length. He suggests that above some certain minimum size threshold, the distribution is largely independent of length. The frequency of output behaviour is plotted for varying program sizes for three different problem domains

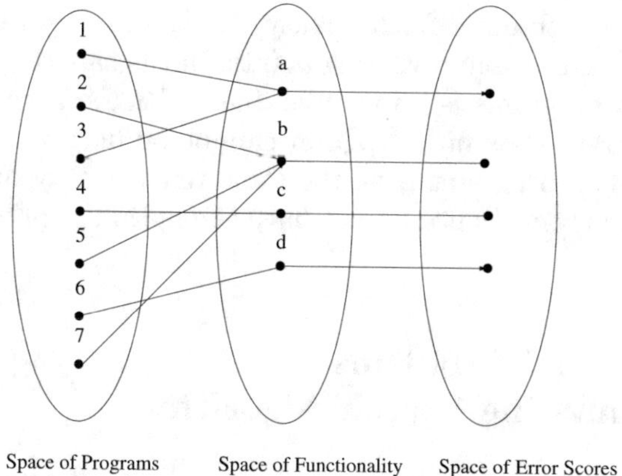

Fig. 2. A space of programs maps to a space of functionality. This mapping is many to one and is related to the universal distribution. A free lunch exists between these two spaces. The space of functionality maps to a space of error scores, between these two spaces NFL still holds.

(the Boolean problems, symbolic regression, evolving agent) and demonstrates that they each tend towards a limiting distribution and that the distribution is not uniform. While these problem domains do not use Turing Complete instruction sets he states that is seems reasonable that a similar result will also apply to big trees including iteration or recursion and memory (i.e. Turing Complete systems).

So where does the universal distribution leave NFL? Figure 2 shows a space of enumerated programs. There are 7 programs in this space. Imagine algorithm $A \equiv \langle 1, 2, 4, 6, 3, 5, 7 \rangle$ and $B \equiv \langle 1, 3, 2, 5, 7, 4, 6 \rangle$. The programs A visits have functionality $\langle a, b, c, d, a, b, b \rangle$. The programs B visits have functionality $\langle a, a, b, b, b, c, d \rangle$. Within 4 evaluations A has sampled all of the functionality avaliable, while B requires 7 evaluations. Whatever the target functionality is A cannot do worse than B. This diagram demonstrates that there is a free lunch in the situation where there is a non-uniform many to one mapping between spaces as there is with program induction.

There are three spaces involved in program induction (see figure 2). A space of programs maps to a space of functionality and this space maps to an error space. If one could directly search the space of functionality we would face a NFL distribution. One can see this by imagining an error function that returns true only if all test cases are passed. This will give a needle in a haystack function and over all functionality it has been show that this obeys NFL [3]. Alternatively the error function could return the number of test cases failed and this would give a binomial distribution. Over all functionality NFL holds for this method of measuring error. We are confined to search the space of programs as we cannot directly access the space of functionality.

One might try to rescue NFL by adding a clause to the theorem excluding programs that have functionality which have been seen before (i.e. by only counting programs with novel functionality). This would be like adding memory to search algorithms to avoid revisiting points. In the case of program evolution, weeding out such programs is impossible due to Rice's Theorem, which states that non trivial properties of a program cannot be decided. The only way we can determine if two programs have the same functionality over the set of test cases is to execute them. Hence do not have the option of patching up the NFL theorem.

5 Combinatorial Problems and Terminating Search Algorithms

The idea of terminating the testing of a solution can be applied to combinatorial problems were the goal is to minimize a certain quantity. For example in TSP the goal is to minimize the total round trip distance. Another well know combinatorial problem is the knapsack problem, but here the idea is to maximize a quantity. The idea of termination can be applied to combinatorial problems where the goal is minimize a quantity.

To illustrate the idea of termination TSP is used as it is probably the best documented. The goal is to visit all the cities stated by the shortest route. Presented with a number of candidate routes, the round trip distance of each one could be calculated in turn and the best selected. A route is evaluated by accumulating a running total as each city is visited. If at any time the running total of a potential route is greater than the shortest route seen so far, further examination of that route is unnecessary and can be discarded immediately. Hence a route could be ruled out before the total distance has been calculated.

What does the space of these problems look like? Some functions are not available, for example a needle in a haystack function does not exist. A single TSP problem can be represented as a table of cities and distances. From a given scenario other problems can be generated simply by re-labelling the cities. If there are n cities, there are $n!$ ways of re-labelling these cities (i.e. all permutations). Whitley [10] has pointed out that NFL holds for permutations of functions. Strictly speaking each permutation must be distinct. Hence when evaluating a complete route in one evaluation NFL holds.

Assuming we have a search algorithm that can terminate examination of a route when it is possible to do so - do we still have a NFL situation? The aim of the next section is to establish a NFL for terminating search algorithms.

6 Extending the Framework for Terminating Search Algorithms

The current framework needs to be extended to allow us to include the case of terminating search algorithms. The framework described above is suitable for scenarios where we can make statements about a point after a single evaluation. We can think of function optimization, a single evaluation tells us the value of a function at that point and we can say if it is a better point than the best so far. We cannot partially evaluate a point, a point is either evaluated or not.

In the case of combinatorial problems it is possible to make a statement about a potential solution after only partially evaluating it. To evaluate a route in the TSP, the distances between each city in the route are summed up to form the total distance. The complete route is the sum of all the distances that compose the route. If at any point during the journey the running total exceeds that of the best route so far there is no point continuing to evaluate that route.

Let us consider a given configuration of cites under the previous framework. There are n cites, each labelled c_i. There are $n!$ routes to try out, which can be labelled R_i and each route maps to a total distance D_i travelled for that route. A search vector is a list of routes $\langle R_1, R_2, \ldots, R_{n!}\rangle$ and this corresponds to a performance vector $\langle D_1, D_2, \ldots, D_{n!}\rangle$.

Extending this framework involves representing a route as list of each of the cities visited in order so we can talk about partially evaluating a route. Thus, for example $R_1 \equiv \langle c_1, c_2, \ldots, c_n\rangle$, represents a route. A search vector $\langle R_1, R_2, \ldots, R_n\rangle$ may be written out in full, explicitly listing each city e.g.

$$\langle\langle c_1, c_2, \ldots, c_n\rangle, \langle c_2, c_1, \ldots, c_n\rangle, \ldots \langle c_n, c_{n-1}, \ldots, c_1\rangle\rangle.$$

This can be called a potential search vector as we may not need to evaluate all points. It represents an ordered list of the cities that may be visited. The potential search vector has a corresponding potential performance vector

$$\langle\langle d_1, d_2, \ldots, d_n\rangle, \langle d_2, d_1, \ldots, d_n\rangle, \ldots \langle d_n, d_{n-1}, \ldots, d_1\rangle\rangle,$$

where d_i is the running total of the journey so far (i.e. the distance travelled in visiting the first i cities listed in the route).

Given a potential search vector, the whole of the first route must be examined as there is nothing to compare it against for the purpose of termination. The second element in the potential search vector lists the second candidate route. If at any point during the journey dictated by this route, its accumulated distance exceeds that of the first, then no more cities are visited and the remaining part of the route need not be examined. Similarly, on subsequent routes, cities towards the start of the route will be visited, but cities towards the end of the route may not be. A list of the cites that are actually visited can be stored in a vector called an actual search vector. For example

$$\langle\langle c_1, c_2, \ldots, c_n\rangle, \langle c_2, \ldots\rangle, \ldots \langle c_i, \ldots\rangle, \ldots \langle c_n, \ldots\rangle\rangle.$$

The dots at the end of each route (except the first) represent the fact that some routes may be partially evaluated. This will have a corresponding actual search vector. For example

$$\langle\ \langle d_1, d_2, \ldots, d_n\rangle, \langle d_2, d_1, \ldots\rangle, \ldots \langle d_i, \ldots\rangle, \ldots \langle d_n, d_{n-1}, \ldots\rangle\rangle$$

To summarize these 4 vectors, a potential search vector is an ordered list of all the points that may potentially be evaluated. A potential performance vector is an ordered list of all the values returned by an evaluation, if all the points are evaluated. An actual search vector is an ordered list of all the points that are actually evaluated (remaining points in a potential search vector are not evaluated due to the ability of the algorithm to terminate). An actual performance vector is an ordered list of the actual returned values of points that are evaluated.

The terminating NFL theorem (TNFL) for combinatorial problems can be stated as

Theorem 2. *TNFL: Every* terminating *search algorithm generates precisely the same collection of* actual *performance vectors when all distinct permutations of a function are considered.*

Proof. Let us consider NFL3 stated in[3] which is: Every search algorithm produces the same collection of performance vectors (when all permutations of a function are considered). Let us restate this in the new terminology for terminating search algorithms. Every search algorithm produces the same collection of *potential* performance vectors. Now let us consider the ability of the algorithm to terminate. If one search algorithm terminates early on some routes on one function then as all search algorithms produce the same collection of potential performance vectors there will be an equivalent skipping of cities towards the end of other routes. But these collections are identical therefore the skips made are identical. Hence two terminating algorithms produce the same set of *actual* performance vector.

This proof is stated in terms of TSP but is of course applicable to any combinatorial problem where the goal is to minimize a quantity.

7 Comments and Discussion

It is the author's hope that by stating the three assumptions under which NFL is stated have cleared up any misunderstanding the reader may have had about NFL before reading this paper. It is perhaps interesting to note that in [5] the following is stated

"We cannot emphasize enough that no claims whatsoever are being made in this paper concerning how well various search algorithms work in practice."

Real algorithms do revisit points but this is undesirable. There are two ways to avoid this problem. The first would be to maintain a list of points visits but this is impractical. A second way would be to construct an exhaustive search algorithm, this is commented on later.

In the NFL framework all functions are considered. What is the distribution of problems in the real world? This is a difficult but fundamental question, so a slightly easier and more formal question may be to ask what problems would we reasonably expect to be able to solve on a computer. One of the aims of program induction is to produce a program with the ability to generalize well from a small set of training data. If the target functionality is incompressible it is impossible to generalize as there is no underlying rule so we can say random functions are unlearnable. It does not make sense to talk about program induction on problems that are incompressible. Generally we are interested in problems with some sort of structure that can be exploited and used to make predictions about input data that was not in the training set. Schumacher [3] has show that NFL results are independent whether or not the set of functions is compressible.

Real search algorithms do revisit points. A list of points visited could be maintained to avoid revisits but this would be impractical for most problems. Exhaustive search algorithms will perform a systematic search without revisiting points. If there are n points in the search space then there are $n!$ ways to visit these points and therefore $n!$ distinct exhaustive search algorithms. In general exhaustive search algorithms will have different lengths and different memory and time requirements. There are many exhaustive search algorithms that cannot be compressed and are essentially just an explicit list of the programs to visit. Other exhaustive algorithms can be written as very short programs, but there are very few of these. Ideally it would be advantageous to visit programs with different functionality but knowing what the functionality of a program is without testing it is undecidable. It appears that some exhaustive search algorithms are better than others.

It is perhaps not surprising that NFL and TNFL hold for combinatorial problems. Combinatorial problems have an intrinsic symmetry and without any knowledge about this beforehand, nothing can be gained.

NFL says all search algorithms perform equally. Now we can say all terminating search algorithms perform equally. This is a restatement of NFL, just at a slightly deeper level. In the standard NFL set up, an evaluation is counted as the evaluation of a candidate solution. In this slightly more refined framework an evaluation counts as evaluation of part of a candidate solution. This different counting system allows us to consider potential savings made by terminating testing early.

8 Summary

NFL is a central but often misunderstood result. NFL holds if revisiting of points is not counted, all functions are considered (or more strictly permutations of a function [10]) and the effort in calculating the next point to visit is ignored. Not revisiting points is unrealistic for most search algorithms, however exhaustive search algorithms are a class of algorithm that only visit points once.

The universal distribution describes the nature of the mapping between the space of programs and the space of functionality. This essentially says there are lots of programs with simply functionality and fewer programs with complex functionality. Due to the universal distribution NFL does not hold for program induction. It seems reasonable that the argument can be extended to other representations (e.g. classifier systems) where the mapping between the representation of a potential solution and its behaviour is a non-uniform many to one mapping. This is backed up the results in Langdon [9]. Attempts may be made to patch up NFL by only counting programs with novel functionality but due to Rice's Theorem this is not possible. Hence, there is a free lunch to be had in program induction, but just how to get at it is not clear.

The idea of terminating search algorithms can be applied to combinatorial problems where the goal is to minimize a quantity. It is shown that there is a terminating version of NFL. This theoretical result may be of little practical importance as the overhead associated with checking the condition for termination may be larger than any potential saving.

Acknowledgements

Michael Vose, Darrell Whitley, Jon Rowe, Xin Yao, Stefano Cattani.

References

1. Droste, S., Jansen, T., Wegener, I.: Perhaps not a free lunch but at least a free appetizer. In Banzhaf, W., Daida, J., Eiben, A.E., Garzon, M.H., Honavar, V., Jakiela, M., Smith, R.E., eds.: Proceedings of the Genetic and Evolutionary Computation Conference. Volume 1., Orlando, Florida, USA, Morgan Kaufmann (1999) 833–839
2. English, T.M.: Evaluation of evolutionary and genetic optimizers: No free lunch. In Fogel, L.J., Angeline, P.J., B"ack, T., eds.: Evolutionary Programming V: Proc. of the Fifth Annual Conf. on Evolutionary Programming, Cambridge, MA, MIT Press (1996) 163–169
3. Schumacher, C., Vose, M.D., Whitley, L.D.: The no free lunch and problem description length. In Spector, L., Goodman, E.D., Wu, A., Langdon, W., Voigt, H.M., Gen, M., Sen, S., Dorigo, M., Pezeshk, S., Garzon, M.H., Burke, E., eds.: Proceedings of the Genetic and Evolutionary Computation Conference (GECCO-2001), San Francisco, California, USA, Morgan Kaufmann (2001) 565–570
4. Wolpert, D.H., Macready, W.G.: No free lunch theorems for search. Technical Report SFI-TR-95-02-010 (1995)
5. Wolpert, D.H., Macready, W.G.: No free lunch theorems for optimization. IEEE Transactions on Evolutionary Computation 1 (1997) 67–82
6. Banzhaf, W., Nordin, P., Keller, R.E., Francone, F.D.: Genetic Programming – An Introduction; On the Automatic Evolution of Computer Programs and its Applications. Morgan Kaufmann, dpunkt.verlag (1998)
7. Kirchherr, Li, Vitanyi: The miraculous universal distribution. MATHINT: The Mathematical Intelligencer 19 (1997)
8. Woodward, J.R.: Modularity in genetic programming. In: Genetic Programming, Proceedings of EuroGP 2003, Essex, UK, Springer-Verlag (2003)
9. Langdon, W.B.: Scaling of program fitness spaces. Evolutionary Computation 7 (1999) 399–428
10. Whitley, D.: Functions as permutations: Implications for no free lunch, walsh analysis and summary statistics. In Schoenauer, M., Deb, K., Rudolph, G., Yao, X., Lutton, E., Merelo, J.J., Schwefel, H.P., eds.: Parallel Problem Solving from Nature – PPSN VI, Berlin, Springer (2000) 169–178

Author Index

Printed in the United States
by Baker & Taylor Publisher Services